HANDBOOK OF FINANCIAL ANALYSIS FOR CORPORATE MANAGERS

With spreadsheet models for decision analysis and performance evaluation applications

Vincent Morrow

PRENTICE HALL
Englewood Cliffs, New Jersey 07632

To Raymond Joseph, Czarina Isoebel, Anthea Rhodora, and Alma Ninfa
for totally supporting this book project.

Prentice-Hall International (UK) Limited, *London*
Prentice-Hall of Australia Pty. Limited, *Sydney*
Prentice-Hall Canada, Inc., *Toronto*
Prentice-Hall Hispanoamericana, S.A., *Mexico*
Prentice-Hall of India Private Limited, *New Delhi*
Prentice-Hall of Japan, Inc., *Tokyo*
Simon & Schuster Asia Pte. Ltd., *Singapore*
Editora Prentice-Hall do Brasil, Ltda., *Rio de Janeiro*

© 1991 *by*

PRENTICE-HALL, Inc.
Englewood Cliffs, NJ

10 9 8 7 6 5 4 3 2 1

Library of Congress Cataloging-in-Publication Data

Morrow, Vincent.
    Handbook of financial analysis for corporate managers : with
spreadsheet models for decision analysis and performance evaluation
applications / Vincent Morrow.
      p.   cm.

    Includes index.
    ISBN 0-13-318346-7
    1. Corporations—Finance. I. Title.
HG4026.M674 1991
658.15—dc20   91-17783
                                  CIP

ISBN   0-13-318346-7

PRENTICE HALL
Business Information Publishing Division
Englewood Cliffs, NJ 07632

Simon & Schuster, A Paramount Communications Company

PRINTED IN THE UNITED STATES OF AMERICA

TABLE OF CONTENTS

DIVISION ONE: ANALYZING
THE PROJECTED PERFORMANCE

Chapter 10   ANALYZING PRODUCT MIX ENHANCEMENT MEASURES 240

Chapter 11   ANALYZING SALES EXPANSION MEASURES 263

Chapter 12   ANALYZING EQUIPMENT
ACQUISITIONS 285

DIVISION TWO: EVALUATING THE PAST PERFORMANCE

Chapter 16   DETERMINANTS OF REPORTED PAST PERFORMANCE

Chapter 22 TRADITIONAL VARIANCE ANALYSIS ... 512

Chapter 23 MULTIVARIANCE ANALYSIS 550

* Product sales deviation used as a basis of the quantity variance of the variable costs.
[†] Input quantity deviation used as a basis of the quantity variance of the variable costs.

PREFACE

This book offers a novel way of understanding and conducting financial analysis. It introduces new techniques to reinforce traditional tools. It illustrates new applications of existing methods. Most important, it leads the readers through a new and faster route to financial analysis practice by exposing them to the spreadsheets of the depth and breadth that are encountered in the business world.

The outcomes of financial analysis work are only as solid as the very foundations upon which they are based: the strategies and implementing measures adopted by the firm, the business environment, the assumptions and manner of preparing the financial projections, and the accounting conventions and formats of financial statements. This book brings a new dimension to the wealth of financial analysis knowledge by examining how these forces define the projected and reported past performance of a firm and its profit- and growth-seeking strategies and measures.

OBJECTIVE OF THIS BOOK AND MEANS TO ACHIEVE IT

The main objective of this book is to enhance the capability of the readers to analyze or comprehend the expected and past performance of measures and business units. The following steps were done to achieve this aim:

- Take an inventory of existing techniques of financial analysis which are most commonly used and which are practical.
- Introduce new techniques to reinforce or supersede current tools which are weak.
- Develop new concepts to facilitate the application of the tools.
- Demonstrate new applications of the techniques to areas which normally are not, but which should be, analyzed.
- Lead the readers through a new and faster route to financial analysis practice.

Inventory of Financial Analysis Techniques. To give the readers a handy reference material, the most commonly used techniques as well as their refinements and ramifications are explained and illustrated in this book.

The tools fall into the following categories: ratio analysis, compound interest methods (internal rate of return and present value techniques), risk analysis (sensitivity, probability, decision tree, break-even point, and crossover point), and variance analysis.

New Techniques.   New techniques are introduced in the book to reinforce or replace the present tools that are flawed. Since the new techniques do not represent radical departures from existing ones but are mere modifications, the readers should be able to easily understand their workings and appreciate their applications. Among the new techniques are integrated management performance ratio which excludes resources not used in the operations, break-even point analysis for raw material cost and wage rates, and variance analysis which can single out deviations in contribution margins arising from changes in industry sales, market share, and collection period of receivables.

New Concepts.   To facilitate the analysis work, new concepts were introduced. For instance, a new cost classification, sales expansion cost, was created to cover advertising and similar expenditures which rise faster than sales and hence cannot be considered as variable cost or fixed cost.

New Applications.   The performance evaluation techniques usually cover the past operations of a firm or operating unit in its entirety. The book introduces a procedure for breaking down the results into the contributions of each major strategy and measure.

Imputed interest is currently used in analyzing proposed measures. The book illustrates a way of applying imputed interest in reviewing the past performance of measures.

New Route to Financial Analysis Practice.   The case analysis in this book simulates actual practice. Hence, the analysis is integrated and comprehensive, the techniques utilized are varied, the worksheets are of sufficient breath and depth, and the figures used are supported by calculations and often rounded off to the nearest thousand dollars.

READERSHIP

This book is intended for those who are interested in appraising or understanding the projected performance or past results of companies, their operating units, and their projects, strategies, and undertakings, including financial analysts, investment analysts, accountants, bankers, general managers, finance officers, marketing and production managers, engineers, staff specialists, entrepreneurs, and all others who are involved in the formulation of business decisions or in the evaluation of the past performance of business firms or in the analysis of the projected performance of measures or projects.

DEVELOPMENT OF THIS BOOK

This work draws upon the diversified financial management experience of the author. He has worked in a broad spectrum of industries ranging from manufacturing, mining, forestry and agriculture, real estate development, and international trading, to investment banking, public accounting, management consulting, and project development.

The author's broad exposure has enabled him to look at the subject from different angles, generate new techniques, and demonstrate the applications of the techniques. The author had the opportunity of brainstorming and applying some of the materials in this book, with his colleagues in several firms.

Many of the techniques, applications, and concepts in this book have been presented to hundreds of participants in business seminars which the author has conducted. The suggestions of the participants have been considered in refining the presentations in this book.

ACKNOWLEDGMENTS

Mr. Joel G. Siegel, CPA, Ph.D, offered helpful suggestions in strengthening the substance of this book and in polishing the style. Mr. Gerald R. Galbo, of the Prentice Hall Business and Professional Publishing Division, encouraged the writing of this text. Jacqueline Roulette and her staff successfully harnessed the resources of Prentice Hall in producing this book. Ms. Sally Ann Bailey painstakingly handled the copyediting of the manuscript.

Vincent Morrow

DISTINCTIVE FEATURES OF THIS BOOK

The book is practical, innovative, and instructional. It is practical because it gives spreadsheet models for typical situations calling for decision making and because it offers the full range of alternative financial analysis approaches.

It is innovative because it reveals new techniques, identifies new situations where the existing techniques may be applied, and offers new concepts.

The publication is instructional because it structures ideas into a tree to show their relationships, relates one technique with another, contrasts and compares one tool with another, and brings out the shortcomings of existing techniques.

PRACTICAL

Analysis of Typical Situations Calling for Financial Analysis. All the applicable techniques are harnessed in attacking business problems. Income tax and inflation are brought into play. The analysis of a problem is done through the use of spreadsheets that may serve as models that may be adopted and modified to suit the particular situation or specific firms. The situations analyzed are:

- Make or buy decision (a cost reduction situation)
- Product deletion (product mix enhancement)
- Sales expansion
- Equipment acquisition, equipment replacement, and lease or buy
- Plant automation
- Loan source selection
- Debt leverage structuring

Illustration of Alternative Treatments. Different situations call for different techniques and the use of different alternatives. The book presents all the alternatives that may be considered in different areas. These areas and their alternative treatments are the following:

- Income statement format
    - Gross profit margin
    - Contribution margin
- Contribution margin format
    - Single contribution margin
    - Multitier contribution margin*
- Interest treatment
    - Loan-based interest
    - Resource-based interest*
- Finished goods inventory valuation
    - Direct costing
    - Absorption costing
- Accounts receivable and accounts payable valuation
    - Accounting valuation
    - Interest-adjusted valuation*
- Project terminal or residual value determination
    - Balance sheet method
    - Capitalized earnings method
- Working capital estimation
    - Balance sheet method
    - Root cost method*
- Past performance evaluation
    - For the total business unit
    - By strategy or measure*
- Project return measurement
    - Internal rate of return (IRR), IRR margin, IRR index
    - Net present value, profitability index
    - Accounting rate of return
    - Cash payoff
- Discount rate determination (for NPV calculation)
    - Weighted cost of capital
    - Cost of specific fund sources
- Cost of stockholders' equity
    - Based on book value of equity
    - Based on market value of equity
- Break-even point technique
    - Sales volume, selling price, unit variable cost or fixed cost
    - Profit, cash, or debt service
- Integrated ratio
    - Current operating assets not segregated
    - Current operating assets segregated*

---

* New technique introduced in the book.

- Historical return on investment
    Accounting rate of return (ARR)
    Residual income
- Accounting rate of return
    Stockholders' equity at book value
    Stockholders' equity at appraised value
    Stockholders' equity at market value
- Variance analysis
    Traditional methods
    Multivariance method*

INNOVATIVE

New Techniques.   The book introduces new techniques in areas where the traditional methods are flawed. The application of the new tools will make the results of analysis work more meaningful. The new techniques are:

- Multivariance method of variance analysis
- Integrated management performance ratio which distinguishes the resources currently used in the business from those which are not
- Root cost method of working capital calculation
- Comparable investment approach in laddering projects where the projects vary in their lives, investment requirements, and cash flow patterns

New Applications.   The publication applies existing tools in situations where the tools are traditionally not applied. These situations are in the following areas:

- Performance evaluation by strategy
- Performance evaluation using imputed or resource-based interest

New Concepts.   The book presents new concepts that will give better guidance in decision making. The new concepts introduced are the following:

- Sales expansion cost as neither fixed cost nor variable cost
- Multitier fixed cost and contribution margin instead of single-level fixed cost and contribution margin
- Interest-adjusted valuation of receivables and payables
- Variable and fixed components of working capital
- Break-even point analysis based on current benefit costs

- Inflation leverage, investors' or temporary leverage, and double leverage

INSTRUCTIONAL

Family Tree Structures.   A family tree arranges the members of a group according to a hierarchy and shows the relationship of one member to another. A tree facilitates the understanding by the readers of the overall relationships. Family tree structures are given for the following:

- Financial analysis techniques (Chap. 1, Ex. 1.1)
- Risk analysis methods (Chap. 7, Part III)
- Financial ratios (Chap. 18, Ex. 18.1)
- Types of risks (Chap. 7, Part I)

Relationships.   A technique is linked to a related technique or method which is more familiar to the reader or which has been previously discussed in the book. The techniques which are linked are:

- Internal rate of return and interest on deposit
- Net present value and IRR
- Certainty equivalent and risk-adjusted discount rate
- Probability analysis and sensitivity analysis
- Decision tree analysis and probability analysis
- Break-even point and crossover technique
- Return on stockholders' equity (ROSE) and residual income
- ROSE and interest spread

Contrasts and Comparisons.   The differences and similarities of related techniques are pointed out for distinction. Contrasts or comparisons are made for the following tools:

- Project cash flow and investors' cash flow
- Effect of net present value and of profitability index
- Conflicting results of IRR, NPV and PI
- IRR and NPV—use as return on investment tools and as risk analysis techniques
- Break-even point sales volume profit area—location in the chart of the profit area for contracting out measures and for inhouse servicing measures
- Front and side debt leverages
- Money leverage and inflation leverage
- Project leverage and corporate leverage

Limitations of Traditional Techniques. A chain is only as strong as its weakest link. The financial analysis chain is composed of the following links: assumptions, financial projections, financial statements, and the individual tools of financial analysis. The weaknesses of the following are discussed in order to give the readers the quality of the results expected of the financial analysis work.

- Assumptions and financial projections
- Financial or accounting statements
- Balance sheet method of working capital calculations
- Loan-based interest
- Weighted cost of capital in discount rate determination and in capital rationing
- Sensitivity analysis
- Probability analysis
- Financial statement ratios
- Traditional variance analysis methods

There is no existing publication on the subject that presents any of these areas in the same depth and breadth as this book does.

Vincent Morrow

Chapter 1

FINANCIAL ANALYSIS FOR DECISION MAKING

Financial analysis determines the character of the investment in a business firm and in its projects or measures, in terms of return and risk. The outcome of the analysis is used in selecting the measures to be implemented or in deciding on the support to be given to the enhancement or disposition of business units.

I. TIME ORIENTATION OF FINANCIAL ANALYSIS

Financial analysis looks at the projected or past performance. See the chart on the inside front cover.

PROJECTED PERFORMANCE (Division One of This Book)

Traditionally, the appraisal of measures is future oriented. The analysis is made to help prepare the most profitable design of promising alternatives and aid in selecting the most feasible option.

In a few cases, the analysis of a company is future oriented, as in connection with its possible sale.

PAST PERFORMANCE (Division Two)

Normally, the analysis of a company, its units, and its products is past oriented. The purpose of the review is to help determine the profitability in the past, usually in terms of the return on investment (ROI). The appraisal is utilized in (1) helping to decide on the future disposition or degree of

1

support to be accorded the company, its operating units, or its products or (2) taking corrective action so as to maximize the ROI.

Missing Link in the Financial Analysis Chain.   Usually, the past performance of *measures* is not evaluated, although the performance of a firm, its units, and its products are reviewed. This lack of evaluation constitutes one of the most severe limitations of current financial analysis practice for the following reasons. First, the absence of review and feedback makes it difficult for management to correct current measures or formulate new ones. Second, since measures constitute one of the major determinants of company performance, it is hard to review the performance of the company, its operating units, or its products without considering the effects of measures implemented in the past.

To help fill this gap in financial management practice, this book devotes two chapters to illustrate how the past performance of measures may be analyzed. See Chapter 24, Evaluating Performance by Strategy, and Chapter 25, Evaluating Performance with Resource-Based Interest.

II. THE ROUTE TO DECISION MAKING

Before any decision is made on any proposed measure, or on the disposition of a company, its units, or its products, the following steps should be taken:

1. Review the impact of the business strategies and their supporting measures on the projected performance or past results.
2. Formulate the underlying assumptions of the financial projections or study the accounting conventions used in the accounting statements.
3. Prepare the financial projections or review the accounting statements.
4. Select the appropriate techniques of analysis to be applied.
5. Analyze the performance.

The flow chart for these steps is on the inside front cover. The steps are briefly described next and examined in more detail in the chapters indicated below and in the chart.

REVIEW THE STRATEGY AND SUPPORTING
MEASURES (Chapters 2 and 16)

The top management formulates the general strategy to be followed by each operating unit. Based on the strategy, supporting measures are drawn up by the operating units and are implemented. The strategy and measures determine the intrinsic projected or past performance of the company and the measures themselves. For instance, a company pursuing a *grow* strategy will report a poor current performance, while a firm on a *harvest* strategy will reveal outstanding results.

This is so since a grow strategy, which is geared to capture market share, involves heavy spending on research and development (R&D), capital investment, and product introduction costs before adequate sales can be generated to recoup these costs and investments. Hence, while the firm is aggressively pursuing this strategy, its investments and costs are high in relation to its sales, thus depressing its ROI.

Thus, unless the underlying strategy is first ascertained and properly considered in the financial analysis work, the outcome of the analysis could be misleading in that it will give credit to units following a harvest strategy and penalize those on a grow strategy.

FORMULATE THE ASSUMPTIONS OR REVIEW THE ACCOUNTING CONVENTIONS (Chapters 2 and 16)

If the analysis is for the projected performance, the assumptions regarding future conditions are developed before the financial projections are constructed. If the analysis is for the past performance, accounting conventions are used in preparing the financial statements.

While the strategies and measures provide the structural framework for the performance, the underlying assumptions and accounting conventions give the final polish to the financial projections and financial statements.

The assumptions and conventions alter the profitability or cash flow of projects or corporations as revealed in the financial forecasts or accounting statements. For instance, the incorporation of inflation in the projected cash flow of a leveraged project raises the project's inflation-adjusted internal rate of return (IRR). The higher the inflation rate employed, the higher the IRR becomes. In like manner, the use of full or absorption costing in finished goods inventory valuation instead of the direct costing, raises the reported net profit during periods of rising inventory levels. This is so since portions of the fixed costs are taken out from the cost of sales in the income statement and shifted to the inventories in the balance sheet.

For this reason, the assumptions and conventions have to be sparingly reviewed. Otherwise, unrealistic projections or statements result.

PREPARE THE FINANCIAL PROJECTIONS OR REVIEW THE ACCOUNTING STATEMENTS (Chapters 3 and 17)

Even given the same assumptions and accounting conventions for the same company or measure, the employment of different methods of calculations or varying formats of financial statements can lead to different outcomes of financial analysis.

For example, the use of the gross profit form of income statement can give erroneous recommendations on the present products to be deleted. The accounting apportionment of overhead to the products may create the illusion that the elimination of a product takes away with it its allocated fixed costs.

The employment of the traditional contribution margin form, which shows the contribution to overhead of specific products, minimizes this limitation since the overhead is not allocated to the individual products. However, it does not fully solve the problem, since it normally categorizes all fixed costs as behaving in only one manner: that the total amount remains fixed within a given range of volume of business. In reality, there are several tiers of fixed cost—the share in the corporate fixed costs, the departmental fixed cost, and the product fixed cost. The deletion of a product takes out only the product fixed cost but usually leaves the other tiers intact.

SELECT THE APPROPRIATE TECHNIQUES OF ANALYSIS (Chapters 4 to 8, 18 to 23)

Given the financial projections and financial statements, the recommendations emanating from the use of the techniques of analysis can still vary, depending upon the specific tool used.

As an illustration, the use of IRR may give the higher ranking to one of two projects. But the project with the lower IRR may have the higher net present value (NPV) if it requires more investment or has a longer duration. In this case, therefore, the application of different techniques may lead to different recommendations. Hence the technique to be used should be selected by considering the objectives, condition, and requirements of the firm. For instance, a conservative firm with limited capital and desiring to maximize its rate of return may prefer to use the IRR. The IRR is the effective rate of return earned on the investment. On the other hand, a growth company which can easily raise financing may opt to employ NPV. This is so since under the NPV approach, projects showing a positive NPV are considered desirable. A project has a positive NPV if its IRR is higher than the cost of capital.

ANALYZE THE PERFORMANCE (Chapters 9 to 15, 24 and 25)

The employment of the same tools based on the same financial projections or accounting statements may still show different outcomes if the tools are applied differently. For example, the use of return on stockholders' equity

(ROSE), or accounting rate of return (ARR) based on the book value of the stockholders' equity may indicate an attractive ROI, probably leading to a decision to support the unit with the infusion of additional financing. This could be a misleading decision if the book value of land and buildings are much lower than the present market values. The utilization of ARR based on book value of stockholders' equity as adjusted upward for the current appraised values of the properties will be much lower and thus may lead to a different decision which may be to dispose the unit.

III. THE TECHNIQUES OF ANALYSIS

FINANCIAL ANALYSIS TREE (Exhibit 1.1)

Exhibit 1.1 presents the financial analysis tree. The tree traces the interrelationships of the techniques of financial analysis to each other, to their roots in the assumptions and accounting conventions, and ultimately to the proposed projects or existing business units where they are applied.

Basis of Financial Statements.   The foundation of the financial analysis tree is composed of the assumptions and accounting conventions. These serve as the basis of the financial statements—the financial projections and the accounting statements. Any change in the assumptions or conventions may also change the financial statements and the outcomes of the financial analysis.

Sets of Statements.   Certain techniques of financial analysis, as the internal rate of return, may use only one set of financial statements. However, sensitivity and probability analysis always require two or more sets since they measure the variability of possible performance.

What is Measured.   The techniques gauge the cost, the return or the risk of projects or firms. The return is the profit or what the owners expect to get in excess of their capital. The risk is the chance that the expected results may not realize.

Purpose of the Study.   The measures of cost, return or risk are used as a basis in (1) deciding on new projects or proposals or (2) judging the past performance of a company and its units. Financial analysis used for the first-named purpose is usually called decision analysis; the one employed for the second purpose is past performance evaluation or simply performance evaluation.

Techniques of Financial Analysis.   Certain tools may be used to measure the return in some applications and risk in others. For instance, the internal rate of return, if calculated from only one set of financial projections, and used in isolation, gauges the return on investment. However, the IRR can be used to measure risk in three ways. First, if it is related to the cost of money, it indicates the relative safety of the firm from risk. The safety is the buffer which is the excess of the IRR over the cost of money.

Second, if IRR is used in sensitivity analysis, the technique indicates how far the IRR might swing under varying conditions. Third, if the IRR is employed in probability analysis, the analysis gives the degree of variability from the most probable estimate of the IRR (the mean).

Number of Proposals or Business Units Where Applied. Generally, the techniques of analysis may be applied either to one or several proposed projects or business units. For instance, the accounting rate of return may be calculated either for only one company or for several firms. If done for several, the return of each is compared with those of the others.

However, there are two exceptions to this. The crossover point technique, whether used alone or in conjunction with either sensitivity or probability analysis, is usually utilized on two proposals. The crossover point cannot be calculated for only one or for more than two proposals.

The other exception is the variance analysis. It is used for only one company or division at a time. Although it may be calculated for more than one business unit, usually the variances of one unit are not compared with those of the others.

Type of Proposal or Business Unit Where Applied. Many of the techniques were designed to measure the overall performance or risk of a company—which includes revenues and returns. Hence these tools are considered as suited for revenue-producing projects. These techniques are the net present value, the internal rate of return, residual income, accounting rate of return, break-even point, variance analysis, and debt/equity ratio.

However, two tools—the present value of cost and the crossover point—are intended to gauge only certain portions of a company's operations. These portions may be cost centers but are not profit centers, as they do not generate revenues.

DISCOUNTED CASH FLOW METHODS (Chapters 4–6)

These methods exploit the concept of compound interest. The principal methods are the internal rate of return and the net present value. The IRR is the compound interest rate which equalizes the present value of the returns with the present value of the investments. The NPV is the excess of the discounted value of the returns over the discounted value of the investment.

The derivatives of the IRR are the IRR margin and the IRR index. The IRR margin is the excess of the IRR over the cost of money, while the index is the IRR divided by the cost of money.

The derivative of the NPV is the discounted return/investment ratio (DRIR), which is commonly known as the profitability index (PI). The DRIR is the ratio of the discounted value of the returns to the discounted value of the investment. Another present value technique is the present value of cost. This is used in projects which do not generate identifiable revenues.

NPV.   The NPV is influenced by the innate IRR of the project, the discount rate or money cost, the size of investment, and the effective project life. Two projects with the same natural project life may have different effective lives if they vary in their return patterns. The one which pays out some of the returns during the early years has shorter effective life than does the one which gives out all the returns at the end of its natural life.

The discount rate used in calculating the NPV may be risk–free or risk–adjusted. The former rate represents the cost of money if the projected cash flow can be received with certainty. The latter incorporates a premium to compensate for the probability that the actual cash flow may deviate from the projections.

Comparable Investment Approach.   Since the IRR is but one of the determinants of the NPV, and since the DRIR and the IRR adjust for the investment size while the NPV does not, the IRR, NPV, and the DRIR may result in conflicting project rankings. This is likely in a situation where the projects being ranked differ in their cash flow characteristics in terms of project life, return pattern, and investment. The application of the comparable investment approach makes these characteristics of the projects comparable, thereby eliminating the conflicting results of the IRR, NPV, and DRIR.

RISK ANALYSIS METHODS

There are five popular methods of risk analysis: sensitivity, probability, decision tree, crossover point, and break-even point.

Sensitivity (Chapter 7).   Sensitivity analysis pertains to the evaluation of the projected performance of a project or company under varying conditions. In sensitivity analysis, varying assumptions are made for the sensitive or critical areas which will materially affect the cash-generating ability or profitability of a firm.

Different sets of assumptions are prepared, each set being used as the basis of constructing the financial projections. The following are some of the critical areas in many projects: sales volume, selling price, and unit costs. Analysis is conducted on the outcome of each set of projections.

Probability Analysis (Chapter 7).   This technique assigns probability factors to the results of the sensitivity analysis under varying assumptions. A weighted average or mean is calculated for all the values under varying assumptions, as adjusted for the probability factors. The variability of each value from the mean is computed in order to arrive at the *standard deviation*. The standard deviation in turn is used as the basis in estimating the *coefficient of deviation* which serves as the index of the project risk.

While the standard deviation or variation measures the deviations from the mean, of both the favorable (upside) and unfavorable (downside) values, the *semivariance* considers the deviations from the mean of only the unfavorable values.

The risk estimated from the probability analysis may be used to reduce the value of the future stream of cash flows. The risk-adjusted cash flow is called *certainty equivalent*.

Decision Tree Analysis (Chapter 7).   This is a specialized application of probability analysis. Decision trees are used where decisions on a project are to be made in several stages and where the later decisions are influenced by the outcomes of the earlier decisions as well as by the intervening events which are beyond the control of management.

Crossover Point (Chapter 7).   Crossover point analysis is used in determining the business volume, interest rate, or similar variable wherein one alternative becomes as good as the other. For instance, it may be employed in ascertaining the cost of money wherein the present value of the acquisition and operating costs of one type of equipment just equals that of the other.

Break-even Point (Chapter 8).   Break-even point (BEP) analysis is used for projects which generate revenues. The traditional BEP is the level of business where the total revenues just equal the total expenses. This may be called the profit BEP sales volume. However, instead of sales volume as the variable, others may be used, such as selling price, raw material usage rate, average wage rate, or interest rate.

A variation of the profit BEP sales volume is the cash BEP sales volume. This refers to the sales volume at which the project will just break even in cash transactions. Another modification is the debt service BEP. This is the sales volume at which a project will generate just enough cash to service the loans. In either case, the sales volume may be substituted by selling price or other critical factor as named in the preceding paragraph.

FINANCIAL RATIOS

A ratio determines the relationship of two figures in an accounting statement. It is used to help determine what happened in the past. In some cases, it is utilized to appraise proposed short-term measures.

Families of Ratios (Chapter 18).   There are five families of financial statement ratios—each covering a business function. The business functions and the covering ratios are (1) mobilization of financing function, covered by the financing structure or debt/equity ratios; (2) investment of the financing in resources, asset allocation ratios; (3) generation of sales through the use of the resources, asset utilization ratios; (4) control of the operations so as to maximize the profit resulting from the sales, sales profitability ratios; and (5) determination of the effectiveness of the total operations, return on investment ratios.

Integrated Management Performance Ratios (Chapter 18). They reveal the total picture of operational and financial management efficiency. A new integrated ratio which is introduced in Chapter 18 ties together the key ratio in each of the five families.

Return on Investment Ratios (Chapter 19). These relate the profit to the stockholders' equity or capital. The most common return on investment (ROI) technique is the return on the stockholders' equity ratio (ROSE), also known as the accounting rate of return (ARR). An alternative to the ROSE is the residual income (RI). The ROSE is internally generated, is expressed in percentage, and is calculated without including the cost of the capital provided by stockholders. On the other hand, the RI uses an external interest rate in imputing the cost of capital, and is denominated in terms of dollars. For as long as there is profit, the ARR is positive. On the other hand, although there is a profit, if it is not enough to cover the cost of capital, the RI becomes negative.

Financing Structure Ratios (Chapter 20). These help in determining the various levels of profitability and risk associated with different levels of debt in relation to equity. If the return on the total investment in a firm is higher than the cost of debt, the use of leverage transfers the differential to the equity holders, thus upping their yield. However, the use of debt also increases the fixed cash outlay for the periodic interest payments and loan principal amortizations, thereby magnifying the risk.

The effects of debt leverage on the profit are analyzed in Chapter 15.

Asset Distribution or Allocation Ratios (Chapter 21). These indicate the portion of the total company funds which are used in (1) productive assets which revolve several times a year, as receivables and inventories; (2) assets which are tied down in operations for several years as land, buildings, and equipment; and (3) those which are not used at all in the current operations—which are the nonoperating assets. For firms in the same industry, those which concentrate their resources on the first type of assets are normally more flexible and profitable, while those which are bogged down by the assets in the third classification show lower returns.

Asset Turnover or Utilization Ratios (Chapter 21). These ratios monitor the effects of the short-term measures as well as point out areas for further improvement. For instance, a turnover ratio can monitor the accounts receivable collection period. A collection period much longer than the authorized sales payment terms may mean that the collection department is lax or the credit department had been too aggressive. On the other hand, a collection period shorter than the sales payment terms may indicate that the prompt payment discount offered by the firm might be too high so as to induce the buyers to avail of the discount.

Sales Profitability Ratios (Chapter 21). These indicate the efficiency of management not only in controlling the costs but also in enhancing the sales. The prevalent concept is that a high net profit in relation to sales is due to the management's success in controlling the costs, that is, cutting down the expense as a percentage of sales. However, the jump in sales without proportionate rise in total cost also creates the same effect.

Statistical Ratios (Chapter 21). All the ratios discussed earlier are de-rived from the financial statement figures. Operating managers may be more concerned with the ratios which incorporate nonfinancial informa-tion. Examples of such ratios are the average cost per labor hour worked, number of units sold per salesperson, and department store sales per square foot of store space.

VARIANCE ANALYSIS

The objective of variance analysis is to pinpoint possible problem areas which may require corrective action. The analysis does this by seeking out the causes of the differences between the actual performance and the budget, or between the actual performance of the last period and that of the prior period. Most of the variances in the net profit arise from devia-tions in the revenues and in the variable costs—in other words, in the contribution margin.

Variance analysis may be employed in manufacturing, marketing, and other types of operations.

Present Techniques (Chapter 22). The four most popular variance analysis methods utilized in reviewing sales and variable costs are (1) the multi-product analysis method, (2) the one-product method that uses a revised budget, (3) the one-product method without the revised budget that uses the sales volume as the basis in calculating the quantity variance of the inputs, and (4) the one-product method without the revised budget that uses the input volume as the basis in estimating the quantity variance of the inputs.

Some of the four tools can pinpoint the effect on the profit, of changes in the sales volume, selling price, and cost per unit of the inputs. However, not one of them can quantify the impact on the profit, of changes in the total industry sales, market share, and operating efficiencies as measured by the usage rate of inputs or labor productivity. This functional deficiency hampers the effectiveness of the current techniques since a windfall rise in industry sales that is not due to management performance could hide even a precipitous fall in market share or deterioration in operating efficiencies, both of which are within management control. In other words, management could still be credited for a basically poor performance, which is camouflaged by an extraneous beneficial event.

New Multivariance Technique (Chapter 23).   A fifth method of variance analysis, which is termed multivariance, is introduced in this book. This new tool seeks to estimate that portion of the deviation in the contribution margin which emanates from changes in each of the following: industry sales, market share, product mix, unit price, sales commission rate, usage rate, raw material wastage, labor productivity, wage rate, interest rate, inflation rate, collection period of receivables, carrying periods of inventories, payment terms of trade suppliers, and practically any other factor, the limitation being set not by the technique itself but by the practical use of the variance which can be derived.

IV. ANALYZING PROJECTED PERFORMANCE

The following measures indicate the types of proposals which need financial analysis prior to the formulation of decision:

Short-term Measures
- *Cost reduction measure*—a proposal to shift to in-house production of goods currently purchased outside, where the production facilities are already available
- *Product mix enhancement*—review of existing products for possibly eliminating submarginal lines
- *Sales expansion measures*—through more aggressive advertising, higher sales commission rates, reduced prices, and longer sales credit terms

Long-term Capital Projects
- *Equipment acquisition*—where the alternatives have different acquisition and annual operating cost and varying useful lives
- *Equipment acquisition financing*—where the options are to buy or to lease
- *Plant automation*—where the automation affects the sales revenues and production costs

Financing Arrangements
- *Loan source selection*—where the sources offer varying amounts, terms, and conditions
- *Debt/equity structuring for long-term projects*—where different types of leverages are available

COST REDUCTION MEASURES (Chapter 9)

This is illustrated by a proposed shift from contracting out a job to in-house manufacturing where the production facilities are already in place.

Rationale.   The logic behind the proposal is that the added fixed cost can be more than recouped by the total decremental variable cost. If the volume is known, the decision is made on the basis of the differential cost—the total cost to make less the total cost to buy. If the total cost to make is lower, then the measure is desirable.

Investment and Return.   The proposal does not call for capital investment. However, it requires additional working capital in the form of raw material and goods in process inventories which are not applicable if the firm continues to buy the finished products.

There are two ways of evaluating the return on this additional investment. One is to follow a path similar to that taken by the residual income approach. An interest cost is imputed on the additional working capital and is added to the variable cost. (Under the traditional RI approach, the interest is imputed not on the assets, but on the amount of the stockholders' equity.) The decision is then based on the differential cost including this interest.

The other method uses the accounting rate of return approach. The additional working capital represents the investment or capital. The total beneficial differential cost represents the savings from the measure or the effective profit. The effective profit is then related to the investment to arrive at the ARR. If the ARR is higher than the cost of financing to be obtained to carry the working capital, then the measure is desirable.

Risk.   Since a firm taking this measure adds on to its fixed cost, it magnifies its risk. A firm loses to the extent that this fixed cost cannot be fully recovered by the savings on the variable cost. The management can be guided on the extent of this risk if the crossover volume is determined—the volume at which the fixed cost just equals the savings on the total variable cost. If the volume goes beyond this crossover point, then the proposal may be justified.

PRODUCT MIX ENHANCEMENT MEASURE (Chapter 10)

A firm enhances its product mix in two major ways: by introducing promising products and by eliminating existing submarginal lines. This book illustrates a case of product review for possible deletion where the firm does not spend much on advertising and product development and where the decision can be implemented in a few months. (Sales expansion measures which require heavy spending on sales expansion costs are treated separately.)

Rationale.   Products are deleted if the revenues derived from them are not enough to cover their costs. Theoretically, the decision is based on the contribution margin (revenues less variable costs). For as long as a product generates a contribution margin, the product should be maintained.

Tiers of Fixed Cost.   The elimination of a product might wipe out certain fixed costs. There are at least two levels of fixed costs: departmental and corporate fixed costs. Bigger organizations might have three or more levels.

The deletion of a product will reduce the fixed costs at the departmental level but normally will not cut down the corporate overhead. Because of this, the use of the traditional contribution margin form of income statement will not suffice, since it lumps into one group all the fixed costs. This format should be modified to show two or more levels of fixed costs and correspondingly two or more contribution margin lines. Decisions can be based on the contribution to departmental overhead in case of a minor product in that department or contribution to corporate overhead in case of a major or sole product.

Investments and Return.   All products require working capital. Product departments need buildings and equipment. There are two ways of establishing the return on these investments. One is by using the ARR. This relates the investment to the appropriate contribution margin. For instance, for a minor product in a department, its contribution to the departmental overhead is related to the working capital.

Another method also uses the ARR as just described. However, the interest on the working capital is imputed first and then added to the variable cost. Interest on the buildings and equipment is added to the departmental fixed cost. Products with negative ARR after imputing the interest have to be deleted.

Risk.   The risk factor is analyzed through the use of the break-even point sales volume (BEPSV) before and after the proposed product deletion. The elimination of submarginal products in this case increases the contribution to overhead as a percentage of sales, reduces the fixed costs, and as a consequence, reduces the BEPSV as a percentage of expected sales.

SALES EXPANSION MEASURE (Chapter 11)

Sales expansion measures are designed to increase market share in established markets. The measures intend to achieve this through more aggressive advertising, higher commission rates, reduced prices, or longer terms of sales.

Rationale.   Sales expansion measures are implemented on the premise that the variable margin (sales less variable costs) of the incremental sales volume is expected to be higher than the additional sales expansion costs. In other words, additional profit can be generated by the incremental sales.

Sales Expansion Costs.   The appraisal of this type of measure has to recognize sales expansion costs as a new type of cost. The traditional cost classifications in relation to the behavior of sales volume are the fixed and variable costs. However, sales expansion costs do not fit into the mold of either variable or fixed costs since sales expansion costs, if used to improve sales in the present market territories, usually rise faster than sales. Hence sales expansion cost has to be added as the third cost classification.

Investment and Return.   The rise in sales pushes up the working capital but at different rates, depending upon the specific type of measure. Normally, the inventories and receivables increase proportionately with the sales. However, if the sales payment terms are lengthened in order to attract sales, then the receivables rise much faster than the sales.

A simple way of determining the profitability of a measure is by imputing interest on the working capital and then comparing the incremental variable margin with the additional sales expansion costs.

Risk.   The BEPSV analysis cannot be used as it is premised on only two types of costs—fixed costs and variable costs. The crossover point method is applied instead. Two types of crossover points may be determined—the crossover sales volume and crossover sales expansion cost. The former is the volume which should be attained after fully spending the budgeted sales expansion costs so that the contribution margin remains the same—either with or without the sales expansion measure. The lower is the crossover volume from the target or budgeted volume, the lower is the attendant risk.

The crossover sales expansion cost is the maximum level of costs which may be spent in order to attain the targeted volume, so that the contribution to overhead remains the same as without the measure. The higher is the crossover cost from the budgeted cost, the less risky is the measure.

EQUIPMENT ACQUISITION (Chapter 12)

Equipment acquisition decisions may involve the choice among equipment with (1) different acquisition and operating costs, (2) different operating lives, and (3) different acquisition financing schemes. The decision may also cover the timing of the replacement of existing units.

Rationale. The selection of an equipment with a higher acquisition cost is made on the basis that the reduced operating costs and the tax reductions arising from the depreciation, both as adjusted for inflation and time value of money, can more than offset the incremental acquisition cost.

Investment and Return. Since an equipment acquisition involves no return or profit but only investments and operating costs, the IRR and NPV cannot be applied. Instead, the present value of cost is used. The acquisition and operating costs as adjusted for inflation are discounted to a certain point in time—usually the proposed date of equipment acquisition. The decision is then made based on the total of the present value of the acquisition and operating costs for each alternative.

Risk. Risk arises from unforeseen fluctuations in interest rate, sales volume, and other factors. The *interest rate risk* may be brought out by calculating the crossover interest rate to be used in discounting the cash flows to the year of equipment acquisition. The crossover rate is the interest rate at which the total present value of all costs of one piece of equipment equals that of an alternative.

PLANT AUTOMATION (Chapter 13)

The hypothetical case of plant automation which is illustrated is assumed to improve the product quality, thus enabling the firm to push up both the sales volume and the selling price. The project also speeds up the production process, thereby cutting down on the inventories.

Rationale. Automation projects require substantial one-time charges in the form of equipment, computer systems, personnel retraining and recruitment, and separation pay to those to be phased out. Furthermore, the annual fixed costs may be raised.

A firm commits to these costs with the expectation of a trade-off in the form of higher revenues, reduced inventories, and lower variable costs per unit. These are expected to raise the contribution margin substantially. Thus the incremental margin should be able to cover up for the increased fixed costs and still generate a fair return on the substantial one-time investments.

Return. Both the IRR and NPV are utilized in evaluating the return. The interest on the investment is not imputed. The use of the NPV automatically incorporates the interest cost.

Debt Leverage. The IRR and NPV are calculated for the project as a whole, irrespective of the financing to be arranged. If the effective cost of debt is lower than the project IRR, the use of debt will enhance both the IRR and NPV. The calculation of the effective cost of debt is discussed in the next section, Loan Source Selection, while the use of leverage is examined in the second succeeding section, Debt Leverage.

Risk.   The heavy additional investment plus the conversion of part of the variable costs to fixed costs intensifies the risk. Hence the project can be justified only if the sales volume or selling prices can be raised, or when the cost of money is relatively low. Because of the uncertain volume, selling price and interest cost, sensitivity analysis is required. Varying sets of assumptions regarding these factors may form the basis of financial projections. IRR and NPV are calculated for each set of projections.

LOAN SOURCE SELECTION (Chapter 14)

Loans available from different sources vary in their amounts, patterns of payment of principal (as payable in equal installments or in lump sum at the end of the term), nominal interest rate, frequency of compounding of interest, timing of payment of interest, upfront fees, and amount and interest earnings on required reserve funds.

Concept of Effective Cost.   Normally, the effective interest cost is the compound interest rate which equalizes the present value of the receipts from the loan with the total payments related to the loan.

This definition is similar to that of the IRR. The only difference is that the IRR pertains to investment, and the effective interest cost, to the loan. The procedure of calculating the effective interest rate is the same as that of the IRR.

Blended Rate.   In some cases, the effective loan proceeds, pattern of payments, or loan duration from alternative loan sources vary. These cases require the ascertainment of the effective cost of the other sources of financing which will supplement the loan with the smaller amount or with earlier repayment. The purpose of this is to bring the total amount available and duration of financing comparable. What should be compared then is the effective cost of the bigger loan or loan with longer duration, and the blended rate of the smaller loan or loan with shorter duration, and its auxiliary financing source. This method of approach is similar to the one used in appraising projects with different investments or durations where the IRR or NPV is employed.

DEBT LEVERAGE (Chapter 15)

Debt leverage is the exploitation of borrowed funds to jack up the residual investors' IRR.

Rationale.   A firm takes on debt for its project if the project's intrinsic IRR (or IRR if the project is without debt) is higher than the effective cost of debt. By exploiting debt, the excess of the project IRR over the cost of the debt pertaining to that portion of total project financing which is carried by the debt is transferred from the lenders to the investors. This value which is transferred enables the investors to earn more than what they could if there were no debt.

Return. The extent to which the investors' IRR can be pushed up depends upon the initial amount of debt in relation to the investors' equity, the duration of the debt, the interest spread, and rate of inflation. The higher or longer are these factors, the higher the investors' IRR becomes. The effect of different types of leverages can be obtained by calculating the IRR of the investors for each type of leverage and comparing this IRR to the IRR of the project if without debt.

Risk. The incurrence of debt raises a firm's cash commitments—for the interest and principal amortization. Risk is created to the extent that the firm may not be able to meet its committed fixed cash outlays. Thus, while debt enhances the investors' IRR, it also magnifies the risk of the project.

Either the sensitivity or the debt service break-even point sales volume (DSBEPSV) may be used in assessing the risk. If the latter is used, the DSBEPSV is related to the expected sales under the worst case scenario. A project is considered to be taking a reasonable risk if there is a very good chance that the expected sales will be higher than the DSBEPSV.

V. ANALYZING PAST PERFORMANCE

Traditionally, the performance evaluation of a firm is made without taking into account the results of the different measures it pursued during the year. Considering that the measures influence the performance of a firm, the appraisal of a firm should be conducted in conjunction with that of its measures. How to conduct such a review is demonstrated in two types of situations:

1. Where a hypothetical firm undertook several short-term and long-term measures. The traditional *loan-based interest* is employed in the net profit and ROI analysis.
2. Where the firm pursued short-term measures only. The *resource-based interest* technique is applied in the gross profit analysis.

EVALUATING THE PERFORMANCE WITH LOAN-BASED INTEREST (Chapter 24)

Current Practice. The conventional evaluation of a company aggregates the results of all measures pursued during the past year. The outcome is the *net* effect of different types of measures implemented in the past:

undertakings which just barely started and those which are already on full steam and measures which require substantial resources but still generate losses and those with minimal investment but produce substantial cash flow. This practice of lumping together the results of all the measures makes it difficult to evaluate the past results, since the results cannot be compared with any of the following: the projected performance of measures as estimated before the implementation, the prior period performance, and the past performance of the other business units.

Illustrated New Application.   The book demonstrates how the results may be segregated by measure and how the results may be compared with prior year performance. The resources and financing of the firm as well as the revenues and costs were assigned to the key projects or measures.

In comparing the results of last year with those of the prior year, the following criteria were used: only the costs and resources which pertain to the generation of the revenues for last year were included in the comparison. Following this guideline, the following were excluded: costs pertaining to earlier years (as settlement of past legal cases), costs benefiting future years (such as R&D), and assets that were not used in past years' operations such as buildings under construction.

The use of these guidelines in the hypothetical case indicated an enhancement in the performance of the firm, whereas the traditional project evaluation techniques reveal otherwise.

EVALUATING THE PERFORMANCE WITH RESOURCE-BASED INTEREST (Chapter 25)

Current Practice.   Under present accounting conventions, the interest charged in the financial statement is based on the loans and is separated from the operating expenses. Furthermore, receivables and payables are carried at accounting values and not at their true economic worth.

This practice gives rise to several flaws in evaluating the past results of a company, its measures, and its managers. For example, the users of the resources are not directly charged for interest on the loan or equity financing used to carry said resources. Hence, there is no direct incentive to maximize the utilization of the resources.

Furthermore, the income reported for a given period may be distorted if there are changes in the beginning and ending balances of receivables and payables. For instance, a company which started a year with $1,000,000 in receivables with average of two months' collection period, and ended the year with no balance, is unduly penalized for the equivalent interest on a $1,000,000 loan for two months.

Illustrated New Application.   The book illustrates an approach which imputes interest on the resources used and charges the interest to the related revenue or cost. Thus, interest on receivables is charged to sales revenues, and interest on merchandise inventories is charged to the cost of sales. The method also discounts the values of receivables and payables to their economic values.

The illustration reveals that the measure to reduce prices but shorten the terms of payments enhanced the profit. On the other hand, the traditional practice shows a deterioration in the results.

EXHIBIT 1.1:
Financial Analysis Tree

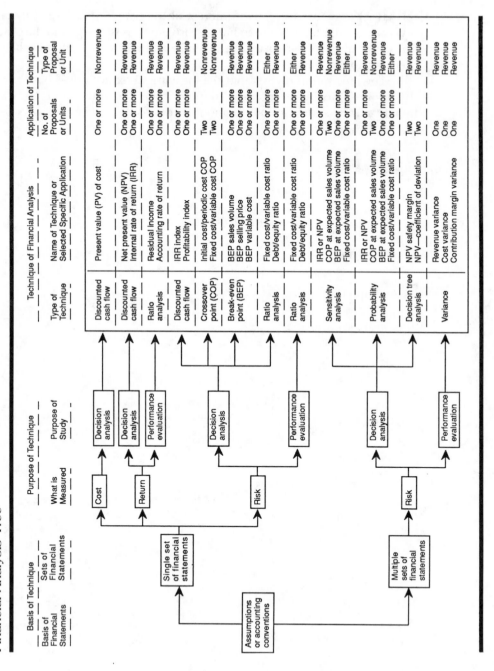

Chapter 2

DETERMINANTS OF PROJECTED PERFORMANCE

This chapter examines how business strategies, the implementing measures, and the underlying assumptions of the financial projections define the future performance of a firm and its specific projects as indicated in the projections.

The strategy pursued by a firm influences the selection of the types of implementing measures. The measures, in turn, help to determine the performance of the firm.

A firm may pursue any of the following general strategies: *grow*, *maintain*, and *harvest*. A grow strategy seeks to capture market share or build up the sales. The functional types of measures necessary to accomplish this objective include new product development and market development. These measures call for substantial investment but do not generate cash at once. Hence, firms on grow strategy show low or negative profit and cash flow.

While strategies and measures determine the innate projected performance of a firm and its projects, the assumptions define the degree of feasibility as revealed in the financial projections. For instance, a rosy assumption on market growth rate will help create an attractive projected cash flow.

I. STRATEGIES AS DETERMINANTS OF PROJECTED PERFORMANCE

The strategies formulated by the corporate or general management dictate the types of measures which may be undertaken and hence indirectly influence the projected performance of a firm.

21

TYPES OF GENERAL STRATEGIES

The alternative general directions which may be taken by the mother organization or main stockholders for a business unit are (1) for the business unit to *grow* or build up its market share or sales, (2) for the business unit just to *maintain* its level of operations or hold its market share, and (3) for the parent organization or stockholders to *harvest* or milk the business unit, that is, get as much cash as possible even at the cost of sacrificing the long-term viability of the unit.

Grow Strategy. Under this portfolio strategy, the corporate mother encourages its division to gain market share. To achieve this, the firm has to concentrate on one or more of the following types of measures: development of new products, expansion to new market areas, or saturation of existing markets. Massive advertising and promotions may be used to saturate present market territories.

Since the cash flow generated by the profit from normal operations is not sufficient to meet the requirements for R&D, market expansion, product introductions, more working capital, and additional physical facilities, the parent has to infuse cash into the division. The cash is supplied either from the other divisions operating under the harvest strategy, which is discussed here, or from the corporate funds coming from new borrowings or additional capital stock issues.

Maintain Strategy. A division in a maintain or hold strategy is allowed to grow but at a gradual phase, along with the growth in the industry. A minimal growth may be allowed.

The advertising budget is just at a level which will allow the company to maintain its market share or sales. The R&D expenditure is just enough to develop new products to replenish the products to be phased out. Capacity acquisition is just adequate to restore the capacity which was weakened by the aging of the buildings and equipment.

Since the measures on product R&D, market development, and capacity acquisition are moderate, the cash required by these projects is usually taken care of by the cash flow created by the operations. The excess cash generation is usually moderate.

Harvest Strategy. A company operating under this strategy skimps on its budget for physical facilities, R&D, product introduction, sales expansion, work force training, public and community relations, and preventive maintenance. It attempts to generate more cash by not putting up new plants, postponing major rehabilitations, and minimizing the acquisition of new equipment. Leasing of physical assets is favored over outright acquisition.

The working capital assets are converted to cash by reducing the inventories even at the risk of interrupting the production schedules or making the products unavailable to customers sometimes. The company reduces the sales credit terms but endeavors to stretch out the purchase payment period. The combined effects of these steps is to extract from the business a substantial cash flow which is then diverted to the units on a grow strategy or is returned to the stockholders.

EFFECTS OF STRATEGY ON INVESTMENT

Firms on a grow strategy have more investments in working capital and physical facilities in relation to sales than do those on maintain or harvest strategy.

Working Capital.   Companies striving to capture market share require more investments in accounts receivable and finished goods inventory if these are used as instruments in expanding sales. For instance, a firm may decide to attract more customers by prolonging its sales credit terms or lowering its sales credit standards. In either way, the collection period is lengthened and the outstanding balance of the receivables in relation to the monthly sales is raised.

A company may also attempt to push its sales by making its products more visible to the customers. Hence it may carry more inventories in its sales outlets. This of course stretches the inventory period and builds up the stocks on hand in relation to the sales.

On the other hand, a firm on a harvest strategy may purposely constrict its sales by cutting short the sales credit terms. This action reduces the collection period and the outstanding balance of the receivables.

Physical Facilities.   A growing business acquires new physical facilities. Initially, these facilities are not fully utilized.

Firms on grow strategy may also have assets which are not currently used in operations but are being held for future use. These include sites for possible expansion, buildings under construction, and major equipment in the process of installation. On the other hand, firms following a harvest strategy scrimp on their capital expenditures and fully utilize the old facilities. They have minimal idle sites or plants.

EFFECTS OF STRATEGY ON SHORT-TERM PROFITABILITY

Firms pursuing a grow strategy incur heavy expenditures on the following: R&D, advertising and promotions, human resource development, and preventive maintenance. Since these expenditures are incurred before any sales result, but are treated outright as expenses, firms with a grow strategy usually incur losses or report minimal profit.

Due to their high investments in both working capital and physical facilities in relation to their sales, growing companies pay more interest per sales dollar than firms on a harvest strategy. Because their physical facilities are newer but have lower utilization rates, growing companies have higher depreciation costs in relation to their sales. This heavy interest and depreciation burden further depresses their current profitability.

On the other hand, firms on a harvest strategy spend minimal amounts on these types of expenditures. They are relying on the products which have been accepted for several years and hence can continue the sale even with minimal market support. Thus, businesses with this strategy normally report handsome profits.

II. MEASURES AS DETERMINANTS OF PROJECTED PERFORMANCE

For an operating unit, planning starts with the portfolio strategy formulated by the corporate mother or by the general management. This strategy is then translated into undertakings for implementation. The types of measures selected help define the future performance of the specific measures. The measures in turn impact on the performance of the firm.

TYPES OF MEASURES BY FUNCTION

A measure, undertaking or project is pursued with the expectation that it will help a firm enhance the return on its capital or provide for growth. Before the measure is approved for implementation, it is subjected to a screening process which includes financial analysis. The financial analysis techniques help the management appraise the profitability, investment requirement, and risk of the project.

This part of the chapter categorizes the different types of undertakings so that, even without applying any technique of analysis, the management can be guided on the relative profitability, investment, and risk of certain types of projects. This chapter will facilitate the drawing up of a preliminary list of possible projects for verification.

Ladder of Functions (Exhibit 2.1).   A proposed measure will boost future performance by providing for long-term growth or short-term profitability. Growth measures involve generating new products through R&D and product introductions, and acquiring the capacity to produce and market. Profitability measures concentrate on improving the production, marketing, and collection functions. Each performance measure initiates or upgrades the activities in one of the business functions in Exhibit 2.1. The measures and functions are characterized by the following features:

1. The implementation of each measure or the performance of each function requires cash infusion.

2. Although each measure or function requires cash infusion, only the last function—collection—generates cash.
3. Therefore, for the measure to be financially successful, it is necessary that the measure itself, as well as all the succeeding functions down to collection, has to be successful—otherwise the cash infusion cannot be recovered.

Performance measures possess varying degrees of risk, investments or costs, time requirements, capital recovery periods, and profit and growth potentials.

Types of Measures Required by Each Strategy. The different strategies call for varying levels of requirements of the different types of measures:

	Level of need for the measure		
Type of measure by function per Exh. 2.1	*Grow strategy*	*Maintain strategy*	*Harvest strategy*
R & D	High	Normal	Low
Product introduction	High	Normal	Low
Sales expansion	High	Normal	Low
Capacity acquisition	High	Normal	Low
Operations	Normal	Normal	Normal

RISK, TIME, AND CAPITAL (Exhibits 2.1 and 2.2)

The higher in the ladder in Exhibit 2.1 is the location of the function which the measure intends to initiate or improve, the longer is the time required before the measure can produce a series of results which will ultimately yield a cash return. Hence, the higher in the ladder is the location of the function,

1. The higher is the required dollar investment or cost.
2. The higher is the level of the risk exposure.

Thus, the measures which can produce cash (1) within the shortest time, (2) with the least dollar cost, and (3) with the least risk are those intended to improve the efficiency of the activities in the last step of the ladder—namely, the collection function. An effort to enhance collection can accelerate the cash flow in a day or week. The success of the collection function does not depend on any other function.

The risk exposure, investment and time requirements, and capital recovery periods of measures for different functions are compared in Exhibit 2.2

RISK (Exhibits 2.1 and 2.2)

By themselves, measures involving product research have the lowest achievability factor. This, even without considering the failure rate involved in the subsequent activities—from product development to collection. Out of so many research projects, only a handful may be considered for possible product development. Achieving a technological breakthrough for a product which is considered practical is quite difficult.

The further down the totem pole is the location of the function which the measure intends to initiate or improve, the higher is the success factor. Thus,

1. The achievability factor for product introduction is better than that of R&D. At least at this stage, there is already a tangible product on hand. However, the measure has still to pass another difficult test—that of consumer acceptance.
2. At the sale expansion stage, the customers have already accepted the product. However the unknown is that the competition may react in such a way as to create a ruinous competition—at least temporarily.
3. For plant expansion or capacity acquisition, the demand for the product has been established already. The only major impediment for success is the subsequent slowdown in the sales that will result in the substantial underutilization of the capacity.

In general, product R&D and market development efforts as a group are more subject to volatile environmental forces and hence are more difficult to control than are the capacity acquisition and operating measures. The first group is basically market oriented and hence subject to the vicissitudes of external forces which are mainly beyond the control of management—the customers and competition. On the other hand, the success of the latter group depends more on attaining efficiency in internal operations and hence is easier to manage.

INVESTMENT AND COST (Exhibits 2.1 and 2.2)

The higher in the ladder is the business function (1) the larger is the investment required to put the measure to a successful completion (that is, until collection), (2) the lower is the liquidation value of the assets resulting from the performance of the function, and (3) the less is the degree of correlation between (a) the cost incurred during the year for the performance of the function and (b) the sales during the year generated by the function.

Cumulative Investments and Costs. A firm undertaking product R&D should be prepared to budget not only for this specific activity, but for subsequent functions—product introduction, sales expansion, capacity acquisition, and operation. Compared with a measure which just concentrates on improving the efficiency of the operations, the cumulative investment in the activity started by an R&D measure is much higher.

Tangible Asset and Liquidation Value.   An unsuccessful R&D effort, product introduction, or sales expansion activity does not result in tangible assets which can yield even a partial recovery of the investment. R&D expenditures and product introduction losses have no financial value rather than as tax-deductible items.

However, the further down the line is the location of the business function, the higher is the realizable value of the assets resulting from the efforts.

Thus, the capacity acquisition function yields physical facilities which can have some sale value. However, they can be liquidated only after deducting a deep discount. One step down the ladder, the manufacturing operations yield finished goods inventories, which give a higher percentage of recovery. The receivables resulting from the selling operations are the easiest and fastest to sell and with the least loss in case of a liquidation. Of course, cash, the result of the last function (collection) is the most liquid asset.

Cost in Relation to Sales Revenues.   The higher is the location of the function in the totem pole, the lower is the degree of correlation between the current year cost of doing that function and the current year sales induced by the performance of that function.

R&D.   If the products being developed this year are not going to be introduced or commercially sold during the same year, then there is no relationship between the development cost and the sales for the current year. There is even no direct relationship between the R&D costs this year and the sales for any subsequent period if the R&D does not result in any sale at all.

New Product Introduction.   While there is a relationship between the cost incurred this year of introducing a new product and the sales this year, the cost is usually out of proportion to the current year revenues of the product. The cost of introducing a product is heaviest during the initial year; on the other hand, the sale during this period is usually the weakest.

Sales Expansion.   The cost of saturating the markets or expanding to new territories has a closer relevance to the current year sales than the product introduction cost has to present year sales of the new products.

Capacity Acquisition.   The fixed costs or capacity costs do not fluctuate in direct relation to the sales. However, since the capacity has been established to correspond to the expected sales, there is some relationship between the two.

VARIABLE OPERATING COSTS.   Variable operating costs such as raw materials, wages of production workers, and sales commissions are directly keyed to the production or sales and hence change in direct proportion to the volume of business. Since these costs vary directly with the fluctuation in production or sales, they are called variable costs. As the operating costs are directly variable, theoretically they do not involve any risk; they can be eliminated if there are no sales.

TIME

The lower is the location in the ladder of the function for which a performance measure is intended, the shorter is the time elapsed between the implementation of the measure and the generation of the cash resulting from the measure. Thus, while it takes a few days or weeks for a collection measure to generate cash, it usually takes years for a product research program to yield cash. Since the latter activity requires so much gestation time, it is naturally subject to a higher probability of delays.

However, while the product development and introduction efforts possess a time disadvantage in producing cash, they also have a distinct advantage: if these projects and the succeeding functions prove successful, the benefits accruing to the sponsoring company resulting from the measure can last for years.

CAPITAL RECOVERY

Since the product development and introduction programs and their succeeding activities require more investment and time to generate cash than operating measures do, they are invariably subject to higher interest charges during the intervening periods. They are also more susceptible to incur costs in excess of the original budget, since cost overrun is a function of time and investment.

Because of their massive capital requirement including accumulated interest and cost overruns, long gestation periods, and prolonged exposure to risks, the product development and introduction undertakings also possess the longest capital recovery periods.

PROFIT, GROWTH, AND RISK

Considering all the factors discussed in the preceding sections, the performance measures are generally characterized as follows:

1. *Short-term measures.* These initiate or improve the activities in the last tiers of the ladder of functions. They usually yield more immediate profit and cash flow and have faster capital recovery. They are also exposed to less risk. However, they do not induce much growth.
2. *Long-term projects.* These are geared toward the activities up in the ladder. They normally encourage growth and create the potential for sizable profit over the long run. However, they also invite more risk.

III. ASSUMPTIONS AS DETERMINANTS OF PROJECTED PERFORMANCE

The specifications of the measures to be implemented, as well as the environment where the firm operates, determines the intrinsic performance in the future of the measures, and as a result, of the firm. However, the financial projections, which is used as the basis of the analysis, is influenced not only by the innate performance of the measures, but also by the assumptions used in preparing the financial projections. Examples of the assumptions are the selling prices, sales volumes, unit costs of production, and inflation and income tax rates.

By way of comparison, the reported past results of a company are molded not only by the innate performance of a business unit, but also by the accounting conventions applied in preparing the financial statements.

For many projects, some of the key factors which may substantially affect the profitability of a project are the project size covered, the gestation period and operating life, the working capital investment, the debt leverage, inflation, sales revenues and operating costs, income tax, and terminal return or residual value.

PROJECT SIZE

A decision on the size of a capacity acquisition project makes a big difference in the financial projections. There are two alternative assumptions which may be made. First, the financial projections are only for the rated capacity that is planned to be initially installed.

An alternative is to run the projections not only for the initial capacity, but also for subsequent expansions. The latter will attain a higher level of economies of scale in that the total fixed costs will not rise as fast as the sales. Hence, the financial projections based on the latter will be much more attractive.

GESTATION PERIOD AND OPERATING LIFE

The gestation period and project life help determine the performance of a project. A long gestation period lengthens the preoperating period, delays the project opening, postpones the capital recovery time, and hence lowers the internal rate of return (IRR) and net present value (NPV).

On the other hand, a longer operating life lengthens the stream of net cash receipts and hence adds to the IRR and NPV.

WORKING CAPITAL INVESTMENT

The investment requirements vary depending upon the assumptions used regarding the collection, inventory, and payment periods. The doubling of collection and inventory periods, say, from two to four months will correspondingly double the cost of money used to carry receivables and inventories. On the other hand, the investment requirement can also be made to appear lower by extending the assumed payment period of the trade payables.

Opportunity Cost of Money.   If the additional receivables and inventories are financed by loans, the cost of money is the actual interest paid to the lenders. If these working capital items are funded by new capital contributions, the cost is the income which the stockholders will forgo due to the shift of their funds from other investment media to the company. If the incremental receivables and inventories are financed by the proceeds from the liquidation of short-term investments of the company, the cost of money is the forfeited income from these investments. In the first case, the cost of money is the actual payment to the lender. In the other two cases, the cost of money is the opportunity cost which is equivalent to the forgone income due to the investment in the working capital.

The opportunity cost is calculated by multiplying the funds involved by the earnings rate which is forgone and by the time duration of the required funding.

Working Capital Calculations.   Two different ways of calculating the working capital—the traditional balance sheet method and the new root cost method—are illustrated in Chapter 10, Analyzing Product Mix Enhancement Measures. The estimation of working capital is also shown in Chapter 9, Analyzing Cost Reduction Measures; Chapter 11, Analyzing Sales Expansion Measures; and Chapter 13, Analyzing Plant Automation Projects.

DEBT LEVERAGE

The extent of debt leverage assumed for a project helps to define the profitability of the project. Where the intrinsic IRR of a project is higher than the effective cost of loans, the higher is the leverage used, the higher is the IRR on the residual investors' capital.

The intrinsic project IRR is the IRR of the project itself, irrespective of the financing structure. IRR is discussed in Chapter 4. The determination of the effective cost of loan is illustrated in Chapter 14, Analyzing Loan Source Selections. The ways of maximizing the investors' IRR through the use of leverage is examined in Chapter 15, Analyzing Debt/Equity Structures.

INFLATION

Inflation changes the results of the analysis based on the financial projections. If all the components of cash streams—receipts and payments—increase with the general inflation rate, and if the project is without debt, the profitability of a project in terms of its IRR is not affected by inflation—except by income tax and any profit-based bonus or management fees. How the IRR is influenced by inflation if the cash revenues rise faster than the costs, or if the project uses debt leverage, is discussed next. The effect of inflation on income tax is discussed in a separate section.

Different Inflation Rates for Revenues and for Costs. For certain projects, it may be justifiable to assume that revenues increase at a slightly higher rate than the costs. As goodwill is gradually built up, the project will be able to increase the prices at a rate higher than the general inflation. On the other hand, as the management gains experience and attains economies of scale, the costs should rise at a rate lower than the inflation. In this case, the inflation-adjusted IRR rises due to the differential in the inflation rate.

The inflation-adjusted IRR is based on the cash flow which employs varying price levels for different periods due to inflation but subsequently deflated to take into account the lower purchasing power. For the procedures of adjusting the cash flow for inflation and then deflating it, see Chapter 12, Analyzing Equipment Acquisitions.

Inflation and Debt Leverage. If the project is partly financed by loans, part of the cash flow streams—the scheduled payments to the lenders—remain untouched by inflation. In case of fixed interest rate loans, the payments on both principal and interest are isolated from inflation. In case of variable rate borrowings, the principal component is free from inflation, while the interest portion may ride with inflation. Since all the cash receipts, but only some of the payments, rise with inflation, the net effect is that the revenue receipts rise at a rate faster than the weighted average rate of the payments consisting of the operating costs and loan amortization. Because of the inflation gap between the receipts and payments, the IRR of the equity holders is enhanced by inflation. This effect is similar to the one cited in the previous case where revenues rise at a rate faster than the costs.

The higher the rate of inflation, or the higher the loan leverage, the higher is the rise in the owners' IRR due to inflation.

Debt leverage and inflation are examined more closely in Chapter 15, Analyzing Debt/Equity Structures.

SALES REVENUES AND OPERATING COSTS

The sales revenue forecast for a company or measure is dependent upon the expected sales volume and selling prices. The quantity, in turn, is based upon the total industry sales and market share. A slight difference in the assumed annual industry sales—say, $11 billion instead of $10 billion— or a slight difference in the estimated market share—say, 11% instead of 10%—could convert a seemingly marginal project into an attractive proposition.

The selling price is another critical variable factor. Although the prices which are current at the time the studies are prepared are well established, the prices which will be prevailing, say, two years down the road when the project becomes operational could easily vary by 5% of the estimates. A 5% price variation can substantially benefit any project. The matter can become more complicated if the project will make a product which is not identical to any product currently in the market. Differences in the specifications could result in a significant price premium or discount relative to the current product.

The production and marketing costs for an expansion program would be relatively easier to calculate and hence subject to less variations in estimates than for a project which will make and sell a new product. In the former, the present unit costs and usage rates can be based on existing operations. However, for the manufacture of a new product, the usage rates have to be calculated by engineers based on laboratory experiments but unconfirmed by commercial runs.

INCOME TAX

The federal income tax rate is 34%. To be added to this is the state income tax which is imposed by many states; the rate varies from state to state. Hence, it is common that the combined income tax easily eats up 40% of the taxable income. Hence, the assumptions regarding the income tax play a significant role in shaping the projected income.

The most important assumption about income tax is the rate in the future. A logical basis is the current rate. However, the rate could change. The effective rate may also vary from the nominal rate due to inflation and the accounting methods used in the financial projections.

Inflation. Inflation silently increases the tax rate in two ways. First, while costs and revenues go up, or the buying power of the dollar goes down, the tax benefit arising from depreciation as a tax-deductible item is held constant. In other words, since the tax benefits are spread out into the future, by the time the benefits are used, the economic value of the benefit by then is lower than that of today due to the declining value of the dollar brought about by inflation. This aspect is discussed further in Chapter 12, Analyzing Equipment Acquisitions, and Chapter 15, Analyzing Debt/Equity Structures.

Second, inflation bloats the nominal dollar value of assets other than receivables. When these assets are disposed of even if no economic or real profit is realized, that is, at the same buying power at which they were purchased, a paper profit arises. The paper profit is taxable. This, in effect, increases the effective tax rate. This is described in detail in Chapter 15.

Combined Effect of Income Tax and Inflation—Illustration. Assume that the projected net profit and tax of a firm for two years are as shown in the first two columns here:

	Year 1 at Year 1 prices	Year 2 at Year 2 prices	Year 2 at Year 1 prices
Net profit	$1,000,000	$1,040,000	$990,476
Tax – 40%	400,000	416,000	396,190
Profit after tax	600,000	624,000	594,286
Loss in value of receivables			476,190
Actual profit			$118,096

Assume further that the inflation during year 2 is anticipated to be 5%, and that the balance of receivables at current prices (before adjustment for inflation) is $10,000,000 as of the end of year 1 and year 2.

With the information given, the after-tax, inflation-adjusted profit in year 2 at year 1 price level is not $624,000 but is $118,096, as calculated in the third column of the table. The net profit, tax, and profit after tax figures in the third column were arrived at by dividing the "Year 2 at Year 2 prices" column, by 1.05, which is 1 plus the inflation rate. The 1.05 is the inflator.

If the face value of the receivables is assumed to remain constant at $10,000,000 in spite of the 5% inflation, the value as of the end of year 2, based on year 1 price level, is $10,000,000 divided by 1.05, or $9,523,810. This indicates that the real loss in value is $476,190. However, this is not deductible for income tax purposes.

Accounting Method for Depreciation. The choice of accounting methods to be used in the financial projections influence the timing of the income tax and hence of the time-adjusted cash flow. For instance, the use of accelerated depreciation in lieu of a straight-line method moves the tax-deductible depreciation charges and hence the tax benefits, closer to the beginning of the project life, thereby raising the IRR. This aspect is discussed in Chapter 12, Analyzing Equipment Acquisitions.

TERMINAL RETURN OR RESIDUAL VALUE

This represents the value of the project as of the last year covered by the financial projections. (The other concepts of terminal return or residual value as well as the balance sheet approach mentioned here are presented in Chapter 4, Internal Rate of Return.) There are two methods used in determining the value: the balance sheet method and the capitalized earnings approach. The results of either method is subject to wide fluctuations depending upon the assumptions used in the calculations.

Balance Sheet Approach.   The balance sheet method assumes the sale of the project as of the end of the planning horizon. The terminal value in this case is equivalent to the balance sheet values of the assets as adjusted, minus the values of the liabilities. The land, buildings, and equipment are the major items subject to value adjustments. The adjustment for the land is required since the land will be worth more than when it was acquired. First, the inflation builds up the value of the land. Second, the growing demand for basically a constant supply pushes up the prices of land.

If the gap between the projected date of land acquisition and the last year to be covered by the projections is, say, 15 years, a 5% assumed annual increase in the value of land will more than double the acquisition cost. However, if a 10% yearly rate were used, the land will more than quadruple in value. A change from 5% to 10% represents a significant change in the financial projections for projects with sizable real estate investments.

Capitalized Earnings Approach.   This uses an earnings rate which is assumed to be desired by possible investors who may be interested in taking over the project at the end of the projection period. This approach capitalizes the projected net income for the last year covered by the financial projections, say, the tenth operating year. For instance, if the projected income for the tenth year is $1,200,000, and the investors desire to earn a 12% return, then the capitalized value of the return is $10,000,000, which is $1,200,000 divided by 12%. In other words, if outside investors pay $10,000,000 for the project by then, they will realize a 12% annual return. From this capitalized value is deducted the projected balance of liabilities as of the same date.

The residual value in this case is dependent upon the assumed capitalization rate. If the rate were lowered to, say, 8%, the residual value rises to $15,000,000.

EXHIBIT 2.1:
Ladder of Functions

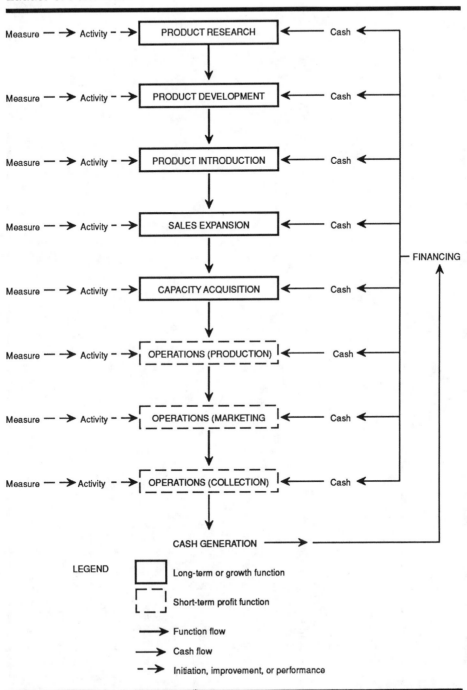

EXHIBIT 2.2:
Measures as Related to the Ladder of Functions—Effects on Investment, Return, and Risk

| | **FUNCTION** | | | |
Factor	*Research and development*	*Market development*	*Capacity acquisition*	*Operations*
Risk				
Type of risk	Product breakthrough	Consumer and industry reaction	Facilities underutilization (capacity risk)	Production interruptions Noncollection
Risk orientation	Market	Market	Internal	Internal
Investment and cost				
Resulting tangible asset	None	None	Physical facilities	Inventories Receivables
Fallback position	4	3	2	1
Type of cost in relation to sale	Product development cost	Sales expansion cost	Fixed costs	Variable costs
Risk due to type of cost	4	3	2	1
Cumulative investment or cost	4	3	2	1
Time				
Cumulative up to collection	4	3	2	1
Probability of delays	4	3	2	1
Duration of benefit	1	2	3	4
Capital Recovery				
Interest cost	4	3	2	1
Probability of cost overruns	4	3	2	1
Capital recovery time	4	3	2	1
Profit/Growth/Risk Potentials				
Immediate profit potential	4	3	2	1
Growth potential	1	2	3	4
Profit size potential	1	2	3	4
Risk potential	4	3	2	1

Note on ranking: No. 1 = most favorable.

Chapter 3 _____

FINANCIAL PROJECTIONS AS BASIS OF ANALYSIS

The projections try to simulate the events which may occur and picture the outcomes of the consummated transactions. Since the forecasts are done before the transactions are effected, it is quite likely that the projected profitability and cash flow statements will deviate from the actual results.

Just as the historical statements try to summarize and present the results of the marketing, production, and financing operations, the financial forecasts attempt to correlate the results of any marketing, engineering, financing, and other studies.

The outcomes of financial projections are contingent upon the specifications of the projects or measures for which the projections are prepared and the assumptions used in the projections. The project specifications include the project size and duration. The assumptions cover the areas which have not been firmed up or which cannot be accurately foreseen. How the assumptions affect the financial projections has been discussed in Section III of Chapter 2.

The financial projections which have been formally adopted by a firm as a basis in evaluating performance are called budgets or targets.

I. NATURE OF FINANCIAL PROJECTIONS

COVERAGE OF FINANCIAL PROJECTIONS

If the financial projections are to be employed as the basis of analysis for deciding on a proposed measure, the projections are just for that measure. If the projections are for appraising the future performance of a firm, the projections are for the firm as a whole.

The degree of completeness of the financial projections required in the analysis depends upon the decision to be made. The evaluation of a make or buy decision concentrates on the cost to make and the cost to buy. This assumes that the choice of one over the other does not impact on the sales volume, selling price, collection period, payment terms for the inputs, and inventory levels.

On the other hand, the appraisal of a self-contained project which will develop and introduce a new product line and have its own manufacturing facilities, will require financial forecasts on the profitability, cash flow, working capital, and capital expenditures—similar to the one illustrated in this chapter.

COMPOSITION OF FINANCIAL PROJECTIONS

The financial forecasts used in decision analysis are usually composed of the following, wherever applicable: (1) statement of assumptions and basic data employed; (2) profitability statement, preferably in the contribution to overhead form; (3) cash flow or statement of expected sources and uses of cash; and in some cases (4) the projected balance sheet. These may be supported by the following: (1) calculation of the working capital required; (2) calculation of the long-term financing requirements for property, plant, and equipment and any R&D; (3) details of sales forecasts; (4) monthly production schedule; and (5) details of the production and other operating costs. These components are discussed in the remaining sections of this chapter.

INFLATION

The financial projections presented in Exhibits 3.2 to 3.6 have not considered inflation. If inflation were incorporated in the financial projections, the (1) tax benefits arising out of depreciation and operating costs, (2) net profit, (3) cash flow, and (4) internal rate of return and net present value will vary. The impact of inflation on the tax benefits is demonstrated in Chapter 12, Analyzing Equipment Acquisitions, while the effect of inflation on taxes, profit, cash flow, and IRR is illustrated in Chapter 15, Analyzing Debt–Equity Structures.

II. STATEMENT OF BASIC DATA AND ASSUMPTIONS

The gathering of the basic data and the formulation of the assumptions represent the first stage in the preparation of the financial projections. The assumptions clarify the foundation upon which the profitability and cash flow estimates are based. The formulation of the assumptions is highly subjective and hence requires sound professional and business judgment.

Illustrative Format (Exhibit 3.1). The purpose of the statement of basic data and assumptions is to give in summary form the following: (1) restatement of the results of the marketing, production, and financing study or assumptions for the items which have not been firmed up in such studies; (2) information from general environmental sources or assumptions if the desired information is not available; and (3) financial assumptions. An illustrative list of the items in the statement of basic data and assumptions used follows:

A. **General project data**
   1. Project size
   2. Gestation period
   3. Operating life

B. **Marketing study**
   1. Sales volume per month or year (in quantity)
   2. Selling price per unit
   3. Advertising and promotional budget
   4. Collection period of receivables
   5. Level of finished goods inventory
   6. Marketing organization and distribution channels

C. **Production study**
   1. Production schedule
   2. Levels of inventories—raw materials and goods in process
   3. Raw materials, labor, utilities, and other inputs—usage rate and cost per unit of material or other input
   4. Equipment— acquisition and operating costs
   5. Plant construction and schedule
   6. Terms of payment for the inputs, equipment, and plant

D. **Financing study**
   1. Type or form of financing to be used, debt leverage
   2. Initial or one-time costs as loan fees
   3. Periodic or monthly costs as interest and mortgage insurance premium

E. **General environmental data**
   1. Inflation rate
   2. Foreign exchange rate
   3. General wage rates

4. Tax rates
5. Capitalization rate

F. **Financial assumptions**
1. Disposition of excess cash
2. Working cash balance to be maintained

For certain items, even an exhaustive study may not be able to give a definite value which may be used directly in the projected profitability or cash flow statements. For instance, a comprehensive market study may give the likely range of annual sales two years hence, say, from 100,000 to 120,000 units. Given this range, an assumption may be made that the sales will be 110,000.

III. PROJECTED INCOME STATEMENT

The projected income statement presents for each month or year covered by the projection period, the revenues, costs, and profit.

Illustrative Format (Exhibit 3.2).   The exact form is dictated by the type of profitability measure or project for which the forecast is prepared. However, for many types of measures or projects, the form in Exhibit 3.2, as modified to suit the specifics of each case, may be used.

The illustrated projected income statement uses the contribution to overhead form. The statement is based on the basic data and assumptions given in Exhibit 3.1.

CLASSIFICATIONS OF COST

In evaluating the measures to enhance the viability of a product or an enterprise, the relevant data on costs are:

1. How much will the costs be if the sales or production volume fluctuates. Hence, the costs should be classified into variable costs and fixed costs.
2. How much will the costs be if the firm attempts to capture market share. Hence, the sales expansion costs should be identified.
3. What part of the costs will require cash outlay or commitment. Hence, the costs should be distinguished into cash and noncash or sunk cost as depreciation.

For certain types of decision analysis, it is necessary to classify all costs including interest and income tax, into variable, fixed costs, and sales expansion costs. This was done in Chapter 10, Analyzing Product Mix Enhancement Measures.

VARIABLE COSTS AND VARIABLE MARGIN

One of the key variables in the financial projections is the sales volume. Since the variable costs fluctuate in direct relation to the sales volume, the variable costs are segregated from the other costs, and are the first ones to be deducted from the sales. This treatment or presentation facilitates the application of risk analysis tools, namely, sensitivity analysis and break-even point. The break-even point analysis uses the variable margin. See Chapter 8, Break-even Point Analysis, for the use of variable margin in break-even point analysis.

The variable margin is also used directly in certain decision analysis, as in the evaluation of product deletion or introduction plans. See Chapter 10.

SALES EXPANSION COSTS

Sales expansion programs, like advertising or promotional programs, are used by management as instruments in introducing new products, invading new market territories, or expanding market share. The costs of these programs are neither variable costs nor fixed costs. The sales expansion costs do not vary directly in proportion to the changes in sales volume. In times when management is trying to capture market share, or introduce new products, the total sales expansion costs rise faster than the sales volume. Thus, as shown in Exhibit 3.2, the firm has to incur a $4,000,000 sales expansion cost in year 1 to establish its product in the market. The sales expansion cost represents 25% of the expected sales in the initial year. Once the product is established, the firm projects its advertising and promotional expenses to be less than 10% of the sales.

The identification of the sales expansion costs is needed in evaluating projects to push the sales volume or raise the selling price. This is demonstrated in Chapter 11, Analyzing Sales Expansion Measures. Sales expansion costs are also described in Chapter 17, Financial Statements as Basis of Evaluation.

TWO-TIER CONTRIBUTION TO OVERHEAD

The income statement in Exhibit 3.2 has one line or level of contribution to overhead. The review of product lines for possible deletion, sales expansion, or introduction, may call for a two-tier contribution to overhead. This is illustrated in Chapter 10, Analyzing Product Mix Enhancement Measures.

A two-tier contribution to overhead presentation requires that the overhead or fixed costs be separated into two levels: at the product departmental level and at the corporate level. The costs at the departmental level are concerned with specific products or product lines. The elimination of all the products handled by a department will wipe out the departmental fixed costs.

ALTERNATIVE INTEREST APPROACHES

In the traditional historical income statement, the interest expense shown is the amount paid or accrued on the loans. In the projected income statement, there are three ways of treating interest: (1) do not show the interest expense, (2) use the loan-based interest approach, and (3) utilize the resource-based interest method. Each of these is described in the paragraphs that follow.

Do Not Show the Interest.   The purpose of this approach is to determine the true viability of the measure or project by itself. This approach is used if the IRR or NPV is calculated for the total financing. This is the method used in Exhibit 3.2 and also in Chapter 12, Analyzing Equipment Acquisitions, and Chapter 13, Analyzing Plant Automation Projects.

Use the Loan-based Interest Approach.   The interest expense is calculated on the expected loans. This follows the treatment in the traditional income statement. This type of treatment is used in (1) preparing operating budgets, (2) calculating the income tax, and (3) preparing financial projections for decision analysis in certain cases.

This approach is used for decision analysis when two conditions are met: first, when the project is a self-contained package with its own financing sources, and second, when the loan sources had been firmed up or when the financing represents a proposal by itself. Hence this approach was used in Chapter 15, Analyzing Debt–Equity Structures. When this approach is applied, the internal rate of return (IRR) or net present value (NPV) which is calculated pertains to the stockholders' equity and not to the total financing for the project.

The degree of project viability will be altered if interest is incorporated since different debt-to-equity ratios, different debt instruments, or different loan sources result in different amounts of interest. The impact of debt-to-equity ratio on the profitability of a project is explained in Chapter 15, Analyzing Debt–Equity Structures.

This procedure is usually used in evaluating past performance. See Chapter 24, Evaluating Performance by Strategy.

Use the Resource-based Interest Approach.   An interest expense is imputed on the entire net financing requirement of the measure, based on the cost of money to the firm. The net financing requirement is the total of the working capital and properties less the trade payables.

This method is usually utilized for short-term measures, since the IRR and NPV are not applicable. This is the procedure employed in Chapter 9, Analyzing Cost Reduction Measures; Chapter 10, Analyzing Product Mix Enhancement Measures; and Chapter 11, Analyzing Sales Expansion Measures.

This approach may also be applied in evaluating past results. See Chapter 25, Evaluating Performance with Resource-Based Interest.

Interest-related Techniques. In addition to the two interest approaches described, the other interest-related tools used in appraising *future* performance are the NPV and IRR.

The other techniques used in evaluating *past* results are the residual income method and intercompany charge procedure. These are examined in Chapter 25. Residual income is illustrated in Chapter 19, Return on Investment Ratios.

INCOME TAX

The presentation of the costs in the profitability statement may not necessarily follow the rules of the Internal Revenue Service (IRS) in calculating income tax. Hence, there may be some differences in the projected income tax liability. If the expected differences are material, a special profitability statement, conforming to the IRS rules, may be prepared just to be used as a basis in calculating the income tax.

Depreciation Methods and Income Tax. The income tax calculated in Exhibit 3.2 is only a rough estimate as it is based on the straight-line method. Although this may be acceptable in preparing financial projections covering several years, the amount may be different if the rules of the Internal Revenue Services regarding the calculation of depreciation are strictly followed.

Inventory Valuation Methods and Income Tax. The valuation of finished goods inventory in Exhibit 3.3, while useful for decision analysis purposes, does not conform with the IRS regulations. Under the IRS regulations, the inventory should cover all costs which include depreciation. However, to simplify the calculations, depreciation was disregarded.

Financial projections for long-term decision analysis should use the direct costing method in valuing the inventory. This method is discussed in detail in Chapter 17, Financial Statements as Basis of Analysis.

Income Tax as Fixed Cost or Variable Cost. In Exhibit 3.2, the income tax was presented as only one line item. In certain types of decision analysis work, it is advisable to calculate the income tax or income tax reduction, at different levels. For instance, in Exhibit 10.2 the income tax was deducted from (1) the contribution to departmental overhead, and (2) the departmental overhead. This type of treatment facilitates the analysis of the implications of deleting or introducing products and abandoning or establishing product departments.

IV. PROJECTED CASH FLOW

Working Capital Requirements (Exhibit 3.3).   Before the cash flow may be prepared, the working capital requirements have to be estimated. Several profitability measures, such as product introduction and deletion, sales expansion, and subcontracting of production operations, impact on working capital. Exhibit 3.3 presents a simplified way of calculating the working capital. Chapter 10, Analyzing Product Mix Enhancement Measures, examines the traditional balance sheet method of calculating working capital and introduces a new approach, which is called in this book the root cost method.

The working capital requirements in Exhibit 3.3 were determined by referring to the relevant income statement figures in Exhibit 3.2 and the working capital duration period given in the statement of assumptions in Exhibit 3.1. Thus, the accounts receivable is based on the sales for one month. Similarly, the raw materials inventory is based on the raw materials usage for two months.

Project Cash Flow (Exhibit 3.4).   Two cash flow statements may be prepared: (1) one from the viewpoint of the project itself, called the project cash flow, and (2) the other from the viewpoint of the equity investors, called the investors' cash flow. Exhibit 3.4 demonstrates a typical project cash flow.

Year 1 is the first year of operations. Year 0 is the preoperating period. Year -1 is the year before year 0. The years as indicated are not necessarily calendar years nor do they represent the company's fiscal year. However, they are usually for a 12-month period each.

Cash Requirements.   For the preoperating period, and during the operating period when the project is expected to incur operating cash deficits, the scheduled payments or cash requirements have to be calculated ahead of the sources or receipts of cash. The cash requirements for land, buildings, and equipment were taken from the statement of basic data and assumptions in Exhibit 3.1.

The working capital requirement of $1,970,000 in year 0 is the amount of financing to be provided before the end of year 0 for the buildup of working capital the following year, as calculated in Exhibit 3.3. The

$1,870,000 cash requirement in year 1 is the required increase in the year 2 working capital.

In year 1, the project is expected to incur a cash deficit from operations of $1,508,000. This amount was taken from Exhibit 3.2.

Since the cash flow is constructed based on a 100% equity financing, all the expected cash payments have to be met by investors.

Cash Returns. For years 2 and 3, the project is scheduled to generate an annual operating cash flow of $1,804,000.

In the same manner that all cash requirements during the first three years will be met by the investors, all the cash generation for the last two years—represented by the operating cash flow and the terminal value—will go to the investors, which is the corporate sponsor in this case.

Terminal Value. The company may decide to keep and operate the project beyond year 3, or it may sell the project as of the end of year 3. In either case, a terminal value has to be calculated—to represent the earnings beyond year 3 if the project were to be kept by the project sponsor or to represent the selling price if it were to be disposed of.

If the project continues to generate $1,804,000 a year, and if the buyer requires, say, a 16% return on its investment, the value of the project as of the end of year 3 is $11,275,000. This is the amount which can earn 16% or $1,804,000 a year. The $11,275,000 is the terminal or residual value, and the 16% is the capitalization rate. Terminal value was examined in detail in the prior chapter.

Investors' Cash Flow (Exhibit 3.5). The investors' cash flow, as illustrated in Exhibit 3.5, reflects the equity holders' investments in, and returns from, the project. The investments and returns are shown in the project and investors' cash flows as follows:

	Presentation in the	
	Project cash flow	*Investors' cash flow*
Investments	As receipt	As payment
Returns	As payment	As receipt

The purpose of the investors' cash flow is to show the expected pattern of the investors' financial relationship to the project. This pattern or stream of cash flow is used in determining the internal rate of return and the net present value of the project from the viewpoint of the investors. Thus, based on the net cash flow in Exhibit 3.5, the IRR is 16% and the NPV is $1,388,000 at 10% discount rate. For the illustrations on the use of investors' cash flow, see Chapter 15, Analyzing Debt/Equity Structures. The procedures for estimating the IRR and the NPV are explained in Chapters 4 and 5.

V. ESTIMATED BALANCE SHEET

Illustrative Format (Exhibit 3.6).   The estimated balance sheet presents the expected value of the assets in the future. The assets are in the form of working capital and property, plant, and equipment. The balance sheet also shows how the assets are financed, that is, how much is funded by the stockholders and what portion is financed by the lenders. The assets and financing are shown as of the date when the first investment is scheduled to be made and at the end of every 12-month period thereafter, and as of the start of operations and at the end of every 12-month period thereafter. In the illustration in Exhibit 3.6, the first investment is assumed to be made as of the end of year -1.

The estimated balance sheet has two purposes. First, it serves as a basis in evaluating the financial condition of the business in the future. For instance, the expected current and debt-to-equity ratios may be calculated based on the estimated balance sheet. Second, the balance sheet ties in the income statement with the project cash flow.

Working Capital.   The net working capital of $1,970,000 shown as of the end of year 0 in Exhibit 3.6 represents the cash to be provided in order to fund the buildup of the working capital up to the end of year 1. The amount is calculated in Exhibit 3.3 under the year 1 column.

Property, Plant, and Equipment.   The land, buildings, and equipment shown in the estimated balance sheet were taken from the project cash flow.

Stockholders' Equity.   The annual contributions by the stockholders and the regular dividends indicated in the balance sheet were brought forward from the project and investors' cash flow statement. The net profit which was added to the stockholders' equity in the balance sheet were carried from the projected income statement.

VI. SALES FORECASTING

Sales forecasting means predicting the future level of sales—in terms of quantity, value, or both. Although the procedures described here are for sales forecasting for an existing operation, many of the techniques are equally applicable to new projects or new products.

SALES FORECASTING APPROACHES (Exhibit 3.7)

Many of the approaches in sales forecasting may be categorized into three groups: the economy-based method, the company sales–based procedure, and the salespeople-based approach. While the applications of the forecasting procedures outlined here vary from industry to industry and from company to company, the description presents the general pattern of sales forecasting methods.

The size of a firm may affect the type of forecasting method used. For instance, a large, multinational firm, may resort to all three approaches described. Its forecasting method definitely includes a study of the world economy. On the other hand, a very small company may completely disregard the economy-based forecast. In between these two extremes, a medium-sized, regional firm may dispense with the world economic forecast, and start with the U.S. demographic and economic study.

Economy-based Approach.   For bigger firms the sales forecast is made after studying the possible future developments in the world economy, the national economy and demography, and the industry in which the firm is operating. The industrial, financial, and other economic developments in the major European, Asian, and other nations impact on the U.S. foreign trade and capital markets. The U.S. population growth, social behavior, and consumer preferences influence the gross national product. Both the U.S. demography and the world and U.S. economies determine the demand for the products of an industry.

Statistical projection methods are used to forecast the total industry sales, based on historical figures. (Selected projection methods are illustrated in the next part of this chapter.) The projected industry sales resulting from the application of the projection methods are then adjusted to consider the anticipated developments in the demography and economy. A reasonable market share percentage is applied on the total industry sales forecast in order to estimate the company sales in the future.

Sales-based Approach.   A more direct and more simple approach uses the historical company sales as the main basis in determining the future sales. Statistical or arithmetical projection methods are used to project the sales. Adjustments are made in the resulting projected sales in order to take into account the effects of the factors which influenced the past sales and which will impact on the future sales. For instance, an unusually hot summer which drove up the sales of air conditioners or ice cream should not be expected to recur every year.

This sales-based approach, if used in conjunction with the salespeople-based method described next, is advisable for small firms which cannot afford to hire economists or avail themselves of the services of economic forecasting firms.

Salespeople-based Approach.   Instead of using historical figures, the sales forecast may be based directly on present information as adjusted for the expectations of the sales force as to the sales which may be realized in the future. Under this approach, all the salespeople are asked for their opinion as to the sales which each of them will be able to effect.

Integrated Approach. The ideal procedure for the big companies is to use all the three methods described. Since the results of each will be different from those of the others, it is necessary to reconcile the figures and arrive at a sound forecast.

After approval by the management, the sales forecast becomes the sales budget. The budget serves as a basis in drawing up the sales quota for each sales department and salesperson.

MATHEMATICAL FORECASTING METHODS

Statistical and arithmetical sales projection methods have been devised to project historical trends into the future. The following are illustrated in this chapter:

1. Algebraic or statistical straight-line method
2. Algebraic or statistical geometric curve or semilog method
3. Arithmetical centered moving average method

The first two methods are employed in projecting either industry demand or company sales. The last method is used mainly in forecasting company sales.

Several other types of statistical sales forecasting methods are covered in books on business statistics.

STATISTICAL OR ALGEBRAIC STRAIGHT-LINE METHOD (Exhibit 3.8)

This method is so called because it uses a statistical or algebraic formula and the resulting projected demand or sales represents a straight line if plotted in an ordinary chart. In other words, the annual or monthly increase in the projected figure is uniform. Since the value of the periodic increase is constant, the periodic increase as a percentage of the value for the preceding year is declining.

Historical demand or sales may be projected into the future by using the table in Exhibit 3.8. The data in the table are filled in, according to the following sequence:

Year (column 1). This is for both the past years used as the base period for preparing the projections (years 1 to 12) and the future years for which the demand or sales are to be projected (years 13 to 22).

X *(column 2).* This is the number assigned to both the past and future years. The number of past years (12) in this case is even. The number of past years is divided by 2. The first six years (years 1 to 6) are assigned odd, negative (with minus sign) numbers, starting with -1 for year 6 (the co-midyear), then -3 for year 5, and so on up to -11 for year 1. The last six past years are assigned odd, positive numbers, starting with 1 for year 7, (the other co-midyear), then 3 for year 8, and so on up to 11 for year 12.

Each of the future years (years 13 to 22) are assigned a number which is actually a continuation of the numbering system for the last six past years (years 7 to 12). Thus, the first future year (year 13) is assigned 13.

If there were an odd number of past years, as 7, the values to be assigned could be as follows:

Year 1	-3	Year 5	1
Year 2	-2	Year 6	2
Year 3	-1	Year 7	3
Year 4	0		

X^2 *(column 3).* This is the square of the value in column 2. Thus, for year 1, -11 multiplied by itself is 121.

Y *or actual demand (column 4).* The actual or past demand or sales is placed in the table.

XY *(column 5).* The data in column 2 are multiplied by the figure in column 4.

Columns 3, 4, and 5. The sums of the values in these columns are obtained as they are used in the formulas described later.

bX *(column 6).* bX is the product of b and of X. X is already given in column 2. However, b is not yet known. Hence the value of b has to be derived, using the formula

$$b = \frac{\text{sum of } XY}{\text{sum of } X^2} = \frac{36{,}716}{572} = 64.2$$

where:

$$\text{Sum of } XY = \text{sum of column 5}$$

$$\text{Sum of } X^2 = \text{sum of column 3}$$

The value of bX is the product of (1) b, which has a value of 64.2 as derived; and (2) x whose value is shown in column 2.

Yc—*Projected Demand or Sales (column 7).* The value Yc is ascertained through the formula

$$Yc = a + bX$$

where

$$a = \frac{\text{sum of } Y \text{ (column 4)}}{n} = \frac{23{,}168}{12} = 1{,}931$$

n = number of past years used as the base of the projections

Thus the value of Yc for year 13 is 2,765. This is 1,931, which is a, plus bX, which is 834.

STATISTICAL GEOMETRIC CURVE METHOD
(Exhibit 3.9)

Under this method, the periodic increase in the projected demand or sales in terms of units or quantity is always increasing. However, the periodic increase as a percentage of the prior period's value is constant.

The projected demand under this method is normally bigger than the one under the algebraic straight-line method because of the compounding effect of the geometric curve method.

If the projected demand or sales under this method is plotted on an ordinary chart, the demand or sales will be represented by a geometric curve. Hence this method is called geometric curve method. If plotted on a semilog chart, the projected demand or sales is represented by a straight line. Hence this method is sometimes called semilog.

The application of this method is illustrated in Exhibit 3.9. The values in the table are obtained as explained here.

Columns 1 to 4. The values are identical to the corresponding columns in Exhibit 3.8.

Log Y (column 5). The logs in this column are obtained by using a table on common logarithms or a computer.

A log has two parts: (1) the integer, which is the digit to the left of the decimal point, and (2) the decimal part, which is composed of the digits to the right of the decimal point. For the number 1,136 (column 4 for year 1), the log is 3.05538, which is composed of the integer, which is 3, and the decimal part, which is .05538. The integer is computed by counting the digits in a number (as 1,136), to the left of the decimal point, if any, and subtracting one therefrom. Thus, 1,136 has four digits. After subtracting 1 therefrom, the balance is 3, which is the integer. The decimal part, which is .05538 is obtained from a table on common logarithms or a computer program.

X Log Y (column 6). The amounts under column 2 are multiplied by the amounts under column 5.

Log Yc (column 7). The amounts to be placed under this column are the results of the formula

$$\log Yc = \log a + X \log b$$

Log a and log b are computed as

$$\log a = \frac{\text{sum of log } Y}{n} = \frac{39.271}{12} = 3.27258$$

The value 39.271 is the total of column 5. n is the number of past years covered, which is 12.

$$\log b = \frac{\text{sum of } X \log Y}{\text{sum of } X^2} = \frac{8.749}{572} = .015294$$

The value 8.749 is the total of column 6. The value 572 is the total of column 3.

The log Yc for year 13 is computed as

$$\begin{aligned}
\log Yc &= \log a + X \log b \\
&= 3.27258 + 13(.015294) \\
&= 3.27258 + .19877 \\
&= 3.471
\end{aligned}$$

where

$$13 = \text{value of } X \text{ in year } 13$$

The 3.471 is then placed under column 7.

Yc—Projected Demand (column 8). The amounts are the antilogs of the logs in column 7. Finding the antilog of a log is the reverse process of finding the log of a number (number = antilog). For year 13, the log (3.471) has an integer of 3 and a decimal part of .471. A table on common logarithm shows that a log with a decimal part of .471 corresponds to a number or antilog of .296, 29.6, 2.96, 2,960, and so on. The integer 3 fixes the number at 2,960 since 3 plus 1 equals 4 decimal places in the number of 2,960—2,960 units, therefore, is the projected figure for year 13. The projected figures for the other future years may be similarly computed.

CENTERED MOVING AVERAGE METHOD

The centered moving average (CMA) method of sales projection is usually used in short-term or intermediate-term sales forecasting, that is, from one to five years, where quarterly or monthly breakdowns are required. It is utilized in projecting company sales.

Applicability (Exhibit 3.10). The CMA method is ideally suited to a situation in which there is both seasonal fluctuation and annual change in the sales. This case is demonstrated in the first part of Exhibit 3.10, where the sales for the second quarter are more than double the turnover for the third quarter and where the annual sales rise by 8–10%.

If the statistical straight-line or geometric curve method were applied on the historical quarterly sales, the projected quarterly sales will be evened out; that is, the quarterly fluctuations will be eliminated.

The purpose of the CMA method is to determine the annual growth of sales and then use this as the basis in projecting the quarterly, monthly, or even weekly sales.

CMA—Quarterly Sales (Exhibit 3.11).   The CMA for a quarter is the total sales of that quarter plus that of the preceding one and a half quarters and that of the succeeding one and a half quarters divided by 4. Thus, the CMA for year 1, quarter III, based on the data given in the first part of Exhibit 3.11, is calculated in the second part of that exhibit.

The CMA sales of other quarters are given in Exhibit 3.11. The CMA sales for the last two quarters of year 4 cannot be calculated due to the absence of information for the first two quarters of year 5.

Note that while the actual quarterly sales from year 1, quarter III to year 4, quarter II indicates a violent fluctuation (Exhibit 3.11, column 3), the CMA sales for the identical period shows a smooth trend (Exhibit 3.11, column 4).

Annualized Sales.   The next step in sales forecasting is to annualize the sales based on the quarterly figures. This is done in Exhibit 3.11, column 5, which multiplied by 4, the CMA quarterly sales in column 4.

Sales Growth Rate.   The growth rate in the CMA quarterly sales is next obtained. See Exhibit 3.11, column 6. The simple average quarterly growth rate is 2.1%.

Historical Quarterly Sales as Percentage of Annualized Sales.   The actual quarterly sales is then calculated as a percentage of the annualized sales— see Exhibit 3.11, column 7.

Projected Quarterly Sales as a Percentage of Annualized Sales.   The projected quarterly sales as a percentage of the annualized projected sales is estimated based on the past percentages. The historical quarterly sales as a percentage of the annualized sales as calculated in Exhibit 3.11, upper table, column 7, may be recast as shown in Exhibit 3.11, lower table. The lower table also indicates the percentages which may be used in preparing the projections. The percentages were rounded off.

Projected Quarterly Sales (Exhibit 3.12).   The quarterly sales for year 5 are projected in Exhibit 3.12, last column. The projections utilize a 2.1% annual increase in the annualized sales, and use the year 4, quarter II historical sales as the starting point. The quarterly sales as percentage of annualized sales were taken from Exhibit 3.11, bottom table, last column.

CMA—Monthly Projections (Exhibits 3.13 and 3.14). The prior illustrations make use of the CMA quarterly sales. The same techniques may be applied to monthly sales. The CMA monthly sales is the total of the sales for that month, plus the sales for the preceding five and a half months, and the sales for the succeeding five and a half months, divided by 12. This is demonstrated in Exhibit 3.13.

The CMA monthly sales for a consecutive 12-month period are shown in Exhibit 3.14. Note that although the actual monthly sales fluctuated violently, the CMA sales grew gradually.

VII. PRODUCTION SCHEDULING AND COSTING

The purpose of production scheduling and costing is to determine the most feasible production plans; synchronize the production plans with the personnel and raw materials requirements; and estimate the labor and materials costs, overhead, discretionary expenses, and sales expansion costs. The plans and estimates, once approved by management, become the budgets which are used as the standards of performance.

PRODUCTION SCHEDULES

After the sales forecast has been prepared and approved, the number of finished goods to be manufactured is estimated. This estimate is called the production schedule. The working out of this schedule considers the sales budget, the desired levels of finished goods inventory, the production capability, and the costs under alternative production schedules.

If there are no pronounced monthly sales fluctuations, and if the production costs are composed primarily of pure fixed costs and variable costs, the quantity to be produced should equal the projected sales volume as adjusted for the desired changes in the finished goods inventories. For instance, if the present inventory is unusually low, the production will be initially higher than the sales budget in order to bring the inventory level to the normal requirement.

If the sales are highly seasonal, the profitability of alternative production schedules have to be studied. The two alternatives which represent the extreme options are:

1. The uniform production schedule—this attempts to attain a uniform monthly production volume but results in highly fluctuating finished goods inventory level.

2. The uniform finished goods inventory level schedule—the production schedule attempts to approximate the monthly sales and therefore results in a more stable or constant finished goods inventory level.

These two alternatives are demonstrated in Exhibit 3.15. The illustrations are based on the assumptions that (1) the ideal production volume is 3,500 units a month and (2) the required minimum finished goods inventory level is 1,000 units irrespective of the monthly sales volume.

Uniform Production Schedule.   This type of schedule, which is Alternative A in Exhibit 3.15, is ideal from the viewpoint of the production department. The uniform schedule is conducive to an orderly manufacturing operation and hence results in lower factory cost compared with the other option.

However, since this alternative requires the buildup in finished goods inventory in preparation for the sales during the peak months, this alternative carries a high level of finished goods inventory. For instance, this alternative requires an average inventory level equivalent to nine months' sales, as compared with the one month's sale under the other alternative.

The high level of inventory brings with it high inventory carrying costs and inventory-related risks. The inventory costs include the financing charges, warehousing expenses, and insurance premiums. The risks cover those arising from possible abrupt changes in consumer tastes and physical loss of the inventory due to fire and similar causes.

Uniform Finished Goods Inventory Level.   To attain the minimum finished goods inventory, the monthly production volume should approximate the sales volume. However, in companies where the demand is highly seasonal, the adherence to this alternative results in a widely fluctuating production schedule.

The variable cost per unit of output during the peak production months is likely to be higher than the variable costs during the periods of normal production. This applies, for instance, to labor cost since substantial overtime and nighttime premiums have to be paid.

Furthermore, if part of the production requirements cannot be met by the company's own capabilities, some of the production has to be contracted out. The cost of contracting, if done for a few months is normally higher than if done on a more regular basis.

FIXED COSTS AND VARIABLE COSTS

The production costs are tied in with the production schedule while the marketing costs are dovetailed with the sales budget. The procedures for estimating the important elements of costs—raw materials, direct labor, and other costs of the production and marketing operations—are discussed in this section.

Raw Materials (Exhibit 3.16). The raw material budget is based on the production schedule, the usage rate per unit of output, and the cost per unit of material. A simplified material cost budget is shown in Exhibit 3.16. This assumes that the usage rate is two units of materials per unit of output and that the raw material cost per unit is $110.

Direct Labor (Exhibit 3.17). The production schedule is converted into the number of direct labor hours. Assuming a straight rate of 10 direct labor hours for every unit of output, the total labor hours required is indicated in Exhibit 3.17.

The exhibit also shows the total direct labor cost, assuming that the rate for the first 35,000 hours a month is $10, and for the excess, $15. The labor in excess of the 35,000 hours a month may be provided by the present employees or by temporary workers, or it may be contracted out.

If the factory is currently producing 3,500 units a month according to the alternative A production schedule outlined in Exhibit 3.15, but would like to shift to the alternative B production schedule, management have to reschedule the direct labor requirements.

One way of working out the labor requirements is illustrated in Exhibit 3.18. This assumes that an average worker puts in an effective working time of seven hours a day, net of absences and idle time. Under this arrangement, the factory requires a year-round work force of about 75 men. Temporary workers will reach a peak of 605 men in June. This requirement can be reduced if the core workers put in some overtime hours or if some of the operations are contracted out.

Other Fixed Costs and Variable Costs. The budget for the other costs is prepared with monthly breakdown. The costs are classified in accordance with their behavior in relation to changes in the production or sales volume.

The other variable production and marketing costs include fuel, supplies, and parts. They can be easily calculated by referring to the production schedule and projected sales and the estimated unit costs.

The fixed production and marketing costs are used to support a given plant rated capacity and marketing capability. These costs include salaries and benefits of managers, rental, and depreciation. These costs can easily be estimated by referring to the amounts in the past. The amounts do not change much from period to period unless there is a variation in the rated capacity or capability.

DISCRETIONARY EXPENSES AND SALES EXPANSION COSTS

The discretionary expenses and sales expansion costs for a given period do not bear a direct relationship with the projected sales or production schedule for the period. Furthermore, these costs are not directly linked to the production rated capacity or marketing capability. Hence, these costs do not lend themselves to the traditional methods of forecasting or budgeting.

Zero-based Budgeting.   One way of estimating the future discretionary expenses and sales expansion costs for a going concern is through the zero-based budgeting approach.

Under this method, decision units are identified. A unit may refer to a function, activity, department, profit or cost center, responsibility center, or any component thereof. The following are examples of the major decision units: product R&D, sales expansion program, and collection program.

For budgeting purposes, the different levels of possible expenditures for each unit is divided into decision packages, the first package being the most important in the unit. Thus, the R&D activity may be divided into the following decision packages:

1. Construct a prototype for product B $400,000
2. Continue applied research on product C   600,000
3. Conduct general product research   350,000

For the sales expansion program the packages may be

1. Expand sales in present market territories $550,000
2. Develop new marketing territories   450,000

The collection program may consist of only one package:

1. Expand the collection department $300,000

Assume that the company has set the budget for the preceding decision units at only $1,000,000. The management, therefore, has to select only so many of the packages such that the total becomes $1,000,000 or less. The ultimate decision depends upon the cash flow projections and return and risk analysis for each of the packages. However, the particular situation of the firm also plays a major role. For instance, if the company is running low on cash, it may have to approve first the $300,000 collection department expansion program, followed by the $550,000 sales expansion in the present markets.

If the firm has sufficient cash flow, but its products are aging, and if the company sees a bright prospect in products B and C, then the firm may throw the entire $1,000,000 on the R&D for these products.

VIII. COMPUTERIZED FINANCIAL PLANNING MODELS

A financial planning model expresses the relationships of a set of data in order to project the possible outcomes in the future of transactions or events. A computer software is used in modeling. A model may be for (1) an entire corporation or one of its divisions or (2) specific projects.

Corporate Planning Model. The model for a corporation or a division is used on a continuing basis. It is used in planning or in deciding such issues as the dividend payment rate, corporate growth rate, financing sources, plant expansion schedule, or even personnel hiring program.

Specialized Models. The model for a project is used as the need arises. For instance, an equipment lease or buy model may be utilized in deciding whether to rent or purchase an equipment.

How an integrated corporate planning model and specialized models work are described next.

INTEGRATED CORPORATE PLANNING MODEL

The integrated model is made up of eight components: (1) basic data, (2) assumptions, (3) external marketing, (4) corporate marketing, (5) production, (6) financing, (7) financial projections, and (8) financial analysis.

Basic Data and Assumptions. The integrated corporate model accepts basic data on the economy and financial markets, the industry and competition, the sales and product history of the firm, the number and compensation of its employees, the capacity of its plants and delivery units, and similar environmental and corporate subjects. Where information on the past and present are believed not adequate to serve as the basis of making projections about the future, the management has to input the assumptions which influence the future sales and costs. A simplified list and illustration of the basic data and assumptions were given in Section II and in Exhibit 3.1 of this chapter.

Economy and Industry. The primary purpose of this component is to project the total industry demand, possible selling prices, and competitive pressure within the industry.

For large corporations with sophisticated computer modeling software, the integrated model may incorporate an economic and industry forecasting model. Economic and industry forecasts were described in

Section VI and Exhibit 3.7 of this chapter. This component may include a statistical projection formula for the industry demand. Two statistical projection methods are illustrated in Exhibits 3.8 and 3.9.

Corporate Sales and Marketing.   This part of the integrated model transforms the industry demand and competition into the corporate sales, selling prices, advertising, and other marketing expenses. Based on the projected sales volume and revenues, the required sales personnel, warehousing spaces, delivery units, and accounts receivable, and finished goods inventory levels are worked out. The model may incorporate a formula for estimating the sales in the near future. An example of such a method is the centered moving average, which is explained in Section VI of this chapter and illustrated in Exhibits 3.10 to 3.14.

Production.   The production model converts the sales projection into a production schedule, and then works out the purchasing and production personnel recruitment programs based on the production schedule. The results of a formula for estimating the labor requirements based on the production schedule are shown in Exhibit 3.18.

The marketing and production components of the model should feed management with the information on the required physical facilities expansion and anticipated personnel recruitment in the future.

The model may be designed so as to optimize the production schedule—selecting the schedule that will give the company the highest return, considering the monthly sales fluctuations, advantages of stable production runs, and the cost of carrying finished goods inventories.

Financing.   The financing portion estimates the total cash requirements for working capital, capital investments, and loan repayments and offers alternatives for possible funding sources. The requirements are calculated based on the sales revenues, production costs, and other inputs from the corporate sales and marketing and production components.

Data previously input into the computer, as on interest rates and debt/equity ratio desired by management, are also availed of during the calculation operation.

The financing component of the corporate model may be so created so that it will facilitate the selection of the best combination of the following factors which will most nearly meet the requirements set by management in terms of return on the stockholders' equity and growth and risk of the company. The factors are debt/equity ratio, dividend payout rate (dividend as a percentage of net profit), additional equity infusion, additional loans, and divestment of certain resources. The chosen path will then be used by management in arranging for additional financing.

If rapid growth will dilute the return per share, then management may decide to slow down the rate of business expansion. This information is then fed into the marketing model.

Financial Models. This part of the model integrates the results of the other components, into the projected income statement, complete cash flow statement, and the resulting balance sheets. These financial projections were described earlier in Sections III, IV, and V of this chapter. Illustrations of these statements are in Exhibits 3.2 to 3.4 and 3.6 and Exhibits 13.1 to 13.4.

Financial Analysis. The integrated planning model may incorporate financial ratios, including integrated ratios which are described in Chapter 18. The ratios may reveal that the management may have to strengthen certain areas. For instance, if the ratio of total assets to sales is low, the management may have to take measures to either liquidate certain non-operating assets or reorient its marketing thrust.

If sensitivity analysis is run on the model, the management may know the impact of changes in sales volume, selling prices, or certain costs on the profitability or cash flow.

This component of the model may also be exploited to inform management on the degree of risk it is taking in the future. For instance, it may reveal the corporation's ratio of fixed costs to variable costs and break-even point. More important, the financial analysis portion may also reveal the company's unhedged positions in (1) excessive receivables without corresponding liabilities, (2) long-term fixed interest rate receivables without the corresponding long-term fixed interest rate liabilities, or (3) foreign exchange receipts without foreign exchange payments in the same currency. These exposed positions may become actual losses in case of fluctuations in prices, interest rates, or foreign exchange rates. See Chapter 7, Sections I and II for inflation, interest, and foreign exchange risks and the use of hedging to minimize these risks.

SPECIALIZED MODELS

Specialized financial models are utilized on a case-by-case basis to help management decide on the most desirable from among competing alternatives. For instance, computerized models will help analyze the data which are needed before deciding on any of the following: (1) make or buy alternatives; (2) product deletions or introductions; (3) sales expansion measures; (4) equipment acquisition, replacement, or buy or lease; (5) automation; (6) loan source selection; and (7) capital structuring. The results of simplified computer models for these areas are given and explained in Chapters 9 to 15.

Relationship of Integrated and Specialized Models. The link of the integrated corporate planning model with special models is illustrated for two types of measures.

PLANT EXPANSION PROGRAMS. The marketing and production components of the integrated model may reveal the need to add to the present facilities. A special model is then used to analyze the IRR, NPV, and risks involved among several alternative ways of adding to the capacity. If an alternative is found and accepted, the cash flows, work force requirements, and other characteristics of the project are then input into the integrated model.

SALES EXPANSION MEASURES.   The integrated model may indicate that the profit may be enhanced if the sales are increased. This is the case where the production fixed costs are high in relation to the production variable costs. A sales expansion cost model, the one described in Chapter 11 may then be used to determine the most cost-effective way of pushing up the sales volume. Based on the runs on this model, management may be able to decide on the combinations of sales expansion measures to be used. This information is then routed to the marketing and production components of the corporate planning model.

EXHIBIT 3.1:
Statement of Basic Data and Assumptions

Marketing aspects

Sales volume and sales expansion costs	*Sales volume in units*	*Sales expansion costs in $1,000*
Year 1	120,000	$4,000
Year 2	240,000	2,200
Year 3	240,000	2,200
Selling price	$100 per unit	
Marketing variable costs	$18 per unit	
Marketing fixed costs	$800,000 per year	
Collection period	1 month	
Finished goods inventory level	1 month	

Production aspects

Production schedule	*Sales*	*Inventory buildup*	*Total production*
Year 1	120,000	12,000	132,000
Year 2	240,000	12,000	252,000
Year 3	240,000	0	240,000
Raw materials inventory level	2 months		
Goods in process inventory	Minimal		
Raw material suppliers—payment	1 month after purchase		

Manufacturing variable costs
  Raw materials $36 per unit of finished good
  Other manufacturing variable costs $15 per unit of finished good
Manufacturing fixed costs $1,200,000 per year
Plant construction period   12 months
Plant cost and payment schedule (in $1,000)
  Land $500 upon start of construction
  Buildings and equipment $2,000 upon start of construction
  Buildings and equipment $2,000 upon completion of construction
Annual depreciation of buildings and equipment—10%.

Other assumptions

Financing	All equity
Income tax rate, federal and state	40%
Terminal value capitalization rate	16%
Excess cash generation	Pay as dividends
Working cash balance	Minimal

EXHIBIT 3.2:
Income Statement (dollars in $1,000), at constant prices

	Year 1	Year 2	Year 3
Sales volume in 1,000 units	120	240	240
Sales	$12,000	$24,000	$24,000
Less: Variable costs			
Raw materials used	4,320	8,640	8,640
Other manufacturing variable costs	1,800	3,600	3,600
Manufacturing variable costs	6,120	12,240	12,240
Marketing variable costs	2,160	4,320	4,320
Total variable costs	8,280	16,560	16,560
Variable margin	3,720	7,440	7,440
Less: Sales expansion costs	4,000	2,200	2,200
Contribution to overhead	($ 280)	$ 5,240	$ 5,240
Cash fixed costs			
Manufacturing	1,200	1,200	1,200
Marketing	800	800	800
General	500	500	500
Total fixed costs	2,500	2,500	2,500
Net profit before noncash costs	(2,780)	2,740	2,740
Noncash costs (depreciation)	400	400	400
Net profit before income tax	(3,180)	2,340	2,340
Income tax	(1,272)	936	936
Net profit	($ 1,908)	$ 1,404	$ 1,404
Cash profit or operating cash flow before working capital			
Net profit	($ 1,908)	$ 1,404	$ 1,404
Add back depreciation	400	400	400
Cash profit	($ 1,508)	$ 1,804	$ 1,804

EXHIBIT 3.3:
Working Capital (dollars in $1,000)

Working Capital	Basis	Duration in months	Year 1	Year 2	Year 3
Accounts receivable	Sales	1	$1,000	$2,000	$2,000
Inventories					
Raw materials	Raw materials used	2	720	1,440	1,440
Finished goods					
Variable costs	Manufacturing variable cost	1	510	1,020	1,020
Fixed costs	Manufacturing fixed cost	1	100	100	100
Gross working capital			2,330	4,560	4,560
Accounts payable	Raw materials used	1	360	720	720
Net working capital			$1,970	$3,840	$3,840
Buildup from prior year			$1,970	$1,870	$ 0

EXHIBIT 3.4:
Project Cash Flow (dollars in $1,000)

Receipts	Year −1	Year 0	Year 1	Year 2	Year 3
Investors	$2,500	$3,970	$3,378		
Operating cash flow				$1,804	$ 1,804
Terminal value					11,275
Total	$2,500	$3,970	$3,378	$1,804	$13,079
Payments					
Land	$ 500				
Buildings	750	750			
Equipment	1,250	1,250			
Working capital		1,970	1,870		
Operating cash deficit			1,508		
Dividends					
Regular				1,804	1,804
Terminal value					11,275
Total	$2,500	$3,970	$3,378	$1,804	$13,079

EXHIBIT 3.5:
Investors' Cash Flow and Return (dollars in $1,000)

	Year −1	Year 0	Year 1	Year 2	Year 3
Investments	($2,500)	($3,970)	($3,378)		
Dividends					
Regular				$1,804	$ 1,804
Sale of project					11,275
Net cash flow	($2,500)	($3,970)	($3,378)	$1,804	$13,079
Internal rate of return	16%				
Net present value as of year −1 at 10% a year					
Year −1 cash flow	($2,500)				
Years 0 to 3 cash flows	3,888				
Total	$1,388				

EXHIBIT 3.6:
Balance Sheet (dollars in $1,000)

Assets	Year −1	Year 0	Year 1	Year 2	Year 3
Net working capital		$1,970	$3,840	$3,840	$3,840
Property, plant, and equipment					
Land	$ 500	500			
Buildings	750	1,500			
Equipment	1,250	2,500			
Total cost	2,500	4,500	4,500	4,500	4,500
Accumulated depreciation	0	0	400	800	1,200
Net book value	2,500	4,500	4,100	3,700	3,300
Totals assets	$2,500	$6,470	$7,940	$7,540	$7,140
Stockholders' equity					
End of prior year		$2,500	$6,470	$7,940	$7,540
Contributions	2,500	3,970	3,378		
Net profit			(1,908)	1,404	1,404
Total	2,500	6,470	7,940	9,344	8,944
Less: Dividends				1,804	1,804
Total equity	$2,500	$6,470	$7,940	$7,540	$7,140

EXHIBIT 3.7:
Sales Forecasting Flow Chart

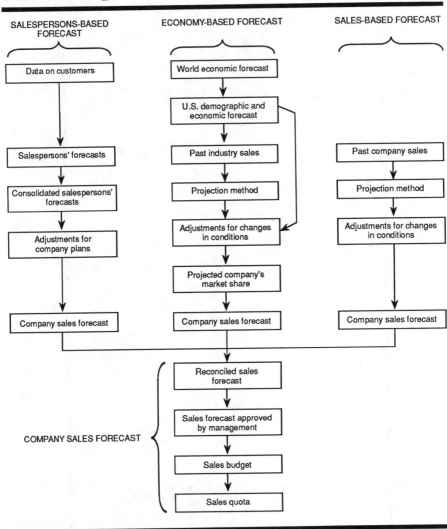

EXHIBIT 3.8:
Statistical Straight-Line Method—Illustration

Year Col. 1	X Col. 2	X² Col. 3	Y Actual demand Col. 4	XY Col. 5	bX Col. 6	Yc Projected demand Col. 7
Year						
1	− 11	121	1,136	(12,496)	(706)	
2	− 9	81	1,329	(11,961)	(578)	
3	− 7	49	1,387	(9,709)	(449)	
4	− 5	25	1,726	(8,630)	(321)	
5	− 3	9	1,953	(5,859)	(193)	
6	− 1	1	1,830	(1,830)	(64)	
7	1	1	2,050	2,050	64	
8	3	9	2,010	6,030	193	
9	5	25	2,271	11,355	321	
10	7	49	2,381	16,667	449	
11	9	81	2,473	22,257	578	
12	11	121	2,622	28,842	706	
13	13				834	2,765
14	15				963	2,893
15	17				1,091	3,022
16	19				1,220	3,150
17	21				1,348	3,279
18	23				1,476	3,407
19	25				1,605	3,535
20	27				1,733	3,664
21	29				1,861	3,792
22	31				1,990	3,921
Sum		572	23,168	36,716		

EXHIBIT 3.9:
Statistical Geometric Curve Method—Illustration

Year Col. 1	X Col. 2	X^2 Col. 3	Y Actual demand Col. 4	Log Y Col. 5	X log Y Col. 6	Log Yc Col. 7	Yc Projected demand Col. 8
Year							
1	− 11	121	1,136	3.055	(33.609)		
2	− 9	81	1,329	3.124	(28.112)		
3	− 7	49	1,387	3.142	(21.995)		
4	− 5	25	1,726	3.237	(16.185)		
5	− 3	9	1,953	3.291	(9.872)		
6	− 1	1	1,830	3.262	(3.262)		
7	1	1	2,050	3.312	3.312		
8	3	9	2,010	3.303	9.910		
9	5	25	2,271	3.356	16.781		
10	7	49	2,381	3.377	23.637		
11	9	81	2,473	3.393	30.539		
12	11	121	2,622	3.419	37.605		
13	13					3.471	2,960
14	15					3.502	3,176
15	17					3.533	3,408
16	19					3.563	3,657
17	21					3.594	3,924
18	23					3.624	4,210
19	25					3.655	4,517
20	27					3.685	4,847
21	29					3.716	5,201
22	31					3.747	5,581
	Sum	572		39.271	8.749		

EXHIBIT 3.10:
Actual Quarterly and Annual Sales

I. Base data

Year	Quarter	Actual quarterly sales	Actual annual sales	Quarterly as percentage of annual sales
1	I	60		20.0%
	II	105		35.0
	III	45		15.0
	IV	90	300	30.0
2	I	69		20.9
	II	112		33.9
	III	53		16.1
	IV	96	330	29.1
3	I	72		20.0
	II	130		36.1
	III	50		13.9
	IV	108	360	30.0
4	I	74		19.0
	II	133		34.1
	III	62		15.9
	IV	121	390	31.0

II. Calculation of centered moving average for year 1, quarter III

Year	Quarter	Actual quarterly sales	Number of quarters	Total
1	I	60	0.5	30.0
	II	105	1.0	105.0
	III	45	1.0	45.0
	IV	90	1.0	90.0
2	I	69	0.5	34.5
Total			4.0	304.5
Divide by number of quarters				4.0
Equals = CMA quarterly sales				76.1

EXHIBIT 3.11:
Actual Quarterly Sales as Percentage of Annualized Sales

Calculations

Year Col. 1	Quarter Col. 2	Actual quarterly Col. 3	CENTERED MOVING AVERAGE Quarterly Col. 4	CENTERED MOVING AVERAGE Annualized Col. 5	Quarterly growth rate Col. 6	Quarterly as percent of annualized Col. 7
1	I	60				
	II	105				
	III	45	76.1	305		14.8%
	IV	90	78.1	313	2.6%	28.8%
2	I	69	80.0	320	2.4%	21.6%
	II	112	81.8	327	2.2%	34.3%
	III	53	82.9	332	1.4%	16.0%
	IV	96	85.5	342	3.2%	28.1%
3	I	72	87.4	350	2.2%	20.6%
	II	130	88.5	354	1.3%	36.7%
	III	50	90.3	361	2.0%	13.9%
	IV	108	90.9	364	0.7%	29.7%
4	I	74	92.8	371	2.1%	19.9%
	II	133	95.9	384	3.4%	34.7%
	III	62				
	IV	121				
				Average	2.1%	

Matrix

Quarter	Year 1	Year 2	Year 3	Year 4	Average	To use
I		21.6%	20.6%	19.9%	20.7%	20%
II		34.3	36.7	34.7	35.2	35
III	14.8%	16.0	13.9		14.9	15
IV	28.8	28.1	29.7		28.9	30
						100%

EXHIBIT 3.12:
Projected Quarterly Sales

Year	Quarter	Actual annualized sale	Projected annualized sale	Quarterly as a percentage of annualized	Projected quarterly sales
1	I				
	II				
	III	305			
	IV	313			
2	I	320			
	II	327			
	III	332			
	IV	342			
3	I	350			
	II	354			
	III	361			
	IV	364			
4	I	371			
	II	384			
	III		392		
	IV		400		
5	I		408	20%	81.7
	II		417	35%	146.0
	III		426	15%	63.9
	IV		435	30%	130.5

EXHIBIT 3.13:
Monthly Centered Moving Average—Calculations

Centered moving average for July of year 1

Year 1	January	18	$\times 0.5 =$	9
	February	20		20
	March	22		22
	April	30		30
	May	45		45
	June	30		30
	July	17		17
	August	12		12
	September	16		16
	October	26		26
	November	40		40
	December	24		24
Year 2	January	25	$\times 0.5 =$	12.5
Total				303.5
Average			303.5/12 mos.	25.3

EXHIBIT 3.14:
Monthly Centered Moving Average—Illustration

		Actual sales	Centered moving average
Year 1	January	18	
	February	20	
	March	22	
	April	30	
	May	45	
	June	30	
	July	17	25.3
	August	12	25.5
	September	16	25.6
	October	26	25.9
	November	40	26.0
	December	24	26.1
Year 2	January	25	26.4
	February	18	26.6
	March	26	26.8
	April	34	27.2
	May	42	27.2
	June	36	27.3
	July	19	
	August	14	
	September	20	
	October	30	
	November	36	
	December	30	

EXHIBIT 3.15:
Alternative Production Schedules (in 1,000 units)

	Sales	Production	Production excess/(shortfall)	Ending finished goods inventory
Alternative A. Uniform production volume				
January	1.0	3.5	2.5	13.0
February	1.0	3.5	2.5	15.5
March	2.0	3.5	1.5	17.0
April	5.0	3.5	(1.5)	15.5
May	10.0	3.5	(6.5)	9.0
June	10.0	3.5	(6.5)	2.5
July	5.0	3.5	(1.5)	1.0
August	2.0	3.5	1.5	2.5
September	1.0	3.5	2.5	5.0
October	1.0	3.5	2.5	7.5
November	1.0	3.5	2.5	10.0
December	1.0	1.5	0.5	10.5
	40.0	40.0		109.0
Average inventory				9.0
Alternative B. constant finished goods inventory level				
January	1.0	1.0	0.0	1.0
February	1.0	1.0	0.0	1.0
March	2.0	2.0	0.0	1.0
April	5.0	5.0	0.0	1.0
May	10.0	10.0	0.0	1.0
June	10.0	10.0	0.0	1.0
July	5.0	5.0	0.0	1.0
August	2.0	2.0	0.0	1.0
September	1.0	1.0	0.0	1.0
October	1.0	1.0	0.0	1.0
November	1.0	1.0	0.0	1.0
December	1.0	1.0	0.0	1.0
	40.0	40.0	0.0	

EXHIBIT 3.16:
Raw Material Cost Forecast
using the Alternative B production schedule

	Production (in 1,000 units)	Material usage (in 1,000 units)	Total material cost (in $1,000)
January	1,000	2,000	$ 220
February	1,000	2,000	220
March	2,000	4,000	440
April	5,000	10,000	1100
May	10,000	20,000	2200
June	10,000	20,000	2200
July	5,000	10,000	1100
August	2,000	4,000	440
September	1,000	2,000	220
October	1,000	2,000	220
November	1,000	2,000	220
December	1,000	2,000	220

EXHIBIT 3.17:

Direct Labor Cost Forecast using the Alternative B production schedule

	Total production	Direct labor hours	NUMBERS OF HOURS			TOTAL LABOR COST (IN $1,000)		
			Base of 35,000 hours	Excess hours		Base of 3500 hours at $10	Excess hours at $15	Combined
January	1,000	10,000	10,000	0		$100	$ 0	$ 100
February	1,000	10,000	10,000	0		100	0	100
March	2,000	20,000	20,000	0		200	0	200
April	5,000	50,000	35,000	15,000		350	225	575
May	10,000	100,000	35,000	65,000		350	975	1,325
June	10,000	100,000	35,000	65,000		350	975	1,325
July	5,000	50,000	35,000	15,000		350	225	575
August	2,000	20,000	20,000	0		200	0	200
September	1,000	10,000	10,000	0		100	0	100
October	1,000	10,000	10,000	0		100	0	100
November	1,000	10,000	10,000	0		100	0	100
December	1,000	10,000	10,000	0		100	0	100

EXHIBIT 3.18:
Direct Labor Staffing Forecast using the Alternative B production schedule

	Total production	Direct labor hours	Working days	Labor hours per day	NUMBER OF REQUIRED WORKERS		
					Total	Core workers	Seasonal or overtime
January	1,000	10,000	22	455	65	75	0
February	1,000	10,000	20	500	71	75	0
March	2,000	20,000	22	909	130	75	55
April	5,000	50,000	22	2,273	325	75	250
May	10,000	100,000	22	4,545	649	75	574
June	10,000	100,000	21	4,762	680	75	605
July	5,000	50,000	21	2,381	340	75	265
August	2,000	20,000	23	870	124	75	49
September	1,000	10,000	19	526	75	75	0
October	1,000	10,000	23	435	62	75	0
November	1,000	10,000	20	500	71	75	0
December	1,000	10,000	19	526	75	75	0

Chapter 4

INTERNAL RATE OF RETURN

The internal rate of return (IRR), also known as the implicit rate of return or discounted cash flow rate of return, is one of the two key tools used in decision analysis for long-term projects. The other is the net present value, which is treated in the next chapter. The IRR is the compound interest rate which equalizes the present value of the returns with the present value of the investments.

This chapter presents the concept of IRR, illustrates how to calculate it, and demonstrates how it is affected by changes in the cash flow stream.

In evaluating the future of long-term projects, the IRR gives more meaningful results than does the accounting rate of return (ARR). The reason for this is that the IRR takes into account the time value of money or cost of money and looks over the entire project life.

The IRR has two practical limitations: bias against, and bias in favor of, long-term projects. Techniques are given to overcome these weaknesses.

This chapter rebukes the two conceptual disadvantages which are normally attributed to the IRR: the assumption regarding the reinvestment rate and the multiple IRRs of certain projects. The prevailing view is that under the IRR concept, the periodic cash returns are assumed to be reinvested at the IRR. The author believes, however, that this is not a limitation of the IRR technique itself since the reinvestment assumption is made for the returns which had been taken out of the project already. The limitation regarding the multiple IRRs is well grounded in theory but is practically nonexistent in the business world.

I. NATURE OF IRR

The internal rate of return is the compound interest rate which equalizes the present value of all the returns with the present value of all the investments, as of a common date. Hence, to determine the IRR, it is necessary to (1) bring all the investments and returns to a common date and (2) arrive at the rate which will equalize the investments with the returns as of said date.

For a new project, the investment is the capital or cash contribution required and the return is the series of dividends or cash drawings. For a stock transaction, the investment is the purchase price and the return is represented by the dividends and selling price. For a bank deposit account, the investment is the value deposited and the return is composed of the withdrawals of the principal plus interest.

IRR is so called because the rate is internally generated; that is, it does not make any reference to a predetermined rate of return, or interest rate, which is derived from external sources. The IRR may be contrasted with the net present value (NPV), which is computed using an external interest rate or money cost which is used as the discounting rate. Net present value is discussed in Chapter 5.

Because of its use of the discounting principle, the IRR is also known as the *discounted rate of return*. Another name is *discounted cash flow* rate of return because it employs data taken from the cash flow statement.

The IRR is sometimes called *implicit rate of return* because the rate is implied from the amounts and timing of the investments and returns of the project.

ILLUSTRATION (Exhibit 4.1)

For project A in Exhibit 4.1, the IRR is the rate at which, if used to discount the following returns to December 31, 1995, which is used as the reference date:

- $58,000 to *a* and
- $67,280 to *b*

the total of the present values *a* and *b* will equal the investment of $100,000 as of December 31, 1995.

The IRR of project A is 16%. At this rate the total present value of the returns equal the investment of $100,000. See Exhibit 4.1, lower panel.

Note that although the IRR is a rate per year, the timing of the transactions—investments and returns—are as of a certain day—which is usually as of the end of the year. For project A, the return of $58,000 for year 1 represents the profit *earned during the year* which is *distributed at the end of the year*, plus a portion of the original investment.

CONCEPT OF IRR (Exhibit 4.2)

In a bank deposit transaction, the depositor places a deposit or a series of deposits. He then withdraws over a period of time from the bank account, until there is no more balance in the account. The withdrawal at any time may represent a return of the original deposit, interest, or a combination of both.

In a business investment transaction, an investment is made in a project, a company, a plant, an equipment, or a profit-making measure. The investment subsequently generates returns in the form of dividends, cash flow, cost savings, or additional profit.

The IRR of a project is similar to the interest rate offered by banks on interest-bearing deposits. For as long as the principal of the deposit remains with the bank, the principal plus any unwithdrawn interest earns the interest rate. In like manner, for as long as the investment stays with the project, the investment plus any unwithdrawn profit earns the IRR.

The deposit-withdrawal cycle is identical to the investment-return cycle as may be noticed from Exhibit 4.2. If a $100,000 deposit is made on December 31, 1995, 16% is the interest rate, which, if compounded annually, will enable the following withdrawals to be made such that at the end of two years, there is no more balance in the account:

1996 $58,000
1997 $67,280

Based on this information, the entries in the passbook are as shown in the table in Exhibit 4.2.

Like the interest on the bank deposit, the IRR refers to the compound interest which is annually earned by an investor in a project. The IRR is applied on the unrecovered original investment plus accumulated unrecovered interest. This means that as long as the investment or part of it is in the project, the investment earns at the IRR rate, compounded annually. Furthermore, the earnings which have not yet been taken out of the project also earn at the IRR rate.

The table in Exhibit 4.2 may be used in checking the internal rate of return as calculated. If the correct IRR is obtained, there should be no balance in the investment account after the last return.

II. ESTIMATING THE IRR

The most practical way to estimate the IRR is to use a computer. Popular software programs for personal computers have formulas for calculating the IRR. However, it is dangerous to use the computer formulas unless the user has a clear understanding of how the formula derives the IRR. The computer formulas follow basically the same procedures as the manual calculations which are described next.

The manual calculations are applied to two projects— first, to project A, for which the data were given in Exhibit 4.1, and then to project B.

PROJECT A (Exhibit 4.3)

The calculations for project A are shown in Exhibit 4.3. The procedures are as follows.

Decide on the Reference Date.   Technically and theoretically, any end-of-year reference date may be used—December 31 of 1995, 1996, 1997, 1998, 2098, or even 500 B.C. The use of any reference date gives the same answer. However, the most practical reference dates to use, in the order of preference, are the date of the first investment, the date of the last investment, and the date of the last return. In the first case, all the values other than the first investment are discounted (their net present values are computed). The first investment is not discounted any more as it is already on the reference date. In the last case, all the values other than the last return are compounded. For project A, we will use first December 31, 1995 as the reference date.

Manually Estimate the Initial IRR.   The closer is this initial estimate to the actual IRR, the less the number of trials needed. The total of the two returns is $125,280. Since the investment is $100,000, the cash profit is the difference of $25,280, which will be earned for an average of one and a half years. Since the year 2 return is only slightly higher than the year 1 return, about one-half of the $100,000 original investment is actually recovered by the end of year 1 and the other half by the end of year 2. In other words, one-half of the investment runs for one year, and the other half, two years. Thus the weighted average life is roughly one and a half years.

Using simple interest (to start with), getting $25,280 in one and a half years on an investment of $100,000 is equivalent to receiving roughly two-thirds of it or $16,862 in a year. The $16,862 amount is 16.9% of $100,000. But 16.9% is a simple interest, and IRR is a compound interest. In this particular instance, the IRR, which is a compound interest, is lower than a simple interest. The initial estimate then is 15%. This rate is used in the first trial. See the exhibit for the calculations for the first trial. At this rate, the total present value of the returns is higher than the investment.

Recalculate the IRR.   The next rate to be tried should be one which will lower the present value of the returns. If the interest rate is raised, the present value factors will be brought down. Hence, a higher rate, say, 16%, is tried next. At this rate, the time-adjusted value of the returns just equal the investment. The IRR is therefore 16%.

PROJECT B (Exhibit 4.4)

Decide on the Reference Date. The reference date which may be used is either the end of 1993, which is the first outlay for the investment, or 1994, the last outlay date. In the calculations, the latter was used (Exhibit 4.4).

Manually Estimate the Initial IRR. To approximate the simple interest rate, determine first the average dates of the investment and returns. Since the investments are made in only two years, take as the average investment year the one with the bigger investment, which is 1994. Next, determine the average return year. By inspection, the average is 1998. The total returns before this (1995 to 1997) is $600,000, which approximates the $550,000 return after 1998. The average time to earn the returns is four years—from 1994 to 1998.

Based on the "given value" column, the total undiscounted returns of $1,450,000 exceed the investment by $550,000. Since it takes an average of four years to earn the $550,000, the average annual gain is $137,500. This yearly increment is roughly 15% of the $900,000 investment. The 15% is the estimated simple interest. A compound interest is lower than a simple interest. Hence we can try for the first trial, a rate lower than 15%, say, 13%. At this rate, the present value of the returns is lower than the compounded value of the investments by $16,000.

Recalculate the IRR. A lower rate is tried next, so that the present value of the returns will go up. At 12%, the present value of the returns is higher than the investments by $17,000, which is about the same amount as the shortfall of the returns compared with the investments at 13%. Hence the IRR is about halfway between 12% and 13%, or 12.5%.

III. EFFECT OF THE CASH FLOW STREAM ON THE IRR

EFFECT OF CHANGES IN THE CASH FLOW

The IRR is based on the stream of investments and returns—their amounts and timing. Any change in the amount or timing will change the IRR.

Changes in the Timing or Project Life (Exhibit 4.5). Consider the alternative cash flow streams in Exhibit 4.5. Based on the initial plans, the cash flow streams may look like the ones in the first column (under base cash flow). The amounts are calculated in Exhibit 4.6. The resulting IRR is 12.5%. If all the investments are made in one year only—1994 (instead of 1993 and 1994)—the IRR jumps from 12.5% to 14.3%. This improvement in the IRR is attained although the total investments and returns remain the same.

If the project life is extended by just one year, the rate of return becomes 15.9% instead of 12.5%.

The IRR is usually calculated on an annual basis. The investments and returns are assumed to occur at one-year intervals, and as of the end of the year.

Quarterly Distribution of Returns.   The IRR may be substantially raised if the returns are distributed throughout the year, say, monthly or quarterly, rather than as of the end of the year and if the IRR calculations are done on a quarterly and not annual basis. The reason is that the investors will be able to use in advance the early returns. If the returns were distributed annually at the end of the year, the use of quarterly compounding will not raise the IRR as there are no interim or quarterly returns whose earnings can be compounded.

Changes in the Amounts (Exhibit 4.5).   Given the same timing as those used in the base cash flow, the rate of return can increase as follows—to 15.6% if the investments are cut down by 10% and 17.7% if the annual cash flows during the full operating years (1997 to 1999) are raised from $300,000 to $400,000.

Of course, in the implementation of projects, the cash flow patterns in terms of amounts and timing can vary a lot. Hence the actual rate of return usually deviate so much from the precalculated rates.

CONCEPT OF INVESTMENTS (Exhibit 4.6)

In determining the rate of return for a project or profitability measure, the investments refer to the cash or cash equivalent used for capital outlay such as land, buildings, and equipment or for intangible expenditures as research and development, introductory advertising and promotion, and other preoperating or start-up expenses. The investment may also be used to fund the working capital and any reserves as for debt service. Furthermore, the investment may be utilized to finance the initial years' operating cash deficits.

The investment requirement is taken from a projected cash flow statement. A condensed statement is illustrated in Exhibit 4.6. The exhibit shows the investment requirements for the two years before the start of operations (year −1 and year 0 in Exhibit 4.6, which are equivalent to 1993 and 1994 in Exhibit 4.5). During the first year of operations (year 1), the project expects to start generating cash as the cash proceeds from sales exceed the payments for operating and other expenses. Hence no additional investment is required.

However, certain projects may continue to require cash during the first few years of operations. These cases occur in instances where the cash proceeds from sales are not adequate to cover the payments for expenses, amortization of debt, and additional working capital. In these instances, periodic or annual cash deficits develop. See Chapter 3, Financial Projections as Basis of Analysis, Exhibits 3.2 and 3.3 for an illustration where an additional investment is required during the first year of operations in order to cover the operating deficit and additional working capital.

CONCEPT OF RETURNS

There are three types of returns: (1) the regular annual returns or cash flow, (2) the terminal or residual value, and (3) the financial transactions return.

Regular Annual Returns. In the projected cash flow statements, the cash generation which may be considered as return to the investors is shown under either one of four classifications:

1. As excess of cash proceeds from sales revenues over payments for operating and other expenses. The manner of disposition as cash payout to the owners, addition to cash balance, or addition to income-earning investment is not indicated. This is the method used in Exhibit 4.6.
2. As cash payout to the owners or business firm undertaking the project, which may be in the form of (a) cash transfers to the mother organization for projects undertaken by an existing firm, (b) cash dividends to stockholders in case of start-ups organized as corporations, or (c) drawings by the owners of a new enterprise.
3. As addition to the cash balance. In this case, the cash balance, which is idle, becomes unusually large toward the end of the project life.
4. As addition to income-earning investments, to be made by the project. These investments include business expansion or passive investments like certificates of deposit and Treasury bills.

Irrespective of the treatment of the cash generation of the project as indicated, the cash generation should be treated as return.

If the annual cash generations are initially treated as yearly additions to cash balance, and not as periodic returns, the computed rate of return will be lower than the correct one, due to the delayed recognition of the cash generation.

Terminal Value. There are three concepts of terminal value or residual value for purposes of determining the IRR:

1. The value of the project as of the end of the project life
2. The value of the project as of the end of the planning horizon or last year covered by the rate of return calculations

3. The sale value of the project

Value at the End of Project Life.   Assume that a project has a 20-year life—from 1991 to 2010. The value of the project as of December 31, 2010 is the terminal value as of the end of the project life. This residual value refers to the liquidating or disposal value of a project.

For a manufacturing enterprise, the residual value consists of (1) the disposal value of the capital investments and (2) the liquidating value of the working capital. The first one includes the resale value of the land and buildings, and the scrap value of the equipment. The second type of value covers the disposal value of the inventories, the collectible value of the receivables, and the balance of the cash in banks as of the last day of operations.

If pro forma balance sheets have been prepared together with the projected cash flow statements, the book values in the balance sheets may be used as the starting point in estimating the liquidating value of the assets. However, the pro forma balance sheet values have to be adjusted for the following:

1. Increases in land value due to inflation. As the balance sheet value is based on acquisition cost, the land value as of the end of the project 20 years later will be much higher.
2. Excess of economic value over the book value of factories. Plants which are fully depreciated in the books may still have an economic value.
3. Liquidation expenses are not shown in the normal projected financial statements. Hence they have to be separately computed.

The balance of unpaid obligations as of the end of the project life is deducted from the expected proceeds of the assets.

The remainder or the terminal value is then added to the regular cash flow for the last year of operations. In Exhibit 4.6, for instance, the terminal value is composed of the expected proceeds from the sale of land, buildings, and equipment of $210,000 and the liquidation of the working capital of $40,000.

Value at the End of the Planning Horizon.   In many cases, the life of a project may cover 20 or even 40 years. It is usually not practical to prepare cash flow projections for 40 years and then estimate the rate of return based on this long duration. The usual practice is to prepare the calculations based on the first 10 operating years of the project. The resulting rate of return will be very low if it includes only the normal annual returns, as no value is placed on the returns after the first 10 years. Hence, it is necessary to estimate the terminal value as of the end of the 10th year. This terminal value represents, in effect, two values: (1) the regular annual returns from the 11th up to the last operating year of the project and (2) the terminal value as of the end of the project life.

There are two alternative approaches used in determining the value as of the end of the planning horizon: (1) the balance sheet approach and (2) the capitalized earnings approach. These approaches are described further in Chapter 2, Determinants of Projected Performance.

The balance sheet approach is based on the resale value of the assets less the liabilities as of this date. This procedure is the same as the one used in estimating the value as of the end of the project life as discussed in the prior section.

Sale Value of the Project. Either the balance sheet or capitalized earnings approach may be used in establishing the sale value. In either case, the commission payable to business broker for effecting the sale, as well as the income tax on the profit from the sale, has to be deducted from the selling price.

Financing Transactions Return. Some long-term loan agreements or bond indentures require the establishment of debt service or other types of funds. The release of these funds and interest earnings thereon to the general funds of the project constitutes a return.

IV. IRR MARGIN AND IRR INDEX

The IRR by itself is an absolute measure of profitability since it is not related to the cost of money. The IRR can be made more useful if it is compared with the hurdle rate or cost of money. The comparison may be done through the IRR margin or IRR index.

Hurdle Rate. Several large corporations have decided on cutoff or hurdle rates for projects. The factors entering in the determination of the cutoff rate include the cost of money, the risks involved, the type of industry, and the corporate strategy. The cost of money is discussed in Chapter 5, Section V, while risk is covered in Chapter 7.

Projects with IRR higher than the hurdle rate are favorably considered. The use of hurdle rates and IRR facilitates the screening of projects.

IRR Margin. The IRR margin is the excess of the IRR over the cost of money as adjusted for risk. Thus, if the IRR is 14% and the money cost is 10%, the margin is 4%. The margin is a measure of both return and risk. The higher the margin, the higher is the return and the higher is the risk which the project can take. The margin represents the possible decline from the expected IRR which the project can take before the project sustains a loss. In the illustration, the project can afford to have the IRR reduced from the expected 14% to 10% before the investors lose from the project.

IRR Index. The IRR index is calculated by dividing the IRR by the risk-adjusted cost of money. Thus the index, based on the figures given in the preceding paragraph, is 1.4. Projects with an index of over one are deemed desirable since the IRR is higher than the cost of money. Like the IRR margin, the index is also a measure of both return and risk. The higher the index, the higher is the return and the higher the risk which the project can absorb.

Debt/Equity Ratio and Risk. Where the money cost is less than the IRR, the IRR, the IRR margin, and the IRR index may be enhanced by upping the debt leverage. This is demonstrated in Chapter 5, Exhibit 5.10, second table. In this instance, the rise in the margin and index does not mean a decline in the risk since such a rise is caused by increasing the debt leverage. Raising the leverage in itself magnifies the risk.

V. EVALUATION OF THE IRR

ADVANTAGES

The IRR facilitates the comparison of competing projects with varying cash flow patterns. This provides the basis of the laddering or ranking of alternative investment opportunities. Furthermore, the IRR as determined can be compared with the money cost or opportunity cost of capital to the investor.

One advantageous built-in feature of the IRR is the lower importance it gives to the values in the distant future. For instance, if the IRR is 16%, the value of a return to be made 10 years from the investment date is less than $0.23 for every $1.00 (in terms of the value of the dollar as of the investment date). In a present value of 1 table at 16%, the present value factor at period 10 is 0.23. The farther away is the time horizon, the bigger is the discount or the percentage of the given value taken off.

The process of progressive discounting of the values automatically takes care of (1) errors in the calculations and (2) risks involved. The farther away is the time horizon, the bigger is the error in estimating the revenue and cost figures included in the cash flow projections. The time distance between the date of the preparation of the analysis and the realization or operation of the project magnifies the risks due to unexpected developments. Thus, the smaller is the ultimate value assigned to the returns from the latter years.

CLAIMED LIMITATIONS

Notwithstanding its apparent sound structure, some claim that the IRR may have certain limitations. These are

1. Practical limitations:
   a. Bias against long-term projects. The severe discounting of values in the distant future, as just explained, may unduly downgrade the significance of long-term projects.
   b. Bias in favor of long-term projects. On the other hand, in spite of values lopped off from the cash returns for the latter years, the IRR may not be a suitable tool for investors who are after fast, quick returns.
2. Conceptual limitations:
   a. Multiple rates of return. The cash flow pattern of certain projects may be such as to result in more than one possible IRR.
   b. Assumed reinvestment rate. When two or more projects are compared, it is assumed that the returns before the final return of the project with the longer project life can be reinvested at a rate which is the same as the IRR.

Bias Against Long-Term Projects. If the IRR is blindly applied, the projects to be selected are those with IRRs higher than those of other projects and higher than the cost of capital or hurdle rate.

Long-term projects, or those which concentrate on the upper end of the ladder of functions in Exhibit 2.1 of Chapter 2, Determinants of Projected Performance, have a longer gestation period, demand more capital, require more capital recovery time, and incur more risk than short-term measures. Naturally they have lower IRR.

Hence, the use of IRR favors short-term projects. This will lead the firm to more profitable operations in the next few years. However, this will stymie growth since short-term measures cannot provide for the development of new products.

Therefore, firms on a grow strategy will have to adopt one of two procedures in order to put promising long-term projects on par with desirable short-term measures although the former show lower IRR.

First, different hurdle rates may be set—generally, the higher is the location of the project in the ladder of functions mentioned earlier, the lower should be the hurdle rate.

Second, a strategic or growth adjustment factor may have to be developed. A project should be credited not only for its IRR but also for its contribution to the growth of the firm. The higher is the location of the project in the ladder of functions, the more should be its credit for the growth factor.

Bias in Favor of Long-Term Projects (Exhibit 4.7). The internal rate of return has automatically provided for bigger discounting (more values taken off) of returns expected in the more remote future. However, in certain projects such a feature may not be enough to take care of unusually high degree of risk involved. Investors in undertakings engaged in fads instead of basic commodities would be interested in the return on the investment just for the first few years. Similarly, investors venturing with very limited finances would consider the performance of their projects for the initial years as very critical.

Because of the foregoing, short-lived, lower-earning projects like project C in Exhibit 4.7 are preferred to longer-term projects with slightly higher overall returns, like project D. If the rate of return is applied to the entire project life, this method will give a higher ranking to project D rather than C. Hence, the application of the conventional IRR can be misleading for high-risk projects or for investors requiring immediate cash generation.

In certain cases, therefore, it is necessary to modify the period coverage of the conventional IRR, by applying the IRR formula only on the returns for the first few years' life of the project, say, five years.

This modified method should be distinguished from the conventional procedure where the IRR is calculated only for the planning horizon which is less than the project life. Under this conventional procedure, a residual value is added to the cash flow for the last year of the planning horizon in order to represent the cash flows expected to be received after the planning horizon period. In the modified method, this residual value is neglected.

Multiple Rates of Return (Exhibit 4.8).   The normal cash flow pattern is composed of negative cash flows (requiring investments in a project or measure) for the initial period or periods, followed by positive cash flow or cash flow stream (representing returns) until the end of the project life. This pattern of cash flow has been illustrated by all the prior examples. Projects having this pattern have only one IRR.

Projects with abnormal cash flow pattern are those which have another negative cash flow after the positive cash flow. Some projects with this pattern have multiple rates of return. Consider the following:

	Year	Project E	Project F
Annual (investments)			
and returns	0	($1,000,000)	($1,000,000)
	1	2,500,000	4,000,000
	2	(1,500,000)	(5,000,000)
	3	0	2,000,000
Project life		2 years	3 years
Internal rates of return		0% and	0% and
		50%	100%

As mentioned earlier in this chapter, an IRR is the rate which, if used to discount or compound the investments and returns to a common date, the total time-adjusted value of the investments equal the adjusted value of the returns. Exhibit 4.8 proves that the IRR of project E can either be 0% or 50%.

The presence of more than one IRR for a project has been advanced as one of the limitations of the IRR method. Although this holds water in theory, this does not present a weakness in practice.

There are very few projects with anticipated abnormal cash flow patterns. The few projects which may fall under this category are those which have substantial cleanup costs upon the termination of the project life, like nuclear plants. For the limited number of projects with expected negative cash flow at the tail of the project life, such negative cash flow is usually funded at the start as it is difficult to arrange for financing when the life of a project is already about to end. For instance, for project E in the illustration, the investment requirement in year 2 would be added to that in year 0. Another arrangement for this project type is to set aside some of the earnings in year 1 to cover the investment required in year 2. Either method eliminates the negative cash flow in year 2, converts the abnormal cash flow pattern to a normal one, and enables the project to have only one IRR.

Assumed Reinvestment Rate (Exhibit 4.9).   The question of reinvestment rate arises when two or more projects with (1) varying recovery patterns or (2) project lives are being compared.

One of the claimed limitations of the IRR is that the project with intermediate returns can attain its given IRR only if the intermediate returns can be reinvested at the same rate as the IRR.

This is illustrated in Exhibit 4.9. Projects A and H have identical investment size and IRR. However they have different lives and recovery patterns. In the case of A, the reinvestment rate applies to its intermediate return, that is, the return before the end of its project life. The intermediate return is the $58,000 expected to be recovered in year 1. The reinvestment period is for one year—year 2, which is the end of the life of A, the project with the longer life.

In the case of H, the reinvestment rate applies to the $116,000 return in year 1. The reinvestment period is also for one year—year 2, for the reason given.

If the $58,000 year 1 return of A can be reinvested at 16%, the return will grow to $67,280 as of the end of year 2. Thus, getting a $58,000 return in year 1 and $67,280 in year 2 is equivalent to getting nothing in year 1 but $134,560 in year 2, if the year 1 return can be reinvested at 16%. In this case, the original investment in A, plus the reinvestment of the intermediate return, earns an overall 16% IRR.

However, if the year 1 return can be reinvested at only 10%, the overall IRR if A declines to 14.49%.

In like manner, if the $116,000 year 1 return of H can be reinvested at

16%, the overall IRR of the investment in project H and in the reinvestment medium remains 16%. However, if the reinvestment rate goes down to 10%, the overall yield of project H and in the reinvestment vehicle whittles down to 12.96%. If the reinvestment rate used for A and H are the same, and the reinvestment rate is lower than 16%, the combined return of project H and its reinvestment vehicle is lower than that of A. The reason is that the lower rate applies to a bigger return ($116,000 for H versus $58,000 for A).

Appraisal of the Reinvestment Issue.   The reinvestment rate issue becomes relevant only because of the attempt to compare projects with different lives or cash flow patterns.

The assumed reinvestment rate issue is almost universally claimed as a limitation of the IRR principle. Actually, it is *not* a weakness of the IRR. By concept, the IRR is internally derived, that is, from data about the project itself. The IRR is applicable only to the investment or part of it while it is in the project. The IRR is only for the unrecovered investment and time while it is in the project. Subsequent investment media can have the same, lower, or higher yields. In project A, the reinvestment rate applies to the $58,000 *taken out of the project* in year 1. Hence the IRR does not apply to this any more. In project H, the reinvestment rate pertains to year 2 earnings, which is *after the life of the project*.

The use of a reinvestment rate, which may differ from the IRR, does not constitute a limitation of the IRR. Rather, it is another tool which is used in forming comparable investment packages out of different projects with varying durations and return patterns. How to use the reinvestment rate in this type of situation is illustrated in Chapter 6.

EXHIBIT 4.1:
Project A—Concept of IRR

I. Given data for IRR calculation

		Reference date *Dec. 31 1995*	*Dec. 31 1996*	*Dec. 31 1997*
Investment	Year 0	$100,000		
Returns	Year 1	*a*	← $58,000	
	Year 2	*b*	←	$67,280
		$100,000		

II. Present value of investment and returns at 16% IRR reference year: 1995

	Calendar *year*	*IRR year*	*Given* *value*	*Present* *value* *factor* *at 16%*	*Present* *value*
Investment	1995	0	$100,000	1.000	$100,000
Returns	1996	1	58,000	0.862	$ 50,000
	1997	2	67,280	0.743	50,000
				Total returns	$100,000

EXHIBIT 4.2:
Project A—Rationale of IRR

BANK DEPOSIT
Interest at 16%

Depositor — Deposit → $100,000 1995 → Bank Deposit — Withdrawals → $58,000 1996 / 67,000 1997

INVESTMENT
IRR at 16%

Investor — Investment → $100,000 1995 → Business Project — Returns → $58,000 1996 / 67,280 1997

DEPOSIT OR INVESTMENT TRANSACTIONS

Year	Balance, start of year	Add interest or return at 16%	Deposit or investment	Less drawings or return	Balance, end of year
1995	0	0	$100,000	0	$100,000
1996	$100,000	$16,000		$58,000	58,000
1997	58,000	9,280		67,000	0

EXHIBIT 4.3:
Project A—IRR Calculation
Reference year: 1995

	Calendar year	IRR year or period	Given value	FIRST TRIAL AT 15%		SECOND TRIAL AT 16%	
				Present value factor	Present value	Present value factor	Present value
Investment	1995	0	$100,000	1.000	$100,000	1.000	$100,000
Returns	1996	1	58,000	0.870	50,435	0.862	50,000
	1997	2	67,280	0.756	50,873	0.743	50,000
	Total returns		$125,280		$101,308		$100,000
	Difference		$ 25,280		$ 1,308		$ 0

EXHIBIT 4.4:
Project B—IRR Calculation
Reference year: 1994

	Calendar year	IRR year or period	Given value	AT 13%		AT 12%	
				Factor*	Adjusted value	Factor*	Adjusted value
Annual investments	1993	−1	$ 400	1.130	$452	1.120	$448
	1994	0	500	1.000	500	1.000	500
	Total investment		900		952		948
Annual returns	1995	1	100	0.885	$ 89	0.893	89
	1996	2	200	0.783	157	0.797	159
	1997	3	300	0.693	208	0.712	214
	1998	4	300	0.613	184	0.636	191
	1999	5	550	0.543	299	0.567	312
	Total returns		$1,450		$936		$965
	Difference		$ 550		($ 16)		$ 17

*The factors used are
For years before 1994 (the reference year)—amount of 1 factor
For years after 1994 (the reference year)—present value of 1 factor.

EXHIBIT 4.5:
Project B—Effect of changes in cash flow streams (dollars in $1,000)

Year	Base cash flow per Exhibit 4.6	WITH CHANGES IN TIMING OR PROJECT LIFE		WITH CHANGES IN AMOUNT OF	
		Investment timing	Project life	Annual Investment returns	
Annual investments					
1993	($ 400)*	$ 0	($ 400)	($ 360)	($ 400)
1994	(500)	(900)	(500)	(450)	(500)
Annual returns					
1995	100	100	100	100	100
1996	200	200	200	200	200
1997	300	300	300	300	400
1998	300	300	300	300	400
1999†	550	550	300	550	650
2000†			550		
Total investments	($ 900)	($ 900)	($ 900)	($ 810)	($ 900)
Total returns	$1,450	$1,450	$1,750	$1,450	$1,750
Internal rate of return	12.5%	14.3%	15.9%	15.6%	17.7%

*Values in parentheses mean investment.
†Excess of returns in 1999 or 2000 over $300,000 represent the terminal value.

95

EXHIBIT 4.6:

Project B—Composition of Investments and Returns (dollars in $1,000)

| | INVESTMENTS AND TERMINAL VALUE* | | | ANNUAL CASH FLOW | | | |
Year	Land, buildings, equipment	Pre-operating expenses	Working capital	Sales revenues	Operating and other expenses	Returns (cash profit)	Net cash flow
−1	($400)						($400)
0	(400)	($100)	($50)				(500)
1	0	0	0	$2,000	($1,850)	$150	100
2	0	0	0	2,500	(2,300)	200	200
3	0	0	0	3,000	(2,700)	300	300
4	0	0	0	3,000	(2,700)	300	300
5	210	0	40	3,000	(2,700)	300	550
IRR							12.50%

*Negative figures (in parentheses) represent investments; positive figures represent terminal value based on assets.

96

EXHIBIT 4.7:
Projects C and D—Comparison of Conventional and Modified IRR

	Period	Project C	Project D
Investment	0	($1,000)	($1,000)
Returns	1	440	220
	2	440	220
	3	440	220
	4	0	220
	5	0	220
	6	0	220
	7	0	220
	8	0	220
	9	0	220
	10	0	220
Internal rate of return			
From year 0 to year 10		15.28%	17.68%
From year 0 to year 3		15.28%	Negative

EXHIBIT 4.8:
Project E—Multiple Rates of Return

		AT 0%		AT 50%	
Year	Current year value	Factor*	Present value	Factor	Present value
Annual (investments and returns)					
0	($1,000)	1	($1,000)	2.25	($2,250)
1	2,500	1	2,500	1.50	3,750
2	(1,500)	1	(1,500)	1.00	(1,500)
Total investments	($2,500)		($2,500)		($3,750)
Total returns	$2,500		$2,500		$3,750

*At 0%, the amount of 1 and present value of 1 factors for all periods are 1.

EXHIBIT 4.9:
Projects A and H—Reinvestment Rate

Project investment	Year	A REINVESTMENT RATE		H REINVESTMENT RATE	
		At 16%	*At 10%*	*At 16%*	*At 10%*
Investment	0	($100,000)	($100,000)	($100,000)	($100,000)
Returns	1	58,000	58,000	116,000	116,000
	2	67,280	67,280	0	0
Internal rate of return		16.00%	16.00%	16.00%	16.00%
Reinvestment					
Investment	1	($ 58,000)	($ 58,000)	($116,000)	($116,000)
Return	2	67,280	63,800	134,560	127,600
Reinvestment rate		16.00%	10.00%	16.00%	10.00%
Total investment					
Investment	0	($100,000)	($100,000)	($100,000)	($100,000)
Returns	1				
	2	134,560	131,080	134,560	127,600
Combined rate of return		16.00%	14.49%	16.00%	12.96%
Composition of year 2 returns					
From project investment (year 2)		$ 67,280	$ 67,280	$ 0	$ 0
From reinvestment (year 2)		67,280	63,800	134,560	127,600
Total		$ 134,560	$ 131,080	$ 134,560	$ 127,600

Chapter 5 _____

PRESENT VALUE TECHNIQUES

There are three commonly used measures which exploit the concept of present value and utilize the company's cost of money: the present value of cost, or simply, the present value; the net present value of returns, or simply, net present value (NPV); and the discounted return/investment ratio (DRIR), which is popularly known by the very general term of profitability index.

The present value of cost represents the discounted value of the stream of costs. It is utilized to appraise the total cost as of a certain date, of acquiring and operating a building, plant, or equipment.

The net present value is the excess of the discounted or present value of the returns of a project over the discounted value of the investment. This chapter explains how the NPV is estimated, how the NPV is related to the internal rate of return (IRR), and how the NPV of a specific project is influenced by its determinants. The determinants are the intrinsic rate of return or IRR of the project, the discount rate, the interest spread (difference between the IRR and the discount rate), the investment or project size, the project life, and the pattern of the returns. The pattern refers to the annual cash recovery from the project.

One claimed advantage of the NPV over the IRR is that the use of NPV promotes growth and maximizes the net profit in terms of dollars, although not necessarily in terms of the rate of return.

The DRIR expresses the relationship between the discounted value of the returns and the discounted value of the investment. Although the DRIR and the NPV use this same set of two figures, the DRIR and NPV can result in the conflicting ranking of projects.

Section IV of this chapter illustrates how confusion can result by using the IRR, NPV, and DRIR in the traditional way. Each of these tools favors a project that is spurned by the other two. The new comparable investment approach (CIA) resolves this confusion in the next chapter.

I. PRESENT VALUE OF COST

Present value, or discounted value, is the worth as of today of sums of money due in the future. The present value is normally computed using as the reference year, the year when the first investment is scheduled to be made.

PRESENT VALUE OF COST METHOD

The present value of cost represents the discounted value or value as of today of the initial and subsequent annual operating costs to be incurred in the future. It is used in comparing alternatives which do not directly generate revenues or cost savings or where the revenues generated or cost savings effected are difficult to measure.

An example of a nonrevenue-producing project is the construction of an administrative building for additional personnel. However, the analysis of the construction of a building to replace a rented one may use net present value as discussed in Section II.

ILLUSTRATION

Consider that a firm is evaluating two types of equipment—both with a life of three years and with the same capabilities. Type I has an acquisition cost of $480,000 and annual operating costs of $50,000. Type II has a much lower first-time cost of $240,000 but higher subsequent yearly costs of $150,000. Thus, the total acquisition and operating costs of type I is $630,000 only, while that of type II is a steeper $690,000. The initial action is to favor type I.

Equipment Cost and Implied Interest (Exhibit 5.1).   However, these figures have not considered the time value of money. Just comparing their total acquisition and operating costs is not enough, since a dollar of acquisition cost payable today is worth more than a dollar of operating cost payable three years hence. Hence the costs have to be adjusted for the value of time, or implied interest.

If the cost of money is 10%, the discounted value of the cost of type I, at $604,000, is still slightly lower than that of type II. However, at a 14% money cost, the time-adjusted total cost of type II is lower. The use of a higher discounting rate favors type II as against type I since the latter has a heavier up-front cost.

At about 12%, the present value of the cost of type I equals that of type II. The 12% is considered as the crossover money cost. At interest costs higher than this rate, type II will have less time-adjusted cost than will type I.

II. NET PRESENT VALUE

Net present value, net discounted value, net discounted return, net present worth, or excess present value is the excess of the discounted value of the returns of a project over the discounted value of the investments. *Net* means after deducting the investments. Hence the NPV is roughly the equivalent of the IRR margin. The margin is the excess of the IRR over the cost of money, which is expressed as a percentage.

A positive net present value indicates that the project will earn more than what it will cost to raise the financing to invest in the project. The higher the net present value, the more desirable is the project.

Both the NPV and IRR margin are utilized primarily to measure return. However, they may also be applied to gauge risk. The NPV represents the dollar amount which may be cut off from the expected present value of returns before the project sustains a loss. Similarly, the IRR margin refers to the interest percentage which may be taken off from the IRR before the project incurs loss from the viewpoint of the investors.

APPLICATIONS

The applications of NPV in three types of situations are illustrated.

Project Without Identifiable Revenues.   The analysis for the construction of an administrative building to replace a rented facility may utilize the NPV. The construction cost is the investment; the rental to be saved less the building-related annual cost such as maintenance and insurance represent the return.

Capital Project.   The NPV concept is commonly used to support capital investment decisions covering the acquisition, expansion, replacement, upgrading, or disposal of physical facilities. In the analysis for these decisions, the acquisition costs, operating costs, and tax credits which extend for several years are discounted to the time when the first cash transaction is made. The NPV also proves a handy tool in major automation programs, where the cost structures, sales volume, selling prices, and inventory and receivable levels are changed. The applications of NPV in equipment acquisition decisions are demonstrated in Chapter 12, while the use of NPV in automation decisions is examined in Chapter 13.

Business Unit.   The NPV is also applied in the decision analysis for the establishment, expansion, or disposition of whole enterprises or business units. In these cases, the future capital expenditure programs, operating cash flows, and residual values are taken into the analysis.

In deciding on the future of a division, the cash flow which serves as the basis of the NPV calculations is first prepared. A simplified form follows.

Year	Capital expenditures	Operating cash flow	Residual value	Net cash flow
Year 0	($30,000,000)			($ 30,000,000)
Year 1		$40,000,000		40,000,000
Year 2	(10,000,000)	44,000,000		34,000,000
Year 3		48,000,000		48,000,000
Year 4	(10,000,000)	53,000,000		43,000,000
Year 5		59,000,000	60,000,000	119,000,000

In this illustration, the financial projection period is only 5 years. In many instances, it may be preferable to have one for 10 years.

If the cost of money to the firm is 10%, the total value of the above net cash flow as of year 0 is $174,000,000. Thus, if the firm is offered $200,000,000 for the division, the offer may be accepted on purely financial considerations. However, other factors may have to enter the picture. For instance, the division may be considered as a good portfolio risk as far as the other investments of the company are concerned. (See Chapter 7, Section I for a discussion of the portfolio risk.) The general strategy of the firm may also influence the decision on the disposition of the firm. (See Chapter 2, Section I.)

CONCEPT OF NET PRESENT VALUE

Illustration (Exhibit 5.2). As exemplified by Project A in Exhibit 5.2, part I, the NPV is the excess of the present value of the returns in years 1 and 2, over the present value of the investment in year 0, using a given discount rate. If year 0 is used as the reference year, and 10% is the discounting rate, the $58,000 projected return in year 1 is discounted at 10% to year 0 in order to establish the value a; the $67,280 return in year 2 is likewise discounted to year 0 to arrive at the value b. Values a and b are then added up to c, and c is deducted from the $100,000 investment in order to arrive at the NPV. The NPV is calculated at $8,331 (Exhibit 5.2, part II).

If the returns are discounted at a rate higher than 10%, the NPV will be lower than $8,331. For instance, if 16% is used, the NPV becomes zero (Exhibit 5.2, part III).

Estimating the NPV. The computations in Exhibit 5.2 make use of the present value factor (present value of 1) taken from a compound interest table. If the current values of the returns are uniform, thus forming an annuity, the present value of 1 *per period* from an interest table may be used instead.

Computer spreadsheet software incorporates a formula to obtain the net present value directly. However, in using the software, the reference year used in the software formula should be checked. For instance, in one software, if the values of years 0, 1, and 2 are entered to determine the NPV, the NPV which will result will be as of year -1, which is one year before year 0, and not as of year 0, which is the presumed reference year in Exhibit 5.2.

Comparison with the IRR.   In calculating the NPV, the discount rate used is the cost of money. It is given. It is obtained outside of the NPV formula. On the contrary, the IRR technique determines the effective earnings rate of a project, which is the IRR. The IRR is internally generated, hence the word internal in internal rate of return.

IRR (Exhibit 5.3, part I).   The IRR is 16% because if this rate were used to discount the $116,000 return to year 0, the discounted value equals the investment of $100,000. In other words, the 16% IRR converts a $100,000 investment in year 0 to a $116,000 return in year 1.

NPV (Exhibit 5.3, part II).   A positive NPV emerges when the IRR exceeds the discount rate used. The 16% IRR converts the $100,000 year 0 investment into a $116,000 year 1 return. When this return is discounted back to year 0, not at the 16% IRR but only at 10%, the assumed cost of money, the discounted value of the return, is $105,455, which is higher than the original investment. The $5,455 excess is the NPV.

Comparison with the Interest Spread (Exhibit 5.3, part III).   In a banking transaction, the profit is created by the spread between the lending and borrowing rates. (Interest spread is also discussed in Chapter 19, Return on Investment Ratio Analysis, Section VI.) Similarly, a NPV is created by the interest spread—the excess of the earning rate (the IRR) over the cost rate (the discount rate). The spread represents the profit. In the illustration, the spread is 6% (16% IRR less 10% discount rate). This spread enables the $100,000 investment in year 0 to generate a net earnings $6,000 in year 1. However, this year 1 earning has to be brought back to year 0 to make it comparable with the timing of the investment. Hence it has to be discounted at the cost of money rate. The discounted value of the $6,000 is $5,455, which is the same as the NPV.

Exhibit 5.3 uses a one-year project life. A more involved case arises when the life is over one year. This is shown in Exhibit 5.7.

DETERMINANTS OF THE NET PRESENT VALUE

Dimensions of NPV (Exhibit 5.4).   The NPV of a project approximates the cubic volume of the box in Exhibit 5.4. Just as the volume of a box is measured by its dimensions of height, width and length, the NPV of a project is determined by the interest spread, investment size, and project life. Thus, if one of these NPV dimensions is raised, the NPV is also upped. However, the NPV is more difficult to gauge because in addition to these three dimensions, there are other determinants: the IRR, the discount rate, the timing and amounts of the returns before the end of the project, and the compounding effect of interest. The last two factors are applicable only to multiperiod projects. Thus, the NPV of a given project will vary if any one of these is changed.

Due to the factors affecting the NPV in addition to the IRR, projects with the same IRR can have varied NPVs. Furthermore, there are projects with high IRRs but with low NPVs or vice versa.

Interest Spread (Exhibit 5.5). Given the investment size, project life, and IRR of a project, the NPV decreases as the discount rate increases. At zero discount rate (just for discussion purposes), the discount factor is one; that is, the return is not discounted at all. At 10% discount rate, the NPV of Project H is $5,455, as explained earlier. When the discount rate equals the IRR (16% in the example), the NPV becomes zero. At discount rates higher than the IRR, the NPV becomes negative.

The decline in the NPV due to the rise in the discount rate is due to two causes. The primary one is the thinning out of the interest spread. As noted in Exhibit 5.3, part III, the spread is actually the factor which creates the NPV. Without the spread, there is no NPV. Thus, the smaller the spread, the smaller the NPV.

The decrease in NPV due to the increase in discount rate is demonstrated by the box in Exhibit 5.4. Given the same investment size, project life, and IRR, the increase in discount rate cuts the interest spread, thereby shrinking the cubic volume of the box which represents the NPV.

The other contributory factor is the discount rate itself. Even given the same spread, the higher the discount, the lower is the NPV for projects with normal cash flow patterns. The effect of discount rate on the NPV, given the same spread, is explained in a separate subsequent section.

Investment Size (Exhibit 5.6). An increase in the investment size will raise the net present value. For instance, project J, which has 1.4 times the investment of project H but has the same IRR and project life, has 1.4 times the net present value.

The increase in the investment size proportionately magnifies the cubic volume of the box in Exhibit 5.4, thereby correspondingly increasing the NPV.

A substantial advantage in the magnitude of investment more than offsets a slightly lower IRR.

Project Life (Exhibits 5.3, 5.6 and 5.7). Given the same investment size and IRR, the project with the longer duration has the higher NPV—

assuming the IRR is higher than the discounting rate. This is due to the longer time with which the investment can generate earnings.

The lengthening of the project extends one of the dimensions of the box in Exhibit 5.4, thereby bloating the volume of the box which represents the NPV. Thus while projects H and K as compared in Exhibit 5.6 have an investment of $100,000 each, and a 16% IRR, H, with a one-year life, has a $5,455 net present value while K, with a two-year life has $11,207, which is about double.

The difference in their net present value may be explained by a comparison of their investment growth and interest spread. See Exhibit 5.3, part II, for project H and Exhibit 5.7 for project K. Project H's $100,000 investment is converted to a $116,000 return as of the end of its one-year life. On the other hand, project K's $100,000 investment, which becomes $116,000 after one year, has another year to grow to $134,560. The .826446 discounting factor for the $134,560 return is less than the .909091 for project H's $116,000 due to the longer discounting time (two years). However, the discounted value of K's $134,560 is still much higher than the time-adjusted value of H's $116,000.

Return Pattern or Investment Recovery (Exhibit 5.6). Given the same investment size, IRR, and project life, the project which has more cash returns during the earlier years has a lower net present value—assuming the IRR is higher than the discounting rate. The reason for this is that the earnings which are taken out of the project in the form of the cash returns do not earn for the project any more.

This is shown graphically in Exhibit 5.4. Any returns before the end of the project life will be chopped off from the box. Hence the NPV will represent the cubic volume not of the entire box but only of the remaining part.

This concept is demonstrated by a comparison of projects A and K in Exhibit 5.6. Both projects have the same investment, project life, and IRR. Project A has a lower NPV because it has a cash return in year 1 while Project K has none.

Discount Rate (Exhibit 5.6). Given the same investment size, project life, return pattern, and interest spread, the project with the lower discount rate (and hence also lower IRR), has the higher NPV—assuming the IRR is higher than the discount rate.

Take the case of projects K and L in Exhibit 5.6. Project L, with a lower discount rate and IRR, has the higher NPV.

III. DISCOUNTED RETURN/INVESTMENT RATIO

The discounted return/investment ratio is the ratio of the present value of the returns to the present value of the investment. The DRIR is commonly known by a very broad term, profitability or ranking index. The DRIR is applicable to cases where the NPV may be used.

The DRIR is roughly the equivalent of the IRR index, which is the ratio of the IRR to the discount rate. Although both the DRIR and IRR index are mainly used to measure return, they may also be utilized to gauge the risk. In both instances, the excess of the DRIR or IRR index over the value of one, represents the portion of the present value of returns or of IRR which may be chopped off from the present value of returns or from the IRR, before the project sustains a loss.

CONCEPT OF THE DRIR
(Exhibit 5.8).

The DRIR is calculated by dividing the present value of the returns by the present value of the investments. Project DD in Exhibit 5.8 has returns whose present value as of year 0 is $222 million. Its DRIR is 1.11, which is $222 million divided by the $200 million investment. The higher the DRIR, the more attractive is the project. Theoretically, a project with a DRIR higher than one will ultimately generate economic profit to the investor.

DRIR compares the present value of the returns with that of the investments. This automatically considers the investment size disparity among projects. The NPV does not provide for this disparity. Hence if the objective of a firm with limited funds is to maximize the return in terms of absolute dollar, the DRIR seems to be a fairer measure than the NPV. Hence some authors favor the use of DRIR in project ranking.

Section II of this chapter has revealed that a project with a much smaller IRR or interest spread but much longer project life, much bigger investment, and much delayed return pattern may have a much higher NPV than another project with a higher IRR. This condition is illustrated by projects CC and DD in Exhibit 5.8. DD, with a slightly lower IRR has a much higher NPV since it has double the investment. This situation results in contradictory project ranking—the NPV favoring DD and the IRR, CC.

STRENGTHS AND LIMITATIONS OF THE DRIR

Differences in Investment. The supposed objective of the DRIR is to correct this limitation of the NPV. The DRIR has succeeded in this mission—it recognized the superiority of CC over DD, and hence has assigned a higher DRIR to CC. The DRIR has succeeded in this case since the DRIR, by formula, recognizes the differences in the investment sizes of the projects.

Differences in Project Lives. However, the DRIR, like the NPV, disregards differences in project lives in comparing the desirability of projects. For instance, as between AA and BB in Exhibit 5.8, the DRIR favors BB although AA has a higher intrinsic profitability rate as measured by the

IRR. The DRIR gives a higher rating to BB because it has three times the life of AA, and hence it has a longer opportunity to generate a cash flow for BB. However, the DRIR did not give credit to the earnings to be made in years 2 and 3 by the year 1 return of AA.

Differences in Return Patterns. Furthermore, the DRIR, like the NPV, does not take into account the differences in the return patterns of projects. Between BB and CC in Exhibit 5.8, the DRIR prefers CC. Although CC has a lower IRR, it has a higher DRIR because its returns are delayed compared to those of BB. However, DRIR failed to consider the income to be earned by the years 1 and 2 returns of BB.

IV. CONTRADICTORY LADDERING OF PROJECTS

Although the IRR, NPV, and DRIR are all time-adjusted techniques, their application in ranking the viability of projects could result in conflicting priorities—with each of them giving the highest rating to a project which was not the first choice according to the other two methods. This situation is exemplified by the four projects in Exhibit 5.8. The NPV gives the first priority to Project DD, the DRIR prefers CC, the IRR favors Project AA, and both the DRIR and the IRR give the second ranking to BB. Project AA, the first choice under the IRR, is the last under the NPV and DRIR; DD, the first under the NPV, is the last under the IRR.

Three questions arise from this erratic project ranking. The first: Since the three methods give different results, are all the techniques basically defective?

The second: Is one of them sound? If so, may the other two be disregarded?

The last: Can the differences in the results of the IRR, NPV, or DRIR be reconciled?

Differences in Applications (Answer to the First Question). All the three methods are basically sound in concept. The IRR is also sound in application, since the IRR automatically considers differences in the cash flow characteristics in terms of the investment size, project life, and return pattern. The DRIR is not sound in application since it disregards disparities in project life and return pattern. The NPV is worse in application since it does not incorporate variations in the three cash flow characteristics. Since the three techniques have differences in what they consider among the cash flow characteristics and what they do not, it is but natural that they produce different results.

Utility of the Three Methods (Second Question). The IRR determines the intrinsic return of a project. It is sound in both concept and application. Hence it should be used in decision analysis.

The NPV gives a different measure of project desirability. While the IRR measures the profitability in terms of a percentage or the rate of profitability, the NPV denominates it in terms of absolute dollars. Hence the IRR should be complemented by the NPV. However, the application of the NPV should be modified so that it considers disparities in investment size, project life, and return pattern.

The DRIR is a hybrid between the IRR and NPV. As may be noticed from Exhibit 5.8, the projects given the first two rankings by the DRIR were given second or third rankings by the IRR and NPV.

Reconcilability of the Differences (Third Question). If the NPV and DRIR consider differences in the cash flow characteristics of the projects, the NPV and DRIR will normally give substantially the same results. Since the NPV and DRIR will have the same results, it is redundant to use DRIR if NPV is also used.

Even if the NPV incorporates the differences in the cash flow characteristics, its results will still be different from that of the IRR since they are calculated in different manners. However, although their results will be different, the differences will be substantially reduced.

Comparable Investment Approach. Chapter 6, Section III, illustrates a way of making the investment proposals comparable in their cash flow characteristics so that the right decisions may be made. The CIA also minimizes, if not eliminates, the differences between the IRR and NPV.

V. CASH FLOW, MONEY COST, AND FINANCING LEVERAGE

It is a matter of common practice that (1) in determining the NPV and DRIR, the cash flows are discounted, using the money cost as the discount rate, and (2) the cash flows are used to internally generate the IRR, and the IRR is compared with the hurdle rate, which, in turn, is partly determined by the money cost.

BASIS OF CASH FLOW AND MONEY COST
(Exhibit 5.9)

Notwithstanding the foregoing, the following issues have seldom been raised and resolved:

Project Cash Flow. Does the project cash flow pertain to (1) the *total project investment*, which is the project equity to be put up by the corporate sponsor and project debt (Exhibit 5.9, alternative 1), or (2) just the *project equity* (alternatives 2 and 3)?

Corporate Money Cost. If the investment just pertains to the project equity, should the money cost to be used as the discount rate or as a basis of the hurdle rate (1) be the cost of the *corporate equity,* which is equivalent to the stockholders' equity of the corporate sponsor (alternative 2), or (2) the weighted average of the *corporate money cost,* which refers to both the corporate equity and the corporate loans (alternative 3)?

The chosen treatment of these issues substantially affects the computed NPV, DRIR, IRR, and hurdle rate, thereby influencing the direction of the decision on the proposals.

CASH FLOW AND MONEY COST—ALTERNATIVE TREATMENTS (Exhibit 5.9)

There are three alternative treatments regarding the project cash flow and corporate money cost to be used. The alternatives are

1. The project cash flow pertains to the project total investment, and the corporate money cost pertains to the weighted average of the corporate equity and corporate loans.
2. The project cash flow refers to the project equity portion only, and the corporate money cost refers to the corporate equity only.
3. The project cash flow represents the project equity portion only, but the corporate money cost represents the weighted average of the corporate equity and corporate loans.

Alternative 1—With Corporate Leverage. This alternative is applicable if the project is to be undertaken by a division and the corporate parent is the one arranging all the financing. The assumption here is that the parent will fund the project from its common pool of funds, which is from both equity and loans.

This treatment may also be used for divisions or projects which will obtain loans on their own but such loans have not yet been arranged, or if the management would like to determine the operating NPV, DRIR, or IRR, that is, the NPV, DRIR, or IRR of the project itself, without the benefit of project debt leverage.

Alternative 2—With Project Leverage. This alternative is used if loans will be obtained directly for the project and if the corporation's equity in the project will be funded by additional stockholders' capital contribution to the corporation.

Alternative 3—With Double Leverage. This is the same as alternative 2 except that the corporation's equity in the project will be financed by both additional stockholders' capital contribution to the corporation and corporate loan. An assumption is made that this corporate funding is in the same proportion as the present corporate financing structure.

Although the alternatives vary in their treatment of project cash flow and corporate money cost and hence in the resulting NPV, DRIR, and IRR, in practice such distinctions are usually not clearly brought out. The differences in the NPV, DRIR, and IRR arising from each alternative are revealed in the succeeding section.

EFFECT OF LEVERAGES ON THE RETURNS
(Exhibit 5.10)

Assume that a one-year project requires a $100,000,000 total investment, of which $60,000,000 will be financed by a 10% loan. Without the loan financing the project gives a 20% IRR, and with the loan, 35%.

The corporate sponsor has a loan cost of 8%, and the stockholders desire an 18% return on their investment. Based on the financing structure shown in Exhibit 5.10, the average money cost is 13%.

Alternative 1—With Corporate Leverage. Based on total equity financing for the project, and with the equity to come from additional corporate capital contributions and corporate loans (and not project loans), the project will have a NPV, DRIR, IRR, and debt/equity ratio as shown in Exhibit 5.10, part II.

The effective debt/equity ratio of 50:50 is the same as the present corporate debt/equity ratio since all the project financing will come from the corporation based on the current proportion of corporate debt to corporate equity.

Alternative 2—With Project Leverage. The 60:40 financing structure ratio is the same as that of the project since the funds which the corporation will supply to the project as its equity contribution will all be taken from additional corporate capital contributions.

The IRR of this alternative is better than that of Alternative 1 due to the use of debt leverage in the project.

The DRIR is better because the increase in the IRR (from 20% in alternative 1 to 35%) is much higher than the climb in the discount rate (from 13% to 18%).

Notwithstanding the improvement of alternative 2 over 1, the NPV declined because of the smaller corporate investment in the project (small investment size).

Alternative 3—With Double Leverage. The debt/equity ratio is 80:20 because of the 40% project equity, only 50% is to be supplied by corporate equity. All the profitability indicators are better for alternative 3 because of the use of double financing leverage—the combined exploitation of the leverage at the project level and at the corporate level.

The other types of leverages are explained in Chapter 15.

MONEY COST CALCULATIONS

Average Cost Versus Cost of Specific Sources.   In practice, the cost of money used as the discount rate or as a basis in determining the hurdle rate normally represents the weighted average cost of the capital, loans, and other funding sources of the corporate sponsor. The soundness of this practice depends upon the specifics of the corporation and its projects and upon the purpose of the analysis.

If the corporate sponsor intends to raise funds in the same financing mix it has at present, or if it intends to finance its projects from a common pool of fund, or if the analysis is made in connection with a preliminary study, then the weighted average cost of existing funds may be used.

However, the use of weighted average has its drawbacks. First, this assumption may be contrary to what the actual sources of funds will be for future projects. For instance, the company may decide to finance future projects mainly with equity because of the restrictions placed by present loan covenants on additional borrowings. Or the corporation may have decided to obtain mainly debt financing in the future in order not to dilute the per share earnings or so as to maximize the shareholders' earnings through leverage.

It is also possible that certain special fund sources may be available for a project but not for the general operations of the corporate sponsor. Thus, a plant to be located in an economic development zone may qualify for a low-interest rate loan.

In these instances, the actual cost of money to be used by the corporate sponsor for the project will be different from the present weighted average cost of funds for the corporation.

A major disadvantage of the use of weighted average money cost is that it will lead to the approval of undesirable projects. The average cost will bring down the higher cost fund sources such that the calculated average money cost to be used as the discount rate will be lower than the IRR of the project. This situation will result in the recommendation for implementation of this project although its IRR is lower than the highest cost fund source to be utilized. (See Chapter 6, part IV, for an illustration of this.) This anomaly can be remedied if specific fund sources are identified for each project.

Historical Versus Expected Money Cost.   Whether the money cost to be used represents average money cost or cost of specific funds, the cost may be calculated based on historical cost or book cost, or expected or projected cost. The first method is more readily available. However, the latter is more specific and hence more reasonable.

Using the expected money cost will also force the management to pinpoint the possible sources of funds for the projects early in the planning stage. It prods management to analyze which idle bank deposits may be tapped, which banks may be approached for new loans, which equity investors may be sounded for additional capital contribution, which existing investments may be liquidated, or how the operating cash flow for the next few years or months may be allocated.

Cost of Fund Sources.

COST OF LOANS. The cost of loans do not refer just to the interest payments, but to loans fees, deposit requirements, and other terms which influence the effective cost of financing. These terms are discussed in detail in Chapter 14. Inflation, and the income tax reduction due to the use of interest and other loan-related costs as tax-deductible items, have also to be factored in.

COST OF STOCKHOLDERS' EQUITY. The manner of estimating the cost of stockholders' equity is more complicated. Several ways of calculating the cost are offered. The two most simple are the book cost approach and the market earnings approach. A method which is gaining acceptance is the capital asset pricing model (CAPM). These three approaches are explained next.

BOOK COST APPROACH. Under this approach, the cost of the equity represents the net profit earned during the latest accounting period, expressed as a percentage of the stockholders' equity per books. The cost under this method is equivalent to the accounting rate of return (ARR) or return on stockholders' equity (ROSE) as explained in Chapter 19, Section I. The various ramifications under this method are also revealed in that chapter. Although this method is both easy to understand and seemingly objective, this may not give the best estimate.

MARKET VALUE APPROACH. Under this method, the total cost to the company is the total income of the stockholders during the latest 12-month period. Their total income is composed of two parts: the appreciation in the market value of the shares during the period and the dividends. Their total income, expressed as a percentage of the market value as of the beginning of the period, represents the cost of equity.

Although this approach is better than the book cost method, this has three limitations. First, it is difficult to obtain the market value of shares where the issuer is not listed on the stock exchanges. Second, due to the wide fluctuations in the stock prices, the calculated cost may be subject to aberrations. In fact, where there is a substantial decline in the prices during the year, this method can result in a negative return. Third, this method gives the historical cost, which may be used only as a takeoff point in estimating what the shareholders desire as their income in the future.

CAPITAL ASSET PRICING MODEL.   This model builds the investors' risk into the cost of equity. The method recognizes two types of risks assumed by an investor in the stock market: (1) the *company risk*, which is known in the CAPM as the unsystematic or diversifiable risk, and (2) the *industry risk*, which is known as the systematic or undiversifiable risk. The company risk pertains to a specific firm, as its reliance on few suppliers, weak financing support, or strained production facilities. These risks influence the return on, and market value of, the shares of stock of the firm.

The industry risk refers to the industry itself, as competitive structure and response of the market to economic cycles. Industry risk impacts on the return and market value of the firms in the industry.

The first type of risk can be eliminated by diversifying an investor's portfolio among different firms in the industry; the industry risk cannot be eliminated by this type of diversification—hence the term undiversifiable risk.

This approach assumes that the shareholders of a company have diversified portfolios and hence the company risk is not applicable to them. Therefore the CAPM considers only the industry risk.

Under the CAPM, the cost of equity of a firm, or the rate of return desired by its shareholders is determined by the following formula:

desired return = risk-free rate + (beta × general stock market
risk premium)

The risk-free rate is the return on government securities, as Treasury bills.

The total return on the general stock market is considered as composed of two items: the risk-free return and the risk premium. The risk premium is the excess of the total return over the risk-free rate.

The beta is the relationship of the variability of the return of stocks of firms in the industry to the sensitivity of the return on the stocks traded in the stock market in general. The variability of the return is considered as the risk. A beta of 1 means that the industry behaves in step with the general market. A beta of less than 1 means that the industry is more stable than the other industries in general, and therefore the risk premium for the industry should be less than that of the general market. Consequently, the desired return for a company in the industry is also lower.

The use of CAPM in determining the cost of equity has two practical limitations. First, the CAPM does not consider the risk pertaining to specific companies (unsystematic risk). This corporate risk is just as significant as the industry risk. See Chapter 7.

Second, the calculations of the beta and general market risk premium are based on historical data, while the resulting cost of equity is used in discounting future cash flows. Industry performance in the past, as when the industry was in the maturity stage, will be different from its future performance when it will be in the declining phase.

COST OF ACCOUNTS PAYABLE. If the historical average money cost has to be used, the accounts payable has to be included as a funding source. Since the payable is superficially interest free, its inclusion will bring down the average money cost.

In reality, accounts payable has a cost in terms of higher suppliers' prices. See Chapter 25 for this concept and application in analysis.

Accounts payable may be utilized to fund projects to the extent that the payables exceed the raw material inventories.

EXHIBIT 5.1:
Equipment Types I and II—Present Value of Cost
(dollars in $1,000)

	TYPE I			TYPE II		
	Current year value	*Present value of 1 factor**	*Present value*	*Current year value*	*Present value of 1 factor**	*Present value*
At discount rate of 10%						
Year 0	$480	1.000	$480	$240	1.000	$240
1	50	0.909	45	150	0.909	136
2	50	0.826	41	150	0.826	124
3	50	0.751	38	150	0.751	113
Total	$630		$604	$690		$613
At discount rate of 14%						
Year 0	$480	1.000	$480	$240	1.000	$240
1	50	0.877	44	150	0.877	132
2	50	0.769	38	150	0.769	115
3	50	0.675	34	150	0.675	101
Total	$630		$596	$690		$588

*At interest rate of 10% or 14% as indicated. Taken from a compound interest table.

EXHIBIT 5.2:
Project A—Concepts of Net Present Value

I. Net present value	Reference year = year 0		Year 1	Year 2
Investment	$100,000			
Present value of returns				
Year 1	*a*	10% discount rate for 1 year	$58,000	
Year 2	*b*	10% discount rate for 2 years		$67,280
Total	*c*			
Net present value	$?			

	Year	Current value	Present value factor	Present value
II. NPV at 10% discount rate				
Investment	0	$100,000	1.000	$100,000
Returns				
Year 1	1	$ 58,000	0.909	$ 52,727
Year 2	2	67,280	0.826	55,603
Total		$125,280		108,331
Net present value				$ 8,331
III. NPV at 16% discount rate				
Investment	0	$100,000	1.000	$100,000
Returns				
Year 1	1	$ 58,000	0.862	$ 50,000
Year 2	2	67,280	0.743	50,000
Total		$125,280		$100,000

EXHIBIT 5.3:
Project H—NPV in Relation to IRR and Interest Spread

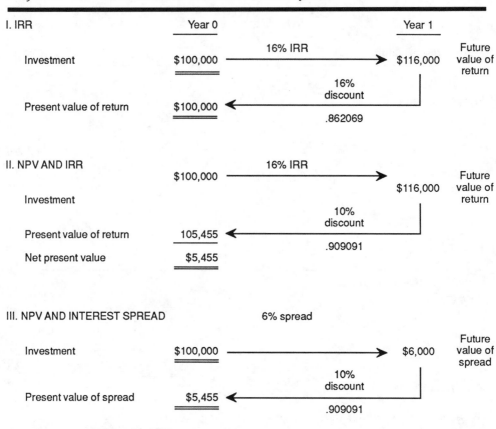

EXHIBIT 5.4:
Determinants of NPV

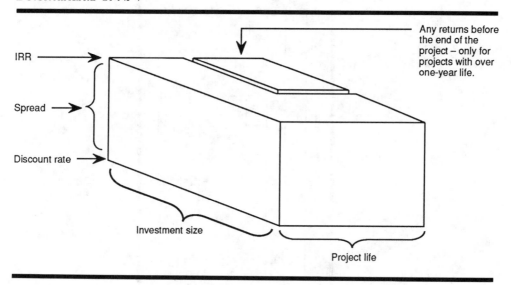

IRR

Spread

Discount rate

Any returns before
the end of the
project – only for
projects with over
one-year life.

Investment size

Project life

EXHIBIT 5.5:
Project H—Effect of Interest Spread on NPV

			Interest spread		
Interest spread		16%	6%	0%	–2%
Discount rate		0%	10%	16%	18%
Investment	Year 0	$100,000	$100,000	$100,000	$100,000
Return					
Current value	Year 1	$116,000	$116,000	$116,000	$116,000
Discount factor		1.000	0.909	0.862	0.847
Present value	Year 0	$116,000	$105,455	$100,000	$ 98,305
Net present value	Year 0	$ 16,000	$ 5,455	$ 0	($ 1,695)

EXHIBIT 5.6:
Factors Affecting NPV

| | | Base | EFFECT OF CHANGES IN | | | |
| | | | Project size | Project life | Recovery pattern | Discount rate |
		Proj. H Exh. 5	Proj. J	Proj. K Exh. 7	Proj. A Exh. 2	Proj. L
Internal rate of return		16%	16%	16%	16%	14%
Interest spread		6%	6%	6%	6%	6%
Discount rate		10%	10%	10%	10%	8%
Discount factors	For year 1	.909	.909	.909	.909	.926
	For year 2	.826	.826	.826	.826	.857
Investment	Year 0	($100,000)	($140,000)	($100,000)	($100,000)	($100,000)
Returns at current value	Year 1	116,000	162,400	134,560	58,000	129,960
	Year 2	0	0	0	67,280	0
Returns at discounted value	Year 1	105,455	147,636	111,207	52,727	111,420
	Year 2	0	0	0	55,603	111,420
	Total	105,455	147,636	111,207	108,331	111,420
Net present value		$ 5,455	$ 7,636	$ 11,207	$ 8,331	$ 11,420
Internal rate of return		16.00%	16.00%	16.00%	16.00%	14.00%

EXHIBIT 5.7:
Project K—NPV in Relation to IRR and Interest Spread

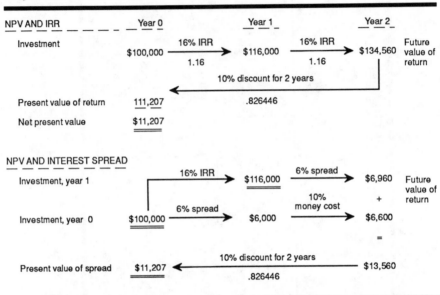

NPV AND IRR ‒ ‒ ‒ ‒ ‒ ‒ ‒ Year 0 ‒ ‒ ‒ ‒ ‒ ‒ ‒ ‒ ‒ ‒ Year 1 ‒ ‒ ‒ ‒ ‒ ‒ ‒ ‒ Year 2 ‒ ‒

	Year 0	Year 1	Year 2	
Investment	$100,000	16% IRR → $116,000	16% IRR → $134,560	Future value of return
		1.16	1.16	

10% discount for 2 years

| Present value of return | 111,207 | .826446 |
| Net present value | $11,207 | |

NPV AND INTEREST SPREAD

Investment, year 1		16% IRR → $116,000	6% spread → $6,960	Future value of return
			10% money cost	+
Investment, year 0	$100,000	6% spread → $6,000	→ $6,600	
				=

| | | 10% discount for 2 years | |
| Present value of spread | $11,207 ← | .826446 | $13,560 |

EXHIBIT 5.8:

Time-Adjusted Return Techniques—Conflicting Results

		PROJECT			
		AA	*BB*	*CC*	*DD*
Project life in years		1	3	3	3
Investment	Year 0	($100,000)	($100,000)	($100,000)	($200,000)
Returns	Year 1	$122,000	$ 20,000		
	Year 2		$ 70,000		
	Year 3		$ 60,000	$164,000	$312,000
Discount rate		12%	12%	12%	12%
Present value of return		$108,929	$116,368	$116,732	$222,075
NPV		$ 8,929	$ 16,368	$ 16,732	$ 22,075
DRIR		1.09	1.16	1.17	1.11
IRR		22%	20%	18%	16%
Project ranking according to					
NPV		4	3	2	1
DRIR		4	2	1	3
IRR		1	2	3	4

EXHIBIT 5.9:
Basis of Corporate Money Cost and Project Cash Flow

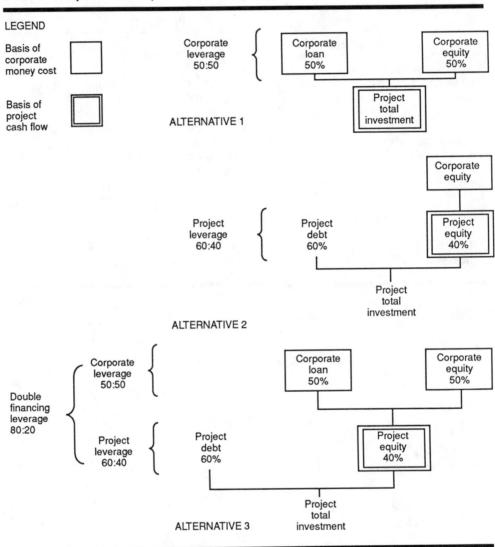

EXHIBIT 5.10:
NPV, DRIR and IRR of Alternative Treatments (dollars in $1,000)

I. Project cash flow and corporate money cost

	Investment	Total return	Net return	IRR
Project cash flow (at project level)				
Loan	$ 60,000	$ 66,000	$ 6,000	10%
Equity	$ 40,000	$ 54,000	$14,000	35%
Total	$100,000	$120,000	$20,000	20%

	Investment	Desired return	Money cost
Corporate money cost (at corporate level)			
Loan	$300,000	$24,000	8%
Equity	$300,000	$54,000	18%
Total	$600,000	$78,000	13%

II. Project NPV, DRIR, and IRR

		ALTERNATIVE I	II	III
Project cash flow		Total	Equity	Equity
Corporate money cost		Total	Equity	Total
Project cash flow				
Investment	Year 0	$100,000	$40,000	$40,000
Return	Year 1	$120,000	$54,000	$54,000
Corporate money cost/discount rate		13%	18%	13%
Present value of return		$106,195	$45,763	$47,788
NPV		$ 6,195	$ 5,763	$ 7,788
DRIR		1.06	1.14	1.19
IRR		20%	35%	35%
IRR margin		7%	17%	22%
IRR index		1.54	1.94	2.69
Effective debt/equity ratio for the project		50:50	60:40	80:20

Chapter 6 _____

PROJECT RANKING AND CAPITAL RATIONING

One of the principal areas of decision analysis is capital budgeting, which covers the evaluation and financing of long-term projects. These projects are usually called capital investment projects or capital projects.

The original tools of capital investment decision analysis—the accounting rate of return (ARR) and the cash payback period—have been superseded in practice by the time-adjusted techniques of the internal rate of return (IRR), IRR margin, IRR index, net present value (NPV), and the discounted return/investment ratio (DRIR), commonly known as the profitability index.

However, these time-adjusted methods still have basic flaws and usually give conflicting project rankings. Their weaknesses and resulting contradictory project ladderings arise from their failure to consider the differences in the cash flow characteristics of the projects being evaluated and ranked. The characteristics are in terms of the investment size, project life, and return pattern. This chapter introduces the comparable investment approach (CIA) in decision analysis for capital projects. This approach exploits the strengths of the IRR and NPV but eliminates their weaknesses in their traditional applications by making the investment projects under consideration comparable in their cash flow characteristics. To make them comparable, the CIA incorporates the cost of money which the NPV also uses as the discount rate. However, the CIA goes a step farther. It exploits, as the reinvestment rate, the earnings rate of other investment opportunities which will utilize the financing that cannot be used by the projects under consideration.

The NPV and CIA assumes that the projects will be funded from the general funds of a business firm. This assumption leads to the use of the weighted or average cost of money which is used as the discount rate. In some cases, however, the financing sources for different projects may not be completely identical. How to apportion the funds to different projects is illustrated in the last part of this chapter.

I. CAPITAL BUDGETING

Capital budgeting is the selection of long-term projects and the allocation of funds therefor.

Long-term projects are undertaken in order to increase sales, expand the capacity to produce, reduce cost, assure the supply of inputs, replace existing facilities, or diversify the business. An R&D effort to develop new products or improve existing ones is aimed to meet the first-named objective. A plant expansion program is intended to add to the rated capacity, while an automation program is designed to expand the capacity, reduce the cost, replace existing facilities, or enhance the sales due to improved product quality.

Contingent Project. A contingent project is one which is dependent or contingent upon the implementation or outcome of another project. The construction of a plant that will make a new product which is the subject of research and development is a contingent proposal. The same thing is true with the provision of working capital for the buildup in the inventories and receivables for the new product. For decision analysis purposes, contingent proposals should form part of the complete package. Thus, the capital project in the given illustration includes the R&D, plant construction, working capital provision, as well as the advertising and promotional costs which are needed in order to introduce the new product.

Capital Budgeting and Inflation. Since it takes time to implement capital projects, and longer time still to recover the investment, the capital expenditures budget, the financial projections, and the financial analysis should incorporate the gradual increase in costs, expenses, and revenues due to inflation.

Inflation in general was discussed in Chapter 2, Section III. The application of inflation in equipment acquisition decisions is examined in Chapter 12, while the impact of inflation on financing schemes is revealed in Chapter 15.

II. EVALUATION OF THE TRADITIONAL RANKING TECHNIQUES

There are two groups of traditional project ranking techniques: those that are time adjusted and those that are not.

TIME-UNADJUSTED METHODS

There are two methods under this classification: the accounting rate of return and the cash payback period method.

Accounting Rate of Return. This method is popular among accountants. The ARR divides the net profit as shown in the projected income statement by the investment in order to arrive at the rate of return. The higher the percentage, the higher is the ARR and the more desirable is the project.

The ARR has four variations: (1) the average ARR for the entire project life, (2) the annual ARR based on the stockholders' investment (paid-up capital), (3) the annual ARR based on the total stockholders' equity as of the beginning of every year, and (4) the annual ARR based on the average total stockholders' equity for every year.

AVERAGE ARR FOR THE ENTIRE LIFE. In this method, the net profit for the entire life or for the entire period covered by the financial projection is estimated. The total is then divided by the number of operating years in order to arrive at the average profit. The average profit in turn is divided by the investment required in order to determine the ARR.

ANNUAL ARR BASED ON STOCKHOLDERS' INVESTMENT. The annual net profit as shown in the financial projections is divided by the investment put in. Since the net profit fluctuates annually, the ARR also varies yearly.

ANNUAL ARR BASED ON TOTAL STOCKHOLDERS' EQUITY AS OF THE BEGINNING OF EVERY YEAR. The ARR is computed on a yearly basis like the preceding method. However, the net profit is divided not just by the investment put in, but by the total stockholders' equity, which is composed of both the investment plus the retained earnings as of the beginning of every year.

ANNUAL ARR BASED ON THE ANNUAL AVERAGE TOTAL STOCKHOLDERS' EQUITY. This is similar to the preceding technique except that the net profit is divided by the average stockholders' equity for the year, and not as of the start of the year. The average equity is computed by adding the beginning and ending equities and dividing the total by 2.

The ramifications of the ARR or return on stockholders' equity (ROSE) as a tool of performance evaluation are examined in Chapter 19.

EVALUATION. The ARR has five severe limitations which render it ineffective in project evaluation. The limitations are in the following areas: (1) concept of return, (2) adjustment for time value of money, (3) applicability of the calculated rate, (4) value of the project after the projection period, and (5) relation to the cost of money (discount rate).

1. *Concept of return.* ARR is based on calculated net profit and not cash. Investment decisions require cash or other real assets and expect a

return of cash and not paper or book profit. Cash can be invested, but profit per se cannot be.

2. *Adjustment for time value of money.* ARR is not adjusted for time. Under the ARR concept, a calculated dollar of profit 1 year hence is considered identical to a calculated dollar of profit 10 years hence.

3. *Applicability of calculated rate.* The ARR as calculated is normally for each year and not for the entire project life.

4. *Value of the project after the projection period.* If the financial projections are for the first 10 operating years, the ARR is calculated for this period. The profit after this period is normally disregarded.

5. *Relation to the cost of money.* The ARR is estimated without considering the actual cost of money. Hence it has still to be compared with the money cost.

Cash Payback Method. This is also called the cash payout period method or investment recovery period technique. This method compares the cash and other assets to be invested in a project, with the cash and other assets which the investment will yield. The result is the number of years or months it will take to recover the investment fully. The shorter the payback period, the faster can the investment be recovered and the better the project.

ILLUSTRATION. Assume that two projects have the following projected cash flow:

		Project AA	*Project BB*
Investment	Year 0	$100	$ 100
Returns	Year 1	100	50
	Year 2	0	50
	Year 3	0	1,000

Project AA has a payback period of one year since the full $100 investment can be recouped in year 1. BB, on the other hand, has a two-year payback. Under this method, AA is more desirable than BB.

EVALUATION. This method has eliminated the first and third limitations of the ARR. The cash payback is based on cash, not profit. Furthermore, the payback period is not for a particular year but for the project as a whole.

However, the payback has retained all the other flaws of the ARR.

1. *Adjustment for time value of money.* The payback is not time adjusted. The $50 year 1 return of Project BB is given the same importance as the $50 year 2 return.

2. *Value of the project after the payback period.* For Project BB, the $1,000 year 3 return is totally ignored since the year 1 and 2 returns are enough to recover the investment fully. This limitation caused the payback period to favor AA although by inspection BB is much better.

3. *Relation to the cost of money.* Like the ARR, the payback has not covered these. In this respect, the payback method is worse than the ARR since the payback period in years cannot be compared with the cost of money which is denominated in percentages.

TIME-ADJUSTED TECHNIQUES

The time-adjusted techniques—IRR, NPV, and DRIR as discussed in the preceding two chapters—have removed the first four limitations of the ARR. These time-adjusted techniques are based on cash flow, consider the time of money, apply for the entire project life, and take into account the value of the project after the period covered by the financial projections. The last-mentioned limitation of ARR was corrected by the time-adjusted methods through the inclusion of the residual value in the cash flow for the last year in the financial period.

However, due to the differences in the way in which the IRR, NPV, and DRIR are calculated, there are often conflicts in project ranking when two or more of these techniques are used. See Chapter 5, Section IV.

III. COMPARABLE INVESTMENT APPROACH

RATIONALE

The comparable investment approach (CIA) transforms the projects with differing cash flow characteristics in terms of project lives, return patterns, and capital requirements into projects with comparable characteristics before applying the IRR and NPV. Hence, the CIA avoids all the limitations of all the traditional tools and minimizes conflicts between the IRR, NPV, and DRIR in project ranking. The CIA

1. Is based on cash instead of net profit.
2. Is adjusted for time value of money, just like the IRR, NPV, and DRIR.
3. Calculates one rate for the entire project life, and not annually like the ARR.
4. Considers all the cash flows of a project, unlike the payback method, which disregards the cash flow after the payback period.
5. Relates to the cost of money (discount rate), like the NPV in its traditional usage.

6. Adjusts for differences in the lives, return patterns, and capital requirements of competing proposals, unlike the NPV.
7. Facilitates the calculation of the crossover discount and reinvestment rates.
8. Promotes congruence between divisional and corporate goals, unlike the IRR.
9. Minimizes conflicts among IRR, NPV, and DRIR in project ranking.

The CIA marries the advantages of the IRR and NPV and reconciles their differences. Since their differences arise from variations in the lives, return patterns, and capital requirements of the competing projects being evaluated, the CIA approach equalizes these qualities, thus making the comparison on a purely apple-to-apple basis.

Where the projects vary in their lives, return patterns and capital requirements, the CIA evaluates their relative financial merits by extending the analyses beyond the projects themselves (the core projects) to cover also the peripheral investments—the reinvestment vehicles and the side projects. Reinvestment vehicles are used if the core projects differ in their duration; side projects are used if the core projects vary in their investment needs.

Reinvestment vehicles and side projects have to be added to the core projects to form the total investment packages so as to make up for the disparities of the core projects in size, duration, and recovery patterns. The IRR and the NPV evaluation techniques are then applied to the entire packages and not to the core projects alone.

INVESTMENT VEHICLES

An investment package, for purposes of the analysis in this chapter, is composed of the core project, the reinvestment vehicle, and the side project. Each of these is described presently.

Core Projects. The comparative analysis of projects with similar cash flow streams is an easy task. Take the following case:

	Year	Project K	Project M
Investment	0	$100,000	$100,000
Return	1	0	0
	2	134,560	129,960

Since the projects have the same investment size and project life and all the returns are made only once, which is at the end of the project life, the advantage of project K is apparent. No assumptions on the discount rate or reinvestment rate is needed. The IRR and the NPV need not be computed.

However, there are few situations where the projects have similar cash flow characteristics and hence consistent IRR and NPV rankings. Projects usually have varying cash flow streams and hence may have conflicting IRR and NPV rankings.

As illustrated in Chapter 5, Net Present Value, Exhibit 5.4, the IRR is only one of the determinants of the NPV, the others being the discount rate, the investment size, the project life, and the return pattern. Return pattern is the timing and distribution of the returns. Hence, a project with a lower IRR can still build up a higher NPV by utilizing a bigger investment over a longer life. This situation creates a problem in deciding as to which of the two projects should be given priority—the one with the higher IRR or the one with the bigger NPV.

Reinvestment Vehicles (Exhibit 6.1, cases I and III).   A reinvestment vehicle is needed if some or all of the returns of one or both projects is received before the end of the life of the project with the longer duration. This is demonstrated in Exhibit 6.1, case I. Since project H has only a one-year life, while M has double that term, the two projects are not directly comparable. Hence we have to create another investment vehicle, which will be piggybacked to core project H. This trailing vehicle will receive as its capital, the yield of H upon the termination of its life in year 1. This reinvestment medium will then allow the reinvested amount to grow until the end of year 2, which is the life of the other project, M. The reinvestment medium extends the life of core project H so that the initial investment, plus the reinvestment medium, run parallel to M from start to finish. The introduction of the reinvestment medium enables us to compare rectangles of the same sizes and shapes as shown in Exhibit 6.1, case I.

Another type of reinvestment vehicle is demonstrated in Exhibit 6.1, case III. Although the two projects have the same size and duration, they do have different return patterns. Project A expects to start generating a return right in year 1. Hence A needs a reinvestment medium to receive the year 1 return of project A, and bring it, together with its earnings, to year 2, which is the end of the lives of both A and K.

In case IV, each of the projects needs a reinvestment vehicle.

Side Projects (Exhibit 6.1, case II).   A side project has to be assumed where two projects of different investment sizes are being evaluated. Consider case II in exhibit 6.1. Core project H requires a $100,000 investment; P needs $140,000. What should be compared in this situation are (1) the $140,000 investment in P and its return, and (2) the $100,000 investment in core project H plus an investment of the $40,000 differential, to be made in the H side project, and the combined returns of these investments. In this case the side project is created in year 0.

Side Projects and Reinvestment Vehicles (Exhibit 6.1, case IV)   A more complicated situation is one where the projects have varying sizes, durations, and return patterns. See Exhibit 6.1, case IV. A side project and a reinvestment medium have to be piggybacked to core project H, while a reinvestment vehicle has to be joined to Q.

Investment Packages. An investment package is composed of one core project plus a side project and/or a reinvestment vehicle. Thus, in Exhibit 6.1, case IV, investment package H is composed of a core project, a reinvestment vehicle, and a side project. The investment packages to be compared should be of the same size. Hence, H and Q are of equal sizes.

Investment Rates. The earning rates to be assessed for the reinvestment media and side projects are those expected to be earned by them. Expanding conglomerates or companies actively acquiring and divesting businesses constantly generate projects, and hence would generally have higher investment or reinvestment rates than would industrial firms in matured markets and with stabilized, structured operations.

The reinvestment and side project investment rates will be lower than the IRR of the core projects if the latter are deemed to be exceptionally good and hence difficult to replicate.

However, the reinvestment and side project investment rates should be higher than the cost money. The business of a firm is not to generate projects which will just break even, but to make a profit by having an interest spread over the cost of money.

If the reinvestment rate or side project investment rate is above the discount rate but lower than the IRR of the core project, the NPV of the total investment package will be higher than that of the core project alone. However, the blended IRR of the package will be lower than that of the IRR of the core project. The NPV of the investment package will be higher because the interest spread of the reinvestment vehicle or side project will generate additional NPV. On the other hand, the blended rate will be lower since the lower return of the reinvestment vehicle or side project will be averaged with the higher IRR of the core project.

The reinvestment issue is applicable only if the intermediate returns have to be reinvested or left with the corporation. If the objective is to maximize the immediate payout to the stockholders via dividends, then the issue becomes moot.

EVALUATION OF INVESTMENT PACKAGES

Guidance on the appraisal of projects with varying cash flow streams is offered in the following situations:

1. Where the projects have substantial IRR variation and substantial life and investment differential
2. Where the projects have minimal IRR variation but substantial life differential
3. Where the projects have minimal IRR variation but substantial life and investment differential

The methodologies in analyzing projects with these differences may be followed in appraising options with other types of discrepancies, as those with varying return patterns.

Projects with Substantial IRR Variation (Exhibit 6.2).   In some instances, the choice between two projects with conflicting IRR and NPV rankings may be made after taking a casual look at their features. Take the case of projects H and N in Exhibit 6.2.

Project N may look as good as H since N's shortcoming in the IRR is made up in its NPV advantage. In fact, some may recommend N, since its higher NPV means that it will be able to maximize the firm's net profit in terms of dollars.

However, a closer comparison of the two alternatives reveals that project H is actually six times more efficient or profitable than N. There are two indicators of this. First, H has an interest spread of 6% (16% IRR less 10% discount rate or money cost) while N has a spread of only 1%.

Second, while the NPV of H and of N are almost the same—the difference is less than 1%—it takes H only 100,000 dollar-years to generate the given NPV, whereas it requires N 600,000 dollar-years ($200,000 × 3 years) to earn almost the same NPV.

In this case, the $49 incremental NPV of project N cannot justify the doubling of the investment dollar and the tripling of the investment time. The $49 incremental NPV represents a very inefficient return (1% of 1%) on the incremental 500,000 dollar-years. Furthermore, it magnifies the risk in terms of much greater investment and time exposure.

Capital investment analysis basically boils down to an evaluation of the input-output efficiency of the investment. The input is in terms of the dollars to be sunk in and the time required to develop the return.

Projects with Minimal IRR Variation but Substantial Life Differential. As shown in the preceding section, a project with a much lower IRR may end up having a higher NPV due to its bigger investment requirement and longer project life. In certain cases, the IRR differential may not be much and hence the projects may require further analysis.

Core Projects (Exhibits 6.3 and 6.4).   Take the case of project H with a 16% IRR and M with 14% as presented in Exhibit 6.3. At 12.035% money cost, the NPV of H and M are the same. At this rate, the NPV of H crosses that of M as illustrated in Exhibit 6.4.

The crossover discount rate is 12.035% because at this rate, the interest spread advantage of H is crossed out by the dollar-years benefit of M. At this discount rate, the interest spread of H is 4%, which is twice that of M's 2%. However, the dollar-years available to M to earn its NPV is 200,000 which is twice that of H.

At money cost lower than 12.035%, M has a higher NPV.

The lower the discount rate, the higher are the NPVs of the two projects as the discount factor of 1 applied goes up. Although the NPV of both projects rise with the decline in the money cost, the NPV of M rises faster than that of H such that the lead of M becomes more pronounced. The NPV of M is more sensitive to changes in money cost since the discount factor is applied for two years, versus only a year in the case of H. M has a two-year life while H has only one.

Conversely, the higher the money cost, the lower are the NPVs of the projects. When the rate is raised from 12.035%, the NPV of M goes down faster than that of H. At 14% the NPV of M disappears while that of H is $1,754. M has no NPV at 14% discount rate because 14% is also its IRR. In like manner, the NPV of H is zeroed at 16% which is its IRR.

The interrelationships of the IRRs, discount rates, and NPVs of H and M are charted in Exhibit 6.4. At zero discount rate (used here for discussion purposes only as money has always a cost), M has a $29,960 NPV while H has $16,000. At the crossover discount rate of 12.035%, either project has a $3,539 NPV. At a discount rate from 0% to 12.035%, the NPV of M is higher than that of H. Also note from the chart that the NPV of M is zeroed at the 14% discount rate, and that of H, at 16%.

Based on the table in Exhibit 6.4, the degree of the relative desirability of a project is affected by the discount rate. Thus, at discount rate of over 12.035%, project H is definitely more financially feasible since it has higher IRR and NPV. However, at a money cost below 12%, the project ranking according to the IRR conflicts with the results of the NPV since H has a higher IRR but lower NPV. At money cost between zero and 12.035%, the disadvantage of M from the lower interest spread is more than made up by its advantage in time duration.

Reinvestment Vehicle (Exhibit 6.5). This conflict can be resolved by an analysis of the IRR and NPV of H not only during its one-year core project life but also during the year after (reinvestment vehicle life). Hence the H reinvestment vehicle has to be introduced. This two-year analysis of H will make the results comparable to that of the two-year life of M. See Exhibit 6.5. The core project investment data in Exhibit 6.5 were taken from Exhibit 6.3. For project H, the return of the core project investment is assumed to be reinvested at the rate indicated.

Total Investment Package (Exhibit 6.5). The investment in the H core project and the return of the successor reinvestment vehicle are combined to become the investment and return of the total investment package H.

For H, the combined rate of return is the blended rate of the IRR during the one-year core project life and the reinvestment rate of the reinvestment vehicle.

Exhibit 6.5 shows that a reinvestment rate of 12.035% gives project H an effective IRR or combined rate of return of 14%, which is the same as the IRR of M. At this 12.035% reinvestment rate and a discount rate of 10%, the NPV of the two projects are the same—which is $7,405. As long as the IRR and reinvestment rate remain constant, the NPV of either project will equal that of the other, irrespective of the discount rate used. Thus, using 12.035% as the discount rate, the NPV of either project becomes $3,539. The reason for the equality in the NPV is that the projects have the same original investment, and at the end of two years, each of the project has a return, before discounting, of about $129,960. If the discount rate is lowered, the NPV will rise—but to the same extent for the two projects.

The crucial factor in the appraisal of this situation then is the reinvestment rate to be applied for project H. At a reinvestment rate higher than 12.035%, H has higher rate of return and NPV than M. On the other hand, at a reinvestment rate lower than the crossover reinvestment rate of 12.035%, H will have lower IRR and NPV than M.

Core Project Crossover Discount Rate, and Crossover Reinvestment Rate (Exhibit 6.6).   Based on the information given on the two projects, the crossover discount rate for the core project which is 12.035% (Exhibit 6.3) is also the crossover reinvestment rate (Exhibit 6.5).

This equality in the crossover rates is explained in Exhibit 6.6. According to the first part of the exhibit, the crossover *discount rate* brings the $116,000 year 1 return of project H to $103,539 in year 0. The same rate carries the $129,960 year 2 return of M to $116,000 in year 1 and thence to $103,539 in year 0. This makes the NPV of M identical to that of H.

An inspection of Exhibit 6.6 shows that the crossover *reinvestment* rate of H should be such as to carry its $116,000 year 1 return to $129,960 in year 2, so that this matches with the year 2 return of M.

Since 12.035% is the rate which can bring the $129,960 year 2 value of M to $116,000 as of year 1 (upper chart), it is also this same rate which can move the $116,000 year 1 return of H to $129,960 in year 2 (lower chart). Hence 12.035% is also the crossover reinvestment rate of H.

The lower chart of Exhibit 6.6 shows how the 16% and 14% IRRs of H and M, respectively, together with the crossover discount and reinvestment rates, results in identical NPVs for the two projects.

As usual, any variation in the discount rate changes the NPVs of these projects. However, the use of any discount rate will result in the H core project and its reinvestment vehicle combined having the same NPV as that of M. This is so because these projects have the same investments as of year 0 ($100,000) and same undiscounted returns as of year 2 ($129,960).

Projects with Minimal IRR Variation but Substantial Life and Size Differentials.   Projects H and Q reflect a real-life situation—except that the project durations have been shortened. This case requires an extended analysis for two reasons: (1) the projects vary in both investment size and project life, and (2) one of the projects has a higher IRR but lower NPV.

Investment Packages (Exhibit 6.1, case IV).   Since H and Q are of different sizes and durations (Exhibit 6.1, case IV), it is necessary to repackage each of them so that they become comparable. For H, it is necessary to create a side project which will absorb the $50,000 investment differential of H and Q. The side project will have to run for the entire life of Q, which is two years. Second, a reinvestment vehicle is needed. This will extend the life of H core project, so that the extended life will be coterminus with that of Q.

On the other hand, a reinvestment medium will be formed to accept the year 1 return of the core project Q and generate the return up to the end of the life of Q.

The side project and reinvestment vehicles, when added to the core projects, will make the H and Q investment packages totally comparable in terms of investment requirements and durations.

Analysis. The specific steps to be followed are described next.

A. Core Projects H and Q (Exhibit 6.7, Part I)

1. Obtain the investment requirements and return data of core projects H and Q. Calculate their IRRs and NPVs.

B. Side Project H (Exhibit 6.7, part I)

1. Obtain the investment differential or the difference in the investment requirements of the two core projects. The investment differential is $50,000. Assume that this will be placed in a side project, which is distinguished from the core project H. This will be added to the core project H, so that the total investments of the core and side projects H equal that of Q. This enables us to compare investment packages of equal sizes. The side project will run up to year 2 alongside the core project H and the latter's extension in the form of the reinvestment vehicle which is discussed shortly. Year 2 is the end of the life of the core project with longer life, which is Q.

2. Ascertain and apply a possible investment or earning rate which will apply to the side project from year 0 to year 2. In the illustration, it is assumed that the investment rate or IRR of the side project is 12.5%.

C. Reinvestment Vehicles (Exhibit 6.7, part II).

1. Create two reinvestment vehicles—one to receive the $116,000 year 1 return of core project H, and the other, the $52,500 year 1 return of core project Q.

2. Ascertain and apply the possible investment rate for the two reinvestment vehicles. In the illustration, it is assumed that the reinvestment rate is also 12.5%.

D. Investment Packages (Exhibit 6.7, part III)

1. The two completed investment packages are comprised of the following: the core projects, the side project, and the reinvestment vehicles. Determine the IRR and the NPV of the packages. The combined or

blended IRR and the combined or total NPV as calculated are shown.

2. Compare the blended IRR and combined NPV of the two investment packages.
   a. Take the package with the higher IRR and NPV.
   b. If the NPV of one package is higher, but its IRR is slightly lower, then consider the one with higher NPV if
      (1) Its IRR is above the hurdle rate.
      (2) The main objective of the company is to increase the total profit in terms of dollars, and not necessarily the IRR.

   Assuming an IRR of 12.5% for side project H, and the same 12.5% as the reinvestment rate for H and Q, the blended IRR of the investment package H is 13.66% as against 14.62 for Q. The NPV of H is $10,150 as against $12,862 of Q. Hence Q is preferable to H.

3. To facilitate sensitivity analysis, calculate the crossover reinvestment rate of the two options. This is discussed presently.

Crossover Reinvestment and Investment Rates (Exhibit 6.8).   The crossover investment rate of the side project and reinvestment vehicles is 14.3545%. The use of this rate will make the two-year IRR or combined rate of return of the two investment packages the same—at 14.9%. Since these two sets of investment packages have the same investment requirements, the same lives and the same IRR, their NPVs, are also the same—at $13,666 using 10% as the discounting rate. Thus, investing in one option will be as financially good as taking the other.

A decline in the reinvestment vehicle and side project investment rates from 14.3545% favors Q in relation to H. H as a package is more affected by any change in the reinvestment and investment rate as this rate is applicable to the following:

1. Side project H—year 0 investment of $50,000.
2. Reinvestment vehicle H—year 1 investment of $116,000.

On the other hand, the reinvestment rate applies only to the reinvestment vehicle Q Year 1 investment of $52,000.

Thus, the use of a reinvestment and investment rate, such as the 12.5% in Exhibit 6.7, which is lower than the crossover rate of 14.3545% makes the IRR and NPV of Q higher than that of the total investment package H. This was shown earlier in Exhibit 6.7.

IV. CAPITAL RATIONING

The preceding discussions have treated the evaluation of projects by assuming (1) that they will be financed from a common pool of fund which has only one actual or imputed cost which cost can serve as the discount rate and (2) the projects are mutually exclusive.

This part of the chapter demonstrates alternative methods of analyzing a situation where these two assumptions do not hold true, and hence (1) the funding of projects will come from separate sources with varying costs and (2) two or more projects may be implemented at about the same time.

Assume that the projects available for implementation and the available funds are as given in Exhibit 6.9.

NPV Approach—Without Risk (Exhibit 6.9). The most common method, but the one which may produce disastrous results, is the traditional NPV approach. According to this method, the returns of the projects are discounted based on the money cost to the firm. The money cost used is usually the weighted average of the funds. In many cases, no risk premium is added to the money cost. For as long as there are funds available, all the projects with positive NPV are implemented.

The average money cost of all the funds available is 13%. Since this is lower than the 14% IRR of the project with the lowest IRR (project U), all the projects in the exhibit have positive NPV. Since all the projects require a total investment of $900,000,000 while the total funds available is $1,050,000,000, all the projects will be pushed through. This illustration has demonstrated that the use of the average money cost has resulted in the tapping of a fund source with a 16% cost (capital stock) to fund a project with a 14% IRR.

This exercise has revealed one of the limitations of NPV: the determination of the discount rate. If the NPV were to be used in ranking the projects, it is difficult to pinpoint beforehand which project will be funded by what financing source. The specific source is necessary in order to pinpoint the money cost and hence the discount rate to be applied. Since the specific source cannot be identified, the average cost will have to be used—hence the defect.

IRR Approach—Without Risk (Exhibit 6.9). An improvement over the NPV approach is the IRR approach. Because the calculation of the IRR does not depend on an external interest rate (or discount rate for the NPV), each project can be traced to a specific financing source.

Under the IRR approach, the rule is that the projects are selected for their implementation based on the descending order of their IRRs, while the funding sources are chosen for their availability based on the ascending order of their interest or money cost. In other words, the first project to be taken is the one with the highest IRR, and the first financing to be availed of is the one with the lowest cost. As many projects as possible are taken, for as long as (1) the funding is available and (2) the IRR of the least profitable project taken is higher than the interest rate of the most costly funding source availed of.

Under this method, only projects R and S are taken. Since their combined capital is $700,000, all the funding sources except the stockholders will be utilized. If this is done, the IRR of the project with the lower IRR (Project S) is 16%. This is still higher than the 14% interest on the most costly financing source to be availed of—unsecured loans.

IRR Approach—With Risk (Exhibit 6.9).   If project risk is built into the analysis, only project R will pass the test. Its $450,000,000 in capital requirements will be supplied by the following, in the order named: bank deposits, future cash flows, secured loans, and unsecured loans. The 16% IRR incorporating risk is still higher than the most costly financing source to be tapped—14% for the unsecured loans.

If project S is implemented in addition to project R, the 14% risk-adjusted IRR of this project is not higher than the most costly funding source to be utilized—the 14% unsecured loan.

IRR and Selective Funding Approach—With Risk (Exhibit 6.9).   The prior approach has attempted to match the IRR of the projects with the financial cost of the financing sources. If the cash generation of the projects is sure to materialize and is realizable on an annual basis equivalent to the IRR, then the method is adequate. Otherwise, the method is faulty.

A better approach is one which considers in addition to the IRR and money cost, the quality of the projects and the fund sources. Getting loans to fund new projects may be risky on two counts. First, if the projected cash flow of the project is not realized, then the loan cannot be repaid. Second, the cash generation of new projects for the first few years do not equal the calculated IRR which is for the entire project life. In other words, a project with a 16% IRR usually does not generate a cash flow equivalent to 16% of the capital. Therefore, a new project will not be able to meet the interest payments on the loan financing.

Hence, if project R is implemented, the $450,000,000 required capital should come only from the following sources: present bank deposits, future cash flow, and stockholders. In this case, the 16% risk-adjusted IRR of the project is not higher than the 16% money cost of additional capital stock. Hence, it may not be advisable to undertake this project—or any of the other projects in Exhibit 6.9.

EXHIBIT 6.1:
Investment Packages

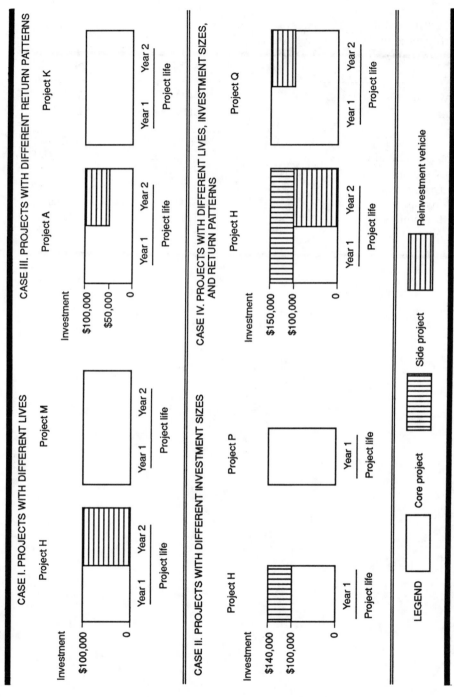

CASE I. PROJECTS WITH DIFFERENT LIVES

Project H   Project M

CASE III. PROJECTS WITH DIFFERENT RETURN PATTERNS

Project A   Project K

CASE II. PROJECTS WITH DIFFERENT INVESTMENT SIZES

Project H   Project P

CASE IV. PROJECTS WITH DIFFERENT LIVES, INVESTMENT SIZES, AND RETURN PATTERNS

Project H   Project Q

LEGEND

Core project   Side project   Reinvestment vehicle

EXHIBIT 6.2:
Projects H and N

	Year	Project H	Project N
Investment	0	($100,000)	($200,000)
Returns	1	$116,000	$ 0
	2		$ 0
	3		$273,526
Internal rate of return		16%	11%
Net present value	0		
Discount rate		10%	10%
Investment	0	($100,000)	($200,000)
Discounted return	0	$105,455	$205,504
NPV	0	$ 5,455	$ 5,504

EXHIBIT 6.3:
Projects H and M—Core Projects

	Year	DISCOUNT RATE				
		16%	14%	12.035%	10%	0%
Project H						
Investment	0	($100,000)	($100,000)	($100,000)	($100,000)	($100,000)
Returns	1	$116,000	$116,000	$116,000	$116,000	$116,000
	2	$ 0	$ 0	$ 0	$ 0	$ 0
Internal rate of return	0	16%	16%	16%	16%	16%
Net present value						
Discount rate		16%	14%	12.035%	10%	0%
Investment	0	($100,000)	($100,000)	($100,000)	($100,000)	($100,000)
Discounted return	0	$100,000	$101,754	$103,539	$105,455	$116,000
NPV	0	$ 0	$ 1,754	$ 3,539	$ 5,455	$ 16,000
Project M						
Investment	0	($100,000)	($100,000)	($100,000)	($100,000)	($100,000)
Returns	1	$ 0	$ 0	$ 0	$ 0	$ 0
	2	$129,960	$129,960	$129,960	$129,960	$129,960
Internal rate of return	0	14%	14%	14%	14%	14%
Net present value						
Discount rate		16%	14%	12.035%	10%	0%
Investment	0	($100,000)	($100,000)	($100,000)	($100,000)	($100,000)
Discounted return	0	$ 96,581	$100,000	$103,539	$107,405	$129,960
NPV	0	($ 3,419)	$ 0	$ 3,539	$ 7,405	$ 29,960
NPV differential						
Excess of H over M		$ 3,419	$ 1,754	$ 0	($ 1,950)	($ 13,960)

EXHIBIT 6.4:
Projects H and M—Crossover Discount Rate

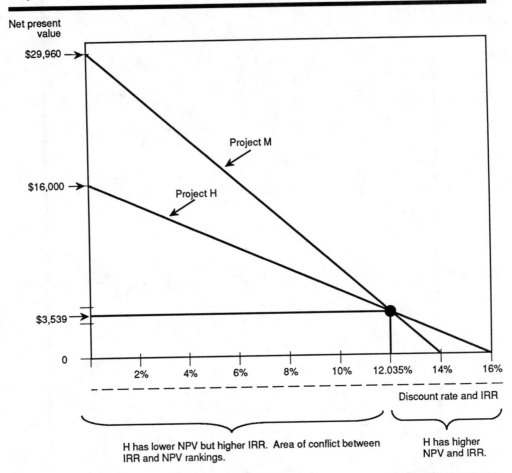

H has lower NPV but higher IRR. Area of conflict between IRR and NPV rankings.

H has higher NPV and IRR.

EXHIBIT 6.5:
Projects H and M—Investment Packages

	Year	PROJECT H reinvestment rate				PROJECT M reinvestment rate 14%
		16%	14%	12.035%	10%	
Core project						
Investment	0	($100,000)	($100,000)	($100,000)	($100,000)	($100,000)
Returns	1	$116,000	$116,000	$116,000	$116,000	0
	2	$ 0	$ 0	$ 0	$ 0	$129,960
Internal rate of return		16%	16%	16%	16%	14%
Net present value						
Discount rate		10%	10%	10%	10%	10%
Investment	0	($100,000)	($100,000)	($100,000)	($100,000)	($100,000)
Discounted return	0	$105,455	$105,455	$105,455	$105,455	$107,405
NPV	0	$ 5,455	$ 5,455	$ 5,455	$ 5,455	$ 7,405
Reinvestment vehicle						
Reinvestment	1	($116,000)	($116,000)	($116,000)	($116,000)	
Return	2	$134,560	$132,240	$129,961	$127,600	
Reinvestment rate		16%	14%	12.035%	10%	
Total investment package						
Investment	0	($100,000)	($100,000)	($100,000)	($100,000)	($100,000)
Returns	1	$ 0	$ 0	$ 0	$ 0	$ 0
	2	$134,560	$132,240	$129,961	$127,600	$129,960
Combined rate of return		16.00%	15.00%	14.00%	12.96%	14.00%
Net present value at 10% discount rate						
Discount rate		10%	10%	10%	10%	10%
Investment	0	($100,000)	($100,000)	($100,000)	($100,000)	($100,000)
Discounted return	0	$111,207	$109,289	$107,405	$105,455	$107,405
NPV	0	$ 11,207	$ 9,289	$ 7,405	$ 5,455	$ 7,405
Net present value at 12.035% discount rate						
Discount rate		12.035%	12.035%	12.035%	12.035%	12.035%
Investment	0	($100,000)	($100,000)	($100,000)	($100,000)	($100,000)
Discounted return	0	$107,203	$105,355	$103,539	$101,658	$103,539
NPV	0	$ 7,203	$ 5,355	$ 3,539	$ 1,658	$ 3,539

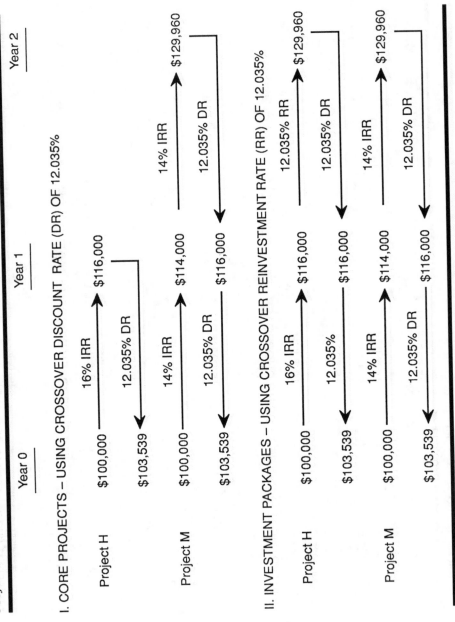

EXHIBIT 6.7:
Projects H and Q—at Assumed Reinvestment Rate

| Discount rate | Year | INVESTMENT PACKAGE H | | | PROJECT Q |
		Core project 10.00%	Side project 10.00%	Combined 10.00%	10.00%
I. Original investments					
Investment	0	($100,000)	($50,000)	($150,000)	($150,000)
Returns	1	$116,000	$ 0	$116,000	$52,500
	2	$ 0	$63,281	$63,281	$138,000
Internal rate of return		16.00%	12.50%	14.26%	15.00%
Net present value					
Investment	0	($100,000)	($50,000)	($150,000)	($150,000)
Discounted return	0	$105,455	$52,299	$157,753	$161,777
NPV	0	$5,455	$2,299	$7,753	$11,777
II. Reinvestment vehicles					
Reinvestment	1	($116,000)		($116,000)	($52,500)
Return	2	$130,500		$130,500	$59,063
Reinvestment rate		12.50%		12.50%	12.50%
III. Investment packages					
Investment	0	($100,000)	($50,000)	($150,000)	($150,000)
Returns	1	$ 0	$ 0	$ 0	$ 0
	2	$130,500	$63,281	$193,781	$197,063
Combined rate of return		14.24%	12.50%	13.66%	14.62%
Net present value					
Investment	0	($100,000)	($50,000)	($150,000)	($150,000)
Discounted return	0	$107,851	$52,299	$160,150	$162,862
NPV	0	$ 7,851	$ 2,299	$ 10,150	$ 12,862

EXHIBIT 6.8:
Projects H and Q—At Crossover Reinvestment and
Side Investment Rates

| | | INVESTMENT PACKAGE H | | | PROJECT Q |
| | | Core project | Side project | Combined | |
Discount rate	Year	10.00%	10.00%	10.00%	10.00%
I. Original Investments					
Investment	0	($100,000)	($50,000)	($150,000)	($150,000)
Returns	1	$116,000		$116,000	$52,500
	2		$65,385	$65,385	$138,000
Internal rate of return		16.0000%	14.3545%	15.1787%	15.0000%
Net present value					
Investment	0	($100,000)	($50,000)	($150,000)	($150,000)
Discounted return	0	$105,455	$54,037	$159,492	$161,777
NPV	0	$5,455	$4,037	$9,492	$11,777
II. Reinvestment vehicle					
Reinvestment	1	($116,000)		($116,000)	($52,500)
Return	2	$132,651		$132,651	$60,036
Reinvestment rate			14.3545%	14.3545%	14.3545%
III. Investment packages					
Investment	0	($100,000)	($50,000)	($150,000)	($150,000)
Returns	1	$ 0	$ 0	$ 0	$ 0
	2	$132,651	$65,385	$198,036	$198,036
Combined rate of return		15.1743%	14.3545%	14.9017%	14.9017%
Net present value					
Investment	0	($100,000)	($50,000)	($150,000)	($150,000)
Discounted return	0	$109,629	$54,037	$163,666	$163,666
NPV	0	$ 9,629	$ 4,037	$ 13,666	$ 13,666

EXHIBIT 6.9:
Capital Rationing

	In $1,000,000		IRR	
	Capital required	*Cumulative*	*Without risk*	*With risk*
Projects Available				
Project R	$ 450	$ 450	20%	16%
Project S	250	700	16	14
Project T	150	850	15	13
Project U	50	900	14	12
	Funds available	*Cumulative*	*Money cost*	
Funding Available				
Present bank deposits	$ 100	$ 100	6%	
Future cash flow	50	150	6	
Future long-term loans				
Secured	200	350	12	
Unsecured	400	750	14	
Additional capital stock	300	1,050	16	
Total	$1,050		13	

Chapter 7 _____

RISK
ANALYSIS

Investment risk is the chance or probability that the expected cash flow or return on the investment is not realized or that the actual results will vary from the projected performance. The greater is the chance of the nonrealization of the cash flow or return, or the greater is the variance of actual results from the projections, the greater is the risk.

Investment decisions are based partly on the expected performance as estimated from the financial projections and outcomes of financial analysis. However, in many instances, the actual results are far from the expected performance. This gap is due to (1) changes in the general business environment or economic situation as rise in inflation and interest rates, (2) developments within the industry as emerging demand of consumers or entry of new competitors, (3) failure of management to perform within the framework of the changed environment, (4) unexpected events as raw material shortages or natural calamities, and (5) plain errors in formulating the assumptions, preparing the financial projections, or conducting the financial analysis.

This chapter identifies the different types of risks, presents methods of minimizing them, and explains and illustrates the techniques of analyzing them.

I. TYPES OF INVESTMENT RISKS

GENERAL CLASSIFICATIONS OF RISKS

Risk may be classified generally in two ways which interlock: (1) according to the level of their applicability and (2) according to the position level of the party concerned with the risk.

Levels of Applicability. Classified according to their scope of applicability, the risks may be at the corporate, industry, or business environment level.

CORPORATE LEVEL. Risks at the corporate or project level affects a specific firm or project only. Examples of such risks are those arising from a high debt/equity ratio and underutilized production facilities.

INDUSTRY LEVEL. Risks at the industry level impacts on all the firms in an industry. Declining product cycle, dependence on energy, and rapid technological development are of concern to all the firms in the affected industry.

ENVIRONMENTAL LEVEL. Business environmental risks, as those relating to the economy, influence the performance and risk of all industries operating within the economy.

The corporate, industry, and environmental risks, as well as their component risks, are studied in the subsequent sections.

Position Levels. There are three general position levels concerned with risks: at the divisional or operating management level, at the corporate management level, and at the corporate equity investor level.

The divisional management is concerned with project risk; the corporate management, portfolio risk; and the investor, security market risk.

The two general classifications of risks interweave to a matrix which follows:

Level of applicability	**Position Level of Party Concerned with Risk**		
	Project risk	*Portfolio risk*	*Security market risk*
Corporate level	Corporate risk	Corporate risk	(Not covered)
Industry level	Industry risk	Industry risk	Systematic risk
Environmental level	Environmental risk	Environmental risk	General security market risk

PROJECT RISK. Project risk pertains to the project itself, in isolation, without considering the relationship of the risk of this project to those of the other existing or proposed projects or investments of the firm. Project risk is influenced by several determinants. Among the significant determinants are developments in (1) the surroundings in which the project operates (environmental risk), (2) the industry where it is in (industry risk), and (3) the corporate entity itself which undertakes the project (corporate risk).

PORTFOLIO RISK. This is the risk of the project in relation to the risk of the present investments.

According to the classical portfolio risk theory, the ideal project is one that behaves contrary to the trend in the performance of the existing investments. In other words, a sound undertaking is one that reaps so much profit while the others incur heavy losses, or vice versa. In this case, the particular project tends to stabilize the total results of the portfolio including the new project.

Thus, the difference between project risk and portfolio risk lies in the perspective taken: project risk considers only the particular project under consideration; portfolio risk views the particular project in relation to the other proposals under consideration as well as existing investments. Both project and portfolio risks cover the three levels of risks: corporate, industry, and business environmental.

SECURITY MARKET RISK.   According to the capital asset pricing model (CAPM), an investor in the common stocks of corporations incur two types of risks: the general securities market risk, which is influenced by developments in the general business environment, and the systematic risk (industry risk), which is the result of developments in both the industry and the business environment. The CAPM was previously examined in Chapter 5.

Risks According to their Levels of Applicability.   The risks classified according to their level of applicability, as well as their components, are as follows:

I. Business environmental risk
    A. Economic risk
        1. Economic cycle risk
        2. Inflation risk
        3. Interest rate risk
        4. Foreign exchange risk
    B. Locational risk
        1. Political risk
        2. Natural calamities risk
        3. Socioenvironmental risk
        4. Ethnic risk
II. Industry risk
    A. Industry-type risk
    B. Product cycle risk
        1. Declining industry risk
        2. Starting industry risk
    C. Market risk
        1. Social risk
        2. Purchasing power risk

        D. Resource supply risk
           1. Capital investment risk
           2. Labor risk
           3. Energy risk
        E. Industry development risk
           1. Ease of entry risk
           2. Oligopolistic market risk
           3. Government regulation risk
           4. Technological development risk
   III. Corporate risk
        A. Project-type risk
           1. Project objective risk
           2. Asset type risk
        B. Business risk
           1. Customer risk
           2. Supplier risk
           3. Price commitment risk
           4. Production facilities risk
        C. Financial risk
           1. Financing risk
           2. Cost structure risk
           3. Cash flow matching risk
           4. Liquidity and default risk

BUSINESS ENVIRONMENTAL RISK

A corporation interacts with the other sectors of the economy and plays a role in its locality. These environments present two types of risks: the risks which are brought about by the general economic forces (economic risk) and the risks which affect only a certain location (locational risk).

Economic Risk. The profitability of a firm is affected by the developments in the general economy. Hence it is subjected to different types of economic risks. Some of the causes of the risks are movements in the economic cycles and fluctuations in the inflation and interest rates.

ECONOMIC CYCLE RISK. In case of a recession, the economic activities slow down, the buying power of the population declines, and their purchases drop. This naturally curtails the sales, and thence reduces the profit or transforms the profit to a loss.

INFLATION RISK. If there is an inflation, those with investments in physical assets such as inventories, land, buildings, and equipment ride with the inflation, since the prices of these resources go up with the rise in prices. However, those with substantial receivables, bond investments, and deposit accounts with the banks lose part of their investment. The real value of these resources decline because the purchasing power of the cash which can be recovered from these investments decline.

INTEREST RATE RISK.   Borrower-firms with short-term loans or variable interest rate long-term loans (liabilities of the borrowers), and whose interest cost is high in relation to their total cost, are vulnerable to upward swings in interest rates.

On the other hand, deposit-taking and lending institutions with short-term or variable interest rate deposits from customers (liabilities) but with fixed interest rate long-term lendings (assets) are most likely to plunge when interest rates jump. This is precisely what happened to the savings and loan industry and to one of the largest commercial banks.

FOREIGN EXCHANGE RISK.   This is created when a firm will generate receipts or earnings denominated in a foreign currency or has commitments to pay in another. Take a company which exports to Germany with the contracts denominated in marks. A drop in the value of the mark in relation to the dollar will reduce the dollar earnings, since the firm gets fewer dollars for every mark in export.

This foreign exchange loss is worsened if the same firm is committed to import Japanese materials and if the yen rises relative to the dollar because it then pays more dollars for every yen it imports.

Locational Risk.   Locational risk is taken when a firm operates in a particular geographical area. The area refers to a city, state, or another nation. By locating in an area, the firm is subjected to the political, natural, socioenvironmental, and ethnic hazards of that place.

POLITICAL RISK.   An American firm faces a grave political risk when it operates in a foreign nation where the government is in the hands of an authoritarian leader. Sudden appearance of new laws without prior public hearings, especially those on the nationalization of foreign-owned companies without adequate compensation, generates a loss for the American owners. Frequent or unexpected changes in the government through coups add to the political instability.

NATURAL CALAMITIES RISK.   Agricultural firms are especially vulnerable to harsh weather conditions such as drought, frost, and storms. However, industrial firms are not spared from natural hazards. Sustained heavy rains could cause the collapse of dams, which in turn, can flood the communities downstream.

SOCIOENVIRONMENTAL RISK.   This occurs when certain segments of society in a particular region are very concerned with the damage to the environment. This public concern leads to legislation which can diminish the profit of firms in certain industries. Examples of these laws are those that restrict (1) the logging operations in forests which are inhabited by endangered species, (2) the extraction of oil from natural preserves, and (3) the dumping of harmful chemicals in landfills which are near populated areas.

ETHNIC RISK.   An ethnic hostility may erupt in an area where a substantial proportion of the population has an ethnic background which is different from that of the owners, managers, or employees of a firm. In its mild manifestation, the antipathy can lead to the boycott of the products of the company. In its more militant form, the movement can physically harm the personnel, customers, or physical resources of the firm.

INDUSTRY RISK

The risk level of an industry is determined by the type of industry itself (industry-type risk), the stage of product maturity (product cycle risk), the response of the customers (market risk), the sources of supply of the inputs of the firms (resource supply risk), and the speed of developments in the industry (industry development risk).

Industry-type Risk.   The type of industry influences the risk of a project in that industry. For instance, an oil exploration project in general is more risky than a commercial property leasing agency.

Product Cycle Risk.   The stage in the product cycle in which the industry is situated helps define the degree of fluctuations of the profitability in that industry. An industry which has already matured has more stabilized market and more established players than does an industry which is just starting or which is already declining. Hence, a new industry as bio-technology is more risky than is an established one as food processing.

DECLINING INDUSTRY RISK.   A declining industry, as the cigaret or minicomputer, is risky in that the drop in the demand may accelerate. Hence the economic lives of the capital investments may outrun their physical lives. Furthermore, some declining industries run a big chance of being stocked up with inventories which will take a longer time to dispose of.

STARTING INDUSTRY RISK.   On the other hand, starting industries, as the biomedical industry, are also risky because of the unproven markets and technologies and long lead times in developing the technical know-how.

Market Risk.   This is the chance that the demand for the products in the future may be less than what is anticipated. There are two major components of this risk: the probability that the consumer tastes of society will change overnight (social risk) and that the buying power of the customers may be diminished in the future (purchasing power risk).

SOCIAL RISK.   The social behavior affects the demand for consumer goods like clothes. The sudden change of what is in vogue may render huge inventories of goods out of style. Fast changes in fashion, on one hand, and slow corporate response time, on the other, collaborate to aggravate the risk. Response time refers to the period elapsed from the date the fashion changes to the time the new designs are stocked in the retail outlets.

PURCHASING POWER RISK.   This risk materializes into a loss if the disposable income of the consumers is not enough to enable them to buy the goods offered by a firm. This happens if the actual costs overshoot the target or if the market survey was not able to gauge properly the economic strata of the potential buyers.

Resource Supply Risk.   This type of risk is influenced by the key factors used in the production of goods. An industry whose inputs emphasize one type of resource is subject to the vicissitudes affecting that resource. Thus, industries which are capital or labor intensive, or which consume so much energy, are more risky than those which are not so dependent on any one of these resources.

CAPITAL INVESTMENT RISK.   Projects calling for huge capital outlays entail much risk due to the magnitude of the financing tied in to one specific undertaking. Furthermore, capital-intensive projects usually need a long gestation period. The longer the capital recovery time, the higher the level of risk.

LABOR RISK.   Legislations on labor as those prescribing the minimum wage or setting work standards can push up the effective labor cost overnight, thereby enhancing the probability that labor-intensive operations will flounder. Substantial upward adjustments in medical insurance premium rates can produce the same effect.

ENERGY RISK.   Metal smelting plants, airlines, and other industries consuming substantial volumes of energy are susceptible not only to the price movements of this commodity but also to the possibility of a short supply. This is so since the United States is a net importer of oil.

Industry Development Risk.   The speed by which major events in an industry is shaped influences the profitability or capital recovery of the projects in the industry since the companies do not have time to adjust to the fast-changing environment. Convulsions in the industry may be caused by the ease of industry entry, the presence of a few major players in the industry, tight government control, and leapfrogging of technological developments.

EASE OF ENTRY RISK.   If new firms can easily enter an industry, the industry can be easily saturated by competitors. An entry is facilitated if the capital requirement is not massive, if no special technology is required, or if there are no government restrictions. New competitors, in their bid to gain a foothold, are apt to offer low initial prices. The proliferation of firms can convert the product into a commodity, as what is happening in the desktop computer industry.

OLIGOPOLISTIC MARKET RISK.   If there are few players in an industry, an aggressive move by one of them can disturb the market equilibrium. This will induce the firms to fight each other more fiercely, thereby reducing their profitability. Thus, when one airline started offering free tickets or tickets at reduced rates a few years ago, in consideration of the mileage previously accumulated by the passengers, the other firms fought back and the financial performance of the industry took a nosedive.

GOVERNMENT REGULATIONS RISK.   Excessive government regulations influence the way an industry operates. Sudden changes in the regulations can disrupt the normal operations in the industry, since the firms are not given enough time to change to the new rules. The sudden loosening of the regulations can also cause firms in the industry to plunge. Witness the demise of several savings and loan associations after the dismantling of the rules on interest rates and allowable investments.

TECHNOLOGICAL DEVELOPMENT RISK.   If products are offered and accepted based on the success of new technologies, the firms in the industry may lose overnight or reduce their profitability if a competitor has leapfrogged their technology. This is happening or has happened to the computer workstation and supercomputer industries where the players are racing to develop the fastest products at the most reasonable prices.

CORPORATE RISK

Unlike the industry or business environmental risk which affects a broad range of enterprises, the corporate risk pertains to a particular company. The survival of a firm is dependent not only on the condition of its environment but also on the specific type of project it has selected (project-type risk), the ways it conducts its business (business risk), and the manner in which it has financed its resources and structured its costs (financial risk).

Project-type Risk.   The type of project undertaken influences the risk of the activity. The project-type risk is composed of the project objective risk and the asset-type risk.

PROJECT OBJECTIVE RISK.   Firms in the same industry but undertaking measures with different objectives incur different levels of risk. A project which seeks to capture market share is more risky than is one which aims to automate the manufacturing operations. In the former type of undertaking, the competitors are likely to fight back, and hence force the firm to spend more on advertising or to reduce prices.

An R&D program is more risky than is a program to speed up the collection. The chance of getting benefits from the collection efforts is contingent on just one factor: the realization of receivables into cash. On the other hand, the possibility of getting an advantage from the R&D efforts hinges on the successful accomplishment of all the following events: the invention of a technologically sound product, the market acceptance of the discovery, the profitable commercialization of the product, and the ultimate collection of the sales.

ASSET-TYPE RISK.   A project calling for an investment in specialized machinery is more destabilizing than is one with a major investment in a general-purpose building. In like manner, an investment in raw materials is more risky than is one in trade receivables.

Business Risk.   The success or failure of a firm is contingent upon the quality of, and kinds of arrangements it has made with its customers and suppliers. Its type of production facilities also counts. A stable firm is one which has established lasting relations with its customers and suppliers who themselves are also stable in their respective businesses.

CUSTOMER RISK.   If a company does not have a firm hold on the market, its customers may shift to other suppliers. Marketers of commodities incur more customer risk than do the manufacturers of specialized machinery in this regard. The customers of the commodity dealers have more choices in their sources of supply than do the customers of the machinery makers.

A firm with casual customers is in a less secure position than is a company which has established joint or cooperative efforts in technological research and development with its customers, or is providing them with long-term, low-interest financing. A company which is just introducing its products is in a more risky position than is one which has acquired brand loyalty among the users of its products.

SUPPLIER RISK.   A manufacturer which sources its raw materials in the open market is more likely to suffer supply disruptions than is one which has long-term purchase arrangements. A maker which has integrated backward to the sources of materials is in the most stable situation from the viewpoint of material supply. However, said maker has also the greatest risk exposure when the demand for its own products dwindle.

PRICE COMMITMENT RISK.   A firm destabilizes its operations if it commits to long-term sales contracts with fixed prices without the corresponding long-term purchase contracts for its inputs at fixed prices. A subsequent surge in prices of the inputs without corresponding adjustment in the selling price will squeeze out the profit in the transaction.

PRODUCTION FACILITIES RISK.   A firm with a huge unused production facility is in a good position to take advantage of growth in the market. However, it is also prone to incur a loss if its sales declines. The effect can be especially disastrous if the production facility is new and has incorporated the state-of-the-art technology and the firm is still amortizing the loan which was used to acquire the plant.

On the other hand, a manufacturer with very limited in-house production capability may not be able to capitalize fully on a sellers' market. However, its losses in a buyer's market is minimized.

Financial Risk.   While the business risk covers the arrangements and relationships with the customers and suppliers and the size and quality of the production facilities, the financial risks are concerned with the financing, cost, cash flow, and liquidity implications of the arrangements with the customers and suppliers. Financial risk is composed of the financing risk, cost structure risk, cash flow matching risk, and liquidity and default risk.

FINANCING RISK.   Financing risk is determined by the debt/equity ratio and the quality of the debtors and equity holders. The financing scheme for a project influences the degree of fluctuations in its profitability. A firm which is loaded with debt is more likely to have wider swings in its performance than is one with minimal loans. A decline in sales will have a more negative impact on the more leveraged company.

A firm with short-term loans is in a more unstable position than is one with long-term bond financing. An issuer of bonds without conversion features is less secure than is the issuer of debts which most likely will be traded for equity because of its attractive conversion features.

A publicly owned firm whose majority of shares is cornered by a few short-term investors who are in just to make a fast killing is more likely to run into difficulties than is one whose stockholders are after the long-term growth of their investment.

COST STRUCTURE RISK.   The cost structure risk proceeds from the raw material supply commitments, production facilities arrangements, and financing scheme.

A company procuring raw materials in the open market, contracting out most of its production operations, and financing its assets mainly with equity has a much better chance to withstand a market decline than does a competitor which has integrated backward to the sources of raw materials, has acquired a new automated plant with unused capacity, and has funded most of its assets with borrowings. The first firm has lower fixed cost and fixed cash payment commitments than the second concern. A decline in sales volume will depress the variable costs but not the fixed costs.

CASH FLOW MATCHING RISK.   A company with a mismatched cash flow, as one whose maturing obligations cannot be covered by expected receipts from operations and liquidation of assets, is headed for a cash flow problem. A similar situation arises when a parent company has investments in start-ups and growing companies but none in cash cows.

LIQUIDITY AND DEFAULT RISK.   A financing structure which is burdened by short-term debt, a cost structure which is loaded with fixed costs, a cash flow where the payments are not matched by receipts, and an asset structure which is top heavy with office buildings and plant facilities but light on receivables and merchandise and finished goods inventories, will most likely generate for the firm liquidity problems when the sales slow down. This is so because the company has no cash or near-cash reserves with which to pay the cash disbursement commitments for the maturing obligations and high fixed costs. When the firm runs out of cash, it has to default on its obligations to the creditors.

PORTFOLIO RISK

While project risk covers the project in isolation, portfolio risk encompasses not only the project under consideration but also the other investments of the project sponsor as well.

Portfolio risk and project risk cover basically the same three general areas: the industry risk, the business environment risk, and the corporate risk as described earlier. The differences between these two types of risks in specific fields within these areas are illustrated next.

Industry Risk

INDUSTRY-TYPE RISK.   The industry where the new project will enter in relation to the industries where the firm has current investments affects the stability of the company, and hence the degree of the portfolio risk. A new synthetic sweetener project of a sugar plantation company has a lower risk than does an apparel project of the same organization. The first project will help in stabilizing the performance of the sugar company in case of a shift in demand from sugar to sweetener.

PRODUCT CYCLE RISK.   A project entering an industry which is in the introductory phase of the product cycle has a high project risk. However, if it is sponsored by a firm with investments in industries in the maturity or declining phase, as one in the U.S. cigarette industry, the project not only reduces the overall risk of the firm but provides for a good strategy. The new project will gradually replace the old investments. In the meantime, the excessive cash generation of the matured investment which is in the harvest strategy can be used to finance the requirements of the cash-hungry new project which will initially implement a grow strategy. See Chapter 2 for a discussion of the grow and harvest strategies.

The cigarette example can be carried a step farther. While it is suicidal to establish a new cigarette project in the United States which will make traditional cigarette products because of the declining market, it is a good strategy to put up a new cigarette operation in the developing countries because their cigarette industries are still growing. The cash flow from the U.S. investments can be channeled to fund the development of the foreign operations.

Business Environmental Risk

NATURAL CALAMITIES RISK.   The project specifications as location and type of investment affect the overall company results. Adding a new factory in the same compound where the other plants of the company are currently situated, or establishing another store in a city where most of the outlets are now located, enhances the portfolio risk. Accidents or calamities can wipe out most of the plants or retail outlets in one area.

Corporate Risk

PROJECT-TYPE RISK.   A sales expansion strategy sometimes calls for the lengthening of the collection period of sales in order to attract customers. Such a strategy if undertaken by a company with minimal debt and with a big portion of its assets already invested in receivables, will be carrying far more portfolio risk than if the same strategy were to be implemented by a firm with substantial obligations and with fewer collectibles.

The latter firm is in a better position to absorb a loss in the value of its receivables due to inflation since such a loss can be offset by its gain arising from the reduction in the value of its debts due to inflation.

FINANCING RISK.   Two undertakings with identical and high debt/equity ratio have the same level of project risk. However, the one to be implemented by a more leveraged company has the higher portfolio risk.

COST STRUCTURE RISK.   Two projects with fixed costs accounting for 85% of the total operating costs are said to have the same degree of project risk. However, if one of the projects is to be undertaken by a firm with fixed costs equivalent to 80% of its total costs, and the other project is to be sponsored by an enterprise with fixed costs of only 30% of its total costs, the first project has a higher portfolio risk.

II. RISK MINIMIZATION AND RISK-RETURN TRADE-OFF

Some types of risk may be minimized, but some may not. For instance, risk due to excessive government regulations and ease of industry entry cannot be changed by a firm. However, other types of risk may be reduced. The methods of cutting down the risk depends upon the specific type of risk. The major means are diversification and hedging. These, and some other methods, are described in this section.

DIVERSIFICATION

Corporations may reduce their overall risk by engaging in diversified industries. Since different industry types do not necessarily rise and fall together and at the same rate, the decline of some industries may be partly compensated for by the rise of others.

If a firm is in two industries, one capital intensive and the other labor intensive, the rise in interest may pull down the former industry but not necessarily the other.

If a company has an investment in an industry where there is an ease of entry and one which is highly regulated by the government, the former investment may be imperiled by the sudden influx of new competitors, but the second may not be so affected.

HEDGING

Hedging is the matching or balancing of opposing transactions or obligations so that the loss in one is offset or mitigated by a gain in the other. Hedging may be effected through specialized institutional arrangements or through prudent financial management practices. Examples of the first type are a futures contract to buy or sell commodities or a forward exchange contract to buy or sell foreign currencies. An illustration of the second one is the timing of the receipt and payment in the same foreign currency such that both transactions occur at the same time. More risks can be covered by sound financial management practices than by dealing in the commodity futures or forward exchanges. Both types are discussed in the five types of risks which are created by unbalanced positions.

Inflation Risk.   Inflation deflates the buying power of the dollar which may be collected in the future from receivables. Inflation also reduces the purchasing value of cash including those in bank deposits, if they are spent in the future. The higher the inflation rate, the higher the loss. This loss can be hedged by pushing up the levels of the loans, accounts payable, and other obligations. These liabilities create gains due to inflation since they are paid in cheaper dollars.

The losses from inflation may also be reduced by means other than hedging. For instance, the goal may be achieved by holding down the investments in bank deposits, receivables, and bonds. Purchases of materials, equipment, buildings, and other items whose value rises with inflation may be accelerated.

Interest Rate Risk.   Banking institutions with long-term fixed interest rate loans have their positions exposed to interest rate fluctuations. A rise in the interest rate they pay on their deposit liability can wipe out their interest margins. This exposed position may be covered by long-term fixed interest rate deposit liabilities. If this type of liability cannot be obtained, then they have no recourse but to grant long-term variable interest rate loans or short-term loans.

Foreign Exchange Rate Risk.   Firms with mismatched foreign currency positions are susceptible to losses in case of exchange rate fluctuations. Those with earnings, expected receipts, or assets denominated in foreign currencies will incur dollar losses if the value of the foreign currencies in relation to the dollar drops. In similar manner, those with expenditures, expected payments, or liabilities denominated in foreign currencies will incur dollar losses if the value of the foreign currencies vis-à-vis the dollar surges.

The foreign exchange losses can be averted if the earnings, receipts, or assets in foreign currencies can be matched by expenditures, payments, or liabilities in identical currencies. For instance, those with foreign exchange earnings, receipts, or assets in Italian lira should denominate the expenses, payments, or liabilities in lira. If not, the firm should obtain forward exchange contracts to sell foreign exchange. Exposures due to expected payments or liabilities in foreign currencies may be similarly protected.

Price Commitment Risk.   A company which is forced to sign long-term sales contracts at fixed prices should match their exposure with long-term purchase contracts for the materials and labor. If this cannot be arranged, they should hedge their fixed selling price commitments with commodity futures contracts to buy if this is available.

Cash Flow Matching Risk.   Cash flow should be balanced in three ways. First, short-term obligations should be matched with short-term assets which can be realized to pay the obligations. Second, long-term investments should be balanced with long-term fund sources. Third, investments in cash-deficit projects, namely, start-ups or growth enterprises should be balanced with cash-generating investments, as those in matured or declining industries.

OTHER MEANS OF RISK MINIMIZATION

Business Environmental Risk

ECONOMIC CYCLE RISK.   At the operating level, a firm can be made more recession resistant by building up the cash reserves, keeping the inventories down, postponing the acquisition of plants until the existing capacities are fully utilized and maintaining a low overhead.

ETHNIC RISK.   The most effective way of controlling this risk is by taking as employees members of the ethnic group. This employment policy may be augmented by a good community relations program. This will involve organizing tours of company facilities for schoolchildren and neighborhood associations.

Industry Risk

SOCIAL RISK.   The risk due to sudden changes in consumer preferences may be minimized by having a shorter response time from the time the changes in the preferences occur, to the time of the delivery of the goods to the customers. Furthermore, the changes may be anticipated by conducting meetings or consultations with the trendsetters.

BUYING POWER RISK.   This risk may be subdued by targeting products to specific economic groups and then determining their buying power. The risk may also be minimized by pricing the products low enough. However, although this will cut down the risk, this will also reduce the return.

RISK-RETURN TRADE-OFF

The higher the expected return, the higher the risk. The decision to implement a proposal, therefore, invariably involves a delicate balancing of the risk with return.

A firm entering an industry which is at the beginning phase of its product cycle has a chance of reaping attractive profit afterward. However, it is also exposing itself to a high degree of risk (product cycle risk). Companies joining the designer clothes or high-technology industries have the same objectives—seeking high returns—but are also courting high risks—social and technology risks, respectively.

At the corporate level, a firm may try to improve its profit by controlling the supply and cost of its raw materials through backward integration. But by undertaking this measure, it also raises the level of its risk in terms of the investment in the project and higher fixed costs.

A manufacturer which undertakes to raise its return by reducing its manufacturing cost per unit and having extra capacity to spare to cater subsequently to an enlarged market falls into the same trap by raising its exposure to production facilities risk.

Similarly, a company which tries to enhance its return on investment (ROI) by tapping loans with low interest rates, may end up with less or negative ROI if the expected operating profit fail to materialize. This happens if the total return on the total investment by both the owners and lenders turns out to be lower than the interest on the debt. See Chapter 15.

III. TECHNIQUES OF PROJECT RISK ANALYSIS

TYPES OF TECHNIQUES (Exhibit 7.1)

The techniques of analysis and the specific areas of project risk which may be used to evaluate are revealed in Exhibit 7.1.

Techniques to Gauge the Business Environmental, Industry, Project Type, and Business Risks. The business environment, the industry situation, the project type, and the business arrangements influence the variability of the results of a project. Most of the more popular or practical project risk analysis tools try to measure this variability. The tools compare a *benchmark* with (1) the *expected results* or (2) the *range of possible variations* of the expected results. The difference between the benchmark and the expected results or range of possible variations thereof indicates the degree of risk. If the expected results are more favorable than the benchmark, the gap gauges the adequacy of the safety margin of the project. All the following tools of project risk analysis are based on this working principle.

1. The sensitivity analysis, which compares the expected results from the base set of assumptions and projections (the benchmark) with the results based on the varying assumptions (the range of possible variations of the expected results)
2. The probability analysis, which compares the mean or weighted average of all the probabilities (the benchmark) with the expected results of each of the different probabilities (the range of possible variations of the expected results)
3. The decision tree analysis, which compares for each of alternative first-stage decisions the mean of all the probabilities (the benchmark) with the expected results of each of the different probabilities (the range of possible variations of the expected results)
4. The break-even point, which compares the break-even point (the benchmark) with the expected level of sales volume or selling price (the expected result)
5. The crossover point, which compares the crossover sales volume or discount rate (the benchmark) with the expected level of sales volume or discount rate (the expected result)
6. The internal rate of return (IRR), which compares the cost of money (the benchmark) with the expected IRR (the expected result)
7. The net present value (NPV), which compares the present value of the investment (the benchmark) with the expected NPV of the total return (the expected result)

These tools are briefly described and explained in detail in the remaining parts of this chapter and in Chapter 8.

Techniques to Gauge the Financial Risks. These risks can be directly measured. The cost structure risk can be gauged by the ratio of fixed costs to variable costs, while the financing scheme risk can be measured by the debt/equity ratio. These are explained next. The liquidity risk can be gauged by the liquidity ratios discussed in Chapter 20.

Classifications of Techniques. The techniques of risk analysis may be grouped into four classifications according to their working principles. The classes are (1) performance variability methods, (2) point of equality techniques, (3) return on investment methods, and (4) fixed-variable commitment indicators.

PERFORMANCE VARIABILITY METHODS

These techniques use varying sets of assumptions and financial projections. The expected results from these varying sets are compared with the weighted average of the results from each of these sets of assumptions or with the expected results from the base set of assumptions.

Sensitivity Analysis. Under this technique, the cash flow, rate of return, and other indicators of performance are calculated, based on the most likely set of assumptions (the base set). The performance indicators derived from the base set serve as the benchmarks. The assumptions are then varied and other sets of projections are prepared (the varying sets). The indicators of performance derived from the varying projections are then compared with those obtained from the base set. The swings in the values of the performance indicators give management an idea of the possible variability of actual results from the base set. The greater the number of indicators which have substantial deviations from the indicators derived from the base set, the more risky is the project.

Sensitivity analysis is explained in detail in Section V of this chapter.

Probability Analysis. This tool takes off from the outcomes of the sensitivity analysis. This method assigns a probability factor to the cash flow and other indicators of performance derived from the base set of assumptions or projections and from the varying projections mentioned in the preceding section. A weighted average or mean is then estimated for the indicators. An index of variability, called the coefficient of deviation, is then calculated. This index measures the difference between the mean and the indicator from each varying set or probability. The higher the coefficient, the more risky is the project.

Probability analysis is treated in depth in Section VI of this chapter.

Decision tree analysis.   This tool is similar to the probability analysis. The major difference is that the coefficient of deviation is calculated for each of the alternative first-stage decisions of a given proposal. Decision tree analysis is illustrated in Section VII of this chapter.

POINT OF EQUALITY TECHNIQUES

These methods seek to determine the point of equality—between the total costs and total revenues of a project in case of break-even point (BEP) or between the total costs of the project and that of another in case of crossover point (COP). The point of equality is then compared with the expected sales volume, discount rate, or other performance indicators.

Break-even Point.   This technique tries to establish the level of sales volume or selling price at which the total revenues just equal the total costs of a project. The BEP is then related to the expected volume or price.

It is possible that initially, the expected volume or price is lower than the BEP, but ultimately, higher. The excess of the BEP over the expected sales volume measures the risk, while the excess of the expected sales volume over the BEP gauges the degree of protection of the firm from possible declines of the sales volume from the expected levels.

BEP is examined in depth in Chapter 8.

Crossover Point.   This tool is applicable to the evaluation of two projects which do not directly earn revenues. The COP is the level of sales volume or other performance indicators at which the total costs of one proposal equals that of another. The gap between the expected sales volume and the COP sales volume represents the safety buffer which will protect the firm from a possible disadvantageous change in the sales volume before the selected proposal becomes less attractive than the one turned down.

COP is explained further in Section VIII of this chapter.

RETURN ON INVESTMENT METHODS
(DISCOUNTED CASH FLOW)

The internal rate of return (IRR) and the net present value (NPV) are primarily return on investment measures in that they size up the value to be recovered in excess of the investment put in. Their usage in this context was examined in Chapters 4, 5, and 6.

However, the IRR and the NPV can also be used in connection with sensitivity or probability analysis as indicators of performance in gauging the variability of the IRR and NPV from the benchmark as described under sensitivity and probability analysis.

Furthermore, either can be employed in risk analysis if they are related to the capital or cost of capital. The excess of the IRR over the cost of money to the investors (IRR margin) is a safety buffer. The project can afford to have the expected IRR reduced to equal the cost of money before the investors incur a loss.

In like manner, the excess of the NPV over the present value of the capital acts as a loss buffer.

Decision Tree. For each of the alternative first-stage decisions for a project, the excess of the present value of the total returns over the present value of the investment, represents the safety margin. This margin is the extent to which the present value of the total returns may be reduced before the original investment suffers a diminution.

FIXED-VARIABLE COMMITMENT INDICATORS

The techniques for measuring the cost structure and financing scheme risks quantity is the relationship between the fixed commitments and the variable commitments. These techniques directly measure the project risk.

Fixed Cost/Variable Cost Ratio. This ratio relates the total fixed costs to the total variable costs at the expected level of operations. The higher the fixed costs in relation to the variable costs, the higher is the level of the risk. The application of this tool to product deletion decision analysis is illustrated in Chapter 10.

Debt/Equity Ratio. Directly related to the fixed cost/variable cost ratio is the financing scheme or debt/equity ratio. Debt spawns fixed commitments in the form of interest and loan amortization. On the other hand, common equity does not generate fixed commitments since the payments to common stockholders for cash dividends is normally contingent upon the profitability of the firm and availability of cash. Thus, the higher the debt in relation to equity as measured by the debt/equity ratio, the more risky is the project.

The concept of this ratio is explained further in Chapter 20, while the application on project risk is examined in Chapter 15.

IV. TECHNIQUES OF PORTFOLIO RISK ANALYSIS

Although several techniques of portfolio risk analysis have been advanced by others, the author considers the following as the more practical or popular ones: (1) correlation analysis, (2) sensitivity analysis, (3) probability analysis, (4) break-even point analysis, (5) debt/equity ratio, and (6) fixed cost/variable cost ratio. These tools are linked to the different areas of portfolio risk in Exhibit 7.1.

Sensitivity analysis, probability analysis, break-even point analysis, debt/equity ratio, and fixed cost/variable cost ratio operate under the same principles as discussed earlier under project risk analysis. The only difference is that instead of basing the analysis just on the project under consideration, the analysis of portfolio risk is expanded to cover the existing investments of the sponsoring organization.

Due to their very nature, three techniques which are employed to evaluate project risk are not utilized to review portfolio risk. The crossover point is employed to study nonrevenue undertakings and hence is usually not employed in risk analysis for a portfolio which includes revenue-producing operations. The IRR and NPV are used to evaluate proposed undertakings but not ongoing operations. Hence they cannot be utilized to evaluate risk where the portfolio includes companies which are already operational.

CORRELATION ANALYSIS

The possible performance of a project is often related to the expected or past performance of the existing investments of a firm during the different stages of the economic cycle: recession, recovery, and prosperity. If the performance of a project and of the present investments goes up and down together during the different stages, the correlation is $+1$. If the project goes up while the other investments deteriorate, or vice versa, the correlation is -1. If there is no relationship at all, the correlation is zero.

A positive correlation increases the portfolio risk since (1) it enlarges the total loss of a firm in case of an economic downturn and (2) it magnifies the fluctuations of the performance. The higher the value of the positive correlation (the maximum is $+1$), the higher is the risk. In like manner, a negative correlation diminishes the portfolio risk since the loss in the existing investments is partly offset by the gain from the new project. The higher the value of the negative correlation (the maximum is -1), the more attractive is the project.

Limitations. The concept of correlation is sound, and hence the technique should be considered in risk analysis. However, the technique has several limitations in measuring the expected performance of a project in relation to those of existing investments, particularly with reference to the performance of the economy.

The first limitation is that the data on the performance of industries during the ups and downs of economic cycles are not current any more. The current period of prosperity (1990) began almost a decade ago. During this time, substantial changes in demographics and industries have taken place and therefore have rendered less effective the use of data on the performance of different industries during the prior economic cycles. For instance, the portions of minorities and the elderly in the total population have ballooned. Furthermore, Japanese cars became entrenched in the U.S. market, and the savings and loan industry fell.

The second shortcoming is that the measure of performance of an industry may represent the national average. But performance may differ from region to region. For instance, while the real estate market in Houston took a nosedive in 1988–1989, the market in Los Angeles witnessed an unprecedented boom.

The third weakness is that there is no accurate measure of performance for an existing operation in relation to the performance of the economy. One popular measure is sales revenues (in dollars). The problem with this measure is that the type of marketing strategy adopted by a firm and the sales expansion costs budget used to support the strategy blurs the correlation between the trend of the sales and the performance of the economy. During the years when a company is on an aggressive grow strategy to capture market share, with this strategy supported by unlimited funds for sales expansion costs, the sales will be showing record advances. But if the strategy is reversed to harvest strategy, and the sales expansion expenses budget withdrawn, the sales is likely to retreat. See Chapter 2 for the distinction between grow and harvest strategies and Chapter 11 for the nature of sales expansion costs.

Another indicator commonly used to measure performance is profit. This measure, like sales, is influenced by the strategy and sales expansion costs. Furthermore, it is also affected by R&D expenditures and other discretionary expenses which have no bearing at all on operating performance since these expenditures are not properly matched with the revenues. See Chapter 24 for the effects of R&D expenditures on the profit.

Possible Solution.   The correlation of the performance of a project with the performance of existing investments can be measured more precisely if a more specific event is used. For instance, if a sugar plantation is considering a move into artificial sweeteners and apparel, a relevant event is the shift in demand from natural sugar to artificial sweetener. Based on this event, the correlation of the sweetener project to the sugar plantation is -1, while that of the apparel project to the sugar plantation is zero. In this case, therefore, the sweetener project has less portfolio risk and hence is more attractive.

SENSITIVITY ANALYSIS FOR PORTFOLIO RISK

Sensitivity analysis for portfolio risk analysis works in the same way as sensitivity analysis for project risk as discussed in Section V of this chapter. The only difference is in the coverage. In the portfolio risk evaluation, sensitivity analysis includes the existing investments of the firm.

Projections are prepared for each alternative proposal and for the existing investments. These sets and the expected results are illustrated

next. Assume that residual income (RI) is used as the measure of performance and that the first full year of normalized operations of the new project
is used as the basis of analysis. Assume further that the conditions under
the varying set is the same as those in the base set except that there will be
a shift in demand from natural sugar to sweetener.

	RESIDUAL INCOME	
	Base set	*Varying set*
With sweetener project		
Sweetener project (new project)	$100,000	$200,000
Sugar plantation (present investment)	500,000	100,000
Total	$600,000	$300,000
With apparel project		
Apparel project (new project)	$100,000	$100,000
Sugar plantation	500,000	100,000
Total	$600,000	$200,000

A shift in the demand from sugar to sweetener will reduce the decline of
the residual income of the company if the sweetener project is the one
implemented. Hence the sweetener project carries less risk than does the
other project.

PROBABILITY ANALYSIS FOR PORTFOLIO RISK

Assume that there is a 60% probability that the assumptions in the base set
mentioned will be realized and there is a 40% probability for the varying
set. The coefficients of deviation of the two alternatives are as follows:

	Residual income	Probability	Results
With sweetener project			
Base set	$600,000	60%	
Varying set	$300,000	40%	
Mean	$480,000		
Standard deviation			$147,000
Coefficient of deviation			.306
With apparel project			
Base set	$600,000	60%	
Varying set	$200,000	40%	
Mean	$440,000		
Standard deviation			$196,000
Coefficient of deviation			.445

These figures have established that

1. It is more likely that the company will have more residual income if it implements the sweetener project. This is measured by the mean. The possible RI in this case is $480,000, against the $440,000 if the other project is selected.
2. The company will be incurring less risk if it implements the sweetener project as the coefficient of deviation which measures the variability from the mean or weighted average is only 30.6% of the mean as compared with 44.5% for the other project.

If a performance indicator other than RI is used, the coefficient will most likely be different from the one shown.

The procedures for calculating the mean, standard deviation, and coefficient of deviation are described and illustrated in Section VI of this chapter.

BREAK-EVEN POINT ANALYSIS FOR PORTFOLIO RISK

The break-even point as a percentage of the expected sales may be used to gauge the capability of a firm to take on risky projects. Assume that the BEPs as a percentage of the expected sales of a new project and of the present operations of two separate companies are as follows:

Project A (new project)	86%
Company X (present operations)	45%
Company Y (present operations)	83%

Project A itself has a high project risk. However, if its operations are combined with those of Company X, the total operations will have a more acceptable portfolio risk.

However, Project A may not be acceptable to Company Y because of its present high BEP.

FIXED-VARIABLE COMMITMENT INDICATORS

The fixed costs/variable costs ratio and the debt/equity ratio may be used to evaluate the portfolio risk. Consider Project A, a possible undertaking by Company X or Y. The expected ratios are

	Fixed costs/ variable costs ratio	Debt/ equity ratio
Project A (new project)	67:33	70:30
Company X (present operations)	10:90	20:80
Company Y (present operations)	71:29	60:40

Project A has a high project risk because of its relatively high levels of fixed costs and debt. Hence it may not be safely undertaken by Company Y, which also has high ratios. However, Company X will be in a very good position to match the high ratios of project A.

V. SENSITIVITY ANALYSIS FOR PROJECT RISK

Sensitivity analysis is the study of the response of the cash flow, internal rate of return (IRR), net present value (NPV), break-even point, and other indicators of performance to the changes in the sales volume, selling prices, costs, amount of capital, and other operating and investment factors.

The study is conducted in two stages. First, one set of assumptions is formulated. Based on this set, the customary financial projections are prepared, and the other tools of financial analysis as IRR and NPV are applied.

During the second stage, assumptions on the sales volume, capital, and other operating and investment factors are varied, and the cash flow, rate of return, and other performance indicators are calculated. The performance indicators are calculated. The performance indicators derived from the second set of assumptions are compared with those coming from the first set in order to determine how the changes in the sales volume and other operating and investment parameters impact on the performance and investment desirability of the project.

FINANCIAL PROJECTIONS BASED ON ONE SET OF ASSUMPTIONS

In many instances, only one set of financial projections is prepared for purposes of decision analysis. This is the case, for instance, if the product had been established in a stable market, and the production and other internal operations have been stabilized.

Operating Cash Flow (Exhibit 7.2). The preparation of financial projections and the formulation of the underlying assumptions have been discussed in Chapters 2 and 3. A simplified model is shown in Exhibit 7.2, set A. Based on this base set, the one-year project is expected to generate an operating cash flow of $1,000,000.

Return on Investment (Exhibit 7.3). The total return on the $6,000,000 investment is $7,000,000—composed of the operating cash flow and the initial capital. Using these figures and a discount rate of 8%, the internal rate of return is estimated to be 16.7%, and the net present value, $481,000.

In this case, the IRR is the same as the accounting rate of return (ARR) for the following reasons: the project has only a one-year life, the investment is made at the start of the one-year period, and the operating cash flow is equivalent to the net profit.

PROJECTIONS BASED ON VARYING
SETS OF ASSUMPTIONS

If certain key aspects of the market or internal operations have not yet been firmed up, or if the economic environment is very volatile, several sets of projections may have to be prepared.

This is the case, for instance, if the product is still to be introduced. In this situation, its market is still not yet established and the possible response of the competition is still difficult to gauge. Several sets of projections may also have to be used if the framework of the internal operations is still being evolved; that is, the production process, labor productivity, or usage rate of raw materials have not yet been commercially experienced.

The instability of the external economic environment adds uncertainty to the future of a project. Unpredictable inflation rate, erratic interest rate, and pending income tax proposals call for assumptions on varying levels of inflation, interest and tax rates.

Procedures. If it is necessary to determine the impact of only one factor, only the assumptions regarding that factor are varied at a time, while the other assumptions are held unchanged. Thus, in sets B and C in Exhibits 7.2 and 7.3, only the sales volume is changed, while the selling price and other conditions were held constant. In sets D and E, the selling price is changed, while all the other assumptions were kept unchanged.

An alternative practice is to vary two or more assumptions at the same time. For instance, both the sales volume and selling price may be changed simultaneously. See sets F to I in Exhibit 7.3 for the resulting operating cash flow.

Operating and Investment Assumptions. There are two sets of assumptions: those affecting the operating cash flow, some of which are listed in Exhibit 7.2, and those influencing the return on investment. The latter includes the amount of the investment and the money cost or discount rate used in calculating the NPV. The other investment assumptions are those on the timing of the placement of the investment, the reinvestment rate, the pattern of the return or recovery of the investment, and the terminal or residual value of the project. These were discussed earlier in Chapters 4 and 5.

The IRR and NPV may be calculated based on the varying operating assumptions but constant investment assumptions are based on varying operating and investment assumptions. The use of these two types of bases is illustrated in Exhibit 7.3.

SENSITIVE FACTORS

Exhibit 7.3 shows that in this example the selling price is a much more sensitive factor than sales volume. A 10% change in the selling price causes a $600,000 deviation in the operating cash flow and a $556,000 change in the NPV. On the other hand, a 10% change in sales volume brings about only a $200,000 variation in cash flow and a $186,000 fluctuation in the NPV.

In other words, the cash flow changes three times faster for every percentage point change in the selling price than is the case for the same percentage point change in the sales volume. There are two reasons why the selling price is much more sensitive than the sales volume in this example.

First, it is assumed that there are no price-sensitive variable costs, such as sales commissions based on the dollar value of sales. Hence, any increase in the price raises the sales revenue but without correspondingly increasing any of the costs except the income tax. Thus, for every $1.00 increase in sales revenue due to price increase, the posttax profit advances by $0.60.

Second, the effective volume-sensitive variable costs as a percentage of sales (under set A) are very high—at 67%. For every increase in dollar revenue brought about by an improvement in the sales volume, $0.67 is deducted as additional variable cost, so that only $0.33 is added to the pretax profit. The ultimate contribution to the posttax profit is only $0.20. This is just one-third of the $0.60 profit contribution for every dollar increase in sales revenue due to price increase.

Sales volume will be as sensitive a factor as selling price under any one of the following situations: first, if there are no variable costs, in which case all the costs except income tax will be constant, and, second, if there are no volume-sensitive costs like raw materials and sales commissions which are based on the number of units sold.

If all the variable costs are volume sensitive but not price sensitive, the higher the variable costs as a percentage of sales, the more sensitive is the price factor relative to the volume factor. Thus, if the total variable costs figure is 80% of sales instead of 67% as in set A, and the fixed costs are smaller so that the total cost percentage is the same (83% of sales), the change in the cash flow due to a change in the selling price will be five times the change in the cash flow due to a change in the sales volume.

The sensitivity of other factors can best be gauged by preparing different sets of financial projections and varying only one assumption at a time.

THREE-SCENARIO ANALYSIS

There seems to be a growing trend to prepare financial projections based on three sets of assumptions which give varying levels of results: optimistic, realistic, and pessimistic. This three-scenario analysis seems to give an appearance of thoroughness and more objectivity and hence is more convincing to the recipients of the evaluation reports.

In reality, a three-scenario analysis is more subjective than one based on a one-set financial projection and generates more questions than it answers. The questions are raised here.

First, which factors should be varied? The varying of different factors give different results. If the selling price is raised by 10%, the NPV goes up to $1,037,000 (set E in Exhibit 7.3); if the sales volume is upped by 10%, the NPV climbs to $666,000 (set C); if the money cost is lowered by 10%, the NPV shoots up to $529,000 (set A-4); if the capital required is slashed by 10%, the NPV inches upward to $526,000 (set A-2). Which of the four figures represents the optimistic estimate?

Second, with the realistic estimates as the starting point, how many factors should be varied in order to arrive at the high and low estimates? If both the sales volume and selling price are dropped by 10%, the cash flow dives to a negative $204,000 (set F). If the assumptions on the other factors in addition to sales volume and price are made more disadvantageous to the firm, the cash flow will be much worse. Thus, this issue alone will lead to the selection of a pessimistic estimate which widely gyrates depending upon the number of assumptions which are changed.

Third, how far from the realistic estimates should the pessimistic and optimistic assumptions be? In Exhibit 7.2, the optimistic sales volume is pegged at 1,100 units, and the pessimistic, at 900. But are these levels reasonable? Should the higher level be 1,200 units instead, or even higher?

SOPHISTICATED SENSITIVITY ANALYSIS

The illustration in Exhibit 7.2 has varied only two factors—sales volume and selling price—while the financing scheme in Exhibit 7.3 has played around with only two additional assumptions—amount of capital and NPV discount rate.

In an actual case, the number of factors which may be considered for possible changes to determine their effect on the cash flow—NPV, IRR, break-even point, crossover rate, and other indicators of return and risk— is practically limitless. The possible number for a small, simple project can easily reach 100, and for a big, complex undertaking, 1,000 or even 10,000.

The mushrooming of the number of pertinent assumptions which could affect a project is illustrated by the sales volume. While the example in Exhibit 7.2 was simplified so that it made only one straight assumption regarding the sales volume (that it is 1,000 for the one-year project life), the assumptions on the same subject for a real project can cover the following areas: date of start of selling operations, sales volume at normalized level, time duration from the start of selling operations until the attainment of the normalized level, and rate of sales buildup. For a project which will handle different products, assumptions on each of these areas may have to be formulated for each major product.

APPLICATIONS

Some applications of sensitivity analysis are given here.

Proposals to shift the performance of certain functions from outside contractors to in-house departments will alter the cost structure of a firm since in-house performance raises the total fixed costs but lowers the variable costs per unit. One of the most sensitive factors in this type of proposal is the business volume. At a low level of volume, it is more advisable to have the job done outside. The application of sensitivity analysis in this regard is demonstrated in Chapter 9.

The automation of manufacturing operations requires substantial initial one-time costs and adds materially to the periodic operating costs. However, these financial commitments are made because of the expectation that selling prices can be raised due to improved quality, and sales volume can be increased due to faster servicing of the orders. Automation projects of this nature should be subjected to sensitivity analysis by varying the assumptions regarding the selling price and sales volume. How to do this is explained in Chapter 13.

Debt financing requires annual debt service which will add to the fixed costs. Hence the structuring of the total financing package into debt and equity should consider the operating cost structure of the firm, that is, the total fixed costs in relation to the total variable costs. Sensitivity analysis should be run to determine the ability of the firm to generate enough operating cash flow to service the debt at different levels of sales volume and amount of debt. This type of analysis is illustrated in Chapter 15.

VI. PROBABILITY ANALYSIS FOR PROJECT RISK

Probability analysis assigns a specific value to the chance that a given assumption used in the financial projections will happen. Probability analysis is both an extension and refinement of sensitivity analysis. The latter is used as one of the inputs of probability analysis.

Of the tools of decision analysis discussed in this book, probability analysis is the one which requires so much judgment in the application, and therefore it should be handled very carefully. The results of probability analysis is subject to several shortcomings, which may be classified into three types: (1) the shortcomings of financial projections as revealed in Chapters 2 and 3, (2) the limitations of three-scenario sensitivity analysis as discussed earlier, and (3) the weaknesses which are peculiar to probability analysis, which will be covered shortly. All the techniques of financial analysis are subject to the limitations of the financial projections since the techniques utilize the financial projections as their takeoff point.

CONCEPTS (Exhibit 7.4)

Probability Distribution Table.   Probability analysis starts with the results of sensitivity analysis. For instance, sensitivity analysis may give the following estimates on the operating cash flow of a project which has a one-year life (Exhibit 7.2, part II, last line):

	Amount
Pessimistic estimate (set B)	$ 800,000
Realistic estimate (set A)	1,000,000
Optimistic estimate (set C)	1,200,000

Probability analysis gives probability values to each of the three amounts. Assume that the managers and analysts who made the assumptions in the financial projections believe that the pessimistic estimate has a 20% chance of happening, the realistic estimate, 60%, and the optimistic estimate, 20%. These probabilities are placed alongside the corresponding amounts in order to constitute the probability distribution table in the first three columns of Exhibit 7.4 for project A.

Mean.   The probability distribution table serves as the basis of calculating the weighted value of the three amounts ($800,000, $1,000,000, and $1,200,000). The mean, which was calculated as $1,000,000 in Exhibit 7.4, represents the weighted average or central value of the three amounts. It serves as the standard by which the individual amounts are evaluated.

Total Deviation or Variance.   This gives the contribution of each sector (as sectors 1 to 3) to the total risk as measured by the variability of the results. Sector 2 has no variability and hence no contribution to the risk since its amount ($1,000,000) is equivalent to the mean. Since the amounts of sectors 1 and 3 vary from the mean, they have contributions. Their contributions are the same ($8,000,000 each) because their probability of happening, at .2 each, are equal and because the variance of their amounts from the mean are also the same ($200,000).

Standard Deviation.   Standard deviation represents the degree of the variability of the individual amounts from the mean. Given the same mean, a bigger standard deviation means that there is a greater chance that (1) the actual results will *vary* from the mean and (2) the *value* of the variance will be material.

Mathematically, the standard deviation is the square root of the total deviation. The total deviation is estimated in Exhibit 7.4. Thus, 126.49 is the square root of 16,000.

Coefficient of Deviation.   It is difficult to gauge the variability of the individual amounts from the mean based on the standard deviation alone, since the means of different projects could be different. Take project A with a mean of $1,000,000 and a standard deviation of $126,490. Compare it with project X (not in Exhibit 7.4), with a mean of $10,000,000 and standard deviation of $500,000.

Although X has a greater standard deviation, it has a much bigger base or mean. Thus, a better gauge of the variation from the mean is not the standard deviation by itself but the coefficient of deviation. The coefficient is calculated by dividing the standard deviation by the mean. The coefficient of project A is .126, while that of X is .050. Project X is therefore more stable since it has a lower coefficient.

Semivariance. The basic limitation of the total deviation or variance ($16,000,000 for project A in Exhibit 7.4) is that the total variance gives equal weights to the deviations of sector 1 and of sector 3 from the mean ($8,000,000 each), although sector 3 does not represent a risk because the amount ($1,200,000) is better than the mean of $1,000,000.

If risk is defined, not as the possible variability of the results from the mean, but the possible *downward* variability, then the variance should include only those sectors where the amounts are less than the mean. Hence the deviation or variance should be only $8,000,000 (the one pertaining to sector 1) and not $16,000,000. The $8,000,000 is the semivariance.

CONCEPTUAL LIMITATION (Exhibit 7.4)

As may be deduced from the formula in Exhibit 7.4 the standard deviation is the product of two determinants: (1) the *probability* of each value and (2) the difference between each *amount* and the mean, as squared.

Since the value in item 2 is squared, the standard deviation gives much more significance to the amount than to the probability. Herein lies the basic conceptual flaw of standard deviation.

The lopsided importance given to the variations between the amounts and the mean is dramatized by projects B and C in Exhibit 7.4. The probability of sectors 1 and 3 of project C is four times that of B. On the other hand, the gap between the amounts of sectors 1 and 3 from the mean of B is four times those of C. Since the difference between the amounts and the mean is squared, while the probability is not, the standard deviation of B is twice that of C.

APPLICATION LIMITATIONS (Exhibit 7.4)

Probability analysis has four major weaknesses in application: (1) multiple coefficients of deviation for the same project, (2) subjectivity in assigning probabilities, (3) subjectivity in deciding on the number of sectors, and (4) lack of objective formula for measuring the risk.

Multiple Coefficients of Deviations.   In decision analysis, the amounts of sectors 1 to 3 in Exhibit 7.4 may correspond to either one of the following: operating cash flow, IRR, NPV, break-even point sales volume, break-even point selling price, crossover point, sales revenues, sales volume, or a similar value. One project normally does not have one and the same coefficient of deviation for all of these, but different coefficients for each. Thus, while the coefficient of deviation based on the operating cash flow as calculated in Exhibit 7.4 is .126, that based on the IRR is .127, and that based on the NPV is almost double at .244. The resulting multiple coefficients of deviation for one project can cause confusion in determining the degree of its own riskiness or its riskiness in relation to alternatives.

Other Limitations.   The application of probability analysis requires very subjective judgment. For project A in Exhibit 7.4, the following probabilities were assigned: .2, .6, and .2. In practice, these probabilities are as easy or as difficult to support as the following and yet produce different coefficients of deviation: .25, .5, and .25.

In Exhibit 7.4, the entire spectrum of probabilities was divided into only three sectors. The use of three sectors is just as subjective as the use of, say, five, yet they produce different results.

The coefficient of deviation gives an indication of the relative variability of the results. Everyone is agreed that the higher the coefficient, the higher is the variability. However, how to convert a given coefficient into a risk premium percentage has not yet been generally agreed upon.

RISK-ADJUSTED PRESENT VALUE OF CASH FLOW
(Exhibits 7.5 and 7.6)

Risk-free Cash Flow (Exhibit 7.6).   Assume that the project with one-year life described in Exhibits 7.2 and 7.3 is certain to attain the operating assumptions mentioned under set A. Since the operating cash flow will not vary from the projected $1,000,000, the project does not entail a risk. If the cost of money (without incorporating risk) is 8% a year, the present value of the $1,000,000 is $926,000. The latter amount is shown as the "final value of the cash flow" in the first column of Exhibit 7.6.

Risk-adjusted Cash Flow.   The $926,000 may be used in the analysis work if no risk is involved. In many cases, however, it may be advisable to include risk in the analysis.

The risk of a project may cover just its operating cash flow or its total return which is composed of the operating cash flow and the recovery of the original investment. There are four ways of incorporating risk in the present value of the operating cash flow or in the net present value of the investment:

Method I: Risk-free cash flow method or adjusted discount rate method or risk-adjusted discount rate method (*without* probability distribution)

Method II: Risk-free cash flow method or adjusted discount rate method or risk-adjusted discount rate method (*with* probability distribution)

Method III: Risk-adjusted cash flow method (or certainty equivalent method)

Method IV: Risk-free present value of cash flow method

The illustrations in Exhibits 7.5 and 7.6 for methods I to IV assume that the risk covers just the operations. The example used is based on the information for sets A, B, and C in Exhibits 7.2 and 7.3 and project A in Exhibit 7.4.

Method I. Risk-free Cash Flow Method (or Risk-adjusted Discount Rate Method)—Without Probability Distribution. This and the other methods derived its name from the label of the intermediate values indicated in Exhibit 7.5 (second to the last column).

This method uses only one set of cash flow projections, which is set A in Exhibits 7.2 and 7.3—the same as the one utilized as the basis in determining the risk-free cash flow or present value without risk as discussed in the first paragraph of this section. However, instead of using the risk-free discount rate, which is 8% in the illustration in the first column of Exhibit 7.6, a 2% risk premium was added. Thus a 10% risk-adjusted discount rate was applied here. The final present value of the operating cash flow as shown in both Exhibits 7.5 and 7.6 is $909,000.

Method II. Risk-free Cash Flow Method (or Risk-adjusted Discount Rate Method)—With Probability Distribution. The following are the differences between this method and method I. First, method II uses several sets of cash flow and probability distribution. Second, method II utilizes the mean cash flow ($1,000 in the illustration) instead of the projected cash flow in I. Third, the 2% risk premium was based partly on the coefficient of deviation.

The resulting risk-adjusted present value of cash flow under II is the same as that under I for the following reasons: first, the mean cash flow is the same as the projected cash flow; second, the risk premium and the risk-free rates for I and for II are the same.

Method III. Risk-adjusted Cash Flow Method (or Certainty Equivalent). If the value of a cash flow which is subject to possible variation in the future is, say, $1,000,000, its equivalent in cash flow which is certain to be realized is less than this amount. If the cash flow is expected to be realized one year hence, and the perceived risk premium rate is 2%, then the equivalent of the $1,000,000 uncertain cash flow is $980,000 in cash flow with certainty. In other words, $980,000 is the certainty equivalent of $1,000,000 in this case.

Method III is different from method II in that III seeks, as the inter-mediate value, the risk-adjusted cash flow or certainty equivalent. This certainty equivalent is then time discounted at the 8% risk-free discount rate to arrive at the $908,000 risk-adjusted present value of cash flow. This value is slightly lower than the $909,000 corresponding value under II because discounting a figure by 2% and then by 8% produces a lower amount than by discounting the same figure by 10%.

Method IV. Risk-free Present Value of Cash Flow Method.   Methods I to III use as the intermediate value, a cash flow which is not yet discounted for the time value of money. Method IV presents as the intermediate value, the time-discounted cash flow, which is the present value of the cash flow. Method IV is different from method III in the sequence of the use of the discount rates: III discounts the value first by using the risk premium and then by applying the risk-free rate; IV uses the reverse sequence.

The ultimate risk-adjusted present value of cash flow under III and under IV (final value) are the same since the two methods use the same discount rates.

VII. DECISION TREE ANALYSIS

Like sensitivity and probability analysis, decision tree analysis uses vary-ing assumptions on key areas. Like probability analysis, decision tree assigns probability factors.

Decision trees are utilized where decisions are to be made in several stages, and where the subsequent decisions will be influenced both by the prior decisions and the extraneous events which occur after the first deci-sion and which are normally beyond the control of management.

DECISION TREE (Exhibit 7.7)

Exhibit 7.7 illustrates a decision tree. The root of the tree is an opportunity to manufacture and market a new product in two separate markets—the north and the south.

First-stage Decision.   The tree is used to evaluate the alternatives to be considered in the first-stage decision. Assume that there are two serious alternatives:

1. Acquire two plants as of the end of year 0—Plant N to be located in the north to serve the north and Plant S in the south.
2. Acquire one plant as of the same time—Plant N to be located in the north and to serve both markets.

The plants are of one size only. If both markets prove to be strong during year 1, the sales and hence the operating cash flow under alternative 2 will be lower than that under alternative 1 as the sales will be restricted by the limited capacity of only one plant.

Probable Extraneous Events. Assume that there are four probabilities regarding the market performance in year 1. These are named chances A to D in Exhibits 7.7 and 7.8. The operations will be continued in year 2 and subsequent years in the markets which prove to be strong in year 1. The operations will be discontinued in the weak markets.

Second-stage Decisions. If the first decision is to acquire Plants N and S (alternative 1), and if both markets prove to be strong in year 1 (chance A), no second-stage decision is required as of the end of year 1 since the two plants will just be enough to serve the two markets.

Similarly, if the first decision is to have only one plant, Plant N (alternative 2), and if the north proves to be strong and the south proves to be weak in year 1 (chance B), then a second-stage decision is not necessary since the only plant—Plant N—is in the right location.

However, in all other cases, a decision has to be made. The possible decisions are given in Exhibits 7.7 and 7.8.

The expenditures for an additional plant, and the cash proceeds from any disposal of the plants to be acquired at the end of year 0, are assumed to take effect as of the end of year 1.

CASH FLOW (Exhibit 7.8)

The cash flow analysis given in Exhibit 7.8 is for the plants to be acquired in years 0 and 1. To simplify the illustration, it is assumed that the plants have only a three-year life. Hence, under alternative 1, there is no operating cash flow in year 4. Under alternative 2, there is a cash flow in year 4 only if a new Plant S is acquired in year 1.

Alternative 1—Chance A. The cost of acquiring a plant is $8 million. Thus, under alternative 1, the cost to be incurred in year 0 is $16 million.

If two plants are acquired in year 0 (alternative 1), and if the two markets prove to be strong (chance A), the year 1 operating cash flow is $13 million. As of year 0, the present value of this cash flow is $11.8 million at 10% discount rate.

The annual operating cash flow for years 2 and 3 are expected to be maintained at $13 million. As of year 0, the present value of these is $20.5 million.

As of year 0, the net present value of the following cash flows is $16.3 million: (1) year 0 plant costs of $16 million, (2) year 1 operating cash flow of $13 million, and (3) years 2 and 3 operating cash flows of $13 million each.

Since there is only a 25% probability that this $16.3 million is realized (chance A), the weighted average of this $16.3 million is only $4.1 million.

Alternative 1—Chance B.   Under chance B, the better second-stage decision is to sell Plant S as this will give a higher net present value of $12.5 million, which is more than the value under the other decision. Hence, this is the only decision considered for chance B.

Alternatives 1 and 2.   The mean or combined weighted average of the net present value of all the four chances under alternative 1 is $2.4 million. This compares with the $7.1 million for alternative 2. Hence 2 is considered as the more desirable.

DECISION TREE ANALYSIS FOR RETURN AND FOR RISK

When the decision tree analysis is used to estimate the net present value, it is employed as a return on investment technique.

The decision tree may also be applied to calculate the risk—in two ways.

Safety Margin.   The safety margin may be determined as follows:

	Alternative 1	*Alternative 2*
Net present value	$ 2,400,000	$ 7,100,000
Initial investment	16,000,000	8,000,000
Present value of total returns	$18,400,000	$15,100,000
Safety margin	13%	47%

The safety margin was calculated by dividing the net present value by the present value of the total return. The 13% margin for alternative 1 means that the present value of the total returns can suffer a 13% reduction before the full recovery of the $16 million original investment may be jeopardized. Since alternative 2 has a higher margin, 2 is exposed to less risk.

Coefficient of Deviation.   The net present value for each of chances A, B, C, and D of alternatives 1 and 2 (see the second to the last column of Exhibit 7.8) may be used as the amount in the probability distribution table in order to calculate the coefficient of deviation of each of the two alternatives. See Exhibit 7.4 for a sample of the probability distribution table. The resulting coefficient of alternative 1 is 4.0 and of 2, 1.1.

This means that 2 is less risky since it has less coefficient.

Return and Risk.   Based on the foregoing analysis, 2 is more desirable than 1 since 2 has more return and less risk. It has more than twice the net present value of 1, more than three times the safety margin of 1, and about one-fourth the coefficient of deviation of 1.

SOPHISTICATED DECISION TREE ANALYSIS

Exhibits 7.7 and 7.8 present an analysis of a simplified case requiring decisions in two stages. An actual situation may call for decisions in three or more stages. For instance, in addition to the decisions on new plant acquisitions, the case may call for decisions on subsequent plant expansions, plant automations, and plant replacements.

The case as presented has limited the decisions to those on acquiring, relocating, and disposing of the plants. A model may be constructed to consider other decisions over a long period of time, starting with the initial research efforts, followed by the development of prototypes, market testing, contracting out the manufacturing, setting up the company's own plants, construction of regional warehouses between the plants and the markets, and subsequent expansions and replacements of the plants and warehouses.

The cash flow in Exhibit 7.8 covers only three operating years and has disregarded inflation. A more realistic model should span at least 10 operating years and should incorporate inflation.

VIII. CROSSOVER POINT ANALYSIS FOR PROJECT RISK

The objective of crossover point (cop) analysis is to determine the level of sales volume, interest rate, or similar variable factor, at which the advantage of one proposal over a competing alternative is converted into its disadvantage.

Among the tools of decision analysis, the COP is the simplest and the one applicable to the widest range of subjects—not only in financial analysis but even in engineering, marketing, and other disciplines.

This book cites several illustrations in different areas of financial analysis—fixed costs/variable costs analysis, initial costs/periodic costs appraisal, loan interest/loan amount evaluation, and IRR-NPV comparison. The diversity of these illustrations should enable the reader to determine where and how he or she can apply COP analysis in his or her own work.

FIXED COSTS/VARIABLE COSTS ANALYSIS IN RELATION TO BUSINESS VOLUME (Exhibit 7.9)

The COP may be applied to a proposal which will alter the fixed costs and variable costs. Variable costs are those which change with the sales or production volume while fixed costs are those which normally do not change. Variable and fixed costs are discussed in detail in the next chapter, Break-even Point Analysis.

There are two types of proposals as far as their effects on the cost structure are concerned: (1) one which will result in higher fixed costs but lower variable costs per unit and (2) the other which will produce the opposite effects. These two types of proposals are discussed now.

Increase in Fixed Costs. At low volumes of operations, the proposal which will increase the fixed costs but lower the variable costs per unit turns out to be less profitable. However, at a certain point as the volume goes up, the total costs of one option equal the total costs of the other. This is the COP. Beyond this point, the proposal which will increase the fixed costs comes out cheaper.

An illustration of this type of proposal is the in-house performance of a function which is currently contracted out—as the sales operations. Assume that at present the sales are handled by independent dealers, with the following costs: monthly fixed costs of $100,000 and variable costs of $4,000 per unit of sales. If the company operates its own sales organization, the costs will be monthly fixed costs of $1,000,000 and variable costs of $1,000 per unit. Current monthly sales hover between 200 and 300 units, but there is a strong possibility that the sales will hit 600 units in one year. The questions are (1) is it worthwhile for the firm to approve the proposal and (2) what is the sales volume which will justify the proposed measure.

The COP sales volume (COPSV) in units may be calculated as

	At present (contracted out)	Proposal (in-house)	Difference
Total monthly fixed costs	$100,000	$1,000,000	$900,000
Variable costs per unit	$ 4,000	$ 1,000	$ 3,000
COPSV			300 units

The COPSV was obtained by dividing the differential fixed costs by the differential variable costs per unit.

At the possible maximum sales of 600 units, the net benefit of the proposal will be $900,000:

	At present	Proposal	Difference
Total monthly fixed costs	$ 100,000	$1,000,000	$ 900,000
Total variable costs	2,400,000	600,000	1,800,000
Total	$2,500,000	$1,600,000	$ 900,000

The COPSV is graphically shown in Exhibit 7.9, chart I. It shows that the proposal will result in a net loss until the sales volume hits 300 units. Beyond that, the proposal becomes attractive.

Decrease in Fixed Costs. The reverse of the situation just illustrated is one wherein a company plans to contract out a function which is currently being done by a department within the company. Assume, for instance, that the expenses of the collection department and the possible costs of having the collection function performed by an outside agency are

	At present (in-house)	*Proposal (contracted out)*	*Difference*
Total monthly fixed costs	$600,000	$0	$600,000
Variable costs as a			
percentage of sales	2%	4%	2%
COP collection volume			$30,000,000

The COP collection volume in dollars was calculated at $30,000,000 by dividing the fixed cost differential by 2%.

The COPSV is graphically shown in Exhibit 7.9, chart II. It shows that the proposal will be worth pursuing only if the collection volume drops below $30,000,000. Otherwise, the proposed contracting to the outside collection agency becomes unattractive.

Contrast—Profit Area. Charts I and II are very similar in that each chart relates two lines—each line representing the total costs of an alternative. Furthermore, the COP is the point where one line crosses the other.

However, there is one big difference between the two charts—the location of the profit area of the proposal. In chart I, the profit area is to the right of the COP, which is the same as the location of the profit area in a BEP chart (see Exhibits 8.2 and 8.4). In chart II, the profit area is to the left of the COP. The reason for the difference is that in chart I, the proposal increases the total fixed costs but reduces the variable cost per unit. Hence the proposal becomes profitable only after the COP is achieved. On the other hand, in chart II, the proposal takes out the overhead but raises the variable cost per collection volume. Hence it is viable only if the volume is lower than the COP.

INITIAL COSTS/PERIODIC COSTS ANALYSIS
IN RELATION TO INTEREST RATE (Exhibit 7.10)

The COP may be applied to a situation where two or more proposals differ in their initial or acquisition costs, and in their annual or operating costs. It is possible that, at very low interest rates, the present value of the total costs of a proposal with less initial costs but heavier periodic costs is more than that of a competing measure. However, at a certain point, as the interest rates go up, the total costs of the option with fewer initial costs equals that of the other. At money costs higher than this COP, the alternative with fewer initial costs becomes more attractive.

Consider that a firm has two alternatives on how to acquire equipment: buy for cash at the start of year 1 or end of year 0 or lease with the

188

Chapter 7

annual payments being at the end of each year. Assume that the equipment has a life of four years. The comparative schedules of payments are

	Year	Buy	Lease
Acquisition cost	0	$475,500	
First-year rent	1		$150,000
Second-year rent	2		150,000
Third-year rent	3		150,000
Fourth-year rent	4		150,000

If the cost of money to the firm is 9%, the present value of the four rental payments as of the end of year 0 is $486,000. In this case, it is advisable to buy as this will cost the firm only $475,500. However the lease alternative is benefited by an increase in interest rate. A high money cost environment is advantageous to an option with delayed payments since the firm can, in the meantime, earn more interest on the money which will subsequently be used to make the payments.

At 10%, the present value of the payments under the lease plan equals the cash buying price of $475,500. At a money cost of 11%, the present value of the cost of the lease plan dips to $465,400, thus making it the cheaper alternative. Exhibit 7.10, chart III, presents the relative costs of the two options in relation to the cost of money.

This analysis disregarded the effects of income tax and inflation. A more detailed appraisal is illustrated in Chapter 12.

INTEREST RATES ANALYSIS IN RELATION TO AMOUNT OF LOAN (Exhibit 7.10)

The COP may be used in deciding on the financing source to be tapped. Assume that a firm is planning to obtain a secured loan from either Bank A or Bank B. Bank A is offering a $12,000,000 loan at 9%. Bank B is giving a lower rate of 8%. However, the possible amount from Bank B is less than $12,000,000. If the loan is obtained from Bank B, the company can get the balance of its $12,000,000 cash requirement from another source at 11%. The question is: What should be the amount of Bank B loan so that the blended rates of this loan and of another financing equals the 9% of Bank A?

If the firm gets only $6,000,000 from Bank B, its blended rate will be 9.5%—which is the average of 8% on the $6,000,000 Bank B loan and 11% on the balance.

If the firm obtains the entire $12,000,000 from Bank B, its cost will be only 8%. If the Bank B loan is $8,000,000, the blended rate will be 9%—the same as the interest on the Bank A loan. The COP can be better appreciated by looking at Exhibit 7.10, chart IV.

NPV-IRR ANALYSIS IN RELATION TO DISCOUNT RATE

The COP is usually used in determining the discount rate at which two projects with different IRRs and initial NPVs will have identical NPVs. This situation arises when the project with more returns concentrated during the earlier years of the project has the higher IRR but lower initial NPV. This is illustrated in Chapter 6, Exhibit 6.4, where project H, with the higher IRR at 16%, has the lower initial NPV at $5,455,000 based on a discount rate of 10%. If the discount rate is raised to 12%, the NPV of both projects will become $3,539,000. In this case, 12% is the COP discount rate.

COMPARISON WITH BREAK-EVEN POINT ANALYSIS

COP has several similarities with, and differences from, the break-even point, which is examined in the next chapter. Both are used to determine the level of a variable factor as sales volume or interest rate, at which the total costs equal the total revenues (in the case of BEP) or at which the total costs or benefits of one option equal those of an alternative (COP).

The BEP, in its traditional concept, involves an analysis of the behavior of revenues, variable costs, and fixed costs, while the COP, in one of its applications, covers the evaluation of the behavior of variable costs and fixed costs (revenues are not covered). This BEP-COP relationship is similar to that of the net present value/present value of cost link: the net present value is used on projects which generate revenues, while the present value of cost is applied on undertakings which do not directly earn revenues.

There are many situations where the BEP, but not the COP, may be used, and vice versa. The BEP cannot be used in relating IRR to NPV, but the COP can, as illustrated earlier. On the other hand, BEP is suited for an analysis where there is an interplay of revenues, fixed costs, and variable costs, while the COP normally does not fit into this type of application.

Notwithstanding their differences in many applications, there are cases where both the BEP and COP may be used to appraise the same set of alternatives. For instance, a firm deciding to contract out its collection function to an outside agency instead of performing it in-house may use the COP to analyze the comparative fixed costs and variable costs under present company practice and under the proposal, and then to determine the level of business volume which will justify the proposal. The COP is used since the collection function by itself does not generate revenues. (The use of COP in this area was illustrated earlier.) Simultaneously, the BEP may also be used in this particular case to appraise the overall company picture which covers not only the fixed costs and variable costs included in the COP analysis but also the other costs of the company, as well as its revenues. In this case, the BEP is calculated under two alternatives: one under the present practice and another assuming the proposal is implemented.

190

Chapter 7

EXHIBIT 7.1:

Types of Risk and Selected Risk Analysis Techniques

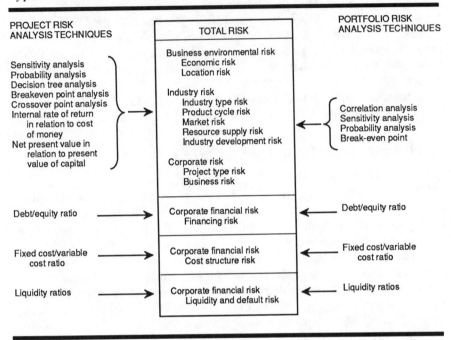

EXHIBIT 7.2:
Cash Flow Under Varying Assumptions

| | | VARY ONE ASSUMPTION AT A TIME | | | |
| | BASE | VARY THE VOLUME | | VARY THE PRICE | |
	Set A	Set B	Set C	Set D	Set E
I. Given Data					
Sales volume	1,000	900	1,100	1,000	1,000
Selling price per unit	$10,000	$10,000	$10,000	$9,000	$11,000
Variable costs per unit	6,666	6,666	6,666	6,666	6,666
II. Income statement/cash flow (in $1,000)					
Sales	$10,000	$9,000	$11,000	$9,000	$11,000
Variable costs	6,666	5,999	7,333	6,666	6,666
Contribution margin	3,334	3,001	3,667	2,334	4,334
Fixed costs	1,668	1,668	1,668	1,668	1,668
Profit before tax	1,666	1,333	1,999	666	2,666
Tax at 40%	666	533	800	266	1,066
Operating cash flow	1,000	800	1,200	400	1,600

III. Other assumptions

All the financing is to be supplied by equity capital; hence there is no interest expense in the income statement.

All the equity is to be used in operations as working cash balance only; no balance will earn interest.

There will be no investments in property, plant, and equipment; hence there will be no depreciation.

All transactions will be for cash; hence there will be no receivables, payables, and inventories.

All volume-sensitive variable costs per unit and total fixed costs as given are at a constant rate irrespective of the sales volume or selling price. There are no price-sensitive variable costs.

There are no sales expansion and other types of costs.

EXHIBIT 7.3:
Cash Flow and Return Under Varying Assumptions

Set	Sales volume (in tons)	Selling price per unit	Operating cash flow ($1,000)	IRR	Total return ($1,000)	Present value ($1,000)	NPV ($1,000)
Varying operating assumptions							
Based on investment of $6,000,000 at 8% money cost							
Base set							
Set A	1,000	$10,000	$1,000	16.7%	$7,000	$6,481	$ 481
Sales volume is varied							
Set B	900	$10,000	$ 800	13.3%	$6,800	$6,296	$ 296
C	1,100	$10,000	$1,200	20.0%	$7,200	$6,666	$ 666
Selling price is varied							
Set D	1,000	$ 9,000	$ 400	6.7%	$6,400	$5,926	($ 74)
E	1,000	$11,000	$1,600	26.7%	$7,600	$7,037	$1,037
Both sales volume and selling price are varied							
Set F	900	$ 9,000	$ 260	4.3%	$6,260	$5,796	($ 204)
G	900	$11,000	$1,340	22.3%	$7,340	$6,796	$ 796
H	1,100	$ 9,000	$ 540	9.0%	$6,540	$6,056	$ 56
I	1,100	$11,000	$1,860	31.0%	$7,860	$7,278	$1,278
Varying investment assumptions							
Based on investment of $6,600,000 at 8% money cost							
Set A-1	1,000	$10,000	$1,000	15.1%	$7,600	$7,037	$ 437
Based on investment of $5,400,000 at 8% money cost							
Set A-2	1,000	$10,000	$1,000	18.5%	$6,400	$5,926	$ 526
Based on investment of $6,000,000 at 8.8% money cost							
Set A-3	1,000	$10,000	$1,000	16.7%	$7,000	$6,433	$ 433
Based on investment of $6,000,000 at 7.2% money cost							
Set A-4	1,000	$10,000	$1,000	16.7%	$7,000	$6,529	$ 529

EXHIBIT 7.4:
Coefficient of Deviation Based on Operating Cash Flow

	PROBABILITY DISTRIBUTION TABLE			CALCULATION OF STANDARD DEVIATION					
Sector	Probability	Amount	Mean	Probability	Amount	Mean	Total deviation	Standard deviation	Coefficient of deviation
Project A									
Sector 1	.20	800	160 = .20	.20	(800	$-$ 1,000)^2	= 8,000		
2	.60	1,000	600 = .60	.60	(1,000	$-$ 1,000)^2	= 0		
3	.20	1,200	240 = .20	.20	(1,200	$-$ 1,000)^2	= 8,000		
			1,000				16,000	126.49	.126
Project B									
Sector 1	.10	600	60 = .10	.10	(600	$-$ 1,000)^2	= 16,000		
2	.80	1,000	800 = .80	.80	(1,000	$-$ 1,000)^2	= 0		
3	.10	1,400	140 = .10	.10	(1,400	$-$ 1,000)^2	= 16,000		
			1,000				32,000	178.89	.179
Project C									
Sector 1	.40	900	360 = .40	.40	(900	$-$ 1,000)^2	= 4,000		
2	.20	1,000	200 = .20	.20	(1,000	$-$ 1,000)^2	= 0		
3	.40	1,100	440 = .40	.40	(1,100	$-$ 1,000)^2	= 4,000		
			1,000				8,000	89.44	.089

EXHIBIT 7.5:

Risk-Adjusted Present Value of Operating Cash Flow—Chart
(dollars in $1,000; cash flow = net operating cash flow)

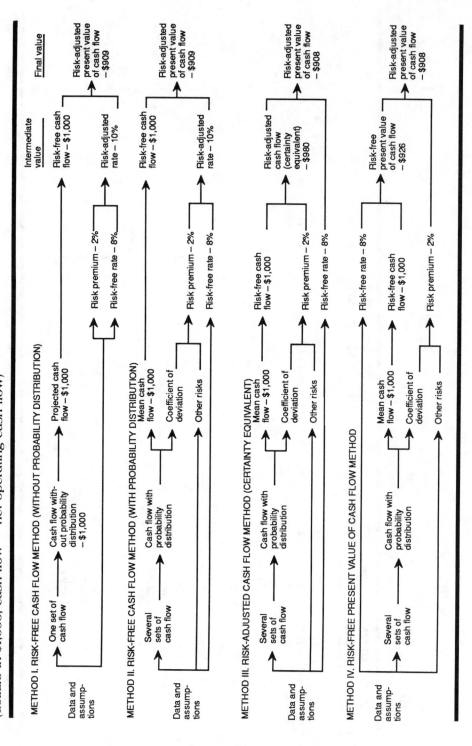

EXHIBIT 7.6:

Risk-Adjusted Present Value of Operating Cash Flow
(dollars in $1,000; cash flow = new operating cash flow)

		WITH RISK		
	Risk-free	*Method I* *Method II*	*Method III*	*Method IV*
Discount rate				
Risk free rate	8%	8%	8%	8%
Risk premium	0%	2%	2%	2%
Risk-adjusted rate	8%	10%	10%	10%
Present value of 1 factor (1 divided by discount rate)				
Risk free rate	0.926	0.926	0.926	0.926
Risk premium	0.000	0.980	0.980	0.980
Risk-adjusted rate	0.926	0.909	0.909	0.909
Operating cash flow	$1,000	$1,000	$1,000	$1,000
First discount rate				
Risk-free rate				.926
Risk premium			.980	
Intermediate value of cash flow*	$1,000	$1,000	$ 980	$ 926
Second discount rate				
Risk-free rate	.926		.926	
Risk premium				.980
Risk-adjusted rate		.909		
Final value of cash flow[†] (after second adjustment)	$ 926	$ 909	$ 908	$ 908

*Corresponds to the second to the last column of Exhibit 7.5.
[†]Corresponds to the last column of Exhibit 7.5.

EXHIBIT 7.7:
Decision Tree—Chart

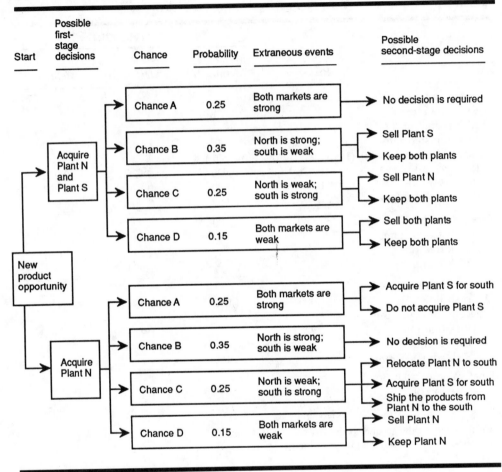

EXHIBIT 7.8:
Decision Tree—Present Value of Operating Cash Flow

| | | FIRST-STAGE DECISION AND OUTCOME | | | POSSIBLE SECOND-STAGE DECISIONS AND OUTCOME | | | | | | FIRST AND SECOND DECISIONS | |
| | | Plant cost year 0 | OPERATING CASH FLOW | | | Plant cost year 1 | OPERATING CASH FLOW | | | Net present value year 0 | Net present value year 0 | Mean |
Chance	Probability		Cash flow year 1	Present value year 0	Decision		Year 2	Year 3	Year 4			
Alternative 1. First decision: Acquire plants N and S												
A	.25	($16.0)	$13.0	$11.8	Decision not required	$0.0	$13.0	$13.0	$0.0	$20.5	$16.3	$4.1
B	.35	($16.0)	$6.0	$5.5	Sell Plant S	$1.6	$7.0	$7.0	$0.0	$12.5	$2.0	$0.7
					Keep both plants	$0.0	$7.0	$7.0	$0.0	$11.0		
C	.25	($16.0)	$5.0	$4.5	Sell Plant N	$1.6	$6.0	$6.0	$0.0	$10.9	($0.5)	($0.1)
					Keep both plants	$0.0	$6.0	$6.0	$0.0	$9.5		
D	.15	($16.0)	($2.0)	($1.8)	Sell both plants	$3.2	$0.0	$0.0	$0.0	$2.9	($14.9)	($2.2)
					Keep both plants	$0.0	$0.0	$0.0	$0.0	$0.0		
										Total for Alternative 1		$2.4
Alternative 2. First decision: Acquire plant N only												
A	.25	($8.0)	$7.9	$7.2	Acquire Plant S for south	($8.0)	$13.0	$13.0	$6.0	$17.3	$16.5	$4.1
					Do not acquire Plant S	$0.0	$7.0	$7.0	$0.0	$11.0		
B	.35	($8.0)	$3.7	$3.4	Decision not required	$0.0	$7.0	$7.0	$0.0	$11.0		
C	.25	($8.0)	$2.0	$1.8	Relocate Plant N to south	($3.0)	$6.0	$6.0	$0.0	$6.7	$6.4	$2.2
					Acquire Plant S for south	($8.0)	$6.0	$6.0	$6.0	$6.3		
					Ship the products from Plant N to south	$0.0	$5.0	$5.0	$0.0	$7.9		
D	.15	($8.0)	($2.2)	($2.0)	Sell Plant N	$2.0	$0.0	$0.0	$0.0	$1.8	$7.9	2.0
					Keep Plant N	$0.0	$0.0	$0.0	$0.0	$0.0	($8.2)	($1.2)
										Total for Alternative 2		$7.1

EXHIBIT 7.9:
Crossover Point
Fixed Costs-Variable Costs Analysis

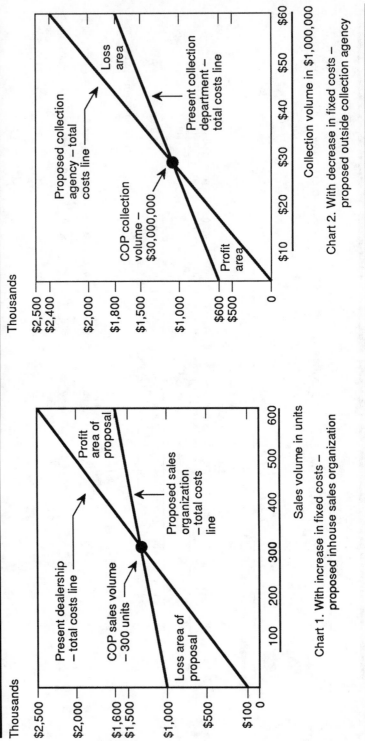

Thousands

Chart 1. With increase in fixed costs –
proposed inhouse sales organization

Chart 2. With decrease in fixed costs –
proposed outside collection agency

EXHIBIT 7.10:
Crossover Point
Other Applications

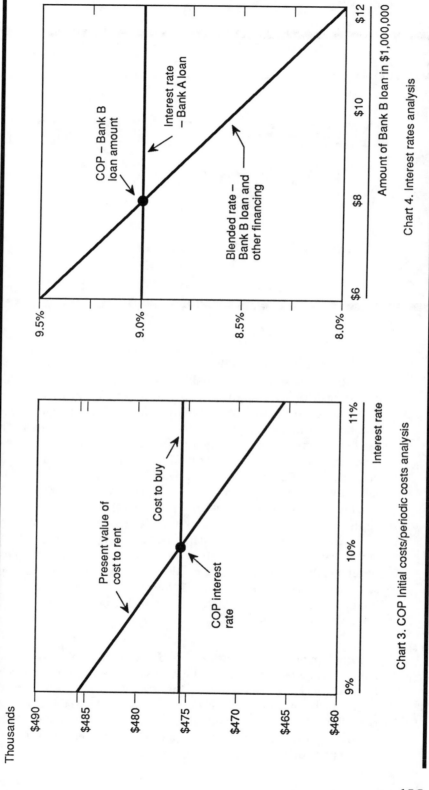

Thousands

Chart 4. Interest rates analysis

9.5%

9.0%

8.5%

8.0%

$6 $8 $10 $12

Amount of Bank B loan in $1,000,000

COP – Bank B
loan amount

Interest rate
– Bank A loan

Blended rate –
Bank B loan and
other financing

$490

$485

$480

$475

$470

$465

$460

9%   10%   11%

Interest rate

Chart 3. COP Initial costs/periodic costs analysis

Present value of
cost to rent

Cost to buy

COP interest
rate

199

Chapter 8 ─────────────────

BREAK-EVEN POINT ANALYSIS

The break-even point (BEP) of a firm represents the level of its sales volume, selling price, unit variable cost, or total fixed cost at which its net loss or cash deficit is transformed into a net gain or cash generation.

The flexible nature of BEP analysis makes it suitable for use in making investment, financing, production, and marketing decisions. The BEP is used to appraise proposed measures or study the future performance of a product, a company, or any of its units. If utilized to evaluate short-term measures, the BEP analysis is applied usually on a monthly basis until the sales volume, selling price, or unit variable cost will have stabilized. If employed to appraise long-term projects, the BEP is calculated on an annual basis until the operations will have normalized.

The BEP becomes particularly useful if compared with related figures. For instance, a project with a profit break-even point sales volume (PBEPSV) that is much lower than the projected sales volume is considered safe. A firm with a PBEPSV that is lower than the other companies in the industry is in a very competitive position. A measure that will lower the PBEPSV of a firm is usually considered viable.

Application in Risk Analysis.   The BEP can be used as an effective tool in helping management identify the levels of risks of alternative measures in three ways. First, it determines the level of sales volume or unit selling price which it has to attain, or the amount of unit variable cost or total fixed cost which it must not exceed, in order that it may not incur a loss. Second, it indicates the percentage drop from the forecasted sales volume or unit selling price or percentage rise from the budgeted unit variable cost or total fixed cost, before the firm loses. Third, it warns management if the total fixed cost as a percentage of total cost goes beyond a reasonable level.

Application in Profit Planning.   The BEP can also be utilized as a technique in profit planning in three ways. First, it indicates the level of profitability or cash flow at varying amounts of sales volume, unit selling price, unit variable cost, or total fixed cost. Second, it reveals the incremental profit or cash flow which may be generated by every unit change in sales volume or dollar difference in unit selling price, unit variable cost, or total fixed cost. Third, it gives the degree of change in profit or cash flow for given amounts of sales volume or unit selling price for every possible proportion of total variable costs to total fixed costs.

Limitations.   But while BEP analysis has almost unlimited application potentials, its traditional usage is also burdened with application limitations. The weaknesses of BEP as currently applied may be classified into two groups: (1) the shortcomings arising from the adoption of the accounting concept of profit and (2) the weaknesses arising from the recognition of only two types of costs: the variable and fixed costs.

The adoption of the accounting concept of profit has resulted in the inclusion of irrelevant costs compounded by the exclusion of relevant ones. The accounting concept includes depreciation and other sunk costs but excludes imputed interest.

Since BEP recognizes only two types of costs, sales expansion costs, which are neither fixed nor variable costs, are forcibly treated as fixed or variable costs. This chapter explains how these shortcomings can be corrected.

I. FIXED COSTS AND VARIABLE COSTS

Basically, BEP analysis involves an interplay of sales revenues, fixed costs, and variable costs. Hence, before the PBEPSV may be calculated, the costs have to be classified into fixed costs and variable costs.

FIXED COSTS AND VARIABLE COSTS—DISTINCTIONS

Fixed costs are so called because their total monthly or annual amount remains constant or fixed irrespective of the level of sales or production volume. Variable costs are so termed because their total amount changes or varies in direct proportion to the volume of business. The fixed costs per production or sales unit go down in inverse proportion to the rise in the volume. On the other hand, the variable costs per unit remain constant.

Certain costs are distinguished into fixed costs and variable costs as follows:

Cost item	Fixed cost	Variable cost
Compensation	Basic salaries of managers	Sales commissions
Depreciation	Depreciation calculated on a straight-line basis	Depreciation based on quantity produced
Purchases	Office supplies	Raw materials and merchandise
Insurance	Insurance on equipment	Insurance on merchandise variable inventory (on top of base stock)
Rental	General office rental	Warehouse for materials if calculated on space actually occupied
Interest on loans	On loans to finance land and buildings	On loans to finance variable finished goods inventory

TOTAL FIXED COSTS—CHANGES

A fixed cost is both a capacity cost and a period cost. Hence the total fixed cost does not change, irrespective of the volume of business, if the volume is within the given capacity and if the time frame is within the given period. Otherwise, the total fixed costs change.

As Capacity Cost—Range Limitation.   Fixed costs are incurred to support a given level of capacity. The higher the capacity, the higher the fixed costs. For instance, the bigger the factory, the higher the levels of the depreciation, plant insurance, and interest on the loan used to finance the factory.

If the production capacity of a plant is 10,000 a month, the total fixed costs is supposed to be constant if the production ranges from zero up to 10,000. However, if the production is raised beyond 10,000, the fixed costs will be increased. A second shift may have to be added, requiring additional overhead. Or the firm may have to lease additional facilities, thereby raising the fixed costs.

As Period Cost—Time Frame Limitations.   In BEP analysis, fixed costs are incurred with the passage of time, for a given period, say, a year. For instance, once the physical facilities have been set up and the managers hired, monthly depreciation charges and monthly salaries start to accrue.

The fixed costs will hold true only for a given period. The buildings and equipment will gradually wear out, thus requiring higher maintenance expenses. Salary adjustments will raise the compensation of monthly personnel.

Fixed Costs as Variable Costs.   Prolonged low production levels in relation to the capacity will prod management to curtail the capacity by reducing the number of shifts, closing some of the plants, or reducing the managerial salaries, thereby cutting the overhead. On the other hand, increased production volume and bright business prospects will lead the company to expand capacity or automate the operations, thereby adding to the fixed costs. In this sense, fixed costs become variable costs in the long run in that the fixed costs ultimately adjust to the sales volume.

VARIABLE COST PER UNIT—CHANGES

In the BEPSV model, the total variable costs rise or fall proportionately with the business volume, while the variable costs per unit of product remain constant. Although this is generally true, in practice the cost per unit of product of certain variable costs may change.

Changes in the Short Run. The gearing up of production to a level which is higher than normal transforms the total cost structure including the variable costs. For instance, the direct labor cost per unit of product may rise if overtime payments including overtime and nighttime differentials exceed the hourly rate based on the total compensation package which includes benefits; otherwise, the direct labor cost per unit drops.

As production volume initially goes up, the raw material cost per unit may decline due to volume discounts or outright reduction in the buying prices and economies of scale in the procurement and storage. However, if the volume goes up to abnormally high levels, and the firm procures in the open market, it may drive up the prices.

Changes in the Long Run. A continued high level of production may lead the firm to go into the automation of operations and backward integration to the sources of the raw material. This will decrease the variable cost per unit of production and raw materials. However, the automation and integration will also substantially add to the fixed costs.

II. PROFIT BREAK-EVEN POINT SALES VOLUME—APPROACHES, CALCULATIONS, AND ASSUMPTIONS

The most popular type of break-even point is the one that determines the level of sales volume at which the total revenues of a firm, its division, or a product just equals the costs. In other words, at BEP, the business unit or product just breaks even in profit. To distinguish this type of BEP from the other types described in this book, this BEP is called the profit BEP sales volume.

PBEPSV APPROACHES (Exhibit 8.1)

There are two approaches in determining the BEP. The approaches vary only in the manner of presentation and calculation; their results are identical.

The traditional or total cost approach is represented by the total cost form of income statement shown in Exhibit 8.1, part II, column C. The statement shows that at the PBEPSV of 189.5 units, the total sales revenues of $4,168,000 equals the total costs.

The contribution margin approach in Exhibit 8.1, part III, column C, indicates that at the PBEPSV, the contribution margin of $1,800,000 equals the fixed costs.

To facilitate the calculation of the BEP, it is necessary to gather information on the projected sales volume, unit selling prices, unit variable cost, and total fixed cost. This information may be prepared in the form as shown in Exhibit 8.1, column A.

PBEPSV CALCULATIONS

There are three methods of calculating the break-even point: through a formula, through a chart, and through trial and error using a computer. Each of the methods may follow either the total cost or the contribution margin approach. The first two methods are described next.

PBEPSV FORMULA

One formula based on the contribution margin approach is

$$PBEPSV = \frac{TFC}{UCM} = \frac{\$1,800,000}{\$9,500} = 189.5 \text{ units}$$

where

PBEPSV = Profit break-even point sales volume

TFC = Total fixed costs

UCM = Unit contribution margin or contribution margin per unit

The figures are taken from Exhibit 8.1, column A.

BEP CHART (Exhibits 8.2 and 8.4)

The BEP point may be estimated from a chart. The chart using the total cost approach is illustrated in Exhibit 8.2. The figures shown to the right of the chart were taken from Exhibit 8.1, column B. The chart utilizing the contribution margin approach is in Exhibit 8.4.

PBEPSV—ASSUMPTIONS

The PBEPSV analysis is effective if it is done for only one product. If done for several products, it is assumed that if the sales volume changes, the product mix is maintained. The constant product mix assumption is explained in Section III of this chapter.

The other assumptions which are used to simplify the calculations are

1. The unit selling price, unit variable cost, and total fixed cost are constant. Variable costs and fixed costs were illustrated earlier in Section I.
2. All the costs are tax deductible. This aspect is discussed in Section IV.
3. The finished goods inventory level does not change—if the absorption method of costing the finished goods inventory is applied. If there are changes in the inventory, the direct costing method should be used. These two methods were compared in Chapter 17.

III. TYPES OF BEP AND APPLICATIONS

The prior discussions have touched on only one kind of BEP: profit BEP sales volume for one product. Different applications or situations call for different types of BEP analyses.

The BEP techniques may be classified in three general ways: (1) according to the variable factor which the BEP technique seeks to determine, (2) according to the definition of the profit, and (3) according to the number of products to be covered in the analysis.

Variable Factor. In the PBEPSV, the variable factor is the sales volume since this BEP technique tries to pinpoint the sales volume at which the firm will just break even. The selling prices, variable costs, and fixed costs are held constant. In certain instances, the selling prices, variable costs, or fixed costs may be used as the variable factor.

Profit. The profit used in the PBEPSV is the accounting profit. This may be advisable in performance evaluation, but usually it is not recommended for decision analysis. The appraisal of proposed measures should normally be based on cash profit. In special circumstances, the profit to be utilized is cash profit after amortization of debt.

Number of Products. The PBEPSV illustrated is only for one product. In many cases, the analysis may have to cover several products as a group.

VARIABLE FACTOR

The BEP is used to ascertain the level of the variable factor at which the firm will break even in profit or cash. The variable factor may be sales volume, selling price, or variable cost. The variable factor used is the one which, at the time the study is prepared, is the most unsettled item.

Sales Volume (BEPSV).   If the sales volume cannot be reasonably forecast, but the prices and cost structure can be confidently estimated, the BEP seeks to determine the break-even point sales volume. The BEP, if related to relevant information, provides the key to decision making.

COMPARISON WITH THE EXPECTED SALES VOLUME.   A typical application of the BEPSV is in plant modernization which increases the total fixed costs but reduces the unit variable costs, or in a capacity expansion measure which increases the total fixed costs. The sales volume is projected and then compared with the expected BEP. A projected sales volume which is lower than the BEPSV means that the company will not be able to generate adequate sales volume to cover the increased costs due to the modernization or expansion. In this case, the proposal will result in a loss and hence has to be aborted.

COMPARISON WITH THE LOSS BUFFER OF PRESENT OPERATIONS. Proposed measures to improve existing operations should be compared with present operations. An increase in the BEPSV by itself does not necessarily mean that the proposal has to be turned down. The expected sales may rise at a faster rate due to improved product marketability or enhanced manufacturing capability. In this case, the loss buffer may increase notwithstanding the rise in the BEPSV. The following figures illustrate this possibility.

	Present operations	*Present plus proposal*
Sales	$100,000	$120,000
BEPSV	$ 85,000	$100,000
Loss buffer	$ 15,000	$ 20,000
Buffer as a percentage of sales	15%	17%

COMPARISON WITH THE LOSS BUFFER OF THE COMPETITION.   The common concept is that the higher its BEP, the more vulnerable is the firm. Based on this rule, Company B in the following table would appear to have the weakest position, and C, the strongest (dollars in $1,000,000):

	Company A	*Company B*	*Company C*
Present sales	$100	$150	$50
BEPSV	$ 85	$120	$45
Loss buffer	$ 15	$ 30	$ 5
Buffer as a percentage of sales	15%	20%	10%

A clearer perspective will be obtained if the loss buffer is related to the sales. If this is done, Company B will emerge as the strongest, and C, the weakest. The loss buffer percentage represents the drop in the expected sales before the firm incurs a net loss. Thus Company B has the strongest position because it can take the highest risk as measured by the percentage decline in the sales which the firm can afford.

COMPARISON WITH THE MARKET. The BEPSV information will become more interesting if it is related to the expected industry sales, market share, and company sales. Take the case of a firm with a calculated 1,800-ton BEPSV and a 2,000-ton expected sales based on a 20,000-ton industry sales and 10% market share. This firm has a 10% buffer for possible sales reduction from the expected sales to protect it from loss.

The 1,800-ton BEPSV can mean the firm will not start losing until one of the following events occurs: a 10% drop in the market share, a 10% reduction in industry sales, or a combined 5% decline in industry sales and 5% loss in market share. These figures are supported by the following table.

		POSSIBLE BEPSV SITUATIONS		
	Projected	*A*	*B*	*C*
Industry sales (tons)	20,000	20,000	18,000	19,000
Market share	10%	9%	10%	9.5%
Company sales (tons)	2,000	1,800	1,800	1,805
Buffer = reduction in				
Industry sales			10%	5%
Market share		10%		5%
Company sales		10%	10%	10%

COMPARISON WITH THE CAPACITY. The foregoing illustrations have shown that the loss buffer, if related to the expected sales, indicates the degree of safety of the firm. But limiting the comparison just to this information gives an incomplete picture and may lead to the wrong decision. Take the case of equipment X and Y in the following table:

	Equipment X	Equipment Y
Risk situation		
Immediate expected sales	$100,000	$100,000
BEPSV	$ 60,000	$ 70,000
Loss buffer	$ 40,000	$ 30,000
Buffer as a percentage of sales	40%	30%
Operational flexibility		
Rated capacity	$120,000	$160,000
Immediate expected sales	$100,000	$100,000
Immediate capacity utilization	83%	63%
Profit potential		
BEPSV as a percentage of capacity	50%	44%
Unused capacity	$ 20,000	$ 60,000
Unused capacity as a percentage of immediate expected sales	20%	60%

If we look at just the first part of the preceding table, we will be inclined to take equipment X since it has a lower BEPSV and therefore has a higher loss buffer.

However, while equipment Y is the more risky between the two, it has the higher operational flexibility and higher profit potential. Based on the immediate expected sales, Y will be operating at only 63% of its capacity.

This means that it has more ability to absorb rush orders as for seasonal demand. Furthermore, it can easily make up for lost production time due to equipment breakdowns as well as raw material shortages and labor relation disruptions.

Since the BEPSV of Y is only 44% of its rated capacity, the equipment has the potential to generate higher profit if the demands approximate the rated capacity. This advantage of Y is also indicated by its higher unused capacity which at 60% of the immediate expected sales is three times that of X.

The analysis of the profit potential is specially useful in businesses where the capacity cost is high. This is true, for instance, in real estate industry—such as hotels, commercial rentals, office buildings, and apartment units. Once the BEPSV is reached, the profit generation per unit becomes very attractive due to the wide contribution margin.

OTHER APPLICATIONS.   In case of decisions on possible product deletions, the BEPSV in relation to the expected sales may be calculated on two bases: one without, and the other with, the proposed deletions. This comparison will point out the relative risks of the options. This application is illustrated in Chapter 10.

The BEPSV may be used in studying the amount of debt which a firm may reasonably take in relation to equity. The BEPSV in relation to the projected sales may be estimated on varying debt/equity ratios in order to determine the risk level which the firm is willing to take considering its desired return. This aspect is examined in Chapter 15.

Selling Price (BEPSP) (Exhibit 8.3). In certain instances, at the time the proposal is prepared, the selling price may have not yet been firmed up. This is true, for instance, if a new kind of product will be introduced. In this case, two BEP analyses may be conducted: one will determine the break-even point selling price (BEPSP), given an assumed volume; the other, the BEPSV, will pinpoint the break-even sales volume, at an assumed selling price per unit.

The BEPSP is also particularly useful in a situation where there is an impending price war. The management may be interested to know how far it can slash its prices before it starts losing.

Another scenario where the BEPSP may be employed is when the firm had reformulated its products, thereby dramatically altering its cost structure. In this case, the firm may like to know the level of its selling price where it will break even.

Like the BEPSV, the BEPSP cannot be fully appreciated unless it is compared with the projected selling price. The selling price loss buffer should also be calculated. Furthermore, the BEPSP, projected selling price, and loss buffer as a percentage of the projected selling price should be compared with those of the competitors, other projects, and present operations.

VARIABLE COSTS IN BEPSV AND IN BEPSP. In calculating the BEPSV, the variable costs are defined as those which change in direct proportion to the sales volume. However, in estimating the BEPSP, the variable costs take on another meaning: those that vary with the selling price. Some costs, as sales commissions calculated as a percentage of sales dollars, can be considered as variable in relation to both SV and SP. However, some costs can be considered as variable in relation to SV but not in relation to SP. For instance, raw materials vary with the change in sales volume but not necessarily with the change in the selling price.

ILLUSTRATION (EXHIBIT 8.3). The BEPSP of $15,590 per unit is calculated in Exhibit 8.3. The figures in the first column of the exhibit were taken from Exhibit 8.1, column B, except that the $5,000,000 total variable cost in Exhibit 8.1 is segregated into the $1,936,000 variable costs and $3,064,000 fixed costs in Exhibit 8.3.

Variable Cost (BEPVC). If the sales volume and selling prices are fairly stabilized, a company may find the BEP tool useful in studying its variable costs. This is true, for instance, if a firm was able to obtain a firm sales order which sets forth both the delivery quantity and selling price. The purpose of the BEP analysis here is to determine the level of variable costs at which the company will break even. The BEP variable cost (BEPVC) is used.

The BEPVC may also be particularly useful to a firm that is negotiating with its raw material suppliers, labor union, commission sales persons, or dealers. The firm may find it worthwhile knowing the extent to which it could raise its raw material costs, wage rates, sales commission rates, or dealer discount rates before its profit is converted to a loss.

A company which carries a high level of receivables or inventories, as a retailing organization, may find the BEPVC interesting. This is particularly true if the working capital is financed by loans with variable interest rates. The BEPVC will inform management the extent to which an upswing in money cost will eat up all its profit margin.

The BEPVC may be calculated by using a form similar to that presented in Exhibit 8.3. However, some adjustments have to be made.

DEFINITION OF PROFIT

The BEP as calculated under current practice may vary depending upon the definition of the profit used. The term profit means accounting profit, cash profit, or cash profit less debt service.

The author believes that a BEP based on accounting profit has limited utility. The results of BEP analysis may be more appreciated if the profit is derived: before deducting sunk costs and past benefit costs and after deducting actual and imputed interest and risk premium. This aspect is discussed in the last part of this chapter, Limitations and Solutions.

Accounting Profit (PBEP).   Traditionally, profit as used in PBEP means accounting profit, which is after depreciation and other noncash items. Under this concept, the fixed costs in Exhibit 8.1 include depreciation. A BEP method using this concept and seeking to determine the BEPSV is called profit BEPSV or PBEPSV. This is the most popular type of BEP, although not necessarily the most useful.

The utilization of PBEP for planning purposes represents one of the many anomalies in the field of financial analysis. For while the planning tools are usually based on outlay costs and imputed costs, PBEP is premised on accounting costs and book profit. Although accounting profit has a more universal application in performance evaluation, it has no room in financial planning and decision analysis.

Cash Profit (CBEP, Exhibits 8.1 and 8.4).   At PBEP, a firm still generates cash from operations due to the inclusion of noncash costs in the calculations. Hence, management might be interested to know the bare-bone BEP, that is, the level of sales volume, selling price, or variable cost at which its cash receipts from revenues just equal its cash payments for the expenses. The tool which is used in this application is the cash BEP or CBEP. The costs used in this application are just the cash costs.

Assuming that $600,000 of the $1,800,000 fixed costs in Exhibit 8.1 is represented by depreciation, the amount of the cash fixed costs is only

$1,200,000. The income statement at CBEPSV is shown in Exhibit 8.1, column D, while the chart is in Exhibit 8.4.

Cash Profit Less Debt Service (DSBEP, Exhibits 8.1 and 8.4). The CBEP may suffice for cash planning purposes if the firm has no maturing obligations. However, if the firm is retiring some debts, its management may be interested to know the level of sales volume, selling prices, or variable costs so that its cash generation from sales revenues will just be enough to pay its cash expenses including interest, as well as amortization of loan principal.

Using the data in Exhibit 8.1, column F, the contribution margin (CM) at the DSBEPSV may be determined by the following formula:

$$CM = debt\ service + cash\ fixed\ costs + tax$$

where

$$tax = tax\ rate\ [CM - (cash\ fixed\ costs + noncash\ fixed\ costs)]$$

The CM may be obtained as

$$
\begin{aligned}
CM &= \$1,000,000 + \$1,200,000 \\
&\quad + .4[CM - (\$1,200,000 + \$600,000)] \\
&= \$2,200,000 + .4CM - \$720,000 \\
.6CM &= \$2,200,000 - \$720,000 \\
CM &= \$2,467,000
\end{aligned}
$$

The DSBEPSV is

$$
\begin{aligned}
DSBEPSV &= \frac{CM\ at\ DSBEPSV}{unit\ selling\ price} \\
&= \frac{\$2,467,000}{\$9,500} = 259.7
\end{aligned}
$$

The income statement at DSBEPSV is in Exhibit 8.1, column E, while the chart is in Exhibit 8.4.

NUMBER OF PRODUCTS (Exhibit 8.5)

So far in this chapter, the BEP analysis has been applied to one product only. The BEP may also be used on a multiproduct operation.

Assume that the projected sales and costs information for products A, B, and C are as given in Exhibit 8.5, parts I and II. The PBEPSV may be derived by the following formula:

$$\frac{PBEPSV}{(in\ dollars)} = \frac{total\ fixed\ costs}{total\ contribution\ margin} \times \frac{projected\ sales}{in\ dollars}$$

$$= \frac{\$1,820,000}{\$2,820,000} \times \$8,700,000 = \$5,615,000$$

The BEPSV of $5,615,000 is 64.54% of the projected sales of $8,700,000. This percentage may be used to convert the projected sales volume in pounds in Exhibit 8.5, part I, to the BEPSV in pounds in part III.

Since the three products in the illustration have different variable costs as a percentage of sales, the BEP technique has to assume that the product mix used in calculating the projected sales (Exhibit 8.5, part II) is maintained at the BEPSV (part III). This assumption makes the BEP for a group of product less effective than that for one product alone.

IV. LIMITATIONS AND SOLUTIONS

The purpose of this last part of the chapter is to pinpoint the limitations of BEP analysis as currently practiced and show how these shortcomings may be corrected. Most of the issues discussed here have not been covered in other publications on financial analysis.

The results of BEP analysis are subject to limitations in two areas: (1) the selection of costs to be included and (2) the classification of costs according to their behavior.

If these limitations are not remedied, the BEP analysis can give misleading signals to management which could result in wrong decisions. However, if these weaknesses are corrected, the BEP can be converted into a very effective tool of risk analysis.

Like the other tools of decision analysis, BEP is also subject to the limitations arising from the assumptions used in the financial projections as discussed in Chapters 2 and 3.

SELECTION OF COSTS FOR INCLUSION

In Section III of this chapter, it was pointed out that traditionally, BEP may refer to break even in accounting profit, cash profit, or cash profit less debt service. Since the use of accounting profit represents a basic flaw in BEP practice, it has to be corrected by changing the types of costs which are normally used in determining the accounting profit. Sunk costs, past benefit costs, and future benefit costs are normally included in the BEP calculation at present. On the other hand, actual and imputed interest and some profit-dependent costs are usually not included. The improper inclusion or exclusion necessarily produces erroneous break-even points that can lead to disastrous decisions. These are illustrated in the paragraphs that follow.

Sunk Costs. The depreciation of equipment acquired in the past, as well as the amortization of costs previously incurred are, under current practice, usually included as fixed costs in calculating the BEP.

If the purpose of the analysis is to help management decide on proposed measures, as on closing plants, the inclusion of such costs will bloat the fixed costs and artificially push up the BEP. If the expected sales is lower than the reported BEP, the tendency of management is to close the plant. However, closing the plant will not take out the sunk costs.

In this situation, it could be possible that if the sunk costs were not included, the expected sales could be higher than the BEP. If this were the case, then the inclusion of the sunk costs will lead management to forfeit the profit.

Past Benefit Costs. The preceding case has illustrated that sunk costs should be excluded in the BEP analysis. But it does not necessarily follow that all kinds of outlay costs (those still to be paid in the future) should be included. Payments to be made in the future, for costs which benefited the past, should not be included in the BEP analysis for the future.

Settlements of legal cases arising from past transactions as well as retirement or medical benefit payments to present and retired employees pertaining to services rendered in the past should not cloud the picture of the future. Their inclusion as costs in the calculations will, like the sunk costs, raise the BEP to unreasonably high levels, and might lead management to abort profitable undertakings.

Future Benefit Costs. In order to improve the factory operations and develop new products, firms have to spend on R&D, management development, and labor training. Presently, these are usually treated as fixed costs although they are not. In good times the expenditures on these items rise, and in bad times, fall. These are not variable costs either because they are not related to the sales volume of the period in which they are incurred.

There are three alternative treatments of future benefit costs. First, future benefit costs which will be used to generate sales or reduce costs in the future should be included in the BEP estimates only to the extent that they benefit the period covered in the analysis. For instance, expenditures for R&D efforts which will not produce results until five years from now should definitely not be added to the costs in deriving the BEP for next year.

Under the second alternative, all these costs should not be included in the BEP calculations. At BEP, the firm will not have enough profit or cash left to fund discretionary expenditures.

Under the last option, all the discretionary expenses should be included, and in full at that. By nature, discretionary expenses are committed to provide for the long-term continuity of the company. Without them, the company will surely fail. Hence, although in practice management has the discretion to cut down on their spending, in reality they are necessary for the future survival and growth of the company.

Of the three options, the first seems to be the most logical. A BEP is for a specific period, and it cannot reflect the correct situation unless the costs are properly matched with the revenues.

Actual Interest.   Interest cost is sometimes disregarded in BEP analysis. The exclusion produces dire consequences. This is particularly true of businesses where the profit margin is very thin, as in trading operations where the firm finances both the receivables and inventories. The exclusion of interest will present a losing venture as if it were a profitable operation. The promise of a profit once the BEP mark is breached, will prod management to keep on expanding the sales volume. However, as they push up the sales, the losses pile up since the actual profit margin is not enough to cover the interest expense.

Imputed Interest.   While imputed interest has been accepted as a cost component in estimating the net present value, present value of cost, incremental costing, and hurdle rate (to be compared with the internal rate of return), it has not yet found its way into the BEP analysis.

The inclusion of actual interest on loans is not enough if part of the resources are financed by equity capital. If only the actual interest is included, the BEP of two otherwise identical operations except for their financing scheme will be different. The one with more equity financing will show a lower BEP. Under this basis, therefore, there is a likelihood that an operation with high equity funding will be implemented due to its apparently low BEP.

Risk premium is sometimes added to the risk-free money cost in calculating the net present value and hurdle rate. Although risk premium does not traditionally enter into BEP analysis, the addition of risk premium to the imputed money cost will make the BEP of proposals with varying degrees of risks more comparable.

Fixed Costs.   Fixed costs are composed of several layers—the topmost is composed of the product fixed costs, followed successively by the departmental, divisional, and then by the corporate fixed costs. In some organizations, there may be five or more layers.

The tiers of fixed costs to be included in the analysis depends on the coverage of the BEP. If it is for just a product, then the fixed costs to be included will be only the product fixed costs. If the BEP is for a department, then the fixed costs will include only the first two tiers.

The tiers of fixed costs are discussed further and illustrated in Chapter 10.

Profit-dependent Costs.   These are the expenditures which are contingent

upon, or calculated based on, the net profit or cash generation. Examples
are income tax, profit-sharing bonus, management and franchise fees
based on profit, and cash dividends. The general rule is that, by definition,
there are no profit-dependent costs at the BEP and that all profit-
dependent costs start to accrue or are paid once the BEP is hit. However,
this holds true only if all the following conditions are met: (1) all the costs
used in the BEP calculations are tax-deductible, (2) all the tax-deductible
costs are included, and (3) all the profit-dependent costs are based on
taxable profit. If any of the requirements do not apply, then there may be
some profit-dependent costs at the BEP, or some profit-dependent costs
may not start to accrue at the BEP.

Tax Deductibility of Costs Used in BEP.   If imputed interest or payment
of loan principal as in DSBEP is included in calculating the BEP, then this
BEP is higher than the income tax BEP. The result is that the income tax
starts even before the attainment of the DSBEP. See Exhibit 8.4, where the
DSBEP is at 259.7 units, while the tax starts to accrue at 189.5 units.

   Of course, the effect of including imputed interest or loan amortization may be partly or more than offset by the elimination of certain tax-
deductible costs as described next.

Inclusion of All Tax-deductible Costs.   Depreciation and amortization are
not included in deriving the CBEP and DSBEP. The effect of excluding
these tax-deductible items is to lower the cash BEP in relation to the tax or
accounting profit BEP. Thus the income tax will not start at the CBEP of
126.3 per Exhibit 8.4, but at the tax BEP which is at a higher level of 189.5
units.

Profit-dependent Costs Based on Taxable Profit.   Even if all the costs used
in the BEP calculations are tax deductible, and all tax-deductible items are
considered as costs, some profit-dependent costs may not start to accrue at
the tax BEP as they are not based on taxable profit. For instance franchise
fee may be based on profit before the general overhead.

CLASSIFICATION OF COSTS ACCORDING
TO THEIR BEHAVIOR

The costs which are commonly misclassified are the interest and sales
expansion costs. The misclassification results in erroneous BEP.

Classification of Interest Cost.   Under present practice, if ever interest is
included as a cost, it is classified either as fixed or variable cost. The
classification depends upon the maturity date of the loan or the balance
sheet classification of the assets financed by the loan. If based on maturity
date, interest on short-term loans is usually wrongly treated as variable
cost, and those on long-term loans as fixed cost. If based on the assets

financed by the loan, interest on loans used to carry property or equipment is considered as fixed costs, and those used to finance current assets, as variable cost.

This classification is often not accurate for two reasons. First, the classification as practiced is related to the loan or asset and not to the expense itself. Second, the interest pertains to the loan only, that is, without imputed interest on the equity.

In calculating the BEPSV, interest on financing used to carry fixed costs should be treated as fixed costs. Thus, interest on financing used to fund the manufacturing overhead (a fixed cost) while the goods are still worked on (goods in process inventory), while the completed goods are still unsold (finished goods inventory) or while the sales have not yet been collected (accounts receivable) should be treated as fixed cost.

The calculation of the overhead component of working capital is facilitated by the use of the root cost method of estimating the working capital. This is explained in Chapter 10.

Similarly, interest on financing used to carry the variable costs component of working capital should be treated as variable costs.

Interest on loans utilized to finance the lengthening of the collection period of receivables, if part of a strategy to expand the sales, should be treated as sales expansion costs and not as variable or fixed costs. See the next part of this chapter, and also Chapters 11 and 17.

Classification of Sales Expansion Costs.   In calculating the BEPSV, all the costs are classified into fixed or variable costs. This classification is suited for established manufacturing operations. For a given time frame and within a given production range, the fixed costs are incurred at pre-established rates. For a given production order, variable costs are incurred at standard costs, usually with allowable variance.

When firms start aggressively to capture market share or develop markets for their products, they spend heavily on advertising, promotions, and other sales expansion costs. This creates an entirely new breed of animal which was not anticipated when the BEP idea was conceived—and hence will not fit into the prehistoric cages of fixed costs and variable costs.

Sales expansion costs are sometimes treated as fixed costs, based on the expectation that the expense budgeted for the year will be fully spent. But in reality, when the sales response is not as good as expected, and does not produce enough margin to justify the expense, the sales expansion cost is held back. On the other hand, when the response is very high, the sales expansion effort is accelerated or, if the firm cannot meet the orders any more, cut down.

Sales expansion costs are not fixed costs because they vary not only with the sales response, but also with the cash flow of the firm and the strategies and measures undertaken.

In certain cases, sales expansion costs are erroneously considered as variable costs if they are budgeted as a percentage of sales. Again, the actual amount to be spent usually does not agree with the plan since it is adjusted to reflect the reality of the evolving marketplace.

They are not variable costs within the classic context of the term because sales expansion costs are spent or committed before the sale occurs. By comparison, sales commission is spent after the sale; raw materials are committed after a sales or production order is received. Hence a dollar in sales expansion cost is as likely to produce 10 dollars in sales as it is to generate 50 cents. Sales expansion costs fluctuate widely, but with the fluctuations not in direct relation to the sales volume.

Notwithstanding these concepts, sales expansion costs are considered either as fixed costs or variable costs in current practice for the simple reason that these are just the slots available.

Sales expansion costs are further explained in Chapter 17.

If a firm is engaged in an aggressive sales expansion strategy and the sales expansion costs represent a significant portion of the total costs, the employment of BEP analysis can normally be misleading, and hence is not advisable. The method explained in Chapter 11 may be used for this purpose.

EXHIBIT 8.1:
Break-Even Point Sales Volume

		PBEPSV			CBEPSV	DSBEPSV	
		Col. A	Col. B	Col. C	Col. D	Col. E	Col. F
I. Sales volume							
Number of units		200	400	189.5	126.3	259.7	400
II. Total cost form monthly income statement ($1,000)							
Sales		$ 4,400	$ 8,800	$ 4,168	$ 2,779	$ 5,713	$ 8,800
Less: Costs	56.8%						
Variable costs		2,500	5,000	2,368	1,579	3,246	5,000
Fixed costs		1,800	1,800	1,800	1,200	1,200	1,200
Total costs		4,300	6,800	4,168	2,779	4,446	6,200
Pretax profit		$ 100	$ 2,000	$ 0	($ 0)	$ 1,267	$ 2,600
III. Contribution margin form monthly income statement ($1,000)							
Sales	56.8%	$ 4,400	$ 8,800	$ 4,168	$ 2,779	$ 5,713	$ 8,800
Variable costs		2,500	5,000	2,368	1,579	3,246	5,000
Contribution margin		1,900	3,800	1,800	1,200	2,467	3,800
Fixed costs		1,800	1,800	1,800	1,200	1,200	1,200
Pretax profit		100	2,000	0	(0)	1,267	2,600
Income tax	40.0%	(40)	(800)	0	(0)	(507)	(1,040)
Tax reduction due to depreciation						240	240
Posttax profit		$ 60	$ 1,200	$ 0	($ 0)	$ 1,000	$ 1,800
Loan principal payment						$ 1,000	$ 1,000
IV. Contribution margin per unit							
Selling price per unit		$22,000	$22,000	$22,000	$ 22,000	$22,000	$22,000
Variable costs		12,500	$12,500	12,500	12,500	12,500	12,500
Contribution margin		$ 9,500	$ 9,500	$ 9,500	$ 9,500	$ 9,500	$ 9,500

EXHIBIT 8.2:

Break-Even Point Sales Volume Chart using the total cost form approach

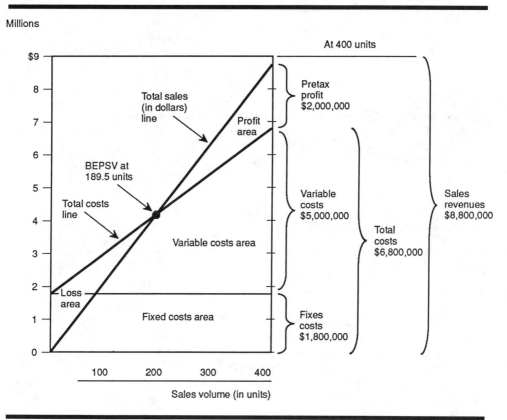

EXHIBIT 8.3:
Break-Even Point Selling Price (with price-sensitive variable costs)

		Projected selling price	PBEPSP
I. Sales volume			
Number of units		400	400
II. Contribution margin form monthly income statement (in $1,000)			
Sales		$ 8,800	$ 6,236
Price-sensitive variable costs			
as a percentage of sales	22%	1,936	$ 1,372
Contribution margin		$ 6,864	$ 4,864
Fixed costs in BEPSP			
Variable costs in BEPSV (not price sensitive)		3,064	3,064
Fixed costs in both BEPSV and BEPSP		1,800	1,800
Total fixed costs		$ 4,864	$ 4,864
Pretax profit		$ 2,000	$ 0
III. Contribution margin per unit			
Selling price per unit		$22,000	$15,590
Price-sensitive variable costs			
as a percentage of sales	22%	4,840	3,430
Contribution margin	78%	$17,160	$12,160
IV. Calculation of BEPSP			
Total fixed costs (in $1,000)			$ 4,864
Divide by contribution margin as a percentage of projected selling price			78%
Equals total sales revenue at BEPSP (in $1,000)			$ 6,236
Divide by projected number of sales units			400
Equals BEPSP per unit			$15,590

EXHIBIT 8.4:
Break-Even Point Sales Volume Chart
using the contribution margin approach

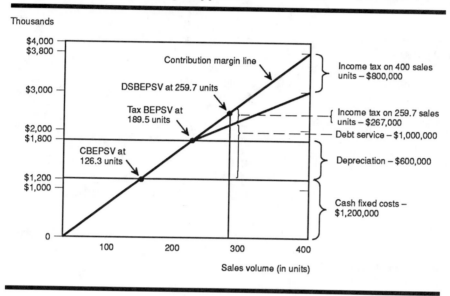

Thousands

EXHIBIT 8.5:
Break-Even Point Sales Volume for a Multiproduct Operation

		Product		
	A	B	C	Total
I. Given data				
Projected sales volume (in pounds)	1,000	2,500	1,100	$4,600
Price per pound	$4,000	$1,000	$2,000	$7,000
Variable costs as percent of sales	63.08%	60.68%	83.64%	67.59%
II. Monthly income statement at projected sales volume (dollars in $1,000)				
Sales	$4,000	$2,500	$2,000	$8,700
Variable costs	2,523	1,517	1,840	5,880
Contribution margin	$1,477	$ 983	$ 360	$2,820
Fixed costs				1,820
Pretax profit				$1,000
III. Monthly income statement at BEPSV (dollars in $1,000)				
Sales volume				
As a percentage of projected sales	64.54%	64.54%	64.54%	64.54%
At break-even point (in pounds)	645	1,613	710	2,969
Price per pound	$4,000	$1,000	$2,000	
Total (in $1,000)				
Sales	$2,582	$1,613	$1,420	$5,615
Variable costs	1,628	979	1,188	3,795
Contribution margin	$ 953	$ 634	$ 232	1,820
Fixed costs				1,820
Pretax profit				$ 0

Chapter 9 _____

ANALYZING COST REDUCTION MEASURES

Short-term cost reduction or cost containment measures seek to improve the profitability of a firm by slashing the costs but without impairing the revenues or long-term performance. Unduly deferring equipment maintenance work is not a cost reduction measure. Although it reduces the costs for the current year, it compromises future performance. Using inferior materials in product manufacture reduces the cost of production but sacrifices product quality and hence impairs the sales.

Cost reduction measures can be implemented, and will affect the operations, immediately. They do not involve long-term expenditures or commitments as for physical facilities or product R&D.

Types of Cost Reduction Measures. Prominent short-term cost cutting measures include the following:

Production

1. Buying products versus making them in-house where the production facilities already exist,
2. Using parts versus subassemblies as the raw materials,
3. Hiring daily laborers versus subcontracting the work.

Marketing

1. Using distributors versus selling directly, where no long-term costs are involved,
2. Paying the salespeople on commission basis versus paying them a monthly salary.

This chapter demonstrates the analysis of a make or buy decision with short-term implications. A typical case is a proposal for the in-house production of goods where the production facilities are already in place and where the company is currently buying the goods. This type of measure is undertaken in the hope that the rise in the fixed costs can be more than covered by the decline in the variable costs. The procedures for the analysis of other short-term measures are similar to those of this make or buy alternative.

Techniques Used. The analysis applies the following techniques and concepts: return on investment, residual income, resource-based or imputed interest, sensitivity analysis, and crossover analysis. The chapter introduces differential cost analysis, which involves incremental and decremental costs.

The analysis of the measure is confined to fixed cost, variable cost, and working capital. More sophisticated evaluation of programs affecting the sales volume or selling prices, or involving sales expansion costs, long-term costs, and multiple tiers of fixed costs is reserved for subsequent chapters.

I. NATURE OF COST REDUCTION MEASURES

COST BEHAVIOR

Short-term cost reduction measures impact on variable costs, fixed costs, or both. Variable costs are those costs where the total amount varies directly in proportion to the sales or production volume. A sales commission based on a flat rate is a variable cost; if the sales go up, so does the total commission expense. On the other hand, a fixed cost is an expense item where the monthly total does not change irrespective of the sales or production volume as long as the volume is within a given range.

The measure analyzed in this chapter requires incremental total fixed cost but results in decremental unit variable cost. The total fixed cost is raised since the in-house performance of a function invariably requires a fixed overhead. The variable cost per unit is reduced since the variable cost of doing the function in-house is lower than that of contracting the function to other firms.

If the quantity of the product required is relatively low, it is usually advisable to buy from the outside. Once the requirement goes up beyond a certain level, the firm can boost its profitability by taking over the manufacturing.

RATIONALE

The in-house performance of a function can be justified if at the expected level of production, the savings in variable cost (or the decremental variable cost or variable cost advantage) is going to be higher than the total incremental fixed cost (or fixed cost disadvantage).

The incremental fixed cost brings in an element of risk in that if the total variable cost advantage cannot fully recoup the incremental fixed cost, the firm will lose instead of gain from the implementation of the measure. However, this risk is accepted on the expectation that there is a high probability that the total variable cost savings will exceed the incremental fixed cost, thus enhancing the profitability of the firm.

Hence, the comparative evaluation of alternatives with these cost features involves a delicate balancing of the variable cost advantage against the fixed cost disadvantage.

II. INTEREST AND RETURN ON INVESTMENT APPROACHES

There are two ways of introducing the cost of capital used to finance the incremental assets to the decision-making picture: (1) the return on investment approach and (2) the residual income method.

The former determines the rate of return on the incremental resources and compares the rate with the cost of money. The latter imputes an interest charge which is added to the fixed costs and variable cost. These approaches are described in the paragraphs that follow.

Rate of Return Approach (Without Imputed Interest). This approach does not add interest to the cost. This relates the cost savings, before interest, arising from the "make" proposal, to the incremental assets required by the proposal. This method tries to determine how much profit the incremental resources are going to generate, or what is the percentage rate of return on the incremental resources. This procedure is similar to the accounting rate of return employed in performance evaluation and the internal rate of return utilized in the review of long-term programs.

Residual Income Approach (With Imputed Interest). The cost of capital invested in the incremental resources is imputed into the cost comparison by taking it up as a cost in the make or buy alternative. The resulting differential cost represents the cost savings and serves as the basis of the decision.

An interest expense is estimated by applying an appropriate interest rate to the differential resources used. The interest rate is the cost of additional capital to be raised to finance the differential resources. A firm that has collateralized bank loans at 10% but has to obtain unsecured loans at 12% for the additional financing will use the latter rate in the analysis. In Exhibit 9.4, the assumed cost of incremental financing is 12%.

This technique is consistent with the residual income ratio (see

Chapter 19, Return on Investment Ratio Analysis), the resource-based interest approach in performance evaluation and the intercompany capital charge method (Chapter 25, Evaluating Performance with Resource-Based Interest), and the present value and internal rate of return concepts employed in long-term project appraisal (Chapters 4 to 5).

III. ANALYSIS BASED ON THE RATE OF RETURN APPROACH

DIFFERENTIAL COST ANALYSIS WITHOUT IMPUTED INTEREST (Exhibit 9.1)

In differential cost analysis (Exhibit 9.1), the incremental (additional) or decremental costs are calculated. The differential cost may be in the form of fixed cost or variable cost. If the proposed measure results in a net decremental cost, then the measure is accepted.

Decisions affecting short-term costs are based directly on accounting records as adjusted for current or projected costs. Thus, in a make or buy decision, the variable costs and fixed costs for each alternative are listed down, and the decision is based on the option offering the lower cost.

Take the case of a company that is currently purchasing every month 500 units of a product for resale. Assume that the present purchase price is $2,500 per unit. On the other hand, if the firm makes the product itself, it will incur $2,092 per unit to produce, plus $200,000 in monthly fixed costs.

If the firm has to make the product, it has to use materials, labor, and utilities. Warehousing and inventory insurance have to also be arranged. All these costs are variable costs in that if the production is changed from 500 units a month, the total monthly variable costs will correspondingly jump or decline. The cost also includes the product overhead but excludes any share in the general overhead.

Product Overhead. This is the fixed cost that is currently not incurred as the firm is just buying the product. However, if the firm makes the product, it has to hire a production manager and other employees who will be paid monthly salaries. These salaries will not be affected by any fluctuations in the volume of production.

Share in General Overhead. The product should not be charged for any share in the general production costs as these are already being incurred. These costs include the salaries of the general manufacturing manager and his staff, as well as expenses of the general office. This also includes the depreciation of the buildings and equipment which are commonly used in the manufacture of all the products. If the company just buys the product, the total general overhead is distributed to the present products. If it makes the product under proposal, the overhead cost should not be redistributed to all the products, including the product under consideration.

Common sense dictates that if the general overhead is not going to be increased by the proposed manufacture of the product, no part of the existing overhead should be charged to the product.

Results of the Analysis. Based on the incremental analysis, it is theoretically cheaper to make the product, as it will save $4,000 a month for the 500 units. However, this difference is so minimal that it is of little practical significance. Still, the proposal should be seriously considered.

VOLUME SENSITIVITY ANALYSIS WITHOUT
INTEREST (Exhibit 9.2, part I)

The analysis in Exhibit 9.1 considered the costing in the short run only, based on 500 units a month. If the quantity is over 500 units, the cost advantage of making the product could increase. Conversely, if the quantity is below 500 units, the advantage will lessen or will be totally lost.

In sensitivity analysis, certain key assumptions are varied, usually one at a time, in order to determine the effect of a different assumption. For instance, in this case, the key assumptions are the number of units a month, the material and labor cost per unit, and the product overhead. For the moment, only the quantity of production is changed. This is done in Exhibit 9.2, part I.

The analysis shows that the decremental cost or savings can be effected by the make decision if the monthly requirement builds up from 500 to 600 units and grows from a paltry $4,000 a month to $45,000.

A decision based mainly on the current level of requirements (500 units) may not prove to be intelligent. Thus, if the analysis uses just one figure as 500 units in the example, the firm may decide to drop the idea of making the product as the cost difference is minimal.

The sensitivity analysis not just points out to the management the possible impact on profitability of varying conditions, but also broadens managerial perspective. For instance, the sensitivity analysis illustrated has indicated that cost savings under the make option accumulates fast after the crossover quantity of 490 units as shown in Exhibit 9.2, part I, is breached. Because of this, management will be encouraged to reconsider its position if there is a strong probability that the actual requirement in the future could be higher than the crossover quantity.

Results of the Analysis. The volume sensitivity analysis has explored the results if the volume varies from 500 units. At 600 units, it is much cheaper to make.

DIFFERENTIAL RESOURCE ANALYSIS (Exhibit 9.3)

The review so far has not factored the value of money to be used to finance the incremental resources (Exhibits 9.1 and 9.2). Before the money cost may be estimated, it is necessary to determine the amount of resources required by the alternatives.

Different options require different levels of assets. The resources involved are the working capital items which are composed of inventories net of trade payables or suppliers' credit.

For manufacturing operations, if all the raw materials are purchased as needed, then no additional resources are tied up in the material inventory. Furthermore, if the materials are paid for upon delivery, the company will not be able to avail of the interest-free financing from the suppliers. However, these assumptions seldom occur in practice. A certain level of material inventory is invariably maintained, and suppliers are usually not paid upon delivery.

The differential resource requirement is determined by calculating first the assets required by each alternative, and then comparing the two. In the example, the resource requirements of the make option in the form of the inventories of raw materials, goods in process, and finished goods are estimated. From the total the suppliers' credit is deducted to arrive at the net capital requirements.

The working capital requirements are estimated by using the traditional balance sheet method. This method is discussed and examined in more detail in the next chapter. An alternative is the root cost technique which is introduced in the next chapter.

Raw Material Inventory. This is applicable only to the make alternative. The illustration has provided for a three months' supply of raw materials. In other words, on the average, the inventory of raw materials on hand will be good for three months' usage. Since the material requirement per unit is worth $900, every unit to be added to the monthly production schedule requires a $2,700 addition to the inventory. The $2,700 inventory is not per unit but per unit per month. If the monthly production is only one unit, the average raw material inventory at any one time is worth $2,700.

Suppliers' Credit. The trade credit, which is created when the suppliers are paid after delivery, reduces the capital requirements for inventories. In the example, the assumptions on the suppliers' credit are as follows:

1. Under the make option, the credit for the raw materials is presumed to be one month.
2. Under the buy option, the credit for the purchased goods is half a month.

Goods in Process Inventory—Raw Material Component. The goods in process inventory refers to the materials already worked on but not yet completed. Upon completion, the costs are transferred to the finished goods inventory. Like the raw materials inventory, this applies only if the goods are made in-house. In Exhibit 9.3, the processing time is assumed to be two months, with most of the materials being required at the start of the process.

This assumption will require, at any time, a goods in process inventory, just for the raw material component alone, of $1,800 per additional unit of production a month. The $1,800 refers to the raw materials input into the production process in the preceding two months, but with the production not yet completed.

Goods in Process Inventory—Labor and Other Components. The laborers will be working on the units under production on an almost uniform basis for the two-month production period. The accumulated labor cost will gradually grow from zero upon the start of production to $1,100 upon the completion. For the two-month processing time, therefore, the average accumulated labor spent on a unit is $550 (zero value upon the start of production plus $1,100 upon completion divided by 2). Since the processing time is two months, the work in process inventory at any one time, based on a production of one unit a month, is $1,100. This is equivalent to a two-month inventory with the average being $550. Based on this, each additional unit to be manufactured every month will raise the labor component of the goods in process inventory by $1,100.

The other manufacturing cost components of the goods in process inventory can be similarly computed.

Finished Goods Inventory. The finished goods inventory will be considered in a make or buy decision if (1) the production cost is different from the buying price and/or (2) the finished goods inventory duration is not the same under the two options.

The inventory duration will vary if there is a difference in the stability of supply. For instance, if the in-house manufacture will give a more steady supply of goods, the finished goods inventory level can be reduced. In the illustration, it is assumed that the in-plant production will provide a more regular delivery of goods, thereby cutting the average inventory level from one month and one week's sales, under the buy option, to only one month.

Due to the differences in the cost and in the inventory duration under the two options, the capital to be tied into the inventory is estimated in Exhibit 9.3.

Variable and Non-variable Resources. It is usually advisable to segregate the working capital component which fluctuates with the production volume from the component which does not. Raw materials inventory, as well as the raw material, labor, and other variable cost components of the goods in process and finished goods inventories, rides with the changes in the business volume. On the other hand, the overhead or fixed cost portion of the goods in process and finished goods inventories remain constant irrespective of the volume, provided the volume is within a given range.

The overhead component of the inventories represent the capital used to pay for the overhead expenses while the goods are still being worked on or while the finished goods have not yet been sold.

Accounts Receivable.   In this particular case, there is no differential capital tied into the accounts receivable. It is expected that both the selling price and collection period remains the same under either option. For the treatment of receivables where there is a difference in the selling price, see Chapter 13, Analyzing Plant Automation Projects, and where there is a variance in the collection period, refer to Chapter 11, Analyzing Sales Expansion Measures.

RETURN ON DIFFERENTIAL RESOURCES
(Exhibit 9.2, parts II and III)

At 490 units the capital required to finance the incremental resources cannot earn any return as the total cost to make before interest just equals the total cost to buy. At 570 units, the $3,255,000 additional assets earn just $33,000 a month or 1%, and nothing more.

Beyond 570, the $5,009 incremental variable investment per additional unit per month (Exhibit 9.3, part III) earns $408 before imputed interest (Exhibit 9.2, part I). This amount is the variable cost savings or decrease in cost if the company will make the goods rather than buy them. This variable cost savings before allowing for the imputed interest, amounts to 8.1% a *month* based on the $5,009 incremental variable investment per unit.

However, this seemingly attractive return should be balanced with the total incremental fixed and variable investment of $3,255,000 which is needed to finance the production of the first 570 units a month which just earns 1% a month (see Exhibit 9.2, parts II and III), as well as the possible loss if the production becomes less than 570.

Result of the Return on Increment Asset Analysis.   At 490 units or lower, it does not pay to make the products. Beyond this level, it depends on the current cost of money to the firm. The money cost should be lower than the return on the incremental asset.

IV. ANALYSIS BASED ON THE RESIDUAL INCOME APPROACH

Every unit of manufactured good necessitates an investment of $6,884 in net working capital (see Exhibit 9.3). This is the average outstanding balance of the net working capital if monthly production is one unit. If the interest cost based on the cost of money to the firm is 1% a month, then $69 has to be added to the $2,092 variable cost to make per Exhibit 9.2. The result is shown in Exhibit 9.4.

Similarly an interest has to be added to the average monthly balance of the overhead cost component in the work in process and finished goods inventory. Since the average balance is $400,000 per Exhibit 9.3, the monthly interest is $4,000.

In like manner, since the option to buy needs an average net working capital of $1,875 for every one unit to be purchased every month per Exhibit 9.3, a 1% interest or $19 has to be incorporated in the cost to buy.

VOLUME SENSITIVITY ANALYSIS WITH IMPUTED INTEREST (Exhibit 9.4)

The sensitivity analysis will forewarn management of the possible consequences if the level of volume or costs varies from the expected level. The imputation of interest into the analysis in Exhibit 9.4 produces the following effects:

1. At the immediate expected monthly requirement of 500 units, it transforms the $4,000 total monthly cost savings under the make plan per Exhibit 9.2 to a $25,000 cost disadvantage per Exhibit 9.4,
2. It raises the crossover volume from 490 units a month before interest (Exhibit 9.2) to 570 after interest.

Result of the sensitivity analysis with imputed interest. At 500 units, it is cheaper to buy. The result of this is the opposite of the prior sensitivity analysis which disregarded the interest.

CROSSOVER QUANTITY

The crossover quantity is the turning point from a loss position to a profit situation. Thus, conceptually, the crossover quantity is the point at which one option is dropped in favor of another. The crossover quantity in the illustration is the monthly quantity at which the cost of buying the products equals the cost of making them. As may be noticed from the sensitivity analysis sheet in Exhibit 9.4, if interest were included, it is cheaper to buy if the company needs 500 units a month, but cheaper to make if it requires 600 units. Thus, the crossover rate should be between these two levels.

There are four methods of determining the crossover quantity: the variable cost advantage analysis technique, the variable cost advantage chart, the total cost chart, and the algebraic equation. The first two tools are illustrated, using interest at 12%.

Variable Cost Advantage Analysis (Exhibit 9.4)   Making the products gives the firm a variable cost advantage of $358 per unit, as the variable manufacturing cost is only $2,161 compared with the $2,519 buying price. See Exhibit 9.4, first column. On the other hand, the decision to make the product brings with it a fixed monthly charge of $204,000, irrespective of the level of production.

Thus, for every unit the company manufactures, it can recover $358 from the monthly fixed cost. To fully cover the $204,000, the company has to make 570 units ($204,000 divided by $358). At this level of production, the variable cost advantage of $358 per unit is just offset by the $204,000 fixed cost disadvantage. At 570 units, the differential cost analysis is:

	Variable cost per unit	Total cost for 570 units
Cost to make		
Variable cost	$2,161	$1,232,000
Product overhead		204,000
Total cost to make		1,436,000
Cost to buy	2,519	1,436,000
Differential cost	$ 358	—

Variable Cost Advantage Crossover Chart (Exhibit 9.5).   The decision to make carries with it the risk that should the production be lower than the crossover quantity, the company losses. On the other hand, the decision generates a profit area which can be realized if the production exceeds the crossover quantity. This risk-profit balance is demonstrated by the variable cost advantage chart in the Exhibit 9.5.

If the firm produces 1,000 units, a $358,000 variable cost advantage is generated. However, from this is deducted the $204,000 monthly fixed costs, giving a net cost savings of $154,000.

The crossover quantity is the point where the total variable cost advantage line of the make option crosses the total fixed cost disadvantage line. The crossing is at 570 units. At the 570 crossover production units, the total variable cost advantage is just enough to cover the fixed costs.

The savings will be enhanced, at the rate of $358 per unit, if the production volume goes beyond the crossover point. On the other hand, if the company decides not to produce in any single month, it loses the $204,000 fixed costs.

V. OTHER CONSIDERATIONS

Cost Structure Risk Analysis.   The analysis should consider the options not in isolation but also in relation to the overall company operations. For instance, if the company has currently a very small percentage of fixed costs in relation to total costs, the company could still afford to add to its fixed costs and therefore consider the make option more favorably.

On the contrary, if the company has a very high level of fixed costs, adding the fixed costs for the make option may unduly increase the risk level of the firm.

If the incremental resources are financed by debt, the debt/equity ratio may be substantially changed, thus magnifying the financial risk.

Value of Intangible Benefits.   Any decision has to include not only the factors cited, but other intangible benefits and disadvantages as well. For instance, the analysis has not yet considered the impact of a more steady supply of products or finished goods inventory, and the possible additional sales due to the more ready availability of the product.

Furthermore, the in-house manufacture may also lead to higher product quality. This, in turn, may bring up the demand for the product and, consequently, enable the firm to raise the selling prices. These factors are discussed in Chapter 13, Analyzing Plant Automation Projects.

The incremental analysis used in the make or buy decision as illustrated is of a short-run nature. This means that no long-term costs are involved. Long-term costs are those which will benefit over several years, like the purchase of equipment or R&D work. If there are significant amounts of long-term costs the incremental analysis will require the use of the time value of money approach. This subject is discussed in Chapter 12, Analyzing Equipment Acquisitions.

EXHIBIT 9.1:
Differential Cost Without Imputed Interest

	Cost per unit	Cost for 500 units in $1,000
Cost to make		
Variable costs		
Raw materials	$ 900	$ 450
Production labor	1,100	550
Utilities and other variable costs	92	46
Total variable costs	$2,092	$1,046
Fixed costs—product overhead		200
Total cost to make		$1,246
Cost to buy	$2,500	$1,250
Incremental (decremental) cost to make		
Total		($ 4)
Variable cost only	($ 408)	

EXHIBIT 9.2:
Volume Sensitivity Analysis Without Imputed Interest

	Variable cost per unit	TOTAL COST (dollars in $1,000)						
		400 units	490 units	500 units	570 units	600 units	1000 units
I. Incremental cost								
Cost to make per month, interest excluded								
Variable cost	$2,092	$ 837	$1,025	$1,046	$1,192	$1,255	$2,092
Fixed cost		200	200	200	200	200	200
Total cost		1,037	1,225	1,246	1,392	1,455	2,292
Cost to buy per month	2,500	1,000	1,225	1,250	1,425	1,500	2,500
Incremental (decremental) cost to make	($ 408)	$ 37	$ 0	($ 4)	($ 33)	($ 45)	($ 208)
II. Incremental net resources								
Net resources if to make								
Variable	$6,884	$2,754	$3,373	$3,442	$3,924	$4,130	$6,884
Fixed, Exhibit 9.3		400	400	400	400	400	400
Total if to make	$6,884	$3,154	$3,773	$3,842	$4,324	$4,530	$7,284
Net resources if to buy	1,875	750	919	938	1,069	1,125	1,875
Incremental resources if to make	$5,009	$2,404	$2,854	$2,905	$3,255	$3,405	$5,409
III. Return on incremental investment								
Monthly return on investment	8.1%	-1.5%	0.0%	0.1%	1.0%	1.3%	3.8%
Annual return	97.7%	-18.4%	0.0%	1.7%	12.0%	15.8%	46.1%

EXHIBIT 9.3:
Incremental Resource Analysis

	Cost per manufactured unit (Exhibit 9.1)	Average inty	Duration in months	Resources
I. Resources required to make the product				
Variable resources per unit per month				
Raw materials	$ 900	$ 900	3	$ 2,700
Goods in process inventory				
Raw material component*	900	900	2	1,800
Labor component†	1,100	550	2	1,100
Other components†	92	46	2	92
Finished goods inventory	2,092	2,092	1	2,092
Total inventories				7,784
Less: Suppliers' credit	900		1	900
Net variable resources per unit				$ 6,884
	Required per month			
Total fixed resources				
Goods in process inventory				
Fixed cost component	$200,000	$100,000	2	$200,000
Finished goods inventory				
Fixed cost component	200,000	200,000	1	200,000
Total fixed resources				$400,000

EXHIBIT 9.3:
Incremental Resource Analysis (*continued*)

	Cost per manufactured unit (Exhibit 9.1)	Average inty	Duration in months	Resources
II. Resources required to buy the product				
Variable resources				
Finished goods inventory	$ 2,500	$ 2,500	1.25	$ 3,125
Less: Suppliers' credit	2,500	2,500	0.5	1,250
Net variable resources per unit				$ 1,875
III. Incremental net resources				
Incremental resources to make				
Variable resources, per unit per month				$ 5,009
Fixed resources, per month				$400,000

*All raw materials are required at the beginning of the production process. Hence the average inventory level is the same as the requirement per unit.

†The inputs are required in staggered amounts and spread out evenly throughout the production process. Hence the average inventory is one-half of the requirement per manufactured unit.

EXHIBIT 9.4:
Volume Sensitivity Analysis with Imputed Interest (dollars in $1,000)

	Variable cost per unit	400 units	490 units	500 units	570 units	600 units	1000 units
Cost to make							
Variable cost							
Before interest, Exhibit 9.1	$2,092						
Interest*	69						
Total	2,161	$ 864	$1,059	$1,080	$1,232	$1,297	$2,161
Product overhead							
Before interest		200	200	200	200	200	200
Interest		4	4	4	4	4	4
Total		204	204	204	204	204	204
Total cost to make		$1,068	$1,263	$1,284	$1,436	$1,501	$2,365
Cost to buy							
Variable cost							
Before interest, Exhibit 9.1	$2,500						
Interest*	$ 19						
Total	$2,519	$1,008	$1,234	$1,259	$1,436	$1,511	$2,519
Incremental (decremental) cost to make	($ 358)	$ 61	$ 29	$ 25	($ 0)	($ 11)	($ 154)

*Interest cost is computed at 1% a month based on the incremental net resources per Exhibit 9.3.

EXHIBIT 9.5:
Make Option Variable Cost Advantage Crossover Chart with Imputed Interest

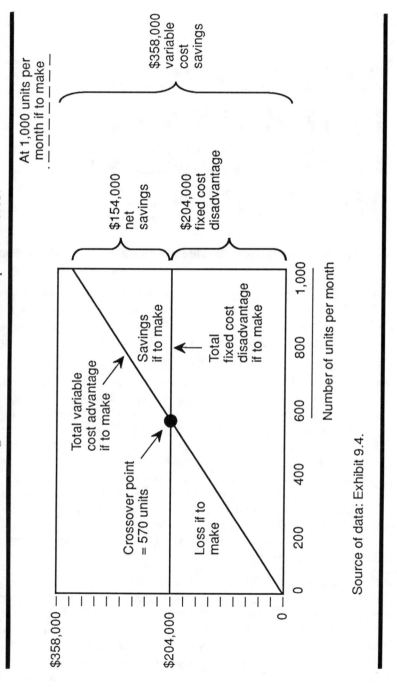

Source of data: Exhibit 9.4.

Chapter 10 _____

ANALYZING PRODUCT MIX ENHANCEMENT MEASURES

The purpose of product mix enhancement measures is to develop a group of healthy product lines that will improve the profitability of a firm.

There are two general types of short-term product mix measures: the deletion of unprofitable products and the introduction of promising ones.

Rationale.   The deletion of a product is effected on the premise that the reduction in the costs will exceed the decline in the sales revenues. The deletion will eliminate the sales revenues and its variable costs. Furthermore, if a department carries only one product, the deletion will also take out the departmental fixed costs. If the department handles several products, the elimination of a minor product may have minimal effect on the departmental fixed cost. In many cases the elimination of a product will not even dent the fixed costs at the corporate level.

The introduction of a new product will create the opposite effect. The introduction will add revenues and variable costs. It will add product departmental fixed costs if a new department will handle the product. The introduction of a new product is justified if the incremental revenues exceed the incremental costs.

Techniques Used.   This chapter introduces four new techniques which sharpen the analysis of product mix decisions. First, instead of having only two levels of costs, namely, the variable and the fixed costs, it uses three tiers—variable cost, departmental fixed cost, and corporate fixed cost. Second, instead of having only one contribution margin, it utilizes two— the contribution to departmental fixed cost and the contribution to corporate fixed cost. Third, it assigns interest and income tax to these three levels of costs. Fourth, it presents the root cost method of estimating working capital which is more refined than the one commonly used—the balance sheet method.

This chapter illustrates the applications of financial analysis techniques in the review of existing product lines to identify those for possible deletion. The appraisal of new products for possible introduction which do not call for heavy development and product introduction costs will follow the same procedures.

The techniques illustrated here are based on the assumption that the sales are fairly stable and that there are no measures to expand the sales. The evaluation of market expansion measures is demonstrated in the next chapter.

I. APPLICATIONS OF THE TECHNIQUES

Comparison With the Analysis of Short-term Cost Reduction Measures.
The analysis of product mix enhancement decisions is similar to that of cost reduction measures in that it involves fixed cost, variable cost, working capital, and imputed interest. However, in addition to these factors, the study of product mix decisions involves sales revenues.

For product mix enhancement measures, the relevant decision basis is not the differential cost or cost savings as in the case of cost reduction measures, but the contribution margin which is sales revenues less the variable costs. The contribution or profit margin determines the financial contribution of each product.

The evaluation of the products for possible deletion may be compared with that of cost reduction measures as follows:

	Cost reduction measures	*Product deletion review*
Number of options compared at a time	Usually two	Two or more
Revenues, costs, and resources evaluated	Fixed costs, variable costs, and working capital	Sales revenues, fixed costs, variable costs, and working capital
Major technique used	Differential cost analysis	Contribution margin analysis
Supporting techniques	Return on differential resources	Return on resources used
	Crossover quantity analysis	Break-even point analysis

Organizational Structure.   The application of the techniques are based on the following assumptions regarding the organizational arrangements within the firm:

1. The product departments are A, B, and C. Each department handles its own manufacturing and marketing operations.
2. The general management and administrative services are done for the corporation as a whole. The covering expenses are called corporate overhead.
3. The physical facilities are used mainly in the manufacturing operations. The facilities are shared by all the product departments.

II. CONTRIBUTION TO OVERHEAD ANALYSIS

The key intermediate profit figures are the contribution to departmental overhead and the contribution to corporate costs. The first is calculated by deducting from the sales revenues, the variable costs.

Tiers of Fixed Costs and Contribution Margin (Exhibit 10.1). The contribution to overhead analysis may produce distorted results unless all fixed costs are identified with the different organizational levels at which they are incurred.

Instead of lumping all fixed costs into one group, as is done under current practice, the fixed costs in Exhibit 10.1 are assigned to two tiers: (1) at the departmental level, and (2) at the corporate level.

Likewise, instead of having the typical one contribution to overhead line, the illustrated form has two: (1) the contribution to departmental overhead and (2) the contribution to corporate overhead. This two-level contribution to overhead line can be used effectively as follows:

1. Decisions on products made in multiproduct departments, as on products A1, A2, and A3 in the example, will focus on the contribution to departmental overhead. As long as a product has a contribution to departmental overhead, the product is profitable.
2. Actions on products of single-product departments, as on products B and C will be based on the contribution to the corporate overhead.
3. Decisions on product departments is based on the contribution to corporate overhead. As long as a department gives a contribution to corporate costs, it is feasible.

A profit in the appropriate contribution to overhead line indicates that the product or product department is financially desirable in the short term.

The departmental manufacturing and marketing overhead of Department A is not allocated to the products in the department as the amount of the overhead will not be affected by the elimination of any of the products. For similar reason, the corporate overhead is not allocated to the three departments.

Interest (Exhibit 10.1)   Interest is a cost. Like the other costs, it should be segregated and classified into the three categories of costs: variable or product cost, departmental overhead, and corporate cost.

The total interest included in Exhibit 10.1 is $733,000:

	Total	*Actual*	*Imputed*
Variable interest	$370,000	$370,000	$ —
Departmental interest	93,000	93,000	—
Corporate interest	270,000	70,000	200,000
Total interest	$733,000	$533,000	$200,000

The $533,000 actual interest represents the actual payments to creditors. The $200,000 imputed interest was calculated on that portion of the resources used which is financed by stockholders' equity. The $733,000 total interest is based on the total resources utilized.

Depreciation.   Depreciation is a sunk cost. By itself, it is irrelevant in the decision analysis for short-term measures. Hence it was not factored in Exhibit 10.2. However, it was considered in calculating the income tax as described next.

Income Tax.   The income tax reduction due to corporate overhead may be calculated as illustrated:

Deductible expenses	
Corporate overhead (assumed amount)	$2,400,000
Actual interest as shown in the above table	70,000
Depreciation (assumed amount)	200,000
Total tax deductible expenses	$2,670,000
Income tax reduction due to the deductible expenses—40%	$1,068,000

Results (Exhibit 10.1)   The contribution analysis as illustrated in Exhibit 10.1 highlights the following:

1. The profitable products are A1 and A2—see their contributions to departmental overhead. Because of their high profit margin, further studies should be made to ascertain the feasibility of enhancing the overall company profit by providing added support to these products so that their share in the total company sales could be augmented.
2. The marginal products—those with negligible profit or loss—are A3 (based on its contribution to departmental overhead) and B (based on its contribution to corporate overhead). Studies should be made to determine if costs can be reduced or sales volume or selling prices

raised. The performance of these products should be closely mon-
itored and decision to eliminate them should be made periodically.

3. Product C is a heavy loser (based on its contribution to corporate
overhead) and should be immediately discarded, unless it is a new
product with potential for growth.

The short-term contribution to general overhead can be increased from
$1,714,000 as shown in Exhibit 10.1, to $2,005,000 by eliminating the losing
products A3 and C:

Net profit before product deletions per Exhibit 10.1	$1,714,000
Additional profit to be realized by eliminating the following products:	
Product A3 per Exhibit 10.1	14,000
Product C per Exhibit 10.1	278,000
Net profit after product deletions per Exhibit 10.2	$2,005,000

Note: Figures may not add due to rounding.

The contribution margin statement after deleting the two products is
shown in Exhibit 10.2.

III. RESOURCE REQUIREMENTS ANALYSIS

Short-term decisions do not involve long-term assets as land, buildings,
and equipment. Hence the resource analysis is limited to working capital.
   Contribution margin analysis is usually not complete unless the cost
of interest on loans used to carry the working capital is added. If a firm has
no loans, then the stockholders are entitled to a yield on their investment,
part of which is used to finance the working capital.
   Before the interest can be estimated, or the return on the stockholders' equity calculated, it is necessary to approximate the value of
working capital used for each product.
   There are two ways of determining the working capital: (1) the balance sheet method, which is the traditional method, and (2) the root cost
technique, a new one. The balance sheet method estimates the total value
of each asset classification in the balance sheet, for example, the receivables, inventories, and payables. The root cost technique, which gives
more reasonable and refined results, calculates the individual cost composition of each asset, for example, the raw material, other variable manufacturing cost, variable marketing expenses, manufacturing and marketing
overhead, and other components of the inventories and receivables.
   Although the asset method is universally known and used, it has

severe limitations which could lead to disastrous decisions as will be illustrated later.

BALANCE SHEET METHOD (Exhibit 10.3)

Traditionally, the working capital requirements of existing operations or proposed programs are based on the receivables, payables, and inventories. These are the items appearing in a balance sheet; hence the term balance sheet method. Based on this method, the working capital requirements of product C are estimated in Exhibit 10.3.

Raw Materials Inventory.   The inventory represents the value of the materials from the time they are purchased up to the time they are issued to the production. The monthly cost of raw materials used is multiplied by the average time the inventories are held. The result is the raw material inventory at any one time. Thus, for product C, where the cost of raw materials used per month is $800,000, and the average inventory period is three months, the inventory at any one time is $2,400,000. This means that the inventory can supply the requirements for the *next* three months.

Accounts Payable for Raw Material Purchases.   If the monthly production and the inventory duration do not fluctuate, the value of raw materials used in any month will be the same as the value of the purchases. If the suppliers give a payment term of one month, the unpaid payable at the end of any month is equivalent to the purchases for the *past* month.

Since the effect of the suppliers' credit is to finance the raw materials inventory, the value of the payables is deducted from the inventory. The result is the net amount which requires financing from the banks or stockholders.

In the illustration for product C, the inventory duration is three months and the payment term is one month, thus giving a two-month inventory for $1,600,000 requiring financing.

Goods in Process Inventory.   The inventory value accumulates the costs from the time the materials are issued to the production process and the manufacturing expenses are incurred, up to the time the production is completed. Upon completion of the process, the costs are converted into finished goods inventory.

The monthly manufacturing cost or cost of sales for product C is $1,260,000. In the illustration it is assumed that these costs are gradually inputted into the production over a two-month production process period. For costing purposes, this is equivalent to putting in these costs at the middle of the production process, which is one month before the goods are completed. Hence the average duration is one month. Thus, to arrive at the average goods in process inventory, the monthly production cost is multiplied by the average duration of one month and not the manufacturing process duration of two months. Since the average duration is one month, the inventory is equivalent to the value of the inputs for the *past* month.

Finished Goods Inventory. This inventory is the value of goods produced but not yet sold. Since it takes two months for product C to stay as finished good inventory, the inventory at any time represents the cost of the goods expected to be sold during the *next* two months.

Accounts Receivables. This is the value of the sales, at *selling price* and *not at cost*, which have not yet been collected. At the time of the sale, the finished goods inventory, plus a markup, is converted into accounts receivables. As it takes three months to collect, the receivables at any time is equivalent to the sales for the *past* three months.

Time Reference. If the monthly prices, costs, and production and sales volumes do not fluctuate from month to month (which is an unusual case), the assets and liabilities may be estimated by applying the average duration period to the values of monthly raw materials used, cost of sales or sales, of either the past or future months. Otherwise, the following distinctions, noted earlier and contrasted here, should be observed.

Working capital item	Basis
Raw materials inventory	*Future* usage of raw materials
Accounts payable	*Past* purchases
Goods in process inventory	*Past* manufacturing cost
Finished goods inventory	*Future* product sales—based on the cost of the products
Accounts receivables	*Past* sales

In times when the volume of sales or production rises, the value of goods in process inventory and accounts receivables estimated by using the value of *future* manufacturing cost or sales will overstate the working capital requirements. Similarly, during a business downturn, the use of *past* material usage or cost of sales in determining the raw material or finished goods inventories will overstate the cash requirements.

THE ROOT COST METHOD

Concept (Exhibit 10.4). There are two perspectives of viewing the working capital requirements:

1. From the origins or roots of the costs (raw materials, other manufacturing variable costs, marketing variable costs, overhead, and others)
2. From the various stages of operations (inventory storage, production process, marketing operations, collection) where the costs are being held up prior to the collection of the sales

These perspectives are illustrated for Product C in Exhibit 10.4.

In the exhibit, the root costs are represented by the horizontal lines. The raw material cost line stretches for nine months—from the raw material storage all the way to the collection function. Hence, there is a raw material cost component in the working capital requirement during the following stages of operation:

Stages of operation	*Corresponding balance sheet item*
Raw material storage	Raw material inventory
Production	Goods in process inventory
Sales operations or finished goods storage	Finished goods inventory
Collection operations	Accounts receivable

Raw Material Component (Exhibit 10.5).   At any one time, the raw material cost component of the working capital (inventories and receivables) is $7,200,000. This amount represents the value of raw materials tied in for nine months from the time the materials are purchased, up to the time the sale is collected. The $7,200,000 is equivalent to the $800,000 monthly raw material usage, multiplied by the nine-month total duration. However, one out of the nine months' float is financed by the suppliers. This financing support takes out one month from the nine. Hence the net financing required for raw materials alone is eight months' requirements, which is $6,400,000. This is the amount shown in Exhibit 10.5.

Production Process (Exhibit 10.5).   Although the length of the production process is two months, the equivalent working capital requirement for materials and other manufacturing variable costs is only one month, as shown in the exhibit. This is so because the materials and other costs are brought into the process in uniform amounts throughout the entire process and not just at the start of production.

Sales Operation or Finished Goods Storage (Exhibit 10.5).   The average finished goods inventory storage time is two months. The average selling time is also two months. Since the selling effort is distributed throughout this period, the equivalent selling time for calculating the working capital requirement for marketing overhead is only one month. There is no working capital requirement for the marketing variable cost as most of this, as the sales commission is incurred as of the time of sale.

Collection (Exhibit 10.5).   All the manufacturing and marketing expenses are not reimbursed until collection. The collection process adds another three months to the working capital cycle.

As calculated in the exhibit, the last stage, which is collection, holds up a total of $4,350,000 in costs. These costs come from the different root costs—raw materials, other manufacturing variable costs, and others.

The working capital required by the various stages of operations as represented by the bottom line in Exhibit 10.5 is $9,790,000.

EVALUATION OF THE TWO METHODS

Limitations of the Balance Sheet Method.   The working capital derived from the balance sheet method has two key shortcomings: (1) the result is usually over- or understated and (2) the amounts are not segregated into that portion which is for variable cost and that which is for fixed cost.

MISSTATEMENT OF THE AMOUNT (EXHIBIT 10.3).   The working capital computed in the exhibit does not accurately represent the real cash *costs* to be financed.

The finished goods and work in process inventories and receivables include depreciation. Depreciation is not a cash cost and therefore is not going to be financed. What requires financing is the acquisition of the building or equipment which gives rise to the depreciation. Hence depreciation should be taken out from the working capital requirement.

Another item which bloats the financing requirement is the allocated general overhead. This is an allocated cost, and hence any decision on product C should disregard this cost. The total general overhead remains fairly the same, whether the production of product C is changed or abolished.

On the other hand, in cases where the operations result in a loss, the cash requirement for accounts receivable, which is based on sales, is not enough to cover the financing for all the costs, since the total of the costs is more than the sales. This is the case of product C.

Conversely, in instances where the sales revenues exceed the costs, as in product A1, the computed accounts receivable include an element of profit. This, of course, inflates the cash requirements since profit does not require financing.

The key limitation of the balance sheet method is that the cash required during the collection period is based on the selling price of the products, and not on the cost. What requires financing is the cash cost (which is the basis of the cash payments) and not the sale. The changes in the selling price do not affect the cash required for the working capital, except for costs which are dependent on the selling price such as sales commissions.

VARIABLE AND FIXED COSTS.   In traditional practice, interest is usually considered a fixed cost. In the few instances where interest is detailed into fixed and variable expenses, interest on loans used to finance receivables and inventories is usually considered as variable cost since receivables and inventories fluctuate with sales volume.

However, some of the cost components of inventories and receivables are actually fixed costs—as manufacturing and marketing overhead. The interest on the working capital required for the fixed cost should be treated as fixed cost. However, this distinction is not provided for by the balance sheet method.

ROOT COST METHOD AS A PLANNING TOOL (EXHIBIT 10.5). The root cost table is an effective visual tool in anticipating the changes in the working requirements and interest charges arising from fluctuations in the root costs or in the duration periods. For instance, a $100,000 increase in the monthly raw material cost translates to an $800,000 rise in the working capital requirements as the total duration period of the raw material cost, from the date of the purchase of the materials up to the collection of the accounts receivables is eight months. This duration is after the one-month purchase credit.

Similarly, a one-month reduction in the collection period of receivables cuts down the working capital required by $1,450,000. This is one-third of the $4,350,000 requirement for a three-month collection period.

Applicability of the Two Methods. The balance sheet method is ideal for use in analyzing other companies, based mainly on the published financial statements, primarily the balance sheets. Detailed financial information, which is required by the root cost method, are usually not available to outsiders.

For internal use, the balance sheet method may be used for long-term forecasting, where the year-to-year discrepancies in the calculated amounts may not be so material. The method may also be used in rough short-term analysis, where only preliminary estimates are desired. This is the method used in the analysis of sales expansion measures in Chapter 11.

The root cost method is best suited for evaluation of short-term options in cases where some or all of the following are present: (1) the differences in the profitability, capital requirements, and risk of the alternatives are quite close and (2) the profit margins (difference between sales and cost of sales) do not vary widely from product to product. In both cases, more refined estimates are required.

IV. INTEREST AND RETURN ON RESOURCE APPROACHES

BASIS OF THE INTEREST CHARGE AND RETURN ON INVESTMENT

The foregoing discussion illustrated the tools used in determining the working capital needs of product C. The working capital requirements for the variable costs of products A1, A2, A3, and B, as well as for the departmental manufacturing and marketing overhead of Departments A and B may be similarly computed.

The land, buildings, and equipment shared by the three departments are best valued at imputed cost, which is the price at which they could be sold. The total assets to be financed, based on the root cost method for working capital are summarized in part I of Exhibit 10.6.

The resources required in product deletion decisions are used in (1) calculating the imputed interest charge which is factored into the cost of the products or (2) determining the rate of return on the resources.

IMPUTED INTEREST

The capital requirements are used in charging the interest to the different products and departments. For the purpose of the exercise, the products and departments are charged 1% a month for the use of capital.

The 1% is assumed to represent the cost of money to the firm. This is either the cost of borrowing or the minimum return before tax expected by the stockholders.

Since the working capital required for the variable costs of product C is $7,330,000, as computed in Exhibit 10.5 and summarized in Exhibit 10.6, a variable interest cost of $73,000 a month is included in the product costing in Exhibit 10.1. Similarly, a departmental interest cost of $25,000 a month, or 1% of the $2,460,000 working capital required for fixed costs of Department C, is added to the departmental costs.

The $2,670,000 corporate overhead in Exhibit 10.6 includes a 1% monthly interest charge on the $24,000,000 imputed value of the land, buildings, and equipment, and the $3,000,000 working capital for corporate overhead per Exhibit 10.6.

RATE OF RETURN ON RESOURCES

The contribution to overhead shown in Exhibit 10.1 is after deducting a 1% monthly charge on the assets employed. The negative contribution to departmental overhead of product A3 and product C implies that the profit margin is not sufficient to cover a 1% monthly interest charge. The positive margin for all the other products means that they can generate a profit on top of the basic imputed interest.

The contribution margins of the different products are summarized and compared with the capital requirements in parts II and III of Exhibit 10.6. This shows that product A1 generates a monthly contribution to overhead of $4,050,000, which is 19.2% of the $21,040,000 investment in variable capital. The 19.2% monthly rate translates into a 231% annual rate after the 12% pretax or 7.2% posttax interest, or 238% including interest. It should be noted that this seemingly high rate of return is before the

Department A manufacturing and marketing overhead and corporate fixed costs.

After deducting the departmental overhead, Department A as a whole contributes only $1,980,000 to the corporate overhead. This contribution, which is after deducting the 12% imputed interest, gives a 68% annual yield on the resources employed in the department.

On the overall, the company generates only $112,000 after interest and income tax, which is 2% on the total value of the capital employed.

Effect of Product Deletions.   The phasing out of products A3 and C will take out (1) the variable costs of these products, (2) the fixed costs of Department C, and (3) the working capital required for these costs. This move will also raise the contribution to the general overhead of the company from $1,714,000 per Exhibit 10.1 to $2,005,000 per Exhibit 10.2.

The deletion of products A3 and C will raise the total corporate return on total capital, after providing for the 12% interest, from 2% per Exhibit 10.6 to 7% per Exhibit 10.7.

V. RISK ANALYSIS

The risks involved in the deletion of products may be evaluated through the use of the cost structure risk analysis and break-even point techniques. These are illustrated next. Sensitivity analysis, which was applied in the cost reduction measures, may also be utilized.

Cost Structure Risk Analysis (Exhibit 10.7).   Generally, the higher the fixed costs in relation to the variable costs, the less flexible is the company, and the higher the risk it takes.

Before the product deletions, Department C has the highest relative fixed costs, which is 43% of its variable cost. This is calculated in Exhibit 10.6. On the other hand, Department B has the lowest at 13%. After including the corporate fixed costs, the total fixed costs for the company is 43% of its variable costs. The deletion of products A3 and C will cause the companywide fixed cost percentage to nudge to 46%. (See Exhibit 10.7) The rise in the percentage is the effect of taking out product A3, which will eliminate all its variable costs but without in any way reducing the departmental or corporate fixed costs.

Break-even Point Analysis for the Entire Company.   The product deletions push up the fixed cost relative to the variable cost, implying that the new cost structure carries more risk. On the other hand, the deletions depress the cash profit break-even point sales volume (BEPSV). Without the product deletions, the BEPSV is 97% of the sales. After the deletions, the BEPSV is reduced to 91%:

	Before deletions	*After deletions**
Projected sales	$23,450,000[†]	$21,275,000
Variable costs	16,300,000[†]	14,104,000
Contribution to departmental overhead	7,150,000[†]	7,171,000
As percentage of sales	30%	34%
Fixed costs	6,963,000[‡]	6,498,000
Break-even point sales volume	22,837,000	19,278,000
As a percentage of sales	97%	91%

*From Exhibit 10.8.

†From Exhibit 10.1.

‡From Exhibit 10.6.

This apparent inconsistency—the rise in the fixed cost relative to the variable cost, accompanied by a decline in the BEPSV—is explained by the substantial improvement in the contribution to department overhead as a percentage of sales. The contribution is 30% before the product deletions and 34% after.

Break-even Point Analysis By Product (Exhibit 10.8).   The foregoing analysis is based on the total company performance. This analysis may be supplemented by one which is on a product basis. An example of a break-even point analysis by product is illustrated in Exhibit 10.8. Note the changing treatment of fixed costs: for each of products A1 and A2, there are no fixed costs since the fixed costs incurred by Department A are for both A1 and A2. These fixed costs are not allocated to the products. On the other hand, all the fixed costs of Department B are charged to product B since the department makes only one product.

Since each of products A1 and A2 has no direct fixed costs, the break-even point for each cannot be calculated. Instead, the break-even point is computed for Department A which markets A1 and A2.

VI. CONTRIBUTION MARGIN BY MARKET TERRITORY

The prior discussions in this chapter are concerned with the analysis for a product deletion decision. The illustrations have assumed that the subject company operates two departments—each department being engaged in the manufacturing and marketing of its products.

The same general principles of analysis may be applied regarding decisions affecting the future of marketing territories or area. However, modifications have to be made to suit the nature of the costs and the organizational structure of the firm.

Contribution Margin Statement (Exhibit 10.9)   Exhibit 10.9 illustrates how the contribution margin statement may be constructed. The statement is based on the following assumptions regarding the operations of the company:

1. The division has only one manufacturing plant and one marketing department.
2. The division operates in two marketing territories.
3. In Marketing Area I, all the salespeople sell the two products—X and Y. In Area II, the salespeople handle only one product—X.

Levels of Variable Costs.   The contribution margin statement has identified two levels of variable costs: those which can be directly traced to specific products, such as raw materials used and sales commissions, and those which cannot be directly identified, such as gasoline of the sales vehicles. In the contribution margin statement, the former class is considered as product cost and the latter, marketing territory variable costs. Since Area II handles only one product, the gasoline of the sales vehicles is considered as product cost.

Levels of Fixed Costs.   The statement uses three levels of overhead: at the marketing area or territory level, at the divisional level, and at the corporate (general overhead) level.

The statement has avoided the allocation of any variable or fixed costs.

Income Tax and Sales Expansion and Future Benefit Costs.   To simplify the presentation, the statement has disregarded income tax, sales expansion costs, and future benefit costs. The income tax may be incorporated in the statement in the way it was shown in Exhibit 10.2.

The analysis of sales expansion cost is demonstrated in Chapter 11, while the accounting for future benefit costs is illustrated in Chapter 24.

EXHIBIT 10.1:
Monthly Contribution Margin for Product Deletion Analysis (dollars in $1,000)

	Company total	DEPARTMENT A				DEPT. B	DEPT. C
		Total	Product A1	Product A2	Product A3	Product B	Product C
Number of units	10,000	9,000	8,000	500	500	500	500
Sales	$23,450	$20,890	$18,400	$1,400	$1,090	$1,475	$1,085
Less: Product or variable costs							
Raw materials	4,550	2,900	1,600	550	750	850	800
Other manufacturing variable costs	9,000	8,620	8,000	470	150	280	100
Marketing variable costs	2,380	2,120	1,840	120	160	150	110
Variable interest	370	285	210	22	53	12	73
Total direct costs	$16,300	$13,925	$11,650	$1,162	$1,113	$1,292	$1,083
Contribution to departmental overhead	7,150	6,965	6,750	238	(23)	183	2
Income tax	2,860	2,786	2,700	95	(9)	73	1
Contribution after income tax	$ 4,290	$ 4,179	$ 4,050	$ 143	($ 14)	$ 110	$ 1
Less: Departmental overhead							
Manufacturing overhead	3,170	2,700				120	350
Marketing overhead	1,030	900				40	90
Departmental interest	93	65				3	25
Total departmental overhead	$ 4,293	$ 3,665				$ 163	$ 465
Income tax	1,717	1,466				65	186
Departmental overhead after tax	2,576	2,199				98	279
Contribution to general overhead	$ 1,714	$ 1,980				$ 12	($ 278)

EXHIBIT 10.2:
Monthly Contribution Margin of Products to be Retained (dollars in $1,000)

	Company total	DEPARTMENT A			DEPT. B
		Total	Product A1	Product A2	Product B
Number of units	12,670	8,500	8,000	500	500
Sales	$21,275	$19,800	$18,400	$1,400	$1,475
Less: Product or variable costs					
Raw materials	3,000	2,150	1,600	550	850
Other manufacturing variable costs	8,750	8,470	8,000	470	280
Marketing variable costs	2,110	1,960	1,840	120	150
Variable interest	244	232	210	22	12
Total direct costs	$14,104	$12,812	$11,650	$1,162	$1,292
Contribution to departmental overhead	7,171	6.988	6,750	238	183
Income tax	2,868	2,795	2,700	95	73
Contribution after income tax	$ 4,303	$ 4,193	$ 4,050	$ 143	$ 110
Less: Departmental overhead					
Manufacturing overhead	2,820	2,700			120
Marketing overhead	940	900			40
Departmental interest	69	65			3
Total departmental overhead	$ 3,829	$ 3,665			$ 163
Income tax	1,531	1,466	0	0	65
Departmental overhead after tax	2,297	2,199	0	0	98
Contribution to general overhead	$ 2,005	$ 1,994	$ 4,050	$ 143	$ 12

EXHIBIT 10.3:

Product C—Working Capital—Balance Sheet Method (dollars in $1,000)

Working capital item	Basis	Monthly cost	Average duration in months	Total required
Raw materials inventory	Raw materials used	$ 800	3	$2,400
Less: Suppliers' credit	Raw materials used	800	1	800
Net financing requirement for raw materials inventory		800	2	1,600
Goods in process inventory	Cost of sales	1,260	1	1,260
Finished goods inventory	Cost of sales	1,260	2	2,520
Accounts receivable	Sales	1,085	3	3,255
Total				$8,635

Source of data: Traditional income statement using the full costing method. The cost of sales includes departmental manufacturing overhead and depreciation.

EXHIBIT 10.4:
Product C—Working Capital Root Cost Chart

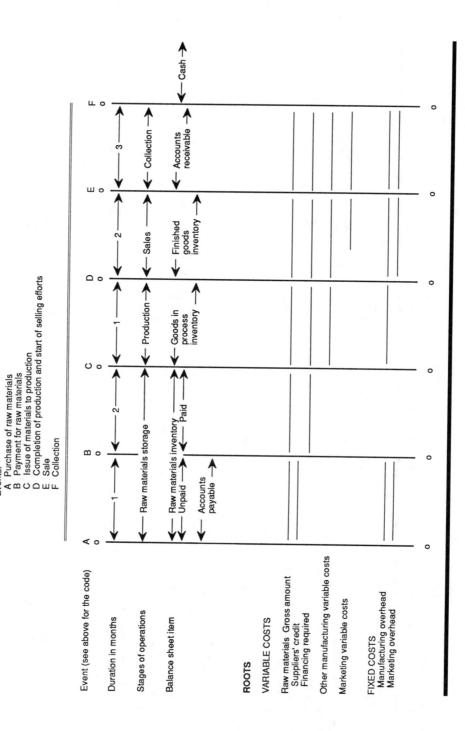

EXHIBIT 10.5:
Product C— Working Capital: Root Cost Method (dollars in $1,000)

				STAGE OF OPERATION				
	Cost basis	Material storage	Suppliers' credit	Production	Sales	Collection	Total duration	Working capital
Duration								
Duration of operation		3	(1)	2	2	3		
Average duration of working capital								
Raw materials	$800	3	(1)	1	2	3	8	$6,400
Other manufacturing variable costs	100			1	2	3	6	600
Marketing variable costs	110					3	3	330
Manufacturing overhead	350			1	2	3	6	2,100
Marketing overhead	90				1	3	4	360
								$9,790
Working capital by operation								
For variable costs								
Raw materials	$800	$2,400	($800)	$ 800	$1,600	$2,400		$6,400
Other manufacturing variable costs	100	0	0	100	200	300		600
Marketing variable costs	110			0		330		330
Total		$2,400	($800)	$ 900	$1,800	$3,030		$7,330
For overhead								
Manufacturing overhead	$350			$ 350	$ 700	$1,050		$2,100
Marketing overhead	90			0	90	270		360
Total				350	790	1,320		2,460
Combined		$2,400	($800)	$1,250	$2,590	$4,350		$9,790

EXHIBIT 10.6:

Products Before Deletions (dollars in $1,000)

	Company total	DEPARTMENT A				DEPT. B	DEPT. C
		Total	Product A1	Product A2	Product A3	Product B	Product C
I. Capital required							
For variable costs	$36,995	$28,460	$21,040	$2,160	$5,260	$1,205	$7,330
For departmental overhead	9,315	6,525				330	2,460
For corporate overhead	3,000						
Property, plant, and equipment	24,000						
Total	$73,310	$34,985	$21,040	$2,160	$5,260	$1,535	$9,790
II. Profit margin after interest and income tax (From Exhibit 10.2)							
Contribution to departmental overhead		$ 1,980	$ 4,050	$ 143	($ 14)		
Contribution to corporate overhead							
Net profit	$ 112					$ 12	($ 278)
III. Return							
Return on top of 12% pretax interest							
Monthly	0.2%	5.7%	19.2%	6.6%	−0.3%	0.8%	−2.8%
Annual	1.8%	67.9%	231.0%	79.4%	−3.2%	9.4%	−34.0%
Return including 12% pretax interest							
Annual	9.0%	75.1%	238.2%	86.6%	4.0%	16.6%	−26.8%
IV. Cost structure before income tax (from Exhibit 10.2)							
Overhead							
Departmental overhead	$ 4,293	$ 3,665	$ 0	$ 0	$ 0	$ 163	$ 465
Corporate overhead	2,670	0	0	0	0		
Total	6,963	3,665	0	0	0	163	465
Variable costs	16,300	13,925	11,650	1,162	1,113	1,292	1,083
Total costs	23,263	17,590	11,650	1,162	1,113	1,455	1,548
Fixed costs as a percentage of variable costs	43%	26%	0%	0%	0%	13%	43%

EXHIBIT 10.7:
Products After Deletions (dollars in $1,000)

| | Company total | DEPARTMENT A | | | DEPT. B |
		Total	Product A1	Product A2	Product B
I. Capital required					
For variable costs	$36,995	$28,460	$21,040	$2,160	$1,205
For departmental overhead	6,855	6,525			330
For corporate overhead	3,000				
Property, plant, and equipment	24,000				
Total	$70,850	$34,985	$21,040	$2,160	$1,535
II. Profit margin after interest and income tax (From Exhibit 10.2)					
Contribution to departmental overhead		$ 1,994	$ 4,050	$ 143	$ 12
Contribution to corporate overhead					
Net profit	$ 403				
III. Return					
Return on top of 12% pretax interest					
Monthly	0.6%	5.7%	19.2%	6.6%	0.8%
Annual	7%	68%	231%	79%	9%
Return including 12% pretax interest					
Annual	14%	76%	238%	87%	17%
IV. Cost structure before income tax (From Exhibit 10.2)					
Overhead					
Product overhead	$ 3,828	$ 3,665		$ 0	$ 163
General overhead (assumed figure)	2,670	0	$ 0	0	
Total	6,498	3,665		0	163
Variable costs	14,104	12,812	11,650	1,162	1,292
Total costs	20,602	16,477	11,650	1,162	1,455
Fixed costs as a percentage of variable costs	46%	29%	0%	0%	13%

EXHIBIT 10.8:
Monthly Break-Even Point Analysis of Products to be Retained (dollars in $1,000)

	Company total	Total	Product A1	Product A2	Product B
			DEPARTMENT A		**DEPT. B**
			Product A1	*Product A2*	*Product B*
Projected sales*	$21,275	$19,800	$18,400	$1,400	$1,475
Variable costs*	$14,104	$12,812	$11,650	$1,162	$1,292
Contribution to overhead*	$ 7,171	$ 6,988	$ 6,750	$ 238	$ 183
As a percentage of sales	34%	35%	37%	17%	12%
Fixed costs[†]	$ 6,498	$ 3,665	$ 0	$ 0	$ 163
Break-even point sales volume	$19,278	$10,385			$1,316
As a percentage of sales	91%	52%			89%

*From Exhibit 10.2.

[†]From Exhibit 10.7, part IV.

261

EXHIBIT 10.9:
Contribution Margin by Product and Market Territory Before Income Tax (dollars in $1,000)

	Company total	Total	AREA I		AREA II
			Product X	Product Y	Product X
Sales	$26,000	$20,000	$15,000	$5,000	$6,000
Less: Product costs					
Manufacturing	12,750	9,750	7,500	2,250	3,000
Marketing	2,600	2,000	1,500	500	600
Interest	1,820	1,400	1,050	350	420
Total product costs	$17,170	$13,150	$10,050	$3,100	$4,020
Contribution to marketing territory variable costs	8,830	6,850	$ 4,950	$1,900	$1,980
Less: Marketing territory variable costs	2,000	2,000			
Contribution to marketing territory overhead	6,830	4,850			1,980
Marketing territory overhead	2,000	1,200			800
Contribution to divisional overhead	$ 4,830	$ 3,650			$1,180
Less: Divisional overhead					
Manufacturing	400				
Marketing	300				
Interest	200				
Total overhead	900				
Contribution to general overhead	$ 3,930				

Chapter 11

ANALYZING SALES EXPANSION MEASURES

Sales expansion measures are the programs that are intended to raise the sales volume by capturing market share or expanding the demand. The sales expansion measures studied here are those whose effects are short-term in nature, that is, those with immediate impact but whose impact is not anticipated to last long after the sales expansion programs have been terminated.

This chapter appraises the profitability of the following types of measures which seek to expand the sales by increasing the advertising budget, increasing the sales commission rates, reducing the selling prices, and extending the sales credit terms. This chapter treats sales expansion costs as a cost classification which is separate from that of fixed costs and variable costs.

Sales expansion cost leverage and crossover sales expansion cost are introduced in this chapter. The other tools employed are the modified contribution margin form of income statement and crossover sales volume.

The factors input in the study are imputed interest, income tax, and risk. Inflation is not included due to the short-term nature of the measures.

I. NATURE OF SALES EXPANSION MEASURES

RATIONALE OF SALES EXPANSION MEASURES
(Exhibit 11.1)

The sales expansion measures analyzed in this chapter are the activities aimed to raise the sales volume by capturing market share in established markets or by building up the demand. The measures used in the illustrations are those which do not have long-term effects; that is, the sales volumes are expected to revert to their original levels once the measures are stopped. These types of measures are applicable particularly to firms dealing in commodities, that is, where brand or customer loyalty is not developed.

Sales expansion measures entail a great degree of risk due to the involvement of two unknown factors: the reaction of the competition and the response of the customers.

Sales expansion measures are pursued on the premise that the variable margin (sales less the variable costs) of the incremental sales units is expected to be higher than the additional sales expansion costs. Thus, in Exhibit 11.1, even if the sales expansion cost is expected to go up by $30,000, this is more than covered by the additional $40,000 improvement in variable margin.

IMPLICATIONS ON UNIT COSTS AND UNIT REVENUES

Specific measures employed to build up the sales usually cause one of the following: (1) escalation in certain costs per unit of sale or (2) decline in sales revenue per unit.

The unit costs which may rise as a result of a sales expansion program are:

1. Advertising and/or promotion
2. Sales commissions
3. Distributors' discounts
4. Warranty
5. Production cost—due to the enhancement of product quality
6. Interest and collection expenses—due to the lengthening of collection period
7. Bad debts—due to the lowering of the sales credit standards

On the other hand, the revenue per unit of sales may be reduced due to the following:

1. Decline in selling price per unit
2. Increase in sales discounts
3. Decrease in interest income from notes receivables arising from installment sales

The escalations in expenses or reductions in revenues listed above are called sales expansion costs in this chapter.

SALES EXPANSION COSTS AS NEITHER FIXED NOR VARIABLE COSTS

The two traditional classifications of costs in relation to their behavior due to changes in the sales volume are the variable and the fixed costs. The total variable cost fluctuate in direct relation to the sales volume changes, while the total fixed cost is constant irrespective of the sales volume. Variable and fixed costs are discussed in more detail in Chapter 8.

Sales expansion costs, when used in building up sales volume, do not fit into the classification of either variable or fixed cost. Sales expansion cost, if used as an instrument of pushing up sales, rises with the sales. However, the rate of change of the cost is usually higher than the rate of increase of the sales. For instance, in Exhibit 11.1, if the present total advertising cost is $30,000 and the firm wants to enhance the sale by 20%, the advertising will have to be pumped up not just by 20% but by a higher rate, which is 100% in the illustration.

Thus, in doing analysis work, or preparing budgets and financial projections, sales expansion costs should be treated differently from the variable costs and fixed costs.

TECHNIQUES USED IN THE ANALYSIS

The analysis of sales expansion measures is divided into two parts: the study of individual measures and the study of the relative merits of all available measures. The analysis for each part is outlined here.

Study of the Individual Measures
- Profitability statements on a monthly basis are prepared under two assumptions: one assuming that the specific measure is undertaken and the other that is not implemented. Since the measures have short-term effects, depreciation is disregarded.
- Where working capital is affected by the measure, the changes in working capital requirements are estimated. The balance sheet method, using direct costing for the finished goods and goods in process inventories, is used. The other methods available are (1) the balance sheet method using the full costing for the inventories, which is the traditional method, and (2) the root cost method, which is discussed in Chapter 10. Direct and full costing methods are covered in Chapter 17.
- A 12% interest charge, representing the assumed cost of money, is imputed based on the working capital requirements. No interest charge is imputed on the investments in property, plant, and equipment, as these long-term investments are not affected by the short-term measures.

- Sensitivity analysis is used due to the unpredictability of the response of sales volume to the sales expansion measures. Crossover sales volume and crossover sales expansion costs are employed.

Comparative Study of all Available Measures
- The alternative measures are ranked according to their crossover sales volume, profitability, and return on investment.

The individual sales expansion measures studied in this chapter are those which expand the sales by increasing the advertising budget, increasing the sales commission rates, reducing the selling prices, and extending the sales credit terms.

II. INCREASING THE ADVERTISING BUDGET

One popular way of expanding sales is by embarking on an aggressive advertising program. The marketing department, with the support of the advertising agency, prepares the advertising program and the budget required to push the sales to a target level. For instance, the advertising budget may have to be doubled in order to raise the sales by 25%. The advertising requirements and the sales forecasts consider the possible response of the customers and reaction by the competition.

To analyze the financial impact of an aggressive marketing program as part of a sales growth strategy, it is necessary to prepare comparative profitability statements as exemplified in Exhibit 11.2. The form of this statement is similar to that used in Exhibit 10.2 of the prior chapter. The only differences are that (1) a new line, sales expansion cost, was added in Exhibit 11.2 of this chapter; (2) the balance after deducting the variable costs from the sales revenues is renamed variable margin; and (3) the income tax is shown in only one line.

Present Operations (Exhibits 11.2 and 11.3). The first column of the income statement shows the current level of monthly revenues, costs, and contribution to corporate overhead after taxes.

The working capital required by the measure is estimated in Exhibit 11.3. To simplify the calculations, the balance sheet method, rather than the root cost technique, is used in estimating the working capital. These two methods are compared in Chapter 10.

The information in the first column of Exhibit 11.2 serves as the starting point in estimating the effects of an accelerated advertising campaign. It is also utilized as the benchmark in evaluating the profitability of the sales expansion measure.

Target Advertising Cost and Target Sales Volume (Exhibit 11.2). The second column of Exhibit 11.2 indicates the amount of the escalated advertising expense ($200,000 a month) and the volume of sales (1,250 units) which is projected to be generated by the beefed-up advertising program. This information is usually supplied by the marketing department.

If the target sales can be achieved based on the advertising budget, then the firm will be able to enhance its contribution to corporate overhead after tax, from $168,000 to $180,000.

Crossover Sales Volume and Target Advertising Cost. In many cases, given the budgeted advertising cost, the sales generated are either under or over the target. It is very difficult to forecast the sales to be realized by an aggressive advertising campaign or, for that matter, any sales expansion measure, due to the unexpected response of the industry and the customers. It is therefore advisable to determine the sales volume level which is required so that the firm may be able to maintain its current level of profitability, assuming that the advertising budget is used up.

This crossover sales volume may be determined by the formula

crossover sales volume = present quantity
+ required incremental quantity

$$\text{required incremental quantity} = \frac{\text{increase in advertising cost}}{\text{variable margin per unit at present}}$$

$$= \frac{\$100,000}{\$480} = 210$$

Hence,

crossover sales volume = 1,000 + 210 = 1,210 units

(Note: As in actual financial analysis work, all the calculations in the exhibits and in the text were rounded off and hence may not tally exactly.)

If the entire expanded advertising budget of $200,000 a month were spent, and the sales hit just the crossover volume of 1,210 units instead of the 1,250 target, the after-tax contribution to corporate overhead is maintained at $168,000 a month. This is proven in the third column of Exhibit 11.2.

Crossover Advertising Cost and Target Sales Volume. There may be instances where the company may decide to exceed the advertising budget so as to achieve the sales target. Just how far the budget may be exceeded without reducing the profit can be easily determined if the crossover advertising cost is known. The crossover cost is the maximum amount which may be spent without reducing the current profit level. At the target sales volume, the crossover advertising expense formula is:

$$\text{crossover advertising expense} = \text{present total advertising expense}$$
$$+ \text{ increase in total variable margin if the target sales volume is attained}$$
$$= \$100,000 + (\$600,000 - \$480,000)$$
$$= \$220,000$$

At the crossover advertising expense level, all the incremental variable margin of $120,000 is used to augment the advertising budget. If the sales target of 1,250 units is attained by spending $220,000 in advertising instead of the $200,000 budget, the contribution to corporate overhead of $168,000 will be maintained. See the last column of Exhibit 11.2.

When to Stop Advertising (Exhibit 11.2).   In cases where advertising produces immediate results, but generates no long-term effects, it is usually good practice to keep on advertising as long as the incremental variable margin is more than enough to cover the additional advertising cost. Once the incremental variable margin falls below the additional sales expansion cost, the advertising program has to be reassessed—and, most likely, stopped.

Thus, after spending $100,000 in advertisements, which generates a sale of 1,000 units and brings in $480,000 in variable margin (first column of Exhibit 11.2), the advertising may be continued by spending another $100,000 only if the incremental expenditure will cause the sale of at least an additional 210 units, which generates an additional $100,000 in variable margin ($580,000 less $480,000). See the third column compared with the first column of Exhibit 11.2.

III. INCREASING THE SALES COMMISSION RATES

Higher sales commission rates may be employed instead of an augmented advertising budget. Where the sales are made through distributors rather than the salespeople, a similar incentive may be given the dealers in the form of a higher discount—or a lower selling price to them.

Present Operations (Exhibit 11.4).   In Exhibit 11.2, sales commission is treated as a variable cost as it varies in direct proportion to the sales. In the example given, it is assumed to always be 5% of sales. However, in Exhibit 11.4, commission is considered as a sales expansion cost, as management will try to lift the sales by hiking the commission rate—from 5% to 10%.

Except for the placement of the sales commissions and advertising expenses, the first column of Exhibit 11.2 is the same as that of Exhibit 11.4. The after-tax contribution to corporate overhead in the first columns of the two exhibits are also the same—$168,000.

Target Sales Commission Rate and Target Sales Volume. The second column of Exhibit 11.4 shows the expected effect on the profitability, if the doubling of the commission rate from 5% to 10% achieves a 25% improvement in sales.

The increased commission rates may be made across the board. As an alternative, the higher commission may apply only to sales per salesperson above a certain level, with the old commission rates being used for the sales below the given level, but with the weighted new commission rate being double the old rate.

Target Sales Commission and Crossover Sales Volume (Exhibit 11.5). Since the hiked sales commission rate may not achieve the target sales volume of 1,250 units, management should know the crossover sales volume based on the new commission rate. The formula for this crossover volume is similar but not the same as the one for the crossover volume at the target advertising cost. The difference is due to the fact that the dollar amount of the target advertising cost is known beforehand. On the other hand, the dollar amount of the target commission is not given; only the rate (10% in this case) is given.

The formula, and the calculation for the 1,154 crossover sales volume at target sales commission rate is shown in Exhibit 11.5. The third column of Exhibit 11.3 reveals that, by using the target commission rate of 10%, and the crossover sales volume of 1,154 units, the after-tax contribution to corporate overhead of $168,000 is the same as that under the present conditions.

Crossover Sales Commission Rate and Target Sales Volume. The crossover commission expense of $158,000 in the fourth column of Exhibit 11.4 is computed in the same manner as the crossover advertising expense at target sales volume. The crossover commission rate is 12.6% of the total sales. This means that even though the overall commission is raised from 5% to 12.6%, and not just to 10%, the company can still maintain its $168,000 monthly contribution to corporate overhead, provided the targeted sales rise of 25% is attained.

IV. REDUCING THE SELLING PRICES

The most effective way of pushing up the sales volume of commodities is by reducing the sales prices. However, the measure could boomerang if the competition will also lower their prices, thus creating a price war.

Effect on Costs (Exhibit 11.6). If the price is lowered, certain other costs will be proportionately scaled down. In the example in Exhibit 11.6, these other costs are:

	Percentage of present sales
Sales commissions	5%
Bad debts	3
Collection expenses	1
Interest on financing used to carry the receivables	2
Total	11%

A 5% reduction in the selling prices cuts down the contribution to departmental overhead before taxes not by 5% of the sales, but by 4.45% of the sales based on present prices.

	Percentage of present sales
Selling price reduction	5.00%
Less reduction in expenses—11% of 5% price reduction	0.55
Net effect on pre-tax profit	4.45%

Target Sales Expansion Cost and Target Sales Volume (Exhibit 11.6). In the second column of Exhibit 11.6, the $63,000 price reduction as a sales expansion cost is 5% of the $1,250,000 sales at present prices. The $7,000 savings in related sales expansion costs is 11% of the $63,000 price reduction or 0.55% of the $1,250,000 target sales at present prices.

Target Sales Expansion Cost and Crossover Sales Volume. If the firm implements the 5% price reduction, the company can still maintain its present profit even though the sales volume will advance by only 13.3% instead of the target 25%. See the third column of Exhibit 11.6.

Crossover Sales Expansion Cost and Target Sales Volume. For the measure to have the same contribution to corporate overhead as at present, the firm can afford to slash the prices by 8.6% as long as the target 25% improvement in sales volume is achieved.

At a sales volume of 1,250 units or $1,250,000 value based on present prices, the $108,000 price reduction in the fourth column in Exhibit 11.6 is 8.6% of the sales.

V. EXTENDING THE SALES CREDIT TERMS

Customers may be attracted not only by lower prices but also by easier terms of payment. However, this measure will build up the receivables faster than the rise in sales since the incremental payment period applies not only to the additional sales attracted by the measure but also to the usual sales.

Effect on Costs (Exhibit 11.7).   Hence, a higher sales volume brought about by a longer payment period has its costs: higher interest expense on the financing used to carry the receivables, more liberal provisions for doubtful accounts or write-off of bad debts, and higher collection expenses.

These expenses are treated as the sales expansion costs in the first column of Exhibit 11.7. The total of $60,000 under the current two-month credit term is 6% of sales.

If the payment term is doubled from two to four months, these expenses as a percentage of sales will also be doubled. Thus, the second and third columns of Exhibit 11.7 show the bad debts, collection expenses, and interest as 6%, 2%, and 4% of sales, respectively instead of the prior 3%, 1%, and 2%.

Crossover Sales Expansion Cost and Target Sales Volume (Exhibit 11.8). The maximum receivable-related expenses that may be spent on the sales of 1,250 units, without diminishing the $168,000 monthly contribution to corporate overhead is $170,000. This is equivalent to the $60,000 receivable expenses based on the current sales at 1,000 units, plus the $110,000 incremental variable margin ($550,000 less $440,000). The $170,000 receivable expenses, which is 13.6% of sales, translates to a collection period of 4.5 months as shown in Exhibit 11.8.

VI. COMPARATIVE PROFITABILITY
OF ALTERNATIVE MEASURES

The profitability and risk of the sales expansion options may be gauged from the following: (1) crossover sales volume (in number of units a month) based on the target sales expansion cost, (2) dollar value of the contribution to corporate overhead based on the target sales expansion cost and target sales volume, and (3) rate of return on the investment in working capital based on target sales expansion cost and target sales volume.

Crossover Sales Volume Based on the Target Sales Expansion Cost (Exhibit 11.9).   This indicates the number of units required to be sold so that the contribution to corporate overhead is maintained if all the budgeted sales expansion cost is spent. If the actual sales fall below the crossover volume, then the company will be in a worse position than if it had not implemented the measure.

The crossover volume of the different options indicates the relative efficiency and underlying risks of the options. As shown in part I of Exhibit 11.9, the price reduction alternative as an instrument of pushing the sales offers the lowest crossover volume. This means that the measure is the most cost efficient or the most profitable as it gives the lowest sales level which will enable the company to equal the current level of profitability, even if the budgeted sales expansion costs were fully spent.

The crossover volume also reflects the degree of risk inherent in the alternatives. The price reduction option has the lowest risk since the crossover volume, which is the lowest, is the most easily attainable.

Contribution to Corporate Overhead Based on the Target Sales Expansion Cost and Target Sales Volume. Part II of Exhibit 11.9 shows the relative profitability of the options, assuming that sales volume as forecast and the costs as budgeted will be achieved. The price reduction program gives the highest level of profitability in terms of the contribution to corporate overhead.

Rate of Return on Investment Based on Target Sales Expansion Cost and Target Sales Volume. Part III of Exhibit 11.9 depicts the ability of the investment in working capital to generate profit in excess of the 1% monthly interest charged to operations. The $3,000 working capital required per unit under the more aggressive advertising and higher sales commission alternatives is calculated in Exhibit 11.3. The working capital under the price reduction measure is $100 lower than that under the aggressive advertising option. A 5% or $50 price reduction translates to a $100 decline in receivables due to the two-month collection period ($50 × 2 = $100).

The investment requirement under the extended sales credit period is $2,000 more than the one under the aggressive advertising program due to the longer collection duration. The $2,000 difference represents the two-month incremental receivable period (from two to four months) based on a sale price of $1,000 per unit.

The posttax contribution to departmental overhead is related to the working capital requirement to arrive at the rate of return on the investment. The price reduction program with an 83% annual return has the highest rating under this criterion. It should be noted, though, that this apparently high return is before deducting both the departmental and corporate overhead.

Ranking the Sales Expansion Measures. The price reduction and increased commission measures have consistently ranked first (most desirable) and second, respectively, in the three criteria used in gauging the return and risk.

VII. SALES EXPANSION COST LEVERAGE

Sales expansion cost leverage is the degree to which the sales expansion cost budget could be augmented in an attempt to push the sales. The higher the leverage, the higher is the probability that the firm can enhance its profitability by raising its sales volume.

Specifically, the sales expansion cost leverage is the ratio of the present variable margin (sales less variable costs) to the present sales expansion cost. The higher the margin, or the lower the current sales expansion cost, the higher is the leverage.

Determinants of Leverage (Exhibit 11.10). Different firms have different leverages; even within the same firm, different products have different levels of leverage. Take the case of Company A and Company B in Exhibit 11.10. These companies have, at present, identical (1) sales, (2) combined variable and fixed costs ($400,000), (3) sales expansion costs, and (4) net profit before tax.

Note, however, that the companies have different fixed-variable cost structures. While Company A has a 1:1 variable cost to fixed cost ratio, Company B has a 7:1 ratio. This discrepancy in the cost structure causes their difference in variable margin—Company A's margin is $300,000 against Company B's $150,000.

This difference in turn accounts for their difference in sales expansion cost leverage. Company A has a 6:1 variable margin to sales expansion cost ratio as against 3:1 for B. This ratio is called the sales expansion cost leverage. The leverage is 6 for Company A since the variable margin at present is $300,000 while the sales expansion cost is $50,000.

Effects of Leverage—If Sales Expand By 20%. If Company A can escalate its sales by 20% from 500 to 600 units by doubling its sales expansion cost, its net profit before tax will rise by 20%. On the other hand, if Company B attains the same sales objective, also by doubling its sales expansion cost, its net profit before tax actually declines. The difference in the comparative performance of the two firms is accounted for by the difference in their sales expansion cost leverage.

Effects of Leverage—If Sales Expand by 100% (Exhibit 11.11). The sales expansion cost leverage calculated earlier is also the extent to which the sales expansion cost can be multiplied to achieve a doubling of the sales volume which will also double the profit.

For instance, Company A in Exhibit 11.11 which has a leverage of 6, can afford to escalate its sales expansion cost budget by sixfold to bring about a doubling of the sales volume. These stepped-up costs and sales will cause the net profit to jump to 200% of the current level.

A similar effect could be made on the net profit of Company B if the sales is doubled by multiplying its current sales expansion cost by its sales expansion cost leverage of 3.

Role of Leverage in Sales Expansion Measures.   Before attempting to expand sales through aggressive advertising, higher sales commissions, reduced prices, or similar means, the cost structure of the product or division should be studied to find out their suitability to competitive sales expansion measures. Naturally, this will be in addition to the appraisal of the market and the competition, as well as to the review of the marketing effectiveness of the specific instruments to be used in capturing market share.

EXHIBIT 11.1:

Improvement in Profit Due to Expansion of Sales Volume
(dollars in $1,000)

	Present *500 units*	*Add* *100 units*	*Future expected total* *600 units*
Sales	$500	$100	$600
Less: Variable costs	300	60	360
Variable margin	200	40	240
Less: Sales expansion cost	30	30	60
Contribution to overhead	170	10	180
Less: Overhead	120	0	120
Net profit before tax	$ 50	$ 10	$ 60

EXHIBIT 11.2:
Increasing the Advertising Budget—Monthly Profitability Statement (dollars in $1,000)

	Present Present	Target Target	Crossover Target	Target Crossover
Sales volume				
Sales expansion cost				
Advertising expense	$ 100	$ 200	$ 200	$ 220
Number of units	1,000	1,250	1,210	1,250
Sales	$1,000	$1,250	$1,210	$1,250
Less: Variable costs				
Raw Materials	300	375	363	375
Other manufacturing variable costs	100	125	121	125
Sales commissions	50	63	61	63
Bad debts	30	38	36	38
Collection expenses	10	13	12	13
Interest on financing of				
Raw materials and work in process inventories	6	8	7	8
Finished goods inventory	4	5	5	5
Receivables	20	25	24	25
Total	520	650	629	650
Variable margin	480	600	580	600
Less: Sales expansion costs				
Advertising	100	200	200	220
Contribution to departmental overhead	380	400	380	380
Less: Departmental overhead	100	100	100	100
Contribution to corporate overhead				
Before tax	280	300	280	280
Income tax	112	120	112	112
After tax	$ 168	$ 180	$ 168	$ 168

EXHIBIT 11.3:

Increasing the Advertising Budget—Working Capital and Interest Expense Per Unit

Working capital item	Basis—cost or revenue	Amount of cost/revenue	Average duration (months)	Working capital	Interest at 1%
Factory inventories					
Raw materials	Raw materials	$ 300	1.5	$ 450	
Suppliers' credit	Raw materials	300	(0.5)	(150)	
Goods in process	Manufacturing variable costs	400	0.75	300	
Subtotal					
Finished goods inventory	Manufacturing variable costs	400	1.0	600	$ 6
Accounts receivables	Sales	$1,000	2.0	400	4
				2,000	20
Total				$3,000	$30

EXHIBIT 11.4:
Increasing the Sales Commission Rates—Monthly Profitability Statement (dollars in $1,000)

	Present Present	Target Target	Crossover Target	Target Crossover
Sales volume				
Sales expansion cost				
Sales commission rate	5.00%	10.00%	10.00%	12.60%
Number of units	1,000	1,250	1,154	1,250
Sales	$1,000	$1,250	$1,154	$1,250
Less: Variable costs				
Raw materials	300	375	346	375
Other manufacturing variable costs	100	125	115	125
Advertising and promotions	100	125	115	125
Bad debts	30	38	35	38
Collection expenses	10	13	12	13
Interest on financing of				
Raw materials and work in process inventories	6	8	7	8
Finished goods inventory	4	5	5	5
Receivables	20	25	23	25
Total	570	713	658	713
Variable margin	430	538	496	538
Less: Sales expansion costs				
Sales commissions	50	125	115	158
Contribution to departmental overhead	380	413	381	380
Less: Departmental overhead	100	100	100	100
Contribution to corporate overhead				
Before tax	280	313	281	280
Income tax	112	125	112	112
After tax	$ 168	$ 188	$ 168	$ 168

EXHIBIT 11.5:
Increasing the Sales Commission Rates—Crossover Sales Volume
Determination

crossover sales volume $=\dfrac{\text{present total contribution to departmental overhead}}{\text{new unit contribution to departmental overhead}}$

where

present total contribution to departmental overhead	=	$380,000
new unit contribution to departmental overhead	=	unit variable margin − (unit selling price × new commission rate)
	=	unit variable margin − ($1,000 × 0.1)
	=	$430 − $100
	=	$330

Hence

crossover sales volume $= \dfrac{\$380{,}000}{\$330}$

$= \$1{,}152$

NOTE: The $1,152 is slightly different from the $1,154 in Exhibit 11.4 due to the rounding off of amounts in the calculations.

EXHIBIT 11.6:

Reducing the Prices—Monthly Profitability Statement (dollars in $1,000)

Sales volume Sales expansion cost	*Present* *Present*	*Target* *Target*	*Crossover* *Target*	*Target* *Crossover*
Selling price reduction	0.00%	5.00%	5.00%	8.54%
Number of units	1,000	1,250	1,133	1,250
Sales at present selling prices	$1,000	$1,250	$1,133	$1,250
Less: Variable costs				
Raw materials	300	375	340	375
Other manufacturing variable costs	100	125	113	125
Advertising and promotions	100	125	113	125
Sales commissions	50	63	57	63
Bad debts	30	38	34	38
Collection expenses	10	13	11	13
Interest on financing of				
Raw materials and work in process inventories	6	8	7	8
Finished goods inventory	4	5	5	5
Receivables	20	24	22	23
Total	620	774	702	773
Variable margin	380	476	431	477
Less: Sales expansion costs				
Price reduction		63	57	109
Savings in related costs		(7)	(6)	(12)
Net sales expansion costs	0	56	50	97
Contribution to departmental overhead	380	421	381	380
Less: Departmental overhead	100	100	100	100
Contribution to corporate overhead				
Before tax	280	321	281	280
Income tax	112	128	112	112
After tax	$ 168	$ 192	$ 168	$ 168
Interest on receivables financing per unit (in $1)	$20.00	$19.00	$19.00	$18.30

EXHIBIT 11.7:

Extending the Sales Credit Terms—Monthly Profitability Statement
(dollars in $1,000)

Sales volume Sales expansion cost	*Present* *Present*	*Target* *Target*	*Crossover* *Target*	*Target* *Crossover*
Sales credit term in months	2	4	4	4.5
Number of units	1,000	1,250	1,189	1,250
Sales	$1,000	$1,250	$1,189	$1,250
Less: Variable costs				
Raw materials	300	375	357	375
Other manufacturing variable costs	100	125	119	125
Advertising and promotions	100	125	119	125
Sales commissions	50	63	59	63
Interest on financing of				
Raw materials and work in				
process inventories	6	8	7	8
Finished goods inventory	4	5	5	5
Total	560	701	666	701
Variable margin	440	550	523	550
Less: Sales expansion costs				
Bad debts	30	75	71	85
Collection expenses	10	25	24	28
Interest on receivables	20	50	48	57
Total	60	150	143	170
Contribution to departmental				
overhead	380	400	380	380
Less: Departmental overhead	100	100	100	100
Contribution to corporate overhead				
Before tax	280	300	280	280
Income tax	112	120	112	112
After tax	$ 168	$ 180	$ 168	$ 168

EXHIBIT 11.8:
Extending The Sales Credit Terms—Receivable-Related Expenses

**I. At present—Based on sales of 1,000 units a month
and a two-month collection period**

	As a % of sales	Amount
Bad debts	3.00%	$ 30,000
Collection expenses	1.00	10,000
Interest on receivables financing	2.00	20,000
Total receivable-related expenses	6.00%	$ 60,000
Total percentage per month	3%	
Number of months	2	

II. Crossover receivable expenses based on 1,250 units a month

	As a % of sales	Amount
Bad debts	6.80%	$ 85,000
Collection expenses	2.27	28,000
Interest on receivables financing	4.53	57,000
Total receivable-related expenses	13.60%	$170,000
Total percentage per month	3%	
Number of months	4.5	

EXHIBIT 11.9:
Profitability of Alternative Sales Expansion Measures

	More advertising	Higher commissions	Reduced prices	Longer sales credit
I. Crossover sales volume based on target sales expansion cost				
Crossover sales volume (in units)	1,210	1,154	1,133	1,189
Contribution to corporate overhead at crossover sales volume (in $1,000)	$ 168	$ 168	$ 168	$ 168
Rank (from best) based on crossover sales volume	4	2	1	3
II. Contribution to corporate overhead based on target sales expansion cost and target sales volume				
Contribution to corporate overhead (in $1,000)	$ 180	$ 188	$ 192	$ 180
Rank	3.5	2	1	3.5
III. Return on investment based on target sales expansion cost and target sales volume				
Working capital				
Per unit	$3,000	$3,000	$2,900	$5,000
For 1,250 units (in $1,000)	3,750	3,750	3,625	6,250
Contribution to departmental overhead (in $1,000)*				
Before tax	$ 400	$ 413	$ 419	$ 400
After 40% tax†	240	248	251	240
Return on working capital—on top of 12% interest*				
Per month	6.4%	6.6%	6.9%	3.8%
Per year	77%	79%	83%	46%
Rank	3	2	1	4

*After providing 1% monthly interest charge on working capital used.
†For federal and assumed state tax.

EXHIBIT 11.10:
Effect of Sales Expansion Cost Leverage on Net Profit—
If Sales Volume Increases by 20% (dollars in $1,000)

	COMPANY A		COMPANY B	
	Present 500 units	Target 600 units	Present 500 units	Target 600 units
Sales	$500	$600	$500	$600
Less: Variable costs	200	240	350	420
Variable margin	300	360	150	180
Less: Overhead	200	200	50	50
Net profit before sales expansion costs	100	160	100	130
Sales expansion costs	50	100	50	100
Net profit before tax	$ 50	$ 60	$ 50	$ 30
Sales expansion cost leverage (variable margin divided by sales expansion cost)	6		3	

EXHIBIT 11.11:
Effect of Sales Expansion Cost Leverage on Net Profit—
If Sales Volume Increases by 100% (dollars in $1,000)

	COMPANY A		COMPANY B	
	Present 500 units	Target 1000 units	Present 500 units	Target 1000 units
Sales	$500	$1,000	$500	$1,000
Less: Variable costs	200	400	350	700
Variable margin	300	600	150	300
Less: Overhead	200	200	50	50
Net profit before sales expansion costs	100	400	100	250
Sales expansion costs	50	300	50	150
Net profit before tax	$ 50	$ 100	$ 50	$ 100
Sales expansion cost leverage (variable margin divided by sales expansion cost)	6		3	

Chapter 12 _____

ANALYZING
EQUIPMENT
ACQUISITIONS

This chapter illustrates the applications of techniques in the evaluation of alternatives in the following situations: (1) selecting among equipment with different acquisition and operating costs; (2) selecting among equipment with different operating lives; (3) deciding whether to replace an existing equipment or not; and (4) deciding on lease or buy alternatives.

A unit of equipment is acquired on the premise that the acquisition cost can be more than offset by the diminished operating costs and by the tax benefits generated by depreciation. Where a choice is to be made among alternative types of equipment, the decision is based on the combined acquisition and operating cost for each equipment.

Because of the long-term nature of the investment in equipment, the acquisition and operating costs have to be adjusted for inflation and time value of money. The inflation adjustment brings the values to a common price level. The time value of money adjustment moves the cash flows to a common date, in the same way that in calculating the IRR, the investment and returns are brought together to a common reference year. The use of price- and time-adjusted values facilitate the comparison of the alternatives.

I. ESTIMATING THE EFFECTIVE ACQUISITION AND OPERATING COSTS

Equipment has two basic types of costs: the acquisition cost or purchase price, which is normally paid upon acquisition, and the operating cost, which is paid throughout the life of the asset. The operating cost includes repairs and maintenance, insurance, compensation of equipment opera-

285

tors, and power. The effective acquisition and operating costs are represented by the actual cash payments for these items, as adjusted for income tax, inflation, and time value of money.

EFFECTIVE ACQUISITION COST

The acquisition cost is not adjusted for inflation and time value of money under the following conditions: (1) the equipment is paid for in cash as of the date of acquisition, which is as of the end of year 0, and (2) year 0 is used as the reference point for both inflation and time value of money. The adjustment is only for income tax, which is derived from the depreciation of the equipment.

Depreciation and Tax Benefits. For accounting purposes, the acquisition cost is periodically charged to operations in the form of depreciation. In the accounting statements, depreciation is an operating expense.

However, since equipment decisions are based on cash flows and not income statements, and since depreciation does not require cash outlay, depreciation by itself does not enter into the financial analysis work. Depreciation is considered only to the extent that it gives rise to an income tax-deductible item which reduces the total cash cost. The Internal Revenue Service has promulgated regulations regarding the methods of depreciation which may be used for tax purposes. One of these methods, the modified accelerated cost recovery system (MACRS), is used as the examples in Exhibits 12.4, 12.6 and 12.8.

If there is no scrap value, all of the acquisition cost of an equipment is transformed into depreciation. Assuming a 40% corporate income tax rate (for both the federal and state taxes), 40% of the total depreciation, and hence, ultimately 40% of the total acquisition cost, is used to reduce the total tax liability of the organization.

Assume that a company buys today a piece of equipment for $3,000. The acquisition cost of $3,000 serves as the basis of determining the annual depreciation of $1,000 a year, or totaling $3,000. To simplify the illustration at this stage, assume first that the straight-line depreciation method is used. (A more accurate result will be obtained if depreciation is based on the MACRS mentioned earlier.) The tax benefit in turn is linked to the annual depreciation. Thus the yearly tax benefit is $400, which is 40% of the $1,000 annual depreciation.

Thus, the company will receive a total tax benefit of $1,200 over the next three years. Hence, the effective acquisition cost (after this tax benefit) is 60% of the purchase price or $1,800. However, this is true only if there were no inflation and money has no time value.

Effect of Inflation and Time Value of Money on Tax Benefits. Due to inflation and time value of money, the effective tax benefit derived from the acquisition cost is lower than the nominal tax rate, which is assumed to be 40% in the illustration.

VALUE OF DEPRECIATION (EXHIBIT 12.1). The $3,000 value of the depreciation for the entire equipment life, which is the basis of the $1,200 tax benefit, is pegged to the acquisition cost, which is paid in year 0 (today), at year 0 price level. The annual depreciation over the years does not grow with the inflation and time value of money. See Exhibit 12.1 for the graphic illustration of the flow and value conversion.

VALUE OF TAX BENEFITS. The tax benefits are received over several years, when the buying power of a dollar is lower than that of a dollar in year 0 due to inflation and interest cost. The tax benefits to be received in the future have to be diluted to today's price level to make them comparable to the value of the dollar used today to procure the asset. Furthermore, the future tax benefits have to be time discounted to today, which is the time the equipment is purchased.

INFLATION (EXHIBIT 12.2). Since inflation pushes up the prices in the future, or reduces the purchasing power of a dollar in the future in relation to the value today, the tax benefits to be obtained in the future have lower purchasing power than do the dollars used to pay the equipment today. In other words, inflation deflates the value of the tax benefits in the future. A 4% inflation rate dilutes the $1,200 tax benefits to be obtained over the next three years, to only $1,110 based on today's price levels. See Exhibit 12.2.

TIME VALUE OF MONEY. The time value of money diminishes further the value of the future tax benefits. Since the benefits cannot be used right away, the company will have to resort to borrowing or forgo interest-bearing investments in order to finance that portion of the acquisition cost which could have been offset by the tax benefits if the benefits were received at once. This imputed interest cost if calculated at 6% a year after tax reduces the $1,110 tax benefits after inflation adjustment to $991. This is just 33% of the $3,000 acquisition cost, against the 40% nominal tax rate. The real acquisition cost, therefore, is $3,000 less $991 or $2,009.

FACTORS AFFECTING TAX BENEFITS. The use of an equipment life longer than the three years in the illustration, or of an inflation or interest rate which is higher than what was used in the example, will further lower the effective tax benefit as a percentage of the acquisition cost.

On the other hand, the application of the modified accelerated cost recovery system depreciation method, in lieu of the straight-line method used in Exhibit 12.2, increases the effective income tax benefit percentage. The application of the MACRS in relation to that of the straight-line method, shifts some depreciation, and hence tax benefit, from the later to the earlier years of the equipment life. Since the price-level deflator and the time value of money discounting rate for the earlier years is lower, the effective tax benefit becomes higher.

EFFECTIVE OPERATING COST

The effective operating cost is the cash outlay, less the tax benefit, as adjusted for inflation and time value of money.

Unlike the tax benefit resulting from the acquisition cost which is obtained a year or more after the purchase price is paid for, the tax benefit derived from operating cost is availed of in the same year that the operating cost is incurred. Hence, there is no adjustment for inflation or time value of money. The effective tax benefit percentage, therefore, is the same as the nominal rate.

Adjustment for Inflation (Exhibit 12.3).   The operating cost in the future is usually calculated by engineers, technicians, and cost accountants, based on today's price level. There are two ways of treating inflation in calculating the total cost as of today—one by considering inflation and another by disregarding it. This is demonstrated in Exhibit 12.3.

In part I of the exhibit, the $500,000 annual operating cost is first estimated based on today's price level. The cost is then inflated to approximate the dollar value at the future price level. Thus, the amount becomes $520,000 a year from now if prices grow by 4% annually due to inflation. The $520,000 approximates the cash outlay to be made by then. Since the cost generates a tax benefit, which is assumed to be 40%, the net after-tax cost is 60% of the $520,000, or $312,000. This is the value based on year 1 prices. This amount is then deflated by 0.96 to bring it to year 0 price level, thus lowering it to $300,000. This is before the adjustment for time value of money.

The $300,000 figure can be arrived at by totally disregarding inflation. The results are the same since deflating the amount as was done in part I cancels out the effect of previously inflating it. See part II of Exhibit 12.3, where the $300,000 was calculated by deducting the 40% tax benefit from the $500,000 cost.

Adjustment for Time Value of Money.   Since the costs are incurred in different years, they are brought forward to year 0 so they can become comparable and addable. The present value factor is applied. This reduces the effective cost since a dollar due one year from now is worth less than a dollar on hand today. Thus the $300,000 after-tax operating cost to be incurred in year 1 as adjusted for time value of money is worth only $283,000 one year earlier.

II. SELECTING AMONG EQUIPMENT WITH DIFFERENT ACQUISITION AND OPERATING COSTS

If two or more pieces of equipment have the same capacity and useful life, the choice will be made on the basis of cost. If one piece of equipment has lower initial cost and annual cost, then the selection of the equipment can be made easily. However, in many cases, the equipment with the higher initial cost has the lower annual cost. Thus, a diesel engine has a higher initial cost but lower operating cost than a gasoline engine. A more mechanized unit has a higher acquisition cost but lower annual cost. A hydroelectric power plant has a higher construction cost but lower operating cost than a thermal plant.

The following streams of costs, based on present day prices, for two pieces of equipment with five-year lives, are illustrative of this situation:

		Equipment A	*Equipment B*
Acquisition cost	Year 0	$ 900	$ 500
Operating cost	Year 1	70	185
	Year 2	70	185
	Year 3	70	185
	Year 4	70	185
	Year 5	70	185
Total cost		$1,150	$1,425

A comparison of the foregoing initially shows that B is more expensive than A. However, no comparison should be made without incorporating income tax, inflation, and the time value of money.

DEPRECIATION AND TAX BENEFITS (Exhibit 12.4)

Assume that, for tax purposes, the company uses the modified accelerated cost recovery system with a half-year convention, according to the Internal Revenue Service Publication 534. Assume also that the equipment is classified as belonging to the five-year property class and that the equipment is to be acquired and paid for as of the end of year 0 and placed in service in early year 1. Assume also that the combined federal and state income tax rate is 40%.

The annual depreciation rates are stated in the first line of Exhibit 12.4. Since the company uses a half-year convention, the company takes as depreciation for the first year or year 1, only half of the depreciation percentage calculated for that year. The half rate is 20% which is the one used for the year. Due to the use of the half-year convention, the scheduled depreciation for tax purposes extends up to year 6, although the actual operating life is only up to year 5.

Since the equipment will be retired by the end of year 5, the equipment will still have a book value by then. Thus, there will be a loss upon the retirement. This loss was added to the year 5 depreciation.

The first column (total) of Exhibit 12.4 shows that the $900,000 cost of equipment A generates a total tax benefit of $324,000 for the five-year period. This benefit is at year 0 prices (that is, after adjustment for inflation), but before adjustment for time value of money. In like manner, equipment B gives a $180,000 tax reduction.

CASH FLOW BEFORE TIME VALUE OF MONEY ADJUSTMENT (Exhibit 12.4)

The total cost of acquiring and operating equipment A, at year 0 price level, is $786,000. See Exhibit 12.4. This amount is composed of $900,000 acquisition cost, $324,000 tax benefit due to depreciation (a deduction), and $210,000 operating cost net of 40% income tax benefit. The comparable figure for equipment B is $875,000. These figures are after adjustment for inflation but before factoring in the time cost of money.

PRESENT VALUE OF COST AT 6% INTEREST— EQUIPMENT A (Exhibit 12.5)

The annual cash flows for the years other than year 0 have to be adjusted for the time value of money. This is accomplished in the exhibit. The purpose of this adjustment is to bring all the cash flow or costs to be incurred, to a common reference point. The reference point used is year 0, the year of the investment.

The further away is the timing of the cost from year 0, the smaller is the time discount factor or the bigger is the value to be taken off. If the cost of money to a corporation is 10%, the effective rate after a combined federal and state income tax of 40%, is 6%. At 6% a year, $1 due one year from now is worth $0.94 today. Hence with year 0 as the reference point, the time discount rate or present value factor used for year 1 is .94.

At 6% interest a year, the value of the costs to be incurred from year 0 to year 5, as of year 0 (and at the price level of year 0) is $799,000. This is the present value of the acquisition and operating costs, net of income tax reduction due to these costs, and as adjusted for inflation and time value of money. The $799,000 is estimated in Exhibit 12.5. For purposes of further analysis, the $799,000 may be broken down as follows: $900,000 to be incurred as of year 0 less the beneficial or favorable cash flow of $101,000 to be derived from years 1 to 5. The $101,000 is represented by the excess of tax benefits due to depreciation and operating costs, over the cash outlays for operating costs. In this case, favorable cash flow means deduction from the cash payments or costs.

PRESENT VALUE OF COSTS—EFFECT OF INTEREST RATE FLUCTUATIONS (Exhibit 12.5)

Using 6% as the after-tax interest rate, the present value of the costs of equipment A, as is noted, is $799,000, and equipment B, $813,000. See Exhibit 12.5. Any movement in the interest rate will change the present value.

Due to the peculiar cost or cash flow structure of equipment A in relation to that of B, any movement in the interest rate will change the present values of the costs of A and B in different directions.

Equipment A. Equipment A has a net favorable cash flow (or net tax deductions) for years 1 to 5 combined. The $101,000 present value of this favorable cash flow as of year 0 is deducted from the $900,000 acquisition cost in order to arrive at the $799,000 net present value of the total costs.

A rise in the interest rate will depress the present value of the years 1 to 5 net favorable cash flow, thereby increasing the combined present value of the year 0 and years 1 to 5 cash flows. For instance, if the interest rises from 6% to 9.6%, the year 0 present value of the unfavorable cash flow stays constant at $900,000, the years 1–5 present value of the favorable cash flows declines from $101,000 to $95,000, and the combined present value of the resulting unfavorable cash flow inches upward from $799,000 to $805,000.

The difference in the present value of the favorable cash flow due to fluctuation in interest will be much more pronounced for equipment with longer life, say, 10 years instead of the 5 in the illustration. This is due to the annual compounding effect of the interest.

Equipment B. On the other hand, equipment B has unfavorable cash flow during the operating years (years 1 to 5), since the income tax reduction is not enough to cover the operating cash costs. Hence the present value of this cash outflow ($313,000 at 6%) is added to the acquisition cost. Any rise in interest rate will slash the present value of the years 1 to 5 unfavorable cash outflow, thus reducing the total present value of years 0 to 5 unfavorable cash flow. For example, if the interest goes up from 6% to 9.6%, the total cost declines from $813,000 to $783,000.

CROSSOVER INTEREST RATE (Exhibit 12.5)

Just which is the cheaper equipment depends on the interest cost to the firm. A firm with a relatively low cost of borrowing or capital (say, 6%), will tend to take equipment with higher up-front or acquisition cost but lower subsequent cost, as typified by equipment A. A company with a 6% interest cost realizes a $14,000 cost saving on equipment A as compared with equipment B.

On the other hand, a firm which obtains funds at 9.6% after tax makes a $22,000 saving on equipment B, which has a lower initial cash outlay but more subsequent cash payments for operating costs.

To a corporation with effective interest of 7.3% the cost of equipment A is the same as that of B. This interest rate represents the crossover rate in this particular case. At this rate, the time-adjusted cost of one equipment is almost the same as that of the other.

III. SELECTING AMONG EQUIPMENT WITH DIFFERENT USEFUL LIVES

There are instances where the choice will be between equipment with a life shorter than that of an alternative. In this instance, the comparative study should span the period which extends up to the end of the life of the more durable equipment. Thus, where equipment C has a life of three years, and D, six years, the analysis should span the following:

Equipment C	
First unit of C	Years 1 to 3
Second unit of C	Years 4 to 6
Equipment D	Years 1 to 6

ACQUISITION COST AND DEPRECIATION (Exhibit 12.6)

The present values of the costs of acquiring two units of equipment C and operating them for six years are calculated in Exhibit 12.6. The acquisition cost in year 0 for the first unit is $500,000. Due to inflation, the buying price in year 3 for the second unit is expected to be $562,000. The depreciation for the first unit is based on $500,000, and for the second unit, $562,000.

Since equipment D has a life of six years, only one unit will be acquired—in year 0.

Equipment C is depreciated under the Internal Revenue Service modified accelerated cost recovery system as a three-year property, and D, as a five-year property. In the exhibit, the loss upon retirement has been included in the depreciation for the last operating year of the equipment.

CROSSOVER INTEREST RATE (Exhibit 12.7)

If the firm has a 6% after-tax interest cost, equipment D offers a cheaper alternative. See Exhibit 12.7.

However, the use of a higher rate may make equipment D more expensive relative to C. This is due to the different cost structures of the options: equipment C has lower year 0 cost, but higher subsequent costs. Any change in the interest rate will not affect the year 0 cost, but will influence the Years 1–6 costs.

Although the use of a rate higher than 6% will reduce the total cost of both alternatives, the reduction of equipment C cost will be more pronounced as it has more years 1–6 cost.

Thus if a 9.6% after-tax rate were used, equipment C will come out cheaper than D. The increase of the rate from 6% slashes the present value of the total cost of C by $92,000, but cuts down the cost of D by only $60,000.

At an interest rate higher than 9.6%, equipment C will be much cheaper than D. At 6.4%, which is the crossover rate, the effective costs of the two pieces of equipment are the same.

IV. DECIDING WHETHER TO REPLACE EQUIPMENT OR NOT

A key decision to be made in equipment management is whether or not to replace equipment—and if so, when. An equipment replacement analysis will have to weigh the differential costs and benefits: (1) the acquisition cost of the new equipment, (2) the tax credit from the depreciation, (3) the tax credit from the write-off of the remaining book value of the present equipment, and (4) the operating costs of both the new and present equipment.

GIVEN DATA (Exhibit 12.8)

A decision analysis sheet is presented in Exhibit 12.8. The evaluation is based on the following:

1. The existing equipment is fully depreciated, with no remaining book value and no scrap value.
2. The new equipment has a useful life for tax purposes of three years; it has no scrap value at any time after installation. The depreciation is based on a three-year life using the modified accelerated cost recovery system of the Internal Revenue Service.
3. The equipment is needed for three years only.

The options considered in the evaluation are:

Option A. Do not acquire any new equipment. Use the existing equipment from years 1 to 3.

Option B. Acquire new equipment in late year 0, to be placed in service in early year 1.

Option C. Acquire new equipment in late year 1, to be placed in service early the following year.

OPTION A: DO NOT ACQUIRE NEW EQUIPMENT
(Exhibit 12.8)

Under this alternative, the only cost involved is the operating cost of the old equipment, less the assumed 40% income tax. As the present equipment is fully depreciated, there is no more tax deduction for either the depreciation or write-off of the equipment.

OPTION B: ACQUIRE EQUIPMENT IN YEAR 0
(Exhibit 12.8)

The cash flows involved are only for the new equipment: (1) acquisition cost; (2) tax reduction due to the depreciation and write-off of the new equipment; and (3) operating cost less income tax. For tax purposes, the property recovery period extends to year 4. However, since the property is used only up to year 3 with no value afterward, the undepreciated portion as of the end of this year is written off. Hence the total depreciation plus the write-off for the first three years equal the acquisition cost.

There are no costs associated with the old unit as it is not going to be used any more during the period covered by the analysis.

OPTION C: ACQUIRE EQUIPMENT IN YEAR 1
(Exhibit 12.8)

Since the equipment will be used for two years only, the acquisition cost remaining after deducting the depreciation for years 2 and 3 will be written off in year 3 for tax purposes.

The operating cost for year 1 is for the old equipment, and for years 2 and 3, for the new unit.

PRESENT VALUE OF COSTS (Exhibit 12.9)

The acquisition and operating costs before adjustments for the time value of money under the three options as calculated in Exhibit 12.8 are converted to year 0 values in Exhibit 12.9.

With an after-tax interest rate of 6%, option B offers the lowest cost. However, if the rate were substantially raised, say, to 9.6%, option A becomes the best choice. In a high-money-cost environment, an option requiring a huge initial cash outlay, as typified by option B, is severely penalized.

V. DECIDING ON LEASE OR BUY ALTERNATIVES

In a lease or buy decision, the difference between the effective cost of the rents and the effective cost of the purchase price is made up of the following: the financial interest charged by the lessor, the income tax deductions, the time value of money pertaining to the tax deductions, and the effects of inflation on the tax deductions and on the annual rents. The tax deductions arise from the depreciation in case of purchase or rent in case of lease.

GIVEN DATA (Exhibit 12.10)

Assume that a firm has two alternative methods of acquiring an equipment: buy for cash or lease with five equal annual rents payable at the start of every year. Assume also that for tax purposes, the equipment, if purchased, is depreciated for five years and has no scrap value. Assume further that if purchased, the price is $1,000,000, and if leased, the annual rent is $275,000. These amounts are entered in Exhibit 12.10.

In this transaction, the seller-lessor is charging a 19% financial interest. From the viewpoint of a buyer whose pretax money cost also happens to be 19%, and whose effective corporate federal and state tax rate is 40%, the posttax cost of money is 11.4% (60% of 19%).

EFFECTIVE COST (Exhibit 12.11)

However, even at 11.4%, the lease arrangement is cheaper. If the payments and tax benefits are discounted at 11.4%, the effective cost under the lease plan is only $685,000 compared with $728,000 under the cash purchase plan. See Exhibit 12.11, last column.

Crossover Rate. Given the specifics of this case, the effective money cost to the firm is 8.4% This is the crossover rate. See Exhibit 12.11, first column. This means that as far as the firm is concerned, the leasing and buying for cash will have the same cost if the firm's cost of money is 8.4%. This is lower than the 11.4% posttax rate earlier computed because of (1) the effects of inflation on the annual rents and (2) the effects of inflation and the time value of money on the tax deductions.

Rents. Due to inflation, the amount of annual rents payable during the latter part of the lease period (in terms of year 0 prices or price levels as of the start of the lease period) is lower than the $275,000 stipulated in the contract. Thus, as of the end of year 4 or beginning of year 3, the amount in terms of year 0 prices is only $235,000 and not $275,000. See Exhibit 12.10.

Tax Deductions. If the company buys the equipment for cash, the tax benefit will be spread over several years from the date of purchase. Although the first tax deduction can be used one year after the cash purchase, the last deduction cannot be utilized until five years after the purchase.

On the other hand, if the firm leases the equipment, all the tax benefits can be utilized just 12 months after each payment of the annual rent. This faster availment of the tax credit under the lease plan favors leasing in two ways: (1) it reduces the erosion of the value of the tax benefits due to inflation, and (2) it trims down the "inventory" of tax benefits waiting to be utilized, thereby correspondingly cutting down the imputed interest on the financing used to carry such inventory.

EXHIBIT 12.1:
Effective Tax Benefit

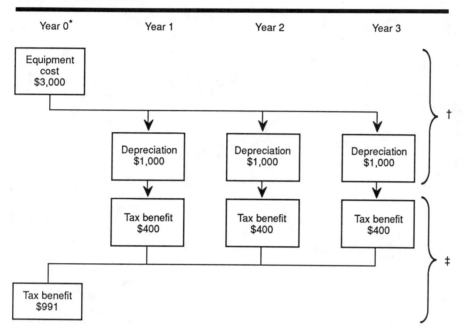

* Year 0 = time of equipment acquisition; Years 1 to 3 =
  operating or equipment usage years.

† When the equipment cost in year 0 is depreciated in Years
  1 to 3, the cost is not adjusted for inflation or time.
  Hence the value of the equipment is the same as the value
  of the depreciation.

‡ However, when the tax benefits in Years 1 to 3 are brought back
  to Year 0, the values are discounted for inflation and time –
  hence the total value is reduced from $1,200 to $991.
  See Exhibit 12.2 for the calculation of the $991.

EXHIBIT 12.2:
Effective Equipment Acquisition Cost (dollars in $1,000)

| | YEAR | | | | |
	0	1	2	3	Total
Given data					
Income tax					
Depreciation rates (assume straight line)		33.3%	33.3%	33.3%	
Federal and state income tax		40%	40%	40%	
Inflation					
Inflation factor at 4%*	1.00	1.04	1.08	1.12	
Deflator at 4%†	1.00	0.96	0.92	0.89	
Time value of money					
Future value (amount of 1) factor at 6%‡	1.00	1.06	1.12	1.19	
Present value factor at 6%§	1.00	0.94	0.89	0.84	
Equipment acquisition cost and depreciation					
Acquisition cost	$3,000				
Annual depreciation		$1,000	$1,000	$1,000	$3,000
Tax benefit, rate		40%	40%	40%	
Tax benefit at current prices		$ 400	$ 400	$ 400	$1,200
Deflator at 4%		0.96	0.92	0.89	
Tax benefit at year 0 prices		$ 385	$ 370	$ 356	$1,110
Present value factor at 6%		0.94	0.89	0.84	
Tax benefit at year 0 prices and as of year 0	$ 991	$ 363	$ 329	$ 299	$ 991
Net acquisition cost at year 0 prices and as of year 0	$2,009				

*This is the price level of any year if price in year 0 is 1. After 4% inflation, the price for any year = 1.04 × price of prior year.

†This is the purchasing power of $1 in any year relative to the purchasing power of $1 in year 0. Deflator for any year = 1 divided by the inflation factor.

‡This is how $1 in year 0 accumulates if interest is 6%. Value in any year = 1.06 of value in prior year.

§This is how much $1 in any year is worth in year 0. Value in any year = 1 divided by the future value (or amount of 1) factor.

298

EXHIBIT 12.3:
Effective Equipment Operating Cost (dollars in $1,000)

	Total as of year 0	YEAR		
		1	2	3
I. With inflation adjustment				
Operating cost at year 0 prices	$1,500	$500	$500	$500
Inflator at 4%		1.04	1.08	1.12
Cost at years 1 to 3 prices		$520	$541	$562
Tax benefit at 40%		208	216	225
Net cost at years 1 to 3 prices		$312	$324	$337
Deflator at 4%		0.96	0.92	0.89
Net cost at year 0 prices		$300	$300	$300
Present value factor at 6%		0.94	0.89	0.84
Net operating cost at year 0 prices and as of year 0	$ 802	$283	$267	$252
II. Without inflation adjustment				
Operating cost at year 0 prices	$1,500	$500	$500	$500
Tax benefit at 40%		200	200	200
Net cost at year 0 prices		$300	$300	$300
Present value factor at 6%		0.94	0.89	0.84
Net operating cost at year 0 prices and as of year 0	$ 802	$283	$267	$252

EXHIBIT 12.4:
Equipment with Different Acquisition and Operating Costs—Cash Flow (dollars in $1,000)

	Total	YEAR 0	1	2	3	4	5
Given data							
Depreciation rates	100.0%		20.0%	32.0%	19.2%	11.5%	17.3%
Inflation factor at 4%		1.00	1.04	1.08	1.12	1.17	1.22
Deflator at 4%		1.00	0.96	0.92	0.89	0.85	0.82
Equipment A							
Equipment acquisition cost	$900	$900					
Annual depreciation	$900		$180	$288	$173	$104	$156
Tax benefit—40%	(360)		(72)	(115)	(69)	(41)	(62)
Tax benefit after 4% deflator	(324)		(69)	(107)	(61)	(35)	(51)
Operating cost at year 0 prices	$350		$ 70	$ 70	$ 70	$ 70	$ 70
After 40% tax benefit	210		42	42	42	42	42
Cash flow	$786	$900	($ 27)	($ 65)	($ 19)	$ 7	($ 9)
Equipment B							
Equipment acquisition cost	$500	$500					
Annual depreciation	$500		$100	$160	$ 96	$ 58	$ 87
Tax benefit—40%	(200)		(40)	(64)	(38)	(23)	(35)
Tax benefit after 4% deflator	(180)		(38)	(59)	(34)	(20)	(28)
Operating cost at year 0 prices	$925		$185	$185	$185	$185	$185
After 40% tax benefit	555		111	111	111	111	111
Cash flow	$875	$500	$ 73	$ 52	$ 77	$ 91	$ 83

EXHIBIT 12.5:
Equipment with Different Acquisition and Operating Costs—Present Value of Costs (dollars in $1,000)

			YEAR			
	0	1	2	3	4	5
Cash flow before time adjustment						
Equipment A						
Total cost at year 0 prices*	$900	($27)	($65)	($19)	$ 7	($ 9)
Present value factor at 6%	1.00	0.94	0.89	0.84	0.79	0.75
Total cost as of year 0	$900	($26)	($57)	($16)	$ 5	($ 7)
Equipment B						
Total cost at year 0 prices*	$500	$73	$52	$77	$91	$83
Present value factor at 6%	1.00	0.94	0.89	0.84	0.79	0.75
Total cost as of year 0	$500	$68	$46	$65	$72	$62

	Interest rate		
Present value			
Interest rate after tax	6.0%	7.3%	9.6%
Equipment A			
Year 0	$900	$900	$900
Years 1 to 5	(101)	(99)	(95)
Total present value of cash flow	$799	$801	$805
Equipment B			
Year 0	$500	$500	$500
Years 1 to 5	313	302	283
Total present value of cash flow	$813	$802	$783
Equipment B is higher (lower)	$ 14	$ 0	($ 22)

*From Exhibit 12.4.

EXHIBIT 12.6:
Equipment with Different Operating Lives—Cash Flow (dollars in $1,000)

				YEAR				
	Total	0	1	2	3	4	5	6
Given data								
Depreciation rates								
Equipment C—first unit	100.0%		33.3%	44.5%	22.2%			
Equipment C—second unit						33.3%	44.5%	22.2%
Equipment D			20.0%	32.0%	19.2%	11.5%	11.5%	5.8%
Inflation factor at 4%		1.00	1.04	1.08	1.12	1.17	1.22	1.27
Deflator at 4%		1.00	0.96	0.92	0.89	0.85	0.82	0.79
Equipment C (two units)								
Equipment acquisition cost	$1,062	$500			$562			
After deflator—4%	1,000	500			500			
Depreciation								
First unit	$ 500	—	$ 167	$223	111	$ 0		
Second unit	562					187	$250	$125
Total	1,062		167	223	111	187	250	125
Tax benefit—40%	(425)		(67)	(89)	(44)	(75)	(100)	(50)
After 4% deflator	(372)		(64)	(82)	(39)	(64)	(82)	(39)
Operating costs	$1,620		$ 270	$270	$270	$270	$270	$270
After-tax benefit—40%	972		162	162	162	162	162	162
Cash flow	$1,600	$500	$ 98	$ 80	$623	$ 98	$ 80	$123
Equipment D (one unit)								
Equipment acquisition cost	$ 880	$880						
Depreciation	$ 880		$ 176	$282	$169	$101	$101	$ 51
Tax benefit—40%	(352)		(70)	(113)	(68)	(40)	(40)	(20)
After 4% deflator	(316)		(68)	(104)	(60)	(35)	(33)	(16)
Operating cost	$1,620		$ 270	$270	$270	$270	$270	$270
After-tax benefit—40%	972		162	162	162	162	162	162
Cash flow	$1,536	$880	$ 94	$ 58	$102	$127	$129	$146

EXHIBIT 12.7:

Equipment with Different Operating Lives—Present Value of Costs as of Year 0* (dollars in $1,000)

	INTEREST RATE		
Interest rate after tax	6.0%	6.4%	9.6%
Equipment C			
Year 0	$ 500	$ 500	$ 500
Years 1 to 6	910	899	818
Total	$ 1,410	$1,399	$1,318
Equipment D			
Year 0	$ 880	$ 880	$ 880
Years 1 to 6	526	519	465
Total	$ 1,406	$1,399	$1,345
Equipment D is higher (lower)	($ 4)	$ 0	$ 28

*Based on the values of cash flow in Exhibit 12.6.

EXHIBIT 12.8:
Equipment Replacement—Cash flow (dollars in $1,000)

| | Total | YEAR | | | |
		0	1	2	3
Given data					
Depreciation rates					
Option B	100.0%		33.3%	44.5%	22.2%
Option C				33.3%	66.7%
Inflation factor at 4%		1.00	1.04	1.08	1.12
Deflator at 4%		1.00	0.96	0.92	0.89
Operating cost of equipment at					
year 0 price level					
New equipment			$100	$120	$150
Old equipment			200	280	380
Option A—do not acquire new equipment					
Operating cost at year 0 prices			$200	$280	$380
After-tax benefit—40%			120	168	228
Option B—acquire new equipment in year 0					
Equipment acquisition cost	$360	$360			
Annual depreciation	$360		$120	$160	$ 80
Tax benefit—40%	(144)		(48)	(64)	(32)
After 4% deflator	(134)		(46)	(59)	(28)
Operating cost at year 0 prices	$370		$100	$120	$150
After-tax benefit—40%	222		60	72	90
Cash flow	$448	$360	$ 14	$ 13	$ 62
Option C—acquire new equipment in year 1					
Equipment acquisition cost	$374		$374		
Annual depreciation	$374			$125	$250
Tax benefit—40%	(150)			(50)	(100)
After 4% deflator	(135)			(46)	(89)
Operating cost at year 0 prices	$420		$200	$100	$120
After-tax benefit—40%	252		120	60	72
Cash flow	$491		$494	$ 14	($ 17)

EXHIBIT 12.9:

Equipment Replacement—Present Value of Costs as of Year 0*
(dollars in $1,000)

	INTEREST RATE	
Interest rate after tax	6.0%	9.6%
Option A—do not replace		
Years 1 to 3	$454	$423
Option B—Replace in year 0		
Year 0	$360	$360
Years 1 to 3	76	70
Total	$436	$430
Option C—Replace in year 1		
Years 1 to 3	$465	$450

*From Exhibit 12.8.

EXHIBIT 12.10:
Lease or Buy Alternatives—Cash Flow (dollars in $1,000)

	Total	0	1	2	3	4	5
					YEAR		
Given data							
Depreciation rates	100.0%		20.0%	32.0%	19.2%	11.5%	17.3%
Inflation factor at 4%		1.00	1.04	1.08	1.12	1.17	1.22
Deflator at 4%		1.00	0.96	0.92	0.89	0.85	0.82
Buy for cash							
Equipment acquisition cost	$1,000	$1,000					
Annual depreciation	$1,000		$200	$320	$192	$115	$173
Tax benefit—40%	(400)		(80)	(128)	(77)	(46)	(69)
Tax benefit after 4% deflator	(360)		(77)	(118)	(68)	(39)	(57)
Cash flow at year 0 prices	$ 640	$1,000	($ 77)	($118)	($ 68)	($ 39)	($ 57)
Lease							
Annual rent							
At current prices	$1,375	$ 275	$275	$275	$275	$275	
At year 0 prices	1,273	275	264	254	244	235	
Tax benefit at 40% of rent							
At current prices	($550)		($110)	($110)	($110)	($110)	($110)
At year 0 prices	(490)		(106)	(102)	(98)	(94)	(90)
Cash flow at year 0 prices	$ 784	$ 275	$159	$153	$147	$141	($ 90)

EXHIBIT 12.11:

Lease or Buy Alternatives—Present Value of Costs of Year 0*
(dollars in $1,000)

Effective Posttax	INTEREST RATE	
	8.4%	11.4%
Buy for cash		
Year 0	$1,000	$1,000
Years 1 to 5	(292)	(272)
Total	$ 708	$ 728
Lease		
Year 0	$ 275	$ 275
Years 1 to 5	433	410
Total	$ 708	$ 685
Lease is lower	$ 0	$ 42

*Based on the values of cash flow at year 0 prices in Exhibit 12.10.

Chapter 13 _____

ANALYZING PLANT AUTOMATION PROJECTS

Chapter 12 demonstrated the analysis of a capital investment decision which does not impact on the sales. This chapter presents a situation where the options vary not only in their capital investments and operating costs but also in the resulting sales volume, selling prices, and working capital requirements.

A decision which exemplifies this situation is one involving the automation of production operations, where the automation (1) enhances the product quality, thereby improving both the sales volume and selling prices, and (2) speeds up the purchasing and production time, thus cutting down the inventories.

I. BASIS OF ANALYSIS

Assume that the alternatives open to a company with an aging plant are:

Option A. Do not automate the plant. Just replace the major equipment.

Option B. Automate the plant operations, so that the company will be able to (1) reduce the production costs due to the streamlined operations, (2) raise selling prices due to improved product quality, and (3) lift the sales volume due to the faster production runs.

Assume that the costs and expected results are as follows:

	Option A: Not automated	Option B: Automated
Acquisition cost	$3,000,000	$12,000,000
Employee training and separation pay		$ 600,000
Operating costs per unit		
Direct labor	$ 180	$ 20
Direct power	20	10
Operating costs per year		
Manufacturing	$ 290,000	$ 800,000
Raw material wastage	20%	10%

Automated operations usually cut down on direct labor costs and raw material wastage, but jacks up the salaried monthly technical personnel and equipment maintenance.

The above costs are the items usually figured out in the traditional cost and benefit analysis. The other significant differences, which although not usually considered should also enter in the calculations, are:

	Option A: Not automated	Option B: Automated
Increase in sales over nonautomated operations		
Increase in sales volume		7%
Premium in selling price		5%
Reduction in inventory periods		
Raw materials	3 months	1 month
Goods in process	3 months	1 month
Finished goods	3 months	1 month

II. NOT AUTOMATED OPERATIONS (OPTION A)

CASH PROFIT (Exhibit 13.1)

The analysis employs the contribution to overhead form of income statement shown in Exhibit 13.1.

Inflation.   Exhibit 13.1 does not show any adjustment for inflation as all the figures use the year 0 price level. Year 0 is the current year, when the decision to automate or not is made and the purchase price for the new equipment or automation paid for. The new equipment or the automated production is assumed to be fully operational by early year 1.

Marketing Costs.   All the marketing costs are presumed to be either variable or fixed cost. It is assumed that there are no sales expansion costs. The annual increase in sales volume is just due to natural industry growth.

Interest and Return on Investment Approaches.   There are two ways of treating the interest cost in the financial projections: (1) the return on investment approach and (2) the postinterest approach.

Like the rate of return on investment approach used in short-term decision analysis described in Chapter 9, Analyzing Cost Reduction Measures, this method disregards the interest expense in the financial projections. See Exhibit 13.1. This method is used if (1) it is desired to highlight the profitability of the project itself, irrespective of the financing scheme used, as the scheme affects the viability of the project, or (2) all the financing is provided for or arranged by the parent company. However, in these cases, although the interest cost is not considered in the income statement, it is subsequently factored in the evaluation when the internal rate of return is calculated and related to the interest rate charged by the parent organization. Furthermore, an external interest rate is used in computing the net present value, which is done in a subsequent part of this analysis.

The postinterest income approach, which is not employed in this chapter, is similar to the residual income method described in Chapter 9. It shows the net income after deducting the interest. This method is applicable to cases where the operating unit plans to obtain the loans directly.

If this method were utilized in the present chapter, the interest on these loans would have to be considered as an expense item in Exhibit 13.1. Since this interest as well as the payments on principal would reduce the annual cash flow during the operating years—years 1 to 6—the corresponding loan proceeds would have to be added to the returns under year 0 in Exhibit 13.4 in determining the internal rate of return. Furthermore, any balance of the loan as of the end of year 6 would be deducted from the terminal return or value of the project.

Depreciation (Exhibit 13.4).   Just as in the analysis of equipment decision in Chapter 12, depreciation by itself does not enter into the analysis process as it is not a cash cost, and hence not a relevant cost. However, depreciation is considered insofar as it affects income tax. The income tax is calculated in Exhibit 13.2, based on depreciation rates for a five-year property, using the modified accelerated cost recovery system.

The acquisition cost of the equipment, which gives rise to depreciation, is a cash cost, and hence is considered in the cash flow in Exhibit 13.4.

Income Tax (Exhibit 13.2).   The income tax is calculated based on the net profit less the allowed depreciation. Since the net profit before tax and depreciation in the illustration use year 0 price level, no adjustment was made for inflation.

However depreciation is used as a basis in calculating the tax benefit derived therefrom. Since the depreciation to be reported in years 1 to 6 are based on the price levels for these years, the depreciation has to be brought to year 0 prices to make it comparable with the revenues and cash costs. Hence the use of the deflator factor.

WORKING CAPITAL REQUIREMENTS (Exhibit 13.3)

The annual increases in the working capital will add to the investment requirements or will be taken from the cash profit generated by operations, thereby diminishing the cash which will go to the investors. The higher the level of working capital or the smaller the amount of operating cash generation, the lower will be the internal rate of return and the net present value.

The working capital requirements for a long-term decision analysis are calculated in about the same manner as that for short-run profitability evaluation. For option A, the working capital requirements for the first three years were projected in Exhibit 13.3. To simplify the calculations, the working capital is estimated using the balance sheet method. (The other method, the root cost method, is discussed in Chapter 10.)

TOTAL CASH FLOW (Exhibit 13.4)

The profitability of a measure is determined by comparing the investments with the returns. The investments and annual returns are listed in Exhibit 13.4. They are all based on year 0 price levels.

Investments.   For either option A or B, the investments are in the following forms: present properties, new equipment to be acquired, present working capital, and additional working capital.

The present properties are valued not at book but at the economic price that they can command in the marketplace. These properties are the land, buildings, and equipment currently utilized and still to be used in the future. The value of the new equipment is the acquisition price of the equipment being considered.

The working capital covers both the requirements based on the present level of operations, which falls under year 0 in Exhibit 13.4, and the annual increases in working capital as estimated in Exhibit 13.3.

Returns.   The return is composed of (1) the operating cash flow, which is represented by the cash profit indicated in Exhibit 13.1, and (2) the terminal value which consists of the properties and working capital at the end of year 6. The present properties and working capital as of the end of the planning horizon in year 6 is considered as a return as they can be used in subsequent periods or converted to cash. The present properties which are land and buildings are presumed to retain their full value. On the other hand, the new equipment to be acquired are assumed to have no value as of the end of year 6 due to obsolescence.

In the illustration, the terminal value is based on the assets as of end of year 6. An alternative way of determining the terminal value is by capitalizing the operating cash flow of year 6. Terminal values in general are discussed in Chapter 2, Determinants of Projected Performance, and Chapter 4, Internal Rate of Return.

III. AUTOMATED PRODUCTION (OPTION B)

The cash profit, income tax, working capital, and total cash flow for option B are worked out in Exhibits 13.5 and 13.6, using the same assumptions used in Exhibits 13.1 to 13.4 under option A, but modified for the following: (1) sales volume is higher by 7%; (2) selling price is higher by 5%; and (3) the raw material, goods in process, and finished goods inventories are for one month only instead of three.

The second column (year 0) in Exhibit 13.5 shows what the cash profit could have been had the automation option been operational as of the start of year 0. This is only for comparative and computational purposes as the automation option, if ever implemented, is assumed to commence at the beginning of year 1.

The total working capital of $3,650,000 indicated at the end of year 0 in Exhibit 13.6 represents the figure under the current level of operations and before automation. The $3,650,000 is the same as that in year 0 in Exhibit 13.3. The purpose of placing this amount in Exhibit 13.6 is to estimate the change in working capital balance during the first year (year 1) of automated operations.

IV. COMPARATIVE ANALYSIS

ANALYSIS BASED ON THE BASIC SET OF ASSUMPTIONS (Exhibit 13.7)

The total cash flow of option A is compared with that of option B in Exhibit 13.7. Although the investment requirement of option B is only 211% of that of A, the cash generation of B is much higher—starting at 521% of A in year 1.

Since the excess of the returns of option B over option A is relatively higher than the excess of investment B over A, B has a higher rate of return. Thus, while option A has an internal rate of return of 15.6%, B is higher, at 17.5%. The incremental investment (excess of B over A) of $9,600,000 brings in an IRR of 20.5%.

At a 6% after-tax (or 10% pretax) cost of money, the $4,200,000 net present value of option A compares with the $7,622,000 of B. If the money cost is raised to 9.6% after tax (or 16% pretax), the net present value of A drops by $1,844,000 compared with the $2,869,000 decrease of B. The higher decline in B is due to its bigger returns in terms of absolute dollars.

Based on the assumptions as given earlier, and the profitability as gauged by the internal rate of return and net present value, option B seems to be the better alternative.

SENSITIVITY ANALYSIS (Exhibit 13.8)

The cash flow streams given in Exhibit 13.7 are based on the set of assumptions enumerated earlier. Although they are supposed to represent the best judgment of management at the time the study is prepared, the outcome in the future is expected to be different.

There are two general types of assumptions: those pertaining to the industry or competitive situation and those referring to the internal operations. The first one includes (1) the additional market share the company can get as a result of automation due to its faster time to service orders, (2) the premium price the firm can gain due to higher quality of the products, and (3) the total industry growth. The internal operational factors are the equipment and production costs. Of the two types of assumptions, the competitive premises are more volatile. It is for this reason that sensitivity runs should be made based on varying market conditions.

The profitability of the two options, based on different market conditions are indicated in Exhibit 13.8. The five sets of projections with varying assumptions result in different degrees of attractiveness of option B over A.

Basic Set of Assumptions.   As stated earlier, based on the basic assumptions stated at the start of this chapter, option B is a clear winner as it has a higher internal rate of return and net present value.

No Increase in Sales.   If the firm fails to increase its sales by 7%, which is expected due to the faster servicing of orders, and if the other assumptions can be attained, the internal rate of return of B will drop down to 15.6%, which is the same as that of A. As B retains its lead in the net present value, it would still seem to be the preferable option under this condition.

No Premium in Selling Price.   If the company will not be able to increase its selling prices at all due to the higher product quality, and if all the other assumptions can be realized, the internal rate of return of option B becomes lower than that of A. However, B still has a higher net present value. Since in this situation the ranking according to the internal rate of return is different from the one according to the present value, the firm will have to study the options more closely. The selection of options wherein one has a higher internal rate of return but a lower net present value is discussed in Chapter 6, Project Ranking and Capital Rationing.

Annual Industry Growth Rate of 2% Instead of 10%.   If instead of the 10% projected annual sales increase due to industry growth the rise is only 2%, but the other basic assumptions are not changed, option A will have a higher internal rate of return. However, at 6% discount rate, B will have the higher net present value. If the money cost glides to 9.6%, A will have a more attractive net present value. This apparent inconsistent behavior is explained as follows:

> *Option A has a higher internal rate of return but lower net present value at 6% discount rate.* This is accounted for by the much bigger investment base of option B. Its disadvantage in the internal rate of return is more than offset by the return on its incremental investment.
>
> *Option A has a lower net present value at 6% but higher value at 9.6%.* The effect of a higher discount rate is to depress the value of the returns, or the cash flow from year 1 to year 6. Since option B has much bigger dollar returns, the effect of the increase in the discount rate is to cut off more from the value of option B than from the value of A.

The selection of the alternative in this case involves two steps. First, decide on which should be given more relative weight under the circumstances—internal rate of return or net present value. The concepts involved and the procedures used, in resolving this issue are treated in Chapter 6. Second, try to refine the estimate on the possible cost of money in the future. It should be noticed that at 6%, the excess of the net present value of option B over A is $713,000, while at 9.6%, the net present value advantage of A is only $22,000. In other words, the net present values of the two alternatives will become identical at a discount rate which is slightly lower than 9.6%.

No Increase in Sales and Annual Industry Growth of 2%.   If the company cannot raise its sales volume in spite of the faster servicing of orders offered by automated production, and if the industry growth is limited to 2% instead of the projected 10%, the firm will be better off without the automation program. Under this scenario, the firm will have a higher internal rate of return and net present value under option A. In other words, the higher investment requirement of the automation program is geared for a high production volume. If the high production level cannot be attained, then the high investment cannot be justified.

CONSIDERATIONS BEYOND THE PLANNING HORIZON

A more important consideration not covered in the financial analysis which spans up to year 6 only is the position of the company beyond the planning horizon. Option B should give the firm a stronger competitive position in terms of bigger market and more customer confidence due to the better service and premium product quality.

EXHIBIT 13.1:
Not Automated Operations—Cash Profit at Constant Year 0 Prices (dollars in $1,000)

	Per unit	ANNUAL TOTAL AT YEAR						
		0	1	2	3	4	5	6
Sales in units—10% annual increase		10,000	11,000	12,100	13,310	14,641	16,105	17,716
Sales	$900	$ 9,000	$ 9,900	$10,890	$11,979	$13,177	$14,495	$15,944
Less: Variable costs								
Raw materials								
At 0% wastage	200	2,000	2,200	2,420	2,662	2,928	3,221	3,543
20% wastage	40	400	440	484	532	586	644	709
Direct labor	180	1,800	1,980	2,178	2,396	2,635	2,899	3,189
Power	20	200	220	242	266	293	322	354
Other manufacturing costs	60	600	660	726	799	878	966	1,063
Marketing expenses	150	1,500	1,650	1,815	1,997	2,196	2,416	2,657
Total variable costs	$650	$ 6,500	$ 7,150	$ 7,865	$ 8,652	$ 9,517	$10,468	$11,515
Contribution to overhead	$250	$ 2,500	$ 2,750	$ 3,025	$ 3,328	$ 3,660	$ 4,026	$ 4,429
Less: Overhead								
Manufacturing		290	290	290	290	290	290	290
Marketing and general		400	400	400	400	400	400	400
Total overhead		690	690	690	690	690	690	690
Net profit before tax		1,810	2,060	2,335	2,638	2,970	3,336	3,739
Income tax per Exhibit 13.2		724	593	579	850	1,070	1,221	1,441
Cash profit at constant year 0 prices		$ 1,086	$ 1,467	$ 1,756	$ 1,787	$ 1,900	$ 2,115	$ 2,298

EXHIBIT 13.2:
Not Automated Operations—Depreciation and Income Tax (dollars in $1,000)

		ANNUAL TOTAL IN YEAR					
	0	1	2	3	4	5	6
Given data							
Depreciation rates	100.0%	20.0%	32.0%	19.2%	11.5%	11.5%	5.8%
Inflation deflator at 4%	1	0.96	0.92	0.89	0.85	0.82	0.79
Income tax at constant year 0 prices							
Net profit before tax at year 0 prices, per Exhibit 13.1	$1,810	$2,060	$2,335	$2,638	$2,970	$3,336	$3,739
Less depreciation before inflation	0	600	960	576	345	345	174
After deflator at 4%		577	888	512	295	284	138
Taxable income*	$1,810	$1,483	$1,447	$2,125	$2,675	$3,053	$3,601
Income tax at 40%—at year 0 prices	$ 724	$ 593	$ 579	$ 850	$1,070	$1,221	$1,441

*After depreciation as adjusted for deflator.

EXHIBIT 13.3:
Not Automated Operations—Working Capital at Year 0 Prices
(dollars in $1,000)

	YEAR		
	0	*1*	*2*
Raw materials inventory			
Raw materials used per year	$2,400	$2,640	$ 2,904
Average duration—in months	3	3	3
Inventory, end	$ 600	$ 660	$ 726
Suppliers' credit			
Raw materials used per year	$2,400	$2,640	$ 2,904
Average duration—in months	1	1	1
Balance, end	($ 200)	($ 220)	($ 242)
Goods in process inventory			
Variable manufacturing costs per year	$5,000	$5,500	$ 6,050
Average duration—in months	3	3	3
Inventory, end	$1,250	$1,375	$ 1,513
Finished goods inventory			
Variable manufacturing costs per year	$5,000	$5,500	$ 6,050
Average duration—in months	3	3	3
Inventory, end	$1,250	$1,375	$ 1,513
Accounts receivables			
Sales per year	$9,000	$9,900	$10,890
Average duration—in months	1	1	1
Receivables, end	$ 750	$ 825	$ 908
Total balance, end of year	$3,650	$4,015	$ 4,417
Increase from prior year-end balance		$ 365	$ 402

EXHIBIT 13.4:

Not Automated Operations—Total Cash Flow at Constant Year o Prices (dollars in $1,000)

				YEAR			
	0	1	2	3	4	5	6
Investments							
Present properties	($2,000)						
New conventional equipment	(3,000)						
Present working capital	(3,650)						
Increase in working capital		($ 365)	($ 402)	($ 442)	($ 486)	($ 534)	($ 588)
Returns							
Operating cash flow per Exhibit 13.1		1,467	1,756	1,787	1,900	2,115	2,298
Terminal value							
Present properties							2,000
Working capital, end of year 6							6,466
Net	($8,650)	$1,102	$1,355	$1,346	$1,414	$1,581	$10,177

318

EXHIBIT 13.5:
Automated Operations—Cash Profit at Constant Year 0 Prices (dollars in $1,000)

	Per unit	YEAR 0	1	2	3	4	5	6
Sales in units—10% increase		10,700	11,770	12,947	14,242	15,666	17,232	18,956
Sales	$945	$10,112	$11,123	$12,235	$13,458	$14,804	$16,285	$17,913
Less: Variable costs								
Raw materials								
At 0% wastage	200	2,140	2,354	2,589	2,848	3,133	3,446	3,791
10% wastage	20	214	235	259	285	313	345	379
Direct labor	20	214	235	259	285	313	345	379
Power	10	107	118	129	142	157	172	190
Other manufacturing costs	60	642	706	777	855	940	1,034	1,137
Marketing expenses	150	1,605	1,766	1,942	2,136	2,350	2,585	2,843
Total product costs	$460	$ 4,922	$ 5,414	$ 5,956	$ 6,551	$ 7,206	$ 7,927	$ 8,720
Contribution to fixed costs	$485	$ 5,190	$ 5,708	$ 6,279	$ 6,907	$ 7,598	$ 8,358	$ 9,194
Less: Fixed costs								
Manufacturing		800	800	800	800	800	800	800
Marketing and general		400	400	400	400	400	400	400
Total fixed costs		1,200	1,200	1,200	1,200	1,200	1,200	1,200
Net profit before tax		3,990	4,508	5,079	5,707	6,398	7,158	7,994
Income tax		1,596	880	612	1,464	2,087	2,409	2,977
Cash profit		$ 2,394	$ 3,628	$ 4,468	$ 4,244	$ 4,311	$ 4,748	$ 5,016

EXHIBIT 13.6:
Automated Operations—Total Cash Flow (dollars in $1,000)

	YEAR						
	0	1	2	3	4	5	6
Investments							
Present properties	($ 2,000)						
New conventional equipment	($12,000)						
Training and separation pay net of tax	(600)						
Present working capital	(3,650)						
Increase in working capital			($ 154)	($ 169)	($ 186)	($ 204)	($ 225)
Returns							
Operating cash flow per Exhibit 13.5		$3,628	4,468	4,244	4,311	4,748	5,016
Decrease in working capital		2,115					
Terminal value							
Present properties							2,000
Working capital, end of year 6							2,472
Net	($18,250)	$5,743	$4,314	$4,075	$4,125	$4,544	$9,264

320

EXHIBIT 13.7:
Automation Decision—Return on Investment (dollars in $1,000)

		Option A Exhibit 13.4	Option B Exhibit 13.6	Increment from A to B	B as % of A
Cash flow stream					
Investments	Year 0	($ 8,650)	($18,250)	($ 9,600)	211%
Returns	Year 1	1,102	5,743	4,641	521
	Year 2	1,355	4,314	2,960	319
	Year 3	1,346	4,075	2,729	303
	Year 4	1,414	4,125	2,711	292
	Year 5	1,581	4,544	2,963	287
	Year 6	10,177	9,264	(913)	91
Internal rate of return		15.6%	17.5%	20.5%	
Net present value					
At 6% after tax					
Year 0		($ 8,650)	($18,250)	($ 9,600)	
Years 1 to 6		12,850	25,872	13,022	
Total		$ 4,200	$ 7,622	$ 3,422	
At 9.6% after tax					
Year 0		($ 8,650)	($18,250)	($ 9,600)	
Years 1 to 6		11,006	23,003	11,997	
Total		$ 2,356	$ 4,753	$ 2,397	
Decline		$ 1,844	$ 2,869	$ 1,025	

EXHIBIT 13.8:
Automation Decision—Sensitivity Analysis (dollars in $1,000)

	OPTION A*			OPTION B*		
	Internal rate of return	NET PRESENT VALUE		Internal rate of return	NET PRESENT VALUE	
		6.0%	9.6%		6.0%	9.6%
Based on basic assumptions (from Exhibit 13.7)	15.6%	$4,200	$2,356	17.5%	$7,622	$4,753
Based on varying assumptions No increase in sales due to faster servicing of orders	15.6%	$4,200	$2,356	15.6%	$6,257	$3,556
No premium in selling prices	15.6%	$4,200	$2,356	14.7%	$5,658	$3,015
Annual growth rate of 2% instead of 10%	11.4%	$2,052	$ 613	10.7%	$2,765	$ 591
No increase in sales due to faster servicing of orders; annual growth rate of 2%	11.4%	$2,052	$ 613	9.0%	$1,718	($ 334)

*The underlined values for the given option are higher than the corresponding values for the other option.

Chapter 14

ANALYZING LOAN SOURCE SELECTIONS

The selection of a loan financing source to be tapped is based, first, on the effective cost of the alternatives and, then, on the nonfinancial factors. The latter includes the development of the relationship with the lender for possible subsequent financing needs, the loan conditions imposed on the lender as participation in the management or attainment of certain ratios before the distribution of dividends, the collateral or security requirements, and the ability of the lender to adjust the payment schedule and other loan requirements to suit the particular needs and capabilities of the borrower.

This chapter analyzes the effective cost of alternative loan sources. The effective cost of financing is the compound interest rate, which, if used to discount (1) the receipts from a financing source and (2) the payments related to the financing, to a common reference date, the total discounted value of the receipts equals the total discounted value of the payments.

The receipts from the loan include the refund of any deposit or reserve required by the financing. The payments cover the loan principal amortization, interest, fees, and other outlays related to the financing, including the establishment of any deposit or reserve fund. The receipts and payments are after adjustments for income tax and inflation.

The definition of effective cost is similar to that of the internal rate of return (IRR). The only difference is that the IRR pertains to investments. The methodology or procedure of calculating the effective cost of financing is the same as that of the IRR. In fact, the personal computer software formula for determining the IRR is the one used in calculating the effective cost of financing.

In the Lotus 1-2-3 software (copyright of Lotus Development Corporation), for instance, the IRR formula, which is also used for the effective cost of financing, is @IRR (estimated IRR rate, range of values).

In the absence of a computer, an alternative procedure of computing the effective cost of financing is by discounting the values to a common reference date using a table on compound interest.

DETERMINANTS OF THE EFFECTIVE COST OF FINANCING

The determinants of the effective cost of a specific loan are

1. The nominal rate of interest
2. The number of days used in calculating periods of less than a year
3. The frequency of the compounding of the interest
4. The timing of the payment of the interest
5. The amount of up-front fees and its relation to the loan amount and loan amortization schedule
6. The reserve requirements
7. The amount of the loan in relation to the total financing needs
8. The loan amortization schedule or pattern of payment
9. The income tax rate
10. The inflation rate

How the effective rate is influenced by these factors is discussed in the following sections.

I. EFFECTIVE INTEREST RATE BASE

NOMINAL INTEREST

The nominal rate serves as the starting point in calculating the effective interest rate. The nominal interest rate is the one stated in the contract. It may refer to the prime interest rate, prime rate plus a certain premium, or a fixed interest rate.

The nominal annual interest rate may be equivalent to the effective annual interest rate only if the following conditions hold true:

1. The interest is compounded annually.
2. The interest is paid at the end of every year.
3. There are no fees and no reserve requirements.
4. The loan amounts and repayment schedules of the financing from different sources are the same.

5. There is no income tax and no inflation.

Since it is very unlikely that the foregoing conditions are fulfilled, the nominal interest rate usually differs from the effective rate.

II. COMPOUNDING, PAYMENT, AND CALCULATION OF INTEREST

The frequency of the compounding and timing of the payment of the interest influences the effective money cost. The more frequent is the compounding, or the more accelerated is the payment, the higher is the effective interest rate.

The effective interest rate for loans with durations of less than a year is increased if the daily rate is calculated on the basis of 360 days rather than 365 days a year.

FREQUENCY OF THE COMPOUNDING OF THE INTEREST (Exhibit 14.1)

Interest is usually compounded daily, monthly, quarterly, or annually. The more frequent the compounding, the higher is the effective interest rate. Take the case of the three loans described here:

	Loan A	*Loan B*	*Loan D*
Nominal interest rate	12%	12%	12%
Compounding of interest	Annual	Monthly	Quarterly
Loan principal	$100,000	$100,000	$100,000
Principal and interest payment at the end of the year	$112,000	$112,551	$112,683
Interest cost—total payment less principal	$ 12,000	$ 12,551	$ 12,683
Effective interest rate	12.000%	12.551%	12.683%

The three loans have the same nominal interest rate, principal, duration (one year), and principal and interest payment pattern (full payment at end of year). However, the loans vary in one aspect: the frequency of the compounding or computing of the compound interest. Hence they have different effective interest rates.

From the viewpoint of the borrower, loan A is the cheapest, or the one with the lowest effective interest rate, since it requires the smallest amount of interest to pay at the end of the year—$12,000. It has the lowest effective interest rate since it has the least frequent compounding of interest—only once. Since the compounding is annual and the duration of the loan is only one year, in effect no portion of the interest bears any interest at all. Hence the 12% nominal interest which is computed on the $100,000 principal alone comes out to just $3,000 a quarter or $1,000 a month.

Loan B has a higher effective interest rate since the interest, although all payable at the end of the year, is computed four times during the year, at 3% per quarter. The interest for the first quarter is calculated just on the $100,000 principal. However, interest for the subsequent quarters are computed based on the principal plus all prior interest. Thus the interest for the fourth quarter is $3,278. This compares with the $3,000 a quarter for loan A. See Exhibit 14.1 for the calculations.

Loan D has the highest effective rate among the three as the interest is calculated monthly. Hence the interest for the last quarter of $3,315 ($1,094 for October, $1,105 for November, and $1,116 for December) is higher than the interest of loan B for the same quarter.

Methods of Computing the Interest.   There are several ways of calculating the effective interest rate for the three loans as described earlier. Three methods are explained here.

The most cumbersome but the most instructional method employs a table similar to that in Exhibit 14.1 in order to arrive at the total principal and interest payable at the end of the term,. and then dividing the interest to be paid at the end of the year, by the principal to be obtained at the beginning of the year.

The second method uses an interest table. For loan B, we divide the annual interest rate of 12% by four quarters to arrive at the quarterly interest rate of 3%. Then we consult the table of "amount of 1" and look for 3%, period 4 (four quarters) to find out the value of 1 earning at 3% for four periods, which is 1.1255 or 112.55%. From this value we take out the value of 1 or 100%, which represents the principal, leaving 12.55% for the effective interest.

Another procedure utilizes the internal rate of return computer software formula but substitutes (1) the investments in the IRR formula, with the proceeds from the loan and (2) the returns in the formula, with the interest and principal payments.

TIMING OF THE PAYMENT OF THE INTEREST
(Exhibit 14.2)

Interest may be required to be paid (1) at the end of the term of the loan, (2) during the term of the loan and at the end of the term, or (3) up front. Paying the interest up front means deducting the interest from the principal, with the balance being the value being released to the borrower.

Given the same nominal rate and other terms except the timing of the payment of the interest, the first arrangement (payable at the end of the term) gives the lowest effective cost. In other words, the later the payment of the interest, the lower is the cost since in the meantime the borrower can make use of the funds which otherwise would be used to pay the interest.

Exhibit 14.2 presents three loans—A, C, and G—with identical terms: nominal interest rate, loan amount, duration, and principal payment pattern. The only difference is in the timing of the payment of the interest. For loan A, the interest is payable at the end of the term; for C, it is at the end of every quarter; and for G, it is up front.

Since the most frequent term of payment is quarterly, the effective interest rate is computed first on a quarterly basis. The quarterly interest may be calculated by discounting the values from quarter 1 to 4 to the reference time quarter 0 so that the discounted values equal the loan principal which is $100,000. The IRR formula may be used.

The quarterly interest is then converted to annual interest by using the calculations shown in Exhibit 14.2, part II.

Loan A—Interest Payable at the End of the Term. The effective annual interest rate of loan A remains at 12%, whether the calculation is made annually or quarterly. The reason is that even if the calculation is compounded more frequently than annually, there is no intervening financial transaction (payment or receipt) to be compounded, since the transactions occur only at the start and end of the year.

Loan C—Interest Payable Quarterly. The nominal rate of 12% a year is equivalent to 3% per quarter. Paying 3% quarterly is equivalent to paying 12.551%, and not 12%. This means that at a money cost of 3% a quarter, paying $3,000 a quarter for a total of $12,000 a year, is just like paying $12,551 at the end of the year. Hence loan C in Exhibit 14.2 has the same effective cost as loan B in Exhibit 14.1. Note that the cumulative values representing principal and interest as of the end of every quarter, for loan B as shown in Exhibit 14.1 and for loan C as indicated in Exhibit 14.2, part II, are identical.

Loan G—Interest Payable Up Front. Obtaining a $100,000 loan and then deducting the 12% nominal interest or $12,000 from the loan proceeds, is just like getting an $88,000 loan and then using $100,000 to pay for both principal and interest at the end of the term. In the latter transaction the interest is $12,000 ($100,000 less $88,000), which is 13.636% of the $88,000 equivalent loan. This rate is the effective interest rate of loan G.

NUMBER OF DAYS USED

The interest for a fractional year is sometimes computed based on a daily interest rate. The daily rate is estimated by dividing the annual interest either by 365 days or 360 days. Of course, the daily interest amount based on the smaller denominator (360 days) gives a higher interest expense:

	Loan H	*Loan J*
Loan principal	$100,000	$100,000
Interest for 1 year at 12%	$ 12,000	$ 12,000
Interest per day		
Based on 365 days per year	$ 32.88	
Based on 360 days per year		$ 33.33
Interest for 1 month of 30 days	$ 986.30	$ 1,000.00

III. UP-FRONT FEES AND RESERVE REQUIREMENTS

Up-front fees and reserve requirements help determine the effective interest rate. The higher the fees or the required reserves, the higher is the effective interest rate.

UP-FRONT FEES AND LOAN AMORTIZATION SCHEDULE (Exhibit 14.3)

Up-front fees are expenses, in addition to interest, which are paid at about the same time as the loan proceeds are released, or earlier. Up-front fees include service fees, inspection fees, registration fees, and credit investigation and legal expenses. Loans and bonds may involve underwriting fees.

Up-front fees are deducted from the financing proceeds. Since the effect of up-front fees is to reduce the proceeds from financing, the effective interest rate is automatically increased.

Because the up-front fees are in effect spread out throughout the life and over the principal of the loan, the excess of the effective interest over the nominal rate is dictated not just by the up-front fees as a percentage of the loan principal, but also by the loan duration and principal payment pattern.

Take the case of loan K in Exhibit 14.3 with the terms as given. Loan K has a 10% effective interest rate, as calculated in the exhibit—using the IRR formula. This effective rate represents a 2% premium over the nominal rate of 8%. On the other hand, loan L with identical terms except that the principal will be amortized over the three-year period will have a 10.9% effective cost or a 2.9% markup.

Loan K has a lower premium because the 5% up-front fee is spread over a loan life of three years, while the fee of loan L is amortized over a shorter effective life of only two years. The interest premium arising from the up-front fee is roughly in inverse relation to the effective loan life. The effective loan life is approximated as follows:

	Year payable	Number of years outstanding	Payments on principal	Dollar-years	Effective loan life (in years)
Loan K	Year 3	3	$100,000	300,000	3
Loan L	Year 1	1	$ 30,803	30,803	
	Year 2	2	33,268	66,535	
	Year 3	3	35,929	107,787	
	Total		$100,000	205,126	2

The dollar-years in the preceding table was obtained by multiplying the number of years outstanding by the payments on principal. The effective loan life was calculated by dividing the dollar-years by the payments on principal.

The effective interest of a loan is affected by the loan life and payment pattern of the principal in the same way that the NPV is influenced by the project life and recovery pattern of the investment or returns. See Chapter 5, Present Value Techniques, Exhibit 5.4.

RESERVE REQUIREMENTS (Exhibit 14.4)

Some loans may require the establishment of a reserve or deposit to guarantee the loan payment or for other purposes. Usually the deposit earns at a rate lower than the loan nominal rate. This interest differential raises the effective interest rate.

Consider Loan M in Exhibit 14.4. If it were not for the reserve requirement, the effective interest rate would be equivalent to the nominal interest of 10%. The institution of the reserve imposes a 1% interest penalty which jacks up the effective interest by 1%. See Exhibit 14.4, part II, for the calculation, using the IRR formula.

The 1% interest penalty in this case is a factor of interest differential between the loan nominal interest and the deposit earning rate, reserve requirement as a percentage of the loan, and net proceeds (loan principal less deposit) as a percentage of the loan principal. The 1% penalty was calculated in Exhibit 14.4, part III, by inputting all these factors.

IV. AMOUNT AND LOAN AMORTIZATION SCHEDULE

In certain instances, the effective cost of a loan may be affected by (1) the amount of loan which may be obtained from a particular source or (2) the amortization schedule of loan principal payment pattern. These cases call for the determination of the effective cost not only of the loans under immediate consideration, but of auxiliary financing arrangements which will be necessary to bring the amounts and payment patterns of the loans under evaluation, comparable.

This method is similar to the comparable investment approach (CIA) used in the evaluation of projects with different investment sizes, project lives, or return patterns as depicted in Chapter 6, Project Ranking and Capital Rationing, Exhibit 6.1, cases II and III. However, the term investment in said exhibit should be changed to loan amount; the project life, loan life; the core project, the loan under consideration; the side project, the supplementary financing; and the reinvestment vehicle, the refinancing loan.

AMOUNT OF LOAN

The amount of loan which may be granted may be restricted by the value of the collateral as determined by the lender. Hence, a decision on loan selection depends not only on the effective interest rate for the loan itself as discussed in the preceding sections but also on the amounts available.

Suppose a company needs a $1,000,000 financing and has physical security to support the loan. Bank N offers a loan for the entire amount at an effective interest of 9.5%. On the other hand, Bank P gives a lower rate, 9%, but can grant only $700,000, which is the loan value it has determined based on the available security.

The analysis of the comparative cost of the loans from the two banks requires additional information: the interest on the $300,000 supplemental financing if the Bank P offer were accepted. If the interest on the additional loan were 12%, then the blended rate of the loan package consisting of the $700,000 Bank P loan and the $300,000 side loan comes out to 9.9%. This is the cost which may be compared with the 9.5% interest on the loan from Bank N.

LOAN AMORTIZATION SCHEDULE (Exhibit 14.5)

The terms of a specific loan can affect the effective cost of (1) that particular loan and (2) a loan package which includes that loan.

Loans with the same amount, interest rate, and repayment period may give different effective interest rates if they have different repayment patterns and if a refinancing loan carries another effective interest rate.

Assume, for instance, that a firm needs $100,000 for three years. The available financing are loans Q and R as described in Exhibit 14.5. The loans have the same amount and features except for the repayment period: the principal of loan Q is payable in lump sum at the end of three years, while loan R calls for equal annual payments which cover both principal and interest. If loan R were taken, a refinancing loan is necessary to bridge the time between the annual payments of principal on loan R and the end of the three years. The 9.19% blended rate of the loan R loan package consisting of loan R itself and the supporting refinancing loan is the one to be compared with the 8% interest on loan Q.

V. INCOME TAX AND INFLATION

In all of the foregoing discussions, the effective interest rate was calculated before considering the income tax and inflation. In an actual case, income tax and inflation should be taken into account. Otherwise, the results could be misleading.

INCOME TAX (Exhibit 14.6, part I)

Since the interest on the loan is deductible for income tax purposes, the income tax benefit reduces the effective interest rate. Take the case of the loan described in Exhibit 14.6. Since the interest rate before tax is 12%, a 40% effective income tax rate cuts the interest rate by 40%, thus reducing the interest to 7.2%.

INFLATION (Exhibit 14.6, part II)

Inflation further reduces the effective interest rate, since the loan is paid in cheaper dollars. If the annual inflation is 4%, and the after-tax interest rate is 7.2%, the postinflation interest rate dives to 3.08%. The 3.08% was calculated by using the IRR formula.

Before applying the formula, the price index is calculated first. At 4% inflation rate, the price for year 1 is 1.04 times that for year 0, the starting point. The price for year 2 is 1.04 times that for year 1, or 1.082 that for year 0.

The deflator factor is then calculated by dividing one by the price index. The deflator factor of .962 in year 1 means that if a dollar in year 0 can buy $1.00 worth of goods in year 0, a dollar in year 1 can purchase only $0.962 worth of commodities in year 0. The difference is due to the decline in the buying power of the currency. The cash flow before inflation is then converted into the cash flow after inflation by multiplying the former by the deflator factor. The IRR formula is then applied to the cash flow after inflation.

EXHIBIT 14.1:
Frequency of Compounding of Interest

	Quarter	Month	Loan A	Loan B	Loan D
Frequency of compounding of interest			Annual	Quarterly	Monthly
Periodic interest			12.00%	3.00%	1.00%
Loan principal	0	0	$100,000	$100,000	$100,000
Interest		1			1,000
End-of-month balance		1			101,000
Interest		2			1,010
End-of-month balance		2			102,010
Interest	1	3		3,000	1,020
End-of-period balance	1	3		103,000	103,030
Interest		4			1,030
End-of-month balance		4			104,060
Interest		5			1,041
End-of-month balance		5			105,101
Interest	2	6		3,090	1,051
End-of-period balance	2	6		106,090	106,152
Interest		7			1,062
End-of-month balance		7			107,214
Interest		8			1,072
End-of-month balance		8			108,286
Interest	3	9		3,183	1,083
End-of-period balance	3	9		109,273	109,369
Interest		10			1,094
End-of-month balance		10			110,462
Interest		11			1,105
End-of-month balance		11			111,567
Interest	4	12	12,000	3,278	1,116
End-of-year balance— principal and interest	4	12	$112,000	$112,551	$112,683
Total interest for the year			$ 12,000	$ 12,551	$ 12,683

EXHIBIT 14.2:

Frequency of Payment of Interest

	Quarter	Loan A	Loan C	Loan G
I. Transactions				
Nominal interest rate		12%	12%	12%
Payment of interest		End of term	Quarterly	Up front
Cash flow				
Loan proceeds	0	$ 100,000	$ 100,000	$ 88,000
Payments	1		(3,000)	
	2		(3,000)	
	3		(3,000)	
	4	(112,000)	(103,000)	(100,000)
Quarterly interest compounded quarterly		2.874%	3.000%	3.247%
Annual interest compounded quarterly (see below)		12.000%	12.551%	13.636%
II. Annual interest compounded quarterly				
Value of principal plus interest, end of quarter	1	1.0287	1.0300	1.0325
	2	1.0583	1.0609	1.0660
	3	1.0887	1.0927	1.1006
	4	1.1200	1.1255	1.1364
Value of interest alone	4	0.1200	0.1255	0.1364

EXHIBIT 14.3:
Up Front Fees

	Loan K	Loan L
Given Data		
Loan proceeds	$100,000	$100,000
Up-front fees—5%	$ 5,000	$ 5,000
Interest—8% a year, payable annually		
Term	3 years	3 years
Payment pattern		
Lump sum at end (balloon payment)	X	
Equal annual amortization—diminishing principal, increasing interest		X

	Year 0	Year 1	Year 2	Year 3
Calculations				
Loan K				
Loan proceeds	$100,000			
Payments—fees	(5,000)			
Payments—principal				(100,000)
Payments—interest		(8,000)	(8,000)	(8,000)
Net receipts (payments)	$ 95,000	($ 8,000)	($ 8,000)	($108,000)
Effective interest rate*	10.0%			
Loan L				
Loan proceeds	$100,000			
Payments—fees	(5,000)			
Payments—principal		(30,803)	(33,268)	(35,929)
Payments—interest		(8,000)	(5,536)	(2,874)
Net receipts (payments)	$ 95,000	($ 38,803)	($ 38,803)	($ 38,803)
Effective interest rate*	10.9%			
Annual amortization		($ 38,803)	($ 38,803)	($ 38,803)
Amortization schedule				
Principal, beginning balance		$100,000	$ 69,197	$ 35,929
Payment—interest		(8,000)	(5,536)	(2,874)
Payment—principal		(30,803)	(33,268)	(35,929)
Principal, ending balance	$100,000	69,197	35,929	0

*Using the IRR computer formula.

EXHIBIT 14.4:
Reserve Requirement

I. Given data

Principal	$100,000
Interest	10.00%
Term—balloon payment at end of three years	
Required reserve	
Amount	$ 20,000
Interest income on the reserve	6% due annually

II. Cash flow and effective interest rate

	RECEIPTS		PAYMENTS		*Excess (deficiency) of receipts over payments*
Year	*Principal proceeds*	*Reserve proceeds and interest*	*Reserve and up-front fees*	*Loan principal and interest*	
0	$100,000		($20,000)		$80,000
1		$ 1,200		($ 10,000)	(8,800)
2		1,200		(10,000)	(8,800)
3		21,200		(110,000)	(88,800)
Effective interest rate (using the computer IRR formula)					11.00%

III. Interest penalty

Loan nominal rate		10.0%
Reserve earning rate	−	6.0%
Interest differential	=	4.0%
Reserve as a percentage of loan	×	20.0%
Interest penalty based on loan principal	=	0.8%
Net loan proceeds (loan principal less reserve) as a percentage of loan principal	/	80.0%
Interest premium based on net loan proceeds	=	1.0%

EXHIBIT 14.5:
Loan Amortization Schedule

	Loan Q	Loan R	
Given data			
Loan proceeds	$ 100,000	$ 100,000	
Annual interest payable annually	8%	8%	
Term	3 years	3 years	
Payment pattern			
Principal at end of year	x		
Equal annual debt service		x	

	Year 0	Year 1	Year 2	Year 3
Loan Q				
Loan proceeds	$100,000			
Payments—principal				($100,000)
Payments—interest		($8,000)	($8,000)	($8,000)
Net receipts (payments)	$100,000	($8,000)	($8,000)	($108,000)
Effective interest rate*	8.00%			
Loan package R				
Loan R				
Loan proceeds	$100,000			
Payments—principal		(30,803)	(33,268)	(35,929)
Payments—interest		(8,000)	(5,536)	(2,874)
Net receipts (payments)	$100,000	($38,803)	($38,803)	($38,803)
Effective interest rate*	8.00%			
Refinancing loan				
Loan proceeds		$ 30,803	$ 33,268	
Payments—principal				(64,071)
Payments—interest			(3,696)	(7,689)
Net receipts (payments)	0	$ 30,803	$ 29,572	($71,760)
Effective interest rate*	12.00%			
Total loan package R				
Loan proceeds	$100,000	$ 30,803	$ 33,268	$ 0
Payments—principal	0	(30,803)	(33,268)	(100,000)
Payments—interest	0	(8,000)	(9,232)	(10,563)
Net receipts (payments)	$100,000	($8,000)	($9,232)	($110,563)
Effective interest rate*	9.19%			

*Using the IRR computer formula.

EXHIBIT 14.6:
Income Tax and Inflation

	Year 0	*Year 1*	*Year 2*	*Year 3*
I. Rate after tax but before inflation				
Loan proceeds	$100,000			
Payments—principal				(100,000)
Payments—interest		(12,000)	(12,000)	(12,000)
Tax benefit on interest		4,800	4,800	4,800
Cash flow after tax but before inflation	$100,000	($7,200)	($7,200)	($107,200)
Effective interest rate*	7.20%			
II. Rate after tax and inflation				
Price index	1.000	1.040	1.082	1.125
Deflator	1.000	0.962	0.925	0.889
Cash flow after tax	$100,000	($7,200)	($7,200)	($107,200)
Cash flow after inflation	$100,000	($6,923)	($6,657)	($95,300)
Effective interest rate*	3.08%			

*Using the IRR computer formula.

Chapter 15 _____

ANALYZING DEBT/EQUITY STRUCTURES

This chapter determines the impact of different types of debt leverages on (1) the internal rate of return of the stockholders in long-term projects and (2) the underlying risk absorbed by the project.

This chapter introduces new concepts of debt leverages, including side leverage, loan size leverage, loan outstanding dollar-year leverage, front leverage, and inflation leverage. Corporate leverage, project leverage, and double leverage were presented in Chapter 5, Section V.

Project cash flow, investors' cash flow, and internal rate of return (IRR) were used in analyzing the return, while debt service break-even point sales volume (DSBEPSV) and sensitivity analysis were employed in assessing the risk. Time value of money, income tax, inflation, and risk were considered in the analysis.

Related to the discussions in this chapter are the following subjects which are covered elsewhere in this book: financial projections (Chapter 3), internal rate of return (Chapter 4), net present value (Chapter 5), sensitivity analysis (Chapter 7), break-even point analysis (Chapter 8), effective cost of debt (Chapter 14), return on stockholders' equity (Chapter 19), and debt/equity ratio (Chapter 20).

I. NATURE OF DEBT LEVERAGE

RATIONALE OF DEBT LEVERAGE

A firm takes on long-term debt for its project if the intrinsic internal rate of return of the project itself, that is, what the total investment in the project can earn over time, is higher than the cost of the available debt. By utilizing debt, the excess of the project IRR over the cost of the debt, corresponding to that portion of the total project cost which is to be financed by the loan is shifted from the lenders to the residual investors. This value which is shifted enables the investors to earn more than the IRR of the project if there were no obligations.

CONCEPT OF DEBT LEVERAGE (Exhibit 15.1)

This concept is graphically illustrated in Exhibit 15.1. Areas A, B, and C represent the total dollar value of the return which the total investment in the project, over a given number of years, can earn. This total dollar value denotes roughly the product of two factors: the project rate of return, which is assumed to be 10% in the illustration, and the dollar-years of investment, which is 15,000.

If the project can obtain a debt at 8%, which will cover 10,000 dollar-years out of the 15,000 total required by the project, the value of area A is shifted from the creditors to the residual investors, where it becomes area D. The total return to be obtained by the investors, then, is composed of two parts: their proportionate share in the project return, which at 10% is represented by area C, and their profit from the debt leverage, which is area D. The leverage in this case enables the investors to gain a 4% increment in their IRR (from 10% to 14%). This is due to the following:

1. The utilization of debt at a cost lower than the project IRR. This passes the 2% time value of money spread to the investors.
2. The utilization of debt with outstanding dollar-year which is twice that of the investors. This multiplies by 2 the 2% time value of money spread in item 1.

IMPLICATIONS ON THE INVESTORS' IRR

From the illustration it is clear that there are two determinants of the investors' IRR: the excess of project IRR over the cost of debt and the dollar-years of debt relative to that of equity. If the excess of the project IRR (time value of money spread leverage) or the dollar-years of debt relative to equity (loan outstanding dollar-year leverage) is magnified, the investors' IRR is enhanced.

These two determinants of IRR are refined in the subsequent discussions. Furthermore, other determinants or other types of debt leverages are also added in the succeeding sections.

IMPLICATIONS ON THE PROJECT RISK

The taking on of debt adds fixed cash outlays—for the interest and amortization of principal. Risk is created to the extent that the firm may not be able to service these requirements in the future. Thus, although debt leverage raises the IRR of the stockholders, it also increases the risk of the project.

TYPES OF LEVERAGES

Although the amount of debt relative to equity, or the loan size leverage, is commonly identified as the only form of leverage, there are several other forms which can also be employed to increase the investors' IRR. The following list presents the various types of leverages.

A. Cost of money leverage
    1. Side or project financing leverage
        a. Loan size leverage
        b. Loan outstanding dollar-year or effective debt life leverage
            (1) Loan payment pattern leverage
            (2) Loan repayment period leverage
        c. Time value of money spread leverage
    2. Front or temporary investors' financing leverage
    3. Project, corporate, and double financing leverages
B. Inflation leverage

Cost of Money versus Inflation Leverage. In a cost of money leverage, the project IRR before debt is enhanced through the exploitation of loan whose cost is lower than the IRR. This is the leverage explained earlier under the concept of debt leverage.

    In an inflation leverage, the creditors lose part of the value of their loans as they are paid in cheaper dollars. This value which they lose is captured by the project or the project's residual investors.

Side versus Front Leverage. Side or project financing is used to fund the project directly. It appears in the projected cash flow statement of the project. Side financing enhances the project IRR, and indirectly, the investors' IRR.

    Front or investors' financing is used to fund all or part of the investors' capital contributions to the project. It is shown in the cash flow statement of the investors and not in the cash flow of the project. Hence it affects the investors' IRR but not the project IRR.

    Most debt leverages refer to side leverage as front financing is a novel form of leverage. Side and front financing are explained further in Section II of this chapter.

Project, Corporate, and Double Leverages. Project leverage is obtained when a project takes on debt. Corporate leverage is attained when a corporate investor obtains debt. Double leverage results if a corporate investor uses a blend of equity and debt to invest in the equity of a project which also obtains loans. These leverages are explained in Chapter 5.

Corporate leverage is of a continuing nature while front leverage is of a temporary duration.

TECHNIQUES USED IN THE ANALYSIS

The appraisal of debt leverage in connection with the analysis of debt/ equity structures is divided into two parts: (1) the study of the effects of leverage on the stockholders' IRR and (2) the evaluation of the impact of leverage on the project risk. The analysis for each part is outlined here.

Study of the Effect of Leverage on the Investors' IRR

- Projected cash flow statements are prepared under varying assumptions regarding the amount and terms of the debt to be taken. Two types of cash flows are prepared: one for the project itself (project cash flow) and another for the investors (investors' cash flow).
- The investors' IRR is determined based on the investors' cash flow. The amount and type of debt giving the highest IRR is considered to be the ideal under the return criterion.

Study of the Effect of Leverage on the Project Risk

- The sensitive operating factors are identified. Several sets of cash flow projections are prepared, one set for each assumption regarding the key sensitive factors. The ability of the firm to service the debt under each set of expected conditions is determined.
- Since sales volume is assumed to be the most sensitive factor in the illustration, the debt service break-even point sales volume is calculated and related to the expected sales under the worst case scenario. A project is considered to be taking a reasonable risk if there is a very good chance that the expected sales will be higher than the DSBEPSV.

II. EFFECT OF DEBT LEVERAGE ON THE INVESTORS' IRR

IRR OF A DEBT-FREE PROJECT (Exhibit 15.2)

Assume that the cash flow of the project with a three-year life is as shown in Exhibit 15.2.

Project Cash Flow.   Buildings and equipment will be purchased as of the start of operations, which is end of year 0. Year 1 is the first year of operations. To simplify the case, the buildings and equipment are to be depreciated for only three years, in equal annual amounts. This treatment is assumed to be used also for income tax purposes. The buildings and equipment are assumed to have no value as of the end of year 3. (For the depreciation methods and rates allowable for tax purposes, consult the Internal Revenue Service Publication No. 534.)

The depreciation is deductible for income tax purposes. Hence, it is deducted from the revenues for purposes of calculating the income tax. However, depreciation by itself does not involve cash flow. Thus, since depreciation is deducted for purposes of estimating net profit before tax which serves as the basis in calculating the income tax, depreciation is added back to the cash profit to calculate the cash flow. The effective federal and state income taxes are assumed to total 40%.

The working capital, to be composed mainly of inventories, will be recovered in full at the end of year 3. All excess cash generation will be given to the investors as cash dividends.

In the meantime, inflation is disregarded.

Investors' Cash Flow.   If all the financing requirements of the project will be met by stockholders' equity, the investors' cash flow will be as shown in the bottom part of Exhibit 15.2. The $3,400,000 equity contribution in the project cash flow is shown as the investment in the investors' cash flow. The dividends in the project cash flow are forwarded to the investors' cash flow as the returns. The resulting IRR is 15.7%.

EFFECT OF SIDE LEVERAGE ON THE IRR
(Exhibit 15.3)

The stockholders' IRR can be increased if debt financing with an effective cost of less than the 15.7% IRR of the debt-free project is obtained. Assume that $1,800,000 out of the $3,400,000 total financing requirement can be supplied by a loan. The principal is payable in three equal annual installments. The interest is 12%, payable at the end of every year. Since the interest is deductible for income tax purposes, the net interest cost after an assumed 40% combined federal and state tax is 7.2% (60% of 12%).

The cash flow in Exhibit 15.2 as modified for the change in financing as just described is presented in Exhibit 15.3.

Investors' Differential Cash Flow.   The effect of the introduction of the debt financing is to cut the equity investment and the returns thereon by the following amounts (in $1,000):

	Year 0	Year 1	Year 2	Year 3
Investments	($1,800)			
Returns	0	$730	$686	$643
Total	($1,800)	$730	$686	$643
Internal rate of return	7.2%			

These figures represent the equity investors' decremental cash flow—or the decline in their cash flow due to the introduction of the $1,800,000 debt financing. The amounts are calculated by deducting the values in the investors' cash flow in Exhibit 15.3 (with $1,800,000 debt) from those in Exhibit 15.1 (without debt).

The loan proceeds are used to substitute for part of the equity, while the debt service less the tax benefits is utilized to reduce the returns to the investors.

The values in the investors' differential cash flow are identical to the amounts in the lenders' cash flow, less the 40% tax savings on interest received by the project. For instance, the $730,000 year 1 reduction in the return to the investors may be calculated as:

Interest—12% of $1,800,000	$216,000*
Less: Tax savings—40%	86,000
Net interest cost	130,000
Amortization of principal	600,000*
Total reduction in return to investors	$730,000

*From the project cash flow in Exhibit 15.3.

Effect of Leverage on the Investors' IRR.   The IRR of the investors' decremental cash flow is 7.2%, which is the same as the posttax or effective interest cost of the loan.

Since the investors are reducing their investment with a debt which costs only 7.2%, which is lower than the overall project IRR of 15.7%, the effect of the leverage is to push up the investors' IRR—to 23% in this case. See the last line in Exhibit 15.3.

EFFECT OF LOAN SIZE LEVERAGE ON THE IRR

If the debt is lower than $1,800,000, the IRR will be lower than 23%. For instance, if the loan is $900,000 only, the IRR will be 18.2%. Conversely, if the debt is higher than $1,800,000, the IRR on the equity will be higher than 23%.

EFFECT OF LOAN OUTSTANDING DOLLAR-YEAR LEVERAGE ON THE IRR (Exhibits 15.4 and 15.5)

Supposing that instead of the $1,800,000 loan in Exhibit 15.3, the loan will be for $1,500,000 but with the terms as described in Exhibit 15.4 under structure C. The cash flow using the $1,500,000 debt is calculated in Exhibit 15.5.

A review of the amount of the debt shown in Exhibit 15.4 reveals a glaring discrepancy: while the amount of debt declines from $1,800,000 in structure B to $1,500,000 in structure C, the IRR rises from 23.0% to 25.6%.

This IRR behavior defies the classic financing structure theory which rules that, if the cost of the debt is lower than the IRR, the higher is the amount of the debt, the higher the IRR becomes. This statement was proven earlier by a comparison of the IRR under the following situations:

With no debt	15.7%
With $900,000 debt	18.2%
With $1,800,000 debt	23.0%

Effect of Loan Pattern Leverage on the IRR.   A study of structures B and C proves that this classic rule, when applied to projects, is subject to this qualification: the debt in the alternatives should have the same repayment pattern and repayment period. The reason why the IRR increases from structure B to C is that, while the original amount of the debt declines from $1,800,000 to $1,500,000, the amount of dollar-years the debts will be outstanding actually rises from $3,600,000 in structure B to $4,500,000 in C, calculated as follows:

	Loan size			*Dollar-years outstanding*
Structure B	$ 600,000	for one year	=	$ 600,000
	600,000	for two years	=	1,200,000
	600,000	for three years	=	1,800,000
	$1,800,000			$3,600,000
Structure C	$1,500,000	for three years	=	$4,500,000

The increase in the dollar-years outstanding was brought about by the difference in the loan principal payment pattern—the loan in structure B is payable in three equal annual installments, while that in C is due in lump sum after three years.

Thus, the term "amount of debt" in the classic financing structure theory, when applied to long-term projects, should be modified to "amount of debt as represented by the dollar-years that the obligation will be outstanding."

Effect of Repayment Period Leverage on the IRR.   The preceding example has demonstrated that the rise in the IRR due to debt leverage is caused not only by the original amount of the loan but also by the payment pattern of the debt. Another determinant of the dollar-years outstanding is the payment period of the loan. Thus, a $2,000,000 loan, due in one year, will generate less leverage than the $1,800,000 debt in structure B. Hence, the IRR with the $2,000,000 loan will be lower than that with the $1,800,000 obligation.

EFFECT OF TIME VALUE OF MONEY SPREAD LEVERAGE ON THE IRR

The bigger the excess of the project IRR over the effective interest cost of the debt, the higher the IRR on the equity. Thus, if the posttax interest on the loan is 6% instead of the 7.2% in structure C, the IRR on the equity shoots up from 25.6% to 26.9%.

This concept is similar to that used in the increase in the return on stockholders' equity (ROSE) due to financing leverage, which is used in performance evaluation and discussed in Chapter 19. This similarity is explained further in the next section.

DETERMINANTS OF LEVERAGE: COMPARISON WITH THE RETURN ON STOCKHOLDERS' EQUITY RATIO AND NET PRESENT VALUE

The concept of the cost of money leverage for project financing is similar to those of (1) the return on stockholders' equity which is used in evaluating past performance and (2) the net present value of projects, which is utilized in decision analysis.

The cost of money leverage for long-term projects represents the total dollar amount that is saved by substituting lower-cost debt for part of the project financing. The savings is passed on to the equity investors, thus enhancing their IRR. Hence, the higher the dollar amount saved, the higher the IRR becomes.

The dollar saved may also be conceived as the cubic volume where the three dimensions are the original amount of the debt, the life of the debt (as adjusted for the pattern and the repayment period of the principal), and the time value of money spread (excess of the overall IRR over the cost of debt). Thus, if one of these dimensions is changed, the IRR on the equity fluctuates.

Similarity with the Return on Stockholders' Equity Used in Performance Evaluation. While the dollar saved in a leveraged project for decision analysis purposes has three dimensions, the dollar value added to the return on stockholders' equity ratio for performance evaluation has only two determinants. These are the amount of the debt relative to the equity and the interest spread (excess of the overall rate of return on the total financing—debt and equity—over the cost of debt). These factors are discussed in Chapter 19, last section—Return on Stockholders' Equity and Interest Spread.

The life of the debt is not considered any more in performance evaluation since the performance evaluation spans only one period. On the other hand, long-term decision analysis spans several years; hence it is a must to incorporate in the calculations the life of the loan.

Similarity with Net Present Value.   The three dimensions of the dollar saved in leveraged long-term project may also be compared with the three dimensions of net present value as follows:

Dimensions of the dollar savings in debt leverage	*Dimensions of the net present value of projects*
Amount of the debt	Amount of the project
Life of the debt*	Life of the project[†]
Time value of money spread	Interest spread[‡]

*As adjusted for the payment pattern of the principal.

[†]As adjusted for the recovery pattern of the investment.

[‡]Excess of the project IRR over the discount rate.

The three dimensions of the NPV are discussed in Chapter 5.

EFFECT OF FRONT LEVERAGE ON THE IRR

Side or Project Financing (Exhibits 15.6 and 15.7).   The typical debt financing for projects, as exemplified by structures B and C in Exhibit 15.4, may be called project or side financing. It is called project financing because the debt directly finances the project. See Exhibit 15.6. Hence the loan proceeds, interest, and principal amortization go to the project cash flow.

It may also be called side financing because it runs side by side with equity financing for several years. See Exhibit 15.7. Thus, the $1,500,000 debt financing in Exhibit 15.5 extends up to the end of the project life, just like the equity investment.

Front or Investors' Temporary Financing.   The normal calculation of the IRR is premised on the assumption that the investors will put in at once cash from their own funds. This is true if there is no front leverage.

However, the investors may further raise their IRR by exploiting another type of leverage—the investors' financing or front leverage. It is called investors' financing because it is used to fund temporarily the investors' contribution to the project. Instead of the investors putting in their money immediately, they borrow first the amount or part of it. Thus, instead of placing cash for 100% of their investment, the stockholders may give out, say, only 20% out of their own funds and arrange an investors' financing to fund temporarily the balance of 80%.

Since this financing is only temporary, that is, it is during the front end of the life of the project, or for the duration of the preoperating period or up to the initial year of operation, this may also be called as front financing.

Technically, the front leverage may or may not be arranged together with a side leverage. In practice, the front leverage is in addition to the side leverage.

The investors' financing shows in the investors' cash flow and not in the project cash flow.

Effect of Investors' Leverage on the IRR (Exhibit 15.8).   Exhibit 15.8 illustrates how a 10%, one-year front leverage for 80% of the equity contribution catapults the 25.6% IRR on equity calculated in Exhibit 15.5 to 41%. The first table in Exhibit 15.8 is the same as the bottom table of Exhibit 15.5.

The middle table in Exhibit 15.8 indicates that the investors will obtain a $1,520,000 front financing, which is 80% of their equity investment. This amount is shown as a return in year 0 as this is a receipt by the investors. The payment of this, plus interest thereon, represents an investment by the equity holders. The 10% IRR in the investors' cash flow with the financing company represents the interest cost.

The last table in Exhibit 15.8 integrates the first two tables and derives the 41% yield on the total investment by the stockholders.

The magnitude of the effect of the front leverage on the IRR is determined by the same forces that define the influence of the side leverage. For the front leverage, these are the amount of the front financing, the duration and pattern of repayment of the principal, and the time value of money spread or the excess of the internal rate of return before the front financing (25.6% in the exhibit) over the interest cost of the financing (10%). If the amount, duration, or time value of money spread is higher than the one used in Exhibit 15.8, then the IRR on the equity after the front financing will be higher than 41%.

EFFECT OF INFLATION LEVERAGE ON THE IRR

The prior sections have discussed how part of the overall return of the project can be shifted from the debtors to the equity holders so as to push the latter's rate of return. The return or IRR in this case is derived solely from the intrinsic profit which the project generates over time, in other words, from the time value of money.

There is another factor which transfers part of the creditors' share in the profit to the stockholders—inflation. Because of rising prices, the creditors are ultimately paid in cheaper dollars. The difference between the value of the original dollar which was borrowed and the value of the cheaper dollar paid, goes to the equity holders. In addition to this phenomenon, inflation also affects the IRR by depressing the net profit or cash flow of the project.

Effect of Inflation on the Nominal IRR of a Debt-free Project (Exhibit 15.9).   Inflation increases the nominal (not real) returns of a project. If all the revenues and cash costs rise at the same rate as the inflation, the cash profit will also rise at the same rate.

Take the year 1 cash profit from the project cash flow in Exhibit 15.2 (in $1,000):

	Year 1		Increase in nominal profit
	Without inflation	With 3% inflation	due to 3% inflation
Revenues	$4,000	$4,120	$120
Cash expenses	2,500	2,575	75
Cash profit	1,500	1,545	45
Tax at 40%	600	618	18
Increase in nominal profit and operating cash flow	$ 900	$ 927	$ 27

The $27,000 rise in nominal operating cash flow shown explains the difference between the year 1 operating cash flow of $1,220,000 if there is no inflation (see Exhibit 15.2) and the $1,247,000 if there is inflation (Exhibit 15.9).

Since the equity investment is the same whether or not there is inflation, but the nominal operating cash flow is higher if there is inflation, the nominal IRR is also higher if there is inflation—18.1% per Exhibit 15.9 compared with 15.7% per Exhibit 15.2.

Effect of Inflation on the Real IRR of a Debt-free Project.   However, the real IRR which is based on real profit is lower if there is inflation. Real profit is nominal profit, which is based on current year prices but deflated to take out the inflation component. This adjusted or real profit is equivalent to the cash flow or profit based on the price level as of the base year which is year 0 in this case.

The decline in the return from the scenario without inflation, to the real return if there is an inflation is due to the higher effective income tax based on year 0 prices. The higher tax is due to the following:

1. Reduction of the real value of depreciation as a tax-deductible item
2. Income tax on the liquidation of working capital, composed mainly of inventories, although there is no real gain in the liquidation

These items are discussed in the paragraphs that follow.

Reduction of the Value of Depreciation as a Tax-deductible Item (Exhibit 15.10).   One of the reasons for the decline in the real IRR is that, one of the tax deductible items, depreciation, is not inflated for tax purposes. Take the comparative figures in Exhibit 15.10. If there will be no inflation, the year 1 operating cash flow will be $1,220,000; see column 1.

If there is 3% inflation, the revenues and cash expenses will rise proportionately. However, the depreciation is held constant at $800,000. The nominal operating cash flow rises to $1,247,000, as in column 2.

However, the real cash flow is smaller $1,211,000 per column 3. This is estimated at $1,247,000 (after inflation) divided by the 1.03 price index for year 1, in order to convert the year 1 cash flow (after inflation) to year 0 price level. The reason why this is smaller than the $1,220,000 cash flow under a stable price scenario (column 1) is that while prices rise at 3%, the depreciation as a tax-deductible item remains the same at $800,000. In other words, the real value of depreciation as a deductible item is actually reduced from $800,000 to $777,000. See column 3 of Exhibit 15.10. As the tax deduction resulting from depreciation declines, the real income tax rises from $280,000 if there is no inflation (column 1) to $289,000 if there is inflation but with the values restated to year 0 price level (column 3).

The effect of inflation on income tax deduction due to depreciation is discussed at greater length and illustrated in Chapter 12.

Income Tax on Liquidation of Working Capital. Another reason for the decline in the real IRR due to inflation is that, when the $1,000,000 working capital, consisting mainly of inventories, which is invested originally at the end of year 0 is liquidated in year 3, the realizable value shoots up to $1,093,000 due to inflation. See Exhibit 15.9. Hence there will be a $93,000 paper profit. Forty percent of the paper profit is taxed. Thus, the net proceeds in year 3 arising from the $1,000,000 investment in year 0 is $1,056,000. Since the price index in year 3 is 1.093 compared with 1 in year 0, the $1,056,000 posttax proceeds is actually worth only $966,000 at year 0 price level. Hence, there is actually a posttax loss of $34,000.

The return to the investors may then be summarized as follows (in $1,000):

	Year 1	Year 2	Year 3
Price index (year 0 = 1.000)	1.030	1.061	1.093
Assuming no inflation			
(from Exhibit 15.2)	$1,220	$1,220	$2,220
Assuming with inflation of			
3% from year 0 (Exhibit 15.9)			
Nominal return	$1,247	$1,275	$2,359
Real return*	$1,211	$1,202	$2,159

*Nominal return divided by the price index.

Effect of Inflation on the Real IRR of a Project with Debt (Exhibit 15.11). The return to the equity holders in a project with fixed interest debt is enhanced in times of inflation since the payments on interest and principal are based on prices as of the date when the loan is granted, that is, the payments are not increased to compensate for inflation. The loan principal and interest are paid in cheaper dollars.

Interest. The posttax interest expense will be lowered by inflation. This is demonstrated in the second table of Exhibit 15.10. In a period of stabilized price levels, the year 1 interest is $180,000. See column 1. The amount is taken from Exhibit 15.5. Since this is tax deductible, the expense is reduced by $72,000, thus leaving a net interest expense of $108,000.

If there is inflation, the annual interest expense remains the same at $180,000, since the interest expense based on fixed interest rate is not adjusted for inflation. See column 2. Since the income tax benefit is pegged to the dollar amount of the interest expense, the income tax on interest also remains constant.

However, both the real interest expense and tax shrink due to the lower purchasing power of the dollar. Thus, if there will be a 3% inflation, the $180,000 interest expense payable in year 1 is worth $175,000 only in terms of year 0 dollars. See column 3. Similarly, the income tax benefit which is pegged at, say, a 40% effective rate is 40% of the $175,000 interest or $70,000. Hence, the real interest expense after tax, which is $108,000 in a no inflation scenario, becomes $105,000 if a 3% inflation creeps in. See column 3.

Therefore, the year 1 net operating cash flow which is $1,112,000 without inflation per the last line of Exhibit 15.10 (column 1) and Exhibit 15.5, is converted to a real cash flow of $1,106,000 after inflation according to Exhibit 15.10 (column 2).

Principal.   Inflation increases the real return to the investors in a debt-financed project in two ways. First, the project achieves a real gain on the amortization of the principal as the loan is paid off in cheaper dollars. Second, this real gain is not subject to income tax. (Contrast this second aspect with the liquidation of inventories at higher nominal prices but at the same real prices—although there is no real gain in the liquidation, there is an income tax).

For instance, if there will be a 3% inflation, the $1,500,000 loan to be obtained in year 0 at year 0 prices per Exhibit 15.11 will be paid with $1,500,000 in year 3, at year 3 prices. However, this payment is worth only $1,372,000 at year 0 price level. The $1,372,000 is calculated by dividing the $1,500,000 by the 1.093 price index for year 3. Hence, the project gains in year 3, through inflation, the difference of $128,000. This value, at year 0 price level, is a net gain since it is not subject to income tax.

III. EFFECT OF LEVERAGE
ON THE PROJECT RISK

The second part of this chapter has demonstrated that the higher the leverage, the higher the return on the equity. This third part of the chapter will show that the higher the leverage, the higher also the risk exposure. Thus, the degree of financing leverage to be obtained involves a balancing of both the desired return with the allowable risk.

SENSITIVITY ANALYSIS

The intrinsic IRR of a project, that is, one without debt, is based on a certain set of assumptions, which include future sales volume, selling prices, and costs. If any of these assumptions is varied, the estimated cash flow, return, and IRR may also change.

If it is expected that all the assumptions will be realized, then the decision will favor the debt/equity structure which will give the highest IRR to the investors.

In reality however, many of the assumptions will turn out to be wrong. Hence, it is necessary to consider not only the IRR to the investors but also the resulting cash flow if the projections will not be realized.

Debt Financing Alternatives. Assume that the alternatives are a $1,800,000 or a $900,000 loan. Both are at 12% and payable in three equal annual installments.

If there is no inflation, the $1,800,000 debt gives the investors a 23% IRR per Exhibit 15.3, while the $900,000 loan yields the investors 18.2%.

Sales as the Uncertain Factor. Since there are several variables that impact on the risk, this chapter will illustrate only one uncertain factor and how it will influence the decision on the debt structure.

Suppose that the sales volume is the most difficult item to establish. Assume further that while it is expected that normally the annual sales will be $4,000,000 or higher, there is also a 20 to 30% chance that the actual volume can go down to only 70% of the expected $4,000,000.

Since sales volume is the uncertain factor, it is necessary to establish the behavior of the operating costs in relation to changes in sales volume. Hence, the first step in the analysis is to break down the $2,500,000 in annual cash operating expenses into fixed costs and variable costs.

Project A—With Cash Operating Fixed Costs of $500,000 a Year. Assume that the cash operating fixed cost is $500,000 a year while the cash operating variable cost is 50% of the sales revenues.

SENSITIVITY ANALYSIS (EXHIBIT 15.12).   Exhibit 15.12 shows that if the project will be able to attain the $4,000,000 annual projected sales, the project will be able to generate enough cash to pay as cash dividends, $855,000 in year 1 if the debt is $900,000 and $490,000 if the loan is $1,800,000. On this basis, it is preferable to obtain a $1,800,000 loan as this produces a higher IRR.

Even if the sales drops down to 70% of the expected $4,000,000, the project can still service fully the $1,800,000 debt; in fact, there will still be $130,000 extra cash left which is available to pay the stockholders.

DEBT SERVICE BREAK-EVEN POINT SALES VOLUME.   It is only when the sales slides to 59.1% of the projected sales that the operating cash flow will just be enough to service the amortization on the $1,800,000 loan. The 59.1% is the debt service break-even point sales volume of project A. See

Exhibit 15.14 for the calculation. At this sales level, the project will incur a net loss before tax. It is assumed that the company will be able to offset this loss against the taxable income from other operations, so that the net loss from the project will be reduced.

If the project obtains a loan for $900,000 only, the DSBEPSV drops down to only 28.7% of the projected sales.

Project B—With Cash Operating Fixed Cost of $2,100,000 a Year (Exhibit 15.13). If the cash operating fixed cost is $2,100,000 instead of $500,000, it will be too risky to take on a $1,800,000 obligation. The risk may be high enough so as not to justify the more attractive IRR.

Exhibit 15.13 shows that if the sales volume drops to 70% of the $4,000,000 projected sales, the project will not have enough cash to service a $1,800,000 loan; the company will then be in trouble. In fact, with this debt load, the sales break-even point is at 77.3% of the expected sales.

DEBT SERVICE BREAK-EVEN POINT
SALES VOLUME (Exhibit 15.14)

The difference in the recommended amount of debt—which is $1,800,000 for project A and $900,000 for B, is caused by the varying amount of operating fixed cash outlays. For project A, the cash fixed costs less the tax benefits arising from the cash fixed costs and depreciation is a favorable $20,000 a year. See Exhibit 15.14.

On the other hand, project B has a high operating fixed cash outlay—$940,000 after-tax benefits. Thus, taking on the high debt loan of $1,800,000 might bring the project to bankruptcy. Hence, project B has to take only $900,000 in debt.

A study of the break-even points in the bottom line of Exhibit 15.14 shows that project A with a $1,800,000 debt takes on about the same risk as project B with a $900,000 debt load. Their sales break-even points as percentages of the projected sales are about the same—59.1% and 60.4%, respectively.

EXHIBIT 15.1:
Concept of Debt Leverage

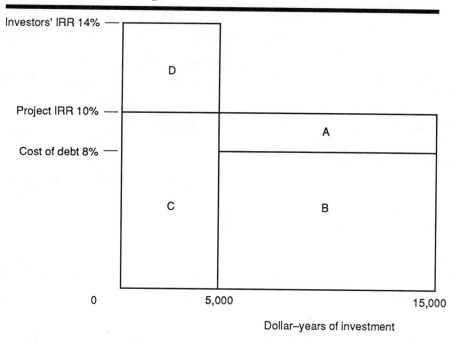

Dollar–years of investment

EXHIBIT 15.2:
Cash Flow for a Debt-Free Project (dollars in $1,000)

	Year 0	Year 1	Year 2	Year 3
Project cash flow				
Cash receipts				
Revenues		$4,000	$4,000	$4,000
Less: Expenses				
Cash expenses		2,500	2,500	2,500
Depreciation		800	800	800
Total expenses		3,300	3,300	3,300
Net profit before tax		700	700	700
Income tax—40%		280	280	280
Net profit		420	420	420
Add back depreciation		800	800	800
Operating cash flow		1,220	1,220	1,220
Equity	$3,400			
Working capital				1,000
Total receipts	$3,400	$1,220	$1,220	$2,220
Cash payments				
Buildings and				
equipment	$2,400			
Working capital	1,000			
Dividends		$1,220	$1,220	$2,220
	$3,400	$1,220	$1,220	$2,220
Investors' cash flow				
Investments	($3,400)			
Returns		$1,220	$1,220	$2,220
Total	($3,400)	$1,220	$1,220	$2,220
Internal rate of return	15.7%			

EXHIBIT 15.3:
Side Leverage—Cash Flow for a Project with a $1,800,000 Debt
(dollars in $1,000)

	Year 0	Year 1	Year 2	Year 3
Project cash flow				
Cash receipts				
Revenues		$4,000	$4,000	$4,000
Less: Expenses				
Cash expenses		2,500	2,500	2,500
Depreciation		800	800	800
Interest		216	144	72
Total expenses		3,516	3,444	3,372
Net profit before tax		484	556	628
Income tax—40%		194	222	251
Net profit		290	334	377
Add back depreciation		800	800	800
Operating cash flow		1,090	1,134	1,177
Equity	$1,600			
Loan proceeds	1,800			
Working capital				1,000
Total receipts	$3,400	$1,090	$1,134	$2,177
Cash payments				
Buildings and equipment	$2,400			
Working capital	1,000			
Loan amortization (principal)		$ 600	$ 600	$ 600
Dividends		490	534	1,577
Total payments	$3,400	$1,090	$1,134	$2,177
Investors' cash flow				
Investments	($1,600)			
Returns		$ 490	$ 534	$1,577
Total	($1,600)	$ 490	$ 534	$1,577
Internal rate of return	23.0%			

EXHIBIT 15.4:
Loan Outstanding Dollar-Year Leverage—Comparative Effect

	STRUCTURE		
	A	*B*	*C*
Financing structure (in $1,000)			
Debt	$ 0	$1,800	$1,500
Equity	3,400	1,600	1,900
Total	$3,400	$3,400	$3,400
Debt/equity ratio	0:100	53:47	44:56
IRR on the equity	15.7%	23.0%	25.6%
Terms of debt			
Interest rate		12.0%	12.0%
Posttax interest rate		7.2%	7.2%
Payment of principal			
In three equal annual installments		X	
At end of year 3			X
IRR on the equity calculated in	Exhibit 15.2	Exhibit 15.3	Exhibit 15.5

EXHIBIT 15.5:
Loan Outstanding Dollar-Year Leverage—Cash Flow for a Project
with a $1,500,000 Debt Payable at the End of Year 3
(dollars in $1,000)

	Year 0	Year 1	Year 2	Year 3
Project cash flow				
Cash receipts				
Revenues		$4,000	$4,000	$4,000
Less: Expenses				
Cash expenses		2,500	2,500	2,500
Depreciation		800	800	800
Interest		180	180	180
Total expenses		3,480	3,480	3,480
Net profit before tax		520	520	520
Income tax—40%		208	208	208
Net profit		312	312	312
Add back depreciation		800	800	800
Operating cash flow		1,112	1,112	1,112
Equity	$1,900			
Loan proceeds	1,500			
Working capital				1,000
Total receipts	$3,400	$1,112	$1,112	$2,112
Cash payments				
Buildings and equipment	$2,400			
Working capital	1,000			
Loan amortization (principal)				$1,500
Dividends		$1,112	$1,112	612
Total payments	$3,400	$1,112	$1,112	$2,112
Investors' cash flow				
Investments	($1,900)			
Returns		$1,112	$1,112	$ 612
Total	($1,900)	$1,112	$1,112	$ 612
Internal rate of return	25.6%			

EXHIBIT 15.6:
Project and Investors' Financing

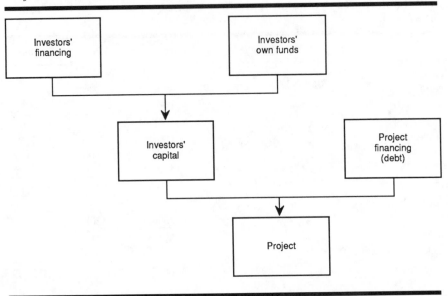

EXHIBIT 15.7:
Side and Front Financing

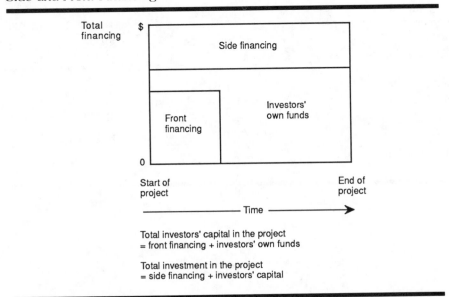

EXHIBIT 15.8:
Front Leverage—Cash Flow for a Project with a $1,500,000 Debt
Payable at the End of Year 3 (dollars in $1,000)

	Year 0	Year 1	Year 2	Year 3
Investors' cash flow with the project*				
Investments	($1,900)			
Returns		$1,112	$1,112	$612
Total	($1,900)	$1,112	$1,112	$612
Internal rate of return	25.6%			
Investors' cash flow with the financing company				
Investments		($1,672)		
Returns	$1,520	$ 0	$ 0	$ 0
Total	$1,520	($1,672)	$ 0	$ 0
Internal rate of return	10.0%			
Investors' total cash flow				
Investments	($1,900)	($1,672)		
Returns	$1,520	$1,112	$1,112	$612
Total	($ 380)	($ 560)	$1,112	$612
Internal rate of return	41.0%			

*Same as in Exhibit 15.5.

EXHIBIT 15.9:
Effect of Inflation—Cash Flow for a Debt-Free Project (dollars in $1,000)

	Year 0	Year 1	Year 2	Year 3
Project cash flow				
Cash receipts				
Price index	1.000	1.030	1.061	1.093
Revenues		$4,120	$4,244	$4,371
Less: Expenses				
Cash expenses		2,575	2,652	2,732
Depreciation		800	800	800
Total expenses		3,375	3,452	3,532
Net profit before tax		745	791	839
Income tax—40%		298	317	336
Net profit		447	475	503
Add back depreciation		800	800	800
Operating cash flow		1,247	1,275	1,303
Equity	$3,400			
Working capital				1,093
Tax on working capital gain				(37)
Total receipts	$3,400	$1,247	$1,275	$2,359
Cash payments				
Buildings and equipment	$2,400			
Working capital	1,000			
Loan amortization (principal)				
Dividends		$1,247	$1,275	$2,359
	$3,400	$1,247	$1,275	$2,359
Investors' cash flow				
Investments	($3,400)			
Returns		$1,247	$1,275	$2,359
Total at current prices	($3,400)	$1,247	$1,275	$2,359
Nominal IRR	18.1%			
Total at year 0 prices	($3,400)	$1,211	$1,202	$2,159
Real IRR	14.7%			

EXHIBIT 15.10:

Effect of Inflation and Tax—Year 1 Operating Cash Flow
(dollars in $1,000)

	Before inflation at year 0 prices (Col. 1)	*After inflation at year 1 prices (Col. 2)*	*Real values at year 0 prices (Col. 3)*
Operating cash flow if without debt*			
Price index	1.000	1.030	1.000
Revenues	$4,000	$4,120	$4,000
Less: Expenses			
Cash expenses	2500	2575	2,500
Depreciation	800	800	777
Total expenses	3,300	3,375	3,277
Net profit before tax	700	745	723
Income tax—40%	280	298	289
Net profit	420	447	434
Add back depreciation	800	800	777
Operating cash flow if with 100% equity financing	$1,220	$1,247	$1,211
Net interest cost if with a $1,500,000 debt			
Interest[†]	$ 180	$ 180	$ 175
Tax benefit at 40%	72	72	70
Net interest cost	$ 108	$ 108	$ 105
Operating cash flow after interest			
Operating cash flow after interest on a $1,500,000 debt[†]	$1,112	$1,139	$1,106

*See Exhibit 15.2 for sources of data in column 1; Exhibit 15.9 for column 2.
[†]See Exhibit 15.5 for sources of data in column 1; Exhibit 15.11 for column 2.

EXHIBIT 15.11:
Inflation Leverage Cash Flow for a Project with a $1,500,000 Debt
Payable at the End of Year 3 (dollars in $1,000)

	Year 0	Year 1	Year 2	Year 3
Project cash flow				
Price index—costs	1.000	1.030	1.061	1.093
Receipts				
Revenues		$4,120	$4,244	$4,371
Less: Expenses				
Cash expenses		2,575	2,652	2,732
Depreciation		800	800	800
Interest		180	180	180
Total expenses		3,555	3,632	3,712
Net profit before tax		565	611	659
Income tax—40%		226	245	264
Net profit		339	367	395
Add back depreciation		800	800	800
Operating cash flow		1,139	1,167	1,195
Equity	$1,900			
Loan proceeds	1,500			
Working capital				1,093
Tax on working capital gain				(37)
Total receipts	$3,400	$1,139	$1,167	$2,251
Cash payments				
Buildings and equipment	$2,400			
Working capital	1,000			
Loan amortization (principal)				$1,500
Dividends		$1,139	$1,167	751
	$3,400	$1,139	$1,167	$2,251
Investors' cash flow				
Investments	($1,900)			
Returns		$1,139	$1,167	$ 751
Total at current prices	($1,900)	$1,139	$1,167	$ 751
Nominal IRR	30.3%			
Total at year 0 prices	($1,900)	$1,106	$1,100	$ 687
Real IRR	26.5%			

EXHIBIT 15.12:

Sensitivity Analysis—Project A with $500,000 in Fixed Costs
(dollars in $1,000)

	ACTUAL SALES AS % OF PROJECTED SALES					
	100%		70.0%		59.1%	
Initial amount of debt	$ 900	$1,800	$ 900	$1,800	$ 900	$1,800
Revenues	$4,000	$4,000	$2,800	$2,800	$2,364	$2,364
Less: Expenses						
Cash expenses						
Variable costs	2000	2000	1400	1400	1182	1182
Fixed costs	500	500	500	500	500	500
Depreciation	800	800	800	800	800	800
Total expenses	3,300	3,300	2,700	2,700	2,482	2,482
Net profit before tax	700	700	100	100	(118)	(118)
Income tax—40%	280	280	40	40	(47)	(47)
Net profit	420	420	60	60	(71)	(71)
Add back depreciation	800	800	800	800	800	800
Operating cash flow available for debt service	1,220	1,220	860	860	729	729
Debt service requirements						
Interest	108	216	108	216	108	216
Less: Tax—40%	43	86	43	86	43	86
Net interest cost	65	130	65	130	65	130
Payment on principal	300	600	300	600	300	600
Total debt service	365	730	365	730	365	730
Available for cash dividends	$ 855	$ 490	$ 495	$ 130	$ 364	($ 0)

EXHIBIT 15.13:
Sensitivity Analysis—Project B with $2,100,000 in Fixed Costs
(dollars in $1,000)

| | **ACTUAL SALES AS % OF PROJECTED SALES** | | | | | |
	100%		*77.3%*		*70.0%*	
Initial amount of debt	$ 900	$1,800	$ 900	$1,800	$ 900	$ 1,800
Revenues	$4,000	$4,000	$3,092	$3,092	$2,800	$ 2,800
Less: Expenses						
Cash expenses						
Variable costs	400	400	309	309	280	280
Fixed costs	2,100	2,100	2,100	2,100	2,100	2,100
Depreciation	800	800	800	800	800	800
Total expenses	3,300	3,300	3,209	3,209	3,180	3,180
Net profit before tax	700	700	(117)	(117)	(380)	(380)
Income tax—40%	280	280	(47)	(47)	(152)	(152)
Net profit	420	420	(70)	(70)	(228)	(228)
Add back depreciation	800	800	800	800	800	800
Operating cash flow available for debt service	1,220	1,220	730	730	572	572
Debt service requirements						
Interest	108	216	108	216	108	216
Less: Tax—40%	43	86	43	86	43	86
Net interest cost	65	130	65	130	65	130
Payment on principal	300	600	300	600	300	600
Total debt service	365	730	365	730	365	730
Available for cash dividends	$ 855	$ 490	$ 365	$ 0	$ 207	($ 158)

EXHIBIT 15.14:
Debt Service Break-Even Point Sales Volume—Projects A and B
(dollars in $1,000)

	Project A		Project B	
Initial amount of debt	$ 900	$ 1,800	$ 900	$ 1,800
Fixed cash outlays				
Operating fixed cash outlays				
Fixed costs	$ 500	$ 500	$ 2,100	$ 2,100
40% tax benefit	(200)	(200)	(840)	(840)
Tax benefit on depreciation	(320)	(320)	(320)	(320)
Total operating fixed cash outlays	(20)	(20)	940	940
Financing fixed cash outlays				
Interest	108	216	108	216
40% tax benefit	(43)	(86)	(43)	(86)
Loan amortization	300	600	300	600
Total financing fixed cash outlays	365	730	365	730
Total fixed cash outlays	$ 345	$ 710	$ 1,305	$ 1,670
Contribution margin at 100% of sales forecast				
Sales	$ 4,000	$ 4,000	$ 4,000	$ 4,000
Variable costs	(2,000)	(2,000)	(400)	(400)
	2,000	2,000	3,600	3,600
40% tax	(800)	(800)	(1,440)	(1,440)
Net contribution margin	$ 1,200	$ 1,200	$ 2,160	$ 2,160
As a percentage of sales	30.00%	30.00%	54.00%	54.00%
Break-even point sales volume				
Amount *	$ 1,149	$ 2,365	$ 2,416	$ 3,092
As a percent of $4,000 sales forecast	28.7%	59.1%	60.4%	77.3%

*Total fixed cash outlays divided by net margin contribution as a percentage of sales.

Chapter 16

DETERMINANTS OF REPORTED PAST PERFORMANCE

Decisions on business units are based on the periodic performance review. However, the results of the review could be tricky. Even given the same degree of competitiveness of two business units, the units are most likely to have different ratings in the review due to forces beyond their control: (1) the strategies formulated by the corporate office and the developments in the business environment, both of which affect the intrinsic performance of the business units, and (2) the accounting conventions applied, which influence the reported performance.

For instance, a strategy calling for heavy spendings on new product introduction can convert an otherwise healthy operation to a paper loss. On the other hand, a windfall rise in industry sales can more than make up for a sluggish company performance as evidenced by declining market share. Furthermore, an accounting practice can give credit to firms which overproduce manufactured goods and then unreasonably build up inventories.

This chapter explains how strategies, environmental forces, and accounting conventions blur the reported past results and then illustrates how new techniques may be used so that due credit may be granted, or penalty imposed on, operating units and their managers.

The last part of this chapter brings out the differences in the techniques of measuring and evaluating reported past performance from the tools employed in projecting and analyzing future performance.

I. STRATEGIES AND SUPPORTING MEASURES AS DETERMINANTS OF PERFORMANCE

The general management formulates the broad or portfolio strategies followed by its operating units. The major strategies are (1) for the business unit to "grow," (2) for the unit just to "maintain" or hold its present level of operations, and (3) for the parent company to "harvest" or milk the division. These strategies are described in Chapter 2, Determinants of Projected Performance.

Different strategies affect the investment and profitability differently. For instance, a grow strategy requires substantial investment but initially contributes losses. On the other hand, a harvest strategy needs minimal investments but generates a high level of cash flow and profit.

Under normal reporting and appraisal techniques, the effects of these strategies are not isolated from the results of established operations. This practice deprives both top and operating management of the information required to monitor the performance of the new strategies as well as that of the established operations. The absence of adequate feedback makes it difficult for management to veer their strategies in consonance with the changing currents of the competition and environment.

RECOMMENDED FINANCIAL ANALYSIS TECHNIQUE

The return on investment (ROI) of firms under a grow strategy is squeezed in two ways. First, they have high advertising and promotions, interest, depreciation, and R&D expenses. Second, they have high investments in both working capital and physical facilities.

Current-year versus Prior-year Comparison (Exhibits 16.1 and 16.2). The traditional review of the results as exemplified in Exhibit 16.1 indicates that the current year performance deteriorated from prior year since the net profit and accounting rate of return dropped. However, if the performance is evaluated not only against the prior year results but also in relation to the strategy, it is evident that the comparable operations (established products only) actually improved in the current year.

In a situation like this, the current year performance should be segregated into two—one based on established operations and the other based on the new strategy. See Exhibit 16.2. By doing this, it is apparent that the net operating profit of the established operations actually improved from $2,500,000 to $3,000,000 and the ROI from 12.5% to 15%.

Chapter 24, Evaluating Performance by Strategy, demonstrates how to segregate the performance of key measures from that of the established operations.

II. ENVIRONMENTAL FORCES AS
DETERMINANTS OF PERFORMANCE

Fluctuations in industry demand, prices, interest rates, and income tax rates, are the major environmental factors that help mold the profitability of firms in a broad spectrum of industries. Usually, the impact of these extraneous forces are not segregated from the effect of managerial actions. As a consequence, management is erroneously charged, or credited, for forces beyond their control. Furthermore, the results of measures themselves, that is, before considering the effect of the changes in the environment, would be hard to gauge.

How environmental factors can cloak the innate performance of a company and how the effects of these factors can be segregated for performance evaluation purposes are illustrated in this section.

INDUSTRY DEMAND (Exhibits 16.3 and 16.4)

A company may perform poorly by losing market share and allowing its costs to soar, but still report an improvement in the net income. This is illustrated in Exhibit 16.3.

The intrinsic current year performance deteriorated: market share dropped to 9.75%, the fixed costs rose by $1,000,000, and variable costs edged to 61% of sales. Notwithstanding these miserable operating results, the reported profit before tax zoomed to $6,815,000. The reason for the conflict between the poor operating performance and the excellent reported profit is the windfall improvement in industry sales.

Recommended Financial Analysis Technique. The $1,815,000 apparent improvement in the net profit is due to the following causes:

Favorable environment change	
—Increase in industry sales	$3,803,000
Less: Poor management performance	1,987,000
Improvement in reported net profit	$1,815,000*

*Total does not add due to rounding.

The $3,803,000 gain in net profit due to increased industry demand is the proportionate market share of the company in the incremental industry sales, less its variable costs. See Exhibit 16.4.

The $1,987,000 cost of poor management performance represents the decline in profit before tax if there were no rise in industry sales. This is the difference in the net profit shown in the first column of Exhibit 16.4 and that indicated in the second column.

How to determine the impact on profit of changes in industry sales, market share, and costs, is explained in Chapter 23, Multivariance Analysis.

INFLATION (Exhibits 16.5 and 16.6)

Inflation, if not properly recognized, reveals an illusory improvement in the reported performance. Consider the data in Exhibit 16.5. The price levels increased by 5% during the current year due to inflation. Exhibit 16.5 reveals the following favorable trends that pushed up the ROI: (1) increase in the net profit and (2) decline in the investments.

Recommended Financial Analysis Technique (Exhibit 16.6). However, the analysis in Exhibit 16.5 contains the following flaws:

1. Due to the 5% inflation, the sales, costs, and working capital in the current year are overstated to this extent if compared with the figures for last year. Hence, the current year figures should be deflated by dividing them by 1.05 (1 for the base year and 0.05 for the inflation).
2. Due to the depreciation, the investment in property, plant, and equipment declined. Hence, the inclusion of these assets distorts the ROI. To make the results comparable, these assets and the depreciation should be eliminated.

The comparable figures are indicated in Exhibit 16.6. The adjusted figures showed deterioration in the following: (1) decline in sales, (2) increase in costs, and (3) increase in the investment in working capital. Because of these, the net profit and the return on working capital deteriorated.

III. ACCOUNTING CONVENTIONS AS DETERMINANTS OF REPORTED PERFORMANCE

The ROI is calculated by dividing the net income by the investment which was utilized in generating that income. Hence, the ROI as the key indicator of management is valid only if (1) all the revenues and costs are duly measured and the investments are properly valued and (2) the investments were actually utilized to benefit the current year operations. The ROI is flawed to the extent that these conditions are not applicable.

This section discusses how the limitations of the accounting conventions regarding the following items distort the ROI and what remedies may be taken: (1) the valuation of the receivables and payables and (2) the classification of certain resources which are implied to be used in operations but actually are not.

How other accounting conventions influence the financial statements are dissected in Chapter 17, Financial Statement as Basis of Evaluation.

VALUATION OF RECEIVABLES AND PAYABLES

Receivables and payables are valued in the accounting statements based on the past transaction which originated them, and not on the amount to be received or paid in the future. Take the following receivables, both dated today:

Account receivable—due 6 months from now—	
without interest	$1,000,000
Note receivable—due 12 months from now—	
with simple interest at 2% a month	$1,000,000

Each of the account and note receivables are carried in the financial statements at $1,000,000.

Recommended Financial Analysis Technique. Assume that the company's effective income tax rate is 40% and the effective cost of money is 1% a month before tax or 0.6% after tax. As of today, the real values of the receivables, assuming minimal collection expenses, credit risk, and inflation, are

	Book and face value	Collectible when due	Value as of today	Built-in gain (loss)
Account receivable	$1,000,000	$1,000,000	$ 965,251	($34,749)
Note receivable	1,000,000	1,144,000	1,067,164	67,164

Since the account receivable has no interest, the amount to be collected six months from now is still $1,000,000. However, at 0.6% monthly simple interest after tax, the $1,000,000 due then is worth only $965,251 today. In other words, $965,251 plus 0.6% per month or 3.6% for six months is $1,000,000.

On the other hand, the $1,000,000 note will give $1,240,000 after 12 months, or $1,144,000 after paying the 40% tax on the $240,000 interest. At 0.6% monthly simple interest, the $1,144,000 due in 12 months hence is worth $1,017,682 today.

If these receivables originate on the last day of the current fiscal year, the effect of the present accounting method of valuation for the account receivable is to overstate the current year profit by $34,749 and understate next year's profit by the same amount. Conversely, the current year profit will be understated by $64,164 due to the note receivable, and next year's profit will be overstated.

The limitations in the valuation of the receivables under current accounting practice have a great impact on the measurement of the year-to-year performance of business units and their managers. The managers who will be inheriting receivables bearing no interest income or with interest at below money cost will be penalized right from the start. On the other hand, those who will be starting off with receivables which yield interest income at above the market rate will receive a built-in but invisible bonus.

The interyear transfers of payables will have the opposite effect. Managers who assume payables with interest at below-market rates will benefit from the transfer.

It is necessary, therefore, that for purposes of performance evaluation, the receivables and payables be restated at their economic values (values as of today).

How the improper valuation of receivables and payables can give misleading signals to management is revealed in Chapter 25, Evaluating Performance with Resource-Based Interest.

NONOPERATING ASSETS

Usually, the net assets (total assets less liabilities) or stockholders' equity of a business unit or company is compared with the net income in arriving at the ROI. Included in the assets are those which are not fully utilized in current operations: (1) carryovers from prior years which represent *past* mistakes and which were not actively used in current year operations and (2) new investments to be used in *future* operations. In the first category are slow-moving inventories, delinquent receivables, idle plants, and nonrelated stock investments. Forming part of the second group are physical facilities just completed or acquired which are intended to be used in the future but not utilized at present. This group includes sites of expansion programs, buildings under construction, major equipment in the process of installation, and inventories which were built up in preparation for a step up in production or marketing. To a certain extent, expensive, showpiece corporate headquarters may also be treated as nonoperating investments if the building carrying costs—interest, depreciation, insurance, and maintenance—are much higher than the prevailing commercial rents for a more austere office space.

Recommended Financial Analysis Technique (Exhibit 16.7). The inclusion of these nonoperating assets depresses the ROI and hides an otherwise superior performance. Consider the information in Exhibit 16.7. Under traditional accounting and financial analysis, the amount of the net assets is considered to be $25,000,000, yielding an 8% ROI. However, the net assets actually used in the current operations to generate the $2,000,000 in profit is only $13,000,000. Hence the real ROI is not 8% but 15%. If the firm uses 10% ROI as the benchmark in disposing of marginal operations, the use of the traditional practice may mislead management to sell the unit.

Due to the growing importance of unutilized resources, new ratios have been designed to reflect the real financial performance and condition. A new integrated management performance ratio which purposely segregates the nonoperating assets is introduced in Chapter 18, Integrated Performance Ratio Analysis. Turnover ratios based on operating assets are given in Chapter 21, Operating Ratios.

IV. PAST PERFORMANCE—DIFFERENCES FROM PROJECTED PERFORMANCE

Past performance almost always deviates from projected performance due to two causes: failure of the conditions to occur as anticipated and variations in the techniques used in measuring and evaluating past performance from the methods employed in projecting and analyzing future performance.

Differences in Evaluation Techniques (Exhibit 16.8).   This part of the chapter treats the deviations of the past performance from projected performance due to the differences in the techniques. The variations in the techniques include the projects and time coverage, basis of analysis, and types of costs utilized. These variations are compared in Exhibit 16.8.

COVERAGE OF THE APPRAISAL

Although decision analysis covers alternative strategies or measures at a time, only one of these is usually implemented. The analysis is for the entire life of the project, which may range from a few months to several decades.

Except in comparative project analysis, decision analysis usually covers only *one project* at a time. On the other hand, performance evaluation is focused on one division or company which has *several ongoing projects.* Furthermore, while the projects covered by decision analysis span *several years*, performance evaluation is only for one performance period, which is usually a month, quarter, or a *year*.

Cross Coverage (Exhibit 16.9).   The cross coverage between decision analysis and performance evaluation is illustrated by the chart in Exhibit 16.9. Based on the presentation in the chart, decision analysis has a horizontal coverage. For instance, the decision analysis for project 2 spans several performance evaluation periods. On the other hand, performance evaluation has a vertical coverage. The evaluation for one performance period as year 3 covers the results for that year of four operational projects.

Because of the discrepancy in the coverage, the results of decision analysis, which is for one project for several years, cannot be directly compared with results of performance evaluation, which is for several projects for one year. The only way of comparing the results are

1. First, by cutting the projected results of a project into different accounting or performance evaluation periods. For example, the projected results of the plant expansion measure may be broken down into year 3 (first year of implementation) and subsequent periods.
2. Second, by segregating the performance results of one period into the different projects. For instance, the performance of year 3 may be segregated into the results of the raw material substitution measure, the plant expansion measure, and the measures implemented during the prior years. (Performance evaluation by measure is explained in Chapter 24, Performance Evaluation by Strategy.)
3. Third, by comparing the projected results of one measure for one performance period, with the actual results of the same measure for the same period. Thus, the projected results of the plant expansion measure for year 3 may be compared with the actual results.

APPRAISAL TECHNIQUES AND BASIS

Resulting Dollar Amount or Rate. Since decision analysis spans the entire project life, the rate given by the internal rate of return (IRR) and the net dollar amount representing the net present value (NPV) is for the *entire life* of the project. There is no annual breakdown. On the other hand, the accounting rate of return (ARR) and the residual income (RI) give the rate of return or net dollar amount for *one year* or other evaluation period only. The rate or amount fluctuates from year to year.

Financial Statement Used. Decision analysis for projects with life of over one year, such as those involving the construction of plants or the acquisition of equipment, is usually based on *cash flow* statements which represent *forecasts*. Performance evaluation is based on the *income statements*, which are composed of *historical* figures.

Adjustment for Time Value of Money. As the cash flow forecasts used in decision analysis are for several years, the values are *time adjusted*; that is, they are discounted to the time when the decision is made or when the capital is invested. A dollar of income during the first year of operations is worth more than a dollar in the second year.

The income statements used in performance evaluation are *not time adjusted*. If the performance period is one year, a dollar of income earned in January is equivalent to a dollar of income in December.

Adjustment for Inflation.   Since the cash flow forecasts cover a number of years, the values are adjusted for inflation. The inflation assumed every year is usually a constant rate.

The income statements are not inflation adjusted although prices change from year to year due to inflation. Hence a slight increment in RI for one year may actually be lower than the inflation for the period.

Changes in Working Capital.   These items are deducted from the cash flow statement used in decision analysis but are not deducted from the income statement employed in performance evaluation. However, they affect the ARR and the RI since they raise the capital base.

Value at the End of the Period.   Where the project operating life is over 10 years, the IRR or NPV is usually calculated based on the cash flow for the first 10 years. The operating cash flow beyond the 10-year period is usually assumed to be represented by the possible sale or capitalized value of the project at the end of 10 years. This value is sometimes called *terminal value*. As the terminal value is added to the cash flow during the 10-year period in determining the IRR or NPV, the terminal value influences the IRR or NPV. (See Chapter 4, Internal Rate of Return.)

In performance evaluation, the ARR and RI are based on the income statement for one year or other rating period. Costs incurred during the period are allocated (1) to those that belong to the period, and hence are deducted from the revenues in the income statement, and (2) to those that will benefit future periods, and hence are placed in the *balance sheet* as of the end of the period. To the extent that some costs are transferred from the income statement to the balance sheet, the cost transfers affect the ARR or RI.

COSTS USED IN THE APPRAISAL

Basis of Costs.   The costs used in preparing the cash flow forecasts are based on the current or *market* prices. The costs in the income statement represent *historical* or past prices. In some cases, the historical prices may be much lower than the market values. For instance, the historical price of land purchased 10 years ago may be only 10% of the current prevailing price.

Imputed Costs.   The cash flow statements for decision analysis may include imputed costs. An example is the fair market rental value of properties that a division is using but that are owned by the parent company, although the parent is not actually charging the division a rent. Imputed costs are not included in the income statement for performance evaluation.

Sunk Costs. On the other hand, historical income statements include sunk costs, such as depreciation. These type of costs are not incorporated in the projected cash flow statements although the acquisition costs of the depreciable property are included in calculating the IRR and NPV. See the following section.

Property, Plant, and Equipment. The acquisition of these items are figured at the *current prices* in the cash flow forecasts.

However, in performance evaluation, these are carried at *net book value*, which is at the much lower historical acquisition costs, less the depreciation which has been charged off through the years. It is even possible that many of the buildings and equipment which are still being used have been fully depreciated in the books, that is, being carried in the books at no value at all.

Equipment may have been overdepreciated due to the use of the accelerated method which takes off from the books large chunks of the acquisition cost during the first few years. Hence, the capital base used in performance evaluation is much lower than the one employed in decision analysis. The low capital base jacks up both the ARR and RI.

Depreciation Method. The projected cash flow statements include the acquisition cost of property, plant, and equipment but not the annual depreciation since depreciation by itself does not involve cash. Depreciation may be considered only in estimating the income taxes to be paid.

On the other hand, the income statement for the past periods usually includes depreciation. Usually, the depreciation is based on the accelerated method since this method maximizes the tax deductions and since many companies use the same depreciation method for tax purposes as for performance evaluation. Under this method, the annual depreciation for the initial years in the life of the building or equipment is much higher than the ones in the later years.

Valuation of Inventories. In the projected cash flow statements, the acquisition of materials or merchandise, including those to be used in building up the inventories are figured at *current prices.*

For a company that uses the last-in, first-out costing method (LIFO), the inventories are carried in the balance sheet at *historical cost.* Since LIFO reduces the income tax liabilities, many companies are using it, not only for tax purposes but for performance evaluation as well.

Treatment of R&D and Product Introduction Expenses. For decision analysis purposes, these are considered as part of the *total cost of the project* and hence do not diminish the annual cash flow from operations.

For performance evaluation requirements, these are *expensed* off or deducted from the operating revenues in order to arrive at the net income that is used as the basis of calculating the ARR or RI.

EXHIBIT 16.1:
Impact of Strategy on Profit—Traditional Analysis
(dollars in $1,00)

	Prior year	Current year	Increase (decrease)
Sales			
Existing products	$14,000	$15,000	$ 1,000
New products	0	1,400	1,400
Total	14,000	16,400	2,400
Costs and expenses			
Existing products	11,500	12,000	500
New products		2,000	2,000
Total	11,500	14,000	2,500
Net profit	$ 2,500	$ 2,400	($100)
Average investment			
Existing products	$20,000	$20,000	
New products		5,000	5,000
Total	$20,000	$25,000	$ 5,000
Accounting rate of return	12.5%	9.6%	

EXHIBIT 16.2:
Impact of Strategy on Profit—New Analysis
(dollars in $1,000)

	Prior year	Current year	Increase (decrease)
Established operations (existing products)			
Sales	$14,000	$15,000	$1,000
Costs and expenses	11,500	12,000	500
Net profit	$ 2,500	$ 3,000	$ 500
Average investment	$20,000	$20,000	$ 0
Return on investment	12.5%	15.0	
Grow strategy (New products)			
Sales		$1,400	
Cost and expenses		2,000	
Net profit (loss)		($ 600)	

EXHIBIT 16.3:

Impact of Industry Sales on Net Profit—Traditional Analysis
(dollars in $1,000)

	Prior year	Current year	Increase (decrease)
Market data			
Industry sales	$500,000	$600,000	$100,000
Market share	10.00%	9.75%	−0.25%
Summary income statement			
Sales	$ 50,000	$ 58,500	$ 8,500
Less: Costs and expenses			
Fixed costs	15,000	16,000	1,000
Variable costs	30,000	35,685	5,685
Total costs	45,000	51,685	6,685
Net profit before tax	$ 5,000	$ 6,815	$ 1,815
Variable costs as % of sales	60.00%	61.00%	66.88%

EXHIBIT 16.4:

Impact of Industry Sales on Net Profit—New Analysis
(dollars in $1,000)

	Prior year	CURRENT YEAR (*)	CURRENT YEAR (†)	Total
Market data				
Industry sales	500,000	500,000	100,000	600,000
Market share	10.00%	9.75%	9.75%	9.75%
Summary income statement				
Sales	$50,000	$48,750	$ 9,750	$58,500
Less: Costs and expenses				
Fixed costs	15,000	16,000	0	16,000
Variable costs	30,000	29,738	5,948	35,685
Total costs	45,000	45,738	5,948	51,685
Net profit before tax	$ 5,000	$ 3,013	$ 3,803	$ 6,815
Variable costs as % of sales	60.00%	61.00%	61.00%	61.00%

*Based on last year's industry sales.
†Due to increase in industry sales.

EXHIBIT 16.5:
Impact of Inflation on Net Profit—Traditional Analysis
(dollars in $1,000)

	AT CURRENT PRICES	
	Prior year	*Current year*
Profit		
Sales	$10,000	$10,450
Less		
Cash costs	7,000	7,380
Depreciation	1,000	1,000
Total costs	8,000	8,380
Net profit before tax	$ 2,000	$ 2,070
Investments		
Working capital	$ 6,000	$ 6,600
Property, plant, and equipment	4,000	3,000
Total	$10,000	$ 9,600
Accounting rate of return	20.0%	21.6%

EXHIBIT 16.6:
Impact of Inflation on Net Profit—Inflation Considered
(dollars in $1,000)

	Prior year	*Current year at prior year's prices*
Profit		
Sales	$10,000	$9,952
Less: Cash costs	7,000	7,029
Cash profit	$ 3,000	$2,924
Working capital		
Working capital	$ 6,000	$6,286
Return on working capital	50.0%	46.5%

EXHIBIT 16.7:

Impact of Nonoperating Assets on ROI
(dollars in $1,000)

	Total investments	*Operating assets*
Working capital		
Actively used in operations	$10,000	$10,000
Old receivables and inventories	1,000	
Property, plant and equipment		
Actively used in operations	28,000	28,000
Idle plants, construction in progress	7,000	
Stock investments	4,000	
Gross investments	50,000	38,000
Liabilities	25,000	25,000
Net investments or stockholders' equity	$25,000	$13,000
Net profit	$ 2,000	$ 2,000
Accounting rate of return	8%	15%

EXHIBIT 16.8:
Decision Analysis and Performance Evaluation—Differences

	Decision analysis	*Performance evaluation*
General		
Purpose	Appraisal of measures, projects or strategies	Review of measures, units, products, or managers
Time orientation	Future performance	Past results
Coverage of appraisal		
Measures covered	One	Several
Time covered	Several years or months (entire project life)	One year, quarter, or month
Appraisal techniques and basis		
ROI techniques	IRR or NPV	ARR or RI
Resulting dollar amount or rate	One dollar amount (for NPV) or one rate (for IRR) for entire project life	Dollar amount (for IRR) or rate (for ARR) is calculated for every quarter or year
Financial statement used	Cash flow (forecast)	Income statement (historical)
Adjustment for time value of money	Adjusted for long-term projects	Not adjusted
Adjustment for inflation	Adjusted for long-term projects	Usually not adjusted
Inflation rate used	Constant rate usually	Not applicable
Changes in working capital and buildings	Cash flow is affected	Income statement is not directly affected
Capitalized value at end of period	Based on annual cash flow	Based on balance sheet
Costs used in the appraisal		
Basis of cost	Market or current price	Historical price or cost
Imputed cost	Included	Excluded
Sunk cost	Excluded	Included
Property, plant and equipment	Market or curren tprice or cost of the asset	Historical price or cost less the depreciation
Valuation of inventories	Market or current price or cost	Historical cost if the LIFO is used
R&D and product introduction costs	Capitalized as part of the project cost	Charged to revenues

EXHIBIT 16.9:
Coverages of Performance Evaluation and Decision Analysis

	Year 1	Year 2	Year 3	Year 4 and beyond	PERFORMANCE EVALUATION: VERTICAL COVERAGE
Project 1 Establishment of the company	/////	/////	/////	/////	
Project 2 New product development		/////	/////	/////	
Project 3 Plant expansion			/////	/////	
Project 4 Raw material substitution				/////	
Project 5 Price reduction				/////	
Other projects					

DECISION ANALYSIS: HORIZONTAL COVERAGE →

Chapter 17 _____

FINANCIAL STATEMENTS AS BASIS OF EVALUATION

The gross profit form of income statement, which shows the gross profit as the intermediate profit figure, was initially used as the primary basis of performance evaluation. This format is geared for trading firms where the expenses consist primarily of fixed costs. For this type of operation, the gross profit conveniently separates the variable costs, which are the cost of sales, from the fixed costs, which are the operating expenses. The variable costs are shown above the gross profit, and the fixed costs, below.

The advent of manufacturing industries revealed the shortcomings of the gross profit form. Since the cost of sales of manufacturers include not only variable costs but also fixed costs, the contribution margin form was devised to separate the variable from the fixed costs. This shows the contribution margin as the intermediate profit figure. All variable costs are placed before the contribution margin, and the fixed costs, below.

However, while the contribution margin form is adequate for smoke-stack, stabilized, manufacturing operations with matured products in an established market, it is not tailored to the growing companies with substantial expenditures on R&D and market development. These expenditures do not fit into the mold of fixed and variable cost and hence reveal the weakness of the contribution margin form.

This chapter illustrates the two traditional income statement formats, reviews their effectiveness in performance evaluation, and suggests an alternative form.

I. GROSS PROFIT FORM OF INCOME STATEMENT

The traditional gross profit form shows the gross profit as the intermediate profit figure. Although generally not advisable for use in the evaluation of manufacturing concerns, this form is nonetheless frequently utilized for this purpose.

INCOME STATEMENT FORMAT (Exhibit 17.1)

The income statement shows the gross revenues, cost of sales and expenses required to generate the gross revenues, and the resulting profit. A typical form is illustrated in Exhibit 17.1.

Gross Profit. In many cases, meaningful information is given by the intermediate profit figure, which result after deducting from the sales revenues, only the cost of sales. Thus, in Exhibit 17.1, the gross profit figure indicates how much money is made before subtracting the selling and general and administrative expenses, interest, and income tax. This information is useful in evaluating the performance of specific products and in determining which products to be pushed, assuming their selling expenses are about the same.

Operating Profit. The operating profit, which is the gross profit less the operating expenses but before subtracting the interest and income tax, is used in evaluating the performance of operating units and in planning the sources of financing to be tapped. For instance, a firm with a high operating profit can afford to support a high level of borrowing.

Net Profit. The income statement indicates the net profit that results after deducting the interest and income tax from the operating profit. Since this is the final profit or the bottom line, this figure is usually relied upon as one of the most significant bases of performance evaluation.

COSTS AND EXPENSES

The costs and expenses may be classified in different ways:

1. By nature, as salaries or depreciation,
2. By department, as manufacturing (which includes the salaries of manufacturing personnel and depreciation of factories) or marketing,
3. By the behavior of the expenses in response to changes in the sales volume, which are fixed costs (as depreciation normally) and variable costs (as wages of daily workers in the production line), or

4. By basic function, as (a) employee services (which includes salaries and depreciation of employee service facilities as recreational and lunch rooms) and (b) building occupancy (which includes the salaries of building maintenance crew and the depreciation of the buildings).

Classification by Department (Exhibit 17.1).   The costs in Exhibit 17.1 are generally arranged by department and then by nature. The items under cost of goods manufactured and sold are those incurred by the manufacturing department. The first six items under the selling, general, and administrative expenses are spent by the marketing department; the seventh item, by the administrative and corporate departments; and the last, by the R&D department.

Classification by Behavior.   Another form of income statement, the contribution margin form, classifies the expenses initially according to their behavior in relation to changes in the sales volume (variable and fixed costs) and then by nature. The classification by behavior is treated in Section III of this chapter.

Fixed costs are those whose total amount remains constant even through the production or sales volume changes within a given range. Variable costs are those whose total amount varies with the changes in the volume.

USE IN PERFORMANCE EVALUATION (Exhibit 17.1)

If used to appraise the performance of a corporation or business unit, the income statement is compared with the income statement of a prior period, another division, a similar company, or with the budget. Thus, in Exhibit 17.1, the results of year 2 are compared with those of year 1. The comparison in the exhibit shows that the performance in year 2 is better than that of the prior year in terms of both the dollar sales revenues and net profit.

The comparison is aided by the use of variances and percentages. The increase from year 1 to year 2 may be calculated and then computed as a percentage of year 1 amount. This analysis indicates that the net profit has improved faster than the sales: while the sales grew by 19.2%, the net profit jumped by 30.8%.

Certain profit ratios may be derived. Some of the common ratios which are based solely on the income statement are the gross profit rate, the operating profit rate, and the net profit rate. These are computed by dividing, one at a time, the gross profit, operating profit, and net profit after tax by the sales. All these ratios reveal an improvement in the performance: the gross profit rate accelerated from 50.0% in year 1 to 55.7% in year 2; the operating profit, from 14.2% to 15.4%; and the net profit, from 6.8% to 7.5%. Generally, the higher the rate, the more profitable is the firm or the better is its performance.

This seemingly improved performance is based on the results *as reported* in the income statement. However, this form of statement has several limitations as discussed later. Hence, any conclusion based on this form of statement could be misleading.

ADVANTAGES

The use of the gross profit form for performance evaluation is generally advisable only for merchandising firms that buy all the goods they sell, but not for manufacturing firms that make their own goods. The reason is that in a merchandising firm, the total cost of sales is considered variable cost, while in a manufacturing concern, only part of the cost of sales is variable cost.

Hence the form is ideal for use by merchandising firms that place significance not only on the sales and net profit but also on the gross profit.

LIMITATIONS

While the traditional form is simple enough to be understood by the layperson, it also has severe limitations for manufacturers: (1) it does not distinguish the fixed costs from the variable costs, and (2) it is geared for the use of absorption costing in the valuation of finished goods inventories of manufacturers.

Retailers whose selling costs are mainly fixed costs are not materially affected by these limitations. First, their cost of sales are 100% variable. These are segregated from the selling costs as the cost of sales are deducted first from the sales in order to arrive at the gross profit margin. Their variable costs are therefore differentiated from their fixed costs.

Second, they do not carry finished goods inventories; what they have are merchandise or purchased inventories. Since retailers do not manufacture goods, the use of absorption costing and its attendant shortcoming is not applicable to them.

Cost Classification According to Behavior.   The costs in this income statement form are usually classified by departments as manufacturing costs (manufacturing department). Such classification may not be so meaningful. A more functional grouping would be by cost behavior. From a companywide evaluation and planning perspective, departmental breakdown is not necessary as the costs of carrying out a certain objective are not compartmentalized by departments; costs cut across departmental boundaries. For instance, a program to improve the overall profit and at the same time maintain the sales may involve the slashing of advertising, accompanied by extending the terms of payments of the receivables. This measure reduces the advertising cost, a selling expense, but jacks up the credit and collection expenses, which is an administrative expense, and pushes up the interest on the financing used to carry the extended collection periods.

If the costs are not arranged according to their behavior, it is difficult to appraise performance or to plan profitability measures intelligently, since variable costs get lost among fixed cost when the sales volume changes. For instance, according to Exhibit 17.1, sales increased by 19.2%, cost of goods sold by 5.7%, and selling, general, and administrative expenses by 33.8%. This indicates that the cost of goods sold tends to be much more of a fixed cost than a variable cost, while the general and administrative expenses seems to be more volatile than variable costs since they increased at a rate faster than that of the sales.

If costs are identified and classified as fixed or as variable, it is easier to assess performance and plan for the future. Fixed cost should normally not increase higher than, say, 2–5% of prior period cost, after adjusting for inflation and changes in the way the business is being operated. On the other hand, variable cost is expected to vary 100% with the sales, as adjusted for price changes.

The absence of segregation also presents difficulties in planning. For instance, it would be time consuming to forecast the costs in preparing financial projections and budgets. Furthermore, it is difficult to apply incremental analysis, sensitivity, crossover, and break-even point analysis since these tools use variable costs and fixed costs.

II. ABSORPTION VERSUS DIRECT COSTING

There are two methods of costing the finished goods inventories: absorption or full costing and direct costing. The choice influences the reported inventory, net profit, and income tax.

ABSORPTION COSTING METHOD (Exhibit 17.1)

The traditional financial statements of manufacturing firms use the absorption or full costing in the valuation of its finished goods inventories. Under this method, the finished goods which are not sold and hence remain in the inventory are valued based on the cost of the raw materials and other variable costs, together with a proportionate share in the depreciation and other fixed costs. As shown in Exhibit 17.1, 14.1% or $10,408,000 of the total manufacturing cost in year 2 is not deducted from the sales revenues as costs, but rather forwarded to the balance sheet as assets; only the remaining $63,410,000 is deducted as cost of sales.

The effect of this is to reduce by 14.1% the depreciation and factory overhead expenses incurred in year 2, which are included in the cost of goods sold although in fact these expenses were not increased by producing the additional units for inventory as these expenses are fixed costs.

In other words, in reality, through the use of absorption costing, the cost of sales in year 2 is understated by 14.1% of the manufacturing depreciation and factory overhead. This is equivalent to $4,540,000 (14.1% of $32,200,000; $32,200,000 = $27,200,000 + $5,000,000). This overstates the net profit before tax, and the value of finished goods inventories in the balance sheet, by the same amount.

Thus, the total depreciation and factory overhead charged to cost of sales in year 2 is only the remaining $27,660,000 (after deducting the $4,540,000) instead of the full $32,200,000. The $27,660,000 for year 2 may be compared with the $30,000,000 total manufacturing depreciation and factory overhead in year 1 which are all charged to cost of sales. The discrepancy here is apparent. Although the year 2 sales is 19.2% higher than the year 1 sales, the depreciation and overhead charged to cost of sales in year 2 is lower than that in year 1.

DIRECT COSTING METHOD (Exhibit 17.2)

The erroneous valuation of both the cost of sales and finished goods inventories under absorption costing is clearly brought out if the results under this method are contrasted with the outcome under the direct costing technique. Under direct costing, only the variable manufacturing costs are proportionately allocated between the cost of sales and increase in finished goods inventories; all the fixed manufacturing costs are considered as cost of sales or period costs.

These two methods of costing are compared in Exhibit 17.2. The sales, cost of goods manufactured and sold, and gross profit of year 2 shown in Exhibit 17.1, which uses absorption costing, are replicated in column 1 of Exhibit 17.2. Column 2 of Exhibit 17.2 shows the same conditions obtained as in column 1, but using the direct costing. The difference in the cost of sales and in the value of the increase in the inventories between the two methods is $4,540,000, which is 14.1% of the fixed manufacturing costs.

The last two columns of Exhibit 17.3 show what would have been the cost of sales if the production volume is just enough to cover the sales—in other words, no change in the finished goods inventories. The cost of sales in the last two columns is the same as the cost of sales in column 2. This proves that the cost of sales in column 1 is understated by the portion of the fixed costs which is charged to the inventories—$4,540,000.

EFFECTS OF THE CHOICE OF THE METHOD
(Exhibit 17.3)

The employment of the full costing method creates adverse effects on the following: valuation of inventories and cost of sales, inventory levels and inventory costs, and income tax and dividends.

Valuation of Inventories and Cost of Sales.   Exhibit 17.3 demonstrates that (1) in periods when the finished goods inventories are rising, the use of absorption costing results in understated cost of sales and overstated inventories, and (2) in periods when there is no change in the finished goods inventories, the absorption costing does not produce any misstatement of the costs. Since during periods of rising inventories, full costing understates the cost of sales, conversely, during periods of falling inventories, this costing method overstates the cost of sales. This method, therefore, has the effect of transferring part of the costs from one period to another.

Inventory Levels and Inventory Costs.   Since during periods of rising inventories, full costing understates the cost of sales or overstates the profit, the use of full costing in performance evaluation in effect gives credit to the business units and managers with growing finished goods inventories. Unless rising inventories are justified, the use of this inventory costing method is dangerous since it encourages managers to stock up on finished goods inventories. As a result, the use of this method expands the inventory-related costs, namely, interest on financing used to carry the inventories, warehousing and other storage costs, inventory insurance, and inventory obsolescence and other expenses.

Income Tax and Dividend.   Income tax and dividends are usually based on the profit using the full costing method. In periods of rising finished goods inventories the impact of the full costing method is to increase the reported net profit and hence the effective tax and dividend rates as the percentage of the profit which is computed on the direct costing method. For instance, the use of direct costing in year 2 resulted in net income before tax of $13,321,000 (See Exhibit 17.4.) The application of full costing hiked the pretax income by $4,540,000 (see Exhibit 17.2, last line), to $17,861,000 (Exhibit 17.1). The actual tax at an assumed 40% effective rate based on the $17,861,000 reported profit is $7,144,000. This $7,144,000 tax comes out to be 53.6% of the actual net income of $13,321,000.

Thus, the use of full costing in this case boosted the effective tax rate from 40% to 53.6%—or by 34% (increment of 13.6% as a percentage of 40%). The bigger is the overstatement of the inventories in relation to the taxable income, the higher is the effective tax and dividend rates.

III. CONTRIBUTION MARGIN FORM OF INCOME STATEMENT

INCOME STATEMENT FORMAT (Exhibit 17.4)

This type of income statement, which is illustrated in the exhibit, highlights as the first intermediate profit figure, the contribution margin. This margin is the profit after deducting from the sales revenues the variable manufacturing and variable selling expenses. The contribution margin is sometimes called the contribution to overhead, or contribution to fixed costs. All the items below the contribution margin are considered fixed costs except the income tax.

Certain decisions can be made using the contribution margin figure. For instance, products or market territories which have negative contribution margins may be dropped off unless they have potentials for growth.

ADVANTAGES

This income statement form has two improvements over the gross profit income statement: it distinguishes the fixed costs from the variable costs, and it is geared for the use of the direct costing method.

Direct Costing. Since the contribution margin income statement is geared for the use of direct costing, the overstatement of the increase in the finished goods inventory, and the understatement of the cost of goods sold in year 2 have been removed.

The $28,600,000 raw materials used and $7,150,000 other direct manufacturing costs in Exhibit 17.4 are the same as those shown in Exhibit 17.3, part I, column 2.

The $4,694,000 raw materials used and $1,174,000 other direct manufacturing costs in Exhibit 17.3, part II, column 2 are not shown any more in Exhibit 17.4 as they do not affect the net profit. In other words, the raw materials and other direct manufacturing costs shown under the variable costs in Exhibit 17.4 are only those going into the cost of sales. Contrast this with the ones shown in Exhibit 17.1, which includes those going into the increase in the finished goods inventories. The method of treatment in Exhibit 17.4 simplifies the presentation and facilitates both performance evaluation and financial forecasting.

Fixed Costs and Variable Costs. The contribution margin format groups together the variable costs, irrespective of the departments involved. Hence, in Exhibit 17.4, the raw materials used, other direct manufacturing costs, and sales commissions are presented together. As noted in Exhibit 17.4, last column, each of these costs grew at 19.2% from year 1 to year 2, which is the same as the sales growth rate.

Compare this with Exhibit 17.1, which shows that the raw materials used and other direct manufacturing costs grew at 38.7% during the same period. These growth rates are higher than the 19.2% because the year 2 figures in Exhibit 17.1 include those which became part of the increase in the finished goods inventory.

LIMITATIONS

Just as the gross profit form of income statement is suited for a merchandising firm whose selling costs are mainly fixed costs, the typical contribution margin format is effective for the matured, smokestack manufacturing firm which is heavy on day-to-day production operations but not aggressive on marketing, product innovation, and expansion. When the contribution margin form is used by growing firms, complications in the use of the income statement develop due to the failure to recognize or treat properly the following which are neither variable nor fixed costs: discretionary costs and sales expansion costs. These costs are described in Section IV of this chapter.

Alternative to the Contribution Margin Form (Exhibit 24.1). A financial statement form which builds on the strengths of the contribution margin statement but eliminates its shortcomings has been designed. Its form and use is illustrated in Chapter 24, Evaluating Performance by Strategy. In addition to the fixed cost and variable cost classifications, the new form has sales expansion cost and long-term cost groupings. A new intermediate profit figure, current operating profit, is shown. This shows the results of current operations, and hence excludes costs related to past transactions or to future growth strategies.

CONTRIBUTION MARGIN FORM AND DIRECT COSTING METHOD

Advantages. The combined use of the contribution margin form and direct costing method has three distinct advantages over the utilization of the gross profit form and absorption costing method.

First, the first pair of techniques is useful in decision making. Illustrations of the situation where the tools may prove handy are in

1. Deciding whether to perform in-house certain functions or have them contracted out. (See Chapter 9.)
2. Deciding whether to continue an operation or shut down a facility.
3. Deciding whether to accept a sales order at below the normal selling price if there is unused capacity.
4. Deciding whether to introduce new products or delete existing ones. (See Chapter 10.)

Second, the pair of tools may be used in evaluating the performance of business segments and their managers, and on the disposition of the units.

Third, the pair facilitates the employment of the other techniques, like the break-even point analysis which also distinguishes the fixed costs from the variable costs. (See Chapter 8.)

Limitations. However, the direct costing method also has its limitations. First, the method does not include in the finished goods inventory, the fixed costs, or overhead. Hence it is not allowed for income tax purposes. Because of this disallowance, it is not normally used also for reporting to the outside stockholders and the banks.

Second, it may be difficult in practice to separate the fixed costs from the variable costs.

IV. DISCRETIONARY EXPENSES AND SALES EXPANSION COSTS

DISCRETIONARY COSTS

Discretionary costs are those over which management has a leeway in determining (1) the amount to be incurred and (2) the timing of the incurrence. Illustrations are advertising, sales promotions, R&D, and management development.

The classification of costs into fixed costs and variable costs is ideal for established factory floor operations. All variable costs such as raw materials or production wages are tied to specific goods produced. All fixed costs such as the basic salary of the production manager remain substantially constant. Management does not have much flexibility as to the amount and timing of the payment of these variable and fixed costs. The raw material and labor costs are dictated by market prices. Negotiations and forward purchase contracts may cut the costs by a few percentage points. Payments may be delayed only by a few weeks.

On the other hand, there are certain costs that management may drastically cut without substantially affecting current month or even current year operations. The reduction of long-term R&D efforts will not hamper the profitability of a firm for a month or even years. The abandonment of quality control programs for an industrial machinery firm will not affect the operations until a number of weeks. The same thing is true with management and skills development programs, productivity studies, and preventive maintenance. Although all of them are intended to generate sales, raise productivity, or save on costs, they are all incurred before the corresponding sales, production, or cost reduction occur. Hence there is no firm commitment to spend these costs.

Since these costs are not directly related to actual sales, they are not variable costs. Since the amount of these costs can easily be raised, reduced, or totally eliminated by management, or their timing postponed, they are not fixed costs either. Take the case of R&D expenses in Exhibit 17.4. This jumped by 194% from year 1 to year 2, which rate is over 10 times the 19.2% rise in sales. Definitely R&D is neither a fixed nor a variable cost.

These costs, called discretionary costs, should be treated differently from the fixed costs and variable costs for the following reasons:

1. Discretionary costs behave differently from the fixed and variable costs.
2. Discretionary costs can easily be cut or expanded by management without materially adversely affecting present operations. If they are treated as variable or fixed costs and then deducted from the profit like the variable and fixed costs for purposes of appraising management performance, the management will skimp on them, thus sacrificing future growth and profitability. Since they are dispensable insofar as present operations are concerned, the unwise slashing of these costs will not be noticed immediately.
3. Discretionary costs benefit mainly the future, not the present operations. Hence it is but fair that they should be charged to the future and not to current operations.

SALES EXPANSION COSTS

These are the costs incurred to push the sales: introduce new products, invade new market territories, or gain market share. Some sales expansion costs, such as advertising expenses, are incurred before the corresponding sales. Others are spent after the sales. For instance, where an attempt is made to expand sales by prolonging the payment terms for the sales, the following sales expansion costs are incurred after the sales: additional interest on loans to carry longer payment terms and incremental bad debts and collection expenses due to prolonged terms.

Sales expansion costs incurred before the sales are discretionary costs in that management can still change the amount any time. On the other hand, costs incurred after the sales are not discretionary costs any more. However, they cannot be classified as fixed costs. In the case of the interest as mentioned, their amounts rise due to the lengthening of the terms of sales. On the other hand, they cannot be considered variable costs because their amounts do not vary with the sales. They increase much faster than do the sales. Consider the following figures (dollars in $1,000):

	Year 1	Year 2	Increase	Increase as a percentage of year 1
Annual sales	$1,200	$1,440	$240	20%
Payment terms in months	1	2		
Outstanding receivables	$ 100	$ 240	$140	140%
Annual interest at 10%	$ 10	$ 24	$ 14	140%

Assume that after attaining an annual sales of $1,200,000 with sales terms of one month, the company decided to gain on sales by doubling the payment period. As a result, the sales rose by 20%. However, with money cost at 10%, the interest cost rose by 140%.

Another sales expansion strategy is to make the products more available to the public—which means carrying more inventory per location, or increasing the number of locations with inventories or both. This strategy involves sales expansion costs in the form of inventory carrying costs: inventory financing interest, insurance, obsolescence. While interest on extended payment terms of receivables are not discretionary costs since they are incurred *after* the sales, interest on extended finished goods or merchandise inventory periods are discretionary costs because they are incurred *before* the sales are made.

Sales expansion costs should be distinguished from the fixed costs and variable costs because

1. Sales expansion costs behave differently from fixed costs and variable costs. Some sales expansion costs may rise faster than sales.
2. Sales expansion costs which are incurred before the sales and hence are also discretionary costs can easily be cut, increased, or eliminated by management, unlike fixed and variable costs.
3. While sales expansion costs benefit the year during which they are incurred, they also benefit future periods, unlike fixed costs and variable costs, which normally benefit only the current period.

Sales expansion costs are discussed further in Chapter 11, Analyzing Sales Expansion Measures.

EFFECTS ON THE REPORTED NET INCOME AND PROFITABILITY RATIOS

Although the incurrence of discretionary and sales expansion costs is normally beneficial to the company in the long run, such expenditure depresses the reported income for the year the expenses are incurred. (See Section VI of this chapter.)

Consequently, these expenditures also pushes down the return on investment (ROI) and other profitability ratios. Hence, in the analysis of a firm which has committed to a sales expansion program or R&D effort, the traditional ratios should be supplemented by the discretionary costs to sales ratio. (See Chapter 21, Section III.)

V. CONVENTIONAL BALANCE SHEET

FORMAT AND PRESENT USES (Exhibit 17.5)

The balance sheet or statement of financial condition shows the financial resources, obligations, and residual interest of the stockholders in a firm as of a certain date, usually as of the end of a month, a quarter, or a year. The conventional form of balance sheet is illustrated in Exhibit 17.5. As currently practiced, the balance sheet is not given as much significance as the income statement in performance evaluation and decision analysis. Performance evaluation is based primarily on the income statement, while decision analysis relies so much on the cash flow statement.

The balance sheet is used mainly to support the two other financial statements. Thus, the only figures used in the balance sheet to determine overall past performance are the value of the stockholders' equity and the value of the total assets. The former is related to the net profit to arrive at the return on investment, while the latter is compared with the net profit to determine the return on assets.

The changes in each of the balance sheet items, from the beginning to the end of a period, are utilized only in constructing the cash flow statement. The changes by themselves are normally not reviewed in studying the company performance.

The balance sheet is locked into the income statement. The net income after tax shown in the income statement, less the dividends, represents the change in the retained earnings or accumulated earnings during the year. The increase in the finished goods inventory in the income statement which is deducted from the cost of sales is the same as the increase in the inventory in the balance sheet.

ADVANTAGES

The conventional form has two basic advantageous features: (1) it is the most popular form to managers, analysts, accountants, and laypersons, and (2) it conveniently segregates the assets and the liabilities into short term or current, and long term. Because of the second characteristic, the derivation of ratios which are used to determine the degree of liquidity of a firm is facilitated. These ratios, which include the current ratio and the quick ratio, are discussed in Chapter 20, Financing Structure Ratios.

The changes in the balance sheet items, if traced to their underlying causes, and related to the resulting profit or cash generation, can give insights into the past and future operations of a firm just like the income and cash flow statements. For instance, the increment in the receivables and inventories could be segregated as due to the following: (1) management inefficiencies or errors, such as for the changes resulting from lax collection practices and inventory problems; (2) implementation of strategy to expand sales; and (3) inflation. The escalations in assets due to the sales expansion strategy could then be related to the profit or cash flow resulting from this strategy.

Incremental operating assets—accounts receivables and inventories— may be related to sales to help analyze the past performance. This type of analysis is explained in Chapter 21, Operating Ratios.

LIMITATIONS

The limitation of the traditional format lies in its inconsistency with the two other financial statements: the income and cash flow statements. Furthermore, the classification of the liabilities in the balance sheet does not conform with that followed in certain ratios.

Inconsistency with Conventional Income Statement Presentation. While the assets and obligations are classified according to the time the assets are converted to cash (current assets and property, plant, and equipment) or the time the obligations are paid (current or short-term and long-term debts), the costs in the income statement are classified by function or department (manufacturing, selling, administrative, and finance) and not by timing of the incurrence of costs (as short term and long term).

While one of the key figures in the income statement is the net operating income for the year, the balance sheet does not show the net assets used in operations during the year. Idle pieces of land, buildings under construction, heavy equipment being installed, and abandoned factories are not segregated from the land, buildings, and equipment that were utilized during the year.

Furthermore, slow-moving inventories and long-overdue receivables are not separated from current stocks and active accounts that generate the business.

Inconsistency with Certain Ratios. In ratio analysis, certain relationships which involve liabilities consider only loans; that is, the trade credits are disregarded. This is true, for instance, in deriving the debt-to-equity ratio, which is the ratio of loans to stockholders' equity. On the other hand, in the balance sheet, the trade credits are lumped together with short-term loans.

VI. LIMITATIONS OF FINANCIAL STATEMENTS

The financial statements are almost always relied upon as a key source of information to be utilized in reviewing the past results of businesses and in projecting their performance. The analytical ratios and variance analysis as

calculated using the formulas in Chapters 18 to 23 give the semblance of
hard facts which are difficult to dispute. This assumes, however, that the
figures inputted into the calculations are rock solid and crystal clear.
However, the figures on gross revenues, costs or expenses, assets, liabilities, and the derived net income and stockholders' equity indicated in
the financial statements are like mud—spongy and murky. Hence the
financial statements should not be taken at face value.

LIMITATIONS OF FINANCIAL STATEMENTS

While accounting rules and conventions have been established to make the
financial statements as objective as possible, certain weaknesses which
compromise the integrity of the figures in the balance sheet and income
statement still persist.

The weaknesses of the financial statements result from two sources:
the limitations of the underlying accounting practices and conventions
themselves and the failure of the accountants or auditors to uncover
fraudulent transactions designed to incorrectly state the revenues, costs,
assets, or liabilities.

The limitations of the accounting practices are caused by

1. The recognition of different alternative treatments, each treatment
   being in accord with the generally accepted accounting principles
   (GAAP). For instance, there are different methods of valuing the
   inventories, each method producing a different result.
2. The failure of accounting practices to properly recognize or value the
   effect of transactions arising from the implementation of business
   strategies. For instance, the failure of the accounting practice to recognize as an investment the expenditures required to expand market
   share understates the assets and overstates the expenses.
3. The failure of the accounting practice to properly recognize or value
   the effects of changes in the business environment. For instance,
   increases in the value of land due to inflation are usually not recognized in the balance sheet, thereby understating both the assets and
   the income.

These limitations distort the magnitude of the different types of assets and
liabilities and the related incomes and expenses. As a result, the same
transaction with the same economic values involved may be assigned
varying accounting values in the financial statements. Conversely, different transactions with different economic values may be given identical
accounting treatments and values. These are illustrated in the paragraphs
that follow.

ACCOUNTING FOR FUTURE BENEFIT COSTS AND DEFERRED PAYMENTS

Accounting conventions do not accurately present in the financial statements, future benefit costs, and deferred payments that arise from the implementation of selected business strategies. Future benefit costs are incurred as a result of sales expansion and R&D programs which are part of a grow strategy, while deferred payments are brought about by a deferred maintenance program under a harvest strategy.

Future Benefit Costs. Accounting practice governs the proper recording of expenditures on equipment as investments since the equipment is a cost which will benefit the future. However, expenditures on promotions and advertising to expand market share, as well as R&D which results in patents, both of which will benefit the future, are expensed outright and not booked as investments.

Deferred Payments. The accounting conventions correctly consider the money taken from others as borrowings if they will be paid back in the future. However, postponed maintenance of equipment is not taken up as liability, although it will require payments in the future.

Accounting for Strategies. Thus, under current practice, the more a firm tries to build up its market share or develop technology which results in patents, the more its net income and ROI declines. Similarly, the more a company runs its factories to the ground—that is, without current maintenance—the more its ROI rises.

Hence, if the underlying financial statements and business strategies are not studied in relation to the ratios and other tools of financial analysis, and if the managerial performance is tied in to the results as reported in the financial statements and shown in the ratios, the management which is under pressure to report acceptable current earnings may steer to destruction the very companies they are supposed to nourish.

(See Chapters 2 and 16 for a discussion of how business strategies influence the performance of a firm.)

ACCOUNTING FOR PROPERTIES

Accounting conventions are deemed to be inadequate to cope with the valuation of properties and accounting for unutilized properties for financial statement purposes.

Valuation of Properties. The generally accepted accounting method of valuing the land, buildings, and equipment based on the original acquisition cost, less accumulated provisions for depreciation, distorts the financial statements in two ways. First, this valuation method disregards the gradual increase in the values brought about by the inflation. Second, it fails to recognize the distinction of depreciation for tax purposes, which uses mainly the accelerated depreciation, and the depreciation for economic valuation purposes, which considers the economic life, which is longer than the tax life. These limitations work to understate the properties and stockholders' equity, thereby understating the accountabilities of the managers for the assets placed at their disposal. The effect of this is to overstate the ROI.

The use of original cost or gross cost will not solve this weakness since the gross cost is not keyed to the current economic value of the properties. Only the use of the replacement value will remedy the situation.

Under current accounting conventions, a company using properties acquired five years ago will be reporting less depreciation expense than will another firm with newer buildings and equipment. The first company has a lower depreciation base since it acquired the properties at lower cost and some of the properties which are already fully depreciated do not show depreciation charges any more in the income statement. Thus, while the two concerns have access to the same equipment, the one with newer assets is penalized due to its higher investment base and bigger depreciation expense.

Accounting for Unutilized Properties. Firms with excess plant capacities or obsolete equipment which is not yet fully depreciated and not yet retired show higher total assets and higher depreciation charges than do those with fully utilized equipment.

ACCOUNTING FOR INVENTORIES

The choice of the inventory valuation method or accounting practice gives varying levels of reported performance.

Inventory Valuations. The GAAP sanction is the use of either the last-in, first-out (LIFO) method or the first-in, first-out (FIFO) method of valuing inventories of raw materials, goods in process, finished goods, merchandise, or supplies. The LIFO method gives lower inventory values but higher cost of sales than does the first-in, first-out method. Hence two firms with identical actual results will report different amounts of net profit if they use different inventory methods.

Finished Goods Inventory Valuations. Section II of this chapter has shown that, when the finished goods inventory of manufacturing concerns are building up, those using the absorption costing method of valuing their finished goods inventories show higher inventory values in the balance sheets and lower cost of goods manufactured sold in the income statement.

Thus, if two divisions utilize different methods, the choice of the method could account for part of the difference in their performance.

Inventory Write-offs or Write-downs. Companies which do not promptly write down or write off their slow-moving or obsolete inventories display higher inventories and lower cost of sales than do those which are conservative in their accounting practice.

ACCOUNTING FOR RECEIVABLES

The financial statements do not give the factual values of the receivables. The estimated future losses on the collections is very subjective. Furthermore, the future interest on the receivables is not recognized.

Estimated Losses on Collections. Two firms with the same quality and face value of trade receivables will report different amounts of receivables in the balance sheet and different amounts of allowance for possible losses in the collection if one of the firms is more conservative than the other in estimating the amounts which will be ultimately collected.

Future Interest on Receivables. A firm with two notes receivable of the same amount and same maturity dates and due from the same debtor values the two notes at the same amount for balance sheet purposes, although one of the notes carries a higher interest rate and therefore has more economic value.

ACCOUNTING FOR SHORT-TERM INVESTMENTS

Inconsistencies are apparent in the valuation of investments and in reporting the profit from the appreciation therefrom.

Valuation of Investments. Take two companies with investments consisting of the same number of shares in the same firm. One firm has acquired the shares at a much lower price than the prevailing market value, while the other company has just purchased the stocks at the current market value. Although they have identical investments, their investments are valued differently in their respective balance sheets. Since they acquired the investments at different costs, they are valued differently.

Profit from the Appreciation of Investments. Take another pair of companies with investments consisting of the same number of shares in the same firm. They acquired their investments at the same acquisition cost. The difference is that one firm just sold its investment at a profit and the other did not. The price did not change from the time of the sale. Although the two companies made the same profit due to the appreciation in the value of their investments, the one that sold the shares will report a net profit from the investments, while the one that held on will not.

ACCOUNTING FOR HUMAN RESOURCES

The value of human resources—either in manufacturing operations or in professional firms is not recognized under current accounting practice.

Resources of Labor-intensive Manufacturing Operations. If the financial statements or ratios derived therefrom are used to compare the performance of different industries, companies, or segments, the degree of automation, labor intensity, and employee loyalty among the subjects to be compared should be considered. While the expenditures for the acquisition of modern factory is taken up as an investment, the cost of training the workers and building up their loyalty is considered an expense. Thus, the return on investment ratios of a labor-intensive operation is overstated due to the understatement of the capital base indicated in the balance sheet.

Resources of Professional Firms. In a professional organization, the most important resources are the business contacts of the partners and the skills of the professional staff. These are not assigned any value at all in the balance sheet. The investment in the office space, furniture, libraries, and laboratories, the ones appearing as assets in the balance sheet, is minimal compared with the value of the contacts and skills. Hence the rate of return ratios in this type of organization are not only irrelevant but outright misleading.

ACCOUNTING FOR OTHER ASSETS

There are several other types of assets which are not recognized in the balance sheet. Examples are leases and tax loss carryforward benefits.

Accounting for Leases. Even firms with the same equipment may not show the same values of the equipment in the balance sheet and may have different amounts of costs or expenses in the income statement. Firms that are using equipment under operating leases do not include the equipment in their balance sheets. Hence they tend to have lower total assets than do those firms that purchased their own equipment. Furthermore, the equipment rentals and other incidental expenses usually vary from the depreciation and other expenses which are required by the purchased equipment.

Accounting for Tax Loss Carryforward Benefits. Past losses may be used to reduce the income tax liabilities in the future. However, the losses are taken at full value to reduce the stockholders' equity, when in fact only part of the book losses should be recognized as such since part of the losses can be used to diminish the future income tax liabilities.

ACCOUNTING FOR LIABILITIES

The traditional accounting practice misstates the treatment of certain types of liabilities. Illustrations of these are liability from lawsuits, unfunded obligations, future interest expense on loans, and convertible bonds.

Liability from Lawsuits. Pending the rendering of a court judgment or the amicable settlement of pending lawsuits against it, a firm may or may not book the cases as liabilities. The action is based on subjective judgment of the management on the probable outcomes of the cases.

Unfunded Obligations. A company which has the legal obligation to pay for the medical insurance premium of its retirees may not recognize such a liability in its books and therefore defer the taking up of the expenses.

Future Interest Expense on Loans. A borrower with two loans with the same amounts will assign identical valuations to the loans for purposes of financial statement preparation, although one loan is more onerous than the other because of higher interest rate and higher security or collateral requirements.

Convertible Bonds. A concern with convertible bonds usually treat the obligation as a liability, although it is very likely that most of the bond-holders will subsequently convert the bonds to common stock because of attractive features. Such features may include the relatively low valuation of shares which can be exchanged with the bonds.

EXHIBIT 17.1:
Conventional Income Statement (dollars in $1,000)

	Year 1	Year 2	Increase	Increase as a percentage of year 1	COMMON SIZE Year 1	COMMON SIZE Year 2
Sales	$120,000	$143,000	$23,000	19.2%	100.0%	100.0%
Cost of goods manufactured and sold						
Raw materials used	24,000	33,294	9,294	38.7%	20.0%	23.3%
Other direct manufacturing costs	6,000	8,324	2,324	38.7	5.0	5.8
Depreciation—manufacturing	5,000	5,000	0	0.0	4.2	3.5
Factory overhead	25,000	27,200	2,200	8.8	20.8	19.0
Total manufacturing cost	60,000	73,818	13,818	23.0	50.0	51.6
Less: Increase in finished goods inventory—14.1%	0	10,408	10,408		0.0	7.3
Cost of goods sold	$ 60,000	$ 63,410	$ 3,410	5.7	50.0	44.3
Gross profit	$ 60,000	$ 79,590	$19,590	32.7	50.0%	55.7%
Less: Operating expenses						
Sales commissions	6,000	7,150	1,150	19.2	5.0	5.0
Advertising expenses	10,000	17,400	7,400	74.0	8.3	12.2
Freight out	1,800	2,259	459	25.5	1.5	1.6
Bad debts and collection expenses	1,200	1,898	698	58.2	1.0	1.3
Marketing overhead	15,000	17,600	2,600	17.3	12.5	12.3
Depreciation—marketing	1,000	1,000	0	0.0	0.8	0.7
Administrative expenses	7,000	7,280	280	4.0	5.8	5.1
R&D expenses	1,000	2,940	1,940	194.0	0.8	2.1
Total	43,000	57,527	14,527	33.8	35.8	40.2
Operating profit	17,000	22,063	5,063		14.2	15.4
Less: Interest expense	3,347	4,202	855	25.5	2.8	2.9
Net profit before income tax	$ 13,653	$ 17,861	$ 4,208	30.8	11.4	12.5
Income tax—40.0%	5,461	7,144	1,683	30.8	4.6	5.0
Net profit	$ 8,192	$ 10,716	$ 2,525	30.8	6.8	7.5

EXHIBIT 17.2:

Year 2 Gross Profit—Using Absorption Costing and Direct Costing
(dollars in $1,000)

		WITH INCREASE IN FINISHED GOODS INVENTORY		WITHOUT INCREASE IN FINISHED GOODS INVENTORY	
		Absorption costing (col. 1)	*Direct costing (col. 2)*	*Absorption costing (col. 3)*	*Direct costing (col. 4)*
Sales		$143,000	$143,000	$143,000	$143,000
Cost of goods manufactured and sold					
Variable manufacturing costs					
Raw materials used		33,294	33,294	28,600	28,600
Other direct manufacturing costs		8,324	8,324	7,150	7,150
Total variable costs		41,618	41,618	35,750	35,750
Fixed manufacturing costs					
Depreciation		5,000	5,000	5,000	5,000
Factory overhead		27,200	27,200	27,200	27,200
Total fixed costs		32,200	32,200	32,200	32,200
Total manufacturing cost	100.0%	73,818	73,818	67,950	67,950
Less: Increase in finished goods inventory	14.1%	10,408	5,868	0	0
Cost of goods sold	85.9%	$ 63,410	$ 67,950	$ 67,950	$ 67,950
Gross profit		$ 79,590	$ 75,050	$ 67,950	$ 75,050
Difference			$ 4,540		$ 75,050

403

EXHIBIT 17.3:
Year 2 Cost of Goods Sold and Increase in Finished Goods Inventory—Using Absorption Costing and Direct Costing
(dollars in $1,000)

	WITH INCREASE IN FINISHED GOODS INVENTORY		WITHOUT INCREASE IN FINISHED GOODS INVENTORY	
	Absorption costing (col. 1)	Direct costing (col. 2)	Absorption costing (col. 3)	Direct costing (col. 4)
I. Composition of cost of goods sold				
Variable costs				
Raw materials used	$28,600	$28,600	$28,600	$28,600
Other direct manufacturing costs	7,150	7,150	7,150	7,150
Total variable costs	35,750	35,750	35,750	35,750
Fixed costs				
Depreciation	4,295	5,000	5,000	5,000
Factory overhead	23,365	27,200	27,200	27,200
Total fixed costs	27,660	32,200	32,200	32,200
Cost of goods sold	$63,410	$67,950	$67,950	$67,950
II. Composition of increase in finished goods inventory				
Variable costs				
Raw materials used	4,694	4,694	0	0
Other direct manufacturing costs	1,174	1,174	0	0
Total variable costs	5,868	5,868	0	0
Fixed costs				
Depreciation	705	0	0	0
Factory overhead	3,835	0	0	0
Total fixed costs	4,540	0	0	0
Increase in finished goods inventory	$10,408	$ 5,868	$ 0	$ 0
Total cost of goods manufactured	$73,818	$73,818	$67,950	$67,950

EXHIBIT 17.4:
Contribution Margin Income Statement (dollars in $1,000)

	Year 1	Year 2	Increase	Increase as a percentage of year 1
Sales	$120,000	$143,000	$23,000	19.2%
Less: Variable costs				
Raw materials used	24,000	28,600	4,600	19.2%
Other direct manufacturing costs	6,000	7,150	1,150	19.2
Sales commissions	6,000	7,150	1,150	19.2
Advertising expenses	10,000	17,400	7,400	74.0
Freight out	1,800	2,259	459	25.5
Bad debts and collection expenses	1,200	1,898	698	58.2
Total variable costs	49,000	64,457	15,457	31.5
Contribution margin	71,000	78,543	7,543	10.6
Less: Fixed costs				
Depreciation	5,000	5,000	0	0.0
Factory overhead	25,000	27,200	2,200	8.8
Marketing department overhead	15,000	17,600	2,600	17.3
Depreciation—marketing	1,000	1,000	0	0.0
Administrative expenses*	7,000	7,280	280	4.0
R&D expenses for future products	1,000	2,940	1,940	194.0
Interest expense	3,347	4,202	855	25.5
Total fixed costs	57,347	65,222	7,875	13.7
Net profit before income tax	13,653	13,321	(332)	−2.4
Income tax—40%	5,461	5,328	(133)	−2.4
Additional tax		1,816	1,816	
Total tax	5,461	7,144	1,683	30.8
Net profit	$ 8,192	$ 6,176	($ 2,015)	−24.6

*The amount for year 2 includes $1,040,000 for legal settlement of cases arising from prior years' operations.

EXHIBIT 17.5:
Conventional Balance Sheet (dollars in $1,000)

	END OF			INCREASE DURING THE YEAR		AVERAGE DURING THE YEAR	
	Year 0	Year 1	Year 2	Year 1	Year 2	Year 1	Year 2
Assets							
Current assets							
Cash	$ 100	$ 200	$ 200	$ 100	$ 0	$ 150	$ 200
Trade receivables*	40,000	40,000	63,120	0	23,120	40,000	51,560
Inventories							
Finished goods†	10,000	10,000	20,408	0	10,408	10,000	15,204
Raw materials‡	6,000	6,000	5,891	0	(109)	6,000	5,946
Total	$56,100	$56,200	$ 89,619	$ 100	$33,419	$56,150	$ 72,910
Property, plant, and equipment							
Buildings and equipment at cost	45,000	45,000	45,000	0	0	45,000	45,000
Accumulated depreciation	(15,000)	(21,000)	(27,000)	(6,000)	(6,000)	(18,000)	(24,000)
Net book value	30,000	24,000	18,000	(6,000)	(6,000)	27,000	21,000
Construction in progress			18,000	0	18,000	0	9,000
Land	5,000	5,000	5,000	0	0	5,000	5,000
Total	$35,000	$29,000	$ 41,000	($ 6,000)	$12,000	$32,000	$ 35,000
Other assets							
Long-term investments	6,400	3,300	3,300	(3,100)	0	4,850	3,300
Total	$97,500	$88,500	$133,919	($ 9,000)	$45,419	$93,000	$111,210

EXHIBIT 17.5:
Continued

	END OF			INCREASE DURING THE YEAR		AVERAGE DURING THE YEAR	
	Year 0	Year 1	Year 2	Year 1	Year 2	Year 1	Year 2
Liabilities and stockholders' equity							
Current liabilities							
Accounts payable	$ 6,000	$ 6,000	$ 12,698	$ 0	$ 6,698	$ 6,000	$ 9,349
Bank loans—short-term	8,500	447	35,595	(8,053)	35,148	4,473	18,021
Current portion of long-term loans	5,000	2,500	0	(2,500)	(2,500)	3,750	1,250
Total current liabilities	19,500	8,947	48,293	(10,553)	39,346	14,223	28,620
Long-term loans, noncurrent portion	35,000	30,000	27,500	(5,000)	(2,500)	32,500	28,750
Total liabilities	$54,500	$39,947	$ 75,793	($15,553)	$36,846	$46,723	$ 57,370
Stockholders' equity							
Capital stock	33,000	33,000	33,000	0	0	33,000	33,000
Retained earnings							
Beginning balance	5,200	10,000	16,553	4,800	6,553		
Net profit during the year	6,000	8,192	10,716	2,192	2,525		
Dividends—20% of profit	(1,200)	(1,638)	(2,143)	(438)	(505)		
Ending balance	10,000	16,553	25,126	6,553	8,573	13,277	20,840
Total stockholders' equity	43,000	49,553	58,126	6,553	8,573	46,277	53,840
Total equity and liabilities	$97,500	$88,500	$133,919	($ 9,000)	$45,419	$93,000	$111,210

*Includes receivables believed to be collectible (and hence not written off) but over one year old; timing of collection not yet ascertained. Amount—$200,000.

†Based on absorption costing method.

‡Includes materials still usable (and hence not written off), but the bulk is not needed in the next few months. Amount—$400,000.

Chapter 18 _____

INTEGRATED PERFORMANCE RATIOS

This introductory chapter on ratio analysis presents the five different families of ratios that examine the five financial and operating functions of a business firm. The functions and the corresponding types of ratios used to dissect them are (1) mobilization of capital—financing structure ratios, (2) investment of the mobilized capital in the different types of resources—asset allocation ratios, (3) generation of sales through the utilization of the resources—asset utilization ratios, (4) controlling the operations so as to maximize the profit resulting from the sales generated—sales profitability ratios, and (5) determination of the attractiveness of the overall operations and investment—return on investment ratios.

The chapter introduces a new integrated management performance ratio which cuts across the boundaries of the five financial and operating functions and interlocks the key ratios in each of the functions. The interlocking ratio is the return on stockholders' equity. Unlike the traditional integrated ratios, this management performance ratio recognizes a new dimension which has recently emerged from the contemporary business scene: the proper treatment of assets not currently used in the main operations which could be idle plants, buildings under construction, slow-moving receivables, or unrelated investments.

The effectiveness of ratio analysis is enhanced if the ratio of a business unit is compared with (1) the past ratios of the same unit (time comparative ratios), (2) ratios of other units of the corporation (interdivisional comparative ratios), and (3) ratios of competing companies (industry comparative ratios).

I. FAMILIES OF RATIOS

OBJECTIVE

The objective of ratio analysis is to determine what happened in the past and what might take place in the future. Ratios are used to measure the improvements made in the past in operating and financing efficiencies and indicate the possible changes in the future.

Ratios are calculated in order to help evaluate the past performance of a corporation, a business unit, products, and managers. Thus, a business unit with a higher return on investment generally indicates, but not conclusively, that it has a better performance.

Ratios are also used in designing alternative profit enhancement programs for the future. For example, sales expansion measures usually give a higher accounting rate of return and build up sales faster than does a corporate office construction project. Hence, the former should be given priority.

Among sales expansion measures, one using prolonged terms of credit may give a higher net operating profit rate (based on sales) than one relying upon advertisement, but it may also have a lower net profit rate after taking into account the interest expense on the additional loan used to finance the incremental receivables.

NATURE AND GENERAL TYPES OF RATIOS

A ratio is a numerical relationship between two figures. For instance, the return on investment is calculated by dividing the net profit by the investment or stockholders' equity.

There are two general types of ratios: the financial statement ratios and the statistical or operational data ratios.

The financial statement ratios, as illustrated by the return on investment, are based primarily on historical or projected financial statements and related information. These ratios relate one figure or set of figures from one financial statement with another in the same or another statement. The ratios enable one to read "between the lines" in the financial statements.

Statistical or operational data ratios are based exclusively or partly on operating figures such as number of employees, labor hours, sales units, or floor areas. Sales per store floor area is an operating ratio.

The financial ratios are explained in Chapters 18 to 21, while the operational ratios are revealed in the latter part of Chapter 21.

FAMILIES OF FINANCIAL STATEMENT RATIOS
(Exhibit 18.1)

The financial ratios as grouped according to their place in the sequence of business functions outlined in the introductory paragraph of this chapter and in Exhibit 18.1 are

1. *Financing structure ratios.* These ratios reveal the financing sources which were mobilized by a firm. The ratios show how the total funding of the firm is proportioned to the stockholders' investments or equity, bank loans, and trade or suppliers' credit. This proportioning or financing mix influences both the return on the stockholders' equity as well as the risk exposure of the firm as a whole.
2. *Asset allocation ratios.* These ratios show how the total financing as mobilized is distributed to the different operating assets as inventories and receivables, and nonoperating assets as buildings under construction and unutilized factories.
3. *Asset utilization ratios.* These indicate the extent to which the resources were used to generate and support sales.
4. *Sales profitability ratios.* These reveal the degree of operating efficiency as indicated by the level of the costs of generating and servicing the sales in relation to the sales.
5. *Return on investment ratios.* These summarize the overall efficiency of the operations and the forms of financing. These show how much the owners get from their investment.

As may be noticed in Exhibit 18.1, these types of ratios are based on the balance sheet and income statement.

The financing structure ratios and asset allocation ratios are based on the balance sheet alone and hence are called balance sheet ratios. The sales profitability ratios are calculated by using the data from the income statement only and therefore are known as income statement ratios. The return on investment and asset utilization ratios are based on both the balance sheet and the income statement and hence are also called interstatement ratios.

The financing structure and return on investment ratios are also called financial ratios. These are discussed in detail in Chapters 19 and 20. The other three types of ratios are operating ratios. They are explained and illustrated in Chapter 21.

FINANCIAL STATEMENT FIGURES USED IN THE RATIOS

The figures used in the derivation of the ratios are as follows:

Income Statement Figures. The sales, costs, and profit figures from the income statement are for the period covered by the review.

Balance Sheet Figures. The figure to be used depends on the type of ratio—whether it is a balance sheet ratio or an interstatement ratio. See Exhibit 18.1 for the coverage of these ratios.

BALANCE SHEET RATIOS. These ratios use figures which are taken from the balance sheet only. The amounts are usually as of the end of the period and sometimes as of the beginning.

If these ratios are linked with the ratios in the other families, then the figures should be based on the beginning or average of the beginning and ending balances so that these ratios will be on a basis consistent with that of the asset utilization and return on investment ratios which are described shortly.

For instance, in the integrated management performance ratio described in part II of this chapter, the stockholders' financing leverage ratio, which is a balance sheet ratio, uses the average balance since this ratio is linked to the operating assets turnover which is an asset utilization ratio. (See Exhibit 18.2.)

INTERSTATEMENT RATIOS. These ratios utilize figures taken from both the balance sheet and income statement. The figures are normally as of the beginning or represent the average for the period. For most purposes, the average is based on the beginning and ending balances. However, more accurate estimates can be obtained if the values refer to the daily or monthly average balances. This is particularly true if there are substantial changes in the balances during the year, specifically if most of the changes took effect toward the beginning or end of the year.

II. INTEGRATED MANAGEMENT PERFORMANCE RATIOS

A running account of what happened to the different aspects of operations and financing is revealed if an integrated set of ratios is used. An integrated set is composed of interlocking ratios which are drawn from each of the five families of ratios named earlier.

ONE-YEAR PERFORMANCE RATIOS (Exhibit 18.2)

An integrated ratio is illustrated in Exhibit 18.2. The figures were taken from Chapter 17, Exhibit 17.1 (for the income statement) and Exhibit 17.5 (for the balance sheet).

The illustrated integrated ratio interlocks because

stockholders' financing leverage × operating assets ratio = Stockholders' operating assets leverage

operating assets turnover × net profit rate = return on operating assets

stockholders' operating assets leverage × return on operating assets = return on stockholders' equity

The different components of the integrated ratio are explained next.

Return on Stockholders' Equity

$$\frac{\text{Net profit}}{\text{stockholders' equity}}$$

The return on stockholders' equity (ROSE) relates the stockholders' equity with the profit. Thus, the two determinants of the ROSE are the amount of the stockholders' equity that is composed of the original investment and unwithdrawn profit and the net profit for the period under review.

There are two ways of directly improving the ROSE: by pushing up the net profit and by reducing the stockholders' equity. However, although the formula indicates these general ways, it does not give any clue on how the ROSE could had been, or may be, improved by more specific means as through more efficiency in the utilization of the resources, reduction of operating costs, use of more trade credits or low-interest loans, or cutting down of the nonoperating assets.

To help management analyze the past or future effect of these operating and financial measures, the ROSE formula may be segregated into two related ratios: (1) the stockholders' operating assets leverage (SOAL) and (2) the return on operating assets (ROA).

These two ratios have introduced another determinant of the ROSE but one that is not a direct part of the ROSE formula: operating assets.

Return on Operating Assets

$$\frac{\text{Net profit}}{\text{operating assets}}$$

Operating assets have more direct relevance to the net profit. What produces the profit is not the stockholders' equity as is but rather the use of the operating assets. The operating managers are not directly concerned with the stockholders' equity; that is the domain of the finance managers.

The operating managers use the operating assets which are in the form of receivables, inventories, and physical facilities to produce the profit. However, operating managers do not deal with nonoperating or nonmoving assets. These type of assets represent either (1) preparations for future growth, (2) errors and inefficiencies in the past, or (3) investments in unrelated undertakings. The first group includes buildings under construction, land held for future development, and expenditures for future product development. The second category covers slow-moving inventories, old receivables, and underutilized production capacities. The last classification involves stock investments in undertakings and other financial investments as those in promissory notes which are not connected with the operations.

Therefore, the performance of the managers and operating units can be better gauged by the return on operating assets rather than by the ROSE.

As indicated by the ROA formula, the ROA can be improved in two ways: by building up the net profit or by slashing the operating assets. However, management will be guided better if they are informed of more specific measures, such as increasing sales in relation to the operating assets and getting more profit out of every dollar of sales.

Operating Assets Turnover

$$\frac{\text{Sales}}{\text{operating assets}}$$

Although the operating assets are used in creating a profit, there can be no profit in the first place unless the assets can generate sales. Normally, the higher the sales, the more attractive is the profit. Hence, an indicator is required to measure the sales generated for every dollar of operating asset utilized. This is supplied by the operating asset turnover (OAT) ratio. The OAT indicates how efficiently management was able to utilize the resources to produce the maximum sales.

However, there are admittedly severe industry limitations to which sales could be increased in relation to the available resources. New high-technology companies, as those in biotechnology, require massive investments in R&D while their sales are still very low if not negligible.

In contrast, merchandise retailing operations, especially those with leased store premises, can easily convert their investments, which are mainly in receivables and inventories, into annual sales that are higher than their operating assets.

Notwithstanding these industry features, steps could be taken by individual firms to maximize the sales in relation to the deployed resources. For instance, the collection of receivables could be accelerated, or the turnaround time of inventories cut down.

The employment of the OAT enables management to examine the degree of success achieved by past measures in slashing the levels of outstanding receivables, inventories, and other resources, as well as determine the extent to which further improvement is possible.

Net Profit Rate

$$\frac{\text{Net profit}}{\text{sales}}$$

Net profit may be increased not by pushing sales per se, but profitable sales, namely, sales that can bring in profit after deducting the costs and expenses. The net profit rate (NPR) determines how much profit is left for every dollar of sales.

Since sales commission is an incentive to the marketing force to bring in sales, the commission should be structured so as to bring more profitable sales and less of the sales with marginal profit.

The net profit rate can be improved by pushing down the costs and expenses as a percentage of sales. This can be brought about by reducing expenses at a rate faster than the reduction in sales or by increasing the sales at a rate faster than the rise in costs.

Stockholders' Operating Assets Leverage

$$\frac{\text{Operating assets}}{\text{stockholders' equity}}$$

The SOAL in Exhibit 18.2 indicates that every dollar of stockholders' equity has made available to the firm $1.83 in operating assets. The $1.83 or 1.83 is the leverage in this case. Usually, the higher the leverage, the higher the ROSE becomes, since the higher is the total of the operating assets which the company can utilize to produce sales. However, this premise holds only if the firm is not paying too much for borrowed money since the interest is deducted from the sales to arrive at the net profit.

There are two ways of magnifying this leverage: by pushing up the nonequity financing available, namely, the loans and trade credits, and by expanding the operating assets component of the total assets. These methods are explained in the two succeeding sections.

Stockholders' Financing Leverage

$$\frac{\text{Total financing}}{\text{stockholders' equity}}$$

The stockholders' financing leverage (SFL) in Exhibit 18.2 shows that a total financing of $2.07 was raised for every $1.00 of stockholders' equity. The balance of $1.07 is from loans and trade credits.

This ratio determines the soundness of the financing mix used for the firm. The mix is the proportion of the stockholders' equity to the other forms of financing. This proportion influences both the ROSE as well as the risk involved.

A firm which is mainly financed by stockholders or with a minimum of bank loans and trade credits is usually financially stable. Its fixed payments to the suppliers of funds—in the form of interest and principal amortizations on the loans—are nominal. In normal times, a bigger portion of its payments to the fund suppliers—in the form of dividends on capital stock—are contingent upon the generation of profit and availability of cash. Since dividend payments are contingent, they can easily be reduced if not totally eliminated when business downturns convert the profit into loss and transform the cash surplus into cash deficit. Furthermore, a low-leveraged firm has a higher chance of obtaining additional financing than does a high-leveraged company.

However, a firm with a low leverage also has a disadvantage: it does not maximize the use of financing leverage which derives from money from loans with interest lower than the cost of stockholders' equity or ROSE. The lower the leverage, the less is the share *per unit of capital stock* in the excess of the firm's operating profit over the interest paid to the creditors. The lower the share per unit of capital stock, the less is the ROSE.

An evaluation of the ratio therefore requires a consideration of the trade-off of a high return of a highly leveraged financing with the minimal risk of a low-leveraged structure. This trade-off of return and risk is illustrated with figures in Chapter 15.

Operating Assets Ratio

$$\frac{\text{Operating assets}}{\text{total assets}}$$

The OAR, which is 88% in Exhibit 18.2, indicates the operating assets as a percentage of total assets. The ratio ascertains how the total financing was distributed to operating and nonoperating assets. The former is composed of currently moving working capital as receivables and inventories and property. The profitability of a firm is lowered if a sizable portion of the financing is invested in resources which are not actively used in current operations.

A substantial investment in currently unproductive assets tend to depress the ROSE. The reason is that, while these types of assets do not benefit the present operations, the interest charges on the loans used to finance them are paid out of or charged to the operations. Furthermore, if stockholders' equity is used to fund these assets, this portion of the equity receives no current return, and hence the overall return on the total equity is lowered.

COMPARATIVE RATIOS (Exhibit 18.3)

The ratios calculated for a firm or business unit for a past period can serve management better if they are compared with the corresponding ratios for a prior period, the budget, other divisions in the company, or other companies in the industry:

1. The comparison of ratios for a past period with ratios for prior periods may reveal a trend.

2. The comparison of ratios for past periods with ratios based on the budget may indicate some problems which can be analyzed for possible correction or may show some limitations in the budget itself.

3. The comparison of ratios based on financial projections or budgets with historical or current ratios will help determine the reasonableness of the forecasts.

4. The checking of ratios of one division with those of another unit within the same organization will help in the evaluation of the divisions and of their managers.

5. The comparison of ratios of one company with another in the industry will help in determining the competitiveness of the firm.

6. The comparison of past performance ratios, such as the collection period of receivables, with the prescribed business practices, such as the credit terms or terms of sale, will determine compliance with the policies or the efficiency of the department concerned.

For instance, meaningful results will be revealed if the ratios in Exhibit 18.2, which are for year 2, are compared with those of the preceding year. This is done in Exhibit 18.3.

Stockholders' Financing Leverage.   This slightly increased from 2.01 in year 1 to 2.07 in year 2, or by about 3%. This is due to the rise in the total liability as a percentage of total financing (liabilities and stockholders' equity). The biggest increase in the liabilities is in short-term loans—which jumped from $4,473,000 in year 1 to $18,021,000 in the following year.

Operating Assets Ratio.   However, the 3% increase in stockholders' financing leverage (a favorable development) was more than offset by a decline in the operating assets ratio, from 0.94 to 0.88 or a drop of about 6% (an unfavorable change). This drop is due to the construction in progress in year 2, which had an average balance of $9,000,000. In other words, although the firm was able to obtain more financing from nonstockholder sources, the percentage of the total financing going to operating assets dropped at a higher rate but in the other direction (unfavorable development).

Stockholders' Operating Assets Leverage.   Consequently, there is a net decline in the stockholders' operating assets leverage from 1.89 to 1.83 or about 3.5% (an unfavorable variance). This is the combined effect of the favorable change in the stockholders' financing leverage and the bigger unfavorable variation in the operating assets ratio.

Operating Assets Turnover.   The firm was able to marshal substantial operating efficiencies. It was able to improve its utilization rate of the operating assets since it raised the operating assets turnover from 1.37 to 1.45, a respectable 6% jump. The higher turnover was achieved because the improvement in the sales of 19% was higher than the rise in the operating assets of 12%.

Net Profit Rate.   Another factor that contributed to the enhancement of the return on operating assets is the substantial climb in the net profit rate or net profit as a percentage of sales—from 6.8% to 7.5%, or an almost 10% rise.

Return on Operating Assets.   The improvement in both the operating assets turnover and the net profit rate collaborated to give a substantial lift to the return on operating assets of over 16%—from 9.4% to 10.9%.

Return on Stockholders' Equity.   In summary, the slight decline in the stockholders' operating asset leverage of almost 4% (an unfavorable variation) was more than offset by the terrific rise in the return on operating assets of over 16% (a desirable change), thus resulting in an attractive enhancement of ROSE of 12%—from 17.7% to 19.9%.

III. DUPONT FORMULA

An integrated performance ratio, the Dupont formula, which was originally applied by E. I. du Pont de Nemours, is more simplified than the one shown in Exhibit 18.2. The formula ties in the profit margin with the return on the total assets. This relationship is expressed as follows:

$$\text{return on total assets} = \text{profit margin} \times \text{total assets turnover}$$

where

$$\text{return on total assets} = \frac{\text{net profit}}{\text{total assets}}$$

$$\text{profit margin} = \frac{\text{net profit}}{\text{sales}}$$

$$\text{total assets turnover} = \frac{\text{sales}}{\text{total assets}}$$

Hence

$$\frac{\text{net profit}}{\text{total assets}} = \frac{\text{net profit}}{\text{sales}} \times \frac{\text{sales}}{\text{total assets}}$$

The modified Dupont formula added the stockholders' financing leverage so that

$$\frac{\text{return on stock-}}{\text{holders' equity}} = \frac{\text{return on}}{\text{total assets}} \times \frac{\text{financing}}{\text{leverage}}$$

Hence,

$$\frac{\text{net profit}}{\substack{\text{stockholders'} \\ \text{equity}}} = \frac{\text{net profit}}{\text{total assets}} \times \frac{\text{total assets}}{\substack{\text{stockholders'} \\ \text{equity}}}$$

Thus, the complete modified Dupont formula becomes

$$\frac{\text{net profit}}{\substack{\text{stockholders'} \\ \text{equity}}} = \frac{\text{net profit}}{\text{sales}} \times \frac{\text{sales}}{\text{total assets}} \times \frac{\text{total assets}}{\substack{\text{stockholders'} \\ \text{equity}}}$$

A comparison of the formula with the one in Exhibit 18.2 shows that the modified Dupont formula does not include the operating assets ratio (operating assets divided by total assets).

IV. LIMITATIONS OF RATIOS

Ratios have two general limitations: those pertaining to the financial statements upon which the ratios are based and those inherent in some of the ratios themselves.

To the extent that the financial statements are distorted, the ratios become misleading. The limitations of the statements were discussed in the last section of Chapter 17. The limitations inherent in certain ratios are revealed in Chapters 19 to 21.

Ratio analysis becomes more meaningful if they are related to the ratios of the same company or business segment for prior periods or to the other companies or segments of the same period. In addition to the general limitations of ratios mentioned in the preceding two paragraphs, comparative ratios are subject to additional restrictions. These are revealed in the following paragraphs.

LIMITATIONS OF TIME COMPARATIVE RATIOS

Time series ratios for the same enterprise or division can become misleading unless adjustments are made for the following: changes in accounting treatments, changes in strategy, and inflation.

Changes in Accounting Treatments. In the same way that changes in accounting practices can distort the comparative financial statements, they can also disrupt the meanings of time comparative ratios. For instance, if a company changes its inventory valuation method from LIFO to FIFO, the ratios may indicate a sudden jump in the profit although in reality the profitability has remained flat or even declined.

Changes in Business Strategy. A shift from a harvest to a grow strategy reduces the reported profit and hence the profitability ratios, although the economic performance of the firm might have improved. Business strategies are discussed in Chapter 2.

Changes in Assets. The disposal of a piece of equipment that has not been used for several years improves the return on investment (ROI) after the disposal. Conversely, the acquisition of new equipment which is not fully utilized at once depresses the ROI.

Inflation. Inflation bloats both the dollar figures displayed in the financial statements and the attractiveness of the resulting ratios. If the figures are deflated to reflect constant purchasing power, the profitability of a firm over a period of time as reflected in the statements and ratios may show a downward trend although the opposite is exhibited before the adjustment.

LIMITATIONS OF INTERDIVISIONAL AND INTERCOMPANY COMPARATIVE RATIOS

The interdivisional or intercompany comparison of ratios is made less effective if the divisions or companies being reviewed have varying accounting treatments, follow opposite business strategies, have different capacity utilization percentages of their plants or other facilities, have acquired their properties under different arrangements, or have different acquisition years for their major properties.

Furthermore, the usefulness of the comparative ratios is weakened if the fiscal years of the businesses under review end in different quarters. For instance, other things being equal, if the ratios of a firm with fiscal year ending on December 31 is compared with an enterprise with fiscal year ending on March 31, the former firm will show a higher profit due to the advance in inflation for three quarters.

EXHIBIT 18.1:
Types of Ratios and Their Relationships

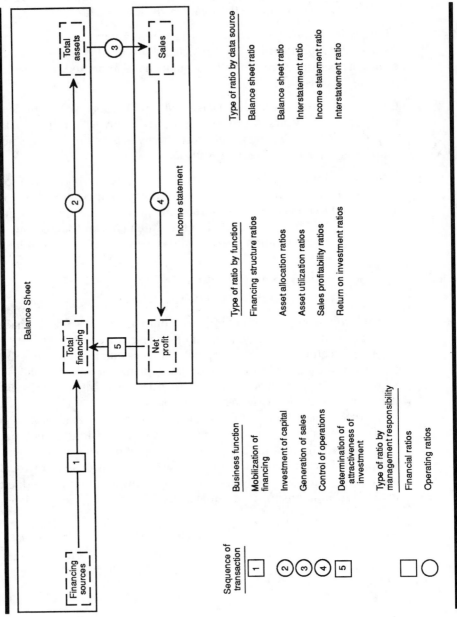

EXHIBIT 18.2:

Integrated Management Performance Ratio—Year 2 (dollars in $1,000)

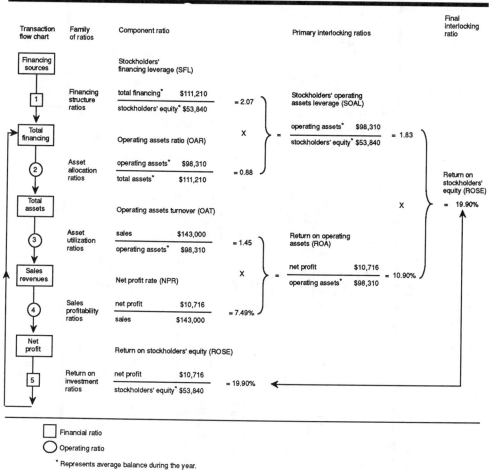

☐ Financial ratio

◯ Operating ratio

* Represents average balance during the year.

EXHIBIT 18.3:
Comparative Integrated Management Performance Ratios (dollars in $1,000)

Name of ratio	Formula	BASE DATA			RATIO		Year 2 as a percentage of year 1
		Year 1	Year 2		Year 1	Year 2	
Stockholders' financing leverage	total financing* / stockholders' equity*	$ 93,000 / $ 46,277	$111,210 / $ 53,840	=	2.01	2.07	102.8%
Operating assets ratio	operating assets* / total assets*	$ 87,550 / $ 93,000	$ 98,310 / $111,210	=	0.94	0.88	93.9
Stockholders' operating assets leverage	operating assets* / stockholders' equity*	$ 87,550 / $ 46,277	$ 98,310 / $ 53,840	=	1.89	1.83	96.5
Operating assets turnover	sales / operating assets*	$120,000 / $ 87,550	$143,000 / $ 98,310	=	1.37	1.45	106.1
Net profit rate	net profit / sales	$ 8,192 / $120,000	$ 10,716 / $143,000	=	6.83%	7.49%	109.8
Return on operating assets	net profit / operating assets*	$ 8,192 / $ 87,550	$ 10,716 / $ 98,310	=	9.36%	10.90%	116.5
Return on stockholders' equity	net profit / stockholders' equity*	$ 8,192 / $ 46,277	$ 10,716 / $ 53,840	=	17.70%	19.90%	112.4

*Represents average balance during the year.

Chapter 19 _____

RETURN ON INVESTMENT RATIO ANALYSIS

There are three types of returns: the return on the equity investment, the return on the loans, and the return on the combined equity and loans. The first two types of returns highlight the degree of profitability and safety of the stockholders' or lenders' investments. The return on their combined investment discloses the overall viability of the enterprise irrespective of the debt/equity mix.

Technically, the return on investment (ROI) may mean the return (1) on the equity of the stockholders or (2) on the investments of both the stockholders and the lenders. In usage, however, ROI has been used to refer to the return on stockholders' equity.

[For the sake of clarity, this chapter uses the term return on stockholders' equity (ROSE) or investment for the first connotation (the return on the investment of the stockholders alone) and the term return on total investment for the second meaning.]

The return on equity techniques may be further classified into (1) the return on stockholders' equity or accounting rate of return (ARR) and (2) the residual income (RI).

This chapter presents a new way of calculating the ROSE: one which breaks down the ROSE into two components—the shareholders' proportionate share in the total return on the total investment and their share in the profit arising from the loan leverage. This ROSE formula is different from the one introduced in Chapter 18, which interprets ROSE as the ratio that interlocks the other components of the integrated management performance ratio, namely, the financing leverage, the operating assets ratio, the assets turnover, and the sales profitability rate.

I. RETURN ON STOCKHOLDERS' EQUITY OR ACCOUNTING RATE OF RETURN

There are two common techniques employed in evaluating the return on the investment of the stockholders: the ROSE or ARR, which is expressed as a percentage, and the residual income, which is denominated in dollars. The former is more popular.

RETURN ON STOCKHOLDERS' EQUITY

$$\frac{\text{net profit}}{\text{stockholders' equity}}$$

The ROSE measures the profit for the period under evaluation as a percentage of the stockholders' investment and accumulated unwithdrawn profit. The profit for the period may be taken out as dividend or retained in the business as additional stockholders' equity.

If the IRR is used in decision analysis, the ROSE or ARR should be utilized in performance evaluation since the IRR is compatible with the ROSE. Both are *rate of return techniques* that are denominated in terms of a percentage rate. They are internally generated and hence are not keyed in to the cost of the capital.

VARIATIONS IN THE APPLICATIONS OF THE ROSE (Exhibit 19.1)

Due to the variations in the procedure of calculating the ROSE, six different rates may be derived for the same company or division, for the same period. This is due to the differences in:

1. The method of valuing the stockholders' equity, that is, whether at (a) book value as shown in the balance sheet; (b) appraised value, which is book value as adjusted for the appraised value of land, buildings, and equipment and sometimes inventories; or (c) market value of the shares of stock
2. The date of the stockholders' equity to be used, that is, whether (a) as of the beginning of the period or (b) the average for the period

Hence, before applying the ROSE formula, the method of valuation and the date of stockholders' equity should be decided first.

The three ways of calculating the ROSE, utilizing different bases of valuing the stockholders' equity, but all using the average balance, are illustrated in Exhibit 19.1.

ALTERNATIVE VALUATIONS OF STOCKHOLDERS' EQUITY (Exhibit 19.2)

The three alternative valuation bases differ in the following: the subject being valued, the basis of the valuation, the determinants of the value, the revisions of the value, and the acceptability of the results. These features are summarized in Exhibit 19.2 and are discussed in the paragraphs that follow.

Subject Being Valued.   Both the book value and appraised value methods place a value on the assets. The liabilities are then deducted from the assets. This practice has a drawback: the assets are not fully valued since part of their value lies in their ability to produce income in the future.

The market value approach tries to correct this weakness. It recognizes that the future earnings are just as important as the present assets. Hence it includes both in valuing the stockholders' equity.

Basis of Valuation.   The book value method uses historical cost for the assets, based on consummated transactions, less accumulated depreciation in the case of buildings and equipment. Since for many companies most of the land, buildings, and equipment were acquired several years ago, when prices were much lower than now due to inflation, the book value is far below the current prices. The use of accelerated depreciation which is allowed for tax purposes has widened the gap between the book value and the current prices.

The appraised value method corrects this deficiency of the book value basis. The values of the land, buildings, and equipment are adjusted to reflect their current or appraised values. In few instances, the book values of inventories which are carried on last-in, first-out basis (LIFO) are also raised to reflect the prevailing prices.

Determinants of the Value.   In the case of the book value method, the total assets less the liabilities is equivalent to the stockholders' equity. The equity, in turn, is equal to the capital contribution plus net profit less dividends. Therefore, the capital contribution, profit, and dividends determine the book value of the stockholders' equity.

The appraised value method has added another determinant: the excess of the appraised value of the land, buildings, and equipment (and sometimes inventories) over their net book value.

The market value of the shares is determined by the present and prospective investors. They judge, among others, the future dividends to be paid by the company, the future appreciation in the market value of the shares, the prospects of the economy in general, and their own requirements and positions. Hence, the determinants of the market value are much broader but at the same time more blurred than those of the two other methods. For the shares listed in the stock exchange, the market value is the price of the transactions. For those not listed, the value is the price which the present owners can get for their shares.

Revisions of the Value.   The amount of the stockholders' equity under the book value or appraised value method is adjusted every month or quarter—every time the financial statements are prepared. On the other hand, the market value of publicly held shares may change any time during the trading hours. The value of shares which are not listed are determined at irregular intervals as offers are received.

The book or appraised value is more stable than the market value for two reasons: first, they do not change as frequently; second, they do not fluctuate violently.

Acceptability of the Results.   The book value method is the most accepted among the three for general purposes. The book value of stockholders' equity is the one which is usually incorporated in the official balance sheet which forms part of the annual report to the stockholders. The appraised value of land, buildings, and equipment is usually not incorporated in the balance sheet but is referred to only in the footnotes. The market value of the shares is not placed at all in the balance sheet.

Evaluation of the Three Methods of Valuing Stockholders' Equity

ROSE AT BOOK VALUE.   Although the valuation of stockholders' equity at book value is subject to severe limitations as discussed earlier and summarized shortly, the ROSE at book value is the most commonly used tool in performance evaluation and investment analysis. Among the factors favoring its application are (1) the ready availability of the information on the value of stockholders' equity, (2) the impression of reliability since the figures are taken from the financial statements, and (3) the ease of linking the ROSE at book value to the other ratios in the integrated ratio analysis as discussed in Chapter 18.

The key limitations of ROSE at book value are (1) the understatement of the real value of the land, buildings, and equipment and (2) the failure to assign value to the future earnings. Since the book value understates the value of the resources for which management is held accountable, the ROSE at book value is usually higher than the ROSE at appraised value or at market value. See Exhibit 19.1 for the comparative ratios.

ROSE AT APPRAISED VALUE.   This is ideal for internal use in evaluating the performance of managers and the divisions for two reasons: (1) the use of up-to-date values for the resources and (2) the more stable valuation of the equity.

ROSE AT MARKET VALUE.   This provides the best basis in performance evaluation since the market value represents actual transactions or offers. The market value, therefore, is fairer and more objective than is the appraised value. However, the use of market value has two setbacks: (1)

the market price of shares may fluctuate violently (witness the 22% drop in the stock prices on October 19, 1987), and (2) the market value of the shares of firms not listed in the exchanges may not be as readily available as the book or appraised value.

DATE OF STOCKHOLDERS' EQUITY TO BE USED

The stockholders' equity employed in Exhibit 19.1 represents the average of the beginning and ending balances. An alternative is to employ the balance as of the beginning of the year. The use of this alternative is founded on the premise that since the reckoning of the return is on an annual basis, the profit for the year should be related to the stockholders' equity as of the start of the period.

However, the use of the average balance is justified on the following grounds:

1. The asset turnover ratios (see Chapter 21) utilize the average balances of the resources. Since the stockholders' equity finances the resources, the equity figure to be used should also be the average balance.
2. The interest on loans which are tapped to finance part of the resources are computed on the average balance.
3. The use of average balance provides a more stable basis due to the fluctuations of the balance from time to time.
4. If the results of two or more divisions or subsidiaries are compared, and one gives quarterly dividends while the others pay annually, the results can be made more comparable if the equity balance used is the average for the period. If the beginning balance is used, the unit paying quarterly dividend is penalized, as no credit is given for the advance payments of dividends during the first three quarters. The earlier dividend payments can give additional income until the end of the year.

II. RESIDUAL INCOME

If the net present value (NPV) is applied in appraising projects, the residual income (RI) should be employed in reviewing the results of operations. The NPV and RI are *net dollar return tools* that are denominated in terms of dollars. They are calculated using external money cost rates—discount rate for the NPV and cost of stockholders' investment for the RI.

RATIONALE

In a banking transaction involving borrowing (accepting deposits by a bank) and lending, the gross banking profit is created by the excess of the lending rate over the borrowing rate. The lending rate provides the revenues to the bank; the borrowing rate represents the cost of the money which was lent. The dollar value of the profit obtained from the transaction is the interest spread multiplied by the amount borrowed and then lent, thus

dollar value of profit in a banking transaction
= (lending rate − borrowing rate)
× amount borrowed and lent

Where the lending rate is 12%, the borrowing rate is 10%, the derived interest spread is 2%, and the amount borrowed and then lent is $1,000,000,

$$
\begin{aligned}
\text{dollar value of the profit} \quad &= \quad (12\% - 10\%) \times \$1,000,000 \\
&= \quad 2\% \times \$1,000,000 = \$20,000
\end{aligned}
$$

FORMULA

Net profit less cost of capital

In business operations, the net profit (NP) after income tax shown as the bottom line in the income statement and serving as the basis in estimating the ROSE is not a clean profit because the cost of the capital put in by stockholders has not yet been deducted. The reported net profit is similar to what the bank gets from the lending operation before deducting the interest on deposits. The clean profit, which is called RI, may be computed by the following formula, which is similar to the one for the dollar value of profit in a banking transaction:

FIRST FORMULA

dollar value of the profit or RI = (ROSE − cost of capital %)
× amount of capital

This may be restated as

SECOND FORMULA

dollar value of the profit or RI = NP − (cost of capital %
× amount of capital)

The RI formula may be illustrated by using the following information which is similar to that utilized in the banking transaction example: the capital is $1,000,000, the net profit is $120,000, the ROSE is 12% (net profit divided by the capital), and the cost of capital is 10%. Applying the first formula,

RI: = (12% − 10%) × $1,000,000 = $20,000

Using the second formula

$$RI: = \$120,000 - (10\% \times \$1,000,000) = \$20,000$$

DETERMINANTS OF RI

The first formula brings out the three determinants of RI: (1) the ROSE (stated as a percent), (2) the cost of capital rate (stated as a percent), and (3) the amount of the capital. The ROSE less the cost of capital rate gives the RI or interest spread. Thus, the RI may be represented as the square area of a rectangle where the height is the interest spread, and the length is the investment size or amount of capital. Two projects with varying spreads and investment sizes may have identical RI if the shortage of one project in the spread is made up in the incremental investment.

COST OF CAPITAL

The manner of calculation of the cost of capital depends upon the use of the RI—whether to evaluate an entire company or to appraise a business segment.

Evaluation of an Entire Company.   From the viewpoint of the owners, their equity in the company is just one alternative investment medium. They can sell their shares at the prevailing market price and invest the proceeds in, say, U.S. Treasury bonds. Since their investment in the company carries more risk, their required return from the firm, or the cost to the company of the capital they put in, is higher than is the yield on the government security. Consequently, the cost of capital is based on two factors: (1) the market value of the shares and (2) the required yield rate, which depends upon the return and the risks of the alternative investment opportunities available to the owners.

Evaluation of a Business Segment.   When a parent company supplies its divisions with financing, the cost of the advances, say, to Unit B, may be calculated in the manner demonstrated here (dollars in $1,000):

	Total	Given to Unit B	Rate	Capital charge
Before risk factor				
Cost of capital stock	$ 30,000	$ 3,000	8%	$ 240
Secured loans	50,000	5,000	10%	500
Unsecured loans	20,000	2,000	12%	240
Total	$100,000	$10,000	9.8%	980
Risk factor for Unit B			2.0%	200
Total capital charge			11.8%	$1,180

Thus, the total capital charge for Unit B is $1,180,000 for one year. In the illustration, the cost of capital stock is that of the parent company. The concept of the cost was discussed earlier. The basic capital charge of 9.8% represents the average cost of funds to the parent company. For new projects, the basic capital charge may be based on the cost of the incremental financing to the parent. Thus, if the parent has to obtain all the funding for a new project, Unit X, from unsecured loans, the basic capital charge will be 12% and not 9.8%.

The risk factor may be varied depending on the risk exposure of the business segment itself and of its various types of assets.

ALTERNATIVE VALUATIONS OF STOCKHOLDERS' EQUITY

RI Based on Stockholders' Equity at Market Value (Exhibit 19.3, part I). Asumming that the owners have placed a 12% rate on the market value of their shares as their desired return, the cost of capital or required return for the case illustrated in Exhibit 19.3 would have been $7,157,000 for year 1 and $9,719,000 for year 2. See the exhibit for the calculations.

Although the net profit rose in year 2, the RI did decline. As may be noticed in the exhibit, this fall in the RI is due to the fact that the market value of the shares expanded by 36%, while the net profit after income tax grew by only 31%.

RI Based on Stockholders' Equity at Book Value (Exhibit 19.3, parts II and III). The calculations of residual income and related ratios in the exhibit are based on stockholders' equity at market value. Since most ratios utilize book value, the RI may have to be converted to the book value basis to make them consistent with the other ratios. This was done in Exhibit 19.3, part II. The cost of capital, which is 12% on stockholders' equity at market value, translates to 15.5% and 18.1% based on stockholders' equity at book value for years 1 and 2, respectively. Although the required yield on the equity based on market value remained constant during the two years (at 12%), the cost of capital based on book value rose from 15.5% to 18.1%. This is due to the upswing in the market value premium (excess of market value over book value). See Exhibit 19.3, part III.

III. EVALUATION OF THE ROSE AND RI

While the ROSE or RI of a firm or division gives the semblance of a fact that cannot be disputed, they are actually as tentative and subjective as the accounting statements that yield the information on net worth and income which serve as the foundation of the ROSE and RI. Furthermore the ROSE and RI give varying effects on the profitability, growth, risk, and congruence of corporate and division goals.

The ROSE and RI are both used to attain the same purpose—to appraise the performance of a business firm, its segments, and managers who are assigned the responsibility of maximizing the profitability of these firms and their segments.

APPLICATIONS

The ROSE and RI may be used to evaluate the performance either of an entire company or its segments.

Evaluation of an Entire Company. If used on a firm the ROSE and RI are calculated using the capital base and net income taken from the financial statements. The capital charge utilized in determining the RI was discussed earlier.

The resulting ROSE will be compared with the cost of the capital to the firm. The cost of capital includes the risk add-on.

Evaluation of a Business Segment. The RI for a business unit is based on the net profit after deducting the capital charge as defined earlier. The ROSE is based on the net profit before the capital charge. The net profit should be before the allocation of the general corporate overhead. However, the value of services provided by the service units within the group (as centralized accounting or purchasing) are deducted as costs only if the operating units are charged at cost or the charges are at competitive rates.

THE ROSE AND RI AS TENTATIVE AND SUBJECTIVE MEASURES

The return on investment ratios as calculated using the formula as given earlier in this chapter cannot be disputed if the figures used are final, objective, and reflect the economic values. However, the stockholders' equity and net income indicated in the financial statements are sometimes tentative, subjective, and represent more the historical costs rather than the market values. Hence the ROSE and RI should not be taken at face value.

While accounting rules and conventions have been established in order to make the financial statements as objective as possible, certain weaknesses which compromise the validity of the figures in the balance sheet and income statement still persist. Some of these are discussed here.

Accounting for Business Strategy. Accounting practice governs the proper recording of expenditures on equipment as investments since the equipment benefits the future. The accounting conventions correctly takes the money taken from others as borrowings if they will be paid back in the future.

However, expenditures on promotions and advertising to expand market share which will benefit the future are expensed outright and are not booked as investments. In like manner, postponed maintenance of equipment is not taken up as liability, although it will require payments in the future. Thus, under current practice, the more a firm tries to build up its market share, the more its ROSE and RI declines. Similarly, the more a company runs its factories to the ground—that is, without current maintenance—the more its ROSE and RI rise.

Hence, if the underlying financial statements and business strategies are not studied in relation to the ratios, and if the managerial performance is tied in to the ROSE or RI, the management may steer to destruction the very companies they are supposed to nourish.

(See Chapter 2 for a discussion of how business strategies influence the recorded performance.)

Accounting for Properties.   Section I of this chapter has revealed that if the land, buildings, and equipment are valued using the book value method, the stockholders' equity is understated. This method understates the assets which are placed at the disposal of the business, and its units or managers, and hence overstates both the ROSE and RI.

The use of original cost or gross cost will not solve this weakness since the gross cost is not keyed to the current economic value of the properties. Only the use of the replacement value will remedy the situation.

Accounting for Nonfinancial Resources.   If ROSE or RI is used to compare the performance of different industries, companies, or segments, the degree of automation, labor intensity, and employee loyalty among the subjects to be compared should be considered. While the expenditures for the acquisition of modern factories are taken up as an investment, the cost of training the workers and building up their loyalty is considered an expense. Thus, the return on investment ratios of a labor-intensive operation are overstated due to the understatement of the capital base indicated in the balance sheet.

In a professional organization, the most important resources are the business contacts of the partners and the skills of the professional staff. These are not assigned any value at all in the balance sheet. The investment in the office space, furniture, libraries, and laboratories, the ones appearing as assets in the balance sheet, is minimal compared with the value of the contacts and skills. Hence the rate of return ratios in this type of organization are not only irrelevant but outright misleading.

Other Accounting Limitations. The other limitations that weaken the financial statements and hence undermine the integrity of the ROSE and RI were revealed in Chapters 16 and 17.

EFFECT ON PROFITABILITY

Return on Stockholders' Equity or Accounting Rate of Return. Since the ARR represents the net profit as a percentage of capital, its utilization in performance evaluation generally induces management to invest in projects which give the highest profit as a percentage of capital. This maximizes the return per dollar of investment.

The utilization of this rate of return technique, therefore, is best suited to situations where capital is a scarce resource, and hence the management goal is to get the maximum utilization out of it.

New Investment—Divisional ARR (Exhibit 19.4). However, the use of the rate of return techniques may not necessarily increase the overall ARR of a corporation. If the managers of a division are judged based on the ARR of their operations, they will be induced to take on projects or buy new assets which will give ARRs which are higher than the ARRs of their current operations. This action augments their future ARR.

New projects are evaluated in terms of IRR and not ARR. Since the IRR cannot be converted into ARR, and since managers are evaluated in terms of ARR, managers who are informed on the projected ARR of new projects will use the projected ARR of the new projects as the basis in deciding which proposal to undertake.

Take Divisions I and II in a corporation where the cost of capital is 14% and the average corporate ARR is 16%. The present operations and proposed projects of these divisions can generate the returns shown in Exhibit 19.4.

Division I, with 20% ARR, will reduce its ARR to 19.4% if it takes project D, which has an 18% ARR. Hence the division will let project D go. In reality, the division could make a clean profit out of the project since the latter's ARR is still higher than the 14% corporate cost of capital. The abandonment of this project will rob the corporation of an opportunity to raise its ARR from 16%.

On the other hand, Division II with an ARR from its present operations of 10% is prompted to develop a new project, project F, which has a 12% ARR, which is lower than the corporate cost of capital of 14% and the current corporate ARR of 16%. However, it will raise the divisional ARR from 10% to 10.7%. This action will prejudice the corporate interest since it will lower the corporate ARR.

Divestment (Exhibit 19.5).   Division I may go a step farther. It may yet hike its ARR from 20% to 22% by dropping product B and just concentrating on product A. See Exhibit 19.5. The division may take this move just to boost its ARR although the corporation is still making money out of product B since B's ARR is higher than the corporate cost of capital. Of course, the divestment of product B will lower the ARR of the corporation as a whole since B's ARR of 17% is higher than the corporate ARR.

The corporate error likely to be committed by Divisions I and II is that the decision to invest or divest is made by comparing their present or target ARR with the ARRs of the investment or divestment candidates and not with the ARR of the corporation and its cost of capital.

Residual Income.   When RI is used, the tendency of management is not so much to maximize the profit per dollar of investment as it is to produce the highest profit in terms of total dollars. This is so since the RI is measured in terms of absolute dollars and not as percentage of capital.

If the RI is used, project D in Exhibit 19.4 will be implemented as it will raise the RI, but project F will be aborted as it will depress the RI. Furthermore, product B in Exhibit 19.5 will be retained.

If the RI, instead of the ARR, is utilized, the projects to be implemented will have a lower ARR.

EFFECT ON GROWTH

Return on Stockholders' Equity.   The application of ROSE in performance evaluation will generally constrict growth. To improve the current or budget ARR, the ARR of new projects have to be higher than the current or budget ones. This will therefore limit the number of projects to be implemented.

ROSE is therefore recommended for companies which intend to restrict growth. However, in case of enterprises operating through divisions or subsidiaries, the effect of the ARR might be growth in the wrong direction since

1. It encourages low-performing divisions, or those with low ARR, such as Division II in Exhibit 19.4, to take on more projects with low ARRs which are below the cost of capital and the corporate ARR, but above the divisional ARR.
2. It produces profitable units, or those with high ROI, such as Division I, to forgo with projects or dispose of existing operations with ARRs lower than the divisional ARR. This leads them to stagnation.

Residual Income.   The utilization of RI in performance evaluation encourages the implementation of new projects. As long as the undertaking can earn more than the cost of capital, the RI of the divisions or independent companies will be improved with the operation of new projects.

In a situation where the current ARR is over the cost of capital, the RI but not the ARR method will lead to the implementation of projects with ARR higher than the cost of capital but lower than the current ARR. Hence companies using RI can grow faster and in the right direction than those using ARR.

RI is ideal for the use of companies with unlimited capital and which desire to grow.

EFFECT ON RISK

Return on Stockholders' Equity. Compared to the net dollar return techniques, the ROSE generally tends to minimize the risk factor. Since the ARR are expressed in percentages, it can easily be compared with the cost of capital. The excess of the ARR over the cost can then be considered as the buffer to absorb losses due to risk.

However, the rate of return techniques may also lead divisional managers to plunge their units to actual losses. Divisions whose current ARR is lower than the cost of capital may be motivated to take on projects with returns above their current ARR but lower than the cost of capital. The corporate management, therefore, will be unknowingly taking on risky projects.

Residual Income (Exhibit 19.6). The RI has its own basic defect which could lead those using it to disaster. If carried to the extreme, its application gives a practically marginal operation a superficial advantage over competing divisions or companies. Since the formula for RI is represented by the following,

$$RI = (ARR - \text{cost of capital}) \times \text{amount of capital in dollars}$$

a very thin spread between the ARR, on one hand, and the cost of capital, on the other, if multiplied by a massive amount of capital, is very enticing.

Therefore, the RI encourages firms to take on additional assets for as long as their ARR exceeds the cost of capital. This may lead to the implementation of undertakings with very thin spreads or margins of safety. For instance, a division may be motivated to expand its market share by lengthening its sales credit terms. This leads to the buildup of receivables. For as long as the rise in the collectibles is accompanied by incremental RI, the management will keep on pursuing its sales expansion program. But, at a certain point, the additional RI generated by the additional receivables may become almost marginal. But management may decide to reach this point just so it could increase its RI. The overexposure in the receivable which generates so little RI creates a tremendous risk.

As another example, supposing Division III is considering two mutually exclusive measures—J and K. Their financial information is capsulized in Exhibit 19.6. A literal application of the RI rule favors K since its RI is bigger than that of J. However, a closer examination of the two measures reveals the following:

1. The RI of K, although bigger than that of J in absolute dollars, is almost nonexistent if compared with the capital required—only a quarter of a percent. That of J is 16 times bigger—at 4%.
2. The differential analysis between the two shows that K requires $19,000,000 more capital than J but delivers only an additional $10,000 in RI, which is a bare 0.05% (or 5% of 1%) of the incremental capital.

Definitely, attempting to obtain an additional $10,000 in RI by exposing an incremental $19,000,000 in capital does not make business sense.

The use of RI, therefore, unless handled with caution, will be courting disaster. A very thin interest spread, if coupled with a very sizable investment, can make an otherwise practically marginal project look enticing.

One idea considered to minimize the risk is to include the risk premium into the cost of capital or discount rate. However, incorporating the risk premium into the money cost to be charged the divisions complicates the analysis work since the risk factor changes with the developments in the business environment.

EFFECT ON THE CONGRUENCE OF CORPORATE AND DIVISIONAL GOALS

Return on Stockholders' Equity

Dollar Profit Maximization as the Corporate Objective (Exhibit 19.7). If the corporate objective is to enhance the benefits to shareholders by generating the maximum net income in excess of the cost of capital, but uses ARR to judge the performance of its divisions, there will be conflicts between the corporate and divisional objectives if the current or budgeted ARRs of some divisions are different from the corporate cost of capital.

Take Divisions I and II in Exhibit 19.7 in a company where the cost of capital is 14%. The corporate goal, therefore, is to implement projects with an ARR of over 14% so as to maximize the net profit in dollars.

Since the current ARR of Division I is 20%, its management will accept only projects with ARRs higher than 20% although the cost of capital is only 14%. On the other hand, since the present ARR of Division II is 10%, it will take on projects with ARRs beyond this rate although the ARRs are lower than the cost of capital.

If Division I or II can develop a project with an ARR higher than 20%, say, project C in Exhibit 19.7, its management will be willing to implement it since it will add to its present ARR. Since the rate of the new project is also higher than the cost of capital, the project will also be acceptable to the corporate management.

Similarly, if a project with an ARR lower than 10% is found, such as project G in Exhibit 19.7, there would be no takers as this is lower than the present profitability rates of both divisions. Furthermore, it is lower than the cost of capital.

For projects C and G, there would be no conflict between divisional and corporate objectives as the decision of corporate and divisional managers are the same—accept project C and abort project G.

However, the divergence in goals arises in case of undertakings with projected ARRs between 20% and 10%. If the ARR is between the cost of capital of 14% and the Division I profit rate of 20%, as projects D and E, the measures will be desired by the corporate management as they will advance the total corporate profit. However, they will be spurned by Division I as they will depress its ARR.

Similarly, a project with an ARR between 14% and 10%, as in project F, will be turned down by the corporation but desired by Division II.

Thus, the decisions on projects D, E, and F would present conflicts between the corporate objectives and the divisional actions.

DIVERSION OF CORPORATE FUNDS TO LOSING PROJECTS (EXHIBIT 19.7). This diversity in interest, in certain cases, could lead to the channeling of corporate funds away from projects which the corporation considers desirable, to undertakings which it believe are marginal at best or just not financially viable.

Assume that project D in Exhibit 19.7 is a possible undertaking of Division I but not of Division II. Although in reality it is a good project for the corporation, Division I will make it appear that it has a low IRR and therefore fails to qualify under the corporate standard. On the other hand, project F, a possible measure for Division II, which does not meet the corporate hurdle rate, will be presented by Division II as if it is financially feasible. The net effect of this situation is that the corporate funds which should have been used to push project D could be diverted to project F.

ARR Maximization as the Corporate Objective (Exhibit 19.7). Managerial actions will be compatible with the corporate objective of maximizing the ARR for the enterprise as a whole only if the corporate ARR equals the current or budget ARRs of all the divisions. However, this situation is the exception in practice. To the extent that there is a difference between the corporate ARR and the ARR of the divisions, there will be deviations between the corporate objectives and the divisional decisions.

Using the data in Exhibit 19.7, if the corporate objective is to maximize the ARR rather than the net profit in terms of absolute dollars, the corporate objective will be to reject project E since it will be lower than the corporate ARR. However, Division II's decision is to accept it.

Residual Income

DOLLAR PROFIT MAXIMIZATION AS THE CORPORATE OBJECTIVE (EXHIBITS 19.5 AND 19.7).   Since RI is already net of the cost of capital, a project is considered desirable as long as it produces a RI.

If RI is used in performance appraisal, the operation managers will be motivated to lift their RI. Thus, they will take on projects which produce a RI and turn down those with a negative RI, irrespective of their current level of RI or ARR.

Thus, Division I will implement project D and E in Exhibit 19.7 (instead of turning them down if ARR were used), since the projects will add to the divisional RI. Division I will also refrain from divesting product B in Exhibit 19.5 since it contributes to the divisional RI. Division II will abort project F in Exhibit 19.7 (instead of pursuing it) because of the project's negative RI. Consequently, RI automatically harmonizes divisional actions with the corporate objective if the objective is the maximization of RI.

COMPARABILITY OF RESULTS

Return on Stockholders' Equity.   The ROSE offers one practical advantage over the RI: regardless of the amount of the capital, the ARR of one business unit can readily be checked against that of (1) another division or company, (2) the industry average, (3) another period, and (4) the cost of capital.

The ARR, however, has at least one weakness in performance evaluation that is outside of financial figures. It does not consider the difficulty of managing a big, new, complicated operation. Thus, small or established divisions with slightly higher ARRs than much bigger units or with start-up operations are given more credit.

Residual Income.   The use of RI is particularly convenient when the cost of capital and risk premium constantly fluctuate or when the capital charge and risk premium are being varied from industry to industry, project to project, and even asset to asset. Undertakings in high-risk industries such as those in biotechnology are usually assigned a higher capital charge than are those in low-risk areas such as food distribution. Projects with practically unpredictable results such as those engaged in basic research may be charged a higher capital cost than are those calling for the construction of additional stores. Last, the assets with highly specialized uses such as automated equipment may be required to earn a higher capital charge than are those that can readily be converted to cash such as merchandise inventories, regardless of the division using these particular assets.

However, determining the risk premium component of the capital charge is subjective.

The application of RI may not give readily comparable results. For instance, a business unit with a massive investment is considered preferable to one with a much higher ARR but with less capital requirement.

IV. RETURN ON LOANS

In the same way that the net profit after income tax is considered as the return to the stockholders, the interest expense of the borrower or interest income of the lenders represents the return to the lenders. The interest expense may be compared with the average balance of the interest-bearing obligations in order to arrive at (1) the return on the loans, which is from the viewpoint of the lenders, and (2) the effective cost of the loans, which is from the viewpoint of the borrowing firm. Since trade credits do not bear interest, they are excluded from the calculations. The effective cost which is calculated here is the historical cost. The procedures for estimating the effective cost for deciding on new projects are given in Chapter 14.

The cost of the loans is calculated for two primary reasons: (1) to determine the effective cost of the loans, before and after income tax and (2) to ascertain the ability of the firm to service the interest and the maturing principal obligations. These payments to the lenders may be checked with the profit or the cash flow.

To aid in determining the financing structure, the effective cost of the loans may also be compared with (1) the return on the total investment and (2) the return on the stockholders' equity.

RETURN TO THE LENDERS

Before Income Tax (Exhibit 19.8)

$$\frac{\text{Interest}}{\text{average balance of loans}}$$

This ratio shows the weighted average interest rate paid on the loans. A change in the rate indicates a fluctuation in the interest rates during the period or a change in the mix of loans with varying interest rates. For the firm in the example, the effective cost jumped from 8.2% to 8.8%. This rise was caused not by the change in the interest rates as they remained stable during the period (at 10% for the short-term loans and 8% for the long-term borrowings), but by the growing proportion of the higher interest short-term loans—which composed 11% of the total loans in year 1 as against 37.5% in year 2.

After Income Tax (Exhibit 19.8)

$$\frac{\text{Interest net of income tax}}{\text{average balance of loans}}$$

From the viewpoint of the firm, the ratio in the immediately preceding discussion indicating the return to the lenders may not be so effective because the interest used is before income tax. Since the interest can be used to reduce the income tax liability, only the net amount reflects the real cost. Hence the need for the ratio based on the interest after income tax which is assumed in the illustration at 40% for both federal and state taxes.

INTEREST AND AMORTIZATION COVER FROM PROFIT (Exhibit 19.9)

Interest Cover

$$\frac{\text{net operating profit}}{\text{interest}}$$

The interest cover from profit shows how many times the interest payment is earned. The earning is represented by the net operating profit.

Amortization Cover

$$\frac{\text{net operating profit}}{\text{required amortizations}}$$

The amortization cover from profit indicates how many times the total scheduled payments to banks for both principal amortization and interest is earned. In the illustration it was assumed that all short-term loans may be renewed every year. Hence no provision was made for the payment of the principal.

For either ratio, the higher the ratio, the safer is the position of the creditors since this means that the firm has more money left for income tax and as a buffer for prospective losses.

INTEREST AND AMORTIZATION COVER FROM CASH FLOW (Exhibit 19.9)

The two prior ratios are based on the net operating profit before interest and income tax but after depreciation. These conventional ratios have several flaws. First, interest may not be considered as a preference item over income tax. Second, depreciation, which had been deducted in calculating the net operating profit, does not require cash. Hence, it is more practical to determine the safety of the banks by comparing the net profit after interest and income tax but before depreciation. This is called the net operating cash flow as this represents the cash generation from operations. However, this is before providing for the financing to augment the working capital. The interest and amortization cover from cash flow are illustrated in Exhibit 19.9.

V. RETURN ON TOTAL INVESTMENT

The return on total investment is the

$$\frac{\text{Net profit after tax } + \text{ interest expense less applicable tax}}{\text{stockholders' equity } + \text{ loans}}$$

The prior sections have discussed the return to specific types of financiers—the stockholders and the lenders. This section treats the combined return on the total investment—made up of stockholders' equity and the interest-bearing obligations. The stockholders' equity used in the illustrations is based on book value, although appraised value or market value may be used in certain cases as discussed earlier.

The return on the total investment is better than the ROSE in gauging the overall viability of the enterprise since the former is not influenced at all by the financing structure used. This is similar to the internal rate of return of a project which gives the total return of a project irrespective of the financing structure utilized.

The total return for year 2 is composed of the $4,202,000 interest according to the income statement in Chapter 17, Exhibit 17.1, and the $17,861,000 net profit before income tax. The total of $22,063,000 is the equivalent of the net operating profit. (See Exhibit 19.10, part I, of this chapter.) However, these figures do not represent the final return as these are pretax amounts. Hence, a 40% income tax was deducted in order to arrive at the posttax values. The resulting after-tax return on the stockholders' equity as shown in Exhibit 19.10, part I, is the same as the net profit after income tax.

In Exhibit 19.10, part II, the rate of return (after income tax) was computed by dividing the return after income tax by the average balance of the investments as indicated in part I. The resulting figures are 11.7% in year 1 and 13.0% in year 2. These rates indicate that on the overall, the total investments earned more in year 2.

The exhibit also reveals a great disparity between the rate of return on the loans and that on the stockholders' equity. In year 2, for example, the lenders earned only 5.3% as against 19.9% for the owners. This wide discrepancy may be explained by the two related ratios in part III of the exhibit: while the loans account for 47.1% of total financing, they obtained only 19.0% of the total returns.

VI. RETURN ON STOCKHOLDERS' EQUITY AND INTEREST SPREAD

The prior discussions gave two ways of interpreting the return on the stockholders' equity: (1) ROSE as the factor of net profit and stockholders' equity (see Section I of this chapter) and (2) ROSE as the final interlocking ratio of the integrated management performance ratio, that is, as the factor of financing leverage, operating assets ratio, asset turnover, and net profit rate (Chapter 18).

A third interpretation of ROSE may be added: that ROSE is equivalent to the stockholders' proportionate share in the total return in the total investment (stockholders' equity plus loans) plus the interest spread or gain in the financing leverage.

ROSE as the Factor of Net Profit and Stockholders' Equity (Exhibit 19.1). Section I of this chapter mentioned that the ROSE is the net profit after tax which was earned by using the stockholders' equity. This is represented by the following formula, using the figures for year 2:

$$\text{ROSE} = \frac{\text{net profit after income tax}}{\text{stockholders' equity at book value}} \quad \frac{\$10,716,000}{\$53,840,000} = 19.9\%$$

Any fluctuation in the net profit or stockholders' equity affects the ROSE.

ROSE as the Final Component of the Integrated Ratio (Exhibit 18.2). ROSE was presented in Chapter 18 as the result of four factors: (1) the proportion of total financing to stockholders' equity (stockholders' financing leverage), (2) the proportion of operating assets to the total assets (operating assets ratio), (3) the sales-generating ability of the operating assets (operating assets turnover), and (4) the profitability of the resulting sales (net profit rate). The relationships of these factors are expressed by the following condensed formula, based on year 2 figures:

	Factor	Value
ROSE =	Stockholders' financing leverage	2.07
	× operating assets ratio	0.88
	× operating assets turnover	1.45
	× net profit rate	7.49%
=	19.9%	

Any change in the amount of stockholders' equity, loans, trade credits, operating assets, nonoperating assets, sales, and costs alters the ROSE.

ROSE as the Factor of Total Return and Interest Spread (Exhibit 19.11). Another meaning of the ROSE, which utilizes the return on the total investment, is that the ROSE is composed of two portions: the stock-holders' proportionate share in the total return plus the interest spread on the debt financing. The latter is the excess of the debtors' proportionate share in the total return less what they actually got.

The ROSE is equivalent to the return on the total investment if an enterprise, after trade credits, is 100% financed by the owners. In other words there are no interest-bearing obligations. Thus, if based on the figures in Exhibit 19.10, there were no loans and hence the equity was $101,861,000 instead of $53,840,000 in year 2, the ROSE would equal the return on the total investment of 13% as the profit after tax would have been $13,238,000 instead of $10,716,000.

However, since part of the investment was financed by loans, and the effective interest cost, after tax, is only 5.3%, the stockholders in effect profited from the 7.7% interest spread or interest savings. The 7.7% spread is the excess of the 13.0% return on total investment less the 5.3% actual interest cost for the loans. See Exhibit 19.11.

If the debt/equity ratio in year 2 were 50:50 instead of 47.1:52.9, the ROSE would have been 20.7% instead of 19.9%. The 20.7% is composed of the 13.0% return on total investment plus 7.7% savings on the portion financed by loans. This could have been possible since the 7.7% savings which could have been generated on the $50,930,000 of loans (50% of total investment) would amount to $3,922,000, and this saving could have been passed on to the stockholders with equity of $50,930,000.

But since in reality less than one-half of the total investment was financed by loans, less than one-half of the total investment generated the interest spread, and more than one-half of the investment (represented by the owners) has to share in the smaller savings. Thus, the savings created was a smaller $3,698,000 (7.7% of the $48,021,000 loans), and this savings was spread out over a bigger stockholders' equity base of $53,840,000. Hence the incremental ROSE due to the loan interest savings is not 7.7%, but only 6.9% ($3,698,000 divided by $53,840,000).

Another way of calculating the 6.9% gain from leverage is demonstrated in Exhibit 19.7.

Change in the ROSE (Exhibit 19.11). The appreciation in the ROSE from year 1 to year 2 (from 17.7% to 19.9%) may be explained as the result of two factors: the rise in the return on the total investment (from 11.7% to 13.0%) and the higher gain due to the financing leverage (from 6.0% to 6.9%):

	Year 1	Year 2
Return on total investment	11.7%	13.0%
Gain on leverage	6.0	6.9
ROSE	17.7%	19.9%

The higher gain from the financing leverage, in turn, is accounted for by three collaborating factors (see Exhibit 19.11):

1. *The increase in the interest spread* (from 6.8% to 7.7%). The year 2 rate is 114% of that of year 1. This, in turn, is the consequence of two factors:
   a. The return on total investment, which rose by 10.8%
   b. The interest rate on loans, which also inched upwards (by 6.5%), but at a lower rate
2. *The rise in the loan component of the total investment* (46.8% to 47.1%). The bigger the component, the higher is the dollar value of the savings. The slight change in the loan component (0.7%) further pushed up the effective gain from the leverage.
3. *Complementary to factor 2, the fall in the equity portion of the total investment.* The less the equity, the less will be those who will share in the dollar value of the savings.

EXHIBIT 19.1:
Return on Stockholders' Equity (ROSE)* (dollars in $1,000)

Name of ratio	Formula	BASE DATA			RATIO		Year 2 as a percentage of year 1
		Year 1	Year 2		Year 1	Year 2	
Return on stockholders' equity (at book value)	net profit after income tax / stockholders' equity at book value	$ 8,192 / $46,277	$10,716 / $53,840	=	17.7%	19.9%	112.4%
Return on stockholders' equity (at appraised value)	net profit after income tax / stockholders' equity at appraised value	$ 8,192 / $49,477	$10,716 / $58,440	=	16.6%	18.3%	110.8%
Return on stockholders' equity (at stock market value)	net profit after income tax / stockholders' equity at market value	$ 8,192 / $59,642	$10,716 / $80,991	=	13.7%	13.2%	96.3%

*The stockholders' equity represents average balances.

445

EXHIBIT 19.2:
Alternative Methods of Valuing Stockholders' Equity

	Book value	Appraised value	Market value
Subject being valued	Assets and liabilities	Assets and liabilities	Assets, liabilities, and future earnings
Basis of the valuation	Historical or book value	Appraised value or current prices	Current or discounted future value for assets; discounted future value for earnings
Determinants of the value	Stockholders' contributions, net profit, and dividends	Same as for book value. Add: market price for land, buildings and equipment	Future dividends and future appreciation of market value of stocks
Revisions of the value	Quarterly or monthly	Quarterly or monthly	Any time during trading hours for publicly traded shares
Acceptability of the results	Used in the balance sheet	Referred to in the footnotes to the financial statements	Not referred to at all in the financial statements

EXHIBIT 19.3:

Cost of Capital and Residual Income (dollars in $1,000)

	BASE DATA		Year 1 as a percentage of year 2
	Year 1	*Year 2*	
I. Based on stockholders' equity at market value			
Cost of capital			
Stockholders' equity			
(average balance of market value)*	$59,642	$80,991	136%
Cost of capital			
Percentage (desired return)*	12%	12%	
Amount	$ 7,157	$ 9,719	136
Net profit after income tax	$ 8,192	$10,716	131
Cost of capital per above	$ 7,157	$ 9,719	136
Residual income	$ 1,035	$ 997	96
II. Based on stockholders' equity at book value			
Cost of capital rate			
Cost of capital per above	$ 7,157	$ 9,719	136
Stockholders' equity at book value	46,277	53,840	116
Cost of capital rate			
Percentage	15.5%	18.1%	117
III. Stockholders' equity			
At market value	$59,642	$80,991	
At book value	46,277	53,840	
Market value premium	13,366	27,151	
As % of stockholders' equity			
at book value	29%	50%	

*Assumed to be given.

EXHIBIT 19.4:
Effect of New Projects on ARR and RI (dollars in $1,000)

	Present operations	Project D	Total
Division I			
Capital	$10,000	$4,000	$14,000
Net profit	$ 2,000	$ 720	$ 2,720
Cost of capital at 14%	1,400	560	1,960
Residual income	$ 600	$ 160	$ 760
Accounting rate of return	20.0%	18.0%	19.4%
Residual income as a percentage of capital	6.0%	4.0%	5.4%

	Present operations	Project F	Total
Division II			
Capital	$10,000	$5,000	$15,000
Net profit	$ 1,000	$ 600	$ 1,600
Cost of capital at 14%	1,400	700	2,100
Residual income	($ 400)	($ 100)	($ 500)
Accounting rate of return	10.0%	12.0%	10.7%
Residual income as a percentage of capital	−4.0%	−2.0%	−3.3%

EXHIBIT 19.5:
Effect of Existing Operations on ARR (dollars in $1,000)

Division I	Product A	Product B*	Total present operations
Capital	$6,000	$4,000	$10,000
Net profit†	$1,320	$ 680	$ 2,000
Cost of capital at 14%	840	560	1,400
Residual income	$ 480	$ 120	$ 600
Return on investment	22.00%	17.00%	20.00%
Residual income as a percentage of capital	8.00%	3.00%	6.00%

*Incremental.
†Assuming no part of common overhead is allocated to Product B.

EXHIBIT 19.6:

Limitation of Residual Income (dollars in $1,000)

Division III	Division III —present	Project J	Project K	Differential (excess of K over J)	Total with K
Capital	$10,000	$1,000	$20,000	$19,000	$30,000
Net profit	$ 1,800	$ 180	$ 2,850	$ 2,670	$ 4,650
Cost of capital at 14%	1,400	140	2,800	2,660	4,200
Residual income	$ 400	$ 40	$ 50	$ 10	$ 450
Return on investment	18.00%	18.00%	14.25%	14.05%	15.50%
Residual income as a percentage of capital	4.00%	4.00%	0.25%	0.05%	1.50%

EXHIBIT 19.7:
Conflict Between Corporate and Divisional Goals—If Corporate Objective is Maximizing Profit in Dollars and If ARR is Used

	Present ARR or cost of capital	ROI of project	Project	Division I objective	Corporate objective	Division II objective
		22%	C	Accept	Accept	Accept
Division I ARR—at present	20%	18%	D*	REJECT[†]	ACCEPT[†]	Accept
Corporate ARR	16%	15%	E	Reject	REJECT[†,‡]	ACCEPT[†,‡]
Cost of capital	14%	12%	F[§]	Reject	REJECT[†]	ACCEPT[†]
Division II ARR—at present	10%	8%	G	Reject	Reject	Reject

*Project acceptable to the corporation is rejected by Division I.
[†]Area of conflict.
[‡]Reject if goal is to maximize ARR and ARR is used in performance evaluation; accept if corporate goal is to maximize net profit in terms of absolute dollars and RI is used in performance evaluation.
[§]Project not acceptable to the corporation is accepted by Division II.

EXHIBIT 19.8:
Return to Lenders or Cost of Loans (dollars in $1,000)

	BASE DATA		RATIO		Year 2 as a percentage of year 1
	Year 1	Year 2	Year 1	Year 2	
Preliminary calculations					
Interest					
Short-term loans (assumed to be given)	$ 447	$ 1,802	13%	43%	
Long-term loans (assumed to be given)	2,900	2,400	87%	57%	
Total	$ 3,347	$ 4,202	100%	100%	
Average balance					
Short-term loans	$ 4,473	$18,021	11%	38%	
Long-term loans (including current portion)	36,250	30,000	89%	62%	
Total	$40,723	$48,021	100%	100%	
Interest rates					
Short-term loans	10.0%	10.0%			
Long-term loans	8.0	8.0			
Weighted average	8.2%	8.8%			
Average balance as percent of total					
Short-term loans	11.0%	37.5%			
Long-term loans (including current portion)	89.0	62.5			
Total	100.0%	100.0%			
Name of ratio	**Formula**				
Return to lenders (before income tax)	interest	$ 3,347	$ 4,202		
	loans (average balance)	$40,723	$48,021 =	8.2%	8.8%	106.5%
Return to lenders (after income tax)	interest	$ 2,008	$ 2,521		
	loans (average balance)	$40,723	$48,021 =	4.9%	5.3%	106.5%

EXHIBIT 19.9:
Loan Payments Cover (dollars in $1,000)

		BASE DATA			RATIO		Year 2 as a percentage of year 1
		Year 1	Year 2		Year 1	Year 2	
Preliminary calculations							
Total required payments							
Interest		$ 3,347	$ 4,202				
Scheduled amortization—long-term loans (assumed to be given)		5,000	5,000				
Total required payments		$ 8,347	$ 9,202				
Name of ratio	**Formula**						
Interest cover from profit	net operating profit	$17,000	$22,063	=	5.1	5.3	103.4%
	interest	$ 3,347	$ 4,202				
Amortization cover from profit	net operating profit	$17,000	$22,063	=	2.0	2.4	117.7%
	required amortizations	$ 8,347	$ 9,202				
Interest cover from cash flow	total operating cash flow*	$14,192	$16,716	=	4.2	4.0	93.8%
	interest	$ 3,347	$ 4,202				
Amortization cover from cash flow	total operating cash flow*	$14,192	$16,716	=	1.7	1.8	106.8%
	required amortizations	$ 8,347	$ 9,202				

*Before working capital requirements.

EXHIBIT 19.10:

Rate of Return on Total Investment—Excluding Trade Credits
(dollars in $1,000)

	Year 1	*Year 2*
I. Required data		
Average balance		
Loans	$40,723	$ 48,021
Equity at book value	46,277	53,840
Total	$87,000	$101,861
Return before income tax		
Loans (interest per income statement)	$ 3,347	$ 4,202
Equity (net profit before income tax)	13,653	17,861
Total (net operating profit)	$17,000	$ 22,063
Return after 40% effective income tax		
Loans (interest less 40% income tax)	$ 2,008	$ 2,521
Equity (net profit after income tax)	8,192	10,716
Total return	$10,200	$ 13,238
II. Rate of return on average balance (based on return after tax)		
Loans (return on loans after income tax)	4.9%	5.3%
Equity (return on stockholders' equity)	17.7	19.9
Total investment	11.7%	13.0%
III. Related ratios		
Return sharing ratio		
Loans	19.7%	19.0%
Equity	80.3	81.0
Total	100.0%	100.0%
Debt/equity ratio		
Loans	46.8%	47.1%
Equity	53.2	52.9
Total investment	100.0%	100.0%

EXHIBIT 19.11:
ROSE and Gain Due to Financing Leverage

	Year 1	Year 2	Year 2 as a percentage of year 1
Summary			
Return on stockholders' equity (Exhibit 19.10)	17.7%	19.9%	112.4%
Return on total investment (Exhibit 19.10)	11.7	13.0	110.8
Gain in ROSE due to financing leverage per below	6.0%	6.9%	115.6%
Composition			
Gain in ROSE due to financing leverage (or share in loan rate savings)			
Savings on investment financed by loans	11.7%	13.0%	110.8%
Return on total investment per above	4.9%	5.3%	106.5%
Less: Interest on loans (Exhibit 19.10)	6.8%	7.7%	114.0%
Loan rate savings	46.8%	47.1%	100.7%
Multiply by loans as a percentage of total investment (Exhibit 19.10)	3.2%	3.7%	114.8%
Total savings as a percentage of total investment	53.2%	52.9%	99.4%
Divide by equity as a percentage of total investment (Exhibit 19.10)	6.0%	6.9%	115.6%
Increase in ROSE due to financing leverage			

Chapter 20 _____

FINANCING STRUCTURE RATIO ANALYSIS

This chapter examines the financing structure ratios. These ratios deal with the proportioning of the total company financing into debt and equity and the allocation of the total debt to long-term and short-term loans.

The impact of the debt/equity ratio on the investors' rate of return is probed in two other chapters: Chapter 19 for performance evaluation and Chapter 15 for decision analysis concerning new long-term projects.

The special types of financing structure ratios are also covered in this chapter. These are the solvency and liquidity ratios that relate certain types of assets to short-term liabilities. Bankruptcy ratios, which are often used for credit rating purposes just like solvency and liquidity ratios, are presented in the last part of the chapter.

I. FINANCING STRUCTURE RATIOS

The financing structure ratios in Exhibit 20.1 help to determine the soundness of the allocation of (1) the total financing of the firm into the stockholders' equity and liabilities and (2) the total liabilities into long-term (those due beyond one year) and short-term obligations.

When used by themselves, the financing structure ratios, just like the other ratios, may not be very meaningful. However, if tied in with relevant information, these ratios may reveal weaknesses in the financing arrangements of the company. For instance, a start-up biotechnology company with stockholders' equity comprising 60% of the financing, and bank loans accounting for the balance, is on shaky ground. On the other hand, a diversified food processing company with established brands and stabilized operations, and with a 50% stockholders' equity in its total funding package stands on a sounder financial foundation.

There are special types of financing structure ratios which are used for particular applications. These are the solvency and liquidity ratios which relate only part of the assets to some of the liabilities. These are exemplified in Exhibit 20.2 and are described later.

TOTAL FINANCING MIX

There are two ratios which review the proportion of stockholders' equity to the creditors' interests (liabilities): the stockholders' financing leverage and the debt/equity ratio. Both ratios are estimated in Exhibit 20.1. These ratios recognize the distinction between the stockholders' equity and the liabilities due to their distinguishing characteristics: liabilities require predetermined payments on principal and interest, while equity does not.

There are two reasons for reviewing the financing mix. First, when the overall return on the assets is more than the interest on the loans, obtaining additional loans can increase the effective yield on the equity. In other words, the firm can take advantage of others' capital to magnify the profitability of the stockholders' investment. For instance, a firm which is 100% equity financed and which earns 15% on its total financing gives its equity investors exactly 15%. If the same firm is 50% financed with a loan bearing interest at 10%, the equity investors would be getting a 20% return, since the 5% excess of the 15% total return over the 10% interest goes to the equity holders. This aspect is discussed further in Section VI of Chapter 19.

Second, when the amount of loan is increased, naturally the fixed payments on the principal and interest are also raised, thereby magnifying the vulnerability of the firm to a slowdown in the sales volume. A highly leveraged structure renders the firm overly exposed to risk. Since the payment schedules for loan principal and interest are fixed irrespective of the level of the profitability, the operating income alone may not be sufficient to service the scheduled payments.

A close analysis of the financing structure ratio should indicate the soundness of debt/equity mix followed in the past, as well as guide management in molding and implementing the proper mix of equity and debt funding which maximizes the return on the stockholders' equity at an acceptable level of risk.

Stockholders' Total Financing Leverage (Exhibit 20.1)

$$\frac{\text{total financing}}{\text{equity}}$$

The ratio in Exhibit 20.1 indicates that in year 1, every $1.00 of stockholders' equity enabled the company to raise an additional $0.79 from bank loans and other creditors so that a total of $1.79 was made available to the company.

A change in the leverage impacts on the profitability and risk of the business. Thus, a reduction in the leverage, which is caused by raising the stockholders' equity or reducing the loans, produces three effects:

1. The risk exposure of the company is reduced, as the loan amortizations and interest payments are minimized.
2. The total net profit is enhanced since the interest expense is cut down.
3. The rate of return on the stockholders' equity is reduced if, before the restructuring, the rate of return was higher than the interest on the loan.

Debt/Equity Ratio (Exhibit 20.1)

$$\frac{\text{debt as a percentage of total financing}}{\text{equity as a percentage of total financing}}$$

This ratio reveals the extent to which the total resources are funded by liabilities or debt and the component which is supported by the owners. The debt in the debt/equity ratio shown in part I of Exhibit 20.1 includes all the obligations of the company. The debt in part II excludes the trade credits (accounts payable).

The year 2 debt/equity ratio of 57:43 in part I of Exhibit 20.1 indicates two things:

1. That 43% of the total assets is financed by the owners' contributions and accumulated earnings and the balance is financed by loans, trade credits, and other obligations
2. That from the viewpoint of the creditors, the company could afford to lose 43% of the total assets before the investment of the creditors is diluted or jeopardized

The debt/equity ratio uses the same set of data and is employed for the same purposes—as the stockholders' financing leverage. The only difference between these ratios is the manner of computation.

Evaluation of the Debt/Equity Ratio. In formulating the desired debt/equity mix, management considers (1) the type of industry the company is in, (2) the cost structure of the firm, (3) its access to financing sources, and (4) the requirements of the lending institutions.

A firm in a stable industry such as public utility can afford to have a high debt percentage. On the other hand, those in risky industries, such as those in construction which handle few large jobs, and those producing agricultural or mineral commodities with highly fluctuating prices and with possible production disturbances due to weather conditions, can ill afford to pile up on debt. New firms with unproven market or un-established technology also require substantial equity backing.

A firm whose operating costs is composed substantially of variable costs rather than fixed costs can better survive a decline in sales volume than can one whose costs are composed mainly of fixed costs. The reason is that when the sales volume declines, the variable costs also go down. Hence the former type of firm is more stable than the second type. Consequently, the first type can afford to have a higher debt component.

Free assets or resources which have not yet been mortgaged to banks, possible guarantees by a parent company, and possible financial help by the stockholders enable a firm to take more risks. Consequently, one with easy access to financing may have more debt as a percentage of its total financing than will one without such access.

Some financing institutions require that their borrowers observe certain ratios including debt/equity ratio. Firms with loans from such institutions or which are planning to get assistance from said banks have to follow the prescribed ratios.

Valuation of Debt and of Equity.   The calculation of the debt/equity ratio is normally based on the valuation of both debt and equity at book value since these are the figures used in the financial statements. A more meaningful ratio is one which employs market or economic values. These types of values are examined in Chapter 17, Section VI, and Chapter 19, Section I.

LIABILITY MIX

Long-term to Short-term Liabilities Ratio (Exhibit 20.1)

$$\frac{\text{long-term liabilities}}{\text{short-term liabilities}}$$

This ratio indicates the amount in dollars of long-term liabilities for every dollar in short-term obligations. The long-term liabilities are normally bank loans which mature beyond one year. The portions of long-term loans which are due in less than a year are usually, but not always, reclassified from long-term liability to short-term debt.

Usually, the higher the amount of the long-term liabilities in relation to short-term obligations, the better is the financial position of the firm, as the long-term loans do not require immediate payment. The ratio in Exhibit 20.1, therefore, shows that the condition deteriorated as the ratio dropped from 3.35 to 0.57. In year 2 the long-term debts declined as the loans were gradually paid off. On the other hand, the short-term debts rose due to the demand for more financing which were not met by equity.

On a period-to-period basis, if there is no change in total liabilities, but there is a shift from short-term to long-term obligations, the ratio goes up. This is an improvement as there will be fewer liabilities to be paid off within a year.

DATA BASIS OF FINANCING STRUCTURE RATIOS
(Exhibit 20.1)

The three ratios in Exhibit 20.1 may be calculated on either one of three alternative basis: (1) total financing or total assets, (2) stockholders' equity and bank loans or net assets, and (3) stockholders' equity and long-term loans. There is no such thing as one correct basis. Each has its own advantages and limitations in specific applications.

Total Financing or Total Assets. In this case, the ratios are based on the stockholders' equity, bank loans, and trade credits. The total is represented by the last line of the stockholders' equity and liabilities section of the conventional balance sheet. By balance sheet equation, the total stockholders' equity and liabilities equal the total assets. Hence the total financing and the total assets are interchangeable for purposes of calculating the ratios. The ratios in part I of Exhibit 20.1 use this basis.

The advantage of this basis is that this tallies with the total stockholders' equity and liabilities in the conventional balance sheet. The amount represents the total financing raised for the firm which is equivalent to the total resources made available. This presents the overall picture.

The limitation of this basis is that this includes the interest-free financing provided by the trade suppliers. The inclusion of this trade credit creates an inconsistency between the financing structure ratio analysis and the return on investment (ROI) ratio analysis since the latter distributes the return just to the interest-bearing note holders and the stockholders. The trade suppliers do not share in the profit before interest but share in the burden of financing the assets.

Stockholders' Equity and Bank Loans or Net Assets. The difference between this and the basis mentioned earlier is composed of trade credits and other noninterest-bearing liabilities or credits. The total stockholders' equity and bank loans is usually equal to the net assets, which is total assets less the trade credits and other noninterest-bearing liabilities. The ratios using this basis are shown in part II of Exhibit 20.1. The total net assets used in year 2 is calculated as total assets of $133,919,000 less the $12,698,000 of payables equals the $121,221,000 net assets.

Since the trade credits are excluded in calculating the ratios, this method eliminates the weakness of the first basis. The limitation of the net assets basis is that it includes temporary bank borrowings, which are represented by short-term loans. These loans are closer to trade credits in that their balance fluctuates monthly with the sales volume.

Stockholders' Equity and Long-term Loans.   The ratios using this basis are geared mainly for long-term planning. For instance, the debt/equity ratios of new capital-intensive projects sometimes use this basis.

The disadvantage of this basis is that many firms usually carry short-term loans and credit lines continuously. The short-term notes are periodically renewed, and the credit lines are reavailed from year to year. This practice converts this type of a legally short-term obligation into a practically semipermanent financing.

II. SOLVENCY RATIOS

The solvency and liquidity ratios are special types of financing structure ratios. Broadly, solvency and liquidity ratios are also financing structure ratios in that they also relate certain types of financing sources to the total funding scheme. However, they are considered special since they serve only a very specific purpose.

A firm is solvent if it will be able to pay all its obligations. In other words, its assets exceed its liabilities. It is liquid if it will be able to pay its debts on time. Solvency ratios, therefore, consider all the assets, while liquidity ratios count only the assets which can be converted to cash in one year or a shorter time frame.

Solvency and liquidity ratios are used primarily by lenders who are reviewing the financial soundness of prospective borrowers. They are also utilized by firms needing financing in trying to figure out the form and type of financing to raise, as well as the requirements of the lenders.

MAJOR SOLVENCY RATIOS

The two most popular solvency ratios relate the total liabilities to the total assets.

Total Liabilities Cover From Assets (Exhibit 20.2)

$$\frac{\text{total assets}}{\text{total liabilities}}$$

This solvency ratio tests the adequacy of the total assets to pay all the debts as of a certain date. Hence the figures used are usually as of the end of an accounting period. The average balance is not utilized for this purpose. This ratio gives the value of the assets which the company has for every dollar of liabilities. The liabilities include loans and trade credits.

Naturally, the higher the ratio, the more solid the cover for the creditors in case the company is liquidated. The total liability cover in Exhibit 20.2 shows that the creditors were more protected in year 1 than in year 2 as the cover has declined in the latter year.

Loss Buffer Coverage (Exhibit 20.2)

$$\frac{\text{total assets} - \text{total liabilities}}{\text{total assets}}$$

This is the twin ratio of the total liability cover. Although they are calculated differently, these two ratios are based on identical sets of data.

The ratio illustrated in Exhibit 20.2 shows that in year 1, the company could have suffered a 56% reduction in the value of the total assets due to liquidation or continuing losses of the firm before the position of the creditors could have been jeopardized. In year 2 the buffer percentage had shrunk to 43%.

OTHER SOLVENCY RATIOS

The other solvency ratios determine the adequacy of operating profit or cash flow (1) to meet the maturing interest payments (interest cover or number of times interest is earned), (2) to pay the maturing loan amortizations (amortization cover or number of times amortization is earned), or (3) to retire the total liabilities (total liabilities cover or number of times the total liabilities is earned). The first two ratios are explained and illustrated in Chapter 19, Section IV.

The third ratio is expounded here.

Total Liabilities Cover From Cash Flow

$$\frac{\text{cash from operations}}{\text{total liabilities}}$$

This ratio shows the annual cash generation after paying the operating expenses, in relation to the total liabilities as of a certain date. A ratio of less than 1.0 indicates that the annual cash generation, if not supported by proceeds from the existing assets, is not sufficient to pay all the present obligations. Since in reality, the existing assets are also available to pay the liabilities, this ratio should be used to supplement the total liability cover. Thus, a total liabilities cover from assets of 2.0 and a total liabilities cover from cash flow of 1.5 means that over a period of one year, the firm will have $3.50 in resources to pay every $1.00 of obligations.

STUDY OF THE SOLVENCY OF A FIRM

The evaluation of an enterprise in order to determine its solvency should extend beyond the confines of the solvency ratios discussed, but go to the other areas. For instance, the following should be reviewed: (1) other tools of financial analysis and (2) business strategies and management practices.

Other Tools of Financial Analysis. The solvency ratios should be supplemented by other ratios and other tools of financial analysis. For instance, the following may also be employed: debt/equity ratio, residual income, return on stockholders' equity, capacity utilization percentage, break-even point analysis, sensitivity analysis, and bankruptcy ratios.

DEBT/EQUITY RATIO.   A high debt/equity ratio means that a firm has committed to pay a high fixed periodic amount in the form of interest and loan. The higher the ratio, the higher the risk that the firm has taken, and the higher the probability that it will be insolvent in the future. (See Section I of this chapter and Chapter 15 for a more detailed discussion of debt/equity ratios.)

RETURN ON STOCKHOLDERS' EQUITY.   The higher the ROSE, the more profitable is the firm, the higher is its cash generation from operations, and the higher is the probability that it will be able to pay all its obligations (Chapter 19, Section I).

RESIDUAL INCOME.   The higher the RI, the higher the profitability of a company, and the higher the chance that it can avoid insolvency. However, if the enterprise uses RI in evaluating the performance of its operating units, the firm may be enhancing its risk exposure since its managers may add on assets and liabilities to its operations although the incremental income on the assets is minimal (Chapter 19, Section II).

NET PROFIT RATE.   A low net profit rate shows that a firm is vulnerable even to slight fluctuations in sales volume, selling price, or unit costs (Chapter 21, Section III).

BREAK-EVEN POINT ANALYSIS.   A company whose actual sales volume is lower than, or just above, its break-even point sales volume has a much higher probability of becoming insolvent than does one whose actual sales is much higher than the break-even point (Chapter 8).

SENSITIVITY ANALYSIS.   A sensitivity analysis may be run for a firm to determine how it can withstand certain assumed adverse conditions in the future—such as reduction in selling price, decline in sales volume, or rise in labor costs (Chapter 7).

CAPACITY UTILIZATION PERCENTAGE.   A low-capacity utilization percentage by itself may mean that a firm has so much idle capacity and therefore is not properly employing its resources. This may be translated to a low sales volume, low or negative profit, and difficulty in paying its obligations in the future (Chapter 21, Sections V and VII).

BANKRUPTCY RATIOS.   These are the ratios which have been found to be effective in predicting bankruptcies (Section V of this chapter).

Business Strategies and Management Practices.   An evaluation of the strategies and practices indicates how the management balances both immediate risk and long-term profit with risk. A conservative firm may avoid short-term risk and at the same time maximize its current earnings.

However, by not taking bold moves at present, it may not be able to grow or solidify its position in the future, thereby ultimately weakening its profitability after having cornered by its competitors. This balancing of both risk and profit and of short-term and long-term effects is illustrated in five areas of strategies and management practices: key business strategy, diversification program, general management practices, financing management practices, and insurance practices.

KEY BUSINESS STRATEGY.   Chapter 2, Section I, has dissected the three prime alternative business strategies: grow, maintain, or harvest. In the short run a firm on a grow strategy is at a disadvantage compared with one on a harvest strategy. The firm earns a lower profit but incurs a higher risk. However, in the long run, it normally gains on one with the harvest strategy: it earns more and incurs lower risk. A firm which had been on a harvest strategy for a long time ultimately weakens its competitiveness, thereby reducing its profitability and placing itself at a higher risk of being squeezed out by competition.

DIVERSIFICATION.   An enterprise with an aggressive industry diversification program has lower short-term profit but has more short-term risk than does one that concentrates on its basic business. However, the short-term sacrifices of a diversifying firm may not be rewarded in the long run. The old concept is that diversification reduces the risk of an enterprise since the decline of one industry can be covered by a growth in another. (See also Chapter 7, Section II.) However, this reduction in risk may be more than offset by another type of risk: the failure of management to run another type of business successfully.

MANAGEMENT DECENTRALIZATION.   Decentralization is bringing down the level of decision making, giving more authority to the operating management, chopping off layers in the chain of command or management hierarchy, and trimming down the staff (as against line) functions. Because of faster decision making and reduced general overhead, decentralization is usually accompanied by higher profitability—both immediate and in the long run. However, decentralization also magnifies the risk in that both honest errors and fraudulent moves of the operating managers will not be remedied at once.

FINANCING MANAGEMENT PRACTICES.   A conservative management practice from the viewpoint of the borrowers favored the use of long-term loans and fixed interest rate obligations to short-term loans and variable rate liabilities. This practice was normally considered as the less risky of the two options. However, the gyrations in the interest rates have proven that the use of long-term loans and fixed interest rates is not a guarantee of safety. Falling interest rates can place a conservative borrowing firm at a disadvantage vis-à-vis those availing of short-term loans or long-term loans with variable rates.

INSURANCE.   The standard practice is to obtain full insurance coverage for certain types of risks. In the short run, a company with full coverage exposes itself to less risk. However, because of the premium, it also lowers its profitability.

III. LIQUIDITY RATIOS

MAJOR LIQUIDITY RATIOS

The most frequently utilized liquidity ratios compare selected assets to selected liabilities.

Current Ratio (Exhibit 20.2)

$$\frac{\text{current assets}}{\text{current liabilities}}$$

This liquidity ratio is based on the following premises:

1. Current assets (cash plus resources which will be converted to cash in one year) will be used to pay off the obligations that will mature during the same period.
2. None of the current assets are used to secure any of the long-term liabilities or contingent liabilities as pledges or guarantees.
3. During the year, there will be no other sources of cash that will be added to the current assets, and there will be no new obligations arising from the continuance of operations that will be added to the current liabilities.

The ratio shows the value of current assets which is available for every dollar of current liabilities. Thus, as indicated in Exhibit 20.2, for year 1 there was $6.28 in current assets for every $1.00 in current liabilities. In year 2 the ratio deteriorated as the current liabilities soared by over 400% while the assets climbed by 59% only.

The higher the value of the assets, the stronger is the position of the short-term creditors since there is a bigger chance that the firm will be able to pay the present obligations as they mature. This means that the firm has enough cash at present or enough cash coming from the collection of existing receivables as well as from the sales proceeds of currently available inventories.

CURRENT RATIO IS 1—IMPLICATIONS.   If the current ratio is about 1, which means that the current assets roughly equal the current liabilities, the company may be able to satisfy the current creditors over a one-year period. However, on a monthly basis, and assuming that the current cash flow from operations is on a break-even basis, the firm may still encounter liquidity problems if the maturity schedule of the liabilities is ahead of the expected cash realization of the assets.

For instance, the payment schedule of the debts may be concentrated toward the start of the year, while the cash realization of the assets may be evenly spread out throughout the year. If this is the case, the firm may be forced to discount its receivables and dump its inventories in a fire sale. Although these options will momentarily raise the monthly cash receipts to meet the maturing obligations, it will also dilute the realization value of the current assets. In effect, therefore, the actual value of the assets becomes less than the face value of the liabilities.

CURRENT RATIO IS LESS THAN 1—IMPLICATIONS. A current ratio which is less than 1 indicates that the current assets are not enough to pay the current obligations. Hence the firm is expected to have a liquidity problem, unless some of the long-term and nonoperating assets are liquidated in one year.

Some of the causes of a current ratio of less than 1 are (1) the utilization of part of the current liabilities to finance long-term assets—land, buildings, and equipment and nonoperating assets—and (2) past and present losses.

UTILIZATION OF CURRENT LIABILITIES TO FUND LONG-TERM ASSETS. The firm may be stepping into a financing trap if it uses short-term liabilities to fund long-term assets. This is not a good practice since it takes over 1 year to convert long-term assets to cash. For instance, it requires at least 10 years to fully recover the investment in a building. On the other hand, short-term financing has to be paid within a year.

However, there are some cases in which it may be sound practice to fund the long-term assets with current liabilities. An example is a situation when the firm is able to (1) negotiate with its suppliers for unusually long payment periods for the purchases, (2) cut down the inventories to low levels, and (3) have short collection periods for the receivables. In this case, the outstanding balance of the trade credits may in effect exceed the current assets consisting of receivables and inventories. In this situation the trade suppliers are in effect financing part of the land and buildings.

PAST AND PRESENT LOSSES. If the firm had been losing, it might have been cutting down on its operations, thus diluting its current assets. However, inadequate cash flow might have prevented the firm from correspondingly scaling back its current liabilities.

This situation creates a downward spiral effect on the cash flow: the unpaid trade suppliers demand cash payment or shorter repayment terms; the firm purchases merchandise or materials on smaller orders, thus failing to avail of volume discounts; and the factory produces at less than economic lot sizes. This further aggravates the losses and constricts the cash flow available for payment to the suppliers.

CURRENT RATIO IS MORE THAN 1—IMPLICATIONS.   If there are more current assets than current liabilities, some of the current assets might have been funded by long-term debt. Hence, part of the current assets may be used to pay off some of the long-term obligations.

Quick Asset Ratio or Acid Test (Exhibit 20.2)

$$\frac{\text{quick assets}}{\text{current liabilities}}$$

This ratio is more conservative than the current ratio. It is used to test the liquidity of an enterprise over a period shorter than a year. While the current ratio considers all the current assets as available to pay the short-term creditors, the acid test ratio takes into account only the assets which can be converted "quickly" into cash. These quick assets are the cash, cash equivalents as marketable securities, and receivables. Although inventories are included in the calculation of the current ratio, they are excluded from the quick asset ratio because of the longer time required to convert them to cash.

COMPARISON OF RESULTS WITH THOSE OF THE CURRENT RATIO.   Since the quick asset ratio excludes inventories, this ratio is lower than the current ratio. See Exhibit 20.2. If the quick asset ratio is much lower than the current ratio, then the company is carrying a substantial inventory.

If the current ratio remains constant or improves, but the quick asset ratio deteriorates, this means that the inventory is rising faster than the other current assets.

The following are the possible reasons for an abnormal buildup in the inventory: (1) unusually large purchases to take advantage of low prices, or in anticipation of future price spiral (applicable to merchandise and raw material inventories), (2) preparation for possible exceptional sales increases (for merchandise and finished goods inventories), and (3) preparation for a production stoppage (for finished goods inventories). Another possible reason is the desire of the company to bloat its reported net profit by stepping up the production for inventory. This is applicable if the firm utilizes the full costing method of valuing its finished goods inventory. This aspect is discussed in detail in Chapter 17, Section II.

OTHER LIQUIDITY RATIOS

Accounts Receivables and Inventories to Accounts Payable and Accrued Expenses

$$\frac{\text{accounts receivable} + \text{inventories}}{\text{accounts payable} + \text{accrued expenses}}$$

This ratio is similar to the current ratio or quick asset ratio in that it compares selected assets with selected liabilities. The major difference between this and the quick asset ratio is the exclusion of cash from this ratio. The exclusion of cash weakens the usefulness of this ratio. Hence this is not as popular as the current or quick asset ratio.

Quick Assets to Cash Expenses. For the quick assets turnover, the ratio is

$$\frac{\text{cash expenses}}{\text{quick assets}}$$

For the quick assets duration, it is

$$\frac{\text{number of days in a year}}{\text{quick assets turnover}}$$

This shows the number of days during which the company can continue to pay its expenses from its quick assets. This assumes that during this period the firm will not be able to generate sales.

Sales to Accounts Payable. For the accounts payable turnover, the ratio is

$$\frac{\text{sales}}{\text{accounts payable}}$$

For the sales days to pay the accounts payable, it is

$$\frac{\text{number of days in a year}}{\text{accounts payable turnover}}$$

This reveals the selling period in number of days which is required so that all the gross collections during that period will be enough to pay the existing accounts payable. This ratio disregards three items: the liabilities other than accounts payable, the assets at present which are also available to pay the payables, and the expenses during the selling period which will have to be deducted from the gross collections—in other words, only the net collections will be available to pay the payables.

The accounts payable turnover in this ratio should be distinguished from the accounts payable turnover in Chapter 21, Exhibit 21.6.

Sales to Trade Liabilities (Accounts Payable Plus Accrued Expenses). For the trade liabilities turnover, the ratio is

$$\frac{\text{sales}}{\text{trade liabilities}}$$

For the sales days to pay the trade liabilities, it is

$$\frac{\text{number of days in a year}}{\text{trade liabilities turnover}}$$

This is similar to the preceding ratio except that accrued expenses were added. This is subject to the same limitations as the other ratio.

Sales to Current Assets.   For the current assets turnover, the ratio is

$$\frac{\text{sales}}{\text{current assets}}$$

For the sales days to double the existing current assets, it is

$$\frac{\text{number of days in a year}}{\text{current assets turnover}}$$

This ratio reveals the number of selling days required so that the present current assets can be doubled. This ratio may be utilized to augment the current assets ratio. A current ratio of 2 and sales days to double the existing current assets of 180 days means that in 180 days the current ratio will be 4 (double the present 2).

The limitation of this ratio is that it assumes that during the selling period, there are no expenses. In reality, only the net profit will be available to increase the current assets. Hence, the sales in this ratio should be substituted with net profit.

Operating Costs to Current Assets.   For the current assets turnover, the ratio is

$$\frac{\text{cost of sales, operating expenses, and income tax}}{\text{current assets}}$$

For current assets duration, it is

$$\frac{\text{number of days in a year}}{\text{current assets turnover}}$$

This ratio shows the number of days' essential costs and expenses which can be financed by the existing current assets. This ratio is weak in that it excludes (1) the present liabilities which will also have to be paid out of the current assets, (2) the noncurrent assets which will also be used to pay the essential costs and expenses, and (3) the sales during the current assets duration period which will also augment the current assets.

IV. LIMITATIONS OF THE MAJOR SOLVENCY AND LIQUIDITY RATIOS

The key solvency and liquidity ratios (total liability cover from assets, loss buffer coverage, current ratio, and quick assets ratio) measure the solvency and liquidity of a firm only in a very general way, since the ratios have four peculiar weaknesses: (1) exclusion of future revenues and expenses, (2) valuation of assets and liabilities at other than real values, (3) use of arbitrary cutoff dates, and (4) inclusion of pledged assets. These limitations are discussed next.

Solvency and liquidity ratios are subject to the weaknesses of the financial statements as discussed in Chapter 17, Section VI, since the ratios are calculated using figures from the statements. The solvency and liquidity ratios are also subject to the limitations of ratios in general as explained in Chapter 18, Section IV.

Exclusion of Future Revenues and Expenses. The ratios include in the calculations, only the assets and obligations as of a certain date. Future streams of positive or negative cash flow, increases in assets due to subsequent income, or increases in debts due to subsequent expenses or losses are excluded. From the balance sheet date up to the time when a firm really becomes bankrupt, the subsequent revenues and expenses could be very significant in relation to the assets and debts as of the just preceding balance sheet date. The ratios, therefore, show only a part of the picture.

Valuation of Assets and Liabilities at Other Than Real Values. The assets and liabilities are valued based on the figures appearing in the books of accounts. These values represent historical prices and may have no bearing on the present or future values.

For instance, land acquired 10 years ago should be currently worth more than twice the acquisition cost. Furthermore, a note receivable which bears no interest and which is due 5 years from now is definitely worth less than its face value because of discounting costs or imputed interest. (See Chapter 25, Section VII, for a discussion of imputed interest in relation to the valuation of receivables and payables.)

Use of Arbitrary Cutoff Dates. In calculating the current ratio, all assets convertible to cash in a year, and all debts due in a year, are included. All others are excluded. In deriving the quick asset ratio, only cash and cash equivalents and receivables are considered; inventories are not taken into account, although the finished goods inventories of some companies can be converted to cash earlier than the receivables of other firms.

Inclusion of Pledged Assets. Certain current assets, such as those pledged to secure long-term debts, are not available to pay current liabilities. Hence the current ratios are distorted to the extent that these assets are included in the calculation of the ratios.

Alternative to the Ratios—Statement of Future Cash Flow. A more meaningful aid in gauging the solvency and liquidity of a firm is a schedule which shows, on one hand, the present and future assets realizable in cash and, on the other, another schedule showing the maturing obligations from present liabilities and future expenses, both on a monthly, weekly, or even daily basis. The monthly collections should then be matched with the periodic payments.

The payment schedule should distinguish the liabilities which have to be paid at once, as taxes and wages, and those which can be postponed, such as those due the terminated suppliers.

V. RATIOS FOR THE PREDICTION
OF BANKRUPTCY

Several studies have been made regarding the ratios which may be used to predict business failures. Among these are those by Altman (Z-score), Altman et al. (ZETA), Beaver, and Wilcox. The first three are discussed in the paragraphs that follow. The study by Jarrod Wilcox (gambler's ruin prediction of business failure) was published in 1971 in the *Sloan Management Review*.

Beaver Study. William H. Beaver reviewed the effectiveness of 14 ratios in predicting bankruptcies. The results were made public in 1968 in the *Accounting Review*. Beaver found out that the three most effective indicators of business failures are the following ratios: (1) cash flow to total debt, (2) net income to total assets, and (3) total debt to total assets.

Z-Score. In 1968, Edward I. Altman presented in the *Journal of Finance* his Z-score formula for predicting bankruptcies. The Z-score is the total of the following ratios as multiplied by the adjustment factor: (1) net working capital to total assets, (2) retained earnings to total assets, (3) earnings before interest and taxes to total assets, (4) market value of stockholders' equity to book value of total debt, and (5) sales to total assets.

ZETA analysis. This model was introduced by Edward I. Altman, Robert G. Haldeman, and P. Narayanan in 1977 in the *Journal of Banking and Finance*. This method considers seven factors in predicting bankruptcy. These factors include the following five ratios: (1) earnings before interest and taxes to total assets, (2) earnings before interest and taxes to total interest payments, (3) retained earnings to total assets, (4) current ratio, and (5) common equity to total capital.

EXHIBIT 20.1:
Financing Structure Ratios (dollars in $1,000)

Name of ratio	Formula	BASE DATA*			RATIO		Year 2 as a percentage of year 1
		Year 1	Year 2		Year 1	Year 2	
I. Based on total financing or total assets							
Stockholders' total financing leverage	total financing	$88,500	$133,919	=	1.79	2.30	129.0%
	equity	$49,553	$ 58,126				
Debt/equity ratio	Debt	$38,947	$ 75,793		44%	57%	128.6%
	Equity	49,553	58,126		56%	43%	77.5%
	Total assets	$88,500	$133,919				
Long-term to short-term liabilities	long-term liabilities	$30,000	$ 27,500	=	3.35	0.57	17.0%
	short-term liabilities	$ 8,947	$ 48,293				
Part II. Based on stockholders' equity and bank loans or net assets (excludes trade credits)							
Stockholders' net assets leverage	net assets	$82,500	$121,221	=	1.66	2.09	125.3%
	equity	$49,553	$ 58,126				
Debt/equity ratio	Debt	$32,947	$ 63,095		39.9%	52.0%	
	Equity	49,553	58,126		60.1%	48.0%	
	Total assets	$82,500	$121,221				
Long-term loans/short-term loans	long-term loans	$30,000	$ 27,500	=	10.18	0.77	7.6%
	short-term loans†	$ 2,947	$ 35,595				

*The base data represent year-end balances.
†Includes current portion of long-term loans.

471

EXHIBIT 20.2:
Solvency and Liquidity Ratios (dollars in $1,000)

Name of ratio	Formula	BASE DATA*			RATIO		Year 2 as a percentage of year 1
		Year 1	Year 2		Year 1	Year 2	
Solvency ratios							
Total liabilities cover from assets	total assets / total liabilities	$88,500 / $38,947	$133,919 / $75,793	=	2.27	1.77	77.8%
Loss buffer percentage	Total assets / Total liabilities	$88,500 / 38,947	$133,919 / 75,793				
	Loss buffer	$49,553	$58,126				
	Loss buffer percentage	56%	43%		56%	43%	77.5%
Liquidity ratios							
Current ratio	current assets / current liabilities	$56,200 / $8,947	$89,619 / $48,293	=	6.28	1.86	29.5%
Quick assest ratio	quick assets / current liabilities	$40,200 / $8,947	$63,320 / $48,293	=	4.49	1.31	29.2%

*The base data represent year-end balances.

Chapter 21

OPERATING RATIO ANALYSIS

There are two types of operating ratios depending upon the data base used: those based exclusively on the financial statements and those that use information outside of the financial statements. The first type may be called financial operating ratios; the second, statistical operating ratios. The latter type may or may not use figures from the accounting statements. Operating ratios are of particular interest to those directly involved in running the day-to-day operations of a business firm, for example, operations managers, sales managers, production supervisors, human resource managers, and inventory control supervisors.

The different kinds of operating ratios discussed in this chapter are

Financial Operating Ratios:

1. Asset distribution ratios
2. Asset turnover ratios
3. Sales profitability ratios

Statistical Operating Ratios:

4. Labor time-cost indicators
5. Manufacturing efficiency indicators
6. Sales productivity indicators
7. Building utilization rates

These ratios should be studied over several periods and compared with those of the other divisions. To the extent the data are available, they should also be related to those of the other companies in the industry.

Financial Operating Ratios.   While the financing structure ratios are concerned with the raising of funds, and while the return on investment ratios deal with the ascertainment of the return on these funds, the financial operating ratios evaluate how the funds were used to produce the return. Specifically, operating ratios attempt to (1) develop clues as to how the total funds were allocated to the different assets, (2) how much sales revenues the assets were able to generate, and (3) how much profit was left from the sales revenues after paying for the costs and expenses.

The asset allocation ratios ascertain the soundness and flexibility of a firm by indicating the portion of the funds going into resources which are directly employed in the operations. The asset utilization ratios delve into the operations by helping to determine the reasonableness of the levels of working capital and buildings and equipment. Possible reasons for the fluctuations in the levels of receivables, payables, and inventories are offered. The sales profitability ratios indicate the efficiency of management in terms of the degree to which the costs and expenses were controlled so as to leave sufficient margin for the return to the business owners.

Statistical Operating Ratios.   The statistical operating ratios give management a picture of how its resources—office employees, production workers, sales force, raw materials, equipment, and building space—were utilized to produce goods, generate sales, and earn profit.

The labor time-cost ratios ascertain the time spent by its employees in relation to the employment cost. The manufacturing efficiency indicators determine the degree of efficiency by which the production inputs of labor, materials, and equipment were utilized to manufacture the goods. The sales productivity indicators point out how the time of the salespeople were utilized to generate sales and sales margins and convert the sales to cash. The building utilization rates evaluate how the floor areas of a store, hotel, or commercial building were used to earn profit.

I. ASSET DISTRIBUTION RATIOS

These ratios (Exhibit 21.1) are concerned with the allocation of the total financing raised by the firm to the different types of resources. The resources are the operating and nonoperating assets. The former is composed primarily of the working capital and physical facilities currently used in operations. The latter is represented by the presently nonproductive assets.

An unhealthy asset mix helps to immobilize the operations. For instance, a retailing firm which cannot stock enough merchandise because of huge, illiquid investment in a "showpiece" corporate headquarters building does not have the flexibility of a competitor with rented quarters.

OPERATING ASSETS RATIO (Exhibit 21.1)

$$\frac{\text{total operating assets}}{\text{total assets}}$$

This ratio emphasizes the assets which are *actively used in the current operations*. This asset category excludes those that are (1) future oriented and (2) past oriented. The former are those that are acquired in preparation for business growth or generating future sales. This includes factories under construction and land held for speculation.

The second group accumulates the results of past errors, inefficiencies, or losses due to changes in business plans or the competitive environment, which have not yet been formally recognized in the accounting records. This group includes old receivables, receivables under litigation, nonmoving or obsolete inventories, and idle plants. For banks, this category includes nonperforming or delinquent loans—those without current interest receipts.

The purpose of segregating nonoperating assets is to relieve the current operations of the burden of carrying the cost of past errors and future development programs as these do not benefit the current operations. The presence of nonoperating assets depresses the net profit since the nonoperating assets do not produce any benefit to the current operations—they neither generate sales nor reduce costs. On the other hand, they require financing. If they are financed by interest-bearing loans, the interest charges cut down the profit from the operations. If the assets are financed by stockholders' equity, the total profit is not reduced; however, the rate of return on investment is diminished as a bigger equity base is needed to support not just the operating resources but also the nonproductive assets.

The operating assets ratio in the exhibit indicates that the firm had weakened its position in year 2 since it had only $0.84 in operating assets during the year for every $1.00 of total assets—a drop from $0.96 the prior year.

TOTAL ASSETS COMPOSITION PERCENTAGES (Exhibit 21.1)

$$\frac{\text{working capital, property and equipment or nonoperating assets}}{\text{total assets}}$$

This ratio gives an overall picture of the allocation of the resources to the general asset groups. It shows how the resources are being frozen in nonoperating assets and in long-term assets. Long-term assets are the land, buildings, factories, and equipment currently used in operations.

Although long-term assets are being used in operations, they are not as productive as working capital. This is especially true with investments in office buildings. Furthermore, unlike working capital, long-term assets require relatively more financing and take longer time to reconvert to cash.

The firms which can currently maximize the utilization of their investments generally are those that (1) concentrate their resources primarily on working capital and secondarily on long-term assets and (2) have minimal exposure in nonoperating assets.

The obvious exceptions to this rule are manufacturing firms which require their own production facilities as well as real estate holding companies which are in the business of owning rental properties.

The total assets composition percentages in the exhibit show a healthy change in the operating assets: growth in the working capital so as to meet the requirements of a developing company and gradual decline in property, plant, and equipment due to the periodic depreciation charge.

Nonoperating assets should normally be kept to a minimum. In the illustration, however, the rise in the balance of nonoperating assets is due to the construction in progress, which is apparently in preparation for the increased production in the future. However, outside of the construction in progress, there is one questionable item under nonoperating assets in the balance sheet—long-term stock investment. The advisability of indefinitely holding this should be studied. The benefits to be derived in the future from this investment should be weighed against the bank interest cost and required return on the stockholders' equity which are used to finance this in the interim.

GROSS WORKING CAPITAL COMPOSITION PERCENTAGES (Exhibit 21.1)

$$\frac{\text{cash, trade receivables, or inventories}}{\text{total current assets}}$$

For merchandising and manufacturing firms, the major working capital assets are the receivables and inventories. Assuming that the receivables and inventories are mostly current, that is, with minimal old receivables or slow-moving inventories, a dollar of receivables is usually worth more than a dollar of inventories since it takes a shorter time to convert a receivable to cash. In fact, in computing the quick asset ratio which was explained in Chapter 20, Section III, only cash, cash equivalents, and receivables are included as current assets. Cash equivalents include temporary investments in the stock market that can easily be converted to cash without substantial loss in liquidation.

A possible situation wherein a dollar of inventory is worth more than a dollar of receivable arises when the following holds true: (1) the inventories are easily salable, and (2) the profit on the sale is high enough to cover the selling expenses and carrying costs of the inventories.

For a manufacturing firm, the finished goods inventories are normally more valuable than the raw materials on a dollar-for-dollar basis since it takes a shorter time to convert the finished goods to cash.

For the working capital composition percentages in Exhibit 21.1, the accounts receivable as a percentage of the total working capital declined from 71.6% to 70.7%. Theoretically, this is a bad trend since receivables are more valuable than the inventories. In practice, however, the decline is too small to warrant any attention.

II. ASSET TURNOVER RATIOS

Generally, the asset turnover ratios determine the degree of efficiency with which the resources were utilized to generate sales. The ratios are calculated by relating the total resources to the sales and other business activity indicators like cost of goods sold or cost of raw materials used. Specifically, the ratios in this group indicate how promptly the receivables are collected and how fast the merchandise inventories are sold out.

For discussion purposes, the asset turnover ratios are grouped as follows:

1. *General turnover ratios.* These relate the total assets, operating assets, net operating assets, gross working capital, or long-term operating assets to sales. These ratios reveal the general efficiency with which the assets or groups of assets were used in generating sales.
2. *Accounts receivable ratios.* These disclose the reasonableness of the collection period considering the credit terms.
3. *Finished goods inventory ratios.* The inventory period reveals the adequacy or excessiveness of the finished goods inventories in relation to the sales requirements.
4. *Raw materials inventory and accounts payable ratios.* The raw materials inventory period shows how long the present inventory will last. The accounts payable payment period reveals the number of months it usually takes to pay the suppliers of the materials. The raw materials inventory period, taken together with the accounts payable payment period, shows how much of the inventory is financed by the trade suppliers.

GENERAL TURNOVER RATIOS

These ratios (Exhibit 21.2) ascertain the level of efficiency with which the resources as a whole were used to make the products and close the sales.

Total Assets Turnover (Exhibit 21.2)

$$\frac{\text{sales}}{\text{total assets}}$$

This ratio is the most widely used asset turnover ratio. It relates the sales to the total assets. It shows how much sales are obtained by every dollar of assets. The higher the ratio, the better the utilization of the resources, assuming of course that the sales have the same profitability rate as discussed in Section III of this chapter.

Generally, merchandising firms have higher turnover rates than do manufacturing firms. Among retailing firms, those that do not own their premises, or that just lease them, have higher turnover than do those that own them. In the manufacturing sector, food repackagers have higher turnover rate than do machine tool manufacturers. In the car industry, the assemblers have higher turnover rates than do the manufacturers that fabricate a substantial portion of their parts.

The rationale for using total assets in the ratio is that a firm is held accountable for all its assets in whatever form they may be. The limitation of this ratio is that the total assets, as the term implies, represents an assortment of resources of varying characteristics. It includes those which are used in the business and hence contributed to the production of goods or sales and those which are not. Hence the ratio is distorted to the extent that the assets which were not instrumental in originating and servicing sales are included in deriving the ratio.

Operating Assets Turnover (Exhibit 21.2)

$$\frac{\text{sales}}{\text{operating assets}}$$

This is a refinement of the *total* assets turnover. The *operating* assets turnover indicates the ability of the firm to use the operating assets to manufacture or purchase and sell goods or render service. The nonoperating assets, which did not benefit the operations during the year under review, are excluded. The typical nonoperating assets were listed in Section I of this chapter.

COMPARISON WITH THE TOTAL ASSETS TURNOVER.   If there are nonoperating assets, the total assets and the operating assets turnovers give different results. Thus, as revealed in Exhibit 21.2, during year 1 the total assets turnover is 1.29 while the operating assets turnover is 1.37. This means that while each $1.00 of operating assets was able to produce $1.36 in sales, the inclusion of nonoperating assets diluted the result to $1.29.

While the total assets turnover remained unchanged at 1.29 in year 2, the operating assets turnover showed an improvement from 1.37 to 1.45. The rise in the discrepancy between the two types of turnovers was caused by the decline in the operating assets as a percentage of total assets from 94% to 89% of total assets:

	Average for the year	
	Year 1	Year 2
Total assets	$93,000,000	$111,210,000
Less: Nonoperating assets	5,450,000	12,900,000
Operating assets	$87,550,000	$ 98,310,000
As a percentage of total assets	94%	88%

The nonoperating assets are composed of old receivables and inventories, construction in progress, and long-term investments.

For purposes of evaluating management, it is normally advisable to use the operating assets turnover in lieu of the total assets turnover if the present management is not responsible for the nonoperating assets.

Net Operating Assets Turnover (Exhibit 21.2)

$$\frac{\text{sales}}{\text{net operating assets}}$$

This ratio is similar to the operating assets turnover except that the trade credits are excluded from the operating assets. The trade credits are not included in order to pinpoint the productivity of just that portion of the operating assets which is financed by interest-bearing loans and the stockholders. Both the lenders and stockholders require a return on their investment; trade suppliers do not. The use of the net assets turnover is advisable if the management whose performance is being reviewed is the one responsible for negotiating with the suppliers for the terms of payment.

COMPARISON WITH THE OPERATING ASSETS TURNOVER. Since the denominator in the net operating assets formula is smaller than that in the operating assets turnover, the former shows a higher turnover. Thus, while the former was 1.47 in year 1, the latter was only 1.37. Moreover, while the net operating assets turnover improved by 9.2% (from 1.47 to 1.61), the operating assets turnover rose by 6.1%. The higher are the trade credits as a proportion of the operating assets, the wider is the cleavage between these two types of turnovers.

Gross Working Capital Turnover (Exhibit 21.2)

$$\frac{\text{sales}}{\text{gross working capital}}$$

Although the net operating assets turnover has a more restricted definition of assets than the operating assets turnover, it still includes in its calculations a hodgepodge of resources. Land, which can be used practically indefinitely, is mixed with raw materials inventories which are consumed in a few weeks or months at most. In order to get a more accurate reading of the productivity of the assets, the long-term assets as land, buildings, and equipment may be segregated from the working capital so that the turnover may be computed solely on the working capital. In the illustration, the old receivables and slow-moving inventories were included in the working capital. If these amounts are material, they have to be excluded.

This turnover has useful applications in merchandising firms and lending institutions since their ability to generate revenues is based primarily on merchandise inventories and receivables in the case of retailers and loans in the case of lending institutions. Their revenues are not affected by their ownership of the buildings housing their branches or stores and corporate headquarters. On the other hand, their ownership of these premises hikes their total assets. Thus, if two firms or divisions are compared, one with owned and the other with leased premises, the application of the total assets or operating assets turnover will produce distorted results: the businesses which own their buildings will have a lower turnover. On the other hand, use of the gross working capital turnover will eliminate the distortion caused by the buildings and yield results which are directly comparable.

Long-term Operating Assets Turnover (Exhibit 21.2)

$$\frac{\text{sales}}{\text{property, plant, and equipment}}$$

This reveals the degree to which land, buildings, and equipment are utilized in the operations. Idle properties such as land held for future expansion or plants under construction should not be included. This turnover is practically useful in industries which depend heavily on real estate, structures, and equipment for their operations. Examples of these industries are manufacturing firms, especially those with massive investments in plants, and real estate holding companies that own rental properties.

There are three possible ways of valuing the physical facilities: at net book value, at original cost, or at appraised value. (Related to the valuations of the physical facilities are the valuations of the stockholders' equity which have been discussed in Chapter 19, Section I.)

NET BOOK VALUE.   This is the most common method of valuing the physical facilities. This is due to the following reasons: (1) the value is readily available, and (2) the valuation is consistent with those used in most of the other ratios which also employ book value. However, this valuation has two basic limitations:

1. The annual depreciation charges, which reduce the book value of the buildings and equipment, are usually based on the depreciation method used for income tax purposes. This method generally results in depreciation charges which are higher than the one based on the economic life of the assets. The effect of this is to have the net book value lower than the real value of the assets.
2. The book value of land is usually lower than its current economic value since inflation has raised the real value from the time the land was acquired.

ACQUISITION COST. This valuation tries to correct, but actually does not remedy, the first-named limitation of the net book value method. The historical or acquisition cost of buildings and equipment has no correlation with the economic value.

APPRAISED VALUE. This method attempts to relate to the current market price of the physical resources. However, this has its own draw-back: the difficulty of obtaining objective valuation of specialized resources where there are few similar assets.

Incremental Operating Assets Turnover (Exhibit 21.2)

$$\frac{\text{incremental sales}}{\text{incremental operating assets}}$$

The objective of this ratio is to highlight the productivity, in terms of additional sales, of the incremental operating assets which were deployed during the year. An enterprise should continue to introduce additional resources as long as the resources generate sales which can turn into profits.

The productivity of the incremental operating assets may be compared with the operating assets turnover during the base year as

	Year 1	Year 2	Increment
Sales	$120,000	$143,000	$23,000
Operating assets	87,550	98,310	10,760
Turnover	1.37	1.45	2.14

The attractive 2.14 turnover on incremental operating assets pushed the overall turnover from 1.37 in year 1 to 1.45.

Similar analysis may be made for the turnover of incremental total assets, incremental net operating assets, incremental gross working capital, and incremental long-term operating assets.

ACCOUNTS RECEIVABLE RATIOS

Accounts Receivable Turnover (Exhibit 21.3)

$$\frac{\text{sales}}{\text{accounts receivable}}$$

The accounts receivable turnover is more specific than the working capital turnover. The former shows the dollar value of sales for every dollar of accounts receivable outstanding. The lower the turnover, the lower is the sales, the higher is the outstanding balance of the receivables, or the faster is the rise in the receivables than the rise in the sales. Thus, as shown in Exhibit 21.3, the turnover dropped from 3.0 to 2.8 since the accounts receivable increased by 29% (from $40,000,000 to $51,560,000), while the sales rose by only 19%.

Collection Period (Exhibit 21.3)

$$\frac{\text{number of days per year}}{\text{accounts receivable turnover}}$$

The collection period has two components: the authorized sales credit term and the collection delinquency period. The latter is the excess of the total collection period over the credit term. Variations in either component causes the period to fluctuate. Management may purposely stretch the sales credit term as a measure to retain or gain market share.

The collection period is reduced by the availment of prompt payment discounts. On the other hand, the delinquency period is stretched by lax credit standards, failure of the sales force to produce sales from creditworthy customers, collection inefficiencies, as well as financial difficulties of customers as during an economic downturn. When a firm sells to industrial customers, an industry slump can cause these customers to delay their payments. Excessive raw materials in the warehouses of the customers may also prompt them to skip on the payments.

COSTS OF LONG COLLECTION PERIOD.   The lengthening of collection period has its costs. The lengthening means bloating the outstanding balance. This requires more financing to support the receivables. The probability of noncollection rises, and collection expenses mount.

FURTHER ANALYSIS AND ACTION.   More detailed investigation into the causes of the rise in the receivables in relation to sales should be conducted. Separate collection periods should be calculated for each major product line, market territories, and similar groupings. A review of the aging schedule may disclose that the noncollection of some big accounts has dragged so far out so as to stretch out the overall collection period of all the receivables. The detailed review may lead to the write-off of certain accounts and the creation of a provision for doubtful accounts.

TREATMENT OF CASH SALES AND DEAD ACCOUNTS (EXHIBIT 21.4).   If any part of the sales is for cash, this portion should be excluded in calculating the ratio. Otherwise, the turnover will appear to be higher than the actual, and the collection period will look shorter than real. See the first table in Exhibit 21.4.

Just as the cash sales should be excluded, so should the "dead" and dying accounts: the uncollectibles and the slow-paying customers. The inclusion of the dead accounts will make the turnover lower than what it really is, and the collection period, higher. See the second table in Exhibit 21.4.

Incremental Accounts Receivable Turnover and Collection Period (Exhibit 21.3).   For incremental accounts receivable turnover, the ratio is

$$\frac{\text{incremental sales}}{\text{incremental receivables}}$$

For incremental accounts receivable collection periods, it is

$$\frac{\text{number of days per year}}{\text{incremental receivable turnover}}$$

These show the productivity of the additional receivables—as measured by the incremental sales. This turnover or collection period is particularly useful in two situations:

1. *When the company has introduced prolonged credit terms or sales payment period to retain or expand market share.* In this case, the turnover of the incremental receivables will be unduly low, and the collection period, high, in relation to those of the prior year.
2. *When the firm is short on capital.* In this case, any funding required to carry the additional collectibles will have to be carefully balanced against the benefits of incremental sales and against the benefits from alternative profitability measures.

Generally, the additional receivables is justified so long as the extra cost of financing and collecting the receivables and the risk of noncollection are more than offset by the profit on the added sales and by the value of future benefits to be derived from an expanded market share.

The turnover and collection period of incremental receivables may be checked against those of the base year as follows:

	Year 1	Year 2	Increment
Sales	$120,000	$143,000	$23,000
Receivables	$ 40,000	$ 51,560	$11,560

	Year 1	Year 2	Increment
Turnover	3.0	2.8	2.0
Collection period in days	122	132	183

The low 2.0 turnover on incremental receivables dropped the turnover from 3.0 in year 1 to 2.8.

FINISHED GOODS INVENTORY RATIOS

Finished Goods Inventory Turnover and Inventory Period (Exhibit 21.5). For inventory turnover, the ratio is

$$\frac{\text{cost of goods sold}}{\text{finished goods inventory}}$$

For inventory period, it is

$$\frac{\text{number of days per year}}{\text{finished goods turnover}}$$

See Exhibit 21.5.

A useful tool in assessing the effectiveness of managing the finished goods inventory is the inventory period—the time spent by the inventory in the warehouse. The shorter is the inventory period, the faster the inventory movement, or the faster the goods being sold.

Before the inventory period is derived, the inventory turnover is computed first. This is done by dividing the cost of sales by the average merchandise or finished goods inventory.

Although the ratios illustrated are for finished goods inventories of a manufacturing concern, the procedures may also be used by merchandising firms for their merchandise inventories.

In the illustrations, the inventory figures represent the average of the beginning- and end-of-year balances. More accurate results will be obtained if the figure used is the monthly or even weekly or daily average for the year. This is particularly true for businesses with highly seasonal inventories such as manufacturers and retailers of Christmas gift items.

COSTS OF EXCESSIVE AND INADEQUATE INVENTORIES. An unwarranted overstocking has its costs:

1. *Financing.* The inventories have to be financed. Financing, whether from bank loans or stockholders, carries with it interest.
2. *Obsolescence.* The introduction of competing products or the change in the demand for the products will cause the value of the inventory to decline.

3. *Warehousing*. Storage fees; inventory insurance; depreciation and insurance of warehouses; physical security; humidity and temperature control; fumigation; handling; stock record keeping; and physical losses as due to theft, spillage, and evaporation all add up to the inventory carrying costs.

Just as excessive inventories pull down the profit due to the extra financing, obsolescence, and warehousing costs, inadequate levels of inventories cause stockouts resulting in the nonrealization of potential sales.

Causes of Fluctuations in the Inventory Period. Variations in the inventory period from year to year may be due to changes in the following factors: effectiveness of inventory system, predictability of demand for the products, strategy to capture market share, manufacturing capability and practices, and accounting practices including the use of full or absorption costing.

EFFECTIVENESS OF INVENTORY SYSTEM. An inventory system refers to the people, equipment, and procedures to monitor sales and inventory levels and initiate the manufacture of goods to replenish the stock. An inventory system which promptly orders the goods helps cut down the stock level in the warehouse. The consolidation of regional and local warehouses, as well as the implementation of a faster delivery procedure to the warehouses and ultimately to the sales outlets, also shortens the inventory period.

PREDICTABILITY OF DEMAND. One of the major reasons for an unjustified buildup in the finished goods inventory is forecasting error due to the frequent changes in the demand for the product. For instance, management might have stocked up in anticipation of a brisk sale which did not materialize. This problem is compounded if management does not keep a close tab on the changing and evolving sales patterns.

STRATEGY TO CAPTURE MARKET SHARE. One of the few justifications for a rise in the inventory period is the implementation of a market expansion strategy. This calls for one or more of the following four measures. First, a new product introduction strategy calls for the stocking up of the product in preparation for the sales. Sales are usually slow for new products.

Second, under a market saturation strategy, the firm may decide to replenish the stocks of the retail outlets more frequently or maintain higher inventory level at each outlet so as to minimize the possibility of a stockout.

Third, under the same strategy, the firm may cover more outlets in the same defined market territory. The sales per store of the new outlets may not be as high as those of established ones.

Fourth, under a market territory expansion strategy, the firm will have to stock up not only the new retail outlets but also the new regional warehouses.

MANUFACTURING CAPABILITY AND PRACTICES.   A reduction in the inventory period may indicate a worsening condition. For instance, the situation could have been brought about by the failure to fully replenish the needed inventories due to limited manufacturing rated capacity or due to production interruptions arising from labor disputes, shortages of raw materials, or similar causes.

On the other hand, the firm might have produced in excess of sales due to the practice of having long production runs. The long runs might have been motivated by lower production costs per unit due to the savings in production start-up or changeover costs, labor costs, and material costs.

ACCOUNTING PRACTICES.   The inclusion of old inventories and the use of full or absorption methods in costing the inventories have a tendency to cause the inventory period to fluctuate.

Old, nonmoving, or slow-moving stocks gradually accumulate in the inventories. The inclusion of, say, a one-year-old stock among one-month inventories in calculating the inventory period stretches the overall inventory period. Old inventories should be excluded in determining the inventory period in the same way that dead accounts are not considered in calculating the collection period.

FULL OR ABSORPTION COSTING.   Most companies value their inventories based on the full or absorption costing method as against direct costing. (For definitions of terms and effect on the inventory values and income statement, see Chapter 17.)

When a firm uses full costing and produces more than what it sells, the factory overhead is spread out over a larger number of units. Hence the overhead and total cost per unit of both the sold and unsold units decline. The net effect of this is to transfer a part of the current year's indirect manufacturing costs to subsequent years via the finished goods inventories at the end of the current year. This causes the total cost of goods sold to be lower, and hence the net profit to be higher, than if the company did not raise its finished goods inventory level. Firms under pressure to report a high profit may therefore unduly overproduce and raise their inventory levels. This action reduces the turnover and lengthens the inventory period.

MORE DETAILED ANALYSIS.   The ratios are usually calculated based on the total inventory levels and total cost of sales. More meaningful results may be revealed if the inventory periods are estimated for each product. The detailed analysis may disclose that although the overall inventory period rises, the profitable items are almost always out of stock whereas the products with no or marginal profits keep on accumulating in the warehouse.

Incremental Finished Goods Inventory Turnover and Inventory Period (Exhibit 21.5). For incremental inventory turnover, the ratio is

$$\frac{\text{increase in cost of sales}}{\text{increase in inventory}}$$

For incremental inventory period, it is

$$\frac{\text{number of days per year}}{\text{incremental inventory turnover}}$$

Slight changes in the inventory period may not be noticeable, especially when the cost of sales does not change much. Hence, the inventory period for the incremental stocks, in relation to the incremental cost of sales may be needed in order to (1) make the change more discernible and (2) help ascertain if the additional stocks can be justified.

As shown in Exhibit 21.5, the inventory period rose from 61 days in year 1 to 88 days. This represents a 44% rise. However, for the incremental cost of sales, the inventory period for the incremental inventory is a boggling 557 days. Hence the profit from sales from the incremental inventory may not be able to support the carrying costs.

RAW MATERIALS INVENTORY RATIOS

Raw Materials Inventory Turnover and Inventory Period (Exhibit 21.6). For inventory turnover, the ratio is

$$\frac{\text{raw materials used}}{\text{raw materials inventory}}$$

For inventory period, it is

$$\frac{\text{number of days per year}}{\text{inventory turnover}}$$

The raw material inventory period is calculated in a manner similar to that of the finished goods inventory period (Exhibit 21.6).

The raw material inventory period may fluctuate from company to company, or for the same firm, from time to time, primarily due to the changes in the supply situation and the predictability of the needs for the material. In certain instances, the decline in the inventory period may be due to financial difficulties or the desire of management to inflate the profit if their inventory is valued on a LIFO instead of FIFO basis.

STABILITY OF SUPPLY. The situation in the open market, proximity to the suppliers, delivery arrangements, consistency of the quality of the materials, manufacturing season, and special characteristics of the materials help to determine the length of the material carrying period. These determinants are described in the paragraphs that follow.

An upswing in the inventory period may be the result of a management decision to stock up in the wake of a growing shortage in the market. The action is made more imperative in the presence of spiraling procurement prices. Distance to suppliers helps destabilize the supply line. Consequently, firms which start to source from distant places, such as Taiwan, South Korea, and Hong Kong, have to augment their buffer stock.

Delivery arrangements affect the inventory levels. More frequent deliveries reduce the material requirements between the deliveries. The implementation by manufacturing firms of just-in-time deliveries shrinks the inventories to nominal quantities.

The consistency of the quality of the inputs or the experienced rejection rate has a bearing on the inventory level. A material with a consistent 99% acceptance rate needs a much lower inventory than does one whose rejection rate gyrates between 75% and 95%.

Factories which run for longer periods than the buying season have to stockpile for the production needs when the materials are not available in the market. This situation is applicable to processors of agricultural, fishery, and forestry materials.

Among the few industries which have to carry unusually large inventories are the cigarette companies. They have to allow the tobacco to age for months before using them.

PREDICTABILITY OF THE USAGE RATE. The predictability of the demand for the finished product impacts not only on the inventories of the product but also on the raw materials. However, there is another factor which does not influence the finished goods but which affects the inventory of the raw materials: the specifications of the materials. The discovery of new and better materials may not affect the sale of the finished products, but may slow down the usage rate of the current raw materials inventory, and require the stocking up of the new material. Thus, the combined inventory will be much higher.

FINANCIAL DIFFICULTIES. An increase in the inventory turnover or decline in the inventory period may mean that the firm is running out on financial resources. Due to this, the company should have difficulty in replenishing its stocks.

INVENTORY COSTING—LIFO VERSUS FIFO. If the inventory is valued at LIFO, the most current purchases are assumed to have been the first ones used in the production of goods. If the inventory in the books has not been touched for years, the valuation of the inventory according to the records, which represent the purchase cost, is much lower than are present prices due to inflation. If during the current year the inventory level has dropped, that part of the beginning inventory which had been used in the production is valued at the much lower, old prices. The effect of this is to depress the cost of sales to the extent that the current prices of the old inventory which was used exceed the old acquisition cost.

ACCOUNTS PAYABLE RATIOS

Accounts Payable Turnover and Payment Period (Exhibit 21.6). For accounts payable turnover, the ratio is

$$\frac{purchases}{accounts\ payable}$$

For accounts payable payment period, it is

$$\frac{number\ of\ days\ per\ year}{accounts\ payable\ turnover}$$

A reduction of the payment period could mean that the firm is taking advantage of prompt payment discounts or has used the shorter purchase terms as a leverage in negotiating with the suppliers for the lowering of the purchase price.

On the other hand, an extension of the payment period could warn that the company is in financial difficulties. This could have forced the company to stretch its payments.

Alternatively, the lengthening of the payment terms may indicate that the company is managing the payables well. By delaying the payments, it is hiking the amount of interest-free financing.

Suppliers' Financing Ratio (Exhibit 21.6)

$$\frac{accounts\ payable}{raw\ materials\ inventory}$$

The accounts payable is usually checked against the raw materials inventory to ascertain how much of the inventory is financed by the suppliers. The suppliers' financing ratio is used for this purpose.

A ratio of 1 indicates that the suppliers are providing the financing just for the raw material inventory. Thus, as shown in the last ratio in Exhibit 21.6, where the ratio is 1 in year 1, the trade credits of $6,000,000 just equal the inventory.

A ratio which is more than 1 discloses that the suppliers are financing not only the raw materials but also the goods in process and finished goods stocks. This was the case in year 2, since the accounts payable of $9,349,000 exceeded the raw material inventory.

OPERATING CYCLE

The total of the accounts receivable collection period and inventory periods (for finished goods, goods in process, and raw materials) represent the operating cycle. The cycle is an important point of reference in analysis work since it represents the time necessary to convert the raw materials inventory to goods in process to finished goods to trade receivables and back to cash. Since the cycle is shortened by the accounts payable payment period, the payment period may be deducted in order to arrive at the net operating cycle. The gross and net operating cycles, which are in days, run parallel to the gross and net working capital, which are in dollars. A clearer relationship between the operating cycles and working capital is demonstrated in Chapter 10, Exhibit 10.4.

In period-to-period or division-to-division comparisons, it is necessary to compare not only the collection, inventory, and payment periods, but also the length of the net operating cycle. This is necessary since a longer receivable period of one division may be offset by its shorter finished goods inventory period, or a longer raw material inventory period may be compensated by a longer trade payables payment period.

III. SALES PROFITABILITY RATIOS

These ratios show what percentage of the sales is left after paying off all or some of the costs and expenses. The intermediate profits and the final profit are compared with the total sales. Each of the sales profitability ratios has its own recommended applications and limitations.

The three most popular ratios are illustrated: the gross profit rate, the net operating profit rate, and the net profit rate.

GROSS PROFIT RATE (Exhibit 21.7)

$$\frac{\text{gross profit}}{\text{sales}}$$

The gross profit rate gives, as a percentage of sales, what is available after deducting the cost of sales. An improvement in the profit rate means that the company was able to boost its sales volume or selling price or hold down its costs. It is also possible that there is a substantial reclassification or shift in cost from cost of sales, which affects the gross profit, to selling expenses, which do not influence the gross profit. For instance, the firm might have dropped its cost of sales by downgrading its products but compensating for it by engaging in an aggressive marketing program. In this manner, the use of inferior raw materials, or the reduction of the labor hours required, cut down the manufacturing cost or cost of sales. The intensified marketing program augmented the selling expenses.

A high gross profit rate translates to a large amount available for the selling and administrative expenses, interest, income tax, and net profit. Exhibit 21.7 shows that in year 2, 55.7% of the sales revenues was available for these expenses and net profit.

Implications for a Merchandising Firm.   For a retailer, the gross profit rate of a product department reflects on the performance of the product manager. It indicates his acumen to mark up the goods. The higher the gross profit rate, the more rewarding is his markup.

Implications for a Manufacturing Firm.   For a manufacturer, the gross profit rate represents the results of the combined efforts of both the marketing and the production managers. As in the retailer, the rate exhibits the ability of the marketing manager to markup the goods. However, the rate is partly the result of the efforts of the production manager to fabricate the goods at a low cost.

Industry Differences.   The gross profit rate varies from industry to industry. Manufacturers in general have higher gross profit rates than do merchandisers. Within the manufacturing sector, makers of high-technology equipment yield more attractive margins than do the traditional food processors. In the merchandising field, specialty retailers produce more attractive gross profits than do discounters.

NET OPERATING PROFIT RATE (Exhibit 21.7)

$$\frac{\text{net operating profit}}{\text{sales}}$$

The net operating profit rate reveals, as a percentage of sales, what is left for interest, nonrecurring charges, income tax, and profit for the stockholders. This rate is sometimes used as one of the bases in evaluating the performance of operating managers. The appraisal is before considering interest expense on the theory that the financing is arranged by the finance managers or, in the case of a division or subsidiary, by the head office.

In reality, however, it is difficult to segregate the operating from the financial results. Sales may be boosted by prolonging the collection period of interest-free accounts receivables or by reducing the interest rate on the sales installment notes to levels below the money cost to the company. The impact of this is to lift the revenues and hence the net operating profit rate but at the expense of higher interest cost.

At the buying end, suppliers may be willing to extend the terms of payments if the purchase price is raised. Although in this case the firm is able to reduce its interest cost by availing itself of longer interest-free trade credit, it is paying more for its materials or merchandise. The consequence of this is to shift some costs from the interest expense to the costs of sales, thereby depressing the net operating profit rate.

NET PROFIT RATE (Exhibit 21.7)

$$\frac{\text{net profit}}{\text{sales}}$$

The net profit rate shows the bottom line of the income statement as a percentage of sales. The ratio exhibits how the company was able to capture market share, hike or maintain its selling prices, and control the costs.

This ratio is more stable than is the gross or net operating profit rate since the net profit rate is not affected by the transfers of costs from one section of the income statement to another. On the other hand, since this rate uses the bottom line, it does not divide the overall results into the functional areas of business, namely, (1) the manufacturing department, which is responsible for the cost of sales; (2) the marketing and administrative departments, which have the jurisdiction over the selling and general office expenses; and (3) the finance department, which handles the loans and covering interest expense. Hence the net profit rate is best suited to the evaluation of the performance of the general managers or of the division or company itself, rather than the appraisal of the operating or financial managers and their respective departments.

INCREMENTAL SALES NET PROFIT RATE (Exhibit 21.7)

$$\frac{\text{increase in net profit}}{\text{increase in sales}}$$

This ratio gauges the rate of profit extracted from additional sales. This is particularly useful in helping to analyze the net profit rate of two periods. For instance, the rise in the net profit rate from 6.8% in year 1 to 7.5% in the following year is accounted for by the exceptionally high incremental net profit rate in year 2—which was 11.0%.

CASH FLOW FROM OPERATIONS TO NET PROFIT

$$\frac{\text{cash flow from operations}}{\text{net profit}}$$

This ratio shows how much of the net profit is in the form of cash. Because of the differences in the calculation of the cash flow and net profit, it is very seldom that the ratio is 1. The differences between the cash flow and profit are usually accounted for by depreciation and other noncash charges and changes in net working capital (cash, receivables, inventories, and trade payables).

Ratio of More Than 1—Implications. This means that the cash flow is greater than the net profit. Another interpretation of this is that the increment in the net working capital during the period is less than the depreciation and amortization of costs. There are three major factors which contribute to this type of situation.

First, the operation is more building or equipment intensive than working capital intensive. Hence utilities and owners of buildings for rent usually have a ratio of over 1. Their cash generation is high relative to their net income since they have to recover the cost of their investment in properties. On the other hand, their receivables and inventories are low in relation to their physical facilities.

Second, the buildings and equipment are relatively new. The depreciation charges are high when the properties were recently acquired. If the accelerated depreciation method which is sanctioned for income tax purposes is used, the depreciation charge for the first few years is unusually high. Furthermore, since none of the properties is fully depreciated, the depreciation base is large.

Third, the growth in the business is not substantial. Companies on a harvest or maintain strategy do not materially increase their working capital. Hence their operating cash flow is normally higher than their net profit.

Ratio of Less Than 1—Implications. Growing businesses, especially those which are heavy on working capital but light on property investments, usually have operating cash flow lower than their net profit. For instance, retailers who carry huge inventories and receivables, lease their premises, and who expand their operations are apt to have a ratio of less than 1.

DISCRETIONARY COSTS TO SALES

$$\frac{\text{discretionary costs}}{\text{sales}}$$

Discretionary costs are those which will benefit the future periods but are normally charged as expenses during the current period. Examples are expenditures for R&D, management and personnel development, and sales expansion.

Since the discretionary costs are treated as expenses during the year they are incurred, they tend to suppress the reported profit and the resulting net operating profit rate and net profit rate. Hence, where the discretionary costs are significant, these profit ratios should be supplemented by the discretionary costs-to-sales ratio. A comparison of the performance of two units may reveal that the division with the higher profit rate has lower discretionary costs ratio. A further study may show that the business segment with the higher profit rate (after deducting the discretionary costs in calculating the profit) actually has a lower profit rate before the discretionary costs.

IV. LABOR TIME-COST INDICATORS

Unlike the types of ratios discussed earlier, which use figures exclusively derived from the financial statements, the labor time-cost indicators and all the other ratios treated in the remaining parts of this chapter use information from other sources.

The labor or working time ratios picture the employees' time behavior, their productivity, and their cost to the company. The ratios may lead to investigations which may recommend the hiring of new workers, the shift of the in-house performance of certain functions to outside contractors, or the implementation of measures designed to lift the morale of the workers.

TIME INDICATORS

Attendance Index

$$\frac{\text{total regular hours}}{\text{full attendance hours}}$$

This index indicates the regular hours timed in (overtime excluded) as a percentage of the total hours assuming full attendance. Thus, if there are 100 employees in a section, and the working time is eight hours a day, five days a week, the total hours calculated on full attendance without tardiness is 4,000 hours for a week.

If the regular hours timed in is 3,800, the attendance index is 95%. This is equivalent to 5 workers out for the whole week, or 25 workers out for one day, or the entire work force late for two hours.

A low attendance index might had been caused by bad weather or by several employees taking their authorized leaves at the same time. In this case the low attendance is not a cause of alarm. However, if the index have been slipping over a long period of time, then the underlying causes should be remedied. The cause might have been the deteriorating physical health of the employees or their sagging morale.

Overtime Index

$$\frac{\text{overtime hours}}{\text{regular hours}}$$

This index compares the number of hours for which the personnel are paid overtime pay with the regular hours worked. If the overtime index is consistently high over a long period of time and the cost per overtime hour is higher than the cost per regular hour, then it is time to consider hiring additional workers.

However, there are several constraints to this measure. High training or hiring costs, high employee turnover of new hires, limited working space, or shortage of equipment may not favor the recruitment of new workers.

The overtime index should be related to other indicators. If the rise in overtime index is accompanied by (1) a decline in the productivity rate and (2) an increase in the raw materials usage rate, production reject rate, or sales return rate, then there should be a strong cause for taking new workers in spite of the constraints brought out in the preceding paragraph.

Chargeable Time Index

$$\frac{\text{chargeable hours}}{\text{total hours worked}}$$

The chargeable hours represent the productive time which is charged to specific jobs. The chargeable hours are related to the total hours timed in. The latter is the total of the regular time and overtime.

The index may be calculated either for (1) all the workers in a firm or factory or (2) only for the professional staff in a professional firm or for the production workers in a factory.

In a professional firm, chargeable time is the time billed to clients. In a factory, chargeable time is the time charged to production or job orders. The higher the index, the higher the performance and the higher the level of profitability since the lower is the overhead which drags down the performance.

The nonproductive time represents two components: (1) the time of nonproduction employees as the clerical workers in an office, whose salary is considered as overhead, and (2) the nonbillable time of the production workers or professional staffers in a professional organization.

Nonchargeable Time Index

$$\frac{\text{nonchargeable hours}}{\text{total hours}}$$

This index can be very effective if used only on the production personnel in case of a factory or on the professional staff members in case of a professional office. A high or deteriorating index calls for investigation as to the causes of the high index. Among the possible causes are a lack of business (lack of production orders in a factory or lack of clients for a professional firm), overstaffing, interruptions in the inputs (shortages of materials or equipment breakdowns in a factory), or unexpectedly long retraining periods for employees.

TIME-COST INDICATORS

Cost Per Regular Hour Timed In

$$\frac{\text{total regular time payroll cost for the period}}{\text{regular hours timed in}}$$

This indicator gives the total payroll cost including benefits but excluding overtime cost per regular hour timed in excluding overtime. An increase in cost per hour may indicate a raise in basic pay, enhancement of the benefits, reduced working hours, or more prevalent absenteeism or tardiness.

The cost of one department should be compared to those of other units. A high base pay in one unit may be compensated by low employee benefits or short working hours.

Cost Per Overtime Hour

$$\frac{\text{total overtime cost}}{\text{overtime hours worked}}$$

The cost per overtime hour may be compared with the cost per regular hour. The prevailing view is that overtime cost per hour is higher than the cost per regular hour. However, this concept does not take into account the fringe benefits. If the benefits are included, it may be that the overtime cost per hour is lower than the cost per regular hour.

If the overtime cost per hour is higher than the regular time cost per hour, if the overtime index is high, or if the overtime work is getting to be a normal practice, then it is time to consider getting more regular workers.

Cost Per Chargeable Hour

$$\frac{\text{total employment cost}}{\text{chargeable hours}}$$

Employment cost is the total payroll cost for all personnel. This includes the base pay, benefits, and overtime pay. The chargeable hours were defined earlier.

The cost per chargeable hour incorporates the cost of unproductive time of production personnel as well as the compensation of general, service, or administrative personnel. This unit cost, plus an allowance for nonpersonnel costs such as office rent or telephone expenses, may be compared with the billing rate of professional firms or service organizations or the pricing rate of manufacturing companies. It may also be used in deciding whether to continue performing certain functions in-house, or having them contracted to outside agencies.

Cost Per Hour Timed In

$$\frac{\text{total employment cost}}{\text{total regular and overtime hours timed in}}$$

The personnel and production managers are interested in the three time-cost indicators described above. These indicators may be used as basis in taking corrective measures. However, those at the higher management position levels may be more concerned with the cost per hour timed in as this presents the over-all results. Furthermore, it is less susceptible to period-to-period fluctuations.

V. MANUFACTURING EFFICIENCY INDICATORS

Manufacturing efficiency indicators are used to rate the efficiency by which the manufacturing inputs of labor, materials, and equipment were marshaled to produce goods. Specifically, the indicators are used to relate to the number of units produced: (1) the cost of labor and materials and (2) the labor and equipment time.

Among the possible applications of the manufacturing efficiency indicators are (1) deciding on the bonuses to production personnel, (2) deciding on which production unit will be used as a model in designing work improvement programs and standards, and (3) determining the idle plant capacity which may be utilized to raise the sales volume.

LABOR PRODUCTIVITY INDICES

Labor Productivity Based on Chargeable Hours

$$\frac{\text{total output}}{\text{chargeable hours}}$$

For a factory, the chargeable hours means the productive hours of the production personnel whose labor cost is considered as direct labor. This indicator is especially useful for labor-intensive operations.

One ratio should be calculated for each major type or class of product with similar labor requirements. The grouping in one ratio of products with different labor requirements will dull the effectiveness of the ratio.

The resulting ratios of different periods or different business units, with different degrees of mechanization or automation should be carefully interpreted. Other things being equal, a more automated unit is apt to have a higher labor productivity. Where the level of automation is about the same, a unit with the highest productivity should be entitled to the highest production bonus and should normally serve as a model in improving the work methods of the other units.

Labor Productivity Based on Total Hours Put in by All Employees

$$\frac{\text{total output}}{\text{total hours of all employees}}$$

The labor productivity based on chargeable hours does not take into account two factors: the idle time of the production workers and the hours put in by the nonproduction personnel. A more comprehensive indicator is based on total hours timed in by all employees.

This index is more effective than the prior one in cases where the index is to be used in comparing different periods or different units where there are some differences in the number of nonchargeable hours as a percentage of chargeable time or in the number of nonproduction personnel as a percentage of production workers.

Labor Cost Per Unit of Output

$$\frac{\text{total labor cost}}{\text{total output}}$$

The two labor productivity indices described may be useful for front-line foremen who are concerned just with the output but not with the cost. Higher level managers may find the labor cost per unit of output to be more useful since it includes, in addition to the data built into the labor productivity index formula, the regular pay, fringe benefits, overtime pay, attendance index, and chargeable time index.

RAW MATERIALS PRODUCTIVITY INDICES

Raw Material Usage Rate

$$\frac{\text{total output}}{\text{raw materials quantity used}}$$

This ratio should be computed for each major raw material. This ratio is influenced not only by the production efficiency but also by the raw material specifications and the desired product quality.

The variance analysis for the raw material usage rate is examined in Chapter 23, Section III.

Raw Material Cost Per Unit of Output

$$\frac{\text{total raw material cost}}{\text{total number of units produced}}$$

The reduction of this unit cost is the joint responsibility of the purchasing department, which has jurisdiction over the cost per unit of raw material used, and the production department, which controls the usage rate. The unit cost should be calculated for every major raw material item. If a period-to-period comparison is made, adjustments have to be made for any raw material substitution effected during the periods covered.

EQUIPMENT PRODUCTIVITY INDICES

Equipment Time Per Unit of Output

$$\frac{\text{total equipment running time}}{\text{total output}}$$

This indicates the equipment time required per unit of output. Equipment usage time includes not only the normal equipment running time used in actual manufacturing operations but also the other incidental time required—as retooling, product changeover time, and warm-up or heat-up time. The heating-up time for certain equipment which operates under very high temperatures as cement kilns and glass furnaces is very substantial.

For chemical continuous process equipment such as an oil refinery, there should be no substantial period-to-period variations in the equipment time per output. However, in batch-type physical product operations as sawmill or garment factories, there may be substantial period-to-period variations depending upon the quantity and specifications of the materials as well as the desired types of products.

Equipment Capacity Utilization Percentage

$$\frac{\text{total output}}{\text{total rated capacity}}$$

The rated capacity of a piece of equipment is the maximum quantity of output which the equipment can produce over a period of time. The technical capacity, which is given by the equipment manufacturer, may be different from the commercially attainable capacity. Some equipment suppliers are notoriously known for overstating the rated capacities of their equipment, while some established, conservative makers intentionally understate the rated capacities of their equipment.

For batch-type, physical process manufacturing operation, such as the assembly of cars or computers, the rated capacity may be determined on a one-shift, five-day basis or on a two- or three-shift basis, depending upon the industry practice.

The utilization percentage is used both to assess past decisions and provide information in planning for the future. An unusually low utilization percentage for a piece of equipment five years old means that the firm erred in estimating the market for its product. The capacity utilization percentage may also be used as a starting point of an analysis to formulate a sales expansion scheme to capture market share so as to utilize the otherwise idle capacity.

VI. SALES PRODUCTIVITY INDICATORS

The sales productivity indicators point out the degree of performance of the individual salespeople and different sales units, not only in producing sales but also in collecting the receivables and in generating profit. The indicators can be used in determining the awards and incentives for the sales force and in ascertaining compliance of the marketing department with the corporate strategies.

SALESPERSON NONFINANCIAL PERFORMANCE RATIOS

Number of Calls Per Salesperson-Day

$$\frac{\text{total number of calls on customers}}{\text{number of salesperson-days}}$$

This ratio indicates the level of sales efforts exerted by the sales force. This ratio can be made meaningful if the ratio is obtained on a per salesperson basis and then by department. This process will identify the salespeople and departments which are trying their best.

The ratio can be made more informative if the number of calls by salespeople and departments is broken down into new and old products, new and old customers, and new and old sales territories. The term new has to be defined: an example is a product introduced during the fiscal year or a new customer acquired during the same period.

The information on the new and old products, customers, and territories gives an indication of the direction of concentration which the salespeople and departments are pursuing. This direction should be checked with the company strategy to ascertain compliance.

Sales Quantity Per Salesperson-Day

$$\frac{\text{total number of units sold}}{\text{number of salesperson-days}}$$

Although the number of calls per salesperson-day indicates the level of activity attained in a given period, it does not reveal the results. The salespeople can be making several calls, but the calls can be useless if they do not generate sales. Hence the significance of the sales quantity per salesperson-day ratio.

The sales quantity per salesperson-day should be segregated by salesperson, by department, by new and old products, by new and old customers, and by new and old territories.

SALESPERSON FINANCIAL PERFORMANCE RATIOS

Sales Dollar Per Salesperson-Day

$$\frac{\text{total sales in dollars}}{\text{number of salesperson-days}}$$

The sales quantity per salesperson-day is effective if the salespeople are selling only one type of product and the product has only one selling price. However, this ratio becomes misleading if the salespeople in a department handle products with different selling prices. Hence, a more meaningful ratio is the sales dollar per salesperson-day.

Contribution Margin Per Salesman-Day

$$\frac{\text{total contribution margin}}{\text{number of salesperson-days}}$$

The sales dollar per salesperson-day is a good index if the products have identical profit margins. However, this is seldom encountered in practice. Hence, the sales dollar per salesperson-day has to be reinforced by the contribution margin per salesperson-day ratio.

For a merchandising firm, the contribution margin is defined as the sales less the following: cost of merchandise sold, compensation of the salespeople, and the salesperson's direct or variable sales expenses. The net value of the sales returns may also be deducted from the sales.

For a manufacturing firm, the cost of merchandise sold is substituted with the variable portion of the cost of goods manufactured and sold.

Like the sales quantity per salesperson-day, the contribution margin per salesperson-day may be broken down into margin per salesperson, average margin per salesperson in each department, margin from old and new products, margin from old and new customers, and margin from old and new territories. This information reveals the salesperson, departments, products, customers, and territories that are contributing most to the profit, and hence should be entitled to the greatest rewards and incentives.

Collections Per Salesperson-Day

$$\frac{\text{total collections}}{\text{salesperson-days}}$$

Sales dollars and contribution margins are useless unless the receivables are converted to cash. Hence, the significance of the collections per salesperson-day ratio.

If the salespeople are not engaged in collection, this ratio shows their effectiveness not only in generating sales but also in recommending credit sales. If they are also collecting the sales, the ratio reflects their efficiency in this undertaking as well.

Other information which will help determine the performance of the salespeople in this regard are the size of their receivables in relation to the sales and the aging schedule of their sales receivables.

VII. BUILDING UTILIZATION RATES

The building utilization rates are used to evaluate the operations of real estate-based businesses: store-based retailers, hotels, apartment buildings, office rentals, and shopping complexes. The utilization rates can be used to compare the performance of retailers offering different levels of service and prices, hotels charging varying room rates, or commercial buildings providing different sizes of common spaces.

The proper application of utilization rates provides incentives to the managers of retailing outfits, hotels, or commercial buildings to extract the highest level of profit measured in terms of dollars out of a fixed resource: building floor area measured in terms of square feet.

MERCHANDISING OPERATIONS UTILIZATION RATE

Sales Per Square Foot

$$\frac{\text{net sales}}{\text{store space in square feet}}$$

One objective of merchandising operations is to maximize the sales generated by one scarce resource—the store space. If this is used as a measure of performance of the merchandising managers, the managers will be prodded to offer either high-priced items or fast-moving merchandise.

Operating Profit Per Square Foot

$$\frac{\text{operating profit}}{\text{store space in square feet}}$$

The sales per square foot measure cannot be used to compare the performance of the regular retailers add high markups to their cost, and those of the discounters who sell at much lower prices and offer less service.

Where differences exist in the markup percentage or extent of service, the operating profit per square foot will provide a better guide than will the sales per square foot.

OCCUPANCY RATES

Hotels and Apartments Occupancy Rate

$$\frac{\text{number of unit-days occupied during the period}}{\text{total number of unit-days available}}$$

The hotel room occupancy rate is established by dividing the number of room-days occupied for a month or year by the total number of room-days available for the same period. For an apartment, the number of apartment units is used in lieu of the rooms.

There are two ways of pushing up the occupancy rate of a hotel. One, during the hotel planning stage (before the construction), is by deciding on the appropriate size of the hotel. Too large a hotel size in terms of rooms will result in so many unoccupied rooms. On the other hand, too small a size will not be able to attract enough visitors or justify the common facilities.

The second, during the operating period, is by getting more visitors or hotel guests through sustained marketing efforts.

The occupancy rate may also be increased by accepting short-time occupancy—for less than a day. Since the available number of room-days is determined by multiplying the total number of rooms by the number of days, while an occupancy for less than a day is counted as if it were for a day, a multiple daily occupancy can sometimes push up the occupancy rate to beyond 100%.

Commercial Buildings Occupancy Rate

$$\frac{\text{number of square-foot-days occupied during the period}}{\text{number of square-foot-days available}}$$

For buildings rented out to several offices or stores, the standard of measurement used in hotels and apartments, that is, rooms or units, does not apply because of the great disparity in the sizes of the floor areas leased to each tenant. A more flexible measure is the floor area in square feet. The area leased out is compared with the net rentable area—that is, after deducting the common areas consisting of corridors, elevators, and other common facilities.

RENTAL VALUES PER FLOOR AREA

Average Rental Value Per Square Foot of Net Rentable Area

$$\frac{\text{total rental value per month or year}}{\text{net rentable area in square feet}}$$

The two previously discussed indicators, while universally used, do not incorporate the dollar values. Although they are useful in comparing the performance of a hotel or other type of rental building during one period to the performance during another period, they may not be adequate to compare the efficiency of one building with another. For instance, two hotels in one general area, with the same standard of physical facilities and services and the same level of operating costs, may have different occupancy rates. But it does not necessarily follow that the one with the higher occupancy has better performance unless the room rates they charge are converted to dollar value per square foot. This measure may reveal that the lower occupancy rate of one hotel is more than made up by the higher charge per square foot.

Average Rental Value Per Square Foot of Gross Area

$$\frac{\text{total rental value per month or year}}{\text{gross building area in square feet}}$$

The rent per square foot of net rentable area may not be effective in comparing two or more hotels, apartment buildings, or office buildings with varying levels of common space as a percentage of net rentable space. A building with higher rentable value per net rentable space is not necessarily more profitable if it has provided for liberal common spaces. A measure that incorporates the cost of common spaces is the rental value per square foot of gross area.

EXHIBIT 21.1:
Asset Distribution Ratios (dollars in $1,000)

Name of ratio	Formula	BASE DATA*			RATIO		Year 2 as a percentage of year 1
		Year 1	Year 2		Year 1	Year 2	
Operating assets ratio	total operating assets / total assets	$84,600 / $88,500	$112,019 / $133,919	=	0.96	0.84	87.5%
Total assets composition percentages	Operating assets						
	Working capital	$55,600	$ 89,019		62.82%	66.47%	105.8
	Property, plant, and equipment	29,000	23,000		32.77	17.17	52.4
	Total operating assets	84,600	112,019		95.59%	83.65%	87.5
	Nonoperating assets†	3,900	21,900		4.41	16.35	371.1
	Total assets	$88,500	$133,919		100.00%	100.00%	
Gross working capital composition percentages	Cash	$ 200	$ 200		0.4%	0.2%	
	Trade receivables‡	39,800	62,920		71.6	70.7	
	Inventories	0	0				
	Finished goods§	10,000	20,408		18.0	22.9	
	Raw materials¶	5,600	5,491		10.1	6.2	
	Total current assets	$55,600	$ 89,019		100.0%	100.0%	

*Base data represent end-of-year balances.

Nonoperating assets	Year 1	Year 2
Old accounts receivable	$ 200	$ 200
Slow-moving raw material inventory	400	400
Construction in progress		18,000
Long-term stock investment	3,300	3,300
Total nonoperating assets	$ 3,900	$ 21,900

†Net of $200,000 old accounts receivable.
§Based on full costing method of inventory valuation.
¶Net of $400,000 slow-moving raw material inventory.

EXHIBIT 21.2:
General Turnover Ratios (dollars in $1,000)

Name of ratio	Formula	BASE DATA*			RATIO		Year 2 as a percentage of year 1
		Year 1	Year 2		Year 1	Year 2	
Total assets turnover	sales / total assets	$120,000 / $ 93,000	$143,000 / $111,210	=	1.29	1.29	99.7%
Operating assets turnover	sales / operating assets	$120,000 / $ 87,550	$143,000 / $ 98,310	=	1.37	1.45	106.1%
Net operating assets turnover	sales / net operating assets	$120,000 / $ 81,550	$143,000 / $ 88,961	=	1.47	1.61	109.2%
Gross working capital turnover	sales / gross working capital	$120,000 / $ 56,150	$143,000 / $ 72,910	=	2.14	1.96	91.8%
Long-term operating assets turnover	sales / property, plant, and equipment	$120,000 / $ 32,000	$143,000 / $ 26,000	=	3.75	5.50	146.7%
Incremental operating assets turnover	incremental sales / incremental operating assets		$ 23,000 / $ 10,760	=		2.14	

*Base data for balance sheet items represent average balances.

EXHIBIT 21.3:
Accounts Receivable Ratios (dollars in $1,000)

Name of ratio	Formula	BASE DATA			RATIO		Year 2 as a percentage of year 1
		Year 1	Year 2		Year 1	Year 2	
Accounts receivable turnover	sales / accounts receivable	$120,000 / $ 40,000	$143,000 / $ 51,560	=	3.0	2.8	92.4%
Accounts receivable collection period (in days)	number of days per year / accounts receivable turnover	365 / 3.0	365 / 2.8	=	122	132	108.2%
Incremental accounts receivable turnover	incremental sales / incremental receivables		$ 23,000 / $ 11,560	=		2.0	
Incremental accounts receivable collection period (in days)	number of days per year / incremental receivable turnover		365 / 2.0	=		183	

EXHIBIT 21.4:
Treatment of Cash Sales and Dead Accounts* (dollars in $1,000)

Treatment of cash sales	Cash sales included	Cash sales excluded
Sales		
Credit sales	$60,000	$60,000
Cash sales	20,000	0
Total sales	$80,000	$60,000
Total receivables	$10,000	$10,000
Turnover	8.0	6.0
Collection period in days	46	61

Treatment of dead accounts	Dead accounts included	Dead accounts excluded
Credit sales	$60,000	$60,000
Receivables		
Current receivables	$ 9,500	$ 9,500
Dead receivables	500	
Total	$10,000	$ 9,500
Turnover	6.0	6.3
Collection period in days	61	58

*The figures used in this exhibit are not related to those in the other exhibits in this chapter.

EXHIBIT 21.5:
Finished Goods Inventory Ratios (dollars in $1,000)

Name of ratio	Formula	BASE DATA			RATIO		Year 2 as a percentage of year 1
		Year 1	Year 2		Year 1	Year 2	
Finished goods inventory turnover	$\dfrac{\text{cost of goods sold}}{\text{finished goods inventory}}$	$\dfrac{\$60,000}{\$10,000}$	$\dfrac{\$63,410}{\$15,204}$	=	6.00	4.17	69.5%
Finished goods inventory period (in days)	$\dfrac{\text{number of days per year}}{\text{finished goods turnover}}$	$\dfrac{365}{6}$	$\dfrac{365}{4}$	=	61	88	143.9%
Incremental finished goods turnover	$\dfrac{\text{increase in cost of sales}}{\text{increase in finished goods inventory}}$		$\dfrac{\$3,410}{\$5,204}$	=		0.66	
Incremental finished goods inventory period	$\dfrac{\text{number of days per year}}{\text{inventory turnover}}$		$\dfrac{365}{0.66}$	=		557	

EXHIBIT 21.6:
Raw Materials Inventory and Accounts Payable Ratios (dollars in $1,000)

Name of ratio	Formula	BASE DATA			RATIO		Year 2 as a percentage of year 1
		Year 1	Year 2		Year 1	Year 2	
Raw materials inventory turnover	$\dfrac{\text{raw materials used}}{\text{raw materials inventory*}}$	$\dfrac{\$24,000}{\$\ 6,000}$	$\dfrac{\$33,294}{\$\ 5,946}$	=	4.00	5.60	140.0%
Raw materials inventory period (in days)	$\dfrac{\text{number of days per year}}{\text{raw materials turnover}}$	$\dfrac{365}{4}$	$\dfrac{365}{6}$	=	91	65	71.4%
Accounts payable turnover	$\dfrac{\text{purchases}^\dagger}{\text{accounts payable}}$	$\dfrac{\$24,000}{\$\ 6,000}$	$\dfrac{\$33,185}{\$\ 9,349}$	=	4.00	3.55	88.7%
Accounts payable payment period (in days)	$\dfrac{\text{number of days per year}}{\text{accounts payable turnover}}$	$\dfrac{365}{4}$	$\dfrac{365}{4}$	=	91	103	112.7%
Suppliers' financing ratio	$\dfrac{\text{accounts payable}}{\text{raw materials inventory}}$	$\dfrac{\$\ 6,000}{\$\ 6,000}$	$\dfrac{\$\ 9,349}{\$\ 5,946}$	=	1.00	1.57	157.2%

*Average balance without deducting old inventories.

†Purchases

Raw materials used	$24,000	$33,294
Reduction in raw materials inventory		(109)
Purchases during the year	$24,000	$33,185

EXHIBIT 21.7:
Sales Profitability Ratios (dollars in $1,000)

Name of ratio	Formula	BASE DATA			RATIO		Year 2 as a percentage of year 1
		Year 1	Year 2		Year 1	Year 2	
Gross profit rate	gross profit / sales	$ 60,000 / $120,000	$ 79,590 / $143,000	=	50.0%	55.7%	111.3%
Net operating profit rate	net operating profit / sales	$ 17,000 / $120,000	$ 22,063 / $143,000	=	14.2%	15.4%	108.9%
Net profit rate	net profit / sales	$ 8,192 / $120,000	$ 10,716 / $143,000	=	6.8%	7.5%	109.8%
Incremental sales net profit rate	increase in net profit / increase in sales		$ 2,525 / $ 23,000	=		11.0%	

511

Chapter 22

TRADITIONAL VARIANCE ANALYSIS

The purpose of variance analysis is to pinpoint the causes of the deviations of the actual results of operations from the plan or budget. The causes of the deviations are used as a basis in formulating corrective actions on measures currently being implemented, drawing up new profit improvement measures, preparing more accurate forecasts, or rewarding managers for their performance.

This chapter illustrates the applications of the four common types of conventional techniques of variance analysis. Three of the techniques cover the analysis of a product in isolation; one relates to a product in a group. Of the one-product analysis techniques, two do not incorporate revised budgets in the analysis work and one utilizes a revised budget.

Some of the present tools can pinpoint the deviation in the profit which results from changes in the sales volume, selling price, and cost per unit of the inputs. However, not one of them can quantify the variation in the profit caused by fluctuations in (1) the total industry sales, (2) the market share, and (3) the operating efficiencies. Operating efficiencies are measured by the usage rate of inputs per unit of goods produced as labor productivity or raw material usage rate.

This functional deficiency hampers the effectiveness of the current techniques since a windfall rise in industry sales which is not due to management performance can hide even a precipitous fall in market share or deterioration in operating efficiencies, both of which are within management control. In other words, management can still be credited for a basically poor performance, but one which is camouflaged by an extraneous beneficial event.

I. SALES AND VARIABLE COSTS— RESULTS OF VARIANCE ANALYSIS

The variance analysis techniques are applied to a hypothetical company with two products. The improvement in the total sales from $9,020,000 per budget to $9,648,000 actual, and the corresponding increase in the contribution margin from $3,650,000 to $3,705,000 as shown in Exhibit 22.1 superficially indicates a good performance. However, a closer look at Exhibit 22.1 reveals that, in spite of the apparent good performance, two ominous signs emerged:

1. The contribution margin of product A, the major product in terms of total contribution margin, declined.
2. There is a shift in the product mix—the share of product A, which is the product with the higher margin contribution per unit, dropped from 60% of total company sales per budget to the 52% actual.

In this particular case, the objective of variance analysis is to dig into the major causes of the drop in the total contribution margin of product A. The different existing traditional tools of variance analysis were utilized to determine the causes of the decline:

Type of analysis	Variances revealed	Basis of quantity variance of the inputs	Application shown in
1. One-product	Quantity and price	Sales volume	Exhibit 22.6
2. One-product analysis	Quantity and price	Quantity of the inputs	Exhibit 22.7
3. One-product analysis	Quantity and price; planning and performance	Quantity of the inputs	Exhibit 22.10
4. Multiproduct analysis	Quantity, price, and product mix	Not applicable	Exhibit 22.11

The results of the four methods are summarized in Exhibit 22.12. All the techniques are deficient in that not one of them gives information on the effect on the profit, of changes in the following:

1. Factors normally under the influence of management
   a. Market share

      b. Usage rate or operating efficiency—quantity of input per unit of product manufactured or sold, as raw material yield rate or labor productivity

  2. Factors normally beyond the control of management

      a. Total industry sales

II. SALES AND VARIABLE COSTS— ONE-PRODUCT VARIANCE ANALYSIS

Although the illustrated company has two products, we will start by analyzing one product—product A—in isolation, that is, without any reference to the other product.

Under the conventional method of variance analysis, the differences between the budget and actual performance of the revenues and the individual items of costs are segregated into two categories: quantity or volume variance and price or cost variance. The applicability of this segregation of variances to sales revenues and variable costs are explained in the paragraphs that follow.

SALES VARIANCES

Sales in terms of dollars are determined by the sales volume in physical units and the selling price per unit.

Hence, the total sales variance is composed of the sales volume or quantity variance and the unit selling price or simply price variance. Changes in the selling price may be caused by general price fluctuations, as those due to inflation or industry trends, or due to specific company strategy.

VARIABLE COST VARIANCES

For the cost items as materials used or direct labor, the total cost is determined by three factors: (1) the sales volume; (2) the usage rate, which is the number of units of input required to make or sell one unit of the product; and (3) the price or cost per unit of input.

Thus, there are three factors affecting the total cost of an input. However, the traditional variance analysis recognizes only two types of variances, namely, quantity and price. Hence, under the conventional method, deviations in any two of the three factors are combined into only one variance.

The quantity variance in the analysis of costs may pertain either to the sales volume or the input volume. If the quantity variance refers to the *sales volume*, the *price* variance is composed of two factors: (1) the cost per unit of input and (2) the usage rate, which is the volume or quantity of input required per unit of sale.

If the quantity variance represents the *input volume*, the *quantity* variance is composed of two variables (1) the sales volume and (2) the input usage rate.

Product Sales Volume Deviation Used as the Basis of Calculating the Quantity Variance of the Variable Costs (Exhibit 22.2). The use of the sales volume variance in computing the quantity variance of the raw materials, labor, and other costs of inputs facilitates the analysis of the variances on a productwide basis, cutting across the different cost items. Furthermore, it will relate the costs to the sales revenues. The use of only one benchmark would assure consistency in the evaluation of the deviations.

Under this alternative, the total variance of each cost item is composed of two components: the sales volume variance and the price variance. The latter in turn is affected by (1) the cost per unit of input and (2) the usage rate or the number of units of the inputs (as pounds of materials or hours of labor) required to produce or sell one unit of a product.

In the case of interest, the cost per sales unit is determined by the balance of the outstanding receivables and the monthly interest rate. The outstanding balance of the receivables, in turn, is determined by the selling price per unit and the collection period in months.

Input Quantity Deviation Used as the Basis of Calculating the Quantity Variance of the Variable Costs (Exhibit 22.3). The use of the sales volume variance as the quantity variance of the variable costs may be advisable for product cost analysis in general. However, functional managers like production or human resources managers may prefer to emphasize the facilities they control or the accountabilities they manage. From the viewpoint of a human resources manager, for example, the number of personnel or the labor hours expended are more relevant than the sales volume. Similarly, a purchasing manager will be more concerned with the raw materials used or the merchandise purchased, and the finance manager, with the value of financing required. Hence, for use at their level, the input quantity variance should be used as the basis of calculating the quantity variance of the input costs.

Under this method, the input quantity, as raw material quantity used, is influenced not only by the sales volume but also by the usage rate. The exhibit gives the components of the input volume for materials, labor, and interest.

DETAILED DATA FOR VARIANCE ANALYSIS

Product Sales Volume Deviation Used as the Basis of Calculating the Quantity Variance of the Variable Costs (Exhibit 22.4). The detailed information needed in preparing the variance analysis is given, based on the variance structure in Exhibit 22.2.

Thus, for raw materials, the usage rate or quantity of materials required per unit of sales is multiplied by the cost per unit of material in order to arrive at the material cost per unit of sales. The difference between the cost per sales unit per budget and per actual gives the price variance. The cost per sales unit is then multiplied with the sales volume to arrive at the total raw material cost.

Input Quantity Deviation Used as the Basis of Calculating the Quantity Variance of the Variable Costs (Exhibit 22.5). This uses the same information as in Exhibit 22.4, except that the information was rearranged in order to follow the structure in Exhibit 22.3.

CALCULATION OF THE VARIANCES—METHOD 1

The popular method of estimating the variances using the conventional technique is demonstrated in Exhibits 22.6 and 22.7. In Exhibit 22.6 the quantity variances of the variable costs or inputs, as $86,400 for the raw material, were calculated using the 36 *product sales volume* deviation. The base data in Exhibit 22.6 were taken from Exhibit 22.4.

In Exhibit 22.7, the quantity variances of the inputs, such as $211,200 for the raw materials, were estimated by utilizing the *input quantity* deviation, which is 1,056 for the material, rather than the 36 sales volume variance. The base data were taken from Exhibit 22.5.

The formula for computing the variances in Exhibits 22.6 and 22.7 are

quantity variance = change in quantity × budget price
price variance   = change in price   × actual quantity

Product Sales Volume Deviation Used as the Basis of Calculating the Quantity Variance (Exhibit 22.6).

SALES VARIANCE. The total sales variance is $324,000, which is the difference between the budgeted sales of $5,940,000 and the actual sales of $5,616,000. This variance is not favorable, or reduces the profit, since the actual sales is lower than the budget. Since there is no change in the selling price according to Exhibit 22.4, all this variance is due to the change in the sales volume. The $324,000 quantity variance is computed by multiplying the 36-unit shortfall in sales (660 units per budget compared with the 624 actual) by the budget price of $9,000 per unit. This sales variance is noted in Exhibits 22.6 and 22.7.

RAW MATERIAL VARIANCE. Since there is a change in both the sales volume and the raw material cost per unit of sales, there are two components in the raw material variance: quantity and price. The quantity variance is calculated by multiplying the 36-unit decline in sales by the budgeted material cost per unit of sales of $2,400. The $2,400 was obtained from Exhibit 22.4.

The price variance was estimated by multiplying the $75 increase in cost per sales unit per Exhibit 22.4, by the actual sales volume of 624.

OTHER COSTS—VARIANCE.   The sales commissions expense has no price variance because there is no change in the commission expense per unit of sales. This is due to the fact that there is no change in the commission rate.

Since the product sales volume deviation was used as the basis of the quantity variance of the inputs, all the quantity variances utilize the 36-unit decline in the sales. Furthermore, all the price variances use the 624 actual sales quantity.

FAVORABLE/UNFAVORABLE VARIANCES.   A variance is favorable if it improves the net profit. The decline in the sales of $324,000 is an unfavorable variance since it decreases the net profit or contribution margin. The total decline in the variable costs of $108,216 is favorable because it enhances the profitability. The resulting contribution margin variance is not favorable since the margin became smaller.

Input Quantity Deviation Used as the Basis of Calculating the Quantity Variance of the Variable Costs (Exhibit 22.7).

VARIABLE COSTS—VARIANCE.   The data used in Exhibit 22.7 were taken from Exhibit 22.5. The variances were calculated using the formula as given earlier which are also the same as those used in Exhibit 22.6.

For the interest expense, the quantity variance does not represent any physical unit, but rather the $3,672,000 change in the dollar value of the balance of outstanding receivables. The price variance of 0.1% refers to the change in the monthly interest rate.

Comparison of the Quantity and Price Variances of the Variable Costs (Exhibits 22.6 and 22.7).
Although the total variances of sales and each cost item in Exhibit 22.6 are the same as those in Exhibit 22.7, the quantity and price variances of the inputs of material, labor, and interest are widely divergent. This is caused by the differences in the components of quantity and price variances in the two exhibits:

	Exhibit 22.6	Exhibit 22.7
Used as the basis in calculating the quantity variance of the inputs	Product sales volume deviation	Input quantity deviation
Components of quantity variance	Product sales volume deviation	Sales volume and usage rate deviation
Components of price variance	Cost per unit of input and usage rate deviation	Cost per unit of input deviation

CALCULATION OF THE VARIANCES—METHOD 2
(Exhibit 22.8)

Exhibits 22.6 and 22.7 show one way of calculating the variances. Another method is illustrated in Exhibit 22.8. Under this procedure, the total variable cost, or the total sales revenue, is calculated three times using different assumptions:

Calculation 1: Based on budget quantity and budget price
Calculation 2: Based on actual quantity and budget price
Calculation 3: Based on actual quantity and actual price

The difference between the results of calculations 1 and 2 represents the quantity variance; between those of the 2 and 3, the price variance; and between those of 1 and 3, the total variance.

With the given information, the results of this method and the one illustrated in Exhibit 22.7 are the same.

PLANNING AND PERFORMANCE VARIANCE
(Exhibit 22.9)

The variances that were estimated earlier represent the changes between the budget and the actual results. Budgets are normally prepared before the start of the period that is being evaluated. The differences between the budget and actual performance may be considered as falling into either one of two types of variances: (1) planning variance and (2) performance variance.

Planning Variance. This arises when expected industry or other environmental developments do not materialize. For instance, at the start of the period under review, sales were forecast to be 660 units based on a review of supply and demand. However, due to actual conditions obtaining in the industry, the actual sales realized is only 624. The 36-sales-unit variance may then be considered as a planning error, and not a performance blunder.

The statement that the 36-unit-variance is a planning error is a very simplified statement which may hold for the moment just for the purpose of illustrating the application of this particular method. (In reality, the product sales volume variance is a function of three primary factors: industry sales, market share, and product mix. Of these three, only industry sales is generally considered as beyond management control. Management has some degree of control over the other two. An analysis segregating the effects of each of these three forces is undertaken in the next chapter.)

Performance Variance (Exhibit 22.9). The expected collection period of sales as given in Exhibit 22.4 is 6 months. If the increase in collection period to 7 months is due to inefficiency of the collection department, then the increase in interest rates due to the lengthening of the collection period is a performance variance.

Revised Budget (Exhibit 22.9). Due to the planning error, which usually affects the sales volume, some companies have started to use a second budget, which revises the one prepared at the start of the period. The revised budget is prepared *after* the end of the period covered by the budget. This budget incorporates the actual environmental conditions but retains the standard costs and usage rates contained in the original budget.

The exhibit shows the original and revised budgets, actual results, and variances. The original budget and actual results are the same as in Exhibit 22.1.

The planning variance is the difference between the original and revised budgets. The performance variance is the difference between the revised budget and the actual results.

Variance Analysis (Exhibit 22.10). An analysis of the changes from the original budget to the revised budget and from the revised budget to the actual performance is made in Exhibit 22.10. All the differences due to the sales volume deviation have been removed from the variances of the inputs and are consolidated in the sales quantity variance. This variance of $137,160 was computed by multiplying the 36-unit difference between the original budget sales volume and the actual by the $3,810 contribution to overhead per sales unit per the budget in Exhibit 22.9 (lower table). The $137,160 sales variance is also the same as the total (contribution margin) planning variance in Exhibit 22.9.

Since the effect of the sales volume fluctuation had been taken out from the variances of the material, labor, and interest, the variances of these inputs are comprised of only two items: differences in the usage rate and fluctuations in the cost per unit of input.

The $48,600 quantity variance in sales commissions per Exhibit 22.7 does not appear in Exhibit 22.10 because the commissions' quantity variance, which is based on sales volume deviation, has been absorbed already in the $137,160 sales quantity variance in Exhibit 22.10.

Relationship of Exhibit 22.10 with Exhibit 22.6. For material, labor, and interest, the *combined quantity and price variances* in Exhibit 22.10 are equivalent to the *price variance* for these inputs in Exhibit 22.6. For instance, the total of the quantity and price variances for the raw material is $46,800 per Exhibit 22.10, which is equivalent to the price variance alone in Exhibit 22.6. The reason for this is that for the cost inputs in Exhibit 22.6 (1) the quantity variance is composed of the sales volume deviation and (2) the price variance consists of (a) the usage rate change and (b) the cost per unit of input changes.

On the other hand, in Exhibit 22.10 (1) the product sales volume deviation (equivalent to the quantity variance in Exhibit 22.6) has been completely taken out of the material, labor, and interest variances and included in the $137,160 sales quantity variance, (2) the quantity variance of the inputs refers only to the usage rate change, and (3) the price variance refers to the cost per unit of input change. Thus, for the inputs, the total variance represents the usage rate and cost per unit differences, which is the same as the price variance alone in Exhibit 22.6.

In Exhibit 22.10, the total product sales volume variance of $137,160 was placed under sales quantity variance. In Exhibit 22.6, the equivalent amount was spread out among the five quantity variances, as follows:

Unfavorable variance—decline in revenues		
Sales		$324,000
Favorable variances—decline in costs		
Raw materials	$ 86,400	
Direct labor	32,400	
Commissions	48,600	
Interest	19,440	186,840
Net unfavorable variance		$137,160

Relationship of Exhibit 22.10 to Exhibit 22.7. For the inputs, the price variances in Exhibit 22.10 are the same as those in Exhibit 22.7. The reason is that the price variances in both tables have only one component, that is, the change in the cost per unit of input. This is distinguished from the price variance in Exhibit 22.6, which includes not only the differences in the cost per unit of input but also the changes in the usage rate of the inputs.

III. SALES AND VARIABLE COSTS— MULTIPRODUCT VARIANCE ANALYSIS

The prior discussions centered on the review of a product in isolation, that is, not in relation to any other product. If there are two or more products, the review of the variances may include changes in the product mix, which is the portion of the total company sales or product group volume that one product holds.

Products in a Group (Exhibit 22.11). In many instances, the sale or production of one product adversely affects another one. Thus, a sale of one brand of car may be made at the expense of the sale of a similar car of the same manufacturer. In like manner, where the production capacity is limited, the capacity allocated for the production of one product has to be taken from another.

If the company sells two or more products, the shift from the more profitable products to marginal ones will depress the overall company profit margins, although the firm may be able to attain the budgeted dollar sales. The change in company profitability due to the variation in product mix is called product mix variance.

There are at least two conventional methods of analysis for this situation. The first one is based not on the sales revenues and specific variable cost items like raw materials used and sales commissions, but only on the contribution margin. This method gives three variances: quantity and price like the ones derived from the conventional method for products in isolation, plus a third: product mix variance.

Thus the $216,000 decline in the contribution margin for product A as shown in Exhibit 22.1 may be segregated into the three types of variances as indicated in Exhibit 22.11.

The procedure for calculating the variances in Exhibit 22.11 is the same as that in Exhibit 22.8, except that the mix variance has been added, and the price variance had been substituted with the contribution margin variance.

A second method is based on the averages and totals of the products in the group. This method is not effective since it does not present the quantities for each product, and there are normally material differences in the prices, costs, and quantities involved in the different products. Hence the use of averages does not give a clear picture and is not illustrated here.

IV. SALES AND VARIABLE COSTS— EVALUATION OF CONVENTIONAL TECHNIQUES

DIFFERENCES IN THE RESULTS (Exhibit 22.12)

The use of the four different traditional variance analysis techniques produce different results as indicated in Exhibit 22.12. The discrepancies in the results arise from

1. The failure to recognize and present separately the effects of the three causes of the variances of the variable costs or cost inputs. These causes are sales volume, usage rate, and cost per unit of input.

2. The inconsistency in the coverage of the price and quantity variances. Where the sales volume deviation is used as the basis in calculating the quantity variance of the inputs, the price variance of the inputs include the changes in both the usage rate and the cost per unit. Where the input quantity deviation is utilized as the basis in calculating the quantity variance of the inputs, the quantity variance of the input includes the changes in both the sales volume and the input usage rate.

3. The inconsistency in the bases of calculations. For the analysis of a product in isolation, the variances are computed based on the sales revenues and each item of cost; for the analysis of products in a group, the variance is based on the contribution margin.

In addition to these structural weaknesses, all the conventional methods possess inherent limitations in the way the variances are calculated:

1. *Dependability of the variances on the sequencing of the calculations.* For the analysis of products in a group, the variances are calculated in this sequence: volume variance, product mix variance, and margin variance. If the sequence is changed, the variance for each of these causes is also changed.
2. *Inconsistency in the treatment of combined price and quantity variance.* For the analysis of a product in isolation, the variance resulting from the combined effect of price and quantity is sometimes added to the quantity variance and sometimes to the price variance.

These limitations are discussed next.

FAILURE TO RECOGNIZE AND PRESENT THE THREE CAUSES OF VARIANCES

The total budgeted cost of each input item varies from the actual due to three factors: sales volume, usage rate, and cost per unit of input. Of the four traditional methods, only the technique which uses the revised budget as the standard of comparison (Exhibit 22.10) recognizes as such these three variances. However, although it identifies these three variances, this technique does not properly present the sales volume variance because it lumps together in one amount ($137,160 in the illustration), under the sales quantity variance, the effect of sales volume variance on all the specific input items of materials, labor, commission, and interest.

INCONSISTENCY IN THE COVERAGE OF THE PRICE AND QUANTITY VARIANCES

The variance analysis for products in isolation which do not use revised budgets utilizes only two variances—quantity and price—although in reality there are three variances.

Because of this restriction, the *method which uses sales volume deviation* as the basis of the input or variable cost quantity variance combines in the *price* variance of the inputs the effect of changes in the usage rate and the cost per unit of the input. (See Exhibit 22.2.) Because of this combination of coverage, the price variance under this method (see Exhibit 22.6) is equivalent to the total of the price and quantity variances under the method which uses the revised budget (Exhibit 22.10). For instance, as shown in Exhibit 22.12, the material price variance of $46,800 under the first column is the total of the quantity and price variances for the materials as shown in the last column of the same exhibit.

On the other hand, the *method which uses the input volume deviation* as the basis of the input quantity variance consolidates in the *quantity* variance the results of changes in the sales volume and in the usage rate. (See Exhibit 22.3.)

Because of the inconsistencies in the compositions of the price and quantity variances, the price and quantity variances shown by these two methods are far from each other. See the first two columns of Exhibit 22.12.

The composition of the quantity and price variances and their applicability to sales, variable cost, or contribution margin under the four conventional methods of analysis are summarized in Exhibit 22.13.

INCONSISTENCY IN THE BASIS OF CALCULATIONS

The variance analysis of a product in isolation is done for the sales revenue and each of the variable costs. On the other hand, the analysis of a product in a group is done only for the contribution margin, which is the combined figure for the sales and variable costs. In other words, it does not show the effect on the sales revenues, and each of the items of costs, of the fluctuations in the sales volume, usage rates, and price levels.

DEPENDABILITY OF THE VARIANCES ON THE SEQUENCING OF THE CALCULATIONS (Exhibits 22.11 and 22.14)

In Exhibit 22.11, the quantity, mix, and price (or margin) variances were computed, one at a time, in this sequence. However, there is actually no logic for following this sequence. In reality, the company sets first the selling prices of the products, which affect the contribution margin. The customers then buy the products. The customers' behavior influences the mix and the volume. If the sequence of calculations were changed to conform to this timing of events, the variances will also change, as shown:

	From Exhibit 22.11	*From Exhibit 22.14*
Sequence of calculations		
Calculation 1	Volume	Margin
Calculation 2	Mix	Mix
Calculation 3	Margin	Volume

	From Exhibit 22.11	From Exhibit 22.14
Resulting variances		
Volume	$228,600	$191,568
Mix	(365,760)	(324,192)
Margin	(78,624)	(83,160)
Total	$215,784	$215,784

INCONSISTENCY IN THE TREATMENT OF COMBINED PRICE AND QUANTITY VARIANCE

As stated earlier, the formulas for deriving the variances are

> quantity variance = change in quantity × budget price
> price variance   = change in price   × actual quantity

The use of the budget price and actual quantity in the last column seems to be based more on practice than on logic or convenience. The preceding formulas seem no better than the following:

> quantity variance = change in quantity × actual price
> price variance   = change in price   × budget quantity

Or, as another alternative, the change in quantity and in price may also be multiplied by actual price and actual quantity, respectively, or by budget price and budget quantity.

The following discussions and illustrations prove that in many instances, the use of a traditional formula results in (1) the overstatement of the variances (2) the inadequate presentation of the variances and/or (3) the inconsistent treatment of certain variances.

Reviewed here are the variance analysis of variable or direct labor costs in four situations:

> Situation A—with decline in quantity (or number of workers) from budget to actual, but with increase in price (or in the average monthly compensation per worker)—illustrated in Exhibit 22.15
> Situation B—with increase in quantity but decline in price—Exhibit 22.16
> Situation C—with increase in both quantity and price—Exhibit 22.17
> Situation D—with decline in both quantity and price—Exhibit 22.18

The base figures used in the exhibits are not related to those in the prior exhibits.

Situation A—Decline in Quantity but Increase in Price (Exhibit 22.15). The budgeted payroll is $200,000, and the actual is $198,000. These amounts are represented by the pair of rectangles at the top of part II of Exhibit 22.15.

The purpose of the variance analysis is to determine (1) the difference in the total size of the area of the two rectangles and (2) the sectors or areas where the two rectangles do not overlap.

The difference in the size of the area refers to the total of the quantity and price variances. Each of the sectors or areas where the rectangles do not overlap represents a variance—either quantity or price.

To help us in the review, we place one of the rectangles on top of the other. Sector X is the area where the two rectangles overlap. Sectors A and B are the areas where there are no overlaps.

Sector A is the quantity variance. This area covers $20,000, which is 10 (the horizontal dimension of sector A) multiplied by $2,000 (the vertical dimension).

Sector B is the price variance. This covers $18,000, which is $200 multiplied by 90, which are its dimensions. Sectors A and B are the actual variances since they are based on the actual measurements of the areas.

The table in part II is the quantitative analysis of the chart and hence represents the actual variances.

The results of the conventional variance analysis in part III are the same as the results in the analysis in part II because it just so happens that

1. The budget price which is used in the traditional method in determining the quantity variance is also the *lower* of the budget price and the actual price.
2. The actual quantity used in conventional analysis in determining the price variance is also the *lower* of the budget quantity and the actual quantity.

Situation B—Increase in Quantity but Decline in Price (Exhibit 22.16). This case is similar to that in situation A in that there is an increase in the quantity or price, and a decline in the other. In part II of Exhibit 22.16, the total budget is composed of sectors B and X, and the actual, X and A. The quantity variance is represented by sector A, and the price variance, sector B. There is no variance representing sector C as this is not covered by either of the rectangles representing the budget or the actual. (In situation A, there is also no sector C for the same reason.)

The actual variances based on the chart are in the table in part II. Under the conventional method (part III), both the quantity and the price variances are overstated by the area corresponding to sector C of part II. For instance, the quantity variance in part III, which is covered by sector A, covers the total of sectors A and C in part II.

The overstatement of the quantity variance is equal to the overstatement of the price variance.

Situation C—Increase in Both Quantity and Price (Exhibit 22.17).   The total difference between the budget and the actual is represented by sectors A, B, and C in part II. Sector A is due to the change in quantity, B results from the difference in the price, and C is the combined effect of both price and quantity changes. The correct individual variances corresponding to the dimensions of each of these sectors are calculated in the table in part II.

Under the traditional variance analysis (part III), the price variance (sector B) covers not only sector B in part II which is the true *price* variance, but also C, which is the combined price and quantity variance.

Situation D—Decline in Both Quantity and Price (Exhibit 22.18).   This is similar to situation C, in that the total variance is composed of sectors A, B, and C in part II with C being the combined quantity-price variance.

The traditional method has included sector C of part II under the *quantity* variance. Note that in situation C, this method of analysis has considered sector C as part of the *price* variance. Hence the inconsistency.

V. OVERHEAD—VARIANCE ANALYSIS

Currently, the plant overhead and discretionary costs are treated as a group for purposes of variance analysis. The only segregation is the one between the variable cost component of the overhead and the fixed cost portion. The same thing is true with the marketing overhead. The traditional treatment usually employs either the two-variance or the three-variance analysis method.

TWO-VARIANCE ANALYSIS (Exhibit 22.19)

The overhead analysis is better carried out if an analysis is done for each of factory overhead, marketing overhead, and general administrative expenses. The review of the factory and marketing expenses should distinguish the variable overhead from the fixed expenses. For a factory, the variable overhead includes the cost of electricity and other sources of power as gas, equipment spare parts, and factory supplies. The fixed costs cover the cost of factory management or supervision, rentals and depreciation generally, and building maintenance. A more detailed discussion of variable and fixed costs was covered in Chapter 8. A two-way variance analysis for plant overhead is illustrated in Exhibit 22.19. The evaluation of marketing overhead may follow the same pattern.

Variable Cost Component.   The two-variance analysis details the cost deviation into volume variance and spending variance. The volume variance portion of the variable cost component is due to the change in the production or sales volume from the budget to the actual, while the spending variance is due to the fluctuations in the unit costs or prices.

For the variable cost component of the plant overhead, the volume variance corresponds to, and is determined in the same manner as, the quantity variance of raw materials, direct labor, and other variable costs, where the product sales volume deviation is used as a basis in determining the quantity variance of the variable costs. See Exhibit 22.6. Hence the volume variance, like the quantity variance, is the deviation in the production (or sales) volume multiplied by the budget price or cost.

Likewise, the spending variance corresponds to, and is determined in the same manner as, the price variance of the raw materials and other variable costs. Hence, the spending variance, like the price variance, is the change in the cost per unit of production (or sales) multiplied by the actual quantity.

CALCULATION. The overhead variance may be calculated by using the same format as in Exhibit 22.6, or it may be patterned after the format in Exhibit 22.8. The illustration in Exhibit 22.19 follows the same pattern as in Exhibit 22.8. The procedures for calculating each of the volume, spending, and total variances in Exhibit 22.19 are the same as those for Exhibit 22.8, as explained in Section II of this chapter, One-Product Variance Analysis—Calculation of the Variances—Method 2.

Thus, the volume variance of $40,000 may be estimated in one of the following ways:

1. As the deviation in the production (which is 200), multiplied by the budget cost ($200)
2. As the difference between the total of the variable cost component of the overhead per budget ($800,000) and the total of the actual variable cost component ($760,000)

LIMITATIONS. This method has two limitations.

First, the variances are calculated in this sequence: volume variance and then spending variance. If the sequence is changed, the variance for each of these causes is likely to change.

Second, the volume variance arbitrarily uses the budget price as the multiplier of the change in the volume, and the spending variance, the actual volume as the multiplier of the change in the cost. These limitations, which are also applicable to direct labor and other variable costs, were treated in depth in Section IV of this chapter.

Fixed Cost Component. Some expenses which are called as fixed costs change if the production or sales volume goes beyond a given range. For instance, the number of supervisors required may be constant for a given number of shifts. If a factory adds or deducts from a predetermined number of shifts, the number of supervisors required may change. In the illustration in Exhibit 22.19, the factory was able to reduce the number of plant supervisors due to the decline in production volume. Hence the cost savings due to this was brought about due to the change in the production volume.

The spending variance is due to the unexpected changes in the costs or prices. For instance, the actual building maintenance expense may be higher than budget due to the increases in the charges made by the contract maintenance firm.

THREE-VARIANCE ANALYSIS (Exhibit 22.20)

The three-variance analysis is suited to a firm with a physical process production operation, which uses the job order cost accounting system and which applies its overhead expenses to the production cost on the basis of the number of direct labor hours, major equipment hours, or some other measures. A firm operating on this basis charges the overhead to a particular job, which is either for specific sales order or for inventory, based on the number of labor or equipment hours spent on the job.

Variable Cost Component.   The variable cost portion of the overhead will have three types of variances: volume, efficiency, and spending.

If the firm charges to the job orders the overhead based on the direct labor hours, the firm will have estimated, before the start of the budget period, the following: the total output for the period, the average direct labor hours required per unit of output, the total direct labor hours, and the variable overhead cost per direct labor hour.

At the end of the period, the variation between the budget and the actual will be due to differences in the following causes: (1) the total output, (2) the number of labor hours per output, and (3) the variable overhead cost per direct labor hour. The variance due to the first-named cause is called the volume variance; the one due to the second, efficiency variance; and the one due to the third, spending variance.

Each of the three types of variances may be calculated in either one of the two ways in which the two-way variances may be computed as described earlier. Exhibit 22.20 illustrates the second manner of estimating.

LIMITATIONS.   This method has three basic limitations. First, the method is conceptually faulty. While direct labor cost may be distributed based on the direct labor hours spent on a job, certain types of costs which form part of the variable cost portion of the factory overhead may have no direct relation to the direct labor hours. Examples of such costs are electricity used to run the machines and spare parts for the equipment.

Second, the amounts of each of the efficiency and spending variances could vary from the ones shown in the upper table of Exhibit 22.20 if the variable cost component of the overhead were charged based on other than direct labor hours. For instance, if equipment hours were employed instead, the efficiency variance would be an unfavorable $51,000 in lieu of the favorable $76,000, and the spending variance would be a favorable $58,000 instead of an unfavorable $68,000. See the two tables in Exhibit 22.20.

Third, the variances are calculated in this sequence in Exhibit 22.20: volume variance, efficiency variance, and spending variance. If the sequence is changed, the variance for each of these causes is likely to change.

Fixed Cost Component. If the three-variance method is used as shown in Exhibit 22.20, only two types of variances can be computed for the fixed cost component—efficiency and spending—the same as in the two-variance analysis in Exhibit 22.19. The efficiency variance will be zero since the fixed cost items are usually not affected by the efficiency factors (as number of direct labor hours).

EXHIBIT 22.1:
Budget and Actual Performance

	ORIGINAL BUDGET			ACTUAL RESULTS			VARIANCE		
	Total	Product A	Product B	Total	Product A	Product B	Total	Product A	Product B
Sales volume in units	1,100	660	440	1,200	624	576	100	(36)	136
As a percentage of total	100%	60%	40%	100%	52%	48%	0%	−8%	8%
Total (in $1,000)									
Sales	$9,020	$5,940	$3,080	$9,648	$5,616	$4,032	$628	($324)	$952
Less: Variable costs									
Raw materials	2,552	1,584	968	2,754	1,544	1,210	202	(40)	242
Direct labor	924	594	330	959	498	461	35	(96)	131
Commissions	1,353	891	462	1,488	842	645	135	(49)	183
Interest on receivables					0			0	
financing	541	356	185	743	432	310	202	76	126
Total variable costs	5,370	3,425	1,945	5,943	3,317	2,626	573	(108)	681
Contribution margin	$3,650	$2,515	$1,135	$3,705	$2,299	$1,406	$ 55	($216)	$271
Product overhead	450	250	200	370	150	220	(80)	(100)	20
Product contribution	$3,200	$2,265	$ 935	$3,335	$2,149	$1,186	$135	($116)	$251
Per unit (in $1)									
Contribution margin		$3,810	$2,580		$3,684	$2,441			

EXHIBIT 22.2:
Variances of Sales Revenues and Variable Costs—Product Sales
Volume Deviation used as a Basis of the Quantity Variance
of the Variable Costs

Factors affecting the variances	Types of variances	Total variance
Sales volume ——	Sales volume variance*	
	+	Sales variance
Industry + Strategy	Price variance (selling price per unit)	
Sales volume ——	Sales volume variance*	
	+	Raw materials variance
Usage rate† x Cost per unit of material	Price variance (cost per sales unit)	
Sales volume ——	Sales volume variance*	
	+	Direct labor variance
Usage rate† x Cost per person-day	Price variance (cost per sales unit)	
Sales volume ——	Sales volume variance*	
	+	Commission variance
Unit selling price x Commission rate	Price variance (cost per sales unit)	
Sales volume ——	Sales volume variance*	
	+	Interest variance
Receivables balance x Interest rate	Price variance (cost per sales unit)	

* Quantity variance = sales volume variance.
† Usage rate   = quantity of input per unit of sales.

EXHIBIT 22.3:
Variances of Variable Costs—Input Quantity Deviation Used
as a Basis of the Quantity Variance of the Variable Costs

Factors affecting the variances	Type of variances	Total variance
Product sales volume x Usage rate*	Raw material quantity variance + Cost per unit of material variance	Raw materials variance
Product sales volume x Usage rate*	Person-days variance + Cost per person-day variance	Direct labor variance
Product sales value x Collection period	Accounts receivable balance variance + Interest rate variance	Interest variance

*Usage rate = quantity of input per unit of sales.

EXHIBIT 22.4:
Base Data for Variance Analysis—Product Sales Volume Deviation
Used as a Basis of the Quantity Variance of the Variable Costs

		Budget	Actual	Variance = increase (decrease)
Sales	Product sales volume	660	624	(36)
	Unit selling price	$ 9,000	$ 9,000	$ 0
	Total value (in $1,000)	$ 5,940	$ 5,616	($ 324)
Raw materials	Usage rate (unit or quantity of material per sales unit)	12	11	(1)
	Cost per unit of material	$ 200	$ 225	$ 25
	Cost per sales unit	$ 2,400	$ 2,475	$ 75
	Product sales volume	660	624	(36)
	Total cost (in $1,000)	$ 1,584	$ 1,544	($ 40)
Direct labor	Usage rate (person-days per sales unit)	6.0	5.7	(0.3)
	Cost per person-day	$ 150	$ 140	($ 10)
	Cost per sales unit	$ 900	$ 798	($ 102)
	Product sales volume	660	624	(36)
	Total cost (in $1,000)	$ 594	$ 498	($ 96)
Commissions	Unit selling price	$ 9,000	$ 9,000	$ 0
	Rate	15%	15%	0%
	Commission per sales unit	$ 1,350	$ 1,350	$ 0
	Product sales volume	660	624	(36)
	Total cost (in $1,000)	$ 891	$ 842	($ 49)
Interest— receivable financing	Unit selling price	$ 9,000	$ 9,000	$ 0
	Collection period (mos.)	6	7	1
	Receivables balance per sales unit	$54,000	$63,000	$9,000
	Interest rate per month	1.0%	1.1%	0.1%
	Interest per sales unit	$ 540	$ 693	$ 153
	Product sales volume	660	624	(36)
	Total cost (in $1,000)	$ 356	$ 432	$ 76

EXHIBIT 22.5:
Base Data for Variance Analysis—Input Quantity Deviation Used
as a Basis of the Quantity Variance of the Variable Costs

		Budget	Actual	Variance = increase (decrease)
Raw material	Usage rate (unit or quantity of material per sales unit)	12	11	(1)
	Product sales volume	660	624	(36)
	Total materials quantity	7,920	6,864	(1,056)
	Cost per unit of material	$ 200	$ 225	$ 25
	Total cost (in $1,000)	$ 1,584	$ 1,544	($ 40)
Direct Labor	Usage rate (person-days per sales unit)	6.0	5.7	(0.3)
	Products sales volume	660	624	(36)
	Total person-days	3,960	3,557	(403)
	Cost per person-day	$ 150	$ 140	($ 10)
	Total cost (in $1,000)	$ 594	$ 498	($ 96)
Interest— receivable financing	Unit selling price	$ 9,000	$ 9,000	$ 0
	Collection period (mos.)	6	7	1
	Receivables balance per sales unit	$54,000	$63,000	$9,000
	Product sales volume	660	624	(36)
	Total receivables (in $1,	$35,640	$39,312	$3,672
	Interest rate per month	1.0%	1.1%	0.1%
	Total cost (in $1,000)	$ 356	$ 432	$ 76

EXHIBIT 22.6:
Conventional Variance Analysis—Product Sales Volume Deviation
Used as a Basis of the Quantity Variance of the Variable Costs

Type of variance	Variance*	Budget price†	Actual quantity‡	Value of variance	
Sales					
Quantity variance	(36)	$9,000		($324,000)	
Price variance	0		624	0	
Total sales				($324,000)	Unfavorable
Raw material					
Quantity variance	(36)	$2,400		(86,400)	
Price variance	$ 75		624	46,800	
Total raw material				(39,600)	
Direct labor					
Quantity variance	(36)	$ 900		(32,400)	
Price variance	($102)		624	63,648	
Total direct labor				96,048	
Commissions					
Quantity variance	(36)	$1,350		(48,600)	
Price variance	0		624	0	
Total commissions				48,600	
Interest					
Quantity variance	(36)	$ 540		(19,440)	
Price variance	$153		624	95,472	
Total interest				76,032	
Total variable costs				($108,216)	Favorable
Contribution margin				($215,784)	Unfavorable

*Quantity variance = product sales volume variance in Exhibit 22.4.
Price variance = cost per sales unit variance in Exhibit 22.4.
†Unit selling price or cost per sales unit in Exhibit 22.4.
‡Actual product sales volume in Exhibit 22.4.

EXHIBIT 22.7:
Conventional Variance Analysis—Input Quantity Deviation Used as a Basis of the Quantity Variance of the Variable Costs

PRODUCT A	Type of variance	Variance*	Budget price*	Actual quantity	Value of variance
Sales	Quantity variance	(36)	$9,000		($324,000)
	Price variance	0		624	0
	Total				($324,000)
Material	Quantity variance	(1,056)	$ 200		(211,200)
	Price variance	$25		6,864	171,600
	Total				(39,600)
Labor	Quantity variance	(403)	$ 150		(60,480)
	Price variance	($10)		3,557	(35,568)
	Total				(96,048)
Commissions	Quantity variance	(36)	$1,350		(48,600)
	Price variance	0		0	0
	Total				(48,600)
Interest	Quantity variance	$3,672,000	1%		36,720
	Price variance	0.1%		$39,312,000	39,312
	Total				76,032
	Total variable costs				(108,216)
Contribution margin					($215,784)

*For sales and commissions, same as in Exhibits 22.4 and 22.6.
For materials, labor and interest, same as in Exhibit 22.5

EXHIBIT 22.8:
Conventional Variance Analysis for Raw Materials—Method II*—
Input Quantity Deviation Used as a Basis of the Quantity Variance
of the Variable Costs

Quantity Price	——————▶ ——————▶	Budget budget	Actual budget	Actual actual	
Quantity	(Exhibit 22.5)	7,920	6,864	6,864	
Price	(Exhibit 22.5)	$ 200	$ 200	$ 225	
Total cost		$1,584,000	$1,372,800	$1,544,400	
Quantity variance			($ 211,200)		Favorable
Price variance				$ 171,600	Unfavorable
Total variance				($ 39,600)	Favorable

*The results are the same as in Exhibit 22.7.

EXHIBIT 22.9:
Planning and Performance Variances (dollars in $1,000)

	Original budget (Exhibit 22.1)	Planning variance*	Revised budget (see below)	Performance variance†	Actual (Exhibit 22.1)	Total variance
Sales volume in units	660	(36)	624		624	
Sales	$5,940	($324)	$5,616	$ 0	$5,616	($324)
Less: Variable costs						
Raw materials	1,584	(86)	1,498	47	$1,544	(40)
Direct labor	594	(32)	562	(64)	498	(96)
Commissions	891	(49)	842	0	842	(49)
Interest on receivables financing	356	(19)	337	95	432	76
Total variable costs	3,425	(187)	3,239	79	3,317	(108)
Contribution margin	$2,515	($ 137)	$2,377	($79)	$2,299	($216)

	Budget per unit (Exh. 22.4)	For 624 sales units (in $1,000)

Calculation of amounts in the revised budget

	Budget per unit (Exh. 22.4)	For 624 sales units (in $1,000)
Sales	$9,000	$5,616
Less: Variable costs		
Raw materials	2,400	1,498
Direct labor	900	562
Commissions	1,350	842
Interest on receivables financing	540	337
Total variable costs	5,190	3,239
Contribution margin	$3,810	$2,377

*Planning Variance: sales and variable costs—equivalent to the quantity variance in Exhibit 22.6 with the product sales volume deviation used as a basis in calculating the quantity variance of the variable costs; contribution margin—equivalent to the sales quantity variance in Exhibit 22.10.
†Performance variance: variable cost by item—equivalent to the price in Exhibit 22.6; variable cost total—equivalent to the total variable cost quantity and price variance in Exhibit 22.10.

EXHIBIT 22.10:
Conventional Variance Analysis with a Revised Budget—Input Quantity Deviation Used as a Basis of the Quantity Variance of the Variable Costs

Type of variance		Variance*	Budget price†	Actual quantity	Value of variance	
Sales						
Material	Quantity variance	(36)	$3,810		($137,160)	Unfavorable
	Quantity variance	(624)	$ 200		(124,800)	
	Price variance	$ 25		6,864	171,600	
	Total				46,800	
Labor	Quantity variance	(187)	$ 150		(28,080)	
	Price variance	($ 10)		3,557	(35,568)	
	Total				(63,648)	
Interest	Quantity variance	$5,616,000	1.0%		56,160	
	Price variance	0.1%		$39,312,000	39,312	
	Total				95,472	
	Total variable costs				78,624	Favorable
Contribution margin					($215,784)	Unfavorable

*Selected quantity variances are calculated below; others are from Exhibit 22.5.

		Per unit (Exhibit 22.5)	For 624 units	Variance
Materials	Actual	11	6,864	(624)
	Budget	12	7,488	
Labor	Actual	5.7	3,557	(187)
	Budget	6.0	3,744	
Interest	Actual	$63,000	$39,312,000	$ 5,616,000
	Budget	$54,000	$33,696,000	

†Budget price for sales of $3,810 = budget contribution margin per unit, taken from the lower table of Exhibit 22.9. Budget price and actual quantity for other items are from Exhibit 22.5.

EXHIBIT 22.11:
Conventional Product Mix Analysis

	Volume ⟶ Budget Mix ⟶ Budget Margin ⟶ Budget	ACTUAL Budget Budget	Actual ACTUAL Budget	Actual Actual ACTUAL
Company sales volume	1,100	1,200	1,200	1,200
Mix	60%	60%	52%	52%
Product volume	660	720	624	624
Contribution margin per unit	$ 3,810	$ 3,810	$ 3,810	$ 3,684
Total	$2,514,600	$2,743,200	$2,377,440	$2,298,816
Quantity or volume variance		$ 228,600		
Mix variance			($ 365,760)	
Contribution margin variance				($ 78,624)
Total variance				($ 215,784)

Source of data: Exhibit 22.1.

EXHIBIT 22.12:
Results of Conventional Methods

I. Variance analysis of a product in isolation—without mix variance

| | | WITHOUT REVISED BUDGET | | WITH REVISED BUDGET |
		Sales volume* (Exhibit 22.6)	Input volume* (Exhibit 22.7)	Input volume* (Exhibit 22.10)
Sales	Quantity variance	($324,000)	($324,000)	($137,160)
Material	Quantity variance	(86,400)	(211,200)	(124,800)
	Price variance	46,800	171,600	171,600
	Total	(39,600)	(39,600)	46,800
Direct labor	Quantity variance	(32,400)	(60,480)	(28,080)
	Price variance	(63,648)	(35,568)	(35,568)
	Total	(96,048)	(96,048)	(63,648)
Commission	Quantity variance	(48,600)	(48,600)	0
	Price variance	0	0	0
	Total	(48,600)	(48,600)	0
Interest	Quantity variance	(19,440)	36,720	56,160
	Price variance	95,472	39,312	39,312
	Total	76,032	76,032	95,472
Total variable costs		(108,216)	(108,216)	78,624
Contribution margin		($215,784)	($215,784)	($215,784)

II. Variance analysis of a product in a group—with mix variance

	Without revised budget (Exhibit 22.11)
Sales and cost items	
Quantity variance	$228,600
Mix variance	(365,760)
Price or margin variance	(78,624)
Contribution margin	($215,784)

*Basis of quantity variance for the variable costs.

EXHIBIT 22.13:
Coverages of Conventional Methods—Variances

	METHOD			
	ANALYSIS OF A PRODUCT IN ISOLATION			ANALYSIS OF A PRODUCT IN A GROUP
	WITHOUT REVISED BUDGET		*With revised budget*	
Type of variance	*Sales volume** (Exhibits 22.2, 22.6)	*Input volume†* (Exhibits 22.3, 22.7)	*Input volume†* (Exhibit 22.10)	*Without revised budget* (Exhibit 22.11)
Sales				
Quantity variance	Sales volume	Sales volume	Sales volume‡	Product sales volume
Price variance	Selling price	Selling price	Contribution margin§	
Inputs				
Quantity variance	Sales volume	Sales volume Usage rate‖	Usage rate‖	
Price variance	Cost per unit of input Usage rate‖	Cost per unit of input	Cost per unit of input	
Contribution margin				
Quantity variance and mix variance				
Contribution margin variance				Contribution margin per sales unit#

* Sales volume is used as the quantity variance of the variable costs.

† Input volume is used as the quantity variance of the variable costs.

‡ Variance of inputs due to change in sales volume.

§ Note that in Exhibit 22.10, the sales variance was computed by using the contribution margin of $3,180 per unit as calculated in Exhibit 22.9.

‖ Usage rate = quantity of input per unit of sales.

\# Composed of selling price, usage rate, and cost per unit of input.

EXHIBIT 22.14:
Evaluation of Conventional Method*

	Budget	Budget	Budget	ACTUAL
Volume ⟶ *Budget*				
Mix ⟶ *Budget*	*Budget*	*Budget*	*ACTUAL*	*Actual*
Margin ⟶ *Budget*	*Budget*	*ACTUAL*	*Actual*	*Actual*
Company Sales Volume	1,100	1,100	1,100	1,200
Product A				
Mix	60%	60%	52%	52%
Product volume	660	660	572	624
Margin per unit	$ 3,810	$ 3,684	$ 3,684	$ 3,684
Total margin	$2,514,600	$2,431,440	$2,107,248	$2,298,816
Margin variance		($ 83,160)		
Mix variance			($ 342,192)	
Volume variance				($ 191,568)
Total				($ 215,784)

*Using the same formula as that of the conventional method which was used in Exhibit 22.11 but with the sequencing of the conversion from budget to actual being based on a perceived chronological order.

Source of data: Exhibits 22.1 and 22.11.

EXHIBIT 22.15:
Situation A—Decline in Quantity and Increase in Price

I. BASE DATA

		Budget	Actual	Variance
	Quantity	100	90	(10)
	Price	$2,000	$2,200	$200
	Total cost	$200,000	$198,000	($2,000)

II. RESULTING CHARTS AND VARIANCE ANALYSIS

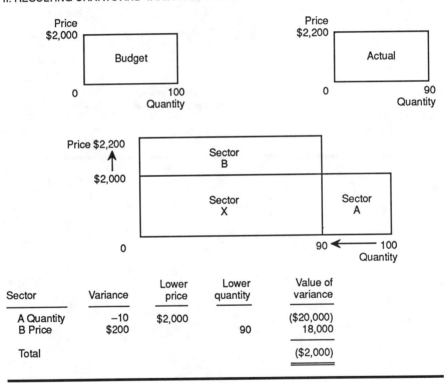

Sector	Variance	Lower price	Lower quantity	Value of variance
A Quantity	−10	$2,000		($20,000)
B Price	$200		90	18,000
Total				($2,000)

III. CONVENTIONAL VARIANCE ANALYSIS AND CHART

CHART–SAME AS TABLE IN PART II

Sector	Variance	Budget price	Actual quantity	Value of variance
A Quantity	−10	$2,000		($20,000)
B Price	$200		90	18,000
Total				($2,000)

EXHIBIT 22.16:
Situation B—Increase in Quantity and Decline in Price

I. BASE DATA

	Budget	Actual	Variance
Quantity	100	110	10
Price	$2,000	$1,800	($200)
Total cost	$200,000	$198,000	($2,000)

II. RESULTING CHARTS AND VARIANCE ANALYSIS

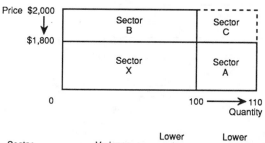

Sector	Variance	Lower price	Lower quantity	Value of variance
A Quantity	10	$1,800		$18,000
B Price	($200)		100	(20,000)
Total				($2,000)

III. CONVENTIONAL VARIANCE ANALYSIS AND CHART

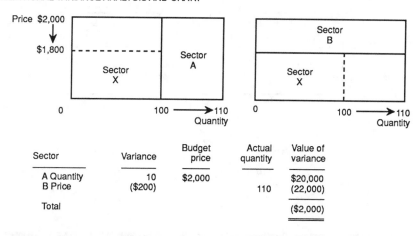

Sector	Variance	Budget price	Actual quantity	Value of variance
A Quantity	10	$2,000		$20,000
B Price	($200)		110	(22,000)
Total				($2,000)

EXHIBIT 22.17:

Situation C—Increase in Both Quantity and Price

I. BASE DATA	Budget	Actual	Variance
Quantity	100	110	10
Price	$2,000	$1,800	($200)
Total cost	$200,000	$198,000	($2,000)

II. RESULTING CHARTS AND VARIANCE ANALYSIS

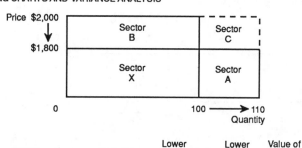

Sector	Variance	Lower price	Lower quantity	Value of variance
A Quantity	10	$1,800		$18,000
B Price	($200)		100	(20,000)
Total				($2,000)

III. CONVENTIONAL VARIANCE ANALYSIS AND CHART

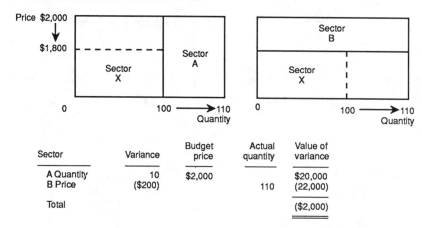

Sector	Variance	Budget price	Actual quantity	Value of variance
A Quantity	10	$2,000		$20,000
B Price	($200)		110	(22,000)
Total				($2,000)

EXHIBIT 22.18:
Situation D—Decline in Both Quantity and Price

I. BASE DATA	Budget	Actual	Variance
Quantity	100	90	(10)
Price	$2,000	$1,800	($200)
Total cost	$200,000	$162,000	($38,000)

II. RESULTING CHART AND VARIANCE ANALYSIS

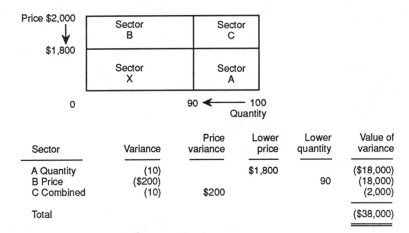

Sector	Variance	Price variance	Lower price	Lower quantity	Value of variance
A Quantity	(10)		$1,800		($18,000)
B Price	($200)			90	(18,000)
C Combined	(10)	$200			(2,000)
Total					($38,000)

III. CONVENTIONAL VARIANCE ANALYSIS AND CHART

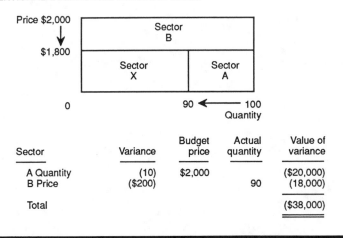

Sector	Variance	Budget price	Actual quantity	Value of variance
A Quantity	(10)	$2,000		($20,000)
B Price	($200)		90	(18,000)
Total				($38,000)

EXHIBIT 22.19:
Plant Overhead—Two-Variance Analysis

	Original budget	Revised budget	Actual
Output	Budget	Actual	Actual
Cost per output	Budget	Budget	Actual
Variable Costs			
Output	4,000	3,800	3,800
Cost per output	$ 200	$ 200	$ 198
Total (in $1,000)	$ 800	$ 760	$ 752
Volume variance		($ 40)	
Spending variance			($ 8)
Total variance			($ 48)
Fixed Costs			
Plant management	$ 50	$ 50	$ 50
Plant supervisors	$ 100	$ 97	$ 97
Building maintenance	$ 30	$ 30	$ 35
Other	$ 20	$ 20	$ 22
Total (in $1,000)	$ 200	$ 197	$ 204
Volume variance		($ 3)	
Spending variance			$ 7
Total variance			$ 4

EXHIBIT 22.20:
Plant Overhead—Three-Variance Analysis

		Original budget	Revised budget	Budget cost at actual hours	Actual
I. Based on direct labor hours					
Output		Budget	Actual	Actual	Actual
Direct labor hour per output		Budget	Budget	Actual	Actual
Direct labor hours					
Cost per output		<u>Budget</u>	<u>Budget</u>	<u>Budget</u>	<u>Actual</u>
Variable costs					
Output		4,000	3,800	3,800	3,800
Direct labor hour per output		2	2	1.8	1.8
Direct labor hours		8,000	7,600	6,840	6,840
Cost per direct labor hour		$ 100	$ 100	$ 100	$ 110
Total	(in $1,000)	$ 800	$ 760	$ 684	$ 752
Volume variance	(in $1,000)		($ 40)		
Efficiency variance	(in $1,000)			($ 76)	
Spending variance	(in $1,000)				$ 68
Total variance	(in $1,000)				($ 48)
Fixed Costs					
Total	(in $1,000)	$ 200	$ 197	$ 197	$ 204
Volume variance	(in $1,000)		($ 3)		
Efficiency variance	(in $1,000)			$ 0	
Spending variance	(in $1,000)				$ 7
Total variance	(in $1,000)				$ 4
II. Based on equipment hours					
Variable costs					
Output		4,000	3,800	3,800	3,800
Equipment hours per output		1.5	1.5	1.6	1.6
Equipment hours		6,000	5,700	6,080	6,080
Cost per equipment hour		$133.33	$133.33	$133.33	$123.75
Total	(in $1,000)	$ 800	$ 760	$ 811	$ 752
Volume variance	(in $1,000)		($ 40)		
Efficiency variance	(in $1,000)			$ 51	
Spending variance	(in $1,000)				($ 58)
Total variance	(in $1,000)				($ 48)

Chapter 23

MULTIVARIANCE ANALYSIS

This chapter introduces the multivariance technique and provides guidelines on the establishment of standards of performance. As a complement, this part of the book offers aids for defining the responsibilities of managers at various levels in the organization chart, for both the favorable and unfavorable variances. The techniques, guidelines, and aids are applied on sales revenues, variable costs, discretionary costs, and sales expansion costs.

The multivariance technique is an innovative method which may be used to determine how much of the change in the profit is attributable to each of the following factors: industry sales, market share, product mix, price or cost, and usage rate. Tracing the variance to each of these causes takes on added significance since industry sales is usually beyond the control of management, market share is partly beyond its control, and the rest are normally influenced by management. The current tools of analysis do not have the capability to identify the effects of industry sales, market share, and usage rate on the profitability.

The multivariance method can attribute the contribution margin variance to each of the named factors not only in totality for each product but also for the sales revenues and each item of variable cost for each product. This information helps management pinpoint both problem areas and opportunities for development.

The multivariance analysis also facilitates the preparation of special studies since the technique possesses the capability to extend the scope of the analysis to causes beyond those enumerated earlier. For instance, it can determine the impact on the profit, of changes in the collection time of receivables, carrying periods of inventories, and payment terms of trade suppliers.

Since the multivariance analysis indicates the determinants of the values of revenues and the cost items, the procedure proves an invaluable tool not only in variance analysis but also in setting the standards of performance and in defining accountabilities or responsibilities and in distributing rewards for performance.

The first four parts of this chapter reveal the concepts and techniques of multivariance analysis and explain the setting of performance standards and accountabilities for the variances as applied to sales revenues and variable costs. The remaining parts illustrate the analysis of discretionary costs, sales expansion costs, and other specialized but significant items of expenses.

I. SALES AND VARIABLE COSTS— MULTIVARIANCE ANALYSIS

The key features of the technique are the following:

1. It decomposes the sales volume variance of both the sales revenues and the variable costs into three components: industry sales volume, market share, and product mix
2. It recognizes three types of variances for materials, labor, interest, or other inputs: sales volume, usage rate, and cost per unit of input.

VARIABLE COSTS (Exhibit 23.1, charts I and II)

Since the new technique recognizes three types of variances for the variable costs, the new technique avoids one of the weaknesses of the conventional method.

The conventional method which does not use a revised budget for variance analysis recognizes only two variances for the cost inputs. The traditional method (1) combines the price and usage variances into one variance only—the price variance (Exhibit 23.1, chart I)—or (2) lumps in the quantity variance and the effects of both sales volume and usage variances to arrive at the quantity or volume variance (Exhibit 23.1, chart II). The traditional variance analysis, therefore, is based on the erroneous assumption that the total cost of any input is influenced by only two factors and that the total cost, therefore, is represented by the square area or product of these two factors.

Actually there are three basic factors influencing the total cost of an input (Exhibit 23.1, chart III). The multivariance method reflects this reality as it recognizes that the total cost of an input is not a square but a cube as it has three dimensions.

Under the new method, the effect of sales volume changes is automatically segregated from the other factors. Hence it is unnecessary to prepare a revised budget just for performance evaluation purposes.

SALES VOLUME (Exhibit 23.1, charts III and IV)

The quantity or sales volume component in Exhibit 23.1, chart III, can be further analyzed into its subparts, namely, industry sales, market share, and product mix (Exhibit 23.1, chart IV). This can be done not only for the contribution margin but also separately for the sales revenues and each item of variable cost.

In computing the variances, the change in the quantity (increase or decrease) is multiplied by the base price which is the lower of the budget or actual price. In the conventional method, the change in quantity is always multiplied by the budget price.

The new method has built-in flexibility to extend the scope of variance analysis to an almost limitless number of factors which produce an impact on the profitability. For instance, the effect of changes in the unit selling prices and in the collection period of receivables, on the interest on loans used to carry the receivables, can readily be ascertained.

The limit to the number of factors is set not by the technique itself but by the usefulness of the variances to be derived considering the particular application.

CALCULATIONS (Exhibit 23.1, charts III and IV)

On the procedural side, the multivariance method is easier to understand since the mathematical calculations of the variances can be directly and visually related to the underlying chart.

In computing the variances, the change in the quantity (increase or decrease) is multiplied by the base price which is the lower of the budget or actual price. In the conventional method, the change in quantity is always multiplied by the budget price.

Under the new technique, the change in the price is multiplied by the base quantity, which is the lower of the budget or actual quantity; in the conventional method, it is always multiplied by the actual quantity.

II. SALES AND VARIABLE COSTS—RESULTS OF APPLICATIONS

The application of the technique to the hypothetical company described in the preceding chapter produced the following results.

OVERALL PRODUCT PERFORMANCE (Exhibit 23.2)

The new technique was able to point out that the $216,000 unfavorable variance is the net result of the $622,000 unfavorable variance due to forces normally within management control, and for which, therefore, management should be charged, and a $407,000 windfall favorable variance for which management should not be credited:

	CAUSES OF VARIANCE		
	Beyond management control	*Can be influenced by management*	*Net*
Unfavorable variances			
Product mix		$344,000	
Market share		203,000	
Unit cost of input		170,000	
Total		717,000	
Favorable variances			
Industry sales	$407,000		
Input usage rate		95,000	
Net contribution			
margin variance	$407,000	$622,000	$216,000
	Favorable	Unfavorable	Unfavorable

The traditional analysis does not bring out the foregoing variances.

VARIABLE COSTS (Exhibit 23.2)

The new technique can detail the variance of each variable cost item—interest, material, and labor—into usage rate, unit cost, industry sales volume, market share, and product mix. The variances for the usage rate and unit cost are illustrated here.

	Interest	*Material*	*Labor*	*Total*
Usage rate variance*	($56,000)	$125,000	$ 26,000	$ 95,000
Unit cost variance*	(34,000)	(172,000)	36,000	(170,000)
Net variance*	($90,000)	($47,000)	$ 62,000	$ 75,000

*Figures in parenthesis represent unfavorable variances.

The variances for interest and material summarized above are accounted for as described in the next sections.

INTEREST (Exhibits 23.11 and 22.4)

Usage Rate Variance. The $56,000 unfavorable usage variance for interest on receivables financing is due to the lengthening of the collection period by one month. Since the selling price of the product is $9,000 per unit and the interest base (lower of budget and actual) is 1% a month, every one-month change in the collection period translates into a $90 interest cost per unit sold. As there were 624 units sold, the total collection period variance (usage rate variance) is $56,000. In an actual case, the $56,000 may be compared with the additional collection expenses needed to accelerate the collection by one month.

Unit Cost Variance.   The interest unit cost variance is caused by the 0.1% rise in monthly interest rate. Since the base outstanding receivables is $54,000 ($9,000 selling price times six months' collection period), the 0.1% swing in interest rate converts to a $54 incremental interest cost per unit of sales. This information gives out the degree of sensitivity of the profit to fluctuations in the interest rate.

MATERIALS (Exhibits 23.13 and 22.4)

Usage Rate Variance.   During the year, the quantity of raw materials used per unit of goods produced was cut down from 12 to 11. Since the base cost of the material (lower of budget and actual) is $200, and 624 units of goods were sold, the operating management should be credited for the $125,000 improvement in the profit due to better material usage.

Unit Cost Variance.   On the other hand, the management should be penalized for the escalation of the purchase cost of the material—from $200 to $225 per unit of material. Since the base raw material usage per unit of finished product is 11, and since 624 units of products were sold, the contribution margin dropped by $172,000 due to this cost change.

Similar analysis may be made for the labor variance.

III. SALES AND VARIABLE COSTS— PROCEDURES OF APPLICATIONS

Product A of Company A which was analyzed in the preceding chapter will be used as an illustration. The product sales volume will be used as the primary quantity variance in the analysis of the inputs. This will assure a uniformity in the calculations of the impact of changes in the industry sales, market share and product mix, for both sales revenues and the variable costs.

SUMMARY OF VARIANCE ANALYSIS (Exhibit 23.2)

The purpose of the variance analysis is to estimate the impact of various factors on the differences between the actual and budget contribution margin. The illustration shows how the total variance in each of sales revenues, commissions, interest, materials, and labor can be traced to the following five factors: industry sales, market share, product mix, input unit per sales unit or usage rate, and price or cost (unit price per input unit). The variances as calculated are summarized in Exhibit 23.2

Impact of Sales on Profit.   The impact of lost sales, that is, the failure to attain the budgeted sales, is to be calculated not only from the perspective of the lost sales revenues but also from that of its effects on the profit which failed to materialize. Hence the factors causing the reduced sales are analyzed in order to determine their effects on the commissions, interest, materials, and labor.

For this matter, the reduction from budgeted to actual sales, as far as it affects the sales revenues and each of the items of costs, are decomposed into industry sales, market share, product mix, usage rate, and unit cost.

Management Control over the Variances.   The industry sales variance is usually beyond the control of management, unless the company controls the industry or is a substantial player in it. Hence industry sales variance is more of a planning variance than a management performance variance.

On the other hand, market share variance is more the responsibility of management. A loss in market share is usually a reflection of poor marketing management performance.

Since industry sales variance is normally beyond the control of management, whereas market share variance is within its control, the company sales variance should be divided between these two components.

Product mix variance is, to a certain degree, within management control. For instance, management can influence the sales of a given product in relation to other products in the group, through the reallocation of the total advertising, promotional, and other marketing budgets, among the product substitutes.

The usage rate is usually controllable by management. For example, the number of hours required to do a certain task may be cut down through improved procedures and incentives.

Price changes—for both the unit selling prices of the products and the procurement costs of the inputs—are partly controllable and partly not. They are not controllable to the extent that they are affected by inflation or general price fluctuations within the industry. They are controllable if they are part of a company strategy or the results of bargaining with the customers or suppliers.

The functional or departmental managers who should be charged or credited for the different types of sales, labor, and raw material variances are identified in Section IV of this chapter.

SALES REVENUES

Stages of Calculations (Exhibit 23.3).   The sales revenue variances, just like the variable cost variances which are discussed later, are calculated in three stages. First, the primary variances, which are the product sales volume and unit selling price, are computed. See Exhibit 23.3. Next, each of the primary variances are broken into the secondary variances. During this phase, the product sales volume variation is decomposed into its components, namely, the company sales volume variance and the product mix variance. In the next stage, the tertiary variances are estimated. The company sales volume variance is segregated into the industry sales and market share variations.

In certain cases, it may also be practical to analyze the unit selling price variance further. For instance, it may be dissected into that portion due to industry or environmental factors, as inflation or general price hikes by the competition and that part which is due to company strategy as a price reduction to gain market share.

The information required in calculating the variances is given in Exhibit 23.4. This is the same as in Exhibit 22.4 except that additional data are given.

Total Sales Variance—Primary Variance (Exhibit 23.5).   As noted earlier, the primary variance analysis breaks down the total sales variance into the quantity and price variances. The first chart in Exhibit 23.5 shows that (1) the budget sales are composed of 660 units at $9,000 per unit or a total value of $5,940,000; (2) the actual sales are made up of 624 units at $9,000, or a total value of $5,616,000; and (3) the price is stable at $9,000. Since the price is stable, there is no price variance. However, the product sales volume changed from 660 to 624, or by 36. Hence the total sales variance is accounted for solely by the difference in the product sales volume.

The *product* sales volume refers to product A. The product sales volume should be distinguished from (1) the *company* sales volume which covers product A and B and (2) the *industry* sales volume.

The product sales volume variance is calculated in the table in Exhibit 23.5. The negative sign indicates that it is a sales volume reduction.

The negative $324,000 variance is accounted for by the product sales volume variance of $-$324,000, which is $-36 \times \$9,000$ per unit (Exhibit 23.5 table and second chart).

Product Sales Volume—Secondary Variance Product Volume (Exhibit 23.6).
The purpose of this exercise is to segregate the total sales variance, which is sector A in Exhibit 23.5, into its two components: company sales volume variance, which is sector A1, and product mix variance, which is sector A2 in Exhibit 23.6.

Note that in the table in Exhibit 23.6, the company sales volume variance (100 units) is multiplied by the base product mix, which is the lower of the budget mix (52%) and actual mix (60%), in order to arrive at the increase of 52 units in the product sales volume due to the deviation in the company sales volume.

Similarly, the product mix variance (8%) is multiplied by the base company sales volume, which is the lower of the budget company sales volume (1,100 units) and the actual company sales volume (1,200), to result in the drop of 88 units in the product sales volume. The net drop of 36 units in the product sales volume is the same as the 36 product sales volume decline per the table in Exhibit 23.5.

The changes in the product sales volume arising from the deviation in the company sales volume and from the deviation in the product mix are both multiplied by the $9,000 unit selling price. If there were a change in the unit selling price, the figure to be used here would be the lower of the price per budget and actual.

The $9,000 price is also the same as the one used in the table in Exhibit 23.5. The $9,000 may also be obtained from the first chart in Exhibit 23.5.

Sectors A1 and A2 in Exhibit 23.6 are just extensions of sector A in Exhibit 23.5. The sector A variance was computed by multiplying the 36 product sales volume variance by the $9,000 price variance. Hence, sectors A1 and A2 should also use the same price.

The total variance in the last column of Exhibit 23.6 is a negative $324,000, which is the same as that in Exhibit 23.5. Exhibit 23.6 divided the $324,000 decline in sales into two parts: the $468,000 increase due to company sales volume and the $792,000 decrease arising from product mix change. See the second chart of Exhibit 23.6 for the correlation of the sectors with the amounts involved.

Company Sales Volume—Tertiary Variance (Exhibit 23.7). The company sales volume variance, which is A1 in Exhibit 23.6, may be segregated further into the industry sales volume variance, which is a planning variance, and the market share variance, which is a performance variance. The industry sales variance is 1,000 units (which is the change from the 5,000 budget to 6,000 actual), and the market share variance is 2% (change from 22% budget to 20% actual). These variances are plotted as A1a and A1b, respectively, in the chart in Exhibit 23.7.

The variances are calculated in the table in Exhibit 23.7. The industry sales volume variance of 1,000 was multiplied by the lower of the budget and actual market share, while the market share variance of 2% was multiplied by the lower of the budget and actual industry sales volume. Note that the net change in the company sales volume of 100 is the same as the 100 company sales volume variance in the table in Exhibit 23.6.

The change in the company sales volume is then multiplied by the 52% actual product mix, which is lower than the budget mix.

The 52% may also be obtained from the chart in Exhibit 23.6 by inspection. Since A1a and A1b in Exhibit 23.7 are just extensions of A1 in the first chart in Exhibit 23.6, and since the company sales volume in Exhibit 23.6 is multiplied by 52% to arrive at the product sales volume variance, the values of A1a and A1b in Exhibit 23.7 should also be multiplied by the same 52%.

The result is the change in the product sales volume, which is 52 units for the combined industry sales and market share variances. This 52 units is the same as the 52 units change in the product sales volume corresponding to the total company sales volume variance per A1 in the table in Exhibit 23.6.

Finally, the change in the product sales volumes in the table in Exhibit 23.7 is multiplied by $9,000, which is the same price used in the tables in Exhibit 23.5 and 23.6. The final result is a total variance of $468,000 for A1a and A1b as shown in the last column of Exhibit 23.7. This is the same as the $468,000 company sales volume variance, which is A1 in Exhibit 23.6.

The table in Exhibit 23.7 has segregated the $468,000 company sales volume variance into an increase of $936,000 due to industry sales volume and decline of $468,000 due to market share drop. See the last chart in Exhibit 23.7.

Analysis of the Decline in Total Sales. The factors causing the $324,000 decline in sales are thus identified as

Factor	Reference	Amount
Industry sales	A1a in Exhibit 23.7	$936,000
Market share	A1b in Exhibit 23.7	(468,000)
Product mix	A2 in Exhibit 23.6	(792,000)
Total increase (decrease) in product sales	A in Exhibit 23.5	$324,000

If the multivariance analysis were not used, the management shortcoming as reflected by the drops in market share and product mix will be more than fully covered by the unexpected bonanza brought about by the rise in industry sales.

The financial impact of the $792,000 decline in sales due to the product mix cannot be appreciated until after the completion of the analysis of the cost factors and the comparison of the relative contribution margin of products A and B. As shown in Exhibit 23.2, the change in the product mix caused a $344,260 reduction in the contribution margin of product A. To this should be added the change in the contribution margin of product B.

COMMISSIONS

The basic data to be used in the variance analysis are summarized in Exhibit 23.4 of the preceding chapter.

Total Commissions Variance—Primary Variance (Exhibit 23.8, part I). Since there are no changes in the unit selling price and commission rate percentage, the variance is due only to the 36-unit drop in the product sales volume as may be noticed from the chart in Exhibit 23.5 multiplied by the $1,350 commission per unit.

Product Sales Volume—Secondary Variance (Exhibit 23.8, part II).   The objective of this analysis is to determine what part of the $48,600 is due to the rise in company sales volume and what portion is due to the fall in the product mix. The variances are computed in Exhibit 23.8, part II. The first three columns (variance, base, and change in product sales volume) are the same as those of Exhibit 23.6. However, instead of using the $9,000 selling price per unit, the $1,350 commissions cost per unit was placed in Exhibit 23.8. The $1,350 commission per unit and the total variance of $48,600 in Exhibit 23.8, part II, are the same as those in part I.

Company Sales Volume—Tertiary Variance (Exhibit 23.8, part III).   The analysis in Exhibit 23.8 part III, breaks up the $70,200 company sales volume variance (A1) in part II into the differences caused by the changes in the industry sales volume and in the market share.

Part III is identical to the table in Exhibit 23.7 except for the last two columns, which are the price per sales unit and total variance in Exhibit 23.7. The commission expense of $1,350 per sales unit and the total variance of $70,200 are the same as those in Exhibit 23.8, part II.

INTEREST EXPENSE

The interest primary variances are due to the changes in the product sales volume and the interest cost per sales unit. (See Exhibit 23.3.) The latter may be decomposed into the receivables balance per sales unit and interest rate variances. The receivables balance variance, in turn, may be factored into the unit selling price and collection period variances.

The data for the analysis of the interest variance are in Exhibit 22.4.

Total Interest Variance—Primary Variance (Exhibit 23.9, chart I, and Exhibit 23.10, part I).   Since the product sales volume is used as the quantity variance of the cost of the inputs, the horizontal axis of sector A in Exhibit 23.9, chart I, is the same as that in the first chart in Exhibit 23.5.

The vertical or price axis in chart I is the interest cost per sales unit. Sector B is the price or interest cost variance. (There is no corresponding sector B in Exhibit 23.5 as the sales does not have a primary price variance since there is no change in the selling price per unit. Furthermore, the commission variance has no sector B as there is no change in the commission rate.)

The interest primary variances are calculated in Exhibit 23.10, part I. The quantity or product sales volume variance is multiplied by the lower of the budget and actual price, and the cost variance is multiplied by the lower of the budget and actual quantity.

Product Sales Volume—Secondary Variance (Exhibit 23.10, part II).   The $19,440 favorable product sales volume variance in Exhibit 23.10, part I is split into the company sales volume variance and product mix variance in part II. The first three columns of the table are identical to those in the table in Exhibit 23.6 and those in Exhibit 23.8, part II. This is so because the sales volume is used as the quantity variance not only for the sales revenue but also for the inputs. Since Exhibit 23.10, part II is an extension of sector A of part I, the changes in the product sales volume column of part II are multiplied by the $540 interest per unit of sales just like in sector A of part I. Naturally, the total variance of $19,440 per part II supports the product sales volume variance in part I.

Company Sales Volume—Tertiary Variance (Exhibit 23.10, part III).   The $28,080 company sales volume variance in part II is broken further into the industry sales volume and market share variances. This was done in part III. This table is the same as the one in Exhibit 23.8, part III, except for the last two columns.

Cost Per Sales Unit—Secondary Variance (Exhibit 23.9, chart II).   The cost per sales unit variance, represented by sector B in Exhibit 23.9, chart I, may be dissected into its three components: receivables per sales unit, interest rate, and combined variances. The analysis is aided by Exhibit 23.9, chart II. The variance area in the chart is divided into three sectors: B1, which is due to the change in the value of receivables outstanding per unit of sales; B2, which is due to the fluctuation in the interest rate; and B3, which is due to the combined effect of these two forces. The total cost per sales unit variance of $95,472 per Exhibit 23.10, part I, is split into these three sectors in Exhibit 23.11.

The $153 total cost per sales unit for the three sectors as well as the product sales volume of 624 units used in Exhibit 23.11 are the same as the figures used in sector B in Exhibit 23.10, part I.

Since there is no change in the selling price, all the $56,160 unfavorable variance (sector B1, Exhibit 23.11) in the receivables outstanding balance per sales unit is due to the lengthening of the collection period. If there were a change in the selling price, the receivables per sales unit variance could be divided into that part arising from the price change and that portion resulting from the collection period increase.

RAW MATERIALS AND DIRECT LABOR

The variances for the raw materials are calculated in Exhibits 23.9, 23.12, and 23.13. The procedures followed are similar to those for interest. The variances for direct labor may be estimated by following similar procedures.

IV. SALES REVENUES AND VARIABLE COSTS— STANDARDS AND ACCOUNTABILITIES

STANDARDS OF PERFORMANCE AND ACCOUNTABILITIES OF MANAGERS

The budgeted revenues and expenses serve as the standard of performance against which the actual results are compared. The deviation of the results from the budgets are traced to their possible causes. If the causes are within the control of management, management is rewarded for favorable variances and is charged for unfavorable deviations.

This budget-results-variance-reward system cannot function smoothly unless the budgeted revenues and costs which serve as the standard of performance are fairly determined and the variances and their causes, which serve as the basis of the reward, are properly determined and identified.

Furthermore, a good system cannot be effective unless the responsibilities for the variances are brought down to the lowest management level in the organization chart. Management is composed not of an individual in the person of the division manager but by a team which includes the marketing, production, finance, human resource, quality control, warehousing, and other managers.

The purpose of this section of the chapter is to discuss how the standards for sales, direct labor, and raw materials may be fairly determined and to help identify those who should be made accountable for the variances. It is expected that the discussions in this section will enable the readers to have the required knowledge in setting up standards and pinpointing the responsible parties not only for the sales revenues, materials, and labor, but for other cost items which vary with sales or production.

How the variances may be calculated have been illustrated in the preceding sections of this chapter.

The setting up of standards and identification of accountable managers for variances of other types of costs are revealed in the remaining parts of this chapter.

SALES REVENUES

The primary sales revenue variances are the sales volume and selling price.

Sales Volume.　　The sales volume refers to the quantity of products sold.

Standard of Performance.　　The projected sales volume which is normally used as a standard of performance is the result of the conglomeration of several factors, many of which are unknown or not measurable at the time the budget is prepared.

The process of estimating the budgeted sales volume is initially based on solid facts, such as the historical sales figures for the past 10 years or detailed information on the orders of each customer for the past year. However, the injection of conjectures transforms the objective character of the projected sales volume into a highly subjective matter.

The conjectures include the opinions of each salesperson regarding the future needs of his or her assigned customers, the underlying assumptions such as on economic growth and demographic movements, the perceived preferences of the buyers for the various products of the company and its competitors, the anticipated acceptance of the new products to be introduced in the market, and the assumed effectiveness of the marketing strategies which each major player in the industry will unleash.

The strategies represent the factors on which the firms rely upon to capture market share such as aggressive advertising and promotion, attractive sales commissions, lenient credit standards, extended terms of sale, minimal interest rates on sales financing, discounted prices, and substantial dealers' help.

The projected sales volume figures, therefore, are very fluid. Hence, although they are adopted formally as the budget and are used as a basis in determining the sales quota, they should not be taken as a rigid framework of reference. What is more important is the analysis which is made after the actual results are in, in order to determine the causes of why the actual sales exceeded or failed to meet the sales targets and pinpoint the accountable managers.

ACCOUNTABILITIES.   The prevailing view is that the deviation of the actual sales volume from the targeted volume is the responsibility of the marketing department. This may be a reasonable assumption if the variance can be controlled by management. Although the sales department plays the most pivotal role in shaping the actual sales volume, the department by itself does not represent a substantial force in influencing the total sales volume.

The first determinant of a firm's sales volume is the total industry sales. This is substantially beyond the control of the firm, unless it happens to be the major player in the industry. For instance, a downturn in the total industry sales, and consequently a decline in the sales volume of a firm, is caused more by the changing preferences and purchasing power of the consumers rather than by the inefficiency of the sales department of a firm.

The second and third determinants are the firm's strategy and competitive strength. These determinants influence the firm's market share—or what part of the total industry sales is captured by the company.

The strategy, which is decided by the top management of big corporations, or by the owners of medium-sized firms, sets the degree of aggressiveness by which the firm will seize market share or the willingness by which it will relinquish it. An enterprise on a fast growth track will blanket its market areas with advertising messages, goad its sales force and dealer network to push the products with fat commissions, and entice the public to buy with predatory pricing policies, relaxed sales credit standards, prolonged sales repayment period, and minimal sales financing interest rates. The top management or owners who approved the strategy are the ones accountable for the success or failure of the strategy.

The strength of a firm lies in the quality, design, and availability of its products and in the effectiveness of its sales organization, in relation to the others in the industry. The building up of these strengths is due mainly to the contributions of its department managers who should be credited accordingly.

Product quality and design.   Product quality is within the provinces of the quality control, production, and engineering departments. Hence the managers of these departments should be credited if the quality is superior to those of the competitors.

Product design is the shared responsibility of the design, production, and sales departments. The last named unit provides the specifications desired by the customers.

Product availability.   A firm whose products are of excellent design and quality and which offers them at competitive price may fail to advance its market share if the products are not available. Thus, the following departments should be penalized for the sales which failed to materialize due to the nonavailability of the goods: the production department if it failed to deliver the units according to the production schedule; the warehousing department if it failed to provide the facilities to stock adequate goods and the market research department if it underestimated the future sales.

Effectiveness of the sales organization.   The sales and human resources departments should be credited if the unusual motivation of the sales force is instrumental in raising the sales volume. The sales and training units should be rewarded for the excellent skills of the salespeople. The market research section should be credited for any intelligence which the sales department was able to capitalize in cornering big sales orders.

Selling Price

STANDARD OF PERFORMANCE.   The selling price which is planned for the budget period is usually based on the historical and current price of the product. Adjustment is then made in order to make the price competitive with those of similar products of the company and of the competitors. This is particularly true where the product is a commodity, or where the products have no peculiar distinctions or do not command brand loyalty. In this case the company competes on price and in many instances may sell at lower than the prevailing prices just in order to obtain a foothold in the doorsteps of the customers of the competitors.

Where the product has special features, a premium is added. Just how much premium to add or how much to undercut the competitors' prices depends upon the strategy adopted by the firm—to grow aggressively and sacrifice current profits, in which case the company is prepared to offer prices which are substantially lower than what the competitors give, or to maximize current earnings and therefore price its products at the highest price which the market can bear.

A firms' pricing policy is synchronized not only with the overall strategy but also with its target sales volume, planned advertisements, commission rates, and sales credit terms.

ACCOUNTABILITIES.   The sales manager is not credited for having effected an actual selling price which is higher than the budget if the rise is due to an industry product shortage. In like manner, the department should not also be charged for a decline in the price if during the period under review the competitors instigated a price war.

However, the sales management should be rewarded even if the actual price just met the target if the management was able to maintain the price during a period of declining industry prices because it has the foresight to obtain long-term sales contracts with fixed prices. But the same management should be penalized if, after obtaining the fixed price sales orders, the market prices dropped.

The selling price variance should be related to the sales volume and sales expansion cost variances, as well as to the changes in product design and quality. A business unit might achieve a highly favorable price variance but at a very high cost in terms of reduced sales volume, rising advertising costs, rising collection periods, and unjustified product redesign and quality control costs.

DIRECT LABOR

Labor Efficiency.   Labor efficiency is measured by the number of direct labor hours that are required to produce one unit of product. It is the equivalent of the raw material usage rate.

STANDARD.   The traditional thinking is that the standard labor efficiency rate is the one set by engineers based on their time-and-motion studies. In practice, the standard used in the budget is the one experienced in the recent past, as adjusted for nonrecurring events and plans of the company. The labor efficiency standard is based on the premise that the work force is highly motivated and properly led.

The standard should be compared with the efficiency rate of the other divisions of the firm as well as of the other firms in the industry, considering the level of workers' qualifications, the efficiency of the equipment, and the degree of automation of the operations. The efficiency to be used may be affected by any restrictions imposed by the labor agreement. If the standard of the company is lower than that experienced by the competitors, then the firm may be headed for trouble.

ACCOUNTABILITIES. A labor efficiency variance is created when the actual management practices, employee morale, working conditions and procedures, workers' skills and physical condition, and equipment type and condition, depart from the assumptions used in preparing the budget.

Management practices. The budgeted labor efficiency can be exceeded if the instructions to the workers are made clearer so there is less time wastage. Closer supervision, especially for new workers or if there are changes in work procedures, can enhance the productivity of the workers. The institution of these practices is the responsibility of the production management. Hence, any improvement in the efficiency should be credited to them.

Participatory management, wherein the workers take an active role in initiating changes in the procedures, can also increase the output of the workers. The general management should be credited for approving participatory management, and the production management, for successfully implementing this.

Paying the workers based on the output rather than hours worked may raise their output per hour. However, this sacrifices product quality, encourages raw material waste, and hence raises the finished product reject rate. The net cost variance arising from these factors should be credited or charged to the managers responsible for the measure.

Employee morale. The introduction of employee benefits programs, such as child care for their dependents, definitely raises the employee morale and boosts their production. The excess of the benefits over the cost should be credited to the human resources department or the general management.

Overtime work, if done for long hours and sustained periods of time, may cause declining productivity due to resulting fatigue and boredom. However, if allowed for limited periods, it may actually improve the labor efficiency in that it builds up their morale, for the workers are given the chance to earn more.

Working conditions and procedures. Improvements in the working space and cleaner and brighter working environment may cause the actual workers' productivity to exceed the budget. However, these improvements also entail some costs.

Reduced workers' motions and shorter distances for the movements of goods while they are being worked on enhance the working efficiency of the workers. The time-and-motion engineers should be rewarded for the savings from these new procedures.

Automation of operations.   The automation of operations normally prove to be advisable in the long run. However, for the first few months, the productivity per worker declines. Added to this cost is the interest on the financing used to fund the new equipment and computer software. In the labor variance analysis, there should be a clear distinction between the labor-hours used in training and the hours spent on actual production.

Cost Per Hour.   The cost includes both the base pay and the benefits. The hour may refer to the hour timed in, or the hour charged to job orders. These terms were defined in Chapter 21, Section IV, which discusses the labor operating ratios.

STANDARD.   The standard cost per hour is what the company strives to attain in the budget period, considering the recruitment and training programs and schedules. The recruitment and training schedules, in turn, are based on the production schedule. The higher the percentage of new workers to the total work force, the lower the average base pay per hour due to the lower wages for the recruits. However, the training cost is higher.

The locale of recruitment influences the initial hiring rate. For instance, recruiting industrial workers in a predominantly agricultural area is normally cheaper than is pirating workers from other factories in an industrial city.

The degree of skills required naturally has a bearing on the hourly rate. Highly automated operations need employees with computer and mathematics expertise.

The presence of a strong labor union may help drive up the wages rates.

ACCOUNTABILITIES.   Those responsible for sales forecasting, production scheduling, and labor recruitment should be held responsible for increases in unit costs due to overtime and nighttime premiums paid in order to gear up production to meet a flood of sales orders. The advantage from lower employee benefit cost per hour worked, arising from the increased total hours worked per person, should be deducted from the wage premiums.

The overall cost of labor on a per hour basis may be cut down without affecting the employee morale by reducing some employee welfare activities and shifting part of the savings to augment the hourly rate. The successful efforts of the human resources development department in this regard should be recognized.

The spiraling of labor costs due to certain causes cannot be blamed on the company management. Instances of the causes are the entry of labor-intensive firms in the area which drives up the wages rates and the steep rises in medical insurance rates which are instituted by the insurers.

RAW MATERIALS

Usage Rate. The usage rate represents the quantity of raw materials used per one unit of output. It is the quantity of raw materials forming part of the finished product, plus rejects, waste, and processing and other losses.

STANDARD. What should be taken as the standard rate is what was achieved in the past, after adjusting for abnormal conditions, and after incorporating the changes which are planned to be made in the future.

The historical usage rate of the business unit under review should be compared with those of the other divisions of the company which are in the same industry as well as other firms in the industry.

The historical usage rate is adjusted for any possible variation in the future due to planned changes which will affect the usage rate in the future. Aging equipment, new and untrained workers, and nighttime and sustained overtime work may cause increased reject rate and hence higher raw material usage.

ACCOUNTABILITIES. The usage rate variance may be due to changes in the raw material quality and design, improvement in equipment efficiency, upgrading of workers' skills, or utilization of alternative production schedule.

Raw material quality and design. The usage rate variance due to changes in raw material quantity is normally the responsibility of the production department. That which is due to variations in the raw material specification is the accountability of the engineering department.

Equipment efficiency. The reject or processing loss rate may be due to the equipment. If the raw material usage rate changes due to the improved or deteriorating state of the equipment, then the maintenance department is responsible for the material usage variance. If the change is due to the use of a new equipment, then the production manager who recommended the acquisition should be credited for this. However, the equipment acquisition also causes unfavorable variances in other expenses, such as higher electricity and interest cost.

Skills of workers. Improved material usage rate may be caused by better skills of the workers. If this is the case, then the human resources or the production department should be commended.

Production schedule. The production schedule has a bearing on the raw material usage rate. Prolonged working hours, especially those running into the early hours of the morning and sustained work under pressure to produce at a rate higher than the normal, may lead to more raw material waste and finished product reject rates.

The influx of unanticipated sales orders may force the recruitment of new workers who need to be trained or the outright contracting of the job at a cost which is higher than what could normally be done in-house.

Increased costs due to these factors are the responsibility of the market research department if it failed to understate the market and the sales department, if it undertook sales expansion activities at a rate higher than the one which was planned and which was communicated to the production department in advance.

The warehousing department can also be blamed if it did not plan out the storage requirements required to even out the production schedule. Naturally, the general management may also be blamed for failing to take the initiative in coordinating and planning in advance the needs of the different departments.

Cost Per Unit.   The cost per unit of raw material used should be distinguished from the cost per unit of output. The latter is a function not only of the cost per unit of material but also of the usage rate.

STANDARD.   In preparing the budget, the cost per unit of raw material is estimated initially based on the current costs. The intentions of present and prospective suppliers are then incorporated. Big manufacturers may also consider possible reduction in price if they develop the suppliers, offer them technical advice, inform them of the requirements way ahead of normal schedule, provide financing support, and give substantial purchase orders.

ACCOUNTABILITIES.   The cost variance may be due to changes in the discounts, new raw material specifications, sourcing from new suppliers, or backward integration.

Discounts.   The raw material cost variance is caused by actions or efforts of several departments. Differences in the purchasing volume discounts are caused primarily by the sales volume variance and secondarily by the lumping of the raw material requirements into small numbers of purchase orders. Bigger purchase orders to take advantage of deeper quantity discounts or lower purchase prices are the work of the purchasing and warehousing managers.

An increase in prompt payment discounts should be credited to the department providing the funding for the purchases. Under traditional practice, this is the finance department.

New raw material specifications.   The unit cost may be cut if raw material substitutes or raw materials with specifications which are different from those originally planned are utilized. This change is normally undertaken by the designing, engineering, or production department. Where the product has to be redesigned, or where the change in the raw material specification affects the product quality, the sales department may have to be brought into the picture.

New suppliers.   The basic purchase cost may be reduced by tapping suppliers which are just starting and which are intent on developing new customers. The sourcing from new suppliers may be initiated by the production or purchasing management. Hence, their efforts should be recognized accordingly.

Backward integration. A substantial unit cost variance occurs when the firm attempts to integrate backward to the source of raw materials. If this is done, there is normally an unfavorable cost variance for the first few months or years of the project, with the expectation that once the project becomes fully stabilized, the unit cost will drop. If this is the case, the management responsible for the project should not be charged for the initial unit cost rise because of the subsequent long-term benefit of the undertaking.

V. PRODUCTION OVERHEAD—VARIANCES AND ACCOUNTABILITIES

TYPES OF COSTS

The last section of Chapter 22 has presented the traditional manner of analyzing production overhead. It was stated that all the overhead items are separated into two groups: the variable overhead and the fixed overhead. All the items in each group are analyzed in the same manner.

The variance analysis can be made more effective if the nature and behavior of the individual cost items with material amounts are recognized and treated accordingly in the evaluation work. Insignificant expenses are better lumped together; it may not be worthwhile to figure out the causes of changes of expenses with very-low-dollar values.

While it is difficult to anticipate all the types of costs in the manufacturing operations of all industries, it is easy to recognize certain types of costs and study their behavior so that the variance analysis work can be done properly. The analysis of three types of costs which are normally considered as part of production overhead are illustrated or explained in this section. It is believed that the presentation of these types of costs can be used by the readers as models in developing the variance analysis methods in their own work.

The three types of costs studied in this part are variable costs, discretionary costs, and fixed costs.

VARIABLE COSTS

Costs with material amounts and which directly vary with production volume or other activities should be treated as variable costs and analyzed in the same manner as raw materials and direct labor as explained in Section III of this chapter. However, certain changes have to be made in order to take into account the peculiar characteristics of the cost item.

Cost of Electricity. One significant item which is normally considered as a factory overhead is electricity. More useful information may be obtained from the variance analysis if the method illustrated here is followed.

ELECTRICITY REQUIREMENT. The total electricity requirement of a factory may be calculated in the manner shown here.

Connected motor load—in horsepower (HP)	
For production equipment	740 HP
To be broken into each major	
equipment unit	
For utilities or services	
To be broken down into each of boiler,	260
water treatment, maintenance shop,	
compressor, lighting and water supply	
Total motor load	1,000 HP
Horsepower to kilowatts (kw) conversion factor	.746
In kilowatts (kw)	746 kw
Load factor or capacity	70%
Operating capacity or adjusted kw	
(basis of electricity consumption)	522 kw

The total electricity consumption of a plant is roughly determined as the adjusted kilowatts multiplied by the number of hours the plant is operated. Thus if the plant with the adjusted 522 kw as illustrated operates for 2,000 hours a year, its total electricity consumption is 1,044,000 kwh (kilowatt-hours).

VARIANCE ANALYSIS FOR PURCHASED ELECTRICITY

(Exhibit 23.14)

The total electricity cost is determined by the total kwh used and the cost per kwh. Hence budget-actual deviations in these two factors constitute the primary variances.

If there is only one power company in the area, the cost per kwh is dictated by the utility company. Hence the user-firm does not have a leeway. Changes in the price imposed by the utility are beyond the control of the management of the user. However, if the utility has a dual pricing structure—one for the electricity peak demand hours and another for the nonpeak periods, the factory management can consider shifting most of its working hours from the peak period.

With emphasis on equipment efficiency (Exhibit 23.14, chart I). The kwh usage is a function of the number of units produced by the factory and the kwh required to produce one unit of output. The latter function indicates the degree of efficiency of the equipment and of the production schedule.

Variations in the kwh required per unit of output is caused by three factors: the engineering efficiency of the machines, the total number of units produced, and the production schedule.

Old machines, especially those which are not well maintained, require more electrical current to produce a given unit of output.

The electricity consumption of the service units (such as lighting and machine shop) does not directly vary with the volume of production. Hence, the higher the production, the lower is the kwh per unit of production for the service units.

The production scheduling can also have a bearing on the kwh required per unit of output. If the production orders are bunched together so that during the production time the production equipment is loaded up, and the production machinery is shut down afterward for a while, then the operating hours and hence the electricity consumption can be minimized. Of course, the production scheduling has to consider not only the electricity consumption and other cost of production, but also the requirements of the market and the financing needs as well. See Chapter 3 for a more detailed examination of production schedules.

With emphasis on operating hours and installed load (Exhibit 23.14, chart II). The analysis based on the first chart in Exhibit 23.14 does not reveal the changes in the number of operating hours and the installed load. This information is incorporated in the second chart. In this presentation, the kwh used is determined by the installed load in kw and the number of operating hours.

Differences in the factory running hours invariably cause a variance in the kwh used. If the factory is operated for a shorter period than projected, the company achieves a favorable cost variance.

The installed load is given by the equipment in place. The acquisition of additional units will naturally raise the total installed load, and hence the kwh. However, if the new units replace the older equipment, and the new units have the same production capacity as the old equipment, the total installed load may decline as the more efficient new units may have lower kw per unit of capacity than the older units.

In the short run, the factory management has control over the number of running hours since they can more easily manipulate the production schedule. However, the installed load is a given factor which they cannot readily change.

Levels of Variance Analysis for Electricity Cost. For a small manufacturing operation, the variance analysis may be made for the total electricity consumption and cost. For bigger operations, two analysis may be conducted—one for the production unit and the other for the service units. For power-intensive industries, the variance analysis may be conducted for each major production unit.

Variance Analysis for Company-Generated Electricity (Exhibit 23.14, chart III). In certain instances, a factory may be generating its own electricity.

In cases such as these, the analysis for the cost per kwh is more exhaustive.

The cost per kwh generated is a function of the total kwh generated and the total cost of electricity produced. The latter, in turn, is the sum of the cost of fuel consumed and the other costs of generating the electricity. The other costs include the depreciation of the generator and the salaries of the electrical engineer and maintenance workers.

Nonfinancial operating ratios may be tied in to the data in the financial analysis. These ratios include the fossil fuel cost per kwh generated and fossil fuel consumption (in quantity) per kwh generated.

DISCRETIONARY COSTS

The discretionary costs which are usually considered as part of the production overhead are R&D, preventive maintenance, labor development, and engineering studies.

Since these costs have no relationship to the current operations, these costs are not affected by the sales. Hence they are not variable costs. On the other hand, they are not fixed costs either, because these expenses can be raised or cut without affecting the operations. Hence the techniques of analysis for variable or fixed costs as described in this and the prior chapters cannot be applied.

A suggested technique of variance analysis of the discretionary costs is exemplified by that for R&D, which is described in the paragraphs that follow.

Research and Development. A comparison of the actual expenditures with the budget may reveal the following as the causes of the variance: changes in the plans and differences in the unit costs.

CHANGES IN THE PLANS. Changes in the plans normally account for a big portion of the variance. The changes are usually caused by (1) shift in the key business strategy, such as from "grow" to "harvest," or (2) the drying up of funds previously earmarked for R&D, or conversely, unexpected cash flow windfalls that become available for R&D and similar efforts. The "grow," "maintain," and "harvest" strategies are described in Chapter 2.

These developments may involve acceleration or deceleration of the R&D efforts, reduction or increase of the magnitude or scope of the work, building up of the in-house R&D capability or subcontracting the work to outside agencies, and participation in joint efforts with other groups such as universities. These changes naturally bring about massive recruitment or disbanding of engineering and scientific teams and the acquisition or disposition of research and development facilities as laboratories, pilot plants, and prototypes. These, in turn, cause a big gap between the budget and actual expenditures.

CHANGES IN THE COSTS. The variance due to the changes in the prices or unit costs is normally much smaller than is the variance arising from the departures from the plans. The cost variance may be due to differences between the actual compensation paid to the R&D staff being different from the anticipated amounts, or increases in the fees paid to professional or research organizations.

OTHER REVIEW TECHNIQUES FOR R&D. Since the continuance of R&D efforts involve future cash outlays and probable cash flow (receipts), the evaluation of R&D expenditures should be supplemented by cash flow, risk including probability, and internal rate of return and net present value analyses. All these techniques were described in earlier chapters.

Furthermore, it is necessary that the financial review be reinforced by qualitative appraisal of the results of the R&D efforts in relation to its prospects.

FIXED COSTS

The fixed costs in the production overhead are those which are not directly related to the volume of production and which are essential to the production operations. The fixed costs include the compensation of factory managers and staff, salaries of plant maintenance and quality control personnel, and equipment costs. Equipment costs cover depreciation, insurance, and property taxes on equipment.

The fixed cost variance is usually due to two factors: production volume and unit cost or price.

Production Volume. If the production volume goes beyond a certain range, or consistently falls below a given level, certain fixed costs will change. Thus, while the rental of warehousing space for raw materials inventory is usually constant, the rental expense goes up if the company has to lease additional space due to the production volume increases.

Similarly, if the production falls below a given level, some of the supervisors may be laid off, or certain manufacturing facilities may be shut down.

Price. The salary of the general manager may change due to a renegotiation of the employment contract or fluctuation in the incentive bonus due to a change in the base of the calculation. This deviation from the budget is represented by a price variance.

VI. OTHER MARKETING COSTS—VARIANCES AND ACCOUNTABILITIES

TYPES OF COSTS

Most marketing expenses may be classified into three types: variable costs, fixed costs, and sales expansion costs. Variable costs and sales expansion costs are similar in that their amounts constantly fluctuate. However, they have a basic difference: variable costs, such as sales commissions and interest on accounts receivable financing as explained earlier in this chapter, are incurred after a sale is made, and therefore vary directly with the sales. On the other hand, sales expansion costs, such as advertising or promotions, are committed before a sale is made, and hence have no direct relationship with sales.

Under current practice, advertising is considered either as a variable or a fixed cost. It is treated as variable cost if the advertising budget is set at a certain percentage of sales; it is called a fixed cost if the budget is for a given monthly amount. In reality, however, it is neither fixed nor variable as it does not fit into the definition of these terms.

In certain cases, the classification of a marketing cost depends more on its purpose or the practice of the sales department rather than on the nature of the cost. Thus, the gasoline of sales vehicles is a fixed cost if there is a given number of salespeople in a territory and they make the same number of trips irrespective of the level of sales—that is, they make a round of all the stores in their area, with the vehicles full or half loaded with merchandise, depending upon the sales volume they make.

The gasoline is considered as a variable cost if the sales are effected at the sales office and the vehicles are used by the salespeople in delivering the goods. Hence, there is no gasoline consumption until after a sale is consummated.

The gasoline is a sales expansion cost if the vehicles are used by the salesmen mainly in offering the goods to new customers. Thus, the vehicles have to make the trips before any sale is effected, and regardless of the volume of any resulting sale.

This part of the chapter reviews the sales expansion costs. The variance analysis of variable cost has been treated earlier by using sales commissions as an illustration. The sales fixed costs may be analyzed in the same manner as the production fixed costs.

SALES EXPANSION COSTS

Sales expansion costs, as advertising, may rise at a rate faster or slower than sales. Sales expansion costs are incurred in order to increase the overall profitability of the firm during the current year and subsequent years.

Visible Sales Expansion Cost: Advertising. Although the objective of advertising is to expand the sales, it is in reality a discretionary cost, like R&D. Hence it has the same budget-to-actual variances: variance due to the changes in the plans and variance due to the changes in the costs.

CHANGES IN THE PLANS. A shift in the basic corporate strategy, such as from "harvest" to "grow," or an exceptionally high or low response of sales to the sales expansion cost calls for changes in the advertising plans.

For print advertisement, the variations in the plans involve changes in (1) the magazine or newspaper media, (2) days of issue (as to come out on Mondays or weekends), (3) page placement (inside page or back page), (4) size of ad, and (5) frequency. For electronic (TV or radio) advertisement, the variation in the plans entail changes in (1) the media (TV or radio station), (2) days of exposure, (3) time of exposure (time of day) or during prime time or off prime time, (4) duration per exposure (in seconds or minutes), and (5) frequency.

CHANGES IN THE COSTS. The price variance constitutes the difference between the budget and the actual, assuming there is no change in the plans. This is due to adjustments in the rates charged by the advertising media.

OTHER REVIEW TECHNIQUES. Although variance analysis is useful in accounting for the differences between the budgeted expense and the actual, it is not adequate in determining the effectiveness of the activity. The advertising cost has to be related to the additional profit or cash flow which is brought about by the incremental sales. This type of analysis is the subject of Chapter 11.

Invisible Sales Expansion Costs. For purposes of financial analysis, there are two types of sales expansion costs: the visible and the invisible. A review of the financial statements will reveal to the readers the advertising and promotional expenses as sales expansion costs. These are the visible sales expansion costs: they can be noticed offhand, and the reader know their purpose.

On the other hand, there are certain sales expansion costs which are hardly visible or completely invisible in that they are not treated as marketing expenses or are not treated as costs or expenses at all. An example of the first one is the use of low financing rates on sales installment notes. The interest on the notes receivables appears on the financial statements as other income (interest income), and the interest on the bank loans which is used to carry the notes receivables shows up as other expenses (interest expense). A completely invisible cost is price reduction. This cost does not register at all as cost or expense, but only as a decline in the selling price. However, the selling price itself does not appear on the financial statement.

Since the invisible sales expansion costs are not properly shown, if at all, in the financial statements and budgets, no budget-actual variance can be readily estimated. Special techniques are required for analyzing sales expansion costs. The technique for reviewing sales expansion costs in general is illustrated in Chapter 11, while the method for appraising interest or time value of money on the financing used to carry receivables is reviewed in Chapter 25.

VII. WAREHOUSING AND OTHER INVENTORY COSTS—VARIANCES AND ACCOUNTABILITIES

TYPES OF COSTS

Inventory costs are the expenses of carrying the stocks of merchandise, finished goods, and raw materials.

Normally, there are three types of inventory costs: variable, semivariable, and fixed. The significant variable costs are the interest on financing used to carry the inventories and the inventory insurance. The more important fixed costs are the rentals or depreciation of warehouse buildings and equipment and compensation of personnel—warehouse operators, inventory handlers, and security guards.

The variance analysis for interest, insurance, and rentals are explained in the discussion that follows. The analysis for the other fixed costs may substantially follow the general procedures for production fixed costs.

INVENTORY INSURANCE (Exhibit 23.15)

One way of applying the multivariance analysis to inventory insurance is by breaking down the total variance into two variances: the insured value variance and the rate variance.

Rate Variance. The rate variance is the difference between the budgeted insurance premium rate (in dollars per $1,000 of insured value) and the average actual rate for the period. The differences in the rate or rate adjustments may be general in character or may be specific to the insured firm.

GENERAL RATE ADJUSTMENT. A major cause of the general rate adjustment is the substantial change in the recent loss experience of the insured with respect to the industry or geographical area where the insured firm is situated. Since this adjustment is beyond the control of the insured, its management should not be accountable for this variance.

SPECIFIC RATE ADJUSTMENT.   A rate adjustment which is peculiar to the insured may be due to the consolidation of insurance coverage, adoption of safety measures, or successful negotiation with a new insurance firm. Since these adjustments are the results of efforts conducted by the management of the insured, the management should be given credit for the rate reductions.

A firm may package together in one policy the different insurable assets, including inventories, of the different divisions which are in different industries and located in different locations. The consolidation of the policy should give the insured substantial discounts not only due to the greater volume of business which it offers its insurance company, but also because of the diversification of risk in terms of asset type and industry and geographical spread.

The installation of safety equipment and procedures, as alarm, sprinkler, and security systems, should also enable the insured to obtain rate concessions from its insurance companies.

Last, the insured may successfully conclude with a new insurer premiums which are lower than its present insurance company could offer. This can be particularly true if the new insurer has sister companies outside the insurance industry and the insured is dealing with the sister companies.

Insured Value Variance.   The other primary variance of inventory insurance is the insured value. A reduction in the insured value invariably reduces the insurance premium and causes a favorable variance. The insured value is composed of two components: the average actual value of the inventories and the margin (excess over the actual value) or the deficiency (underinsurance). The greater the deficiency, the lower is the premium cost, but the higher is the level of risk which the operating company is taking on to itself.

The average actual value, in turn, is a factor of two items: the value per unit of inventory and the average number of units on stock. The value per unit changes due to (1) inflation, (2) variations in specifications, and (3) negotiation with suppliers in case of merchandise and raw materials and negotiations with suppliers and control of production costs in case of finished goods.

The average number of units on stock is indicated by three determinants: (1) the sales volume for finished goods or merchandise inventories or production volume for the raw materials inventories, (2) the inventory turnover or average inventory period, and (3) the production schedule of firms with highly seasonal sales in case of finished goods inventory. Production scheduling is discussed further in Chapter 3, Section VII.

Management should be rewarded for its successful efforts in reducing the inventories by shortening the inventory period or by improving the production schedule.

INVENTORY INTEREST (Exhibit 23.15)

The variance on interest on loans used to carry to inventories may be calculated by following substantially the same procedures as for estimating the inventory insurance variance. The major differences are (1) instead of using the insurance premium rate, the loan interest rate is applied, and (2) the interest rate is based on the actual inventory value rather than on the insured value.

INVENTORY INSURANCE AND INTEREST AS SEMIVARIABLE COSTS

Inventory insurance and interest may be considered as variable cost in that they increase with the rise in sales or production volume. However, they are not variable cost in the same context that raw materials used is a variable cost, since the production or sales volume is not the only factor which changes the quantity of the inventories. As discussed earlier, the quantity is also affected by the inventory periods and production schedules.

In certain cases, inventory insurance and interest may be considered as semivariable cost, since part of the cost is variable and part is fixed.

If the amount is significant it may be advisable to divide the inventories into two parts: the base inventories and the variable portion. The base component represents the minimum level required to sustain operations; the variable part is the one that floats with the production or sales volume on top of the minimum level. Interest on loans used to carry the base inventories and insurance thereon is a fixed cost; interest on loans to finance the other part and insurance thereon is a variable cost.

RENTS ON LEASED WAREHOUSES (Exhibit 23.15)

In many instances, the warehouse rent is composed of two factors: the total floor area in square feet and the rental rate per square meter. The rate is the result of a rate canvass, negotiation with the lessor, and periodic rate adjustment in case of leases previously perfected. Management should not be penalized for rate increases due to inflation. However, the management should be credited for rate reduction if they have relocated the warehouse to a cheaper neighborhood.

For purposes of analysis work, the total area available (in square feet) should be segregated into the average used area and the unutilized space.

A high unutilized space may compensate for a low rental rate. The company may have obtained an oversized warehouse because of the low rental per square foot. While management is credited for low rentals, it should also be charged for the unutilized space.

There are two performance indicators for the utilized space: the number of units stored and the stocking rate. These indicators are very effective if a sizable portion of the inventories is homogeneous, as in the case of raw materials of a cigaret manufacturer—the tobacco is in hogsheads of almost uniform sizes and weights.

The more the company can cut down on the number of units stored, or reduce its inventory levels, the lower will its warehousing space requirements will be, and the lower will be the rental cost in the long run. However a low inventory level does not necessarily mean a low space requirement if the inventories are not properly stacked up—that is, if the number of units in storage is low in relation to the space occupied. Hence the management should be judged not only on how well it is able to keep down the inventory levels, but also on how it is able to maximize the utilization of every square foot of warehousing space.

VIII. ADMINISTRATIVE COSTS—VARIANCES AND ACCOUNTABILITIES

This part covers the three types of administrative costs: discretionary expenses, fixed costs, and allocated costs.

DISCRETIONARY EXPENSES

The variance analysis of the discretionary expenses cannot be generalized, since each type may call for a special treatment. Two types of discretionary expenses are examined here: management development costs and management bonuses.

Management Development Costs. Like the R&D and advertising expenses, the variance of actual expenditures from the budgeted administrative expenses is accounted for mainly by changes in plans and secondarily by variations in price. Thus, management development costs, which include the cost of seminars, formal graduate courses, group discussions and consultants, fluctuate in accordance with the overall management plans regarding corporate growth and diversification, on one hand, and sourcing of executives, on the other.

A firm which adopted during the year an aggressive expansion strategy, coupled with a program to fill up new positions from the inside, will naturally overshoot its management development budget. On the other hand, a company which decided during the year to slow down on its activities and recruit experienced managers from other firms will have an unspent management development cost budget.

It is apparent, therefore, that the performance of management should be judged not on whether it has a favorable or unfavorable variance at the end of the year, but on how sound is the strategy it has adopted during the year and how effective is its management development program in helping attain said strategy.

Management Bonuses. There are two types of management bonuses: contractual and discretionary. The amount of contractual bonus to be received by executives is stipulated in the management contract. The amount is dependent on the achievement of certain targets, as a profit which is defined in the contract or the successful introduction of a given number of products within a period of time. The budget-actual variance of such bonuses, therefore, is mainly due to the error in projecting the attainment of the targets.

On the other hand, the variance of discretionary bonuses is due purely to the difference between the amount of the bonus decided by the executive committee or equivalent body and the amount anticipated by those who prepared the budget.

FIXED COSTS

The variance of a number of office expenses—as salaries of office employees and rental of office spaces—may be divided into quantity variance and price variance. The quantity variance is due to the change in the number of personnel or square footage of office space, while the price variance is due to the variation in the hourly or monthly rate of the employees or in the rental rate per square foot of office area.

The quantity variance of the fixed costs should be distinguished from the volume variance of the variable costs.

ALLOCATED COSTS

It is a normal practice of many organizations to charge the operating divisions with the cost of operating the corporate office. Allocated expenses which are beyond the control of the management of the division should be taken out of variance analysis. The reason is that the objective of variance analysis is to evaluate the performance of a business unit and its managers. Hence the analysis should be restricted to the items which are within the control of the unit which is being appraised.

EXHIBIT 23.1:
Graphic Comparison of Direct Labor Variances

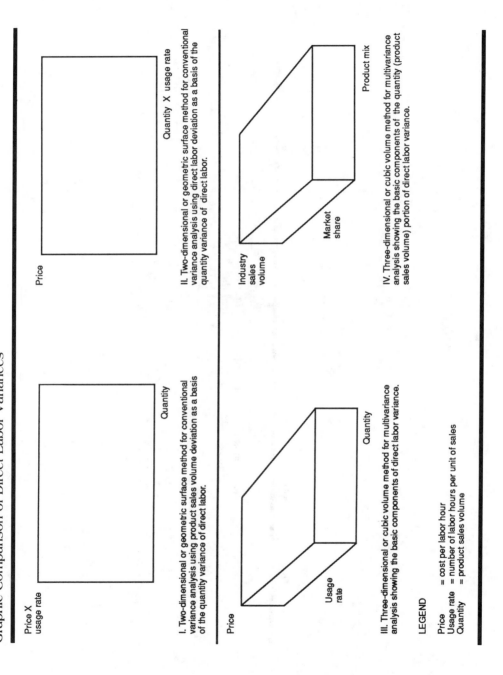

Price X
usage rate

Quantity

I. Two-dimensional or geometric surface method for conventional variance analysis using product sales volume deviation as a basis of the quantity variance of direct labor.

Price

Quantity X usage rate

II. Two-dimensional or geometric surface method for conventional variance analysis using direct labor deviation as a basis of the quantity variance of direct labor.

Price

Usage
rate

Quantity

III. Three-dimensional or cubic volume method for multivariance analysis showing the basic components of direct labor variance.

Industry
sales
volume

Market
share

Product mix

IV. Three-dimensional or cubic volume method for multivariance analysis showing the basic components of the quantity (product sales volume) portion of direct labor variance.

LEGEND

Price   = cost per labor hour
Usage rate = number of labor hours per unit of sales
Quantity   = product sales volume

581

EXHIBIT 23.2:
Summary of Variances (dollars in $1,000)[†]

	Sales (Exhibits 5, 6, 7)	Commission (Exhibit 23.8)	Interest (Exhibits 23.10, 11)	Materials (Exhibits 23.12, 13)	Labor	Total	Contribution margin
EXPENSES							
Total variance							
Per budget	$5,940.00	$891.00	$356.40	$1,584.00	$594.00	$3,425.40	$2,514.60
Actual	5,616.00	842.40	432.43	1,544.40	497.95	3,317.18	2,298.82
Total variance*	($ 324.00)	($ 48.60)	$ 76.03	($ 39.60)	($ 96.05)	($ 108.22)	($ 215.78)
Sales volume variance							
Industry sales volume	$ 936.00	$140.40	$ 56.16	$ 249.60	$ 82.99	$ 529.15	$ 406.85
Market share	(468.00)	(70.20)	(28.08)	(124.80)	(41.50)	(264.58)	(203.42)
Company sales volume	$ 468.00	$ 70.20	$ 28.08	$ 124.80	$ 41.49	$ 264.57	$ 203.43
Product mix	(792.00)	(118.80)	(47.52)	(211.20)	(70.22)	(447.74)	(344.26)
Product sales volume	($ 324.00)	(48.60)	($ 19.44)	($ 86.40)	($ 28.73)	($ 183.17)	($ 140.83)

582

EXHIBIT 23.2:
Continued

	Sales (Exhibits 5, 6, 7)	Commission (Exhibit 23.8)	Interest (Exhibits 23.10, 11)	Materials (Exhibits 23.12, 13)	Labor	Total	Contribution margin
EXPENSES							
Price variance							
Usage rate*			$ 56.16	($ 124.80)	($ 26.21)	($ 94.85)	$ 94.85
Unit price per input unit			33.70	171.60	(35.57)	169.73	(169.73)
Combined variance			5.62	0.00	(1.87)	3.75	(3.75)
Price per sales unit	$ 0.00	$ 0.00	$ 95.47	$ 46.80	($ 63.65)	$ 78.62	($ 78.62)
Combined sales volume and price variance							
Product sales							
volume	($ 324.00)	($ 48.60)	($ 19.44)	($ 86.40)	($ 28.73)	($ 183.17)	($ 140.83)
Price per sales unit	0.00	0.00	95.47	46.80	(63.65)	78.62	(78.62)
Combined volume and price					(3.67)	(3.67)	3.67
Volume and price	($ 324.00)	($ 48.60)	$ 76.03	($ 39.60)	($ 96.05)	($ 108.22)	($ 215.78)

†Figures in parentheses denote unfavorable variances.
*Input unit per sales unit.

583

EXHIBIT 23.3:
Primary, Secondary and Tertiary Variances

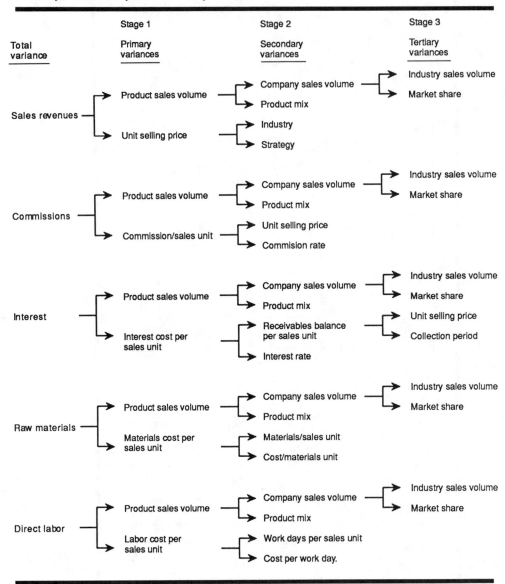

EXHIBIT 23.4:
Base Data For Variance Analysis

	Budget	*Actual*	*Change*
Sales			
Industry sales volume	5,000	6,000	1,000
Market share	22%	20%	−2%
Company sales volume	1,100	1,200	100
Product mix	60%	52%	−8%
Product sales volume	660	624	(36)
Unit selling price	$9,000	$9,000	$ 0
Total value (in $1,000)	$5,940	$5,616	($324)

EXHIBIT 23.5:
Sales—Primary Variance

I. ANALYSIS OF THE CHANGE FROM BUDGET TO ACTUAL (Budget ———▶ Actual)

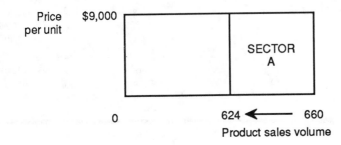

II. CALCULATION OF THE VARIANCE

Sector*		Variance	Base†	Total variance
A	Product sales volume	(36)	$9,000	($324,000)

*Pertains to the area in the chart.
† Lower of the budget and actual.

III. COMPONENTS OF THE SALE VARIANCE

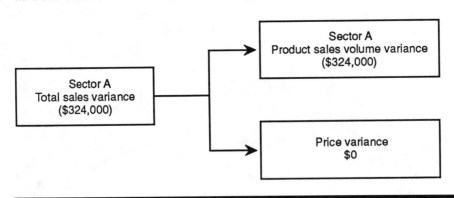

EXHIBIT 23.6:

Sales—Product Sales Volume—Secondary Variances

I. ANALYSIS OF THE CHANGE FROM BUDGET TO ACTUAL (Budget ──────▶ Actual)

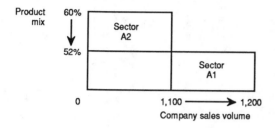

II. CALCULATION OF THE VARIANCES

Sector*		Variance	Base†	Change in product sales volume	Price per sales unit	Total variance
A1	Company sales volume	100	52%	52	$9,000	$468,000
A2	Product mix	–8%	1,100	(88)	9,000	(792,000)
A	Total = product sales volume			(36)	9,000	$324,000

* Pertains to the area in the chart.
† Lower of the budget and actual.

III. COMPONENTS OF THE SALES VARIANCE

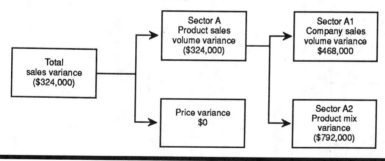

EXHIBIT 23.7:

Sales—Company Sales Volume—Tertiary Variances

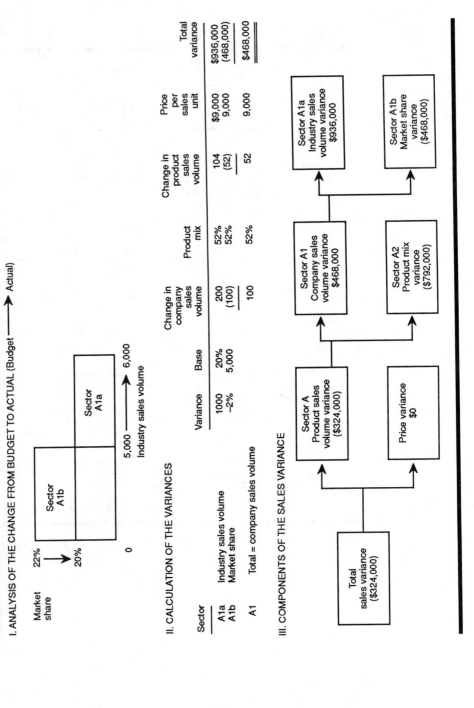

I. ANALYSIS OF THE CHANGE FROM BUDGET TO ACTUAL (Budget ——→ Actual)

II. CALCULATION OF THE VARIANCES

Sector		Variance	Base	Change in company sales volume	Product mix	Change in product sales volume	Price per sales unit	Total variance
A1a	Industry sales volume	1000	20%	200	52%	104	$9,000	$936,000
A1b	Market share	–2%	5,000	(100)	52%	(52)	9,000	(468,000)
A1	Total = company sales volume			100	52%	52	9,000	$468,000

III. COMPONENTS OF THE SALES VARIANCE

EXHIBIT 23.8:
Commissions—Variance Analysis

I. COMMISSIONS – PRIMARY VARIANCE

Sector*	Variance	Base	Total variance
A	Product sales volume		
	−36	$1,350	($48,600)

II. PRODUCT SALES VOLUME – SECONDARY VARIANCES

Sector*	Variance	Base	Change in product sales volume	Commission per sales unit	Total variance
A1	Company sales volume	100	52%	52	$1,350	$70,200
A2	Product mix	−8%	1,100	(88)	1,350	(118,800)
A	Total = product sales volume			(36)	1,350	($48,600)

III. COMPANY SALES VOLUME – TERTIARY VARIANCES

Sector*	Variance	Base	Change in company sales volume	Product mix	Change in product sales volume	Commission per sales unit	Total variance
A1a	Industry sales volume	1000	20%	200	52%	104	$1,350	$140,400
A1b	Market share	−2%	5,000	(100)	52%	(52)	1,350	(70,200)
A1	Total = company sales volume			100	52%	52	1,350	$70,200

*Sector A is the same as in the first chart in Exhibit 23.5, sector A1 and A2 in Exhibit 23.6, and sectors A1a and A1b in Exhibit 23.7. However, instead of the $9,000 shown as selling price per unit in Exhibits 23.5, 23.6, and 23.7, substitute $1,350, which is the commission rate per unit.

EXHIBIT 23.9:
Interest, Materials and Labor

I. INTEREST – PRIMARY VARIANCES

II. INTEREST COST PER SALES UNIT – SECONDARY VARIANCES

Interest
cost per
sales
unit

$693

$540

	Sector B	Sector A

0

624 → 660
Product sales volume

Interest
rate

1.1%

1.0%

Sector B2	Sector B3
	Sector B1

0

$54,000 → $63,000
Receivables per sales unit

III. RAW MATERIALS – PRIMARY VARIANCES

IV. RAW MATERIALS COST PER SALES UNIT – SECONDARY VARIANCES

Cost per
sales
unit

$2,475

$2,400

	Sector B	Sector A

0

624 → 660
Product sales volume

Cost per
unit of
material

$225

$200

Sector B2	
	Sector B1

0

11 → 12
Usage rate or
materials per sales unit

The charts for the product sales volume secondary variances for interest, and raw materials are the same as the first chart in Exhibit 23.6. The charts for the company sales volume tertiary variances for interest, and raw materials are the same as the first chart in Exhibit 23.7.

590

EXHIBIT 23.10:
Interest Variance Analysis

I. INTEREST – PRIMARY VARIANCE
(See Exhibit 23.9, Chart I, for the Sectors A and B)

Sector		Variance	Base	Total variance
A	Company sales volume	–36	$540	($19,440)
B	Cost per sales unit	$153	624	95,472
	Total = product sales volume			$76,032

— Exhibit 23.11

II. PRODUCT SALES VOLUME – SECONDARY VARIANCES
(See Exhibit 23.6, Chart I)

Sector		Variance	Base	Change in product sales volume	Intrest per sales unit	Total variance
A1	Company sales volume	100	52%	52	$540	$28,080
A2	Product mix	–8%	1,100	(88)	540	(47,520)
A	Total = product sales volume			(36)	540	($19,440)

III. COMPANY SALES VOLUME – TERTIARY VARIANCES
(See Exhibit 23.7, Chart I)

Sector		Variance	Base	Change in company sales volume	Product mix	Change in product sales volume	Price per sales unit	Total variance
A1a	Industry sales volume	1000	20%	200	52%	104	$540	$56,160
A1b	Market share	–2%	5,000	(100)	52%	(52)	540	(28,080)
A1	Total = company sales variance			100	52%	52	540	$28,080

EXHIBIT 23.11:

Interest: Cost Per Sales Unit—Secondary Variance

(See Exhibit 23.9, chart II, for the sectors B1, B2, and B3)

Sector	First variance	Second variance	Base	Change in cost per sales unit	Product sales volume	Total variance
B1	$9,000		1%	$ 90	624	$56,160
B2	0.1%	54,000		$ 54	624	$33,696
B3	0.1%	$9,000		$ 9	624	5,616
				$153		$95,472
B	Total = cost per sales unit				624	

*Since there is no change in the selling price, all the $56,160 variance in receivables outstanding per sales unit is due to the change in the collection period.

EXHIBIT 23.12:
Raw Materials Variance Analysis

I. RAW MATERIALS – PRIMARY VARIANCE
(See Exhibit 23.9, Chart III, for the Sectors A and B)

Sector		Variance	Base	Total variance
A	Product sales volume	(36)	$2,400	($86,400)
B	Cost per sales unit	$75	624	46,800
	Total = variance			$(39,600)

— Exhibit 23.13

II. PRODUCT SALES VOLUME – SECONDARY VARIANCES
(See Exhibit 23.6, Chart I)

Sector		Variance	Base	Change in product sales volume	Raw material cost per sales unit	Total variance
A1	Company sales volume	100	52%	52	$2,400	$124,800
A2	Product mix	–8%	1,100	(88)	2,400	(211,200)
A	Total = product sales volume			(36)	2,400	($86,400)

III. COMPANY SALES VOLUME – TERTIARY VARIANCES
(See Exhibit 23.7, Chart I)

Sector		Variance	Base	Change in company sales volume	Product mix	Change in product sales volume	Raw material cost per sales unit	Total variance
A1a	Industry sales volume	1000	20%	200	52%	104	$2,400	$249,600
A1b	Market share	–2%	5,000	(100)	52%	(52)	2,400	(124,800)
A1	Total = company sales variance			100	52%	52	2,400	$124,800

EXHIBIT 22.13:

Raw Materials: Cost Per Sales Unit—Secondary Variances
(see Exhibit 23.9, chart IV, for the sectors B1 and B2)

Sector	Variance	Base	Change in cost per sales unit	Base product sales volume	Total variance
B1	(1)	$200	($200)	624	($124,800)
B2	$25	11	275	624	171,600
B	Total = cost per sales unit		$ 75	624	$ 46,800

EXHIBIT 23.14:
Electricity Cost—Variances

Total variance	Primary variances	Secondary variances	Tertiary variances

I. PURCHASED ELECTRICITY – KEY VARIANCE BASED ON KWH PER OUTPUT

II. PURCHASED ELECTRICITY – KEY VARIANCE BASED ON OPERATING HOURS

III. COMPANY-GENERATED ELECTRICITY

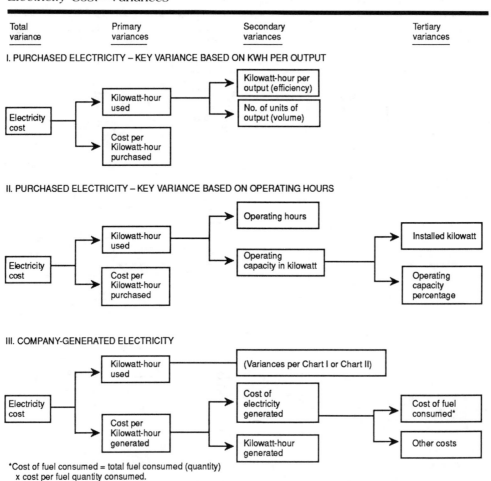

*Cost of fuel consumed = total fuel consumed (quantity) x cost per fuel quantity consumed.

EXHIBIT 23.15:
Warehousing and Inventory Costs—Variances

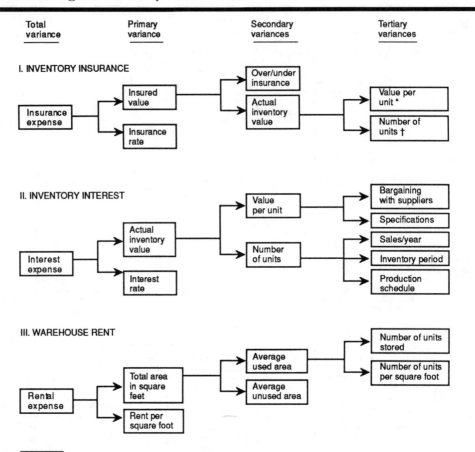

*Value per unit = caused by specifications and inflation.

†Number of units = caused by production schedule (for finished
  goods and raw materials) and by purchase schedule (for merchandise
  and raw materials).

Chapter 24 _____

EVALUATING PERFORMANCE BY STRATEGY

Strategies and programs are the locomotives that drive business firms to growth and profitability. However, while the results of operations are often segregated and reviewed by division and by product, they are usually not separated and evaluated by strategy.

Due to this vacuum in information, it is difficult to gauge and evaluate the performance of strategies and programs. Hence, management will literally be groping in the dark when they strive to take corrective actions or formulate new plans that can improve the operations.

This chapter describes and illustrates the techniques that may be employed to determine the profitability of each major strategy and relate it to the resources which were utilized in the implementation of said strategy.

A new income statement format is used. The new format is suited for a dynamic firm, that is, one that spends heavily on market and product development. This new format improves on the traditional contribution margin form by remedying its limitations which were revealed in Chapter 17, Section III.

I. STRATEGIES AND MEASURES

Assume that the company pursued the following in year 2:

Short-term profitability measures
   1. Cost reduction
   2. Market saturation in existing territories

Long-term strategies
1. Market territory expansion
2. New product development and plant expansion.

The company has to determine the results of each of these programs in addition to those of the normal operations. The normal operations and the measures and strategies are explained in the paragraphs that follow.

Normal operations.   The normal operations cater to a regional market which remains stagnant. The players in the industry just try to maintain their respective market shares. The selling prices and costs inch upward with the inflation rate, which is assumed to be 4%. Under this stable environment, the advertising cost of the firm is held constant. Furthermore, there remains no need to expand the plant capacity.

Cost reduction and management inefficiency.   During the year, the management implemented cost reduction measures. These involved (1) slashing the interest expenses by reducing the raw materials inventory and lengthening the terms of payment for the accounts payable and (2) cutting the administrative costs. However, management inefficiency caused the finished goods inventory to balloon from two months' sales requirements in year 1 to three months in year 2.

Market saturation.   The company undertook a market saturation program to expand the sales volume within the existing geographical territories. The firm accomplished this by lengthening its terms of sales from four to five months and spending heavily on advertisement.

Market territory expansion.   This strategy involves the opening of a new market territory. The program required the establishment of a sales facility in the new area, accompanied by a massive introductory advertising program. Sales operations were conducted for the last four months of year 2. The new sales facility required additional marketing fixed costs. However, no additional manufacturing and general administrative overhead costs were involved.

New product development and plant expansion. The objective of this strategy is to provide for the future, new products, and expanded production facilities. The firm intensified its new product development effort by trebling its R&D expenses in year 2 to $2,940,000. The construction of a new plant was commenced. The covering expenditures during year 2 totaled $18,000,000.

II. PROFITABILITY

Lumping together the results of all the different strategies with that of the normal operations will not give management an idea of the performance of both normal operations and each of the major programs. Hence, the profitability and corresponding resources used for each of these sectors have to be brought out.

FORMAT AND DATA SOURCES (Exhibit 24.1)

The first step is to construct an income statement which clearly shows the sales, costs, and resulting profit for each activity. A detailed income statement which shows the results by strategy is illustrated in Exhibit 24.1.

The year 2 total figures are the same as the corresponding amounts in the contribution margin income statement in Exhibit 17.4 of Chapter 17. However, instead of classifying the costs just into variable and fixed costs, the new format groups the costs into four categories. The new groups cover (1) the sales expansion costs and (2) long-term costs—consisting of the future and past benefit costs and sunk costs. The reasons for these new groups are given later.

SALES (Exhibit 24.1)

The sale of normal operations for year 2 is basically the same as that of the prior year as adjusted for inflation. The sales arising from the implementation of the market saturation measure is the incremental sales in the original market territories. In an actual case, the sales from the new geographic markets can easily be taken from the sales records.

VARIABLE COSTS (Exhibit 24.1)

Since the selling prices and costs increased with the inflation, the variable cost as percentage of sales of year 2 is about the same as for year 1—31.5%.

The freight out which was retained under variable cost for new market territories is based on the equivalent freight for the old territories. The additional freight due to the longer distance was reclassified from variable costs in Exhibit 17.1 of Chapter 17 to sales expansion cost in Exhibit 24.1 of this chapter.

For each of the individual strategies or measures, the advertising, bad debts, and collection expenses were also reclassified. With these reclassifications, each of the remaining variable costs increased at the same rate as the sales—19%.

Since the products sold in the new market territory were made in the old manufacturing facilities of the company, and since the prices in the new market are the same as in the traditional market, the direct manufacturing costs as a percentage of sales is the same as for the normal operations.

SALES EXPANSION COSTS (Exhibit 24.1)

Sales expansion costs are these incurred in connection with programs to push sales beyond the normal levels. These costs are separately shown as these are neither variable nor fixed costs. (For further materials on sales expansion costs, refer to Chapter 17, Financial Statements as Bases of Evaluation, for general discussions, and Chapter 11, Analyzing Sales Expansion Measures, for applications in decision analysis.)

Although sales expansion costs are related to sales, they do not vary in direct proportion to the sales. For instance, these grew by 73% in year 2, compared with the sales and variable costs, which rose by only 19%.

Market saturation measure.   The lengthening of the sales credit terms brought with it added collection expenses. Hence this measure is charged for this incremental cost. The longer credit terms give rise to the build-up in the receivables, which, in turn, necessitates financing. The additional financing raises the interest cost.

Market territory expansion strategy.   Advertising and freight costs in relation to sales are higher than those for the normal operations. The advertising cost is high due to the low initial sales volume and excessive product introduction advertisements in the new area. The freight cost is high because of the longer shipping distances involved.

CURRENT OVERHEAD (Exhibit 24.1)

Current overhead costs are those which were incurred in, and benefited, the period under review. Hence, the current overhead shown in Exhibit 24.1 excludes R&D expenses, legal settlement costs, and depreciation. Legal settlement costs were part of the $7,280,000 administrative expenses in Exhibit 17.4 of Chapter 17. These long-term costs are explained further presently.

The remaining fixed costs were assigned to normal operations, cost reduction, and new market territories. Factory overhead and maintenance are chargeable to normal operations. The overhead of the marketing facilities in the new market territories are assigned to the market territory expansion strategy; the rest of the marketing overhead is for normal operations.

After taking out $1,040,000 legal costs from the $7,280,000 administrative expenses, the balance of $6,240,000 is for current operations. If there were no cost savings in year 2, the amount for this year could had been the $7,000,000 in year 1 plus inflation, or $7,280,000. The difference of $1,040,000, which coincidentally is of the same amount as the legal costs, is the result of cost savings.

CURRENT OPERATING PROFIT (Exhibit 24.1)

The current operating profit shows the revenues earned during the year, as well as the costs which were incurred or committed during the year to earn the revenues. The performance of managers may be based on this figure less the interest as discussed next.

INTEREST (Exhibits 24.1 and 24.2)

The interest expense in Exhibit 24.1 is based on the loans which are used to support the resources utilized by each activity. The interest expense for each activity is calculated in Exhibit 24.2. The loan balances used in the computations were taken from the balance sheet in Exhibit 24.3. The traditional or loan-based method of charging interest to operations was followed. An alternative technique, the resource-based interest approach, is explained and illustrated in Chapter 25.

Cost reduction measure. The $76,000 savings in interest is due to the $1,898,000 reduction in long-term loans at 8% a year for a weighted average duration of half a year.

Market saturation measure. The interest includes that on loans used to carry the receivables in excess of the traditional four months' sales. (The treatment of interest on financing to carry the receivables is explained and illustrated in Chapter 25, Evaluating Performance with Resource-Based Interest, for application in performance evaluation, and Chapter 11, Analyzing Sales Expansion Measures, for use in decision analysis.)
   Because of the jump in the outstanding receivables and in the inventories, the interest expense at $674,000 is a significant 5.4% of the incremental sales. Under normal operations, the interest was only 1.9% of sales.

Future growth strategy. The interest on loans utilized to finance the construction in progress are not charged to normal operations since the current year did not receive any benefits from them. Hence it is shown under the future growth strategy.

LONG-TERM COSTS (Exhibit 24.1)

Although R&D and legal settlement costs in the illustration were incurred in year 2, they did not benefit year 2. R&D will benefit future years, while the legal settlement cost is for cases arising from prior years. Although depreciation benefited year 2, the covering buildings and equipment were acquired in prior years. Since these costs were not incurred in year 2, they may be called long-term costs and hence should be excluded from current costs. Otherwise, current performance will not be properly measured.

Depreciation and past benefit costs are not directly controllable by the management.

INCOME TAX (Exhibit 24.1)

The total income tax in year 2 is $7,144,000. This is 40% of the assumed combined federal and state tax, based on the $17,861,000 taxable income in Exhibit 17.1, Chapter 17 which uses the full costing method for finished goods inventory. However, utilizing the direct costing procedure as done in Exhibit 24.1 of this chapter, the pretax income is only $13,321,000. Hence, the actual tax liability of $7,144,000 comes out to 53.63% of the pre-tax income under the direct costing method. The 53.63% flat rate is then applied to the pretax income of all activities.

See Chapter 17 for a fuller discussion on the differences in the net income under the two methods of finished goods inventory costing.

NET PROFIT (Exhibit 24.1)

Normal operations and saturation measure.   The normal operations were able to achieve a posttax profit of 5.3% of sales. Notwithstanding the rise in the sales expansion costs and interest expense as a percentage of sales, the market saturation measure was able to produce a posttax profit of $2,449,000, which is 19.6% of sales. This impressive profit rate was achieved since the firm was able to implement the strategy without adding to the fixed costs.

Market expansion territory strategy.   The low sales volume, on the one hand, paired with the high start-up costs, on the other, resulted in a massive loss of $3,576,000 after interest on the working capital. However, part of this loss was used to reduce the income tax liability. Thus, the net accounting loss is $1,658,000.

Future growth strategy.   The paper accounting loss arising from this strategy is $1,808,000. This amount includes, in addition to the R&D expenses, interest on the financing for the plant construction, less the reduction of income tax liabilities due to the losses. In reality, the $1,808,000 reported accounting loss is not an economic loss but an investment for the future, since the purpose of the R&D efforts is to seek new products for the future, and since the objective of the expanded manufacturing facilities is to provide for future growth.

III. RESOURCES

ASSIGNMENT OF RESOURCES (Exhibit 24.3)

Each activity was charged with the resources utilized by them. The receivables, inventories and other assets, and payables assigned to each measure are shown in Exhibit 24.3. All the cash balance was charged to normal operations since the strategies during the year did not require any additional working cash.

     The old land, buildings, and equipment were also allocated to normal operations since the new measures did not need any new plants. However, the plant under construction was placed under "future growth strategy" in the balance sheet since the construction will be utilized in the future and hence did not benefit the current operations. Selected resources assigned to certain activities are explained next.

NORMAL OPERATIONS

The normal operations have maintained the following levels of working capital:

Accounts receivable	
Based on number of months' sales	4 months
Finished goods inventory	
Based on number of months' direct manufacturing costs	2 months
Raw materials inventory	
Based on number of months' raw material usage	3 months
Accounts payable	
Based on number of months' raw material usage	3 months

These working capital levels are net of the old receivables of $200,000 and slow-moving raw material inventories of $400,000. These amounts were retained under normal operations since they are not related to any of the strategies pursued during the year. However, since they were not utilized during the year, they were considered nonoperating assets.

     The normal operations had to carry current accounts receivable of $41,600,000 as of the end of year 2. This is equivalent to four months' sales. This amount is shown in the balance sheet in Exhibit 24.3 as the accounts receivable balance as of the end of year 2. This represents an increase of $1,800,000 over the beginning balance.

COST REDUCTION MEASURE
AND MANAGEMENT INEFFICIENCY

The failure of management to monitor and control production closely has led to an unintended rise in finished goods inventory from two months of sales during year 1, to three months in year 2. This added $2,600,000 to the $5,200,000 normal inventory. The $2,600,000 represents the raw material and other direct manufacturing costs component of one months' cost of sales in the normal operations segment.

On the other hand, the company succeeded in reducing the raw materials inventory from three months of raw material requirements to two months. This shaved off $2,080,000 from the usual $6,240,000 inventory. The net effect of these changes in the inventory levels is a $520,000 addition to the total assets. See Exhibit 24.3.

MARKET SATURATION MEASURE

The market saturation program with its corresponding attractive profit was achieved at a high cost in terms of incremental investment in accounts receivable and the resulting risk from possible noncollection of a material portion of the collectibles.

To pursue the strategy, the firm had to allow the receivables to rise by one month from the usual four, not only on the incremental sales due to the measure but also to the sales from normal operations as well. The additional receivable is $15,600,000:

Normal operations	
Sales at $124,800,000 a year or $10,400,000 a month	
Increase in collection period by one month —	
from four to five months	$10,400,000
Incremental sales due to the market saturation strategy	
Sales at $12,480,000 a year or $1,040,000 a month	
Receivables at five months' sales	5,200,000
Total receivables	$15,600,000

The $15,600,000 receivables translates to 125% of the incremental sales of $12,480,000 for the whole year. Another way of sizing up the magnitude of this is to assume that, had the terms of collections on the normal sales been maintained at the usual four months, the terms for the incremental sales would have been 15 months. (For incremental accounts receivable turnover and collection period ratio analysis, see Exhibit 21.3, Chapter 21, Operating Ratios.) In addition to the massive buildup in the receivables, the strategy also resulted in the rise of the finished goods and raw materials inventories of $780,000 and $416,000, respectively. Thus, the total gross working capital requirements reached $16,796,000. However, the company was able to finance part of this by extending the terms of payments to suppliers. This produced an $832,000 accounts payable funding. Thus, the net working capital financed by bank loans and profit from the measure is only $15,964,000.

IV. RESULTS OF PERFORMANCE

RESULTS IN YEAR 2 (Exhibit 24.4, part II)

The normal operations have returned 16% on the net operating assets used in year 2. This is based on the posttax net profit of $6,676,000 as a percentage of the net operating assets of $42,833,000. The latter is equivalent to the working capital and property, plant, and equipment used in the business, less the accounts payable and loans. In other words, net operating assets equal the stockholders' equity less the nonoperating assets. In the given case, the nonoperating assets are the long-term stock investments and old receivables and inventories.

The two short-term measures implemented during the year, namely, the cost reduction and the market saturation programs, have performed much better, having generated a net profit after tax equal to 306% of the net operating assets.

No return on investments were calculated for the long-term strategies—market territory expansion and new product development and plant expansion—since they have not yet attained operational status during the year.

CURRENT YEAR RESULTS IN YEARS 1 AND 2
(Exhibit 24.4, part III, and Exhibit 24.5)

The income statement in Exhibit 24.1 and the return on operating assets in part II of Exhibit 24.4 have been designed to evaluate the comparative performance of the strategies which became operational in year 2. If the results in year 2 have to be reviewed against those of year 1, the net income has to be adjusted for the following items in order to make the net profit and the return on net operating assets for the two years comparable:

1. The legal settlement costs in year 2 have to be deleted since these costs pertain to earlier periods.
2. The R&D in year 1 has to be omitted since these costs will benefit the future periods.
3. The income tax in year 2 has to be recomputed at a straight 40% of taxable income—the same rate as for year 1.

The income statement as adjusted is presented in Exhibit 24.5. As shown in Exhibit 24.4, part III, the resulting year 1 return on net operating assets (RONOA) based on the adjusted net profit is 25% while that for year 2 is 30%. The 30% return for year 2 is only for the normal operations and cost reduction and market saturation measures. The results of the long-term strategies were excluded as they were not operational yet in year 2.

Exhibit 24.4, part III, reveals that there is a fall in the RONOA from 25% in year 1 to 22% for the normal operations alone in year 2. The main cause of this decline is the use of less debt leverage in the latter. In year 1, the average balance of loans was $40,723,000, while the corresponding figure for year 2 normal operations was $28,967,000. (See Exhibit 24.2.) For year 2 normal operations, the cost of the loan was only 8% before tax or 4.8% after tax. Hence, if more debt were used, the return on net operating profit could have been higher than 22%.

The improvement in the RONOA from 25% to 30% may be compared with the favorable change in the return on stockholders' equity (ROSE) from 18% to 20% during the same period. Under traditional method, the ROSE may be calculated as

	Year 1	Year 2
Stockholders' equity*		
Beginning of year	$43,000,000	$49,553,000
End of year	49,553,000	58,126,000
Average	46,277,000	53,840,000
Net profit†	$ 8,192,000	$10,716,000
Return on stockholders' equity	18%	20%

*From Exhibit 5, Chapter 17, Financial Statement as Basis of Evaluation.
†Exhibit 17.1 of Chapter 17.

The difference in the results shown by the RONOA and the one revealed by the ROSE may be accounted for by the discrepancies in the following:

1. *Strategies covered.* The RONOA excludes both the results and net resources of the growth strategies (market territory expansion and future growth—new product development and plant expansion).
2. *Resources covered.* The RONOA excludes the nonoperating assets, which, for the beginning of year 1 alone, consisted of 12.3% of the total assets according to the balance sheet:

Total assets according to the balance sheet in Exhibit 17.5, Chapter 17	$97,500,000
Non-operating assets and other adjustments	
Long-term stock investments	$ 6,400,000
Finished goods inventory adjustment*	5,000,000

Raw materials (slow moving)	400,000
Receivables (old accounts)	200,000
Total	$12,000,000
As percentage of total assets	12.3%

*Fixed cost component of the inventory so as to adjust the valuation from the full costing method to the direct costing basis.

The nonoperating assets were deducted from the stockholders' equity in the RONOA analysis.

3. *Finished goods inventory costing method used.* The RONOA analysis utilized the direct costing method; the traditional ROSE applied the full costing technique.

4. *Long-term costs.* The RONOA excluded the R&D, which is a future benefit cost, and the legal settlement cost, a past benefit cost.

EXHIBIT 24.1:
Income Statement (dollars in $1,000)

				YEAR 2			
	Year 1	Normal operations	Cost reduction	Market saturation	New market territories	Future growth	Total
Sales	$120,000	$124,800	$ 0	$12,480	$5,720	$ 0	$143,000
Less: Variable costs							
Raw materials used	24,000	24,960	0	2,496	1,144	0	28,600
Other direct manufacturing costs	6,000	6,240	0	624	286	0	7,150
Sales commissions	6,000	6,240	0	624	286	0	7,150
Freight out	1,800	1,872	0	187	86	0	2,145
Total variable costs	$ 37,800	$ 39,312	$ 0	$ 3,931	$1,802	0	$ 45,045
Contribution margin	82,200	85,488	0	8,549	3,918	0	97,955
Less: Sales expansion costs							
Advertising expenses	10,000	10,400	0	2,000	5,000	0	17,400
Bad debts and collection expenses	1,200	1,248	0	125	57	0	1,430
Additional collection expenses		0	0	468	0	0	468
Additional freight for new markets		0	0	0	114	0	114
Total sales expansion costs	$ 11,200	$ 11,648	$ 0	$ 2,593	$5,172	$ 0	$ 19,412
Contribution to overhead	$ 71,000	$ 73,840	$ 0	$ 5,956	($1,253)	$ 0	$ 78,543

EXHIBIT 24.1:
Continued

YEAR 2

	Year 1	Normal operations	Cost reduction	Market saturation	New market territories	Future growth	Total
Less: Current overhead							
Factory overhead	25,000	26,000	0	0	0	0	26,000
Additional maintenance		1,200					1,200
Marketing overhead	15,000	15,600	0	0	2,000	0	17,600
Administrative expenses	7,000	7,280	(1,040)	0	0	0	6,240
Total current overhead	$ 47,000	$ 50,080	($1,040)	$ 0	$2,000	$ 0	$ 51,040
Current operating profit	24,000	23,760	1,040	5,956	(3,253)	0	27,503
Less: Interest expense (income)	3,347	2,322	(76)	674	323	959	4,202
Current profit	20,653	$ 21,438	$1,116	$ 5,282	($3,576)	($ 959)	$ 23,301
Less: Long-term and sunk costs							
R & D expenses—future products	1,000	0	0	0	0	2,940	2,940
Legal settlement costs		1,040					1,040
Depreciation—manufacturing	5,000	5,000	0	0	0	0	5,000
Depreciation—marketing department	1,000	1,000	0	0	0	0	1,000
Total noncurrent costs	7,000	7,040	0	0	0	2,940	9,980
Net profit before tax	$ 13,653	$ 14,398	$1,116	$ 5,282	($3,576)	($3,899)	$ 13,321
Income tax (from Exhibit 24.2)	5,461	7,722	599	2,833	(1,918)	(2,091)	7,144
Net profit	$ 8,192	$ 6,676	$ 517	$ 2,449	($1,658)	($1,808)	$ 6,176
Cash flow from operations	$ 14,192	$ 12,676	$ 517	$ 2,449	($1,658)	($1,808)	$ 12,176

EXHIBIT 24.2:
Interest in Year 2 (dollars in $1,000)

| | | YEAR 2 | | | | | |
Interest calculations	Year 1	Normal operations	Cost reduction	Market saturation	New market territories	Future growth	Total
Short-term loans							
Beginning balance	$ 8,500	$ 447	$ 0	$ 0	$ 0	$ 0	$ 447
Ending balance	447	0	0	9,954	6,460	19,181	35,595
Average balance	4,473	223	0	4,977	3,230	9,590	18,021
Interest at 10% a year	447	22	0	498	323	959	1,802
Long-term loans							
Beginning balance	40,000	32,500	0	0	0	0	32,500
Ending balance	32,500	24,987	(1,898)	4,410	0	0	27,500
Average balance	36,250	28,744	(949)	2,205	0	0	30,000
Interest at 8% a year	2,900	2,299	(76)	176	0	0	2,400
Total interest	$ 3,347	$ 2,322	($ 76)	$ 674	$ 323	$ 959	$ 4,202
Loan mix based on average balance							
Short-term loans	11%	1%					
Long-term loans	89%	99%					
Combined							
Average balance	$40,723	$28,967					
Effective interest rate	8.2%	8.0%					

EXHIBIT 24.3:
Balance Sheet (dollars in $1,000)

	Year 1	YEAR 2					
		Normal operations	Cost reduction	Market saturation	New market territories	Future growth	Total
Assets							
Current assets							
Cash	$ 200	$ 200	$ 0	$ 0	$ 0	$ 0	$ 200
Trade receivables	39,800	41,600	0	15,600	5,720	0	62,920
Inventories							
Finished goods							
Raw materials component	4,000	4,160	2,080	624	1,830	0	8,694
Other variable costs component	1,000	1,040	520	156	458	0	2,174
Total	5,000	5,200	2,600	780	2,288	0	10,868
Raw materials	5,600	6,240	(2,080)	416	915	0	5,491
Total current assets	$50,600	$53,240	$ 520	$16,796	$ 8,923	0	$ 79,479
Property, pant, and equipment							
Land	5,000	5,000	0	0	0	0	5,000
Buildings and equipment							
At cost	45,000	45,000	0	0	0	0	45,000
Accumulated depreciation	(21,000)	(27,000)	0	0	0	0	(27,000)
Total property	29,000	23,000	0	0	0	0	23,000
Total operating assets	$79,600	$76,240	520	16,796	$ 8,923	$ 0	$102,479
Non operating assets							
Old trade receivables	200	200	0	0	0	0	200
Old raw materials inventory	400	400	0	0	0	0	400
Construction in progress	0	0	0	0	0	18,000	18,000
Long-term stock investments	3,300	3,300	0	0	0	0	3,300
Total nonoperating assets	$ 3,900	$ 3,900	0	0	$ 0	$18,000	21,900
Total assets	$83,500	$80,140	$ 520	$16,796	$ 8,923	$18,000	$124,379

EXHIBIT 24.3:
(Continued)

| | Year 1 | YEAR 2 | | | | | |
		Normal operations	Cost reduction	Market saturation	New market territories	Future growth	Total
Liabilities							
Current liabilities—working capital							
Accounts payable	$ 6,000	$ 6,240	$2,080	$ 832	$ 3,546	$ 0	$ 12,698
Current liabilities							
Short-term loans	447	0	0	9,954	6,460	19,181	35,595
Current portion of long-term loans	2,500						
Total current liabilities	$ 8,947	$ 6,240	$2,080	$10,786	$10,006	$19,181	$ 48,293
Long-term liabilities							
Long-term loans	32,500	24,987	(1,898)	4,410	0	0	27,500
Less current portion	2,500						0
Long-term portion	30,000	24,987	(1,898)	4,410	0	0	27,500
Total liabilities	$38,947	$31,227	$ 182	$15,197	$10,006	$19,181	$ 75,793
Stockholder's equity							
Capital stock	33,000	33,000	0	0	0	0	33,000
Retained earnings							
Beginning balance	5,000	11,553	0	0	0	0	11,553
Net profit	8,192	6,676	517	2,449	(1,658)	(1,808)	6,176
Dividends	(1,638)	(2,317)	(180)	(850)	575	627	(2,143)
Ending balance	11,553	15,913	338	1,599	(1,083)	(1,180)	15,586
Total stockholders' equity	$44,553	$48,913	338	$ 1,599	($ 1,083)	($ 1,180)	48,586
Total liabilities and stockholders' equity	$83,500	$80,140	$520	$16,796	$ 8,923	$18,000	$124,379

EXHIBIT 24.4:
Return on Operating Assets (dollars in $1,000)

	Year 1	YEAR 2			
		Normal operations	Cost reduction	Market saturation	Total
I. Average net operating assets used during the year					
Beginning balance					
Operating assets*	$85,500	$79,600			$79,600
Less: Liabilities	(54,500)	(38,947)			(38,947)
Net operating assets	$31,000	$40,653			$40,653
Ending balance (from Exhibit 24.3)					
Operating assets*	79,600	76,240	$520	$16,796	93,556
Less: Liabilities	(38,947)	(31,227)	(182)	(15,197)	(46,606)
Net operating assets†	$40,653	45,013	338	1,599	46,950
Average net operating assets during the year	$35,827	$42,833	$169	$ 800	$43,801
II. Total return on net operating assets					
Net profit (from Exhibit 24.1)	$ 8,192	$ 6,676	$517	$ 2,449	$ 9,642
Return on average net operating assets	23%	16%	306%	306%	22%
III. Current year return on net operating assets					
Adjusted profit (from Exhibit 24.5)	$ 8,792	$ 9,263	$670	$ 3,169	$13,102
Return on average net operating assets	25%	22%	396%	396%	30%

*Excludes the following nonoperating assets: old trade receivables, fixed manufacturing costs in finished goods inventories, slow-moving raw material inventories, and long-term stock investments.
†Equals stockholders' equity less nonoperating assets.

EXHIBIT 24.5:
Adjusted Net Profit (dollars in $1,000)

		YEAR 2			
	Year 1	*Normal operations*	*Cost reduction*	*Market saturation*	*Total*
Current profit before tax (from Exhibit 24.1)	$20,653	$21,438	$1,116	$5,282	$27,836
Less: Sunk costs Depreciation— manufacturing	5,000	5,000	0	0	5,000
Depreciation— marketing	1,000	1,000	0	0	1,000
	6,000	6,000	0	0	6,000
Net profit before tax	14,653	15,438	1,116	5,282	21,836
Income tax—at 40% for year 1 and year 2	5,861	6,175	446	2,113	8,734
Net profit	$ 8,792	$ 9,263	$ 670	$3,169	$13,102

Chapter 25 _____

EVALUATING PERFORMANCE WITH RESOURCE-BASED INTEREST

This chapter illustrates how to apply imputed interest in evaluating the performance of a firm which pursued measures affecting its selling prices and procurement costs.

The traditional performance evaluation is based on an income statement which uses the loan-based interest treatment. This recognizes as expense only the interest which have been paid or accrued on loans. Furthermore, the interest is not considered as a cost of operations but rather as a financial expense which does not influence the operating profit.

An alternative approach is to charge the operations with the interest which is imputed on the resources used in the operations, whether such financing is supplied by banks or stockholders. Under this resource-based approach, the sales revenues are charged with the interest calculated on the financing which carried the receivables. This pushes down to the operating management level the incentive to profitably utilize the resources. Furthermore, it impresses on the operating managers the need to consider the money cost in their decisions.

The outcome of these two approaches are compared in a simple case involving sales performance. Consider the following: Divisions A and B sold the same quantity and quality of merchandise and incurred the same costs and expenses. Division A sold the merchandise for $10,000,000 on a six-month sales credit term. Division B shipped out the goods for $9,800,000 on a one-month collection basis. The company borrows at 1% a month. The normal performance review considers Division A the better performer since it sold the merchandise for a higher sales value.

The real results in this case cannot be gauged unless the interest cost of carrying the accounts receivables is imputed and charged to the operations, that is, deducted from the sales revenues. If this approach were used, Division B is considered the superior achiever since it produced more effective revenues:

	Division A	*Division B*
Sales	$10,000,000	$ 9,800,000
Less: Interest cost at 1% a month		
For six months	600,000	
For one month		98,000
Effective sales revenue	$ 9,400,000	$ 9,702,000

This conflict in the outcomes of the evaluation of the relative performance of Divisions A and B was brought about by the use of two different interest approaches.

The evaluation in this chapter has two key differences from the case in the prior chapter: the use of resource-based interest in lieu of the loan-based interest and the focus of the analysis on the gross profit rather than on the net profit.

I. LOAN-BASED INTEREST—NATURE

CONCEPT (Exhibit 25.1, part I)

In the conventional income statement, the interest is not linked to any specific business transaction as sales or merchandise cost. Sales and the cost of sales, together with the selling and general and administrative expenses, determine the operating profit. See Exhibit 25.1.

The interest expense is shown in the income statement as a financial cost which is after the net operating profit and hence does not enter into the determination of the sales revenues, gross profit or contribution margin, and operating profit.

LIMITATIONS

The traditional performance reporting practice is characterized by (1) the use of loan as the basis of interest in the performance evaluation and (2) the segregation of the interest from the operating results. These features create the weaknesses of the method.

Use of loan as the basis of interest. The conventional income statement includes only the interest which is charged by banks on loans. Since the assets of a firm are financed not only by loans but also by stockholders' equity and by trade or suppliers' credit (in the form of accounts payable), the interest cost which is included in the performance evaluation is only a fraction of the total money cost of using the resources of an enterprise.

Since the interest is based on loans, the interest expenses cannot be readily traced to the various resources employed by the different activities of the business. See Exhibit 25.1, part I. This practice, therefore, is inconsistent with the concept of accountability, wherein the manager is held responsible for the resources under his or her command.

Segregation of interest from the operating results. Operating decisions invariably involve financing costs. The institution of sales credit terms or the lengthening or shortening of sales payment period are instruments of augmenting the sales. At the procurement end, arrangements regarding on-time delivery of goods and trade credits influence the effective prices paid the suppliers.

Notwithstanding the marriage of operating decisions and financing considerations, their resulting offspring, namely, the sales revenues and operating costs, on the one hand, and the financing costs, on the other, are not presented together to form the integrated profitability picture. For instance, sales revenues, which are affected by the sales payment terms, are not shown together with the interest on financing which is used to carry the receivables.

The costs of purchases and of merchandise sold, which are influenced by the terms of payments to the suppliers, are shown under cost of sales, while the interest on loans that are used to finance the inventories net of the financing provided by the trade suppliers is presented in another section of the income statement under interest expense.

This separation of sales and operating costs from the interest expense implies that the interest expense does not result from the operating decisions. This is based on the premise that loans, which generate the interest, are within the exclusive province of the finance department, whereas marketing and purchasing functions that give rise to sales and cost of sales are in the jurisdiction of the operating managers.

Possible consequences of the limitations. This practice of basing interest on loans and not charging the cost of using these resources to the related activities creates three cracks in the management plaster.

First, the operating managers will be prompted to make marketing and purchasing decisions without consideration of the financing costs. For instance, the gross profit and operating profit can be bloated at terrific financing costs. By simply offering a liberal collection period to the customers at no or very low interests rates, the sales volume can be substantially raised. However, in reality, the incremental revenue from the sales may not be adequate to justify the additional interest cost.

Second, if the managers or activities are not charged for the money cost of receivables, inventories, buildings, and other resources which they use, or are not given credit for the trade financing which they can haggle from the suppliers, the operating managers are not provided the incentives to squeeze the most out of their resources or to negotiate with their suppliers for longer terms of payment.

Third, since the value of the usage of the resources is not costed and the activities are not charged for the cost of the resources, top management is not placed in an informed position to allocate the resources to the promising activities and properly reward the top performing operating managers.

II. RESOURCE-BASED INTEREST—NATURE

CONCEPT (Exhibit 25.1, part II)

The implementation of profit improvement measures generates sales revenues and incurs costs. These revenues and costs, in turn, call for, or result in, resources and financial obligations. For instance, sale and purchase transactions give rise to accounts receivables and accounts payable, respectively, while increased sales volume necessitates the beefing up of merchandise inventories. Thus, these resource-using activities should be directly charged for the interest cost of carrying the resources. See Exhibit 25.1.

DISTINCTIVE FEATURES

The resource-based interest approach differs from the historical, loan-based interest method in the treatment of (1) interest expense on receivables, inventories, buildings, and equipment; (2) interest income on payables; and (3) year-end adjustments of receivables and payables.

Interest expense. Imputed interest expense representing the money cost of resources utilized in operations is charged to the resource-using activities. Thus, interest on financing used to carry the receivables is deducted from the sales revenues. Interest on inventory financing is added to the cost of merchandise sold. Interest on financing to carry the buildings is charged to the building users. The interest is calculated and applied based on the money cost to the company, although the resource is actually funded by noninterest-bearing financing as trade credits or stockholders' capital contributions.

Interest income. Imputed interest income which compensates for the value of interest-free financing provided by suppliers is credited to the cost of carrying on the operations. Thus, interest income which is imputed on accounts payable is deducted from the cost of merchandise purchased and sold.

Year-end adjustment of receivables. At the end of the year, the face value of the receivables which are forwarded to the following year is marked down to its economic worth. The markdown represents the interest expense to be incurred during the initial months of the succeeding year due to the financing to be used to carry the receivables until they are collected. This markdown reduces the balance sheet value of the receivables and correspondingly increases the interest cost to be deducted from the sales revenues. This aspect is discussed in Section VII of this chapter.

Year-end adjustment of payables. Similarly, the face value of the accounts payable to be forwarded to the following year is reduced in order to reflect its real value. The reduction approximates the value of the utilization of the interest-free funding to be provided by the trade payables during the initial months of the succeeding year until the payables are paid. The reduction in the value decreases the amount of the payables to be shown in the balance sheet and raises the interest deduction or interest income to be offset against the cost of merchandise purchased.

III. INTEREST APPROACHES IN PERFORMANCE EVALUATION

The interest cost under the resource-based interest approach can readily be reconciled with the interest under the other interest-oriented performance review methods, namely, the loan-based interest method, the intercompany capital account procedure, and the residual income technique. To simplify the illustration, assume that the interest rate on the bank loan is the same as that on the stockholders' equity and intercompany account—10%.

The use of the loan-based and resource-based methods in analyzing proposed projects are described in Chapter 3, Financial Projections as Basis of Analysis.

LOAN-BASED INTEREST (Exhibit 25.2, part I)

Except for year-end adjustments of receivables and payables, the two methods should result in the same net interest expense, and hence show the same pretax net profit. This is illustrated in Exhibit 25.2.

Using the figures given, under the resource-based interest approach, a total of $1,200,000 in interest expense is charged to the activities using the $12,000,000 in resources. However, the activities creating the $2,000,000 in accounts payable are credited with the $200,000 interest income. Thus the net interest adjustment to operations is $1,000,000. However, since the stockholders supplied $4,000,000 in financing, the $400,000 interest income on this will be deducted from the total interest cost. The net result is a net interest charge of $600,000, which is equivalent to the actual interest on the $6,000,000 loan.

INTER-COMPANY CAPITAL ACCOUNT CHARGE
(Exhibit 25.2, part II)

The resource-based interest method has a similarity to the present practice of some corporations of charging their divisions for the use of corporate funds.

Currently, large corporations charge their divisions or strategic business units for the funds which the head office transfer to the units. The charge is pegged to the cost of funds to the head office. Sometimes, a premium is added on to represent (1) a required markup or profit by the head office, (2) compensation for risk, or (3) differential in the profit potential among divisions. A unit with a built-in profit advantage, as one handling a matured product in a protected market, is sometimes charged a rate higher than is one that is just introducing its main product.

The amounts in the last column assume that instead of having an independent company with a stockholders' equity, the operations are carried by a division, so that in lieu of stockholders' equity the division has an intercompany account with the head office.

The resource-based method charges to operations a total of $1,000,000 in imputed interest expense. The intercompany method charges the division the same amount—$600,000 in the form of bank loan interest and $400,000 as interest on the intercompany capital. The similarity ends here, since the $1,000,000 interest expense under the resource-based interest method is distributed to sales, cost of sales, and operating expenses. This distribution is not done under the intercompany account method.

RESIDUAL INCOME (Exhibit 25.2, part III)

Under the residual income concept, the net profit shown in the traditional income statement is not final since the interest on the capital provided by the owners has not yet been deducted. Hence, an interest has to be imputed on this equity. Thus, the total interest charged to the company is composed of the sum of this imputed interest plus that historical interest on the bank loans. The total interest in this case, which is $1,000,000, is the same as the interest charged to operations under the resource-based interest approach. (See Chapter 19, Return on Investment Ratios, for a more thorough discussion of residual income.)

IV. LOAN-BASED VERSUS RESOURCE-BASED INTEREST—USE IN COMPARING GROSS PROFIT PERFORMANCE

The results of the two methods are compared by applying them to the evaluation of the sales and gross profit of a merchandising firm which had been in operation for two years. Assume that at the start of year 2, the company instituted the following measures:

1. Reduction in the selling prices by an average of 2%, which was accompanied by the shortening of the sales credit term from five months to one
2. Escalation of the buying price of merchandise by an average of 2%, in return for the lengthening of the terms of payment from one to four months

The evaluation of the results of year 2 relative to year 1 revolves around the profitability of these measures.

SALES, PURCHASES, AND INVENTORIES

The company has set the following inventory levels, collection periods, and payment terms, which were substantially followed during the two years of operations:

	In months	
	Year 1	*Year 2*
Collection period of sales (in months' sales or number of months from date of billing to date of collection)	5	1
Merchandise inventory period (in months' cost of merchandise sold or number of months from date of purchase to date of sale)	2	2
Accounts payable for merchandise purchases (in months' cost of merchandise sold or in number of months from date of purchase to date of payment)	1	4

For the sake of simplicity, it is assumed that the sales and purchases are invoiced at the end of every month and the purchases and expenses are paid at the end of the month.

OTHER INFORMATION

All the annual sales and expenses as shown in the income statement were effected or incurred uniformly throughout each year. Interest is based on the beginning balance of each month. Income tax is assumed to be paid as of the end of the month, for the tax corresponding to the current month's taxable income. The assumption on the tax is made in order to simplify the calculations; in practice, it is paid after the month for which it pertains. Assume also that there is no inflation and that the effective combined federal and state income tax rate is 40%.

As of the start of year 2, the firm sold or discounted all the outstanding accounts receivables, which had a face value of $2,500,000, for $2,440,000, or a discount fee of $60,000.

V. LOAN-BASED INTEREST METHOD—USE IN GROSS PROFIT PERFORMANCE EVALUATION

PROFIT ANALYSIS (Exhibit 25.3)

The outcome of the traditional analysis indicated that the company performance deteriorated during year 2. The conventional income statement shows that although there is a 5.0% improvement in the sales revenues in year 2, the cost of merchandise sold climbed by 9.3%, thereby causing a 4.1% fall in the gross profit.

SALES VARIANCE ANALYSIS

Variance analysis traces the causes of the changes in the gross profit, to the fluctuations in sales volume, selling price, and cost.

The $300,000 rise in sales is accounted for as follows: $429,000 due to increase in sales volume, less $129,000 due to the reduction in the selling price.

Because of the 2% drop in selling prices, the year 2 prices are only 98% of the year 1 prices. Hence the $6,300,000 year 2 sales volume is equivalent to $6,429,000 at the year 1 price ($6,300,000 divided by 98% = $6,429,000).

	Sales at year 1 prices		Percentage of year 1 prices		Sales per income statement
Year 1	$6,000,000	×	100%	=	$6,000,000
Year 2	6,429,000	×	98%	=	6,300,000
Change	$ 429,000				$ 300,000

Since the company handles several products, it is not advisable to use as the volume of sales for variance analysis purposes the number of physical units sold. Hence the sales volume is based on the sales value, using year 1 sales as the reference point.

Under the conventional variance analysis, the $300,000 rise in sales is detailed into quantity and price variances, which are as follows:

Formula

Volume or quantity variance	=	change in volume	×	prior year (year 1) price
Price variance	=	change in price	×	current year (year 2) volume

Application

Volume variance	=	$429,000	×	100%	=	$429,000
Price variance	=	(2%)*	×	$6,429,000	=	(129,000)*
Total sales variance						$300,000

*The figures in parentheses represent deductions.

COST OF SALES VARIANCE

Using the same formula as for the sales variance, but substituting cost variance for the price variance, the $379,000 climb in the cost of sales may be broken down as follows:

Volume variance	=	$429,000	×	68%	=	$292,000
Cost variance	=	2%*	×	$4,372,000	=	87,000
Total cost variance						$379,000

* Average increase in the procurement cost.

The $4,372,000 year 2 cost used in these calculations is equivalent to 68% of the $6,429,000 year 2 sales at year 1 selling prices. The 68% is the cost of sales as a percentage of sales based on year 1 figures.

GROSS PROFIT VARIANCE

The gross profit unfavorable variance of $79,000 is therefore traceable to the following causes:

	Sales	Cost of sales	Total
Volume variance	$429,000	($292,000)	$137,000
Selling price variance	(129,000)		(129,000)
Cost variance		(87,000)	(87,000)
Total variance	$300,000	($379,000)	($79,000)

VI. RESOURCE-BASED INTEREST APPROACH—
USE IN GROSS PROFIT PERFORMANCE
EVALUATION

If the evaluation were conducted purely in terms of the traditional accounting practice, the apparent conclusion is that the measures to alter the terms of payments for the sales and purchases as leverage for the changes in the selling prices and procurement costs have failed. However, conducting the analysis in the light of imputed interest completely reversed the outcome, thus providing support for the strategy.

The application of the resource-based interest has shown that the performance of the firm has tremendously enhanced in year 2, as indicated by sales and gross profit.

GROSS PROFIT (Exhibit 25.4)

The gross profit statement is based on the information which was used in preparing the statement in Exhibit 25.3. There are major differences in the sales and cost of sales as reported in Exhibit 25.3, which uses the loan-based method in the traditional income statement form, and Exhibit 25.4, which utilizes the resource-based approach in a more functional format.

Sales.   While the reported sales increased by only 5% in year 2 before the imputed interest adjustment, the actual sales value after considering money cost jumped by a much higher 9.7%. The difference is due to three items:

1. The imputed interest on financing used to carry the receivables during the year. This is based on the average balance of the receivables.
2. The year-end markdowns in the valuation of the receivables. This is explained in Section VII of this chapter.
3. The discount fee paid in year 2 to liquidate the year 1 receivables. In Exhibit 25.3 this was shown under operating expenses. However, since this arose from the conversion of sales receivables to cash, this was reclassified as a sales deduction.

Year 1 is charged more for interest because during the year, the term of sale was five months; in year 2, it was only one month. Consequently, in year 1 more financing was tied up in the receivables. Hence year 1 is penalized more. The longer collection period in year 1 materially reduced the cash value of the sales.

However, the decline in interest cost due to the shortening of the collection period was slightly eroded by the rise in sales volume.

Cost of sales. While the cost of merchandise purchased under conventional accounting jumped by 9.3%, the cost as adjusted for resource-based interest climbed at a lower 6.1%. The difference is due to the following:

1. The imputed interest income on the trade credits which reduced the cost of merchandise sold
2. The year-end markdowns in the valuation of the payables which decreased the cost of merchandise sold

Year 2 is credited more for interest income on payables because during the year the payables were outstanding for four months compared to one month in year 1. The longer payment period substantially slashed the cash value of the purchases. Furthermore, both the sales volumes and nominal purchase prices jumped in year 2; these required a higher level of purchases and, consequently, more trade payables.

GROSS PROFIT VARIANCE ANALYSIS
(Exhibits 25.4 and 25.5)

According to Exhibit 25.3, which uses the loan-based interest method, the gross profit declined by $79,000 in year 2. As explained earlier, this was traced to the following causes:

		Favorable (unfavorable) variance
Increase in sales volume		
Increase in sales revenues	$429,000	
Increase in cost of sales	(292,000)	$137,000
Decrease in selling price		(129,000)
Increase in cost of merchandise		(87,000)
Total change		($79,000)

On the other hand, Exhibit 25.4, which employs the resource-based interest approach, shows a $297,000 rise in the gross profit. Of this amount, $288,000 is due to merchandise buying and selling operations as accounted for in Exhibit 25.5—see the bottom line of the last column. The balance is caused by nonrecurring transactions. Exhibit 25.5 incorporates the results of the conventional analysis, which are placed under the "sales" and "cost of sales" columns. The combined totals of these two columns indicate a fall in the gross profit of $79,000 ($379,000 less $300,000). As is evident from the exhibit, interest cost has converted the $79,000 decline in gross profit to a rise of $288,000. The $367,000 difference is due to the money cost which was disregarded in the traditional analysis. This represents the imputed interest on accounts receivable, accounts payable, and inventory, which were calculated at 1% a month based on the collection, payment, and inventory periods given in Section IV of this chapter.

Sales volume variance (Exhibit 25.5, part I).   While the normal variance analysis indicates a $137,000 improvement in the gross profit due to the rise in the sales volume, the actual enhancement is only $113,000 (Exhibit 25.5, part I, last column). The interest on the incremental inventory, accounts receivable, and accounts payable ate up the difference. The 1% monthly interest is applied on the year 1 working capital durations.

Selling price variance (Exhibit 25.5, part II).   The strategy to depress the selling prices by 2% and at the same time cut down on the terms of payment from five to one month has actually pushed up the effective selling price. Although the usual analysis shows a $129,000 reduction in the gross profit due to this strategy, the substantial drop in the interest cost coming from the contraction of the outstanding receivables has converted the $129,000 unfavorable variance to a $130,000 beneficial change.

Purchase cost variance (Exhibit 25.5, part III).   Similarly, the plan to negotiate with suppliers to stretch the terms of payment on the purchases from one to four months in return for jacking up the nominal procurement prices by 2% has actually cut down the effective purchase cost. Thus, it added $45,000 to the gross profit. If the added value of the interest-free financing brought about by the extended payment period was not injected into the review equation, the result would show an $87,000 decline in the profit.

VII. THE REVALUATION OF RECEIVABLES AND PAYABLES

RATIONALE

The time value of money is universally recognized in the evaluation of long-term projects. For instance, the internal rate of return and net present value techniques have long been used in the review of capital expenditures, construction of plants, or acquisition of companies.

However, the concepts of the time value of money, which have proven useful in capital budgeting, have not been exploited in performance evaluation. The objective of this section is to lay down the general rationale and procedures involved in the use of time value of money in the valuation of receivables and payables so that revenues in one performance period are properly matched with the corresponding costs. The illustration used is for accounts receivable, although a similar procedure may be applied to accounts payable.

Given data. Consider a company with the following assets, among others:

Cash in banks	$1,000,000
Accounts receivable from Customer A	
Due one month from now (non interest bearing)	$1,000,000
Note receivable from Company B, dated today	
Principal of note	$1,000,000
Interest at 0.5% a month	
Due one month from now, with interest	
Note receivable from Company C, dated today	
Principal of note	$1,000,000
Interest at 1.5% a month	
Due one month from now, with interest	

Under conventional accounting and performance evaluation practice, these assets are valued in the amounts indicated. In reality, the assets should have different values, for two reasons:

1. Cash is available for use today, while the receivables will not be available until one month hence.
2. Varying amounts will be realized from the different receivables. Assuming all of them can be collected in full and there will be no collection expenses, the receivables will generate the following amounts of cash one month hence:

a. Accounts receivable—Customer A	$1,000,000
b. Notes receivable—principal plus interest	
From Company B	$1,005,000
From Company C	$1,015,000

The information given leads to the following:

1. A dollar of cash is more valuable than a dollar of receivable (at face value), even if the receivable is fully collectible and there are no collection expenses.
2. An interest-bearing receivable is more valuable than one which is not interest bearing; a receivable which bears a high interest is more valuable than is one with a lower rate.

Money cost and value of assets. The economic value of a receivable is determined in reference to cash for two reasons: the value of cash cannot be disputed, and cash is available today.

The true value today of the accounts receivable is lower than its collectible value due to the interest in the intervening period.

Assume for the moment that the money cost to the firm is 1% a month. Money cost is determined in several ways, but for practical purposes, the money cost refers to either one of the following:

1. Interest rate on bank loans which the firm can easily obtain
2. Interest, dividend, or profit rate on investments where the firm can easily place its funds and that the company can easily dispose of

If the company needs $1,000,000 today it cannot use directly the receivable as described. Rather, the firm has to do one of the following: (1) obtain a $1,000,000 loan and pay $10,000 in interest expense (1% of $1,000,000) or (2) dispose of some investments and forgo with $10,000 in interest or dividend income or other profit. After one month the firm collects the receivable, and it can then pay off the loan or reinvest the amount. In either case the firm loses $10,000—which is the money cost.

Thus, the real values as of today of the receivables, after considering the interest on the notes and the money cost, may be roughly estimated as shown in Exhibit 25.6.

APPLICATION TO THE CASE—YEAR 1

If all the $6,000,000 sales in year 1 per Exhibit 25.3 were for cash, there would have been no receivables at year end. However, only $3,500,000 of the sales have been collected at the end of the period, so that $2,500,000 remained outstanding as receivables. The $2,500,000 was not collected until year 2.

Although the receivables originated in year 1, and the entire $6,000,000 sales was credited to year 1, the money cost of carrying the $2,500,000 receivables unduly penalizes the profitability of the receiving period—year 2.

By not properly assigning the correct value to the receivables at the end of year 1, the traditional accounting and analysis practice gives full credit to year 1 for the entire sale of $6,000,000, although the initial months of year 2 carried the burden of the interest cost of the financing which was used to fund the $2,500,000 in receivables which originated from year 1.

It is proper that year 1 is charged, and year 2 is credited, for this interest burden. The interest expense is equal to the diminishing balance of the year 1 receivables scheduled to be shouldered and financed during the initial months of year 2, multiplied by the interest rate. Thus, the $2,500,000 receivable to be forwarded to year 2 should be reduced by the $75,000 interest to be incurred in year 2 to finance the $2,500,000 collectible. This $75,000 appears as a sales reduction in Exhibit 25.4.

EXHIBIT 25.1:
Interest Flow Chart

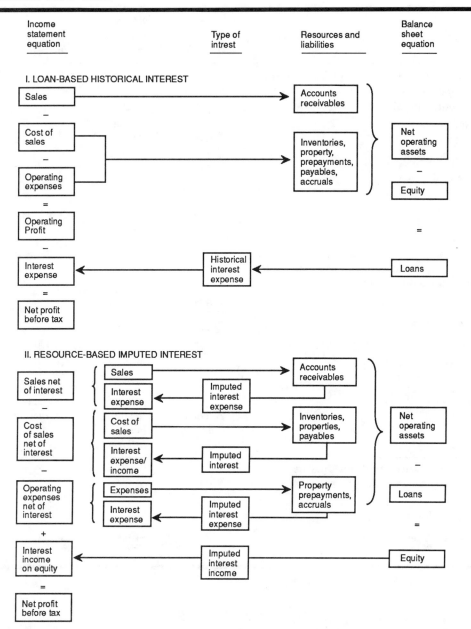

EXHIBIT 25.2:
Comparison of Interest Concepts (dollars in $1,000)

	Average monthly balance	Resource-based interest	Loan-based interest
I. Comparison with loan-based interest			
Operating assets	$12,000	$1,200	
Accounts payable	(2,000)	(200)	
Net assets	10,000	1,000	
Loan	(6,000)		$ 600
Stockholders' equity	$ 4,000	(400)	
Net interest charge		$ 600	$ 600

	Average monthly balance	Resource-based interest	Intercompany capital charge
II. Comparison with intercompany capital charge			
Net assets after trade payables	$10,000	$1,000	
Loan	(6,000)		$ 600
Stockholders' equity	$ 4,000		
Intercompany capital account	$ 4,000		400
Total interest charge		$1,000	$1,000

	Average monthly balance	Resource-based interest	Interest charges in residual income
III. Comparison with residual income			
Net assets after trade payables	$10,000	$1,000	
Loan	(6,000)		$ 600
Stockholders' equity	$ 4,000		400
Total interest charge		$1,000	$1,000

EXHIBIT 25.3:
Conventional Income Statement (dollars in $1,000)

	Year 1	Year 2	Increase	Increase as % of year 1
Sales	$6,000	$6,300	$300	5.0%
Cost of merchandise sold	4,080	4,459	379	9.3%
Gross profit	$1,920	$1,841	($ 79)	−4.1%
Less: Operating expenses				
Salaries	600	600	0	
Depreciation	300	300	0	
Insurance	24	24	0	
Market research for future projects		350	350	
Discount fees		60	60	
Other expenses	180	180	0	
Total expenses	$1,104	$1,514	$410	37%
Operating profit	816	327	(489)	−60%
Interest expense	362	72	(290)	−80%
Net profit before income tax	454	255	(199)	−44%
Income tax at 40%	182	102	(80)	−44%
Net profit	$ 272	$ 153	($119)	−44%

EXHIBIT 25.4:
Gross Profit Statement Using the Resource-Based Interest Approach
(dollars in $1,000)

	Year 1	Year 2	Increase	As a percentage of year 1
Sales	$ 6,000	$ 6,300	$300	5.0%
Interest adjustments				
Interest on receivables outstanding	(225)	(58)	167	
Markdown of receivables at year-end	(75)	70	145	
Discount fee	0	(60)	(60)	
Total adjustments	(300)	(48)	252	
Effective sales value	$5,700	$6,252	$552	9.7%
Cost of merchandise purchased	4,080	4,459	379	9.3%
Interest adjustments				
Interest on payables outstanding	(44)	(145)	(101)	
Mark-down of ending payables	(3)	(34)	(30)	
Total adjustments	($ 48)	($ 179)	($131)	
Effective purchase cost	4,032	4,280	247	6.1%
Interest on inventory	82	89	8	
Total merchandise cost	4,114	4,369	255	6.2%
Gross profit	$ 1,586	$ 1,883	$297	18.7%

EXHIBIT 25.5:
Gross Profit Variance—New Approach (dollars in $1,000)

				INCREASE (DECREASE) IN PROFIT					
	Rate or change	Base	Interest rate	Sales	Cost of sales	Accounts receivable interest	Accounts payable interest	Inventory interest	Total
I. Increase in profit due to increase in sales volume									
At year 1 prices, costs and working capital durations									
Year 2 sales volume (see text, Section V)		$6,249							
Year 1 sales volume		6,000							
Increase in sales volume and receivables interest	68.00%	429	5%	$429		($ 21)			$408
Increase in cost of sales and payables interest		292	1		($292)		$ 3		(289)
Increase in inventory interest		292	2					($ 6)	(6)
Increase (decrease) in profit		$ 137		429	(292)	(21)	3	($ 6)	$113
II. Increase in profit due to increase in effective selling price									
Year 2 sale at year 1 prices and durations		$6,429	5%			321			321
Decline in selling prices	2.00%	129		(129)					(129)
Year 2 sale at year 2 prices		$6,300	1			(63)			(63)
Increase (decrease) in profit				($129)	$ 0	$258			$130
III. Increase in profit due to decrease in effective purchase cost									
Year 2 transactions under year 1 durations									
Year 2 sale at year 1 prices		$6,429							
Year 2 cost of sales at year 1 cost of sales percentage	68.00%	4,371	1%						
Accounts payable interest		4,371					(44)		(44)
Inventory interest		4,371	2					87	87
Year 2 transactions under year 2 durations									
Year 2 cost of sales at year 1 cost of sales percentage	68.00%	$4,371							
Increase in purchase cost	2.00%	87			(87)				(87)
Year 2 cost of sales at year 2 prices		4,459	4%						
Accounts payable interest		4,459	2				178		178
Inventory interest		4,459						(89)	(89)
Increase (decrease) in profit					($ 87)		$135	($ 2)	$ 45
Total gross profit variance due to operations				$300	($379)	$237	$138	($ 8)	$288

EXHIBIT 25.6:
Economic Value of Cash and Receivables (dollars in $1,000)

	Cash	Accounts receivable	Note from Company B	Note from Company C
Face value	$1,000	$1,000	$1,000	$1,000
Add interest on the notes				
Interest rate			0.5%	1.5%
Amount	$ 0	$ 0	$ 5	$ 15
Total collectible upon maturity	$1,000	$1,000	$1,005	$1,015
Less: Money cost—1% of collectible value	$ 0	$ 10	$ 10	$ 10
Economic value	$1,000	$ 990	$ 995	$1,005
Amount of 1 after one month	1.01			
Present value of 1 factor	0.9901			

INDEX